Letters of H. P. Lovecraft

VOLUME 9

LETTERS TO F. LEE BALDWIN, DUANE W. RIMEL, AND NILS FROME

H. P. LOVECRAFT

LETTERS TO
F. LEE BALDWIN,
DUANE W. RIMEL, AND
NILS FROME

EDITED BY
DAVID E. SCHULTZ AND S. T. JOSHI

Hippocampus Press

New York

Published by Hippocampus Press
P.O. Box 641, New York, NY 10156.
http://www.hippocampuspress.com

Cover design and Hippocampus Press logo by Anastasia Damianakos.
Cover production by Barbara Briggs Silbert.

First Edition
1 3 5 7 9 8 6 4 2

ISBN 978-1-61498-157-2

Contents

Introduction

It is no secret that H. P. Lovecraft wrote a lot of letters. The full scope of his correspondence probably will never be known and can only be guessed at. One hint as to its volume is the checklist Lovecraft kept in the summer of 1934, to record to whom he had sent postcards during his travels between April and September (perhaps to avoid duplication of effort). The cards are listed as being sent only from Charleston, South Carolina (visited twice); DeLand, Florida; St. Augustine, Florida; and Nantucket, Massachusetts, although his travels took him to several other places. The list contains 70 names, many being the usual suspects but also a few individuals who still remain unidentified. (Curiously, it names four persons to whom it seems he mailed *no* postcards.) Lovecraft sent a total of 221 cards: 49 from Charleston; 57 from DeLand; 51 from St. Augustine; and 64 from Nantucket. Many individuals received a card from each stop; some got as few as only one. Total cost to mail? At a penny each, $2.21. (This is the amount Lovecraft told Jonquil Leiber he spent on average for food each week!) Cost to buy? At a penny apiece, another $2.21. But the list is only a rough indicator of his mailing habits. First of all, it is for postcards only, not letters. Secondly, it does not list *all* postcards he is known to have sent in the period in question. As one example, he sent numerous postcards to his host of much of the summer, R. H. Barlow, from Washington, D.C., Richmond, and Ocean Grove, New Jersey. He may well have sent cards from those places to other individual as well. It is well known that Lovecraft also wrote letters to people while he was traveling, for we see many from the summer of 1934 with Barlow's address as his own temporary address. And it was during this period that Lovecraft and Barlow mailed their spoof "The Battle That Ended the Century," addressing and affixing postage to a bundle of letters (nearly forty) that were then remailed from Washington, D.C. The point is that, in a period of about four and a half months, Lovecraft must have mailed nearly four hundred items. Had he not been traveling, he may have written numerically fewer items, but one imagines that instead of postcards he likely would have been writing longer letters.

When R. H. Barlow had the sad duty of going to Providence in March 1937 to sort out Lovecraft's effects, having been designated literary executor in Lovecraft's "Instructions in Case of Decease," he composed a list of addresses of persons for August Derleth and Donald Wandrei to contact, presumably regarding acquisition of Lovecraft's letters for transcription for a future publishing project. Presumably, Barlow copied the addresses from documentation kept and used by Lovecraft (now lost—his "death diary"?), and presumably the persons named were all correspondents, ranging from occasional to regular. The list contains 90 names (plus two for whom Barlow did not have addresses). This lengthy list contains names of a few individuals who are not mentioned, or perhaps only very infrequently, in Lovecraft's correspondence. Letters to many of the individuals named have never been seen. Some correspondents, like W. Paul Cook, Samuel Loveman, and Sonia Lovecraft, destroyed their letters from Lovecraft. But Barlow's list also names many of the young fans who started writing Lovecraft after his travels in the summer of 1934.

Simply put, toward the end of his life, and even though he enjoyed writing and receiving letters, Lovecraft was close to becoming overburdened with correspondence. He would tell people from time to time, *in letters,* that he perhaps should cut back on his letter writing. He does not seem to have done so. And in the last six months of his life it seems that the letters he wrote, at least to certain people, were growing longer and longer.

One reason for all the letters was emergence of science fiction fandom in the mid-1930s. New fan publications sprang up faster than a person could count them. With the emergence of the *Fantasy Fan* in September 1933, Lovecraft became a hit among weird fiction fans. He gladly contributed short pieces, mostly unpublished, not only to it but also to the ever more abundant fan publications: *Fantasy Magazine, Phantagraph, Science-Fantasy Correspondent, Science Fiction Bard,* the *Planeteer, Supramundane Stories,* and others, including some that never got off the ground. Prospective publishers learned that Lovecraft was an easy touch for material (though he rarely wrote anything new to be published, instead drawing upon unpublished material or pieces not likely to have been widely seen previously). As Lovecraft slyly explained, "All the kids clamour for MSS., & I keep them quiet by exhuming callow effusions from old amateur papers."[1] Since they had to write him to ask for material, he needed to reply, and often, because of his unbusinesslike and chatty manner, correspondence developed with the young fans. Those who were not content to publish fanzines usually were prospective writers, and they brought not only the burden of letter writing but also of reading and evaluating their fledgling stories and poems. All this was encouraged by Lovecraft, for he invited any and all comers to let him see their writing, and of course each writer gladly obliged, giving no thought to the fact that Lovecraft was a very busy man and that each fan was not Lovecraft's only correspondent. In a sense, Lovecraft was the patron saint of early fandom, for he continually encouraged and boosted new talent; and if talent were deficient, he would ply pen to manuscript to help the writer along.

The three recipients of Lovecraft's letters gathered in this volume were all active in fandom at the time. F. Lee Baldwin and Duane W. Rimel both, oddly enough, lived in the same small town of Asotin, Washington (population 600). Lovecraft often lamented that in the metropolitan area of Provi-

---

1. HPL to Richard Ely Morse, 20 November 1936 (ALS, New York Public Library).

dence, there were nearly half a million residents, and if any shared his interest in weird fiction, he did not know them. And yet in tiny Asotin, there were two such individuals who actually knew each other, and who knew other like-minded fellows as well, as Rimel recounts in his "A Fan Looks Back." The third recipient, Nils Frome, lived still farther from Lovecraft, in Fraser Mills, British Columbia, but that mattered not. He still was an active fan.

Franklin Lee Baldwin was born in 1913. It is not certain how he came to write to Lovecraft. The *Fantasy Fan* made its debut in September 1933, and even though Lovecraft eventually was well represented over the short run of the magazine, the inaugural issue does not even mention him. Baldwin had been reading the pulp magazines of the day, beginning with *Argosy* around 1923 (when he was ten), *Weird Tales,* and *Amazing Stories,* where he first read Lovecraft's "The Colour out of Space" in 1926. Baldwin's first letter to Love-craft, dating also to September 1933, makes the bold proposal to reprint "The Colour out of Space" as a booklet—with Lovecraft's consent, of course. Lovecraft revised the tale slightly for the prospective publication, but the plan never materialized. Nevertheless, Baldwin soon became an active contributor to the *Fantasy Fan,* writing two columns of news notes: "Side Glances" (April, May, September 1934) and "Within the Circle" (June, July, August, October, November 1934; January, February 1935, with a brief resurgence in *Acolyte* for the summer 1943 issue). Much of the information Baldwin recorded, virtually verbatim at times, was from Lovecraft's letters to him, as was the significant early article, "H. P. Lovecraft: A Biographical Sketch," originally scheduled to appear in the *Fantasy Fan* but, following that magazine's demise, published in *Fantasy Magazine* (April 1935). (One notices a theme here—that fan publica-tions tended to be short-lived, and sometimes did not even survive gestation.) Lovecraft, who was something of a yenta at the time, passed along in his let-ters news on what everyone within his circle was up to, and so he was a good source for Baldwin's aptly named column.

Baldwin was not a prolific writer of fiction, although the Bibliography lists a few stories that he wrote. His interest in fandom soon waned following Lovecraft's death, only to be reawakened a few years later when he came to know Francis T. Laney. In his acerbic memoir of his days in science fiction fandom, Francis T. Laney has nothing but glowing praise for Baldwin:

> F. Lee Baldwin did not appear on the scene until December 1942 and made no more than three or four trips to visit me during 1943. Nevertheless, he was a major influence on *Acolyte,* and not just because he was my only "in-the-flesh" fan for nearly a year. He was indefatigable in seeking out new contacts for us, particularly among the professional authors, and was directly responsible for *Acolyte's* contacts with Derleth and the Wandreis. His enthu-siasm and candidly intelligent criticism were worth far more than his gener-ous encouraging. (xi)

In those days, Duane W. Rimel's admiration for Baldwin was equally profound, although Kenneth W. Faig, Jr. has pointed out that the two had "differences" later in life. Baldwin's own copies of Rimel's early professional stories, all signed to Baldwin and published in *To Yith and Beyond*, show true, warm appreciation for his support to Rimel over the years: "For my good friend, F. Lee Baldwin, a staunch believer" (36); "With best regards to my good friend . . . who encouraged me in my hour of need" (11); "Here it is, Lee; I hope you like it. Your kind words in the past have encouraged me no end" (25). His activity in fandom may have been slight, but it was profound.

Baldwin's letters from Lovecraft, presumably like his own to Lovecraft, tapered off over the years. Laney wrote: "When Lovecraft died the heartbroken Baldwin forsook fantasy altogether until *The Acolyte* dragged him back into fandom five and a half years later" (xi). He also observed that Baldwin was "a successful man from the mundane point of view, being foreman of the largest bakery in Central Idaho" (xii). Still, Baldwin retained great admiration for Lovecraft, and with the emergence of the *Acolyte* he published excerpts of one of Lovecraft's letters to him as "Lovecraft as an Illustrator."

Baldwin performed as a musician for his entire adult life. In her book on Baldwin, Josephine Richardson recounts how she and Baldwin had both performed on pianos one afternoon in August 1987, in Moscow, Idaho, and when Baldwin rose to stand following their performance, he collapsed and died—a musician to the end. Various anecdotes about Baldwin are gathered in *Within the Circle: In Memoriam F. Lee Baldwin* by Josephine Richardson and divers hands (Moshassuck Press, 1988).

Duane W[eldon] Rimel was born in 1915. He attended the same high school in Asotin as Baldwin did. The two were friends, and it was Baldwin who introduced Rimel to the weird fiction magazines and who mentioned that he was even corresponding with H. P. Lovecraft. As noted, Lovecraft was an easy touch. On 26 December 1934, merely two months after Baldwin first wrote Lovecraft, Rimel now approached the great author, asking Lovecraft to autograph his bound copy of the tearsheets of Lovecraft's "The Dunwich Horror."

In his letters Lovecraft wrote expansively to Rimel about numerous subjects, offering constant assistance in matters of literary technique. Lovecraft's letter to Rimel of 17 June 1934 includes a segment called "Notes on Writing a Story," one of several different versions of his own "Notes on Writing Weird Fiction" (1933). He read many of Rimel's early stories and revised some of them, including "The Tree on the Hill" and "The Disinterment," and perhaps also "The Jewels of Charlotte." Rimel sold his first story, a juvenile tale, to *Progressive Youth* in 1935, and also two stories to *Weird Tales*. He continued to publish many other stories in fanzines and semi-pro magazines. Lovecraft touched up his poem cycle "Dreams of Yith"; Clark Ashton Smith even lent a hand on one of the stanzas. Rimel's poem was clearly imitative in concept of Lovecraft's *Fungi from Yuggoth,* which he read in manuscript. Even Rimel's linoleum cut heading bore resemblance to that which Hugh Rankin created for appearances of Lovecraft's poem in *Weird Tales.* Ironically, Rimel's poem debuted in the *Fantasy Fan* before four of Lovecraft's sonnets that had inspired it.

Lovecraft wisely suggested that the two boys in Asotin share whatever he might send them. Instead of possibly having to write the same content twice for two letters going to two individuals who lived close by, Lovecraft urged them to read each other's letters. In his very first letter to Rimel, Lovecraft wrote: "If you would care to see more of my stuff, you have an excellent chance right now—since a large assortment of my old tales is at present in the hands of a fellow-townsman of yours—Mr. F. Lee Baldwin—as a loan. I will ask Mr. Baldwin to sub-lend the material to you if you like." It seems not to have occurred to Lovecraft that Rimel had written him precisely because he was friends with Baldwin.

In his so-called death diary, HPL mentions revising Rimel's "From the Sea" in January 1937. Possibly the story is unpublished or lost, but it may ultimately have appeared in print as "The City under the Sea." Rimel briefly spearheaded the Lovecraft fan movement in the 1940s, luring Francis T. Laney into fandom and coediting the *Acolyte* (1942–46), although the *Acolyte* was not by design a fanzine dedicated to Lovecraft and his work. Both Rimel and Baldwin were listed on the masthead as contributing editors. The magazine was first published in Clarkston, Washington (a scant 6 miles distant from Asotin) from Fall 1942 to Fall 1943. Rimel and Baldwin continued to contribute, even after Laney moved to Los Angeles and resumed publication of the *Acolyte* there. In the preface to *Howard Phillips Lovecraft—1890–1937: A Tentative Bibliography* (1943), Laney acknowledged the contributions of both Baldwin and Rimel to the undertaking.

Rimel was also a lifelong musician, but unlike Baldwin he pursued an active career as a writer. Once he learned that he could earn real money by writing, following the acceptance and publication of *The Curse of Cain* (1945), he became a writer of crime novels. In his aptly named "Brief Autobiography," written late in life for *To Yith and Beyond,* Rimel wrote somewhat modestly that he was "listed in *Who's Who in the West* and in *Contemporary Authors.* A former commissioner for the Asotin County Federal Housing Authority [1952–54], he was also active in the labor movement at Lewiston, Idaho for many years. He has published six mystery novels and a number of shorter fictional pieces. Some of his novels were printed in England and other foreign countries" (6). His obituary (he died in 1996) says he also worked in the circulation department of the Lewiston *Morning Tribune* and that he played piano in local dance bands for about forty years. He was briefly president of the Lewiston Chapter of the AFL-CIO musicians union. As for his writing career, the obituary tells a somewhat different story than Rimel himself related, stating that he "wrote 266 novels over a 45-year period" and that the "majority of his works were paperback fiction novels, under various pen names. Some of his mystery novels were printed in Europe." The editors include a lengthy listing of Rimel's novels in the Bibliography but have not even come close to identifying them all. Rimel wrote westerns and soft-core pornography under the pseudonyms Peter Biggs, Eric Leggett, Andre Lemir, and Rex Weldon. Much of his weird short fiction and poetry has now been reprinted in *The Forbidden Room, The Many Worlds of Duane Rimel, The Second Book of Rimel,* and *To Yith and Beyond.*

The fan movement was not limited to the United States. Nils Helmer Frome has been described as a pioneer fan in Canada, though as with many fan publishers, his publication was short-lived. Frome was born in Ratansbryn, Jamtland, Sweden in 1918. His adoptive family brought him to Canada when he was four and he lived there much of his life. He died in Llandudno, Caernarvonshire, Wales in 1962.

Lovecraft's earliest letter to Frome is from October 1935. His surviving letters are all fragmentary, and it is not known when Frome might have sought material from Lovecraft for publication, although Lovecraft mentions the prospective publication in letters from late 1936 and early 1937. Frome's fan publication had the lofty and esoteric name *Supramundane Stories*—perhaps trying to be even more astounding than *Astounding Stories*. He obtained material for it from Lovecraft, Rimel, and Clark Ashton Smith, among others.

It is clear from Lovecraft's replies to Frome that the latter had interest in weird fiction, but also (as did many of the fans of the day) such bogus concepts as telepathy, numerology, and phrenology. Lovecraft was polite, but firm, in his responses, but his true thoughts on the matter was evidenced in letters to others:

> If you want bold & nutty scientific concepts to work on, get in touch with the kid who is about to edit *Supramundane Stories*—Nils H. Frome, Box 3, Fraser Mills, B.C., Canada. Some of his vague & unformulated concepts would do credit to an Einstein or a de Sitter on the one hand, or to an asylum case on the other hand! I've been obliged to decline the honour of collaborating with this fertile young genius—but if you feel like dressing up some highly intricate concepts for *Astounding, Wonder,* or *Amazing,* he's your man! (*Letters to Robert Bloch and Others* 184–85)

Lovecraft's "Notes on Writing Weird Fiction" and "Nyarlathotep" appeared in the second issue of *Supramundane Stories* in Spring 1938, a year after Lovecraft had died. The first issue of Spring 1937 had nothing by Lovecraft. Lovecraft had also submitted "What the Moon Brings," but Frome did not publish it. Frome worked various jobs in logging camps, and ended up as a janitor in Wales, but art was probably his greatest talent.

The letters in this volume offer a narrow but valuable glimpse into Lovecraft's involvement in the burgeoning world of fantasy fandom and into his tremendous industry in letter writing. Some have complained that Lovecraft wasted his time writing so many letters, and yet he did what he enjoyed. It may well be that his generosity to and encouragement of the many youths who approached him as expressed in his work are a greater legacy than his composition of the stories that inspired those youths.

—DAVID E. SCHULTZ
S. T. JOSHI

A Note on the Text

All manuscript letters consulted are held at the John Hay Library. One letter to Duane W. Rimel and one letter to Nils Frome (as well as a few paragraphs from others) derive from the Arkham House transcripts, a set of which is held at John Hay Library.

Acknowledgments
The editors wish to acknowledge the assistance of John H. Stanley and Christopher Geissler of the John Hay Library, Scott Connors, Kenneth W. Faig, Jr., Donovan K. Loucks, Eileen McNamara, and Christopher O'Brien.

Abbreviations

CE	Lovecraft, *Collected Essays*
CF	Lovecraft, *Collected Fiction*
MW	Rimel, *The Many Worlds of Duane Rimel*
NHF	Moskowitz, *Howard Phillips Lovecraft and Nils Helmer Frome*
OFF	Lovecraft, *O Fortunate Floridian!*
SB	Rimel, *The Second Book of Rimel*
SL	Lovecraft, *Selected Letters*
TYB	Rimel, *To Yith and Beyond*
CC	*Crypt of Cthulhu*
FF	*Fantasy Fan*
WT	*Weird Tales*
CAS	Clark Ashton Smith
DWR	Duane W. Rimel
FLB	F. Lee Baldwin
HPL	H. P. Lovecraft
JHL	John Hay Library, Brown University (Providence, RI)
NF	Nils Frome
RHB	R. H. Barlow

Baldwin & Rinel

Letters to F. Lee Baldwin

[1]   [ALS]

[H. P. LOVECRAFT
66 COLLEGE STREET
PROVIDENCE R.I.]

Octr. 2, 1933

Dear Mr. Baldwin:—

It would certainly delight me to have "The Colour Out of Space" reprinted as a booklet, for I like it more than any other of my tales. Possibly you know that Edward J. O'Brien gave it a three-star rating in his "Best Short Stories of 1928."

If you decide to embark on this venture, I wish you would let me correct the copy you use, since the version in *Amazing Stories* is disconcertingly full of misprints. I would attend to the matter very quickly. As for the copyright—I don't think you would have to ask permission for reprinting, since (unless memory plays me false) I sold only the first N. American rights. Regarding the share of proceeds due the author—I really don't know what is customary, since I have never had a book published. Another of my tales ("The Shunned House") is about to be issued in this way, however—in which venture I believe I am to divide equally with the publisher. This, though, is a somewhat informal matter undertaken by an old friend; hence may not represent the prevailing commercial usage. If you can ascertain the customary figures, I shall be glad to abide by them.

With every good wish, & hoping that something may come of the venture, I am

Yrs most cordially & sincerely,
H P Lovecraft

[2]   [ALS]

66 College St.,
Providence, R.I.,
Octr. 16, 1933.

Dear Mr. Baldwin:—

Regarding the copyright on "The Colour Out of Space"—it is of course held by *Amazing Stories,* with my own rights of reprinting (in other than North American magazines) reserved in my arrangements with them. I imagine that the thing to say would be "Copyright, 1927, by *Amazing Stories* (or the name of the company—you might ask them about it, for the magazine has changed hands since that time); reprinted from A.S. Sept. 1927 by permission of the author." *Am. St.* is now issued, I believe, by the Teck Pub. Co., 350 Hudson St., N.Y. City. I'm sorry my information about the matter is not more definite & conclusive—but commercial details never were my specialty!

As to the remunerative plan—the $^1/_3$ of the net proceeds (if any) idea which you suggest is entirely satisfactory to me. I fancy 200 copies would form an edition sufficiently large—although I shall probably order quite a few copies to give away to friends if you can furnish them at a substantial discount under the regular 25¢ price (which seems very sensible).

Regarding the "Shunned House" booklet—it has had an almost amusing set of vicissitudes. Originally printed in 1928 by the Recluse Press of Athol, Mass. (W. Paul Cook), it suffered delay & was never bound—the loose sheets of an edition of some 250 copies laying about neglected after Cook's financial & nervous breakdown in 1930. This year *Walter J. Coates, North Montpelier, Vermont* (publisher of *Driftwind*—with whom Cook is now located) decided to salvage the edition—binding it cheaply in cardboard & trying to market it through the facilities of his Driftwind Press. He still has this intention, although I haven't the faintest notion when the thing will appear. You might ask him about it—he would possibly offer suggestions regarding the marketing of "The Colour Out of Space" (advertising it in *Driftwind*, &c.) Indeed—unless you are yourself a publisher or have a special printer in mind, you could probably get the edition issued by Coates more cheaply than by anybody else. Another good printer of booklets is Charles A. A. Parker, 114 Riverside Ave., Medford, Mass. "The Shunned House" is very well printed. I read proof myself, & there is not a single typographical error. There is a preface by Frank Belknap Long, Jr.[1]

I shall be very glad to see & correct the MS. of the "Colour". I'm afraid this isn't so much generosity as self-defence on my part, since I dread having my stuff misprinted. I'd like to read proofs if it can be arranged. When I don't exercise care, I sometimes find the most humiliating errors in the text of my printed products—for example, in my recent "Witch House" in W.T. there are absurd slips like "magical LOVE" for *magical LORE*, & "HUMAN element" for "KNOWN element."[2] I don't see how these blunders can creep in, but they do—& the printed text of the "Colour" in A.S. is very erroneous.

By the way—in view of your interest in weird material, I enclose a circular of the most remarkable bargain I have ever seen on the market . . . six magnificent tales by Clark Ashton Smith for a quarter.[3] These stories are all better than anything in W.T., & I can conscientiously recommend them to anyone taking a delight in the fantastic & the macabre. The brochure is rather plainly & carelessly printed—but the literary value excuses all that!

With every good wish, & hoping that nothing will interfere with the successful issuance of the "Colour", I remain

Yrs most cordially & sincerely,

H. P. Lovecraft

Notes

1. W. Paul Cook of the Recluse Press printed *The Shunned House* in 1928 but did not bind it. In 1933, Walter J. Coates of the Driftwind Press was going to bind it but never did so. R. H. Barlow acquired 115 copies in 1934 and 150 more in 1935 but bound only a few copies. Arkham House eventually bound and distributed the sheets in the 1960s. The manuscript for the story, sold at auction in 2006, has not been examined, but it appears that HPL is correct in that the printed version is free of typographical errors.
2. *WT,* July 1933; cf. *SL* 4.213–14.
3. *The Double Shadow and Other Fantasies* contains "The Voyage of King Euvoran," "The Maze of the Enchanter," "The Double Shadow," "A Night in Malnéant," "The Devotee of Evil," and "The Willow Landscape." All had been rejected by *WT.*

[3]   [ALS]

66 College St.,
Providence, R.I.,
Novr. 14, 1933.

Dear Mr. Baldwin:—

Glad to hear that the corrected MS. came back safely. It will be a pleasure to have this story printed *right* at last—for the slips in the magazine version have always annoyed me. When Edward J. O'Brien wrote that he was citing it on the Roll of Honour in his Best Short Stories of 1928, I was egotistical enough to send him a table of corrections, so that he might know what the text really was like. Thanks for the proofreading privilege. The more times proofs are read, the better. My "Shunned House" had *5* readings— two of which were by me—& is one of the few 100% perfect texts I know of.[1] No hurry, of course, about the booklet. As to the number of copies I want—I could really use as many as two dozen, for there are innumerable friends who have given me copies of their own books & who therefore merit complimentary copies in return. But unless the price is pretty low, I shall have to limit myself to a single dozen. I couldn't decently get by without giving copies to Smith, Wandrei, Long, & nine or ten others—though I might curtail on some doubtful cases. Years of literary dabbling do give one a tremendous number of fellow-scribbler acquaintances to whom the courtesies of exchange are due. I shall have to do the same thing with the "Shunned House", too, if I ever get it—for most of these acquaintances have given me more than one of their products.

Concerning my earlier tales—& those unpublished ones which you have not seen—here is a list of all the stories which I consider good enough to acknowledge. While I dare not lend any copies from my complete file of W T (the last time I did so the issues in question nearly fell to pieces. Old pulp magazines won't stand the hardships of transportation.), I'll be delighted to mail you cuttings or MSS. of the items in question. The only ones which I can't furnish at present are those marked with an asterisk.

X The Tomb	Herbert West—Reanimator*
X Dagon	Hypnos*
X Psychopompos (in rhyme)	— The Hound
— Polaris	— The Lurking Fear
X Beyond the Wall of Sleep	— The Rats in the walls
— The White Ship	X The Unnamable
— The Doom that Came to Sarnath	— The Festival
The Statement of Randolph Carter	The Shunned House
X The Terrible Old Man	X The Horror at Red Hook
~~The Tree~~	X He
— The Cats of Ulthar	— In the Vault
X The Temple	X Cool Air
Arthur Jermyn	— The Call of Cthulhu
— Celephaïs	X Pickman's Model
X From Beyond	— The Silver Key
X The Picture in the House	— The Strange High House in the Mist
X The Nameless City	The Dream-Quest of Unknown Kadath*
X The Quest of Iranon	The Case of Charles Dexter Ward*
X The Moon-Bog	— The Colour Out of Space
— The Other Gods	— The Dunwich Horror
— The Outsider	The Whisperer in Darkness
X The Music of Erich Zann	At the Mountains of Madness
— The Dreams in the Witch House	The Shadow over Innsmouth
	The Thing on the Doorstep.

There is also a tale collaborated with E. Hoffmann Price but practically mine—"Through the Gates of the Silver Key." Let me know any you'd like to see, & I'll gladly shoot them along. A few of these are about to appear in magazines—["]The Other Gods["] & others in the *Fantasy Fan*, & "Sarnath" & "Celephaïs" in *Unusual Stories*.[2] I enclose circulars of these new periodicals in case you don't know of them. The Price collaboration may possibly appear in W.T. Some of these items have been reprinted in anthologies. Of course, they are uneven in merit, & I am constantly striking stories off the list as not up to the proper standard. If you'd like, you could merely send a list of those you've not seen, & let me do the choosing according to merit.

With every good wish, & appreciation of your favourable opinion of my work, I remain

Yrs most sincerely,

H P Lovecraft

[Enclosed leaflet for the *Fantasy Fan*, on which HPL wrote:] Special offer—18 mo. for $1.00.

Notes

1. HPL maintained that John Ravenor Bullen's *White Fire* (Athol, MA: Recluse Press, 1927), which he edited, also was free of typographical errors.
2. It was in fact William L. Crawford's companion publication *Marvel Tales [of Science and Fantasy]* that printed "Celephaïs" and "The Doom That Came to Sarnath."

[4]   [ALS]

66 College St.,
Providence, R.I.,
Decr. 13, 1933

Dear Mr. Baldwin:—
                    Under separate cover, in two bundles (one of MSS. first class & one of printed matter 3d class), I am sending you a majority of the tales which you list as not having seen. Others will come later as I get hold of copies; though a few seem to be rather inaccessible. "The Dream-Quest of Unknown Kadath" & "The Case of Charles Dexter Ward" are long tales (with almost no sales likelihood) which I have never typed, & which could hardly be deciphered by anybody but myself. I detest the process of typing, & avoid it whenever I can. The ordeal of typing a long story is more than I am willing to face unless marketing chances are at least pretty fair. "Hypnos" is a rather dull tale, & I have no copy except in a magazine in too poor shape to send through the mail. "Herbert West—Reanimator" was a 6-part serial in a cheap little magazine in 1922. It didn't amount to much, but if I can find the file I'll let you see it. I also think I have a MS. of the first three instalments somewhere. "Polaris"—my only MS.—is in the hands of *The Fantasy Fan,* & will be printed before long. "Arthur Jermyn" is lent, but I'll send it when it gets back. "The Shadow Over Innsmouth" & "At the Mountains of Madness" are long tales—72 & 115 pages, respectively. I'll send them later. "The Thing on the Doorstep" is my latest effort.[1] The MS. is now circulating among friends, & I'll have your name added to the list. I hope these tales won't disappoint you—at least, that most of them won't. Some, I fear, are pretty poor; so that if any collection of my stuff were published, I'd exclude them. As it is, I've repudiated & destroyed a number of my efforts. Of my tales, I like best "The Colour Out of Space" & next-best "The Music of Erich Zann." Glad you liked "The Other Gods". This is an old piece—dating from the days when I imitated Dunsany. "Celephaïs" & "Sarnath" also belong to this class.
        As for the issuance of "The Shunned House"—I haven't the least idea about the details. The only one who can tell is the prospective publisher— Walter J. Coates, The Driftwind Press, North Montpelier, Vermont. He is rather hard-pressed financially, & of course always busy with his monthly magazine & book-publishing, but I think he still means to bind & issue my tale.

Cook spoke lately of having the loose sheets sent to him, & of the selection of a very tasteful grey cardboard for the binding. It will be odd to have this thing come out as a Driftwind item, yet with a title-page bearing the Recluse Press (Athol, Mass.) imprint of 1928. Possibly Coates might print a new title-page—though that would mean a lot of work, & some difficulty matching the paper. The text I am sending you is a rather poor galley-proof, but it's my only copy & is probably legible enough.

Glad to hear news of the "Colour" venture, & hope that no unexpected obstacles may develop. I hope that the price of 24 copies will be low enough to let me get that many, for I really ought to present about that number. Also—if I could afford it, I ought to have a few on hand for future presentations.

The first issue of *Unusual* will appear around Christmas. Its format will differ somewhat from that outlined in the circular—the need for economy prompting certain retrenchments. It will be printed on pulp paper & consist of 64 two-column pages, 6 × 9. The price will be *10¢* at the outset. The future depends on how #1 fares. If it goes well—& if arrangements for marketing can be made with the American News Co.—a better grade of paper & a price of 15¢ will be considered. I certainly hope the venture will succeed.

I also think the *Fantasy Fan* fills the proverbial long-felt want. As for the collection of the turbulent young "Effjay Akkamin"—I see no reason to doubt that it is as he represents it.[2] Such material is extremely easy to get, & of no real value owing to the insignificant status of the poor devils—like myself—who scribble for the pulp tripe-sheets. Another & less noisy youth who has a collection of this sort is R. H. Barlow of Florida—who lately acquired a printing press & is slowly getting out an extremely small edition of some of the letters of the late Henry S. Whitehead.[3] If you are in any way a Whitehead admirer you may want a copy of this item—which you could probably get by writing Barlow. His address is Box 88, De Land, Fla.

About the *Science Fiction Digest*—I have never seen a copy of it, hence can shed no light on the story "Cosmos" except to say that I am certainly *not* one of its authors.[4] Science fiction has never interested me as much as straight weird material, although several of the sciences (chemistry, physics, geography, anthropology, & especially astronomy) themselves have formed major interests of mine at various periods. In youth I used to contribute monthly articles on astronomical phenomena to the daily press.[5]

I trust you had a pleasant Thanksgiving. Mine was especially appropriate—for I spent it on the soil of ancient *Plymouth* (less than 40 miles from here), where the first one of all was celebrated some 312 years ago. The day was almost like summer—as high as 68° at 3 p.m.—& I found the old town & surrounding countryside extremely attractive. At present the weather shews a marked contrast—it being so cold that I cannot leave the house. My health does not allow me to be out in temperatures much under 20°—though in compensation, I thrive in the hottest kind of summer weather, 90° being my favourite heat. I may have to move south some day.

With best wishes, & trusting that both packages of tales may reach you safely, I remain

> Yrs most sincerely
> H P Lovecraft

[P.S.] A young friend of mine asks me to enclose these in my correspondence.[6] I can heartily recommend him as a good & conscientious printer if anyone is in need of stationery or similar material.

Notes

1. Written 21–24 August 1933. HPL refused to submit stories to *WT* after it had rejected *At the Mountains of Madness,* and so the story remained unpublished until January 1937.

2. Forrest J Ackerman, whose name HPL lampooned in "The Battle That Ended the Century" (May 1934) and "In the Walls of Eryx" (1936), boasted a large collection of science fiction ephemera, including autographs, manuscripts, and movie stills. He described his collection at length in six installments of "My Science Fiction Collection," *FF* (September 1933–February 1934).

3. RHB printed a few pages of *Caneviniana* but never completed it. In 1942, Paul Freehafer circulated *The Letters of Henry Whitehead* through the Fantasy Amateur Press Association.

4. *Cosmos* was a round-robin novel of seventeen chapters published in *Science Fiction Digest* (July 1933–December 1934/January 1935). The contributing authors were Earl Binder, Otto Binder, Arthur J. Burks, John W. Campbell, Jr., Lloyd Arthur Eshbach, Ralph Milne Farley, Francis Flagg, Abner J. Gelula, J. Harvey Haggard, Edmond Hamilton, David H. Keller, Otis Adelbert Kline, A. Merritt, P. Schuyler Miller, Raymond A. Palmer, Edward E. Smith, Bob Olsen, and E. Hoffmann Price.

5. HPL contributed 20 astronomical articles to the [Providence] *Tribune* (1906–08), 17 articles to the *Pawtuxet Valley Gleaner* (Phenix, RI) (1906; possibly more in 1907–08), and 53 articles to the [Providence] *Evening News* (1914–18).

6. A flyer for The Hampshire Press, 14 Hutchins St., W. Concord, NH.

[5]   [ALS]

> 66 College St.,
> Providence, R.I.,
> Jany. 10, 1934

Dear Mr. Baldwin:—

I have just returned from a fortnight's visit to Frank Belknap Long, Jr. (whose tales you doubtless know) in New York, & have found your two postals & the much-appreciated Christmas card.

Sorry the tales reached you in such bad shape. A few more trips by mail, I fear, will quite finish them unless I pack them in cotton! "The Shunned House" seems to be lost, since I certainly enclosed it (in the form of galley proofs) in the 3d class package. This is unfortunate, though I suppose it will be possible to get more loose sheets from Coates or Cook or whoever has the printed edition. Glad you liked some of the tales, & hope you find most of the rest equally acceptable.

By the way, as coincidence would have it, I have just heard from another person in your town (—Duane W. Rimel, Box 100, Asotin) who seems rather interested in my stuff, & who says he hasn't seen much of it. It occurs to me that you might sub-lend the tales you have to him. There is no hurry about their return, so that either you or he could send them along whenever you are both absolutely through with them.

My visit was very interesting, for besides Long I saw many others connected with the weird writing game—among them the tremendously gifted A. Merritt, whose "Moon-Pool" you doubtless remember. Others were Donald Wandrei, Wilfred B. Talman, T. Everett Harré (who edited the anthology "Beware After Dark"), & the two boys (Conrad Ruppert & Julius Schwartz) who publish the semi-amateur magazine *Fantasy* (formerly *Science Fiction Digest*). I also saw Wandrei's younger brother, who has a story in the current W T, & whose fantastic drawings shew a genius of astonishing maturity.[1] As usual, I enjoyed the museums & bookstalls—& a friend of mine[2] (the one who figured as "Harley Warren" in the dream which gave rise to my "Randolph Carter" story) quite overwhelmed me by presenting me with several things (notably an Egyptian *ushabti* & a Mayan stone idol) for my own modest collection.

With all good wishes, & again thanking you for the card,
  I remain
    Yrs most cordially & sincerely,
    H P. Lovecraft

Notes

1. "In the Triangle." Howard Wandrei also illustrated his brother Donald's collection of poetry *Dark Odyssey*.
2. Samuel Loveman.

[6] [ALS]

         66 College St.,
         Providence, R.I.,
         Jany. 13, 1934

Dear Mr. Baldwin:—
      Your of the 6th crossed my previous letter in the mails, so that by this time you know about my recent trip & about the loss of "The Shunned House" in the mails. I'm not worrying about the latter, since I can always worm loose copies out of Cook or Coates even if they never do anything with the edition as a whole. In the course of time I hope to be able to

let you see it—sorry you couldn't this trip.

As to the two novelettes in MS.—I'm greatly fearful that you could never decipher them in my much-corrected, interlined, & transposed script. I'm not sure that I could make 'em out myself after 7 years! Also—I have grave doubts about their quality. My standards of fiction have changed since 1926–7, & these things are my first attempts at *long* stories anyhow. Thus I'm not at all certain that I'd want them published in their present form. However, I'll get them out as soon as I have a spare moment, & see just what they look like. One of them might not be so bad after a little touching-up & toning-down. And if I think the MSS. are in any way legible, I'll send them along. "Herbert West" is pretty rotten—a connected *series* (not a continuous serial) with a lot of *repetition* at the start of each story in order to make it quasi-complete. Also—the tone is rather cheaply sensational in order to please the cheap editor for whom I wrote the series. I have the file of magazines (a lousy litter!) somewhere, & when I dig 'em up I'll let you see the thing. But it's pretty poor stuff. By the way—I am told that the collaborated "Through the Gates of the Silver Key" will appear in the July W.T. Don't expect too much of it—collaboration is a handicap which always prevents me from doing my best. I trust, incidentally, that you'll let your youthful fellow-townsman Duane W. Rimel see anything I may send; since he seems to be so anxious to do so.

Glad you like "Erich Zann"—which is not as much of a general favourite as I wish it were. It interests me to know that you are a musician—which reminds me that two of my "Fungi from Yuggoth" have been set to music by another specialist in that art farther south along your Pacific Coast—Harold S. Farnese of the Los Angeles Inst. of Mus. Education. If you'd care to see the scores[1] (which I, a rank non-musician, *have never seen*) you might make inquiries of Farnese—whose address is 4001 S. Harvard Blvd., Los Angeles, Cal. I'm also glad you like "Pickman's Model". That description of Boston's squalid & sinister North End was pretty realistic of the time at which the story was written—1926—although a vast number of the ancient houses are now torn down. The especial crooked lane mentioned was stripped of its buildings less than a year after I wrote the tale—I'll never forget how provoked I was when I tried to shew the locale to Donald Wandrei in 1927, during his first trip east. I hadn't been there myself since the preceding year, & had whetted Wandrei's expectations tremendously. Then, when we got to the scene, there was nothing left but a desert of gaping cellars & foundation stones laid open to the prosaic afternoon sun! However, we could still trace the cobblestoned line of the lane—which was called Foster St. The place is now built over with warehouses, factories, or something of the sort. As for "The Horror at Red Hook"—that is a bit too melodramatic to be good art, although the local colour is quite realistic. I lived only 2 years in New York—in Flatbush in 1924, & on Brooklyn Heights in 1925[2]—but came to know its geography & antiquities very thoroughly because of my intensive antiquarian explorations. I think I've mentioned that old-time architecture & antiquarianism in general form my principal hobby. "Cool Air" is set in a 14th St. house which I knew very well—my friend George Kirk having a bookshop on the ground floor.[3] Glad you liked this thing—which Wright rejected, & which never seems to have attracted much praise.

Yes—Barlow is setting up his "Caneviniana" by hand. I tell him that 35 copies is an absurdly small edition in view of the probable demand. If he has the type set up, he surely ought to strike off at least 50 copies—the extra trouble & expense of which would not be great.

As to obtaining a collection of MSS., pictures, signatures, &c. from the poor devils who write for the pulp magazines—the way to go about it is simply to ask each author for what you want. The reason it is easy is that the writers in question are all half-baked "small-timers" like myself—who feel tremendously flattered when anybody thinks their autographs, MSS., &c. are worth collecting. Most of us are so childishly vain that we fall all over ourselves in our eagerness to supply material! Of course, the MSS. &c. of *real authors* like Machen, Blackwood, Dunsany, James, &c. are another proposition entirely. These things *do* cost money, & are by no means easy to get. You'll notice that kid collectors like Ackerman & Barlow never have any items of that calibre. They merely pick up the wholly worthless reliques of the negligible small fry. Most of the pulp magazines sell the original drawings of the "art" work very cheaply—but I wouldn't give a nickel for any picture that ever appeared in any of the damned rags!

"The Turn of the Screw" is the *one* weird product of the eminent American author Henry James—who must not be confused with the living British author Montague Rhodes James. It is a very powerful & subtle piece of work—about the evil effect which the ghosts of a dead servant & governess wrought on the two sensitive & susceptible children. All readers may not like it equally, but no one can deny its power. It can, I think, be obtained for 95¢ in the Modern Library edition—or you could undoubtedly get it at any good-sized city public library. If it isn't available at Asotin I'd be delighted to lend you my copy with no hurry at all about return. Let me know if you'd like to see it. It has a trifle of James's well-known involvedness & preciosity, but not as much as some of his later work has. As you know, James had 3 distinct literary periods—which some wit has called those of James the First, James the Second, & the Old Pretender![4]

I am interested in your idea of personally printing my "Colour"—have you & your colleague a press, or are you planning (like Barlow) to enter the typographical field as newcomers? The rates of professionals are certainly tremendously high, & are likely to get worse & worse as time passes. That is where the boys who issue *Fantasy* & *The Fantasy Fan* are wise—young Conrad Ruppert does all the printing of both magazines himself.

As for magazine payment rates for weird stuff—the best that any of the pulp magazines give nowadays is about a cent a word. I received $140.00 for the "Witch House", which ran to some 32 pages of MS. Price & I will get exactly the same amount for our collaboration. Some other magazines pay much less—especially *Wonder Stories,* whose editor Gernsback is a veritable Shylock. Hugo the Rat (as Clark Ashton Smith & I affectionately call him) never pays at all except under pressure—in fact, one New York lawyer makes a specialty of Gernsback bad debt collection![5] It is really impossible to devise any equitable scale of material recompense for literature, painting, or other forms of aesthetics. Art is so utterly remote from commerce in motivation, psychology, methods, standards, & objects, that no fixed rapport is even conceivable. Payment for commercial fiction is never made on a basis of artistic merit, but is determined solely by the possible financial profit which the work in question can bring the magazine. Thus a miserable mess of sensational hash likely to attract a vast flock of cheap readers is considered more "valuable"—& paid more highly—than a carefully wrought & intrinsically splendid piece of literature which will appeal only to the minority of intelligent & cultivated readers. Under our present economic system there is no reason why this should not be so—since financial value depends altogether upon negotiability. The creation of art must thus be regarded as something absolutely distinct from commercial processes—something as distinct & non-negotiable as excellence of personal character (which is itself a form of art). The only legitimate motive of the aesthetic creator is a high-grade form of personal satisfaction—he must never expect to cash in on his talents, or at least, never expect to cash in in any way proportionate with his intrinsic merit. Of course, some first-rate artists *do* reap good financial rewards when they happen to please a large audience or to acquire in some way an imposing reputation. But this is all a matter of chance. There are more fine artists starving—or supported from other sources—than there are fine artists living on the proceeds of their real creative work. This is a natural condition which we have to accept. There is no reason why it should be otherwise, nor is anything to be done about it. We live in a blind & impersonal cosmos without any such values as "right" or "justice". These picturesque conceptions—& all the high-sounding "oughts" derived from them—are mere inventions & illusions of the gullible & egotistical human brain.

What you say of the weather & physiography of your locality interests me greatly, since my maternal grandfather—the late Whipple V. Phillips—spent a great deal of time in the same general region (in Idaho) in the 1890's. He was president of the Owyhee Land & Irrigation Co., which had for its object the damming of the Snake River & the irrigation of the surrounding farming & fruit-growing region. I was a small boy then; but his trips out there, & his descriptions of the country, interested me prodigiously. In his offices downtown he had all sorts of samples of Idaho minerals & produce, & his occasional letters postmarked "Boise City", "Mountain Home", & "Grand View" (the latter place named by him, & occupying land owned by the company) lent a sense of reality to these exotic specimens. There was considerable trouble about building the dam, & it was twice washed away by floods.[6] When my grandfather died in 1904 his estate was in considerable confusion, so that we were all left poor. His Idaho holdings were closed out—but I have always wondered what became of the Snake River project, & whether his enthusias- tic dreams for the future of the region were ever realised. Your climate seems to be free from the extremes of ours. During the cold spell of Christmas week the mercury was down to 9 below in New York, 11 below in Provi- dence, & 17 below in Boston. I have to keep indoors in such weather— though the N.Y. subway system enabled me to get about during my visit without much exposure to the arctic air.

Yes—I certainly have read—& own—Machen's "Black Seal", which is part of the novel "The Three Impostors". It's great stuff—I wish I could turn out something like it. If there's anything of Machen's you haven't read I'll be delighted to lend it to you—do you know "The White People", "The Great God Pan", "The Terror", & "The Hill of Dreams"? Recently I have heard of a *new* Machen item (though M. once said he had ceased to write weird stuff) called "The Green Round". I haven't seen it, but shall try to do so soon. If it is as good as the old-time Macheniana I shall purchase it—the Argus Bookshop of Chicago offer it for $1.50.

Rainy today, but I must get out for errands. Anything is better than *cold!*

With every good wish, & appreciation of your favourable verdicts on my tales, I remain

Yrs most cordially & sincerely,

H. P. Lovecraft

Notes

1. Farnese set the "The Elder Pharos" and "Mirage" from *Fungi from Yuggoth* (*WT*, February–March 1931) to music, but HPL neither heard nor saw the finished work. The sheet music is reproduced in *Fungi from Yuggoth* (2016), 259–64.

2. At 259 Parkside Avenue and 169 Clinton Street, respectively.

3. 317 West 14th Street, where Kirk was to open his Chelsea Book Shop. The bookshop instead opened at 365 W. 15th Street c. October 1925. Later it moved to 58 West 8th Street.

4. Philip Guedalla, *Supers and Supermen: Studies in Politics, History and Letters* (New York: Knopf, 1924), 45. Guedalla refers to two kings of England and the Stuart "pretender" James [III] (1688–1766). The Young Pretender, Charles [III] (1720–1788), "Bonnie Prince Charlie," was the son of the Old Pretender.

5. CAS had enlisted the services of Ione Weber to to secure $769 in back payments from *Wonder Stories*.

6. For further information, see Kenneth W. Faig, Jr., "Whipple V. Phillips and the Owyhee Land and Irrigation Company," *Owyhee Outpost* No. 19 (May 1988): 21–30; rpt *The Unknown Lovecraft* (New York: Hippocampus Press, 2009): 50–55. Concerning Grand View, see Lin- da L. Morton, "Grand View, the Early Years," *Owyhee Outpost* No. 19 (May 1988): 31–49.

[7]   [ALS]

66 College St.,
Providence, R.I.,
Jany. 31, 1934.

Dear Mr. Baldwin:—

The 3d. class matter duly arrived, & I sent it back almost at once to Rimel, from whom I had just received a letter. I am interested to hear that he is your colleague in the proposed publishing venture. He seems extremely bright & appreciative, & some verses he enclosed indicate that he possesses considerable talent in the field of weird expression. Glad you have let him have the MSS. Before long I hope to be sending my long MSS. for your joint perusal. Meanwhile I am sending under separate cover a parcel with three items—Machen's "Three Impostors" & "House of Souls" (the latter containing "White People" & "Great God Pan"), & my own "Shunned House" in the form of unbound sheets. Trust you'll let Rimel see these items if he wishes to. I learned the other day that Coates's plan for binding & distributing "The Shunned House" has fallen through—so that there will once more be an indefinite delay in the appearance of the thing. It is likely that a young fellow in Florida—R. H. Barlow—will later attempt the issuance of the brochure, binding a few copies at a time. I hope this tale will not disappoint you. To some it may seem rather heavy & excessively full of historical & antiquarian colour. Wright twice refused it for W.T.[1]

I was greatly interested in your account of your environment, & am sure that your home must be delightful despite the effects of that bygone flood. The great maple, the orchard, & the neighbouring creek must combine to form a restful & beautiful scene; & you are to be envied your freedom from the noise & bustle of the town. I have always been fond of the country, though I have never lived there. In my youth I was as used to rural as to urban scenes, since my early home was in a part of Providence not far—in those days—from the open fields & woods. Now most of that country is solidly built up with residential streets; although a small strip of it—the high wooded bluff along the Seekonk River & an adjacent series of ravines—has been preserved in its primitive state as a park reservation. Even today I get out to the country as often as I can. Almost every warm summer afternoon I take my work or reading in a bag & set out for the wooded river-bank or the fields & woods north of Providence—spending the time till dark in one or more favourite rustic spots. My present residence, however, is in the compact part of the town near the college—on the crest of the precipitous hill forming the oldest part of Providence. I like this location very much, since (as I think I told you) ancient houses & colonial street vistas form almost my leading hobby. My greatest delight is in travelling to other old towns (& I've seen most of them, from Quebec to Key West & New Orleans) & observing the different varieties of old-time architecture. In my neighbourhood many of the streets are not greatly changed since the Revolution—there are churches built in 1775 & 1816, college edifices of 1770 & 1820, private houses going back as far as 1742, a schoolhouse of 1769, a market house of 1773, a court & colony house of 1761,[2] & so on. The extreme steepness of the hill has kept off business invasion, & here & there are little bits of almost rustic or village scenery which the city has overtaken & passed beyond without greatly disturbing. The house I live in was built about 1800,[3] & has all the earmarks of old colonial architecture—classic carved doorway, small-paned windows, six-panel doors, wide floor-boards, Georgian mantels, primitive latches, &c. It is situated at the back of a quaint grassy court off College St., just behind the John Hay Library of Brown University. There are old-fashioned gardens on the south & west, & the vista of old-time roofs & steeples & sunset hills from the west windows is exquisite. My aunt[4] & I occupy the upper half of the house—2nd floor & attic—while a school-teacher[5] lives in the lower half—1st floor & basement. I have, as my own personal domain, a large library & small adjoining bedroom on the southern side of the building. The library—where I work—is on the southwest corner, & my desk is at a west window with a splendid view. Around me are the old books & pictures & furniture that I have known all my life, & without which I should scarcely know what to do. I am very much devoted to familiar scenes & objects—this being the reason I have not long ago moved South. Enclosed is a picture of my residence—which you might return at your leisure. The window over the doorway is that of my bedroom, while the two windows on the left are those of my library. The marble wall in the foreground is that of the college library. I wish I could shew you around Providence some time—as a resident of a *new* country, you would find these old houses & marks of almost 300 years of continuous life rather fascinating. (Though perhaps you are familiar with such things through travel.) However, there are other New England towns where older houses exist. Our oldest is 1735, though just across the line in Pawtucket is an old tavern whose original parts may go back to 1640. We have no peaked gabled houses like the "Witch House" of my story, though Salem, Mass. (on which my "Arkham" is based) has many. The oldest house in New England is in Dedham,[6] ¾ of the distance from Providence to Boston. Except for the Spanish houses in St. Augustine, Fla. & Santa Fe, N.M., this is also the oldest private home in the United States, having been built in 1636. The oldest non-Spanish building of any kind in the country is St. Luke's Church in the Isle of Wight Co., Virginia, built in 1632. I have never been to the Old World, hence the oldest structures I have ever seen are those of St. Augustine, Fla. Here some of the houses—built of coquina-stone & wood— go back to 1571 or thereabouts, so that they were fairly well aged when the Pilgrims first set foot on Plymouth Rock in 1620. The St. Augustine P.O. is housed in the old Spanish Governor's palace, built in 1596. But I wish I could see England & the rest of Europe—with mediaeval houses & even the ruins of classical antiquity! Ancient Rome is another hobby of mine.

"Through the Gates of the Silver Key" is a sequel to my old "Silver Key"—although I repeat enough of the former story to make it complete in itself. In several other tales I refer to Randolph Carter, & in one of the long unpublished MSS. ("The Dream-Quest of Unknown Kadath") he is the central figure.[7] As to the manner of collaboration—Price wrote a rough draught of what he thought would be a good sequel & sent it to me.[8] I changed everything to suit myself, added an opening section, appended a whole second half involving interplanetary adventure, & finally put the whole story into my own words. Of Price's share there is now left only the general situation, a few descriptive touches in the central part, & a mathematical theory of time which he was anxious to insert. He wants to have his name omitted as co-author,[9] but I am insisting on its retention, since the tale is not of the sort I would have written without him. But this is the last collaborative job I shall ever attempt.[10] The process is merely a hindrance when one has something of one's own to express. Yes—the "Colour" was my only contribution to *Amazing*. Never contributed to *Wonder* or *Astounding*. These "scientifiction" magazines are often dull, though they have occasional high spots like Smith's work. A. Merritt's latest published work is "Burn, Witch, Burn". He is now working on a sequel whose scene will be the fabulous city of Ys, supposed to have sunk off the coast of Brittany in ancient times.[11] Merritt is in some respects absolutely unique—nobody else can lend such an air of subtly unholy & horrible suggestion to a description of a region. I think I told you that I met Merritt in person for the first time this month. He is a delightful chap; about 45 or 50, stout, sandy, & grey-eyed, & extremely affable, intelligent, & well-read. Besides being an original author, he is associate editor of Hearst's flamboyant Sunday supplement—the so-called "American Weekly." Hope you can get a copy of the Yuggoth music from Farnese. He is composing a sort of music drama in which he may use some of the characters of my artificial mythology—Yog-Sothoth, Azathoth, &c.[12] About "Cool Air"—it was published in 1927 in the short-lived Philadelphia magazine called *Tales of Magic & Mystery*, after having been rejected by Wright. "He" was based on the old Greenwich-Village section of New York City—whose quaintness is now passing almost as rapidly as that of Boston's North End. Like "Red Hook", it expresses something of my detestation of the metropolis. I was in N.Y. in 1924 & 1925, & came to hate it like poison. The cursed rows of unbroken brick & stone without a glimpse of green got my nerves, & I used to take my work in a bag & flee to the nearest suburbs where something like the old Providence atmosphere could be found. Oddly enough, one of my favourite refuges was the present home of *The Fantasy Fan*—Elizabeth, N.J., a delightful old town with wooden colonial houses & plenty of greenery. "He" was written on a bench in Scott Park, Elizabeth—near an old house which in later years was tenanted by Editor Hornig. In those days Hornig & I didn't know that each other existed! Possibly I passed him a dozen times without knowing it.

As to the way I think of—& compose—stories, there is no one general rule. The ideas come from almost anywhere—a dream, a picture, a landscape, a street vista, a newspaper paragraph, another story, a stray thought or impression—& my ways of developing them are just as varied. Sometimes an idea suggests a complete story before I know it, in which case I can set right down & reel the thing off in a single day, but this is not very frequent. Usually I reflect on an idea for several days, letting associative incidents develop in my imagination, & selecting the most effective ones. Then I begin constructing tentative synopses till I hit on one that seems to hold together well & have some degree of dramatic power. When I get that I start writing—& the length of time I take depends on the difficulty of the theme & the length of the text. For a short story of average length, 3 days is perhaps the most common period spent in the actual writing. I revise my stuff very rigorously, & make frequent changes while composing. Often when I'm half through a story a new idea will occur to me, so that I'll pause & change important features—perhaps adding a whole new introduction or extending the action far beyond the limits originally planned. The "Whisperer" took about a fortnight[13]—the "Witch House" somewhat less than a week. As to the value of my stuff—I wish it were as great as you so charitably assume! In reality, however, one must relinquish such pleasant illusions. Of all the W.T. contributors, only a few are likely to break into real literature. Derleth will—though not through his weird work. Smith may. Wandrei & Long very possibly may. Howard has a chance—though he'd do better with traditional Texas material. Price *could,* but I don't think he will because commercial writing is "getting" him. Whitehead was on the way—but death got him too soon. As for me—I doubt if I'll ever get much of anywhere. The verse in W.T. is almost all bad or mediocre—Smith's & Wandrei's & Long's, & occasionally Howard's, being about the only specimens worth reading.

Hope you can get "The Turn of the Screw" locally—if not, I'll be glad to lend it. Look in libraries for the volume called "The Two Magics"—in which the "Turn" is the first story. Yes—this is the James who wrote "Portrait of A Lady". Don't get him mixed with the living weird writer Montague Rhodes James—who is Provost of Eton College & an antiquarian (expert on mediaeval Latin MSS. & cathedral architecture) of note. Machen is one of the high spots of fantastic literature. "The Hill of Dreams" has a good deal of the autobiographical, though it does not literally represent the author by any means. It is perhaps the most exquisite record of literary struggles in existence—& the imaginative parts (the Gwent countryside—the Roman dream-life—the London streets) are of marvellous potency. Lucian is a perfect type of the hypersensitive literary temperament—& I can profoundly sympathise with his always baffled efforts to get on paper just what he wanted to express. "The Black Seal" is part of "The Three Impostors"—the rest of which you can now read. "The White People" & "The Great God Pan" are in "The House of Souls." Later I'll send you "The Terror"—as printed under a slightly expanded title in the *Century* in 1917. I am told that Machen—despite a former resolution to write no more weird stuff—has a new book out . . . . "The Green Round." I must certainly investigate the matter.

Your plans for the issuance of the "Colour" sound very interesting & promising—& I'm sure that the result will be adequate despite your inexperience with typography. As time goes on, you may outdo W. Paul Cook's performances in the field of private publishing. 3 × 5 is amply large enough for a small book page—indeed, in printing a very short item separately it is often better to have a thick booklet with many small pages than a large-paged & painfully thin pamphlet. You can see how much better the format of "The Shunned House" is, than that of Smith's "Double Shadow." Linoleum cuts will be a great asset—& judging from one that I saw, Rimel's are exceedingly neat & clever.

Thanks immensely for the Idaho views, & for the verbal sidelights on a region my grandfather knew so well. So the old dam wasn't finished till two years ago! The last I knew of the project was in 1904—the year of my grandfather's death. The dam was then washed away, & no one knew when it could be replaced. So much of the enterprise depended on my grandfather personally, that the Owyhee Co. eventually went out of existence—at least, as a Rhode Island institution—without attempting to rebuild. Probably the thing was ultimately carried through by a whole new generation of men. The engineer of the original project—in my grandfather's time—was a Mr. Wylie.[14] My uncle Edwin E. Phillips—who died in 1918—was also in the company, & made several trips to Idaho. The beginning of my grandfather's business interest in Idaho was about 1887, & in 1888 he organised (together with his nephew Jeremiah W. Phillips & a group of other Providence men) the Snake River Co., which dealt in land & cattle. Very soon, however, he saw that *irrigation* was the big thing—hence in Oct. 1889 the company was reorganised & reincorporated as a Maine corporation (heaven knows why—the offices & officials were all in Providence!) under the name Owyhee Land & Irrigation Co. My grandfather was General Manager as well as President. It was a tremendous responsibility, & the two successive burstings of the dam virtually wiped the Phillips family out financially & hastened my grandfather's death— at 70, of apoplexy. But he had a great idea of the future of the Snake River Valley under irrigation, & I always take pleasure in learning of the gradual justification of his hopes. In a way, I think he was rather ahead of his time. He thought of agriculture, fruit-raising, land development, irrigation, &c. on a large scale not very common in the 1890's—& yet nowadays similar projects of the vastest magnitude are springing into existence all over the West. I have some of the records of the Owyhee Co. as a sort of family relic—including the minutes of the meeting at which it was incorporated. The Secretary—my grandfather's old friend Clarke H. Johnson of Foster, R.I. (where the Phillipses came from)—later became Chief Justice of the R.I. Supreme Court.[15] Regarding the Idaho Phillipses—they cannot be relatives of ours except in an infinitely distant way, since my grandfather & uncle never *lived* in the west. They were sometimes in Idaho for weeks at a time, but always continued to reside in Providence. The most westerly point at which our family has relatives of any recognisable degree of closeness is *Delavan, Illinois,* where two of my grandfather's uncles, James & Benoni Phillips, settled in the 1820's.

Your column in the F F[16] will probably excite considerable interest, & I trust you may have no difficulty in filling it. Yes—mention the musical setting of the verses & the coming S.K. sequel if you like. The two sonnets set to music are "Mirage" & "The Elder Pharos"—both in the W.T. issue for Feb–March, 1931. As for Ackerman—I fancy he's about 16, & that he attends high-school. Robert E. Howard's occupation is fiction-writing, though he helps his father (a physician) attend to a small farm on the outskirts of Cross Plains, Texas. He is 27 years old, & has led a somewhat roving & adventurous life. Is an amateur athlete & boxer. Fond of fighting, & believes barbarism to be preferable to civilisation. Is a profound historic student, & an authority on the folklore & traditions of the Southwest. Long has studied at N.Y. University & Columbia College. Writing is his sole occupation. His father is a dentist, & he lives with his parents. He is 31. What other writers would you like to know about? I'm in touch with Smith, Price, Wandrei, Derleth, Talman, & a few others. Price has just left New Orleans, & is staying a while at Pawhuska, Okla. He intends to return eventually to his native California. He is 35, a World War veteran, a West-Pointer, & a former cavalry officer. Also superintendent of an acetylene gas machinery plant till about 2 years ago. Now subsists wholly by fiction-writing. Expert Orientalist—connoisseur of Persian rugs—knows Arabic—skilled fencing-master—mathematician. Derleth is 24—U. of Wis. graduate. Lives Sauk City, Wis. Rapidly gaining fame in magazines of select quality with serious reminiscent regional fiction & poetry. His first book will be out next month—I enclose a circular about it.[17] Smith is 40, & a weird poet since boyhood. Protege of late George Sterling. Also fantastic painter of great power. Has translated Baudelaire. Wandrei is 25—U. of Minn. graduate. Sole occupation, fiction. Comes from St. Paul, but now lives in N.Y. His younger brother Howard, who has a story in the Jan. W T, is a weird artist of vast power who will be heard from later. Would you care to see pictures of any of "the boys"? I have quite an assortment of snapshots.

About 2nd hand bookstores—try Dauber & Pine, 66 5th Ave., N.Y. City; Schulte's Bookstore, 4th Ave., N.Y. City; Argus Bookshop, 333 S. Dearborn St., Chicago; Goodspeed's Bookshop, Ashburton Place, Boston, Mass.; J. A. Tyson, Caesar Misch Bldg., Providence; Leary's Bookshop, 9th St., Philadelphia. I'll quote some other names when I think of them.

Well—I hope the books will reach you safely & that you'll enjoy them. No hurry about returning them. Providence is just pulling out of a cold spell—it was down to zero Monday, & I haven't been out of the house for three days.

All good wishes—

Yours most sincerely—

H P Lovecraft

Notes

1. Wright rejected the story in September 1925. There is no record of a second rejection by Wright; HPL may have been thinking of its rejection by Edwin Baird of *Detective Tales*. Only following HPL's death in March 1937 did Wright deign to publish the story.

2. The First Baptist Church (1775) at 75 North Main Street; the First Unitarian Church (1816), 301 Benefit Street; the "college edifices" are University Hall (1770) and Manning Chapel (1820) of Brown University; the Stephen Hopkins House (1743; original cottage built 1707 by John Field), 15 Hopkins Street, formerly stood at the foot of Hopkins Street on South Main Street, moved halfway up the hill in 1804; the Old Brick Schoolhouse (1769), now 24 Meeting Street; the Market House (1773) at 1 South Water Street; the Old State House (Colony House) at 150 Benefit Street (1762).

3. The Samuel Mumford House at 66 College St. (now 65 Prospect St.) actually dates to c. 1825.

4. Annie E. P. Gamwell.

5. Alice Sheppard.

6. The Fairbanks House; cf. HPL's "An Account of a Trip to the Antient Fairbanks House . . ."

7. Randolph Carter also figures in "The Statement of Randolph Carter" (1919), and "The Unnamable" (1923), and is cited in passing in *The Case of Charles Dexter Ward* (1927).

8. E. Hoffmann Price, "The Lord of Illusion," *Crypt of Cthulhu* No. 10 (1982): 47–56.

9. Price felt that only about fifty words of his remained in the story.

10. HPL also collaborated with Kenneth J. Sterling on "In the Walls of Eryx" (1936).

11. *Creep, Shadow!* is the sequel to *Burn, Witch, Burn!*

12. HPL refers to Farnese's proposal c. October 1932 to collaborate with him on a musical drama in one act set on Yuggoth to have been called *Fen River*. HPL declined, and the project was never completed (or, probably, even begun).

13. Actually, HPL began "The Whisperer in Darkness" on 24 February 1930, "provisionally finished" it on 7 May, then extensively revised it and completed on 26 September.

14. The project engineer was A. J. Wiley.

15. Clarke Howard Johnson, whom HPL called his grandfather's best friend and executor of his grandfather's will.

16. Initially "Side Glances" but eventually "Within the Circle." See Appendix.

17. *Murder Stalks the Wakely Family.*

[8]   [ALS]

66 College St.,
Providence, R.I.,
Feby. 13, 1934

Dear Mr. Baldwin:—

Very glad to hear that both my letter & the bundle of books arrived safely. Take your time about the latter, & let Rimel read them if he cares to. Glad you like the "Fungi from Yuggoth"—which are somewhat uneven, though one or two aren't bad. Yes—I think your partner's verses shew a very good grip on the weird, & I don't doubt but that both they & his fiction will develop with practice. I hope to read some of his tales later on. Sorry his "Ladder" came back from W.T.[1]—but that must be expected at first, & to some extent always. My "Shunned House" was rejected not merely once, but twice by the fastidious Mr. Wright. You'll like Machen, I'm sure. In "The House of Souls" the artistically best story is "The White People", while the most dramatically hideous is "The Great God Pan". The short tale at the end of "The Three Impostors"—"The Red Hand" has always seemed especially effective to me.[2] I'm anxious to see the new Machen book—"The Green Round"—but am too broke to buy it at present. Derleth has it, & Smith is ordering it—I'll probably borrow it from the latter. By the way— don't bother to send postage for the various items I forward . . . . I'm no Important Dignitary like the great Effjay Akkamin! His insistence on two-way postage from those he condescends to accept as correspondents is pretty damn good! Now I know why he didn't reply to the second sarcastic letter I wrote him a couple of years ago . . . I didn't send postage!

Glad the picture of #66 proved interesting. No hurry at all about return— let Rimel see it . . . . which goes also for all the snapshots in this letter. I shall be very glad to see some views of your place—which I know must be delightful. I'd like to see the Northwest some time—not only Idaho but the coast. When I was a small boy I read the juvenile novel "Rick Dale", by Kirk Munroe (a boys' author almost forgotten now), & some of the most interesting parts dealt with Seattle & Puget Sound—then hardly past the boom or late-pioneering stage. The region seemed very fascinating to me, & I longed to visit it. Seattle was also mentioned very often in Munroe's Alaskan stories—"The Fur Seal's Tooth" & "Snow Shoes & Sledges." Alaska also captivated my imagination— all the more so because my constitution could never endure cold (I can't go out when it's under +20°). The idea of people actually keeping alive in the arctic region of the Yukon seemed so strange to me that the whole subject of Alaska took on the overtones of mystery & glamour in my mind. I hope you'll be able to get in on some of the exotic expeditions which beckon you. If I were more used to roughing it I'd like to participate in some archaeological venture in Africa, Central America, or the Amazon Valley. I am especially fitted for the tropics, since I don't know what it is to feel too warm. The hotter it is, the more energy & vitality & alertness I seem to have—though I have never encountered any temperature much over 100°. About 90° is my choice for an outdoor temperature. Aside from adventurous expeditions—I hope you'll be able to make that eastern trip in the summer or autumn. You will certainly find much to fascinate you—museums, libraries, & visible surviving relics of all the historic scenes & events which books have made familiar to you. Providence has some world-famous collections, largely connected with Brown University. Two of these—the collection of Lincolniana & the Harris Collection of Am. Poetry—are housed in the John Hay Library next door to me. Not far off is the world's greatest collection of Americana & American books prior to 1800—at the John Carter Brown Library—& a little to the south is the Annmary Brown Memorial Library with America's greatest collection of incunabula.[3] And of course the houses of Old Providence—as of other ancient towns—are worth a study in themselves. Yes—Rimel told me of that rock with Indian or pre-Indian carving, & I'm immensely curious about it. I shall welcome any snapshots you may take. We have similar carved rocks in R.I. & Mass., though their inscriptions usually turn out to be the work either of Indians or of early colonists. There is still a great deal of mystery about the prehistoric period in America. Up to a very recent time it was assumed that no human beings preceded the Mongoloid "Indian" races who came from Asia over Behring Strait; yet within the last 2 years at least one immensely ancient & primitive skull has been dug up. It is still doubtful, though, whether the Indians had any *immediate* predecessors. Even if there were primitive men, they apparently did not survive long enough to leave many traces. All the human reliques which have been discovered seem to be connected with peoples whose skulls ally them with the Indians. However, there were many different divisions among the Indians, so that one group might well be unable to identify the carving or picture-writing of another group.

About "The Moon Pool"—there *is* a sequel to the *original novelette* as published in the *All Story* for June 7, 1918; but this sequel (first printed as a serial in the A-S & entitled "The Conquest of the Moon-Pool") is *included* in the later book version of "The Moon Pool" . . . . which in turn was reprinted in *Amazing Stories*. There is *not* any sequel to the whole *Amazing Stories* & book version of the novel.

I am indeed glad to hear that you like "The Shunned House." I had an actual house in mind when writing the tale a decade ago—a place which *looks* spectral & sinister, although there is really nothing bizarre or unpleasant connected with its history.[4] It belongs to friends of ours, & has never been out of the family since its construction in 1763. The 10 years since the writing of the story have not changed it in the least—I'll shew it to you if ever you get around this way. Benefit St. is only half a block down the hill from this place—though the Shunned House is considerably north of College St. The geographical & historical background of the story is true to fact—only the characters & events being fictitious. Poe was often in Providence, & many anecdotes about him have been handed down in local households. Benefit St., despite a qualitative deterioration, still looks much as it did in his day (1848). The Golden Ball or Mansion House is a rooming establishment, & I get my clothes pressed at the tailor's shop in one corner of it. The 1761 Colony House is wholly unchanged—as are the 1769 school, Shakespeare's Head, & the Quaker Meeting House with its carriage sheds nearby. St. John's hidden churchyard is an ineffably fascinating spot—quite ghoulish at night.[5] But then—everything about the old hill section is fascinating. Providence is a curious old place—keeping many of the outward aspects of a small town even though it is the centre of a compact population (262,000 within city limits, & other large towns on all its borders) of about 500,000. In the midst of the thickest parts there are odd little backwaters—bits of old garden, farmyard, & country lane or village street—which have not changed at all since very old days. I now live in such a spot—to see the grassy court & gardens around this house one could hardly imagine that a busy metropolis stretches away on every side!

Glad things look well for the "Colour" . . . . . 6 × 4 seems like an excellent size to me. For a short tale, small pages & many of them are best. "The Shunned House" will be very pleasing in appearance if Barlow ever binds & issues it. Your "sort of a secret" sounds interesting—& I hope a successful outcome of the venture will enable you to reveal it. "Caneviniana" progresses slowly but surely—acute eye trouble prevents Barlow from working too continuously at literary or typographical projects.

Many thanks for the Idaho views, which I return herewith. That bridge is very extraordinary looking, while the mountain highways are genuinely impressive. I notice that the vehicle shewn is horse-drawn. The Boise City stationery also interested me. To think of a modern building like the Hotel Boise in the town my grandfather knew so well!

Glad the notes on W T writers proved of interest. Why not drop a direct line to those who sound interesting? It ought it help your column. Here are some addresses: (you know Smith's)

> Robert E. Howard, Lock Box 313, Cross Plains, Texas.
> Frank B. Long, Jr., 230 W. 97th St., New York, N.Y.
> Seabury Quinn, 34 Jefferson Ave., Brooklyn, N.Y.
> E. Hoffmann Price (temporary), Pawhuska, Okla.
> August W. Derleth, Sauk City, Wisconsin
> Donald Wandrei, 84 Horatio St., New York, N.Y.
> Wilfred B. Talman, Scotland Post Road, Spring Valley, N.Y.
> Hugh B. Cave, 94 Montgomery St., Pawtucket, R.I.
> Francis Flagg, Fort Huachuca, Arizona.
> H. Warner Munn, Route 1, Athol, Mass.

Concerning Quinn—I think he comes from Kentucky.[6] A trace of Southern accent still remains in his speech. He is a little over 45, dark, good looking, & rather stocky, with a small moustache. Very intelligent, pleasant, & well-read. He is married & has at least one child. He started out in life as a lawyer—writing being merely an avocation. He now edits an undertaker's trade paper—a job he obtained through a curious series of steps. Long ago (when he was in Washington D.C.) somebody sued the paper for some reason or other, & Quinn was the attorney pressing the suit. His side lost, but the editor & publisher were so much impressed with his skill & brains that they looked him up afterward & hired him to conduct a column on the legal aspects of the undertaking profession. After a time his literary & editorial aptitude became so marked that he was given more & more work outside his nominal province—& finally he was made assistant editor . . . . a full-time job which caused him to move to New York & give up his legal practice. Still later he succeeded to the editorship. The magazine (formed by the consolidation of two predecessors) has the rather queer title of *The Casket & Sunnyside*. Quinn's earlier tales were written slowly, carefully, & artistically, & are infinitely superior to anything he writes now. "The Phantom Farmhouse",[7] in an early W T, is his undoubted masterpiece. It was in 1925 that he hit on this glib de Grandin stuff—the first of the series being called "The Horror on the Links."[8] He now grinds them out endlessly for the money he can get—making no pretence of artistic purpose. His work, however, is never slipshod—the form is always polished, & a great deal of real scholarship in the field of obscure superstitions is apparent. He has had work in other magazines—detective & adventure tales—but W.T. remains his principal medium. The walls of his study are covered with the cover designs accorded his stories. Despite his extensive amateur knowledge of medical matters, Quinn has never studied medicine or anatomy. Nor, despite the many French phrases in his de Grandin tales, does he know French.

As for myself—I was born on August 20, 1890, about a mile east of where I live now.[9] My home was then near the edge of the thickly-built district, so that my childish memories cling round rural scenes—fields, woods, farms, brooks, ravines, & the broad Seekonk River with its high wooded banks—as much as they do around urban scenes. The houses in that part of town were only about 30 years old or less, but I used to be fascinated by the ancient houses in the hill section where I now live. *Old* things always impressed me—& when I discovered the very ancient books of the family library in a dark attic room, I read them more than any others. That is how I came to be so familiar with the different sorts of old-fashioned typography. Everything mysterious & fantastic also impressed me—I loved to hear fairy-tales & ghost & witch stories—which latter my grandfather used to tell me. When I began to read at the age of 4, Grimm's Fairy Tales & the Arabian Nights were among the first things I seized on. Later I came across simple books about Greek & Roman mythology, & was still more fascinated by them. When I was 8 I began to take an interest in science—first chemistry (I had a small laboratory in the cellar) & later geography, astronomy, & other subjects—but my liking for myths & mystery never decreased. I first tried writing at 6, & the earliest story I can remember was written at 7—something about a cave of robbers called "The Noble Eavesdropper." At 8 I wrote many crude tales (frightfully crude!), two of which—"The Mysterious Ship" & "The Secret of the Grave" I still have. I also wrote reams of verse, the rules for which I learned from an old book published in 1797.[10] My style in both prose & verse was very old-fashioned, for I always felt a strange kinship with the 18th century—the age of the old books & the old houses I loved. I also felt a strong affinity for ancient Rome. All this time I had a very free hand in choosing my pursuits, since ill health kept me from school much of the time. I had many nervous breakdowns, & in the end was unable to attend college— indeed, my health was never any good till I was 30 years old. I was about 8 or 9 when I first got hold of Poe & adopted him as a model. Virtually all my tales were weird—for nothing has ever fascinated me half so much as the mystery of time & space & the unknown . . . . though I have not believed in religion or any form of the supernatural since I was 8. Remote & inaccessible places like the *antarctic* & other worlds enthralled my imagination. Astronomy in particular attracted me—I had (& still have) a good small telescope, & when 13 began to edit & publish a little astronomical magazine—*The R.I. Journal of Astronomy* on a hectograph. When I was 16, & in high school, I broke into print for the first time—with a monthly article on astronomical phenomena in a newly-founded local daily, & with other astronomical articles in the rural press.[11] At 18 I became dissatisfied with all my fiction, & de- stroyed most of the tales I had written. About that time I turned exclusively to verse, essays, & criticism, & did not write another tale for 9 years. My health was so poor that I led a very inactive life—travelling not at all, & being quite a hermit . . . . . though I always managed to get out to the country (mostly on a bicycle) on fine summer afternoons. In 1914 I joined one of the nation-wide amateur press associations which are so helpful to isolated liter- ary beginners, & was brought into contact with many capable writers who helped to check certain oddities in my style & to redirect my attention to the weird fiction which must always constitute my major form of self-expression. I began my new series of weird tales in 1917—with "The Tomb" & "Dagon". In 1918 I wrote "Polaris", & in 1919 "Beyond the Wall of Sleep". There was then no thought of *professionally* publishing these things, though a few ap- peared in the amateur press. Late in 1919 I first encountered the work of Dunsany, which influenced me profoundly & awaked me to a period of in- tensive production never parallelled before or since. In 1923 the discovery of Arthur Machen further stimulated my imagination. Meanwhile—after 1920— my health began very gradually to improve. I became less of a hermit, tried my hand at travelling (New Hampshire 1921, New York & Cleveland 1922),

& began the intensive exploration of other old towns than Providence. (Salem, Marblehead, &c—which became reflected in my tales as "Arkham" & "Kingsport".) In 1922 I first had a story professionally published—in a small magazine called *Home Brew*, edited by one of the amateur press association members. This was the very poor "Herbert West—Reanimator"—a series of six separate episodes presented in instalments. Later that year the same magazine published my "Lurking Fear" (afterward reprinted by W.T.) as a 4-part serial with illustrations by Clark Ashton Smith—whom I had also met through the amateur association. In 1923 W.T. was founded, & at Smith's urging I sent in 7 stories for consideration. All were accepted[12]—Edwin Baird, more favourable to me than Wright, then being editor—& publication began in October with "Dagon". From then on I have been having things in W.T. I soon encouraged my young friend Frank B. Long (also met in amateur journalism) to contribute—his first tale appearing late in 1924.[13] About this time my increasing health caused me to branch out in the world more than formerly—even to the point of attempting residence in New York, where most of my friends happened to be—but this programme did not prove satisfactory. I grew to hate the metropolis—& in 1926 returned home for good. However, my travelling proclivities continued, & I have been constantly pushing my limits of exploration both north & south. In 1924 I reached Philadelphia; in 1925 Washington & Northern Virginia; in 1927 Portland, Maine & southern Vermont; in 1928 more of Vermont, the Mohawk Trail, Albany, Baltimore, Annapolis, Washington again, & the Endless Caverns in Western Virginia (my first glimpse of the marvellous underground world); in 1929 Kingston & other historic N.Y. spots, Richmond, Williamsburg, Jamestown, & Yorktown in Virginia; in 1930 Charleston on the South & Quebec on the North; in 1931 the whole of Florida, even Key West; & in 1932 Chattanooga, Memphis, Vicksburg, Natchez, New Orleans, & Mobile. Declining finances—now rather desperate—have curtailed my travels. When I had the money I hadn't the health, & now that I have the health I haven't the money. Only cheap 'bus & excursion rates now enable me to get around as I do. Literary revision—which I do in addition to original writing (the late Houdini was among my clients)—has all gone to hell. Unusual events are very rare with me—slow shrinkage being the general rule of life. My family has now shrunk to one aunt & myself, & last May we combined households in this ancient backwater which belongs to the college & has a very cheap rental despite its good location, comfortable spaciousness, & admirable steam heat & hot water. I have always wanted to live in an old house, but never succeeded till poverty drove me to this one! I have become extremely fond of the place—whose size has enabled us to get a good many family things—furniture, paintings, statuary, &c—out of storage. It seems, in some ways, tremendously like the old house on a small scale. I believe I mentioned that my own personal quarters consist of a library & a bedroom—my desk being at a west window with a fine view of old roofs & gardens, distant spires & towers, & the glamourous sunset beyond. My library contains about 2000 volumes, though I have catalogued only the weird section of it. My favourite authors—aside from the Graeco-Roman classics & the English poets & essayists of the 18th century—are Poe, Dunsany, Machen, Blackwood, M. R. James, Walter de la Mare, & others of that type. Apart from phantasy, I prefer realism in fiction—Balzac, Flaubert, de Maupassant, Zola, Proust, &c. I think the French are better adapted than we to the reflection of life as a whole—our Anglo-Saxon specialty being poetry. I dislike nearly all Victorian literature, & believe that such very recent material as escapes freakishness has more promise than most of the stuff immediately preceding it. Ultra-modernism I regard as mainly a blind alley, though it may contribute isolated elements to the main stream. I like conservatism in style, & think recent prose tends to be slipshod & inartistic. In music my taste is very poor—probably as a result of violin lessons forced on me when I was too young—& very rapidly forgotten. I am a frank barbarian, with Victor Herbert[14] as about the upper limit of my real appreciation. In painting my taste is conservative, with landscapes as my favourite subjects. I wish I could draw & paint—as many of my family have done— but I can't. In architecture I hate functional modernism as a bull is supposed to hate a red rag. The classical is my first choice, though I poignantly appreciate a really soaring specimen of Gothic. All told, it is possible that science, history, & philosophy interest me more than aesthetics. Politically I used to be a reactionary—royalist & feudalist—but recent realistic thought has switched me to an almost opposite pole of economic liberalism . . . . government ownership, artificially allocated work, fixed schedules of pay & hours, unemployment insurance, old-age pensions, & so on. But I don't think the people can ever govern themselves. Reforms will have to come through a fascistic rule of the trained few unless they are to peter out in a mess. I am all for the preservation of the main cultural tradition, & have no use at all for radical upheavals like Russian bolshevism. Philosophically I am a mechanistic materialist like George Santayana. I am greatly interested in the mystery of early man—archaeology, anthropology, &c., & am a born antiquarian in every way. Perhaps my most persistent interest is the imaginative recapture of America's 18th century past. Roman history also engrosses me. I can't think of the ancient world except from a Roman point of view, & am especially fascinated by *Roman Britain* (as Arthur Machen is), where the Roman cultural stream meets the stream of my personal ancestry. I shall yet use Roman Britain in fiction— though I don't know just how. I dislike to see great cultural fabrics split up, & am a sincere Tory in my regret for America's separation from the British Empire. I think the differences of 1775 ought to have been settled within the Empire. I admire Mussolini, but think Hitler is a very inferior copy—led astray by romantic conceptions & pseudo-science. At that, though, Hitler may have formed a necessary evil—saving his country from disintegration. In general, I

think any nation ought to keep close to its original dominant race-stock—
remaining largely Nordic if it started that way; largely Latin if it started that way,
& so on. Only in this manner can comfortable cultural homogeneity & continuity be secured. But Hitler's extremes of pure racialism are absurd & grotesque.
Various race-stocks differ in inclinations & aptitudes, but of all of them I consider only the negro & australoid biologically inferior. Against these two a rigid
colour-line ought to exist. As for my own stuff & literary methods & views—I
have outlined these things in former letters, leaving very little to be supplied in
the portrait of myself.* In casual matters, an utter indifference to games &
sports of every kind may be noted. My chief pleasure is seeing old houses &
wandering about ancient & picturesque landscapes on summer days. I'm never
under a roof in summer if the weather permits—but always take my work &
reading in a bag & make for the woods & fields. I love heat & can't stand the
cold—so that I may have to move south some day despite my intense attachment to my native scenery & atmosphere. Walking is my only form of real exercise—& in this pursuit I have developed an almost unlimited endurance in
recent years. I prefer only 2 meals a day, on a flexible schedule. I usually work
best at night. I abhor all sea food with a tremendous & inexplicable violence, &
dote on cheese, chocolate, & ice cream. I don't care for tobacco & have never
tasted intoxicating liquor. In general, I prefer an Apollonian to a Dionysian attitude. I have an inordinate fondness for *cats* of every shape & kind, including the
toughest & most battered old Thomas-warriors. In aspect I am 5 ft 11 in. tall,
weight vacillating on either side of 145, very light complexion, brown eyes,
brown hair turning iron-grey, stoop shoulders, & a phiz as ugly as hell—with
elongated proboscis & lantern jaw. Plain & conservative in attire, & unobtru-
sive & retiring in manner except when I get started on an argumentative conversation. Argument—either oral or epistolary—is something I can't resist.

Enclosed are all the gang pictures I can rake up at the moment—some
being sent to *Unusual Stories* for the staff artist to try his hand on as a basis for
line drawings. If this magazine ever gets going it will publish some writer's
brief biography & portrait each month. I include the late Dr. Whitehead,
since you must be familiar with his work. A reproduction of this picture—
which is a splendid likeness—will from [*sic*] the frontispiece of Barlow's book.
The view of Wandrei is an old one. He's 25 now, & doesn't look quite so
kiddish. The shots of me date from 1931, but I look about the same—&
Long never changes. The Price & Talman views are very typical, & those who
have seen Smith say his is. I include young Barlow, since you've seen his Annals of the Djinns in the F F,[15] & will later see his Caneviniana. And I also
stick in Harry Bates, former *Astounding* & *Strange Tales* editor, since you've

---

*I might add that E. J. O'Brien 3-starred work of mine in 1928 & 1929, & that the
O. Henry mem. annual gave equivalent mention in 1932. Lesser O'Brien & O. Henry mentions have also occurred. Five (5) tales of mine reprinted in anthologies.

doubtless read magazines of his editing. Of the rogues in this gallery, I have met in person all *except* the following: Barlow, Bates, Derleth, Howard, Smith. I may possibly meet Barlow in the spring, for he has invited me to visit him in De Land. It depends on my pocketbook. As for non-portrayed writers—I've met Quinn, but have never seen Cave although he lives near at hand in the border city of Pawtucket. I had a controversy with Cave by letter,[16] & I fear my low opinion of commercial fiction offended him so much that he does not care to meet me! I've never met Farnsworth Wright. Price knows Edmond Hamilton & Jack Williamson (with whom I've never been in touch) & likes them immensely. He is also a close friend of Kirk Mashburn.[17] He hopes to meet Howard & Smith during his present travels. Neither Howard nor Smith has ever met any W.T. writer. As I said before, there's no hurry at all about the return of the snaps. Shew them to Rimel & keep them as long as you like, so long as they come back in the end.

Your old Greek testaments sound extremely interesting, & I should think you'd hate to dispose of them in view of their association with your grandfather. Mastering Greek after 40 is a feat to be proud of—I haven't been able to retain much of the little I got when I was 16 & 17! There used to be a polyglot testament—Latin, Greek, & English—in our old dark attic, but I let it go during one of the later upheavals. Now I'm almost sorry that I did—indeed, I always regret it when I let a book go. I should think you'd try to collect all your grandfather's works, as a family matter if not for literary reasons. My ancestry is shy on writers—unless some of the clergymen (all in England) listed on my charts published sermons or other stuff that I know nothing about. The things I keep for family interest are the paintings by my mother (d. 1921) & elder aunt (d. 1932), which really have marked artistic merit (especially my late aunt's) in addition to the associational value to me. Many were hopelessly spoilt in storage, but some were never stored & others have been successfully touched up & repaired. A great marine view by my aunt now hangs in the large space over the staircase. I also have a very old crayon drawing by my grandmother, & may possibly inherit a painting by a great-aunt later on. It would be much more convenient if my reliques of family talent were compact books instead of large canvases—but I try to hang on to everything as long as I can. I don't care to live at all—& don't intend to—unless I can keep a reasonable number of my accustomed things around me—the tables, chairs, bookcases, pictures, books, & ornaments which I have known all my life, & which have stayed on through five removals. These things spell *home* to me, & I would not know what to do without them.

You are to be envied your freedom from frost—for Providence has just emerged from the worst cold spell in its recent history, during which the mercury broke all minimum records by sinking to *17 below zero*. Nothing like this has been approached before since the establishment of the weather bureau here 30 years ago—the closest being the terrible winter of 1917–18. Probably the nearest parallel is the appalling 1778–9 season, when Narragansett Bay froze over & the Royal troops in Newport nearly perished—having to cut down all the surrounding woods & even demolish certain old houses in order to get fuel enough to keep alive. Of course I didn't leave the house while the worst cold lasted (20 above is the lowest I can stand without developing all sorts of painful symptoms—& eventually losing consciousness)—& it was delightfully warm in here—83° or more at the lowest. The reports I received from Vermont—50 below & worse—were too horrible for my mind fully to grasp! Your climate is obviously milder than ours despite your more northerly situation—just as England's is. After all, latitude is only one factor among many. Providence is in exactly the same latitude as the city of Rome & the northern part of Spain!

As for "latest work"—in the sense of stories, I'm not doing any at present, other tasks having come in ahead of original fiction-writing. I hope, though, that I shall get a chance to finish some tales before very long—if only to apply the research & review in the fictional field which I have been prosecuting for the last half-year. I think I told you that I am gravely dissatisfied with my work, & that I have been experimenting in an effort to find out the best direction to take.

Well—this rambling has gone to atrocious lengths . . . far beyond anything you could have intended when requesting biographical notes. Pardon a natural garrulousness! Don't hurry with the loaned material, & give my regards to Rimel.

With all good wishes—

Yrs most sincerely,

H. P. Lovecraft

Notes

1. Duane W. Rimel, "The Ladder of Thought."

2. The epigraph to HPL's "The Horror at Red Hook" is from "The Red Hand."

3. Annmary Brown Memorial (1907; Norman M. Isham, architect), 21 Brown Street. Now a part of the Brown University Library system.

4. The John Mawney House (c. 1764), 135 Benefit Street. HPL referred to it as the Babbitt House. The house had been owned in the late 1920s by George H. Babbitt and Sarah H. Bullock, and at the time of this letter Sarah Bullock still owned the property.

5. St. John's Episcopal Church (1810), 275 North Main Street. The churchyard is mentioned in "The Shunned House" (1924) and "The Messenger" (1929). It was there that HPL wrote his Poe acrostic, "In a Sequester'd Providence Churchyard Where Once Poe Walk'd" (1936).

6. Seabury Quinn (1889–1969) was born and lived in Washington, DC.

7. "The Phantom Farmhouse" (*WT*, October 1923; rpt. March 1929).

8. "The Horror on the Links" (*WT*, October 1925; rpt. May 1937).

9. I.e., at 454 (formerly 194) Angell Street.

10. Abner Alden, *The Reader*.

11. HPL's first appearance in print was a letter to the *Providence Sunday Journal* (3 June 1906). For his early astronomy columns, see letter 12, n.9.

12. HPL submitted only five stories: "Dagon," "Arthur Jermyn," "The Cats of Ulthar," "The Hound," and "The Statement of Randolph Carter."

13. "The Desert Lich" (November 1924).

14. Victor August Herbert (1859–1924), Irish-born American composer, cellist, and conductor. Best known for composing many successful operettas that premiered on Broadway from the 1890s to World War I.

15. Nine (of eleven) installments of "Annals of the Djinns" appeared in *FF* between October 1933 and August 1934.

16. Cf. HPL to A. W. Derleth, August 1932: "I'm having quite a fight with Hugh B. Cave on the subject of literary motivation. When I mentioned Belknap's resentment at Bates's cuts in 'Space Monsters', he came back with a rather unsympathetic rejoinder, as if an author were an ass to mind the mutilation of his products—at least, in the pulp field—& spoke of writing as a purely commercial game in which no one ought to pay too much attention to what he has written. All this, to me, was as a red rag to the proverbial bull—so I sailed into him & told him that not everybody could be satisfied to grind out colourless junk which could be slashed without harm & forgotten on the morrow. He replied with more hard-boiled arguments, & corroborated old Doc Johnson's Philistine dictum by averring that no one but a genius or an idiot writes from any but a mercenary motive. Naturally, this got Grandpa going again—& in a mild vein. I used you as the classic example of one with the rare gift of writing popular stuff with your left hand while your right turns out genuine literature. At present the combat is rather a draw—for Cave seems to differ less (except emotionally) from my position, at bottom, than either he or I thought he did" (*Essential Solitude* 2.498–99).

17. Edmond Hamilton (1904–1977), Jack Williamson (1908–2006), and W. Kirk Mashburn, Jr. (1900–1968), popular weird or science fiction writers of the day.

[9]   [ALS]

66 College St.,
Providence, R.I,
March 5, 1934.

My dear Mr. Baldwin:—

I am glad to hear that the portraits proved interesting, & do not wonder that some of them were surprises. When some other views are returned I'll shew you a much more characteristic picture of Wandrei—taken last January. Whitehead's picture shews him as he was when I visited him in 1931. At one period he was much stouter, but illness whittled his weight down rapidly in 1930. Your remark about his resemblance to a typical missionary leads me to enclose a view of him in full clerical regalia.[1] He was a very "high-church" Episcopalian or "Anglo-Catholic"—& probably had more sympathy with Roman Catholics than with "dissenters" or Evangelical Protestants. In ancestry he was English & Scotch—old Virginia stock on his father's side, & West Indian planter stock on his mother's. No more fascinating & delightful person ever lived—& his varied interests & accomplishments were almost past counting. He was a classmate of Pres. Roosevelt's at Harvard, & studied under such men as Santayana, Royce, & Münsterberg.[2] Yes—Smith does have a sort of Poesque look; & in his youth, when he was smooth-faced, he reminded many people of Keats. Derleth is 25 this year—the picture is a bit out of date. Incidentally—here's a circular of his new book. Pardon me if I sent one before . . . I can't quite remember whether I did or not. Barlow surely does look like a kid—I don't know his age, but he can't be over 17 unless Florida has acted upon him like the fountain of youth which Ponce de Leon vainly sought. I have a vague hope of getting down to visit Barlow this spring—though finances make it hardly a probability. Your sizing-up of Long is surprisingly accurate—he is indeed very highly strung, & I often accuse him of letting emotion usurp the place of thought in matters of social & political opinion. He went over to communism with a violent thud a couple of years ago. In a way I think he does have the celebrated "inferiority complex"—which he masks with an air of cynical sophistication. He stutters when excited. He is very delicate in constitution, & has consequently led a very sheltered life—depending greatly on his parents. As a result, he seems in many ways like a small boy, though he will be 32 next April.[3] He is exceedingly brilliant, & a poet of very high order. His general scholarship is enormous—including odd corners of scientific as well as literary erudition. Talman is assuredly the Adonis & Beau Brummell of the crowd—extremely handsome, & gifted with a capable savoir faire that most of us lack. Price is an extraordinary & delightful chap—I think I told you about his diverse & unusual gifts. Incidentally—I think you'll soon see a let-up in his hack fiction. He has decided not to enslave himself so abjectly to cheap editors, & has accepted a partnership in a garage business in Pawhuska, Oklahoma—thus securing a reliable source of income & emancipating his literary side. The next few months will shew how well he uses his new-found liberation. And so I look about as I write? Others have said that—although as a matter of fact there is very little connexion between personal appearance & type of activity. All sorts of physical types do all sorts of things—though of course there are certain *roughly* selective influences which tend to steer a few special types into particular pursuits (as, for instance, the primitively atavistic youth gravitates toward prize-fighting). Later on, there are some types of activity which leave a certain telltale impress on the appearance—but this impress is largely superficial—more a matter of mannerisms, expressions, costume, & grooming than a matter of basic physiognomy. Thus all that could *really* be predicted about me from my writings is that I would tend to be old-fashioned & inconspicuous in dress, haircut, habits, & the like. I might be either tall or short, fat or lean, light or dark, so far as my written expression could indicate. As to face—the most one could actually predict would be that I'd be likely to have the settled, unemotional contours of objective contemplation rather than the mobile, perpetually agitated features of violent, capricious, & subjective impulsiveness. By the way—I'll send you a snap of myself for permanent retention as soon as I get some duplicates . . . . . & I won't charge you a dime for it, either, since I am no celebrity like young Effjay Akkamin![4] Thanks for the compliment of requesting it. And incidentally —thanks for the glimpse of the mighty Effjay's likeness. He surely is quite a boy! Actually, there's no real harm in the kid. He's simply a bright, active youth with more than the usual amount of the ebullient egotism of the 'teens. Give him a few years & he'll snap out of it—though meanwhile it does no harm to take him down a peg when his ego begins to encroach on others, as in the F F.[5] His appearance is really very wholesome & prepossessing. I return the pictures as per request—& incidentally, I'd like to see the view of Whitehead again eventually, though there's no hurry about it. I shall welcome views of yourself & Rimel whenever you have any to spare or to lend. And I'd likewise appreciate an autobiographical sketch. Which reminds me—the autobiographical jottings in my earlier letter are certainly yours to use as you please, though they are really in no shape for publication as they stand. I merely rambled along on the spur of the moment, using no care or selectiveness whatever, but just dumping down a lot of data in a shapeless mess for you to pick & choose from. Much of the stuff is wholly irrelevant—trifles about my opinions on this & that question, & even notes on dietary preferences! All this was shoved in merely to round out the picture for yourself. What the readers want is merely the part dealing with my writing & the imaginative outlook behind it. You can easily choose—from the whole rubbish-heap I sent—a few pertinent facts for whatever sketch you write. It ought not to be long, for personal exploitation is out of place in connexion with figures as insignificant as pulp-scribblers. If you'll send me what you prepare, I'll gladly help in pruning it into shape. By the way—touching one detail—my early ill-health didn't merely prevent me from *finishing* college, but prevented me from *attending at all*. I was in a state of almost complete nervous breakdown in the autumn of '08, when I was to have entered. What little health I've had has all been since 1920 . . . . & most of it since 1925. A curious way to grow old—getting a bit stronger instead of weaker each year! By the way—Crawford is planning to use a 900-word biographical sketch of me in about his third issue—if *Unusual* lives that long. That's what he's borrowed so many pictures for—to have his illustrator make a sketch based on several different views. Possibly you'll prefer to choose other biographical subjects in order to avoid duplication—but use your own judgment. It was several months ago that I prepared the article for Crawford, & heaven only knows when—or if—he'll publish it![6] By the way—there's an excellent autobiography of Edmond Hamilton in the January issue of *Fantasy Magazine*,[7] while previous issues (under the old name of *Science Fiction Digest*) have contained articles on still more important figures, including A. Merritt & Farnsworth Wright.

I was glad to learn that Rimel's poem was accepted, & hope his story "The Blue Stone" will also land somewhere. I trust, by the way, that you shewed him the snapshots of "the gang". Yesterday I sent him two books to read—Blackwood's "John Silence" & M. R. James's "Ghost Stories of an Antiquary"—with the request that he pass them on to you when finished. Hope you'll enjoy them when they come your way—no better weird material exists. Meanwhile I am sending you two books—containing Blackwood's famous "The Willows"[8] (perhaps the greatest weird story ever written) & Henry James's "Turn of the Screw." These can be turned over to Rimel when you're through with them—& in the end both shipments (though there's not the least hurry) can be returned to me. I'm glad to hear that you like Machen, & hope that D W R will share your sentiments. Writers of the Blackwood–Machen–James grade are highly valuable influences for young beginners, since they tend to counteract the false standards & cheap methods represented by pulp fiction. Yes—"A Fragment of Life" does drag a bit. If I recall aright, the one strong point is the way it throws a kind of magic around the far-stretching, unexplored old streets of a venerable city. I have always felt the same way about streets, & the influence of the tale gave the exploration of labyrinthine New York a double charm for me. Of all the Machen tales sent I least liked "The Inmost Light"—which seemed to me somehow conventional & undistinctive. I place "The White People" far ahead of "The Great God Pan" because of its greater art & subtlety.[9] Most readers miss the denouement the first time. "G. G. Pan" is marred by excessive dependence on *coincidence*— a very bad thing in fiction. If you like, I'll send you "The Hill of Dreams"— not weird, but full of brooding fancy . . . . . the biography of a sensitive literary mind. Also "The Shining Pyramid"—a collection whose title item is much on the order of "The Red Hand" . . . . dealing with the hellish "little people" of the hills. Machen is at his best on this theme. I haven't yet seen his new book, "The Green Round", though Derleth says it is excellent.

I haven't read "On the Trail of Ancient Man",[10] but have always been keenly interested in the Andrews expeditions which it describes. The bleak uplands of Asia have always fascinated me—& form the prototype of my imagined plateau of elder horror—the hellish region of "Leng". By the way—I have just read for the first time A. Merritt's old tale "The Metal Monster", which deals with a terrain of this sort. This appeared in 1920, but I then passed it over because other readers told me it was dull. That was their mistake & mine! Actually, I'm not sure but that it's the best & most convincing presentation of the starkly alien & utterly un-human that I've ever read. The *human* characters are commonplace & stereotyped puppets of the pulp tradition, but the *scenes & phenomena* are powerful beyond description. There can be no question of Merritt's absolutely unique power, & I wish he would completely break loose from the cheap magazine sphere & its standards. Another thing I'm now about to read is Count de Prorok's book on his archaeological excavations at the site of ancient Carthage—lent me by Clark Ashton Smith.

Yes—if I ever get out to the northwest I shall certainly take in Asotin.

Thanks! And as I said before, if you can get east, I can surely keep you busy sight-seeing! The whole Atlantic & Gulf coast region teems with material of scenic, historical, & antiquarian interest—more, really, than one could exhaust in a lifetime. Even in my own southern New England region I am constantly stumbling on new things—obscure villages remote from public transportation lines, & so on.

I've just read the new W T—which is a very average issue. Smith's illustration to his own tale strikes me as tremendously powerful. The human figure is a bit stiff, but the whole conception—the cyclopean pillared hall, the two nameless corpse-bearers, &c.—is subtly & curiously haunting.

No—long letters never bore me . . . . & I only hope that my own do not bore my correspondents. I lean to the habits of my favourite 18th century in doing a good deal of letter writing. While you are probably right in deeming organised correspondence clubs (where writing must be more or less trivial & perfunctory, I imagine) rather futile, I believe that a really intelligent epistolary contact with persons in widely different regions can sometimes be a very valuable broadening & maturing influence. Only the exceptional individual can have face-to-face contact with enough varied types to give him a representative idea of his own civilisation as a whole, yet with the aid of letters he can exchange opinions & perspectives with minds of every sort. I have found this so myself. As a person of very retired life, I met very few different sorts of people in youth—& was therefore exceedingly narrow & provincial. Later on, when literary activities brought me into touch with widely diverse types by mail—Texans like Robert E. Howard, men in Australia, New Zealand, &c., Westerners, Southerners, Canadians, people in old England, & associated kinds of folk nearer at hand—I found myself opened up to dozens of points of view which would otherwise never have occurred to me. My understanding & sympathies were enlarged, & many of my social, political, & economic views were modified as a consequence of increased knowledge. Only correspondence could have effected this broadening; for it would have been impossible to have visited all the regions & met all the various types involved, while books can never talk back or discuss. Even as it is, I realise that my broadening is only partial—since it does not extend outside the English-speaking world. But at least my perspective & sense of proportion are just a bit improved.[11] However—I realise that such a broadening could never have resulted from a merely casual & promiscuous correspondence. The only correspondence worth having is with persons who really have something to say to one. When an individual has certain highly specialised & uncommon tastes—as, for example, an interest in weird fiction—it almost always requires correspondence to put him in touch with enough people of like tastes to form a circle of discussion. It isn't likely that one could ever encounter more than one or two others with such exceptional tastes within the relatively narrow circle of personal acquaintance in one geographic locality. Which reminds me that the presence of even two genuine weird-tale lovers like you &

Rimel in one rather small town is distinctly extraordinary. I've never come across any thorough weird-tale specialist in Providence.

  With every good wish—

      Yrs most sincerely,

           H P Lovecraft

P.S. The edition of "The Shunned House" is stored at the house of Cook's sister in Sunapee, N.H., & I doubt if he could get a copy now. He is trying to hasten her shipment of the package to Barlow. It would probably be most feasible to wait until Barlow gets the sheets—& then ask him for a set. I'd like to get hold of some more sets myself.

Notes

1. See photo gallery in *Thirty Years of Arkham House* (Sauk City, WI: Arkham House, 1970).

2. HPL refers to the philosophers George Santayana (1863–1952) and Josiah Royce (1855–1916) and the psychologist Hugo Münsterberg (1863–1916).

3. Actually he would be 33.

4. See "The Battle That Ended the Century": "Meanwhile a potentate from a neighbouring kingdom, the Effjay of Akkamin (also known to himself as an amateur critic), expressed his frenzied disgust at the technique of the combatants, at the same time peddling photographs of the fighters (with himself in the foreground) at five cents each" (*CF* 4.521).

5. See "The Boiling Point" (*FF*, September 1933–February 1934).

6. HPL wrote "Some Notes on a Nonentity" (about 3000 words) on 23 November 1933. He later prepared the 900-word version, titled "Notes on a Nonentity"; this version never appeared in *Unusual Stories*. The full version was first published posthumously in *Beyond the Wall of Sleep* (1943). Recently the 900-word version was discovered and appeared in the *Lovecraft Annual* No. 4 (2010): 163–65.

7. "Edmond Hamilton," *Fantasy Magazine*, 2 No. 5 (January 1934): 15–16.

8. In John Gilbert Bohun Lynch, ed., *The Best Ghost Stories*.

9. The four Machen stories are in *The House of Souls*.

10. By Roy Chapman Andrews.

11. The apex of this concept is achieved in "The Shadow out of Time," written later this year, in which minds from the full geographical and temporal extent of earth's history exchange information with members of the Great Race.

[10] [ALS]

         66 College St.,

           Providence, R.I.,

            March 27, 1934

My dear Baldwin:—

      Don't hurry in the least about reading & returning any of

the books. They would otherwise be idle on the shelves—& it is much better for them to be in the hands of those who can enjoy & appreciate them. I'm very glad you like Machen, for he seems to me one of the most important of all weird writers—even if he does overwork coincidence now & then. That is the sort of fiction I am always aiming to write—& you can rest assured that it is the only kind I shall ever aim at. The popular pulp-magazine sort holds not the slightest iota of attraction for me. By the way—I've just read Machen's new book—"The Green Round"—his first weird production in 17 years. Clark Ashton Smith lent it to me. It is really extremely interesting—with some very potent reflections of that persistent sense of the unreal world impinging on the real which many imaginative persons possess. In the usualness & unexplainedness of the phenomena represented, it recalls some of Machen's queer prefaces—such as that to "The Three Impostors". Its faults are—mainly—a certain rambling diffuseness, tameness, & overuse of typical stylistic mannerisms. Also—the poltergeist manifestations depicted tend to be somewhat hackneyed. Hardly one of Machen's greatest—but typically Machenian for all that. I'm vastly glad to have read it, & may buy a copy when I'm less broke. If I do, I'll lend it to you & Rimel. The Argus book Shop of Chicago sells it for $1.50.

As to my own stuff—I can tell better after a little more study & experimenting whether I'd better keep on attempting tales or lie fallow for a while. I may indeed try some more archaeological stuff like "The Nameless City" (& the "Mountains of Madness"—which you'll see before long) in the course of time[1]—although one group of critics constantly urges me to stick close to the New England background.

I have not only read, but own, both Smith's "Ebony & Crystal" & Wandrei's "Ecstasy"—also the latter's "Dark Odyssey", with illustrations by his remarkable young artist-brother. If you haven't these items, I am sure you could still obtain them from their respective authors. You have Smith's address—Wandrei's is 84 Horatio St., Apt. 4B, New York, N.Y. These volumes—published in limited editions & generally cherished by those who possess them—would not be likely to be found in second-hand book shops; though the chances of finding the weird classics (Machen, Blackwood, James, &c) in such places are better.

My recent reading of Merritt's "Metal Monster" was by courtesy of R H. Barlow, who lent me the old magazine instalments containing it. I am sure he would be glad to lend the text to you if you would ask him. "The Metal Emperor" is another version of the same story—by no means so good as the original. Barlow has both—hence I'd advise you to specify the original Argosy form when requesting the loan. Merritt may yet revise this thing again—removing the touches of cheapness inherent in the human characters & some of the incidents. Of Merritt's unique gifts & tremendous power there can be no doubt. He can conjure up a sense of the imminence of strange life & unreal worlds as no other can—& absolutely no one has approached him in the coherent, tangible, concrete, & sustained description of utterly alien & non-human phenomena. The great pity is that he has catered to popular markets instead of following the Machen–Blackwood–James tradition. If he [w]ould only work in a purely artistic vein, he could perhaps surpass any other weird author who has ever lived. Unlike most of the pulp weirdists, who do not care especially for fantasy & write it only for market reasons, Merritt has a deep & abiding interest in the unreal. I think I mentioned that he is a close personal friend of the great Russian mystical painter Nicholas Roerich.[2] It is possible that he may blossom out in later life—he is 50 now—with some really high-grade material. He certainly realises, at last, that his talents have been largely side-tracked through popular catering.

Barlow's book of Whitehead letters comes along slowly but surely. He is hampered by very bad eyesight (blindness was at one time threatened), & cannot work steadily at anything requiring concentrated vision. Did I mention that I may get down to Florida to see Barlow about May 1st? I'm sure he'll be glad to reserve you a copy of "Caneviniana". Have you his address? It is Box 88, De Land, Florida. Yes—Whitehead himself was a great personality—both very studious & very kind. I doubt if I've ever met anybody else quite so *effectively* versatile—that is, so really *good* at many different things. His stories can certainly never be replaced. There are other people who know the West Indies—but no one else who can look at them & reproduce their brooding legendry from just the same angle. I wish someone would collect his best stories in a posthumous volume.[3]

As for the mythical characters—hellish gods & Elder Ones—of Smith & myself—the idea is scarcely original. Bierce occasionally refers to such imaginary background-horrors (Hastur, the Lake of Hali, the Seven Moons,[4] &c.), & Robert W. Chambers has several times used the Bierce background. Dunsany has invented a whole system of gods & legends—with a marvellous array of names. How much of the "Book of Eibon" & the "Necronomicon" will ever appear in concrete form is debatable. Smith has written a chapter from Eibon called "The Coming of the White Worm", but I am under the impression that Wright has turned it down. As to a *novel*—if I said that *Smith* had written one, I made a mistake. The thing meant is undoubtedly *August W. Derleth's* detective novel—"Murder Stalks the Wakeley [*sic*] Family"—published by Loring & Mussey of New York & now on sale. It has been quite well received by reviewers. Wandrei has written two novels—one weird—but neither has found a publisher.[5]

Yes—I certainly would like to meet Smith, who is in some ways the most unusual person I know. I have been a close correspondent of his since August 1922, when I was 'put next' to him by my friend Samuel Loveman (the "Harley Warren" of my "Statement of Randolph Carter"), who in turn got in touch with him through the late poet George Sterling. Smith was born in Auburn, California, in 1893, & has never been out of his native state. He lives with his parents in a cottage on a hill side somewhat outside Auburn village—

within easy access of a rather weird type of mountain scenery (Crater Ridge &c.—cf. "The City of the Singing Flame") which has figured in some of his tales. His family has always been in very straitened circumstances, & his parents are now in the 80's—having married late in life. His father is a gentleman of a very ancient English Catholic family—born in England, & bearing the hyphenated name of Ashton-Smith. (C A S does not use the hyphen) The elder Smith in his youth was something of a soldier of fortune, & travelled in many odd corners of the earth, including the Amazon jungles of South America. Clark probably derives much of his exotic taste from the tales told him by his father when he was very small—he was especially impressed by accounts of the gorgeously plumed birds & bizarre tropical flowers of equatorial Brazil. On his mother's side Smith comes of American Southern blood—Huguenot & English. From childhood he was a poet, artist, & dreamer—obviously something of a boy wonder. He attended ordinary public schools & never went to a university, but has amassed an immense & curious erudition through private study. When 17 he published his first book of poetry—"The Star-Treader"[6]—[you might get a copy of this from my bookseller-friend George W. Kirk—Chelsea Book Shop, West 8th St., New York City. Or I could lend you my copy.] & attracted the favourable attention of George Sterling. At the same time he conducted his original & untutored experiments in art—evolving a fantastic style of drawing & painting which is really ineffably powerful despite its lack of technical smoothness. When he had an exhibition of paintings at Berkeley many critics highly praised his work. Smith's tastes have always inclined toward the cosmic & the fantastic, & his poetry is mainly concerned with bizarre themes despite occasional excursions into more mundane lyrical fields. Much of his verse shews the influence of Sterling; whom he has visited many times, & who wrote prefaces for some of his books.[7] At one per[i]od—when he was about 18—Smith wrote several stories . . . . in a vein somewhat less non-terrestrial than his present work . . . . but he did not keep up the practice. His present series of tales dates from 1925. Until lately he suffered from very poor health—including a now-vanished touch of tuberculosis. During his ill period he displayed the greatest disregard of health rules—exposing himself recklessly to all kinds of weather—but his rashness cured instead of killed him. I believe he was at one time inclined toward a touch of artistic "pose"—wearing a picturesque shock of hair & even growing a full beard—but that is all over now. Naturally, he is rather misunderstood & unappreciated by the provincial villagers among whom he lives, but as he gets into middle age this disturbs him less than it used to. I can see a perceptible mellowing & growth of geniality in him during the last five years. He no longer has the touch of active, cynical bitterness that he once had. At one period Smith conducted a column—largely verse—in his local paper, *The Auburn Journal*. At the age of 32 he took up the study of French—at home, & without a teacher—& in six months was writing French poems of marvellous power. He has since contributed verse to some of the leading Paris maga-zines—the editor of one of which wrote him that he could hardly believe he was not a Frenchman. And yet Smith has never known any French-speaking person, & could hardly *pronounce* the language intelligibly! His translations of Baudelaire—both free paraphrases in verse, & literal ones in prose—are the best I have ever seen, although they have not yet found a publisher.[8] Smith has read the magazine W T from the start—& was the first to direct my at-tention to it. At that period he did not expect to contribute to it, but at my urging he sent in several poems—many of which were accepted.[9] I kept urg-ing the editors—first Edwin Baird & then Wright—to use his art work, but they were very slow to respond. Indeed, it was not till this year that any pic-ture of his was accepted. His new period of fiction writing was very slow in developing. In 1925 he wrote "Sadastor" & "The Abominations of Yondo", but Wright rejected both.[10] Not till about 1930 did he become prolific—& persistent in bombarding editors. Then his success as a fictionist began quite suddenly—both W T & the science-fiction magazines accepting his tales in unlimited quantity. This unfortunately caused him to write many cheap hack tales, but such pot-boiling has never spoiled his real style. When he sets out to write something really serious, he *does* it! His pictorial work would require a chapter in itself. Some of his hideous heads—proboscidian, semi-reptile, semi-insect—are classics of their kind, & no one excels him in drawing un-earthly, abnormal, & poisonous *vegetation*. His large landscapes—scenes on Saturn, & on still remoter worlds—are full of a mysterious spell. If you'd like to see some of Smith's smaller drawings I'll gladly lend you those in my pos-session—as soon as their present borrower returns them. I have met two people who have seen Smith face to face—one friend of his in Auburn who visited the east last year,[11] & one easterner (George Kirk) who visited him in California in 1921. He is very kindly & likeable, & incredibly brave in his life-long struggle against illness, poverty, & misunderstanding. He has at times helped out his revenues by fruit-picking, but is always forced to struggle hard. His home is a very small one, with no running water—just a primitive well outside. He writes in the open a good deal—at a table in his front yard—& takes many walking trips in the picturesque mountains of his region. The re-sponsibility of his aged parents (who are inclined to domineer a bit) has kept him chained rather closely at home—if it were not for them, he would prob-ably manage to see more of the world. Perhaps, though, his localism has been a blessing in disguise—his limited acquaintance with this world (San Francis-co being the only metropolis he knows) giving his imagination all the keener force in depicting other worlds & other universes! Some day I hope I can meet Smith in person—which is not at all impossible in view of the reasona-ble rates quoted by some of the transcontinental 'bus lines.

 Regarding Cave—he frankly admits that his hack work is absolutely no good as art. He regards writing as a business, & thinks wholly in terms of dollars & cents. According to his own standards he is a success, & he slightly looks down upon those who write from a purely aesthetic motive. It is this latter point which drew my criticism & perhaps caused me to say something which grated on him. Actually, Cave is exceedingly brilliant—cultivated & well-read, & a better artist (when he wants to be) than his theories would indicate. Don't judge his capacity by his cheap junk. Once in a while he writes a splendid story in spite of himself—such as "Dead Man's Belt."[12] Several years ago he contributed some poignant & sincere free verse to the local Providence papers, shewing the natural artistic personality which he deliberately suppresses. I knew this work well—hence was immensely surprised about 1930 to see cheap stories with the same signature in the pulp magazines. My brief exchange of letters with Cave was prompted by his efforts to get me into the Am. Fiction Guild (at $10.00 per year), of which he is the New England representative. The fact that I did not join probably did nothing to boost my stock with my talented fellow-Rhode-Islander. No—I haven't read "The Corpse-Maker",[13] & don't think I shall make any effort to do so!

I have never met or corresponded with George Allan England, but have known & admired his work for 20 years & more. "Darkness & Dawn" is a splendid thing—do you know it? "The Thing from Outside" is exceedingly potent—I have read it 2 or 3 times, & have it in my file of the first year of *Amazing Stories*.[14] W. Paul Cook & H. Warner Munn have met England & had many interesting discussions with him. It seems that he owns the plates of the now out-of-print "Darkness & Dawn", & could get out a new edition quite cheaply if any publisher would coöperate with him. Cook had an idea of tackling the job—but just then his general collapse came. Young Barlow is also in touch with England—who, it seems, is in very painful circumstances & poor health (arthritis) at present. I wish D & D could be reissued. If my memory is any good, it is one of the most powerful tales of the remote future ever written.

I'm not working on the actual text of any story just now, but am planning a novelette of the Arkham cycle—about what happened when somebody inherited a queer old house on the top of Frenchman's Hill & obeyed an irresistible urge to dig in a certain queer, abandoned graveyard on Hangman's Hill at the other edge of the town. This story will probably not involve the actual supernatural—being more of the "Colour Out of Space" type . . . . . greatly-stretched "scientifiction". One thing I've done is to prepare a *map of Arkham* in order to avoid slips in allusion.[15] As the Arkham tales multiply, I must be careful to exercise consistency in local geography.

Your brief autobiographical sketch is very interesting, & reveals you to be much younger than I had imagined. It arrived on *March 26th*—very opportunely, to celebrate your coming of age! Let me wish you a happy adulthood, & many pleasant returns of the natal day. I recall when I turned 21—on Aug. 20, 1911. Though in poor health, I attempted an all-day electric-car trip as a celebration—riding westward through the picturesque countryside of my maternal ancestors, eating lunch at Putnam, Conn., going north to Webster, Mass., (near which my first actual *memories* [1892] begin), then turning north-east to Worcester, keeping on to Boston, & finally returning home at night after a virtually record-breaking circuit. I managed to do it without disaster, though having to pause a bit in Worcester to rest. This ride took me not far east of the "Dunwich" country (Wilbraham, Monson, Palmer, Hampden—near Springfield), though I did not behold that strange region till seventeen years later. I surely hope that your travel ambitions may some day be grati-fied—& I don't see why they can't be, since youth, health, enterprise, & re-sourcefulness will go far toward getting one a berth with some of the many exploring & archaeological expeditions of this adventurous & restless age. The abundance of legal talent in your heritage ought to give you a keen ana-lytical faculty & mature judgment! Your musical inclinations evidently come from the maternal side—& I am glad you have been able to utilise them prac-tically. There must be considerable interest & variety in your moderately scat-tered professional engagements—which I hope will, from now on, be more numerous than in February!

I must look up your dusky favourite Duke Ellington on my aunt's radio—an instrument which I don't very often disturb. Though very obtuse in musical matters (as I have previously mentioned), it is likely that I could grasp some of the tonal & rhythmical qualities which you admire. In my youth I liked the sim-ple "coon songs" of the period very much—though of course they made no pretence to actual musical status. In those crude early ballads—"Ain't Dat a Shame", "Oh, Oh, Miss Phoebe", "Good-Bye, Eliza Jane", "Jes' Kiss Yo'self Goodbye", "Bill Bailey, Won't You Please Come Home", &c.—there undoubt-edly existed the beginnings of the complicated syncopations now taken so seri-ously by musical prophets. It's curious to trace the development of the stream; a stream lying wholly within my own conscious lifetime. The earliest syncopa-tion I remember was about coeval with the Spanish War—when the terms "rag-time" & "cake walk" were first heard. "Oh, Oh, Miss Phoebe" is the first thing of the sort I recall—in 1899 or thereabouts. About 1900 or 1901 a flood of this popular stuff appeared—not only songs, but instrumental cake walks like "Creole Belles", "Georgia Camp Meeting", & the like . . . . all of which I used to hum & whistle with zest. The reason I remember so many is that the gang of 10- & 11-year-olds to which I belonged had an organisation called the Blackstone Military Band—we used a queer device of the period called the "zobo" . . . . a brass horn with a membrane at the mouthpiece, which would make the human voice sound like the tones of a band instrument. And were we chronic disturbers of the peace! I was not only one of the zoboists, but the drummer & cymbal-clasher as well—since (pardon the egotistical note!) I was the only member who could keep time accurately. My percussion instruments kept my hands busy, so that I obtained a light cardboard zobo which I could hold with my teeth, & thus be two bandsmen in one! Later—for stationary concerts—I devised a foot-operated mechanism (on the general plan of the trap-drummer's apparatus) which took care of the banging & thumping & left my hands free for ostentatious virtuosity on the fake brass cornets & trombones of my zobo collection. Ah, me—good old 1901! Once in a while I hear stray songs of that era revived, & at such times my memory goes back to the days when the Blackstone band made afternoons hideous with the strains of "Smoky Mokes", "Mah Sunflower Sue", "Cindy", "Creole Belles", & other ditties, marches, & cake walks of the time. The beginners of a great tradition! We got it out of our systems early—not one of us, so far as I know, ever having the least connexion with music in manhood. Later in the century—after 1910— "ragtime" changed entirely in character, so that what came to bear that name was entirely different from the cakewalks of my boyhood. This was the age of "Alexander's Ragtime Band", "Waiting for the Robert E. Lee", &c. Another change set in around 1916 or 1917, when the word "jazz" first began to be heard,[16] & since then (although I haven't kept track of the stream) other changes seem to have taken place. The era of the saxophone apparently developed a type of pseudo-African drone unlike anything previous. I wish you all luck with your original musical composition, & hope to hear "Congo Dawn" some day. I can imagine the suggestions of sinister obeah-magic, & invocations to nameless crocodile-gods, which might be put into such a piece by means of judicious tom-tom beating!

If you're interested in boxing, you ought to correspond with Robert E. Howard—who is not only a pugilistic fan, but a skilled performer in the ring as well. Have you seen his spirited prize fight stories? Some appeared under the pseudonym "Patrick Ervin."

Altogether, you give an interesting & well-rounded picture of a vivid personality well worth knowing—& I hope I may have a chance to greet you face to face some day. Snaps of yourself & Rimel will surely be welcome whenever you have some to spare. Thanks, by the way, for the pleasing specimen of your local flora.

About Old Providence—it is really a tremendously interesting place, where much of the past survives to a surprising extent. I know of no other large city so much like a quaint colonial village. It is the steep precipice dividing the collegiate & residential East Side from the commercial town on the westward stretching plain that saves us from metropolitanism. Business simply can't climb such a vertical slope—so that up here we keep the grassy lanes, walled gardens, & quaint old houses of other days. Providence was founded in 1636 by religious refugees from Massachusetts under Roger Williams. It lies at the head of Narragansett Bay—the eastern shore being the base of our precipitous hill. Nowadays the water at the foot of the hill is all filled in or bridged over, so that the western or business section begins almost immediately there—only a chain of open squares separating the ancient slope from the region of skyscrapers. In 1636, however, the hill descended into a region of coves & salt marshes, with only a narrow shore strip at its base. Roger Williams settled on this shore near a spring (still flowing, & now the seat of a small park) at the base of the hill, & a row of huts sprang up along the shore line—where the Indian trail from the west crossed a fording place & followed the shore till it climbed the hill & crossed the plateau to the next water-crossing—the river Seekonk, where a canoe ferry was maintained. This line of huts marked what was called "The Town Street"—earliest of all our thoroughfares, & still surviving as North & South Main Sts. (a shabby business & lodging-house district today). As time went on, the infant settlement slowly climbed the steep eastward hill against which the first houses were built—having to do this because only water & marshlands & islands lay to the west. At the same time it expanded north & south along the base of the hill—building wharves & better houses, & gradually prospering through the growth of a sea trade founded in 1681. Most of the town was burnt in 1676 during King Philip's War. Beginning around 1700 the marshes across the bay were filled in—largely with earth obtained through the levelling of Weybosset Hill, which rose on the largest bit of dry land there. In 1711 a bridge was thrown across the narrow ford, & a dry land route to the west opened up. Around 1750 streets were laid out in the newly filled region, & the present business section (then residential) began to develop. But the principal old settlers stuck to the East Side & pushed on up the hill—laying out Back or Benefit St. as you have read in "The Shunned House". The houses began to be more &

more substantial—first the gambrel roofed type & later of a simple slant-roofed typed with classic doorway—the latter often having a railed double flight of steps. Of this latter type hundreds  still survive in good condition. Imagine a network of streets—one along the base of the precipice, others dizzily climbing the  slope, still others ranged along the parallel streets (Benefit, Wheaton, & Congdon) forming ledges on the hill, & a few in Prospect Street (laid out 1770), which runs along the summit— with endless rows of houses like these, & you will get a good idea of how Providence looked at the time of the Revolution, & how a good deal of the ancient hill district still looks today. Ambitious public buildings began to go up about 1760, & most of these early landmarks still stand. The colony house built in 1761, the brick school house of 1769, the college edifice of 1770, the Market house of 1773, the Baptist Church of 1775, &c. &c. are all with us today in the best of condition. The town reached the top of the hill about 1800—when this house was built. We have thousands of houses of the period, including such public edifices as the domed Beneficent church (1808), St. John's Church (1809), the Unitarian church (1816), [17] &c. &c.

Providence about 1760, seen from crest of hill. Large tree in upper left marks approximate site of 66 College St. Road half way down hill—in middle distance—is Benefit St. Bulk of town below this. Across the Cove & Bay the newly filled-in West Side can be seen—with a few new houses marking development.

Also, beginning about 1760 large numbers of elaborate brick mansions began to be constructed—the accompanying crude sketch indicating a peculiarly local type evolved about 1774 by the amateur architect Joseph Brown. This house—& most of the other mansions of the period—still exists in good condition—as does the first brick house (1750) ever erected in Providence.[18]

Eastward, over the crest of the hill, the woods & fields stretched across the great plateau which sloped gently downward from the precipice's brink toward the Seekonk River (see sketch on preceding sheet)—ending in a wooded bluff—still preserved as such by the park commission (Blackstone Park, where I played in youth, & where I still take my work

on summer afternoons). Here could be found occasional farm houses (many of which *still exist*, imbedded amidst the solid city streets of later generations) & one great country seat called Elm Grove. This region was crossed by the Wampanoag Trail to the Seekonk ferry—a road later developed by the white men as Angell St. I was born in Angell St.—hence I can boast that my native highway is *older than the colonisation of New England*—an Indian path of unknown antiquity! During the 19th century the solid city streets (a very good residential district with fine houses & gardens, though in ugly Victorian architecture) pushed about ¾ of the way across the plateau toward the Seekonk. My old home lay near the edge of this solid section, so that I could get to the open country in a couple of blocks. Thus I grew up as much a country boy as a city boy. I lived in a city house, & could look *west* over solid streets; but a minute's jaunt to the *east* took me to the woods & ravines & stone walls & farmsteads of ancient New England. Today the solid city has overrun the entire plateau except for the strip of Seekonk river bluff (& the ravine adjacent to this) preserved by the park commission. However—queer oases (such as you'd find nowhere save in Providence) still remain. At one place—in the midst of residential streets—is a five-acre poor-farm surrounded by a stone wall 10 feet high—absolute country inside, just as when it was founded in 1828.[19] At another place nearer the Seekonk is a private farm of perhaps 3 acres—with house, barns, sheds, stone walls, cow pasture, & cornfield exactly as when laid out in 1735. On every side are the smart streets & trim houses (mostly modern colonial) of a recent real-estate development, but within the boundary walls the rural past remains untouched. There must be dozens of overtaken farmhouses & bits of farmyard in the city, but this is the only complete farm I know of in the heart of the best residential streets. Providence certainly is unique!

The filled-in land west of the bridged-over bay (more & more filling & bridging were done after 1750, so that the dry land grew decade by decade) began to develop as a business section (after a residential period) about 1800. Beyond it—on the higher ground farther west—other residence districts developed in the 19th century; some of them becoming very opulent, though they have now relapsed to shabbiness, leaving the ancient eastward hill & the plateau beyond it supreme as a dwelling-place. The main connecting link between the ancient hill & the westward plain is Market Square—the site of the Great Bridge of 1711 & of the Market House of 1773. This lies at the foot of College St.—only a 3-minute downward plunge from where I live. Here is a great bridged open space—with the present head of bay navigation (a fascinating old waterfront) a block south of it. The Market House still stands, but four years ago (against my frantic newspaper protests) a row of splendid old waterfront warehouses (1816) along the eastern shore was torn down.[20] Prior to that wanton demolition, the square had a tremendously ancient aspect. It is still, of course, very ancient—& the new buildings are designed in the old Georgian style. Just across the bridge is the junction still called by its colonial name of Turk's Head (after an old shop sign), & due west stretches the main business thoroughfare—Westminster St., laid out in 1750. Here are most of the skyscrapers—although among them several of the old colonial houses lingered till very recently. One is still there—behind a false facade—& in the cross streets several more are half-hidden. But the oldest visible building in this region is the great pillared Arcade of 1828—in the Greek style, & having as columns *the largest monoliths in the world, except for those in the new Cathedral of St. John the Divine in New York*. That is—the great pillars are *not* made up of short "drums" piled one on top of the other in the usual way. They are each *all in one piece*—quarried in western Rhode Island & brought to town by oxen.[21] Out of my west windows I see the tops of all the skyscrapers, but distance softens their outlines & causes them to blend rather picturesquely with older houses & church towers in the foreground, & with the remote steeple & far western horizon beyond them. The vista at sunset is really marvellous, & makes me wish vainly that I could draw or paint. Just at the foot of College Hill is the massive new court-house—a triumph of *imitation* colonial architecture completed less than a year ago. By breaking up the huge mass into many gables & adding a Georgian belfry, the architect preserved the old-Providence atmosphere. This building has a front at the bottom of the hill in S. Main St. & a rear half way up the hill in Benefit St. So steep is the hill, that what is the *ground floor* at the higher Benefit St. level, is the *5th floor* counting from the S. Main St. level! Many people take advantage of this circumstance to get a free ride half way up the hill—my aunt does since her ankle accident of last year. She enters the court house down town & takes the elevator to the 5th floor—then walking out the back door straight into Benefit St., & more than half way home!

And now for some of the pictures which I promised to shew either you or Rimel some time ago. Let him see them, anyhow. I'm sorry that I couldn't find more, but my files are in rather bad shape just now. From some of these views you can get a pretty fair idea of certain ancient places in Providence & elsewhere in the State. Note especially Market Square as it was a century ago— I've indicated houses still standing. This view doesn't include the stretch where the warehouses were demolished. The building with the two end chimneys at the extreme right is the old Franklin Hotel, built about 1820 & standing at the foot of College St. Up the hill, on the College St. side, is an ancient archway through the building to let coaches into the cobblestoned courtyard & inn-yard. This ancient feature used to be common in all the towns of the colonies—as in Europe—but so far as I know, Providence has the *last* three examples (one of the others a few doors above in College St.) in America save for one deserted & boarded-up specimen in Philadelphia. It paralyses me to think that all these old houses on the N. side of College St. below Benefit are doomed to ulti-mate destruction—being owned by an art school which will eventually erect a building on the site. But I hope I'll be dead before they go![22]

Many of these pictures are marked "please return"—referring to previous loans. However, *only the booklet* need be sent back from this trip. The *other* items are duplicates, & if any especial one appeals to you or Rimel, pray feel at perfect liberty to keep it. The booklet has a good deal of interesting histori-cal data, but is of particular interest because *it shews this house* in its frontis-piece. I have marked #66 & other salient points. This picture gives an excellent idea of the whole College St. neighbourhood—the new court house, the steep hill, & the ancient university on the summit. Note that #66 is set back from the street in a quaint gardened court. I think I've shewed you a close-up snap shot of the house. The courthouse colonnade at the bottom is where my aunt takes the elevator to go home. Half way up, you can see where Benefit St. crosses. The ugly chimney on the hilltop horizon is of the college engineering building—whence steam heat is piped to this house & others owned by the university.

Regarding New England's decaying backwater townships & villages like "Dunwich" (*Arkham*—or Salem—is hardly of this type, being a city of some 40,000 with genteel stagnation & macabre tradition rather than actual *decay* as a keynote)—they are real enough in essentials, & are perhaps most typically found in West Central Massachusetts—near the Connecticut Valley. Vermont & other sections have remote regions culturally & materially on the down grade—for the trend of the more vigorous stock is toward the towns, leaving the country in the possession of the less energetic—but the peculiar psycho-logical disintegration which impresses me so much seems most marked in Massachusetts. There seems to be a slow slipping of the once alert, sturdy, &

responsible-minded yeomanry to the callous, shiftless, & amoral "poor white" state whose southern analogues have been so vividly treated in the tales of William Faulkner & Erskine Caldwell. But the spectacle is even more sombre than in the south, for these retrograding Yankees had the gloomy Puritan tradition with all its repressions, abnormalities, & demoniac legends behind them. Things are *whispered* in a portentous, blood-curdling way peculiar to New England. In Wilbraham, for example (where some amazing cases of crime, incest, repulsive domestic triangles, &c. crop out amongst the ignorant farming populace), they whisper oddly about a certain hill-shadowed street in the neighbouring town of Monson[23] where an abnormal profusion of *suicides* occur from year to year. And so on & so on. That this is a direct legacy of the old Puritan tradition seems fairly obvious. We have more of it in Rhode Island, which springs from the revolt against Puritanism—indeed, I always associate the *sinister* with tight-lipped Massachusetts. However—I don't have to go far to explore Massachusetts . . . . for I've never lived in a house (save for my 2 Brooklyn years) from whose roof Massachusetts is not visible. Massachusetts is to Providence folk what Idaho is to you in Asotin.[24] About a quarter of the cars seen in our downtown section any day have Mass. plates—representing the large section of southern Mass. countryside whose natural metropolis is Providence rather than Boston. We're about 2 miles from the state line on the east. While the latent horror of backwoods Massachusetts always impressed me (cf. "The Picture in the House"), I never had a really close view of it till I visited in Wilbraham in 1928. I then had every chance to study it, for the household of my hosts included a diligent antiquarian & a town official intimately familiar with the rural population & their problems. The story I got out of this glimpse—"The Dunwich Horror"—was undeniably crude & overdone, but I was pleased when O'Brien gave it a three-star rating—my only tale besides the "Colour" to be so honoured.[25]

As for New York—I probably detest it more thoroughly than any other spot with which I am familiar. It is the one place that seems *utterly alien* to me—part of a cultural fabric & line of development in which I have no part & in which America has no part. Cleveland—Philadelphia—the South—all these places are comprehensible to me, & within my radius of sympathy. But Manhattan remains outside. And it is all the more melancholy because certain old houses & street effects reveal that a truly American & comprehensible New York *once existed*. The old New York of brownstone & brick was part of the national fabric. But since 1900 this ancient city has been overwhelmed with a chaos of feverish giganticism & unassimilable Semitic blood which has left almost nothing of the past. Modern commercial-Jewish New York of the dizzying towers is like an alien capital built on the foundations of a lost native city—& what survives of the old is tinged with a sadness & mockery which make one want to leave it soon. Of the faces in the street most are swarthy & Asiatic, & with queer, drawn expressions indicating thoughts & emotions in which Nordic-Aryans can never share. What Hitler fears in Germany has come to pass in New York—an Oriental subject-race has insidiously captured the land from its hereditary stock. Of course, millions of Nordics still live in New York, but the other aggressive millions of pushing Jews stand out as supremely conspicuous & give a keynote to the daily life of the streets. The very milk-bottles left at one's door have bizarre-looking Hebrew characters on the caps—to assure the worthy majority of customers that the fluid is strictly "kosher"—whatever that may signify in the way of chemical purity or sacerdotal blessing! But of course this is only the *massed impression.* Actually, New York is a complex congeries of local units—neighbourhoods & suburbs— some of which remain fully within the Aryan-American stream & are the seat of a tranquil local life not differing in essentials from that of New-England. This is especially true in certain former suburbs—*overtaken villages* in various stages of assimilation. Flatbush, where I spent a year, is now a solid part of Brooklyn, yet retains much of the past—single houses with grassy yards & American inhabitants, & an old church dating back to 1796—while Jamaica & Flushing, also on Long Island, are still independent, old-fashioned villages despite the creeping in of apartment houses. Staten Island is still open country dotted with separate villages—some of which are exceedingly quaint & ancient. In Manhattan itself many colonial houses remain—& there were still more when I first explored the region in 1922. Some regions—especially in the overtaken village of Greenwich, now infested with artists & litterateurs (mostly poseurs, but including a few genuine performers like Wandrei & his brother)—are quite definitely colonial; with slant-roofed brick houses in solid blocks, whose high stoops, pillared, transomed doorways, & projecting dormers mark them as typical. Streets like that in the accompanying sketch are by no means extinct—& are such as Genl. Washington knew when he lived there. This type of house is akin to Georgian town houses in other large American towns & in London—the *high stoop, with its long flight of steps* being the peculiar New York feature. So conservative was the *old* New York (as contrasted with the traditionless & rootless Babel of *modern* New York) that this general design persisted with certain modifications clear down to 1900—the Victorian brownstone houses having the same high stoop, arrangement of door & windows, &c— although the roofs became flat after 1830. None of the old *Dutch* town houses with stepped gables remain, though Dutch *farmhouses* with curving roof line & characteristic gambrel are still common in sections once rural. These—many of which are now overtaken by the city streets—largely date from between 1750 & 1800. Some are kept in good condition & open as public museums—especially one (the Lefferts cottage) at the edge of Prospect Park in Brooklyn & another (the Dyckman farmhouse) far north on Manhattan Island at Broadway & 204th St. This latter makes one think of Providence so far as its setting is concerned, for a bit of ancient farmyard remains around it. There is a Dutch mansion remaining (& open as a museum) in Van

Cortlandt Park, & in 160th St. is an English colonial mansion of 1760. Of ancient public buildings one may mention St. Paul's Church (1766), Fraunce's [*sic*] Tavern (1719), & the City Hall (1812). The old Planter's Hotel at Greenwich & Albany Sts., where *Poe* stopped when he first came to N.Y., is still in good condition. Also, Poe's suburban cottage in Fordham (now a solid part of the Bronx) is preserved & open as a museum.

Of modern New York the chief advantages are (a) the exotic architectural effects produced by the tall buildings when seen from a distance (you've undoubtedly seen hundreds of pictures of these—& the real thing is even more impressive), & (b) the museums, bookshops, art galleries, & kindred advantages. The *museums* are for me the chief attraction—both the great Metropolitan (art) & American (natural history) Museums, & the innumerable special museums—Hispanic, historical, City (historical), Am. Indian, Modern Art, Whitney (mod. art), Brooklyn (art & nat. hist.), & so on. In the Metropolitan is the greatest Egyptian collection in America—whole tombs transplanted stone by stone, mummies, sarcophagi, sphinxes, statues, household articles, ornaments, &c. &c.—everything in incredible profusion. That is what money does. There is no mistaking the importance of New York as a centre of *the tangible instruments of culture* (not culture itself), & it is as desirable a place to *visit briefly* as it is undesirable to *live in.* Two weeks at a stretch is all I can stand—& I'd see it even less than I do, if (by some malign chance) so many of my friends hadn't drifted there. Long is the only one of the gang *born* there, but Wandrei, Morton, & others have settled in the region for one reason or another. Hence whenever I pay the place a visit, I have to make an endless round of calls. One of the things about N.Y. that maddens me is the *utter absence of greenery or any vegetation* in the central districts. Park strips are few & anaemic, & Central Park looks dingily moth-eaten. Brooklyn, however, has Prospect Park (very pleasant) & a Botanic Garden containing an enchanting Japanese section with every detail of the formal Oriental landscape. Up in the

Bronx the Zoölogical Garden is interesting & well-stocked—& in one place on Manhattan Island there is a remaining bit of primitive forest—at Inwood, near the northwest tip. In a still suburban part of Brooklyn—Flatlands, at Mill Basin—stands the oldest edifice in the state of New York—the ancient Schenck house dating from 1656. This is older than any house in Providence. When I was in Brooklyn I used to take my work & go long distances to escape the metropolitan atmosphere.

My favourite retreats were towns with old wooden houses & green gardens— as nearly like Providence as possible—such as Flushing & Hempstead on Long Island, & Elizabeth in New Jersey . . . the latter the future home of our friend the *Fantasy Fan.* I wrote "He" in Scott Park, Elizabeth—in front of the old Scott house (now demolished), & it amused me to learn recently from Hornig that he once lived in that very edifice! Not, however, in 1924 & 1925, when I haunted the region. People in New York tend toward shallowness, artificiality, assumed cleverness, & bad manners. Contrary to popular belief, they are not swift-moving. Although always in a hurry, & eager to save time on car & subway trips, their walking rate seems very *slow* to a New Englander. They tend to be soft & self-indulgent— professing fatigue if forced to walk above a snail's pace for any length of time, & taking a street-car for short distances that anybody else would walk. Their dialect (worse in some individuals than in others) is harsh & barbaric. They reverse the *-oi* & *-er* sounds—pronouncing *coil* as "curl", & *curl* as "coil". Thus if repeating the name *Ernest Boyd,* they would say "Oinest Bird". They would give the phrase "The Earl of Jersey bought oil stock" as "The Oil of Joisy bought Erl stock." They also say "mom*u*nt" for *moment,* & tend to pronounce *sphinx* & *sphere* as "spinx" & "spear". They tend to use the redundant *already* common in the Middle West—saying, for example, "Oh, he's gone home *already*" when they merely mean that someone has gone home. The source of this dialect is a vast mystery to philologists, since it is *not shared* by the neighbouring parts of New York State & therefore cannot be due to Dutch influence. My friend Talman comes from Spring Valley, N.Y.—as Dutch a region as any outside Holland—& has not a trace of "New-Yorkese". He, incidentally, hates Manhattan as badly as I do. He has to work there, but commutes daily from his native & ancestral Spring Valley—a full 2-hour trip! Black Harlem—of possible interest to you as a source of sy[n]copated melody—is impressive to the Easterner chiefly on account of its *size,* since all the eastern towns have large African sections. To many westerners—

as, for instance, a friend of mine in Appleton, Wisconsin,[26] who never saw a nigger till he was in college—it would be quite stupefying. I don't know whether there are any blacks in your part of the world or not—or, if so, how thick they are. In Harlem there must be about as many as there are in all the southern states put together—one realises it unpleasantly in the uptown Broadway subway, one of whose three branchings above 96th St. leads to the black belt. The Bronx trains are bad enough—packed solidly with bulbous-nosed or Mongoloid-faced Jews—but de Lenox Ab'noo trains sho' ain't no place fo' no blond of any kind! Black Harlem itself I know largely from 'bus windows—the coach lines from Providence passing down Lenox or upper 7th Ave. through the heart of the district. It is the *extent* which almost stupefies one . . . block after block after block . . . outdoing anything that Charleston or Richmond or Savannah or Atlanta or New Orleans can produce. You'd never think there were so many niggers in the world, or that there were so many denizens of New York that aren't Jews! I'll bet Senegal & Nigeria look white as compared with that zone from about 150th St. down to 125th & beyond. Africa pushes south all the time—crowding the Jews & impinging on the white Puerto-Ricans (who nosed out the Jews in their region about 1930) of upper 5th Ave. And yet this whole black colony scarcely dates from before 1913, when the blacks of "San Juan Hill" downtown were evicted to make room for the new Pennsylvania station. The dispossessed families found some cheap tenements in upper Harlem (then mainly Nordic-Aryan) & formed a nucleus—quickly spreading as the white families on their borders moved away. How far they will get, no one can tell. The Jews don't retreat before them as rapidly as the Aryans did, but they begin to go when the blacks get very thick in a block. The northern rim of Central Park will probably check them & turn their spread eastward—where they'll displace great Greek & Hungarian colonies. The most amusing parts of Harlem are where the rich blacks dwell—these being almost as neat & spruce as Aryan neighbourhoods. The *houses* include some of the most elegant reliques of the Stanford White period, & the prosperous professional Æthiops keep them spic & span! Amusing in another way are the shop windows of Lenox & 7th Aves. All the drug stores carry rabbit's-foot luck charms, dream books, anti-kink fluid & pomade for the wool of dusky sheiks & sirens, & (also for the rites of Congolese coiffure) devices called "straightening-irons." The clothing-stores feature gaudy & eccentric suits & flaming haberdashery. Sharp social distinctions are said to exist among the blacks—for example, West Indian negroes are disliked by the coons of the continental U.S. Some of the West Indians—who speak with a British accent & have an independent arrogance which grates on Southerners—despise the American blacks as much as the latter hate them. Portuguese negroes—so-called "Bravas" from the Cape Verde Islands, unpleasantly common in Providence & other southern New England ports—appear to be absent from nigger Harlem. While the black belt has no well-defined eastern limit, it is checked abruptly on the west by the rocky precipice of St. Nicholas Heights, atop which are the Gothic quadrangles of N.Y. City College (whose student body is almost solidly Jewish) & the streets of a rather passable & fairly Aryan neighbourhood amidst which can be found (overtaken & packed in among modern city blocks) the old country seat (built about 1800) of Alexander Hamilton, out of whose door he walked to his death on that fatal duel morning in 1804.

Glad the garden is progressing, & that spring in general is getting in motion. I envy you! Wintry blasts still continue, & only last Saturday there was a slight fall of snow. Yesterday it rained, & today it blows! I shall certainly be glad to get to Florida if I can so arrange it. However—there have been a few mitigatingly mild days. A week ago Sunday the mercury rose almost to 70°, & my aunt & I were treated to a motor ride toward Worcester. Patches of snow here & there in the country—& some of the oak forests weirdly *autumnal* looking through their odd retention of last year's withered foliage.

I feel tremendously & undeservedly flattered by your kindly mention of the crude & casual sketch in my letter to Rimel. I've always wished I could draw, but have no natural aptitude for it—so that despite infinite pains my best efforts in that direction are rather ludicrous & pathetic. Odd, too, for my grandmother, great-aunt, mother, & late elder aunt were all accomplished artists—while my father's sketch book attests his very passable skill with a pencil. It makes me green with envy when I see certain naturally gifted persons effortlessly translate a visual impression to paper. When I try the same thing, the result is an awkward mess of forced pen-scratches. Whether I could ever learn how to draw decently with patient special instruction, I really don't know. My poor results in school discouraged me—although perhaps some of the completeness of the failure was due to the fact that I was confined to certain simple objects & problems, & not allowed to have my own way & choose my own methods. It is my weakness that I can't conform to rules & restrictions very well. I have to learn to do things in my own way—as dictated by my especial interests & aptitudes—or not at all. That was probably what turned me against music in childhood—I was confined to the simple drudgery & repeated exercises of orthodox instruction. In drawing it was the same way. All that ever really interested me were landscape & architectural effects—rural vistas, & pictures of houses, & street scenes—but school instruction was very slow in getting to these. Instead, I was chained to vases & cubes & spheres & flowers & all that, & filled full of rules for making lines & handling light & shade. Well, that was all very valuable—but what I wanted were rules of perspective for landscapes & panoramas. The smaller objects did not interest me, & I had no incentive to help me master my natural crudeness of pen-&-pencil manipulation. The few landscapes I was allowed to do were assigned without basic perspective rules—why, I don't know. So I gave up serious drawing as a bad job. In the ensuing years I have often crudely scratched diagrams of things as primitive illustrations, but have realised that pictorial art is not for me. Books of self-instruction are very rare, & I never found one that was a real help—except perhaps a specimen I came upon rather recently, which had some simple perspective rules given more comprehensively than usual. Since studying this, it is possible that my houses look more like houses than like cows or locomotives—but all this comes too late to do me much good. And of course I have not the natural talent to warrant taking time off for serious study. As for a view of the "blasted heath"—that's rather a hard proposition, since my idea was simply a region where all the vegetation had disintegrated to a greyish powder! However, I suppose a view of the *edge* of it would (if I could really draw it) convey some idea of what I had in mind. Stunted trees, dead prostrate trunks, & all that—& a suggestion of the abandoned road & perhaps a farmhouse ruin. But I doubt if I could formulate any pictorial conception that a fastidious editor would care to print! The problems of wide perspective are too complex for an ignorant layman to do more than fumble around with—& then again, I am dolefully weak on the sort of pen-strokes needed to represent light & shade—& various surfaces—properly. But here goes—as an experiment:

Not so hot . . . . not so hot! It takes more than I've got to put across the picture of desolation inherent in the original idea of the blasted heath! And this reminds me that I feel tremendously complimented by your suggestion that I attempt a frontispiece for "The Colour Out of Space"! Ah, me—would that I could! I have always envied authors who can illustrate their own tales—putting into visibility exactly what they have in mind instead of depending on the routine work (often careless, uncomprehending, & unsympathetic) of magazine illustrators—but have scarcely hoped to be able to produce anything suitable myself. Your suggestion tempts me strongly, even though I wouldn't like to have the booklet saddled with any crude sketch likely to detract from the value of the whole undertaking. I may try some experimenting & let you see what you think of the results. However, even if I secured a half-decent pictorial effect, I'm afraid that it would be of a sort hard to reproduce in a cut for printing—since I'm especially poor at getting effects with *no lines*, such as printers generally desire. I seem to have to build a view up with many fine lines & dots in order to make it look even half like anything. However—we'll see. If by any chance I happen on any effect that seems worth trying, I'll send it along for your opinion. But I'm under no illusions as to the ineptitude of my unschooled pictorial blunderings!

Some good exhibitions & lectures recently at the local art museum—including one of the greatest temporary groupings of modern Spanish paintings ever housed under one roof—Zuloaga, Sarolla,[27] & all the other contemporary titans. A series of lectures with lantern slides gave necessary data on the background of Spanish art as a whole, & on the Italian, Flemish, & French sources of that art. I'm lucky to have a museum as my neighbour—it is in that *Benefit St.* of which you've heard so much . . . just down hill half a block & around the corner from 66 College.

Well—I sure have covered a lot of paper, & I trust you can pardon my somewhat senile rambling! Hope you'll find the enclosures interesting—& that you will let Rimel see all of them. Best regards to you both.

Yours most cordially & sincerely—

H P Lovecraft

P.S. If at any time you'd like to see samples of the younger Wandrei's marvellous weird art work, I'll be glad to lend you some *photographs* of his drawings which Donald took & gave me.

Notes

1. It was many months before HPL attempted and completed "The Shadow out of Time" (1934–35).

2. The Russian artist Nicholas Roerich (1874–1947). See FLB 14n3.

3. Arkham House published Whitehead's *Jumbee and Other Uncanny Tales* (1944) (for which RHB wrote a preface) and *West India Lights* (1946).

4. Hastur is mentioned in "Haita the Shepherd"; Hali in "An Inhabitant of Carcosa"; the Seven Moons is not cited in any story by Bierce.

5. See FLB 11.

6. *The Star-Treader and Other Poems* was published when CAS was nineteen.

7. George Sterling (1869–1926) wrote prefaces to CAS's *Odes and Sonnets* (1918) and *Ebony and Crystal* (1922).

8. See Volume 3 (2007) of CAS's *Complete Poetry and Translations* for his translation of *Les Fleurs du mal.*

9. This despite the magazine's initial policy not to publish poetry. CAS's first poems appeared in *WT* in the issue for July–August 1923 ("The Red Moon," "The Garden of Evil").

10. "Sadastor" finally appeared in *WT* in July 1930, but *WT* never published "The Abominations of Yondo."

11. Helen V. Sully.

12. Hugh B. Cave, "Dead Man's Belt" (*WT*, May 1933).

13. Hugh B. Cave, "The Corpse-Maker," *Dime Mystery Magazine* 3, No. 4 (November 1933): 8–57.

14. George Allan England (1877–1936), *Darkness and Dawn, Cavalier* (1912–13); rpt. 1914; "The Thing from—Outside," *Science and Invention* (April 1923): 1162–68; *Amazing Stories* 1, No. 1 (April 1926): 67–73.

15. See FLB 11n12.

16. HPL was no aficionado of jazz, as one might gather from this line from *The Case of Charles Dexter Ward:* "what healthy antiquarian could recall how the creaking of Epenetus Olney's new signboard (the gaudy crown he set up after he took to calling his tavern the Crown Coffee House) was exactly like the first few notes of the new jazz piece all the radios in Pawtuxet were playing" (*CF* 2.313)

17. The Colony House, i.e., The Old State House (1762), 150 Benefit Street (Rhode Island declared its independence from England in the Colony House two months before the Declaration of Independence); [brick school house] (1769) [opposite the Sign of Shakespear's Head in Gaol-Lane] . . . ; the college edifice, i.e., University Hall—the original, and for fifty years the only, building at Brown University (1770); the Market House (1773); the First Baptist Meeting House (1775), designed by Joseph Brown, 75 North Main Street; Beneficent Congregational Church (actually 1809), 300 Weybosset Street; St. John's Episcopal Church (actually 1810), 271 North Main Street; and the First Unitarian Church (1816), 301 Benefit Street.

18. HPL to August Derleth, 2 September 1931: "Behind me is the old gambrel-roofed Richard Brown house—erected 1750 & the second brick house (the very first is also standing in good shape down town) to be built within the corporate limits of Providence" (*Essential Solitude* 1.371).

19. The Dexter Asylum was named for Ebenezer Knight Dexter, who upon his death in 1824 bequeathed a property known as Neck Farm, for a facility to care for the poor, aged and mentally ill of Providence. It operated from 1828 to 1957. Brown University's athletic complex now stands on the former asylum site on Hope Street.

20. "The East India Brick Row."

21. Arcade Providence at 65 Weybosset Street is the nation's oldest indoor shopping mall, currently home to the Lovecraft Arts & Sciences Council, host of NecronomiCon Providence.

22. He was not. The College Building of the Rhode Island School of Design was erected on College Street in 1936. HPL's residence at 66 College was moved to 65 Prospect to make way for erection of the List Art Center of Brown University (1959).

23. Perhaps the inspiration for "VII. Zaman's Hill" of *Fungi from Yuggoth.*

24. Asotin is on the Washington–Idaho border, on the west side of the Snake River.

25. "The Dunwich Horror" received the three-star rating in 1929. Stories that received one-star ratings were "The Picture in the House" (1924) and "The Silver Key" (1929).

26. I.e., Alfred Galpin.

27. Daniel Zuloaga Boneta (1852–1921) and Joaquín Sorolla y Bastida (1863–1923), both Spanish painters.

[11]   [ALS]

Charleston, S.C.,

April 29, 1934.

My dear Baldwin:—

Your very interesting letter of the 15th was forwarded to me at Charleston, in whose idyllic climate & fascinating antiquities I am basking for a week prior to my visit in De Land. This is the most captivating city in North America (with the possible exception of Quebec), & is undoubtedly the place where I shall live if I ever find the northern winters absolutely unbearable. Right now I have three times the energy, physical & mental, that I had in New York four days ago.

I had a pleasant week in N Y with Long—seeing Talman, [Donald] Wandrei, Howard Wandrei, & others. Howard Wandrei allowed me to inspect many more of his marvellous drawings—photographs of which Rimel has doubtless shewed you. Donald, by the way, hasn't any stock of "Dark Odyssey" in N.Y.—but I fancy he could get you a copy if given time. The illustrations include some of Howard's best work. Donald's weird novel is called "Dead Titans Waken". I fancy he *did* try it on W.T., but Wright is very cautious about accepting serials. The later novel—non-weird—is called "Invisible Sun." At present Donald is suspending all work on novels—doing pulp shorts & experimenting with plays. No novel of his has ever been accepted anywhere.

Well—I left New York at midnight, Apr. 22–3, & spent the next morning (Monday) in Washington D.C.—exploring the ancient Georgetown section. This is the quaintest part of the National capital—on a hill across Rock Creek from Washington proper, & being the only part antedating the artificial laying out of the Federal City in the 1790's. Georgetown was founded around 1750, & was in Maryland before the D.C. was established. Many of its 18th century houses remain—largely of brick, with quaint doorways & steps.

Most of it is now a quiet residential section, with brick sidewalks, old trees & vines, & all the other attributes of mellow urban antiquity. On the semi-rural heights farthest away from Washington several old-time country-seats still survive. Near the Potomac waterfront—on a hillside now a slum—can still be found the remains of the old Chesapeake & Ohio Canal . . . . one of many built in the era before railways & later abandoned. The still used (& recently improved) Erie Canal is an exception. Providence has its old canal—leading to Worcester & called the Blackstone Canal . . . . built in the 1820's & abandoned in the 1840's. In Richmond, Va. an old canal has been made into an aqueduct for the city water supply. The old canal in Georgetown still has well-defined locks—with ancient wooden gates that turn on massive cylinders. They are largely rotted now, & could not possibly be worked.

I left Washington at 1 p.m. & had an hour in Richmond—116 miles to the south. This is Poe's real home town, & I know it well. Enclosed is a card shewing the residence of Pres. Davis—a typical Richmond mansion. Just back of this house is a steep wooded declivity leading to the place where Shockoe Creek once ran.

Leaving Richmond at 5:15 p.m., I later had an hour in Raleigh, N.C. Charleston was reached on Tuesday at dawn. Here I secured a room at the Y M C A & at once commenced my explorations. Though I know Charleston well, I never tire of revisiting it. It is fully summer here now—rich green vegetation, hot days, straw hats, & all. In Washington & Richmond it is merely springlike—with delicate young foliage. And in N.Y. it is still wintry, with chill winds & bare boughs. I certainly wish I lived here . . . . . up north I wore an overcoat, but here I sit around the Battery hatless & vestless, picking up a coat of tan! Shall move on to Savannah May 1, & be in De Land May 2, unless plans change. My temporary address for a fortnight or so will be % R. H. BARLOW, BOX 88, DE LAND, FLORIDA. Much as I like Florida, I shall hate to leave old Charleston—for the latter has a charm nowhere else to be found. If ever there was an earthly paradise, this is it! By now you have doubtless received the pictorial folder I sent Tuesday. Give Rimel a look at it—& he'll reciprocate with a glimpse of the booklet I sent him.

This is a pretty old region, even though Charleston is about 40 years later than Providence in point of settlement. The first attempt at colonisation was by French Huguenots under Jean Ribant in 1562—the name Carolina being derived from Charles IX of France. They settled at Port Royal—on the coast below Charleston—but went home in the following year. In 1564 Laudonnière brought out another colony, but the Spaniards from Florida soon wiped it out. Then came a long hiatus—after which, in 1663, Charles II of England claimed the region & made land-grants to a group of noblemen of whom Anthony Ashley Cooper, later Lord Shaftesbury, was the most active. These noble "proprietors" did not themselves come to Carolina, but in 1669 sent out a colony to found a town on the great harbour where the rivers Ashley & Cooper (named for Lord Shaftesbury) join the sea. In 1670 this group of 160 built a "Town of Trade" on the Ashley, between two inlets since called Orange Grove & Old Town Creeks. This town—across the Ashley from the present Charleston, was called at first Albemarle Point & later Charles-Town after Charles II. It was very philosophically governed —its plan of organisation,

called the "Grand Model", being drawn up by the philosopher Locke—a close friend of Lord Shaftesbury. It was a strict agrarian aristocracy, rank being fixed by landholding. Thus a *landgrave* held 48,000 acres, a *cassique* (from Ind. *cacique*) 24,000; & a *baron* 12,000. This system, however, lapsed with the years. The present site of Charleston, on the peninsula between the Ashley & Cooper, was called Oyster Point, & was thinly settled from 1672 onward. In 1679 it was decided to move the town thither—so an area was elaborately laid out & fortified on the Cooper River. The transference occurred in 1680—this being generally accepted as the birth-date of modern Charleston. The name Charles-Town was transferred also—& the old town soon fell into disuse. All through this period the Carolina colony was swelled by new arrivals—great planters from the West Indies who took extensive holdings north of the town, & humbler folk from elsewhere. Slaves were introduced by an early Governor who came from Barbadoes. After the revocation of the Edict of Nantes in 1685 many Huguenots flocked in, giving the town a typical element. Their names linger prominently to this day . . . Manigault, Huger, Pon, De Saussure, Legaré, &c. The new Charles-Town of 1680 was about 4 squares long & 2 wide, & forms the oldest part of the present city. The original walls were soon outgrown, however—the town spreading out on all of its landward sides. New colonists gradually flocked in—Dutch from New-Netherland, Yankees from Massachusetts, Germans & Swiss from Europe. It was the Germans who brought the delicate wrought-iron industry for which Charleston later became so famous. All elements mixed well, & a very refined English culture predominated. On account of the wide swamps separating Charles-Town from the rest of the colonies, communication with them was scanty, while frequent traffic was maintained with England. Eldest sons went to Oxford & Cambridge instead of to the colonial colleges. As a result, Charles-Town was the most maturely civilised city in America. The *accent* of the local speech remained phenomenally pure, so that to this day one never hears the common southern dialect with its negroid influence ("Ah reckon he's gōn dahn to de cote-haouse") in Charleston, despite its universal prevalence in neighbouring Georgia & N. Carolina. Pirates, Indians, & Florida Spaniards often harassed the colony, while yellow fever was a common menace till its eradication in modern times. Autumn hurricanes likewise took their toll till the construction of modern sea-walls curbed their effects.

The Charleston of today—& the Charleston of song & story—crystallised in the 18th century. Houses built in the 1720's still stand, & the typical old-Charleston architecture—with French & West Indian influences—took definitive shape around 1760. General agriculture, rice, indigo, & cotton were successively the source of Charleston's wealth. Plantations were in the malarial island regions, & their owners lived in town as much as possible—thus developing an urban culture not found in mainly rural colonies like Virginia. In 1719 the colony of Carolina was taken from the Lords Proprietors & made a Crown Colony, & in 1729 it was divided into North & South Carolina, with Charles-Town as the latter's capital. Charles-Town began to assume its present aspect in the 1730's. Roof-tiling was introduced in 1735; & soon afterward the brick & stucco houses began to adapt themselves to the climate—acquiring side porches of 2 & 3 stories, with door giving on the street. Charleston's famous walled gardens, with ironwork gates, date from 1740 & afterward. Churches, library, & museum all appear during the 18th century.

During the unfortunate political upheaval of the 1770's, Charles-Town was largely rebel in sentiment despite social conservatism. In 1776 a royal fleet attempting to take the city was repelled by the forts on the harbour islands, but in 1780 Charles-Town fell to Lord Rawdon & Sir Henry Clinton . . . . who occupied the still-impressive Brewton–Pringle house shewn in your folder. After Cornwallis's surrender the town was evacuated, & the rebel army entered it late in 1781. In 1783 the name of the city was officially changed from *Charles-Town* to its present exact form of *Charleston* . . . . & about this time it ceased to be the capital of South Carolina—the inland town of Columbia being laid out to serve that purpose. Society in Charleston was very little changed by the revolution—

remaining cultivated & aristocratic. In 1792 there was a valuable influx of French gentlefolk from St. Domingo—victims of the negro uprisings there.

This period—late 18ᵗʰ & early 19ᵗʰ centuries—was the heyday of Charleston's social glory & material prosperity. The unique local civilisation acquired an intensity & permanence which enabled it to resist change & survive despite war & disaster & poverty. Nowhere in the world does 18ᵗʰ century culture still live so markedly as in Charleston. Architecture escaped the fearful decadence of 1830 & onward which engulfed the rest of America, Georgian designs persisting till the period of the Civil War & even after. In 1800 Charleston was the leading centre of culture on this continent . . . . having the best libraries, theatres, &c. in all the colonies. Relations with *Rhode Island* were especially close, because of our planter class in the south county (with town houses in Newport)—an element unique in New England. The great Newport miniature painter Malbone moved to Charleston, & became the teacher of the famous Charleston miniaturist Fraser.[1]

The great fire of 1861 & the Civil War crippled Charleston badly, & the earthquake of 1886 dealt another blow—yet the old culture survives vigorously. Newcomers who appreciate the climate & architecture & traditions have helped to maintain prosperity, & the tourist traffic steadily grows. Around lower Church St. a sort of art colony is forming. In general, the old families remain in the saddle. Blacks are very numerous, & their street cries form a picturesque element. Foreigners are scarce—just a sprinkling of Jew merchants, Italians, & a few Chinese.

Charleston is shaped like N.Y. City, & the regular layout of the streets promotes the analogy. East Bay, Church, Meeting, King, Legare–Archdale, & Rutledge Ave. are (E. to W.) the leading N & S thoroughfares. Tradd, Broad, Market, Wentworth, & Calhoun (S to N) are the great transverse streets. The tip, as in N Y, is called the Battery—& is the seat of a park with live-oaks & palmettoes. The finest houses (*unlike* N.Y.) cluster about the Battery, & in general lie below Broad St. Tradd St. has the most old buildings. Broad is the financial district, & King above Market is the retail shopping section. Broad & Meeting, at their intersection, mark the civic centre—with City Hall (built 1801), Court House (1786), Hall of Records (1820), & P.O. in close proximity. Here also is St. Michael's Church, built in 1762. At the foot of Broad is the Old Exchange built in 1771. Calhoun St. (line of revolutionary fortifications) was the N. limit of the colonial town, but the modern city has spread far beyond. Old churchyards are numerous & very picturesque. Gardens are everywhere—& the whole town is pervaded with the charm of palmettos, live-oaks, magnolias, azaleas, & fragrant blossoms. The odour of flowers & the song of birds at twilight always charm the visitor. And the sound of sweet bells & the crowing of roosters add to the traditional glamour.

Architecturally, Charleston is absolutely unique. It built up a school of its own in colonial times, & most of the ancient buildings still survive. You'll find a good assortment of views in the material sent to you & Rimel. Brick is the dominant building material, & most of the houses are stuccoed over, giving a very continental aspect. Walled gardens, iron balconies, gates, & grilles, side porches, & pointed roofs are typical features. Steeples tend to be thicker than in New England. Classic colonial doorways are numerous & fine. But for the prevailing *flatness,* Charleston would be the most picturesque of cities.

Late parapet or false attic front having imitation windows & grille work

Typical building effects are here very crudely suggested. These are the private houses. Public buildings tend to have a neo-classic effect with double steps something like this. Note the archway under the steps. This is typically Charlestonian, & is also found in the larger private mansions. But of course nothing short of a treatise could convey any full idea of Charleston architecture. Its nearest analogues are, perhaps, the architectures of Quebec & New Orleans—yet it is really like nothing but itself. This

distinctive architecture, plus the charm of climate & greenery, make of Charleston a thing so fascinating that no words can do it justice.

Yes—keep those books as long as you like. "The Turn of the Screw" certainly is very subtle & involved—needlessly so, I truly believe. Of course no absolutely direct writing could convey all the emotional nuances involved—& yet I think that Henry James was often more complex & vague than he might have been. Take your time & re-read—the tale has a vast & malign power despite its defects. I'm glad you share my high opinion of "The Willows"—which I still call the greatest weird story ever written.

No—"At the Mountains of Madness" is not my latest effort. It was written in the spring of 1931, just before I left home for my long Whitehead visit in Florida. After that comes "The Shadow over Innsmouth"—written in November 1931 as a sort of echo to a Newburyport trip which I took with W. Paul Cook in the preceding month. Both of these tales are now on the way toward you—I have supplied instructions for passing from loanee to loanee. Hope they won't disappoint you too much. They have not proved popular, despite the care I have taken with them. "At the Mts. of Madness" is really my most serious work—crystallising a persistent feeling regarding the Great White South & its lethal desolation which I have had since I was 10 or 11 years old. About the "Randolph Carter" stuff—yes, the "Statement" is the first of the lot. I wrote that in 1919—as a virtually literal transcript of a dream. The next is "The Silver Key." (1926) After that *was* "The Dream-Quest of Unknown Kadath" (1926–7), but on looking over the MS. last month I found it below my normal standard & struck it off the list. However, I have not destroyed the MS., & may take certain bits from it for later use. I have also discarded the other long tale—"The Case of Charles Dexter Ward" (1927). The coming Price collaboration is the third "Carter" tale—& probably the last. As for "The Thing on the Doorstep"—I wrote it last August. It is the latest to date. The circulation copy is going the rounds, & will reach you somewhat later than the other two.

Barlow's "Caneviniana" has been held up by his bad eyesight—a really alarming condition which will take him to New York for medical treatment in the autumn. It is possible, however, that I can help him speed things up when I get to De Land next week. My sight is very good at close distances, & I can probably master the essentials of typesetting without too much trouble. Barlow may take my advice & print more than 35 or 50 copies in the end—he has had several additional requests for the brochure.

No hurry about the "Colour"! Yesterday I dropped the Teck Corporation a line attesting my hearty approval of your venture & giving formal permission for the reprinting, so I fancy that obstacle is removed.

No—the creation of fictitious gods & regions & cults & rituals is nothing new! Poe went some distance in that line—you know his "Dark Tarn of Auber" & "Mt. Yaanek".[2] Machen also contributed—remember the "Aklo Letters", "Voorish Domes" &c. in "The White People"?

My whole collection of Smith's weird drawings is now bound your way . . . . though I forget whether I gave the present loanee (R. F. Searight, 19946 Derby Ave., Detroit, Mich.) your or Rimel's address. If it doesn't shew up in Asotin soon you might drop Searight a line. I know you'll appreciate those vivid grotesques. It's very likely that you could persuade Klarkash-Ton to draw you a Saturnian landscape—why not ask him? You could drop him a line of appreciation after seeing my collection. Meanwhile I'm curious to know what you think of Howard Wandrei's work—as photographed by Donald. When you & D W R are through with this, you might send it to me in Florida—I want Barlow to see it.

Yes—ah sho does lahk coon songs, & my pretensions to musical taste are so non-existent that I make no effort to conceal the fact. Too bad more of the old timers are not revived. The radio has brought sporadic revivals of many of the ballads of my youth, but there are hundreds still forgotten. I'd like to send in a list to some broadcasting company—they could undoubtedly dig the old pieces up in the files of various musical publishing houses or at the copyright office in Washington. I haven't heard the new ones, but will try to repair the omission before long. All that you say on the subject is of great interest, & I have no doubt but that this quasi-negroid element will figure substantially in America's future musical tradition. As for Farnese—I haven't heard from him in a long time. Hope he'll come across with the "Fungi" scores. I may ask for a photostatic copy of the things—for I'd like to hear them played—& if I do, I'll surely lend it to you. Yes—I know the saxophone is an old instrument, & had heard of it before its wild popularity in the 1920's. I rather like it—& don't object to neighbours practicing on it as some do. Still, it is distinctly limited—& can never become a standard instrument like the piano or violin. So you've known & forgotten the banjo! After all, I guess a special technique like that of a musical instrument is pretty easy to forget. Still—I fancy I could still toot a "zobo" of the Blackstone Band variety!

Glad the Providence notes proved interesting rather than boresome—& that you found a map which clears up some of the allusions. Yes—I explored the ancient North [not *Hill*] Burial Ground . . . . indeed, my lately-discarded tale of "Charles Dexter Ward" centred around it! The earliest settlers lie there. As for Swan Point—which opened in 1847, & to which were transferred, ancient headstones & all, the graves formerly existing in the Beneficent Congregation churchyard—all my own recent ancestors rest there, & space is reserved for me! It is a very beautiful cemetery, extending over the wooded hills & dales which end in the bluff of the Seekonk River. The oldest headstone which I have seen (transferred from elsewhere) is dated 1711, & has the skull & crossbones common at that period.[3] Providence is surely a great old town, & I'd surely miss the hills if health forced me to move permanently down here.

I was greatly interested in your notes on your section, & especially in the amazing social recognition accorded to negroes. This latter is unheard-of in the east. Up north negroes use the same vehicles & waiting-rooms as whites, & are allowed in the cheaper restaurants & cinema shews, but never have personal associations with whites except on a master & servant basis. They are tacitly barred from the higher grade of restaurants, theatres, shops, & Pullman cars. Down south here the colour line is absolute—a virtual necessity because of the vast black population. Niggers sit on the rear seats of cars & buses, use the gallery of all theatres, have their own parks & eating places, & are restricted to special "Coloured" waiting rooms in stations. Even the cheapest lunch rooms of Charleston are all-white in clientele. Whenever I've been south a long time & come back north, it makes me shrink a bit to have some big buck nigger sit down beside me in a car or waiting room. Washington is the most southerly place without a strict colour line. Baltimore, farther north, draws the line tightly. In the public parks of the South there is varied usage—usually determined by custom—regarding niggers. Richmond is very liberal—blacks being allowed in all the parks. In Charleston, the Battery seems to be all-white except for the black nurses of white children & for beggars who move on continually. In City Park—by the 1769 statue of William Pitt—niggers are freely admitted, but they always take benches apart from white people. Old southern towns like Charleston have worked out the relations between the races pretty well; & there is no friction as in the inner or "deep" south. The blacks know their place, & the white people behave very kindly & considerately toward them. I never saw a Southerner insult or affront a nigger. These local Charleston blacks are of the "gullah"[4] type—& probably of superior African ancestry. They do not exhibit the lawless qualities of the more heterogeneous inland blacks, & lynching is unknown here. There's a great difference between niggers . . . . the best coming from the African east coast, as distinguished from the cheap guinea blacks that used to flood the New Orleans market. Providence was a great slave-trading town in the old days—I guess I told you about the famous "triangular trade" . . . rum, niggers, & molasses. Our ships frequently traded with Charleston. We gradually abolished slavery in the decades following 1780, but our old Narragansett plantations had hundreds of blacks. One of my ancestors[5] left 133 in his will.

What you say of my crude sketches flatters me tremendously, & I am tempted to try that frontispiece later on. I'll keep in mind the size & details desired. It'll be pretty amateurish stuff at best, though. Unless Barlow has a copy of the "Colour" handy I'll have to wait till I get home before making the attempt, since I never remember all the descriptive details of my junk. Nothing is more provoking than a drawing which contradicts the story it is supposed to illustrate—something which occurs constantly in W T because of the negligence of the alleged "artists."

As for a map of Arkham—fortunately I have my crude one with me, so here is a copy. It really isn't of much interest—the only reason I sketched the original last month was to keep my own geographical references from getting mixed up. My mental picture of Arkham is of a town something like Salem in atmosphere & style of houses, but more hilly (Salem is flat except for Gallows Hill, which is outside the town proper) & with a college (which Salem hasn't). The street layout is nothing like Salem's. As to the location of Arkham—I fancy I place the town & the imaginary Miskatonic somewhere north of Salem—perhaps near Manchester.[6] My idea of the place is slightly in from the sea, but with a deep water channel making it a port. I'll try to dope you out a Cthulhu & a Pickman-thing when I can get at the text of the stories. I fear I've thrown away the Cthulhu sketch which I drew for my own guidance when writing the story in 1926. But for god's sake don't frame such crudities! The best I can do is nothing but a rough diagram in essence. As for signing & dating—I've never done that with any sketches of mine, since I don't recognise them as actually presentable products . . . . but if you wish, I'll do so. By the way—don't be too critical of the crude diagrams in this epistle—done from memory on a knee-propped pad on a bench amidst the rustling sea-winds of Charleston's historic Battery!

And now let me thank you exceedingly for the batch of recent snaps plus the two older ones. All were extremely interesting—& I return the senior two as per request. You certainly were a cute & pretty little rascal at 8! I have some odd old pictures of my younger self somewhere, & I'll later let you glimpse such as I can find. I never was much to look at—a solemn-faced little cuss, even when in the best of spirits. One of my old pictures will make you laugh— taken when I was 19. From the stiff derby hat, high choker collar & conservative black coat you'd judge I was about 90! You'll get another laugh out of a later view—taken when I was fat in 1922. It shews Long (then a lean little shrimp) & me standing in front of Poe's cottage in Fordham.[7] I seem to be bursting out of my clothes! Glad to see the views of your parents. The ones of yourself & Rimel shew up finely under a magnifying glass, & indicate that neither of you has anything to worry about so far as appearance goes. The backgrounds are likewise interesting. What a magnificent tree in the view of you & D W together! The views of the Baldwin & Rimel homes are no less pleasing. Asotin's situation among the hills is delightfully picturesque . . . . . & the apricot trees remind me of my grandfather's old letters, & of the old booklets of the Owyhee L. & I. Co.—of which I still have one copy. If I ever find another of those booklets among old family papers I'll send it to you—we used to have dozens knocking around. I think it would interest you. Yes—I'd be glad to see any views of the Snake River country which you may have handy—& I'm sure that views of your orchestral colleagues would also be of interest.

About Baird's quitting W T—it was in 1924 that Wright superseded him, the November issue being Wright's first. Baird's trouble, I fancy, was lack of business ability. He was tardy with his issues, & tried to make up for the missing ones by publishing a mammoth July '24 number which sold for 50¢. He also accepted MSS. indiscriminately—in excess of the magazine's needs. He got the thing into a frightful tangle, so that authors had to wait aeons for their pay. In the autumn the major stockholder J. C. Henneberger (himself an erratic plunger in his way!) took matters into his hands, settled somehow with the authors [he paid me $60.00 in the form of a book order on Scribner's, which he happened to have. Boy! Did I run riot with bookbuying for once in my life?],[8] appointed Wright editor. Old Farnsworth, with all his faults, has done well. He keeps the magazine afloat while all others of its kind go under. I believe he is now himself the majority stock-holder, Henneberger having faded out of the picture years ago. Much of the stock is held by the firm that prints the magazine—the Cornelius brothers of Indianapolis.

No—I've never read Walpole's "Man With Red Hair", though I've always wanted to. If I don't find it in the library when I get home, I'll be very grateful for the loan which you generously offer. Its reputation has reached my ears several times—& the incident you quote makes me additionally anxious to see it for myself. As for Eli Colter's "Golden Whistle"—not having my W T file with me, I couldn't say what issue it appeared in.[9] Nor do I know anything about Colter himself. I never liked his tales overly well, since to me they seemed to contain just a touch of the mawkish. When I get down to Barlow's I can undoubtedly place the story, since he has an *almost* complete W T file. Regarding old-time authors & their dropping out—I suppose some (like Burks & Suter) turn to other forms of writing, while others die or stop writing. I don't believe Wright's policy alienates many—for despite his caprices he is undoubtedly better than the usual run of editors to deal with. There is something in the nature of editorship which seems to cripple men's judgment & common sense! Many, though, dislike the low pay & delayed cheques lately characteristic of W.T. Magazines published by large corporations like Street & Smith are better to deal with financially. As for the recent trend of W T—you'll be agreeably surprised when you finally read the current issue, since it is distinctly above the average. Two stories—"Black Thirst" & the Burks reprint—are of distinguished excellence, while two more—Smith's "Malygris" & the Howard tale—are far above the average. Four good stories in one issue set something of a record!

As for publicly mentioning my collaboration in stories signed by others—**for god's sake don't!!!!** It would be violating the confidence of clients to reveal that their alleged work isn't theirs, & if it became known that I 'gave away' those who employ my services, I wouldn't be employed any more! I really ought not to have mentioned the facts in these matters to anyone—but the temptation is strong in the case of private individuals who shew interest in my efforts. But I must ask all such to keep mum on the subject. When I accept pay for a revision or ghost-writing job, I naturally sell all rights which I might otherwise possess. The editorial remuneration & auctorial credit alike belong to the one who has bought the rights—& if I publicly 'tell on him' I am robbing him of something he has paid for. It is only privately—among good friends, & with injunctions to secrecy (which latter I perhaps neglected to give in this case)—that I speak of these matters. Incidentally (& confidentially)—did I mention that I wrote the late Houdini's "Imprisoned With the Pharaohs" in the large July '24 W T?[10]

About touching on Wright's rather silly objections to the phrase "cosmic ecstasy"—go ahead with my blessing! There's no need of mentioning me, though the point is that the phrase (whoever wrote it) was needlessly objected to, & that the objection was shewn (it doesn't matter by whom) to be pedantic & invalid. Such a takedown of an editor would be very salutary if Hornig will use it. It could be presented in a perfectly friendly & inoffensive way.

Yes—I like the F F in spite of its crudities & misprints. *Fantasy* is not so interesting to me—largely, perhaps, because it specialises in science fiction, for which I don't care much. Glad you like my article[11]—or such of it as the printer deigns to leave in readable form. No—I haven't written anything of the sort lately. This article certainly forced me into quite a bit of reading—in 1925 & 6, when W. Paul Cook first asked me to prepare it for his short-lived *Recluse.* In giving it to Hornig for reprinting, I have tried to bring it down to date in such places as demand change—including certain notable items published since 1927. If I ever had the time & energy, I'd like to expand this thing into a real treatise. There isn't anything extant covering exactly the same ground.

I suppose you're aware of the hopeful news concerning Crawford's venture. I believe I wrote Rimel about the sheets of my story, which arrived just before I started on my trip, & about Crawford's statement that he had finished printing the issue by hand. It now appears (or so I interpret a hasty phrase in a letter just received from Barlow) that the issue is out, & that it is fairly satisfactory despite a certain amateurishness of aspect. I'll be eager to see a copy—which I'll do at Barlow's. My non-letter mail is not forwarded to me. I'm glad that Crawford has made good. I felt sure that he was sincere & earnest about his project, despite the endless delays & excuses which alienated several of his all-too-few paid subscribers. He is even now badly handicapped through lack of type. I hope he will now receive enough support to allow him to continue the magazine. It is evident that he has not quite as much practical savoir faire & assurance as the group of boys who issue F F & *Fantasy.* Incidentally, he has changed the name of his venture from *Unusual Stories* to *Marvel Tales*—an improvement, I think. There are about a dozen errors in my "Celephaïs", but one can get a sort of idea of what I was trying to write.

Meanwhile I am basking in the 18th century atmosphere of America's most fascinating city. Well as I know it, I continually stumble on little details which I've previously overlooked. Next Sunday I shall have an opportunity to inspect the *interior* of one of the old mansions—which I welcome, since I have so far seen only a few Charleston interiors. I am also doing a bit of research in the old churchyards. Many of the local slabs are of *Newport, R.I.* workmanship—& one stone marks the grave of Joseph Harper, manager of the Providence Theatre, who died in Charleston in 1811.

Well—pardon the crudities of this hasty epistle—written in the open air & under public conditions not very favourable to concentration. Better next time. All good wishes—

Yr most obt hble Servt

H P L

[P.S. on envelope] Have just moved on to Savannah. This town is not as old & quaint as Charleston. It was founded in 1733, & has lost a good deal of its early architecture. But much remains—& the warm, green-shaded streets & innumerable parks & old doorways with railed steps make it tremendously fascinating. Have 8½ hours here—or I may stay over still later & take a night coach to Jacksonville. Then—tomorrow morning, May 2—to De Land. ¶ Savannah is warmer than Charleston—more vines & creepers, & the palmettos grow taller.

¶ Here at last is that promised picture which you can keep. Had it snapped in a dime studio in Charleston yesterday. First in 3 years—Gad, how I've aged in that period! I'll get another one snapped for Rimel before long.

H P L

The Rhode Island General Nathanael Greene is buried beneath a monument in Savannah.

[Enclosure: HPL's map of Arkham, MA.][12]

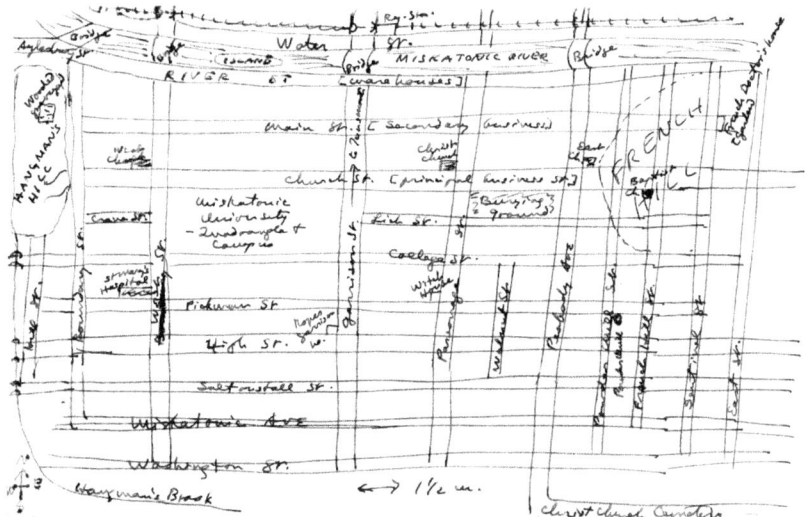

Notes

1. Edward Greene Malbone (1777–1807); Charles Fraser (1782–1860).

2. The references are to Poe's "Ulalume."

3. See *Letters to Alfred Galpin:* "one June day in 1917 I was walking through Swan Point Cemetery with my aunt and saw a crumbling tombstone with a skull and crossbones dimly traced upon its slaty surface; the date, 1711, still plainly visible" (81).

4. Gullahs are descendants of enslaved Africans living in the Lowcountry region of the U.S., which includes both the coastal plain of South Carolina and Georgia and the Sea Islands.

5. Robert Hazard (1635–1710) was HPL's great-great-great-great-great-grandfather. He had a house so large that he was once asked whether he rode from front to back door on horseback.

6. About 8 miles south of Gloucester, on Massachusetts Bay.

7. See *SL* 3, facing p. 70.

8. See *SL* 1.355–56. HPL is misremembering. The $60.00 he received from Henneberger was not for *WT* stories, but for work that HPL had done on a planned humor magazine.

9. Eli[zabeth] Colter, "The Golden Whistle" (*WT,* January 1928).

10. The May/June/July issue of *WT* contained 3 items by HPL: "Imprisoned with the Pharaohs," ghostwritten for Harry Houdini, "Hypnos," and "The Loved Dead," revised for Clifford M. Eddy, Jr.

11. The reprint of "Supernatural Horror in Literature," then being reprinted in *FF*.

12. "Map of the Principal Parts of Arkham, Massachusetts" (HPL's title is on reverse), copied by an unknown hand in the *Acolyte* 1, No. 1 (Fall 1942): 26 (as "Map of Arkham"). Other maps of Arkham are reproduced in *Marginalia* (Sauk City, WI: Arkham House, 1944), preceding p. 279, and *Letters to Robert Bloch and Others*, 169.

[12]   [ALS]

% Barlow, Box 88,
De Land, Fla.
May 16, 1934.

My dear Baldwin:—

So busy do my genial hosts keep me, that I can't possibly do justice to the various letters at hand, including your interesting communication of April 30. However, I must at least drop a brief & grateful acknowledgment. A few days ago I managed to get a line off to Rimel, in which (assuming that he shares his correspondence, as was intended) you will find more or less of a description of my brilliant & genial young host & his pleasant habitat. Barlow has also sent him a package containing "The Metal Monster", "The Blind Spot", & my Dunsany book[1]—all of which are equally meant to be read by you.

I am having a glorious time here—the climate is exactly what is needed to brace me up. You'll learn from my Rimel letter of the various trips & activities which have been under way. Don't yet know how long I'll stay—Barlow always vetoes all talk of moving on. By this time you will undoubtedly have received my long letter from Charleston, & the pictorial material from Savannah . . . . with a snap of my ugly mug enclosed. I was sorry to leave Savannah behind, for that town marks the southern limit of the English Georgian architecture of which I am so fond. Down here, though, I've seen an old Spanish sugar mill antedating 1763, & the ruins of a Spanish mission built in 1696.

The trip to Dunedin seems to be cancelled, & I also doubt if I shall meet Cummings, Hamilton, & Williamson—who are too broke for side-trips, & the latter two of whom may be returning directly north. As for the relative merits of H & W—it seems to me it's largely a toss-up. H surely turns out the worst tripe, yet on the other hand W. never wrote anything approaching "The Monster God of Mamurth."[2]

As I wrote Rimel, Barlow's Canevin book is held up by his bad eyesight & may not be out till winter or next spring. Meanwhile the edition of "The

Shunned House" (115 copies—others lost & damaged) has come from Cook, & gradual steps will be taken toward its binding & issuance. Possibly some copies will be bound in the skins of snakes that Barlow has shot! Yes— Barlow has a really notable collection of books & literary reliques despite a certain amount of pulp trash. Letters from James Branch Cabell, & so on. Regarding the original ms. of the coming "Silver Key" sequel—I regret to say that I've promised it to this selfsame young collector (to add to his trash department); but I'll try to dig up something else before long. Yes—I'll be glad to sign anything which you may happen to have around, although I must warn you that such a signature isn't worth much. Glad you like "The Outpost". I haven't seen it in print yet, since my non-letter mail isn't forwarded, & Barlow doesn't take F M. Wright turned it down 3 or 4 years ago. I got the idea of "The Fishers from Outside" from one of the odd books of the extravagant dreamer Charles Fort.[3] I suppose you know all about him.

About returning books—Providence is the place. My aunt is always ready to receive material. If express is cheaper than parcel post, by all means use it. It's just as convenient for me. Which reminds me—Barlow tried to send his package to Rimel by express, & the agent at De Land wouldn't take it— saying there was no express office at Asotin. Was this a mistake?

I've just seen *Marvel Tales*—Barlow's copy—but haven't had a moment to read it yet. It certainly isn't at all bad, & I hope Crawford can keep it up. The other day I had a note from Eshbach, the other editor. Like you, I prefer the small size. That story of Long's scheduled to appear is one which I consider among his very best, although Wright rejected it. Some of Klarkash-Ton's scheduled tales are also magnificent.[4] I imagine that there will always be enough rejected good stories by the best weird magazine authors to keep all three semi-amateur papers—F F, M T, & F M—supplied.

I haven't seen the account of Wandrei in F M,[5] but imagine it must be interesting. I am sure the corresponding one of me will be as nearly so as the less interesting nature of the subject will permit. As for the details you are seeking— the first fantasy yarn I had published *anywhere* was in the *amateur* press . . . . in *The United Amateur* for . . . . . . 1916. (I can't recall the month.) that was "The Alchemist", which I wrote in 1908. The next was "The Beast in the Cave", an older tale, written in 1905 when I was 14½. This appeared in W. Paul Cook's *Vagrant* some time in 1917. These two were the only ones which I had saved from a general holocaust of my fiction late in 1908. I wrote no stories between 1908 & 1917, being then wholly devoted to verse, essays, criticism, & the natural sciences. The favourable reception of those old tales in the amateur press caused me to resume story-writing—largely through the encouragement of W. Paul Cook & Samuel Loveman. Of the *new* series, the first tale was "The Tomb", & the next "Dagon", both written in 1917. Both of these & other later ones were published in the amateur press.[6] The first tale of mine to appear in a *professional* magazine was something written to order for *Home Brew*, a cheap rag edited by one of the old amateur group. This was "Herbert West—Reanimator", a 6-part series appearing from January to July 1922. A rotten mess, which I have since wholly repudiated. The next thing also appeared in *Home Brew*—a 4-part serial called "The Lurking Fear", appearing early in 1923 & illustrated by Clark Ashton Smith. This was later reprinted in a single number of *Weird Tales*. *Home Brew*, after a change of name, failed in 1924.[7] If this magazine seems too insignificant to notice, you can say that my fictional publication (serious professional) began with "Dagon", in the Oct. 1923 number of *Weird Tales*. As for extremely primitive childhood weird items—the first I recall is "The Noble Eavesdropper", written in 1897 at the age of 7. The earliest surviving infantilia are "The Mysterious Ship" & "The Secret of the Grave", both dating from 1898. None of this stuff, of course, ever was or will be published.

Regarding my "Complete Works"—a good deal of the stuff I have perpetrated is really far too trivial to mention. This is especially true of the verse. All that could possibly be of interest is a list of my mature weird tales, which I enclose, plus perhaps the following items:

Juvenile magazine—*R.I. Journal of Astronomy* (hectographed)—1903–1907

1906–1918—Monthly astronomical articles in *Providence Tribune* & *News*.

1906–7—Astronomical articles in rural papers.

1913–18—Verses of old-fashioned cast in *Providence News*.

1914—Exposé of astrology—*Prov. News*[8]

1915—Serial—"Some Outlines of Astronomy" *Asheville* (N.C.) *Gazette-News*.[9]

1914 & onward—verses, official criticism, & minor articles in amateur press. None notable.

1915–23—Amateur magazine *The Conservative*

1917—Verses—"Nemesis".

1923—Edited poems of J. E. Hoag—wrote preface.

1927—Edited posthumous poems of J. R. Bullen—wrote preface.

1927—article "Supernatural Horror in Literature" in *The Recluse*.

1930—Verses "The Outpost", "The Ancient Track", & "Fungi from Yuggoth."[10]

¶ Best story: "The Colour Out of Space". 2nd best, "The Music of Erich Zann." Poorest stories repudiated & forgotten. "Herbert West—Reanimator", perhaps the worst. Other bad stories: "The Hound", "He", & "Hypnos." Three favourite writers: Poe, Dunsany, & either Machen or Blackwood, with M. R. James in the same class. Favourite pulp writers—A. Merritt, Clark Ashton Smith, R. E. Howard, Frank B. Long, C. L. Moore, E. Hoffmann Price, & others. No connexion whatever with Brown (or any other) university—though I happen to live near it & on property owned by it. Am next door to its John Hay Library, containing the Harris Collection of American Poetry, greatest of its kind in the world. **No**—for Jesu's sake **don't** mention that Klarkash-Ton & I call Gernsback "Hugo the Rat." That would form a thoroughly unjustifiable attack, despite the fact that the damn skunk undoubtedly deserves it! The one striking case of the early rejection of a tale later accepted by another editor & well received is that of "The Rats in the Walls." In 1923 I submitted this to R. H. Davis, then editor of *The Argosy*, & he returned it as being too horrible & unusual for the Munsey publications. It was then accepted by Edwin Baird of *Weird Tales*, printed, & exceedingly praised by readers. In 1930 Wright reprinted it in W T, & in 1931 it was included in the British "Not at Night" anthology. No—it would not do to say that I wrote anything published under Houdini's name. It is always un-ethical to 'give away' a revision or ghost-writing client. You might, however, say that I did research & literary work for Houdini from early in 1924 until his death in October 1926. By the same token, *don't for your life mention* that I wrote "Yig", "Electric Executioner", "Horror in Museum", &c.! *One must never give away a client.* I believe I touched on this point in the letter sent from Charleston. You can say that I have done much revision & ghost-writing, but I don't know that I'd hint about the source of various W.T. items.

Glad to hear that the musical situation has improved, & that you have not found it necessary to play in beer-gardens or other more or less inappropriate places. The engagements in Peck must take on something of the aura of adventurousness in view of the striking situation & sometimes perilous condition of the highway by the Clearwater River. Yes—from what you say I'd imagine that the region is indeed like hilly Vermont with its suggestion of brooding cosmic secrets. The performance at Deary must surely have been interesting . . . . especially the instance of social equality accorded a negro boy. That incident sounds like something in France or other European countries where there is no huge black population to create a special situation. It certainly would not do in the East—& especially the South! Here in Florida niggers have to keep strictly in their place. That quip on the races of N.Y. has a good deal of truth behind it. Despite the plethora of Jews, it is a fact that an Irish clique still controls N.Y. politics—& the coons of Harlem certainly seem to prosper from the existing order! Regarding Jews—they are undoubtedly very superior mentally, & we can absorb a good many of them without damage. The only trouble is when they become too numerous & unassimilable. Their great difference from us is in emotions & inherited ideas of things. They belong to an ancient & deeply ingrained tradition which cannot mix with ours. Negroes, en masse, are undoubtedly biologically inferior despite the achievements of exceptional individuals. Their blood must be kept strictly out of the veins of the white American people.

Congratulations on the new dictionary! The F & W Standard is one of the best. I use the Stormonth's Dictionary (British) which my father used, & also an old edition of Webster's International.

About "The Metal Monster"—the whole set of *Argosy* instalments has gone forward to Rimel from Barlow, & you will behold it ere long. "The Face in the Abyss" in its revised & enlarged form (called "The Snake Mother") ran 8 *Argosy* instalments beginning Oct. 25, 1930. It is also published under its original title in book form. Barlow has the book, & will be glad to lend it to you if you'll let him know. The book of poems by Smith written at 17 & published at 19 is entitled "The Star-Treader". Yes—I've thought of writing a weird novel, but have never actually begun one.[11] If I did, it would deal with the New England scene.

You'll find considerable about my gifted young host in my letter to Rimel. You ought to see the bas-relief of *Cthulhu* which he has just made!

More anon. All good wishes—

Yrs most sincerely—

H P L

[P.S.] Howard Wandrei's stuff is surely magnificent. He has just gone for the summer to Provincetown on Cape Cod (Mass.), & can be addressed in care of Alvin von Hinzmann, 543 Commercial St. Barlow has a plan for publishing 11 × 14 photographic reproductions of his work.

[P.]P.S. [on envelope:] Price is now at his old home—5314 East 12th St., Oakland, Cal. He has just made a trip to Auburn to see C A S—the meeting being extremely pleasant. Like Robert E. Howard, Smith had never met another W T writer in person before.

[Enclosure: HPL's list of stories. Non-extant.]

Notes

1. A. Merritt, *The Metal Monster;* Austin Hall and Homer Eon Flint, *The Blind Spot;* Lord Dunsany, *A Dreamer's Tales.*
2. Edmond Hamilton, "The Monster-God of Mamurth" (*WT*, August 1926; rpt. September 1935).
3. Charles Fort (1874–1932), author of *The Book of the Damned* (1919), *New Lands* (1923), *Lo!* (1931), and *Wild Talents* (1932).
4. Long's "The Dark Beasts" appeared in *Marvel Tales* No. 2 (July–August 1934). CAS had no stories in the magazine.
5. Julius Schwartz and Mortimer Weisinger. "Donald Wandrei Interviewed." *Fantasy Magazine,* 3 No. 3 (May 1934): 10–15.
6. W. Paul Cook (1880–1948) published HPL's juvenile tale "The Beast in the Cave" (1905) in *The Vagrant* in 1916. In the summer of 1917, HPL wrote "The Tomb" and "Dagon," which Cook also published.
7. *Home Brew,* edited by George Julian Houtain, was later renamed *High Life,* but it folded in 1924.
8. HPL refers to various articles and satires (the latter published under the pseudonym "Isaac Bickerstaffe, Jun.") attacking astrology articles by J. F. Hartmann.
9. The series was in fact titled "Mysteries of the Heavens Revealed by Astronomy." All astronomical articles cited here appear in *CE* 3.
10. This list, abridged and adapted by FLB, was published in Francis T. Laney and

William H. Evans, *Howard Phillips Lovecraft—1890–1937: A Tentative Bibliography* ([Los Angeles]: FAPA, Winter 1943), 10.

11. In 1922 HPL did begin *Azathoth,* which he described as a "weird Vathek-like novel" (*SL* 1.185). Earlier, in 1920, he had considered writing a "hideous novel" (*SL* 1.110) called *The Club of the Seven Dreamers* but probably never began it. He apparently did not consider *The Case of Charles Dexter Ward* (1927) or *At the Mountains of Madness* (1931) to be full-fledged novels.

[13]   [ALS]

De Land—

June 3, 1934

My dear Baldwin:—

　　　　　　Your of the 21st, with postscript of the 22nd, duly arrived. By this time you ought to have received the parcel post bundle with The Metal Monster, Blind Spot, &c.—which was sent either to you or to Rimel. Let Barlow know if it didn't reach Asotin—it would be a pity to have it lost in the mails. I note the conditions regarding express shipments, & shall keep them in mind—although possibly the saving on small packages of one or two books might not be extreme. Meanwhile I trust the Klarkash-Ton drawings came from Searight, & that you & Rimel found them enjoyable. Keep them as long as you like—& send them down here to Barlow when you are through with them. There are some of them which he hasn't seen. About the Silver Key—there was no *trilogy*. The coming story is a sequel to *one* only—"The Silver Key", published in the Jany 1929 issue of W.T. I think I've lent this to you in the past—if not, I'll be glad to do so when I get home.

About book bindings—Barlow has *tried* some snake-skin specimens, but has so far produced nothing satisfactory to himself. He hasn't attempted any with human skin as yet—indeed, he hasn't even killed & skinned any human beings experimentally. . . . black or white! Later on I'll send photographs of his Cthulhu bas-relief & elephant-god statuette. As for drawings of my monsters—enclosed is a sketch of Cthulhu which I hope isn't too outrageous. I'll try Pickman's Model later on, when I can get time to read the story & refresh my memory on details.

Don't hurry about the biography—I'm sure Hornig's readers can very well wait. Glad you liked the photograph—which is quite a good likeness. The Florida climate certainly has set me on my feet, & I hate to think of returning north. Before long I must be moving on—probably toward St. Augustine, since hopes of Havana are well-nigh extinct.

Sorry to hear that the good old orchestra has been forced to disband, & hope that you can gather at least a few of the familiar group around you in the new union organisation. What you say of some of the members is surely interesting in the extreme—John Blake must have a vast amount of fortitude & resourcefulness to carry on his gruesome occupation so successfully at his age! Yes—I'll be glad to see views of some of the valiant group. Your present work appears to take you to some rather picturesque places—indeed, Pierce sounds very much like the Wild West towns of popular tradition.

I had not realised that so much of the old west remained—although Robert E. Howard has convinced me that Texas is still "wild & woolly." The good old Snake would appear to include remote reaches where things have not changed much since my grandfather's time. There must be a sort of grim irony in the fake mining operations—which I suppose are carried on just to keep the stock-selling racket technically within the law.

Yes—there are many scenes in Barlow's region which make one think of the real tropics & their jungles. This is especially true of the palm-lined shores of the St. John's river, which is crossed about half way between the house & the village. That river-bank landscape might well be one along the Congo or the Amazon. There are no other human habitations in sight of the Barlow place, & it will be a long time before the suburbs of De Land reach out that far. There is no rural free delivery—the Barlows have to get & deliver their mail in town, where they have a box at the P.O.

West of the Barlows' the ground begins to get slightly hilly—an unusual thing for Florida—& there are some fine views of outspread lakes & forests. At length one reaches Eustis—a very attractive little town on the shore of a sizeable lake of the same name. About 30 miles south of De Land is Orlando, the metropolis of central Florida & one of the most scenically beautiful towns in the U.S. Eastward on the coast are New Smyrna & Daytona, about which I believe I wrote in my previous letter.[1]

My hosts have kept me so busy that I've had no time to do any writing—indeed, I can hardly keep up with my correspondence! However—the tropical atmosphere of Florida would not in any way prevent my writing about Arkham. I wrote the best part of "The Whisperer in Darkness"—a Vermont story—in Charleston, & many authors write in environments wholly opposite to those they describe. Some, indeed, believe that one can best treat a scene when far enough removed from it to make it seem like a distant picture. For example—my extremely local Providence tale, "The Shunned House", was written in Brooklyn, N.Y.[2]

As for Barlow's photographic prints of Howard Wandrei's drawings—I don't know whether he'll try *renting* any. His idea is to *sell* them at $2.00 each . . . . which barely covers the cost. I guess he can fix you up with a "Shunned House" copy bound in snake-skin—or at least with a snakeskin back strip. Write him about it. It will be some months, however, before he can get at the task of issuing the brochure.

Hope you didn't find housekeeping too hard during your mother's absence. I often get meals myself, but rely largely on canned & package goods. Sorry you irrevocably destroyed "Congo Dusk", since it may well have had its strong points. Trust you'll have good luck with the new dance number . . . . which

I hope you'll send along to Barlow as suggested. He could undoubtedly read the music & venture suggestions, though of course he is only an amateur & beginner in musical matters. My own opinion would be valueless—though I'd be glad to give a layman's reaction. However—it isn't likely that I'll be here long enough to be on hand when Barlow gets the music. Some time I trust I can have an opportunity of hearing one of your compositions. You have so much knowledge & experience in this field that I know your work must be delightful.

Got the new W.T. yesterday, but am inclined to think it is not a remarkable issue. The high spot, beyond doubt, is Klarkash-Ton's powerful "Colossus of Ylourgne." Howard's story is so un-typical & below par that I'm inclined to think it a resurrection from early days.[3]

Well—I must cease abruptly & get this ready for the trip to town. More later, when opportunity permits. Barlow sends regards.

With every good wish—

Yrs most cordially,

H P L

[Enclosure: HPL's drawing of Cthulhu]

Cthulhu

June 3, 1934   H. P. Lovecraft

Notes

1. I.e., DWR 11 (13 May 1934).

2. Written 16–19 October 1924, seven months after HPL had been married and moved to Brooklyn.

3. So far as is known, "The Haunter of the Ring" was written only a few months before publication.

[14]   [ALS]

66 College St.,

Providence, R.I.,

July 27, 1934.

My dear Baldwin:—

Yours of the 16th arrived, just as I mailed quite a longish letter to Rimel[1]—hence, assuming that he has shewn you this epistle, you already know the events of my later wanderings & ultimate return home. Your silence needs no excuse—indeed, most of my correspondents have been getting silence from me of late, since my programme is utterly disorganised with piled-up work. Another thing—a whole novel to straighten out & supply with a prologue—arrived this morning, & I really don't know what in hades I can do about it!

Sorry your recent work has proved so arduous, & trust you'll have plenty of opportunities to rest. Glad you copied the list of tales, & trust you'll ask for any you may wish to see. Here is a sketch of Pickman's Model to match the Cthulhu. I sent Rimel one at his request, & this is a duplicate of the general theme—with variations in details. Of course the sketch is crude, but it shews roughly what I had in mind. Rimel made a fine drawing of the Model from imagination—I trust he shewed it to you before sending it along to Providence. What you say of the "Mountains of Madness" cheers me up immensely & strengthens my determination to try to start another writing period later on. Ever since I was 11 or 12 the mystery of the great white Antarctic has haunted me poignantly—almost disturbingly—& this yarn was a very serious attempt to capture the mood & get it off my chest.[2] Wright turned it down, & most of the readers of the MS. disliked it—the whole incident doing more to stop my writing than any other one thing. Glad the city under the ice sounds vivid & convincing. Gad! but I actually *did* roam those primal & terrible corridors when I wrote the thing! They suggested themselves, as through a kind of pseudo-memory. As to the artist who painted a picture of Leng—I must confess that I've forgotten the whole allusion, so that I don't know whether the figure I named was real or fictitious. I don't suppose this has anything to do with the famous artist Nicholas Roerich, to whose strange paintings of Thibetan mountain scenery I frequently allude. Roerich is real enough—there is a whole museum in N.Y. devoted to his work,[3] & he is a personal friend of A.

Merritt. The "Innsmouth" story was suggested by the ancient & decaying town of Newburyport, Mass. Hope you'll like "The Thing on the Doorstep." Don't know when I can ever get around to the writing of that Arkham yarn.

The new F F came out long ago—an excellent issue, it seems to me. Your column is certainly all right—with timely & appropriate paragraphs. I assume it was the printer who metamorphosed Klarkash-Ton's Star-Treader into "Star-Tr*a*der"! Further news—Price is paying C A S a second visit. Robert E. Howard recently explored the gigantic Carlsbad Caverns in New Mexico, & found this glimpse of the nether abyss of utterly stupendous grandeur & nightmare fascination. His letter on the subject is virtually a lyric poem![4] Robert Bloch of Milwaukee has just placed his first story—"The Secret in the Tomb"—with W.T.

Glad you like "The Blind Spot." Though it has its conventional aspects, the whole thing struck me as unusually original & convincing. I understand there is a sequel, though I've never seen it. The descriptive parts of "The Metal Monster" certainly form notable stuff, & I hope Merritt will eventually prepare a new & definitive version, as he half intends to do. "Burn, Witch, Burn" has considerable realism; though the gangster atmosphere is a bit stereotyped, while the events are not quite as richly imaginative as most of Merritt's inventions. As for the new novel—I understand it will begin in the *Argosy* some time during September.[5] I want to pick up the issues containing it. Don't hurry about the books—plenty of time. Derleth has just sent me an anthology—"Strange Assembly", compiled by John Gawsworth—containing two Machen items I never heard of before.[6] Haven't had time to read it yet.

If you saw that jungle stream near Silver Springs, you wouldn't wonder why the Tarzan film was taken there! It looks precisely like all the pictures of tropical jungles that I've ever seen—& the sensation of sailing down it past palms & vines & creepers & trailing moss & coiled snakes & turtles & alligators on logs is indescribably weird. One would swear that it is indeed Africa!

I surely hope you will some day realise your ambition of exploring a genuine jungle country. Your new friend certainly has covered the globe a bit—although I think his tale of negroes crossing with gorillas is a bit exaggerated. Legends of this sort are common in Africa, but are undoubtedly without foundation. Experiments conducted by the Dutch years ago, & more lately the Yerkes foundation in America, prove that gorillas are really very distant from all existing human species—our own simian ancestors having been apes of a wholly different sort. No fertile crossing between gorillas & negroes is possible, & gorillas are not attracted in any way by human beings. However—there's no reason to think that Mr. Graybill is not widely travelled. He probably repeated the legend just as he heard it. It's curious, though, that he mentioned his "membership" in the National Geographic Society as a mark of distinction—since the "members" of this enterprise are merely the subscribers to the *National Geographic Magazine*. Anybody who subscribes is a "member"—& there are no qualifications for "membership." It is as if *Weird Tales* called itself the "National Weird Literature Society" & considered every subscriber a "member." Personally, I think the arrangement is distinctly cheap—& unbecoming in an organisation which really does as much useful work as the Geographic Society does. For of course there *is* a genuine nucleus to the society—a governing board & actually participating members who perform all the functions of a real learned society. The practice of allowing all the magazine's subscribers to consider themselves "members" is undoubtedly a good circulation-getter, since it gives the general public a chance to feel itself part of a dignified fabric. Kids & naive people take their "membership" seriously, but cultivated adults of course realise how little it means. That's why it's a bit odd that this chap parades it seriously. Amusingly enough—to carry out the idea—the advertising matter of the Geographic takes the form of "invitations" to become a "member". Since they generally get names from other subscribers, they say (in a filled-in form-letter) that so-&-so "recommended" you for "membership", & so on. Barlow is a "member"—& so was I once. Every now & then I get an "invitation" saying that somebody or other has "recommended" me as a member. Well—I'd like to subscribe again if I could spare the cash! I hope Mr. Graybill will be able to help you get in touch with an expedition—of course, it is possible that he is actually connected with the *governing body* of the Geographic Society. So he knows Merritt, eh? I'll ask A M whether he recalls Graybill if I get the chance, although he has owed me a letter for a long time. The present Dept. of Labour job would seem to be quite an important & exacting one.

That session of yours at Pierce surely was quite an ordeal, & I trust you won't have anything as arduous as that to cope with for a long time. From your account, Pierce would appear to be a typically hard-boiled & wide-open town of the traditional frontier sort—even if its toughest element did hail from the slums of New York. What you say of the wooden sidewalks is interesting. Wood is quite extensively used for sidewalks in many places—especially Quebec—but the destructive effects of the loggers' boots is something I never heard of elsewhere. Too bad the town had a tough C C C unit wished on it. Some of those companies contain pretty bad material, though others—like the Chicago one you mention—seem to be of vastly higher grade. They probably form a good influence for the boys in them. So Pierce—or Pierce City—was the first Idaho capital![7] I never heard my grandfather mention it, but suppose he must have had dealings there prior to Idaho's statehood in 1890. By the way—I suppose you know that your own neighbour *Lewiston* was the *first* territorial capital. It is so designated in the primary geography (1865) used by my mother in school.[8] The old buildings you mention must be of extreme interest, & I hope they will remain well preserved. They really ought to be public museums—as perhaps they will be some day.

Rhode Island has not had as hot weather as the west—nothing over 90°

so far as I know. There have been several spells uncomfortably cool for me. Glad the St. Augustine folder arrived safely. I certainly had a great trip, as you can see from my letter to Rimel. It would take a volume to describe all the features of it. I was especially pleased to see the Poe cottage in Philadelphia— fitted up exactly as in Poe's time. But I suppose St. Augustine & Charleston were the real high spots. They have a fascination of which one never tires.

Shall be glad to see the snaps when they come. Barlow took an excellent picture of me June 16,[9] when he got his new camera, & I'll send a print when I can get hold of some extras.

With every good wish—
      Yrs most sincerely—
           H P L

[Enclosure: HPL's drawing of Pickman's model]

Pickman's Model — H. P. Lovecraft
July 27, 1934.

Notes

1. I.e., DWR 15 (23 July 1934).

2. In his youth, HPL wrote several nonextant treatises about Antarctic exploration (*Voyages of Capt. Ross, R.N., Wilkes's Explorations*), as well as an *Antarctic Atlas.*

3. The Roerich Museum (then located at 103rd Street and Riverside Drive, now at 319 West 107th Street in New York) was a favorite haunt of HPL.

4. See letter 106 (c. July 1934) in *A Means to Freedom.*

5. *Creep, Shadow!*

6. "The Gift of Tongues" and "The Rose Garden" (from *Ornaments in Jade,* 1924).

7. Actually, Pierce was the first county seat of Shoshone County, established in 1861. When the Idaho Territory was established in 1863, the capital was Lewiston. When Idaho became a state in 1890, the capital was (and is) Boise.

8. Possibly David M. Warren, *A Primary Geography.*

9. The classic dark portrait. See frontispiece, *Selected Letters* 5.

[15]　　[ALS]

Aug. 21, 1934

My dear Baldwin:—

　　　　　Glad the various monsters proved of interest. The originals of Barlow's figures are very clever, & I hope you can see them both some time. If you come east I'll be delighted to shew you Cthulhu, & old Bill Lumley would doubtless take equal pride in exhibiting the Elephant-god. As for my newly-acquired "Bird of Space"—he looks something like this . . . standing about a foot tall. He is carved out of a piece of horn—I don't know of what animal, thought the colour is black—& highly polished & lacquered on the exterior. Wings & feathers—as well as eyes—are suggested through some very delicate engraving. The posture of the bird—as if looking into the sky preparatory to a hop-off for unknown trans-galactic reaches—combined with its generally weird aspect to suggest the title "Bird of Space". I am told that this object represents a type of carving common over a century ago among American sailors on ships trading in the Far East. The Sino-Japanese influence is so strong that there is little doubt who the sailors' teachers were. I've put the Bird on the top of a new low bookcase in company with a Japanese idol & a Kim Lung vase. Loveman was amazingly generous to give me this object. I had admired it for years in his home, but never thought of hinting for it. On the last night of my visit we fell to talking about it, & as I left he pressed it into my hands as a final thunderbolt surprise. That's just like him! Some time I mean to take a photograph of this & other objects in my "museum"—& when I do I'll send you prints. I have an Egyptian ushabti, Mayan images, & other odd & curious things. As for the story, "The Bird of Space", it's distinctly worth reading. If you can't get hold of it, I'll dig it up & lend it to you some time—taking due precautions not to let the magazine get in any worse shape than it is. I read the sequel, too.[1] Hope you'll like "The Thing on the Doorstep", though I have my doubts. It is extremely different from the "Mts. of Madness", & is usually liked by the people who *don't* like the "Mountains". Haven't yet sent the "Thing" to Wright, but may before long.[2] As for sending stuff to other magazines—I've studied these others fairly thoroughly, & don't think that anything of mine would have a chance with them. They all have their artificial conventions, to which my work does not conform. Regarding Wright's ostensible reason for turning down the "Mts of Madness"—I believe it was that the story is "too long" & incapable of effective division into instalments of the proper length. Others complained of the slow development—& that was probably Brother Farny's real reason for rejecting it. He simply didn't like it—for he finds himself able to waste no end of serial space on favourites like Otis Adelbert Kline. I don't know what Wright's reason for turning down "Innsmouth" was—I didn't submit it personally, but Derleth sent it in while it was lent to him. I believe, though, that Derleth said the reason was the same as before—too long, & not well divisible.[3] Yes—A. Hyatt Verrill is one of the best of the scientifictionists. His style isn't notable, but his plots always dovetail well with actual scientific knowledge. He is a noted explorer & anthropologist.

About "The Face in the Abyss"—I have the original 1923 *Argosy* novelette & will be glad to lend it to you; while Klarkash-Ton can similarly supply you with the 1932 addition, "The Snake Mother" . . . . or pardon me, I see by your letter that you have that. I was going to offer you the loan of the bound book formed by the joining of the two—which I'm just acquiring from Barlow on a trade—but if you have "The Snake Mother" you won't want that. Personally, I prefer the 1923 novelette to all the rest. When this part was included in the book something was cut out. That's why I think I'll keep the novelette even though I'm getting the book. But don't be in any hurry to return the magazine. Hope it gets to & from Asotin in good shape despite its age. Yes—I'd vastly appreciate the loan of the Blind Spot sequel, & will promise careful return. Thanks! You might also send the Carthaginian tale, which certainly ought to be worth a skimming. Haven't yet looked for the Walpole volume—I've been in such a constant rush! About "Randolph Carter"—I had a set of tattered, yellowing sheets until very recently, but they now seem to have disappeared . . . . unless they're lent to somebody. I constantly lose things through lending. The tale appeared in W T for *February 1925*. I still have a carbon of the original MS.—now lent to Rimel, who (to my surprise) lately said he had not read it. If my old sheets turn up, you're welcome to them. Otherwise I hope you can get a set elsewhere. Incidentally—here are the Red Hook & Gates sheets duly autographed—to your satisfaction, I trust. You might get Price's autograph on the Gates—his address is 5314 East 12th St., Oakland, California. Which reminds me—Robert E. Howard (Lock Box 313, Cross Plains, Texas) would undoubtedly reply most cordially to any letter he might receive, & would surely be glad to sign any tale of his sent him. He is a delightful chap—though with an odd prejudice against civilisation which causes him to wish he were a primitive Celtic barbarian.

About that mimeographed spoof[4]—I hate to demolish any clever theories, or place any limitations on a free-for-all guessing game, but I must call attention to a few facts which play the very devil with your theories. First— the Eastern members all received their copies *long before I struck Washington.* I was in Washington July 2–3–4, & the hoax was an old story by that time. Indeed, when I heard from Long about it I was still in St. Augustine. Of course, I don't know whether all the circulars were mailed at the same time—but I'd suggest that you compare the postmark on the spoof with that on the thing I sent you from St. Augustine. So far as I know, the circulars were mailed while I was in either De Land or St. Augustine. As for the matter in the circular—of course it is plain that the writer was somebody in close touch with "the gang" . . . . someone to whom I had spoken of your musical pursuits,[5] of Prince Effjay's commercial ego, & of kindred topics. Reviewing my various close correspondents, I might make some interesting guesses—but I don't want to spoil the fun by doing that. Go to it, boys! But as I recently pointed out to Rimel, you undoubtedly err in saying that I was not mentioned in the thing. As I view it, there is no question but that the *reviser* "Horse-Power Hateart" is meant to be myself. "H.P." is the standard abbreviation for *Horse Power,* while *Hate-Art* is an obvious inversion of *Love-craft.* And the reference to the revision business is a clincher. Many prominent writers & fans, however, are omitted. I haven't my copy at hand now, but seem to recall that Donald Wandrei, Edmond Hamilton, Hornig, Rimel, & dozens of others are not touched upon. One odd thing—of all the names cited, only one—Otis Adelbert Kline—is not given in parodied form. Some of the guesses as to authorship have been curious indeed—you & Rimel being among the suspects. Eventually, beyond a doubt, the whole thing will come out. If not exposed from outside, the concocters will probably speak up & claim for themselves whatever credit there is in so essentially insipid & frivolous a venture. Go ahead & guess anything you like in the F F—it all contributes to the general gayety—but I warn you that it will be easy to prove that I was no farther north than St. Augustine at most when the fans began to get their copies of the thing! Meanwhile, good luck with your quest! Yes—the F F does make some appalling misprints. My stories & article are always full of them.

Your change of industrial scene is interesting—& it is surely curious how the forest-fire exodus changed Pierce. Hope the conflagrations can be checked before a maximum of devastation results. I visited a fire-fighters' observation tower in Florida & was greatly interested in the way they sight distant blazes, telephone directions, compare notes, & finally summon out the firemen. Pierce without its usual riotous crowds must seem strange indeed. I've noted Cottonwood on the map, but knew nothing of its nature, industries, & population before. It's only comparatively recently that I've realised how many Hollanders have immigrated to the Northwest & North Middle

West. When I think of a Dutch-American, I still think first of the old 17th century New Netherland stock, from which my friend Wilfred B. Talman is descended. I did, though, realise that a more recent Dutch element exists in Michigan & Wisconsin. One of this group now living in Providence (though I haven't met him in person) is the poet & novelist David Cornel de Jong.[6] It is rather singular that members of the different Northern European nations have a different appearance (as some undoubtedly do, though others don't), since they all belong largely to the same basic race-stock. I suppose the causes are varied—differences in diet & climate, differences in individual settlement [i.e., by chance, certain types of the many shades of physiognomy prevailing throughout any race predominated amongst the settlers of some specific region], & partial amalgamation with different types of natives found in the respective regions of settlement. The last-named cause is probably the most potent; for in the various realms of its wide wandering & settlement our common Nordic stock has met & mixed with races as far apart as the Mongoloid (Lapp–Finn), Slavonic, & Mediterranean, to name only a few. In the British Isles the Mediterranean element is very strong—giving rise to the "Black Irish" type, & to the dark, short people of Wales & Southern England generally. It is curious how much more primitive & persistent the brunet type is than the blond. Introduce a little blond blood amongst a brunet population, & it is wholly lost in two or three generations—as in the case of Italy, which has swallowed up thousands of yellow-haired Celts & Teutons without leaving a trace of them. On the other hand, a little brunet blood can quickly darken half or ¾ of any vast blond population amongst whom it is introduced. There are extremely few blond Italians, Greeks, or Spaniards—& yet there are as many brunets as blonds in all the northern races. British blood has had many odd accessions through the heterogeneous followers of the Conqueror. Also—it contains all the varied elements added to the aboriginal stocks by the diversely recruited Roman legions. The Germans—especially those of the South & East—have vast amounts of Slavonic blood due to the slow westward filtration of Wendish elements. The Prussians are also strongly Slavic—though in their case the Slavonic blood is the original element, the Teutonic coming later. The language called "Old Prussian" is a Slavic dialect. All of the tongues of Europe, however, (except the Lapp, Finn & Magyar descendants of Mongol speech, & the absolutely unclassifiable Basque of the Pyrenees) are more or less remotely derived from the speech of the Nordic or Aryan race, shewing how powerful it must have been in ancient times as distinguished from all others. Paradoxically, the original Aryan *speech* has been retained most closely by a branch whose *blood* has been the most mixed with alien stocks—i.e., the Hindoo. The purest blond representatives of the old race are probably the Scandinavians—especially those of Iceland, where the only mixture has been with Irish Celts of a not dissimilar basic origin. One of the great puzzles of northern ethnology is the origin of the peculiar facial & cranial type associated with the Gaelic Celt of Western Ireland & northern Scotland—the type with the upturned nose, long upper lip, heavy eyebrow-ridges &c. This type has no known analogue anywhere else in the world, & the ethnologist is at a loss to determine how it arose. The races entering into the composition of the Gaels must have been largely Nordic, with a touch perhaps of Alpine (Slav) & Mediterranean. Whence, then, came this peculiar physiognomy? Was there some unknown aboriginal stock in the British Isles of which history has retained no trace? A lesser puzzle—& of a somewhat negative nature—lies within the modern mixture of the Anglo-Saxon race; i.e., why have certain types of physiognomy common in Great Britain failed to reproduce themselves among the purely British stock of the United States? The key to this riddle probably lies in the marked regional variations in the British population, & in the fact that the East Anglian counties (with a purely Saxon basis) were overwhelmingly predominant in the colonial immigration—thus creating a local American type not representative of the whole of Britain. The Celtic element typical of Southern & Western England is especially lacking in the typical Yankee—as is also the dark Cockney type derived from urban London.

Glad to hear that the bulk of the old orchestra is about to reassemble—& many thanks for the attractive miniature snaps, which shew up finely under a magnifying glass. Your colleagues all seem to be very pleasant & prepossessing youths—& you yourself certainly do not suffer by comparison! I herewith return the views designated for that procedure—while keeping with much gratitude the two snaps of yourself. Incidentally—I send another snap of myself for your collection. This was taken by Barlow with his new camera, & turned out to be the most lifelike picture I've had in years. My aunt has even framed her copy—though the thing was purely experimental, & the negative badly spotted through careless developing. Sorry you've lost your undertaker-trumpeter & guitarist, but trust the replacement may prove brilliantly satisfactory.

August W.T. seems a bit above the average—Moore–Howard–Flagg leading. Recently I've discovered—through some books lent by Koenig—a weird author I never appreciated before, but who really deserves (despite some obvious weak points) to rank among the titans of his class. I refer to one William Hope Hodgson & his three volumes "The Boats of the Glen Carrig" (1907), "The House on the Borderland" (1908) & "The Ghost Pirates" (1909). His later book "Carnacki the Ghost Finder"—which I had read before—is vastly inferior. After reading these books I felt obliged to prepare a note on Hodgson & send it to Hornig for incorporation into Chap. IX of my weird fiction article when he gets to it.[7]

Just now I am about to embark on my final trip of the season—first to visit a friend near Boston[8] (incidentally seeing W. Paul Cook) & then to take the boat to ancient Nantucket Island, off the Massachusetts coast, where more of the colonial past is said to survive than in any other part of the United States. I've never been there, but those who have say that the old-fashioned atmosphere is marvellous. Nantucket was a great whaling port in the 18th & early 19th centuries, & grew to be a mighty town with tangles of curving streets, colonial houses, windmills, belfried churches, & all the other appurtenances of an early New England village. Then stagnation overtook it, so that no more new houses were built. To this day it is said to preserve the exact aspect of a seaport of 100 to 150 years ago—& with a *perfect completeness* hardly to be found among even the quaintest & most archaic of the mainland parts. These mainland parts, even when old houses predominate, usually have at least a few new houses which clash with the archaic atmosphere. Nantucket, on the contrary, is said to have absolutely *no* houses newer than 1820 or 1830. It is certainly exactly the kind of place I dote on, & I'd have visited it long before had it not been for the relative difficulty of access. Hope I shan't be disappointed—my expectations are certainly high enough. I'll send you postcards or folders if any are obtainable. I trust to luck to find a place to stop at whose prices won't leave me flat broke! The town is in a great harbour on the northern side of the island. If possible, I shall visit other parts of the island—including the quaint village of Siasconset on the southeastern shore.

Read the new *Terror Tales* some time ago, but find it very poor. Just got the new F F, & deem it an excellent issue. Young Morse is rather a gifted chap—the son of an Amherst professor & an assistant librarian at Princeton.[9] I've met him in person in N.Y.

All good wishes—

Yrs most sincerely—

H P L

Notes

1. Everil Worrell, "The Bird of Space" (*WT*, September 1926); "Cattle of Furos" (*WT*, October 1926).

2. HPL did not submit "The Thing on the Doorstep" to *WT* until the summer of 1936.

3. See Farnsworth Wright to August Derleth, 17 January 1933 (ms., Wisconsin State Historical Society): "I have read Lovecraft's story, THE SHADOW OVER INNSMOUTH, and must confess that it fascinates me. But I don't know just what I can do with it. It is hard to break a story of this kind into two parts, and it is too long to run complete in one part. I will keep this story in mind, and if some time in the near future I can figure out how to use it, I will write to Lovecraft and ask him to send me the manuscript." In May 1931, when HPL had submitted *At the Mountains of Madness* to *WT*, the magazine was being published bimonthly, which would have made the story more difficult to publish as a serial. The magazine resumed monthly publication in August.

4. HPL and RHB, "The Battle That Ended the Century" (May 1934). HPL is being somewhat disingenuous in not denying involvement outright. His assertion that he was not north of St. Augustine at the time of the writing is without merit, for postage-paid envelopes could have been mailed to a person living in Washington, DC (such as Elizabeth Toldridge) for individual posting there.

5. "An appropriate dirge was rendered by Maestro Sing Lee Bawledout on the piccolo" (*CF* 4.524).

6. David Cornel de Jong (1901–1967) was born in the village of Blija in the northern part of the Dutch northern province Friesland. His family emigrated to Grand Rapids in 1914, and he attended Brown University in 1932 but left when his first novel was accepted by Alfred A. Knopf. He wrote at least one novel about Providence: *Benefit Street* (1942). See also his book *With a Dutch Accent: How a Hollander Became an American* (1944).

7. *FF* ceased publication before "Supernatural Horror in Literature" with the note on Hodgson could appear. The article ("The Weird Work of William Hope Hodgson") appeared in *Phantagraph* and then was incorporated into "Supernatural Horror in Literature" as published in *The Outsider and Others* (1939).

8. Edward H. Cole of Wollaston.

9. Richard Ely Morse's "Ebony and Ash: A Tale of Three Wishes" appeared in *FF* 1, No. 12 (August 1934): 189–90.

[16]   [ANS][1]

[Postmarked Providence, R.I.,
1 October 1934]

Blind Spot &c. safely arrived, & I look forward with pleasure to an opportunity for perusal. Returned material also here. Thanks for the loan—hope there's no hurry about return, since I'm utterly inundated with piled-up work & can't get to reading for some time. ¶ Some weird books by W. H. Hodgson are coming to Asotin in the course of circulation—hope you'll enjoy them. Just got new W. T., but no chance as yet to read it. Regards—
H P L

Notes

1. *Front:* The Carrie Tower, Hope, Manning and University Halls at Left. Brown University, Providence, R.I.

[17]   [ANS][1]

[Postmarked Providence, R.I.,
17 October 1934]

Have at last read the two serials so kindly lent, & am returning by parcel post. Let me thank you afresh for sending them. "Spot of Life" has an excellent idea, although it is handled according to the familiar conventions of pulp fiction. It well continues the story of "The Blind Spot", though not quite equalling it. ¶ "The Barbarian" interested me tremendously because of my lifelong feeling of identification with Rome & the Romans.[2] Although cast in the mould of popular romance, this story is very vividly & effectively written. The author seems to have an excellent superficial command of ancient history, though he errs on details—especially regarding Roman names. He also speaks of the *denarius* (a small silver coin roughly corresponding to a dime) as a *gold* coin, &c. But aside from these minor slips, it's an excellent story of its kind. I'm immensely glad to have read both of these tales, & again thank you for the thoughtful loan. Incidentally—you have supplied tremendously clever bindings & decorations. ¶ Autumn is here, & the shadow of hibernation descends upon me. But I shall get a few more outings before November's chill sets in. All good wishes—Yrs most sincerely—H P L

Notes

1. *Front:* Van Wickel [*sic*] Gates, Brown University, Providence, R. I.
2. Apparently a reference to H. Bedford-Jones (1887–1949), "The Barbarian," *Hutchinson's Adventure-Story Magazine* 1, No. 6 (February 1923).

[18]   [ALS]
66 College St.,
Providence, R.I.,
Novr. 2, 1934

Dear Eph-Li:—

Your crowded programme surely more than excuses any apparent tardiness in writing! I trust the post-harvest season will bring you something of a breathing spell.

The biography is surely admirably written—& as interesting as its prosaic subject will allow![1] I've been over it with care, & have given it the few touches which strike me as necessary. Most of the emendations, I fancy, are self-explanatory. In one case, I thought it would be better not to publish, in actual print, the fact that the dream section of "The Horror from the Hills" was not written by Long. As it now stands, I imagine that the MS. is quite in shape to send on to Hornig. Of course, I don't know how much space he'll want to allot to it. Possibly he'll think that $5\frac{1}{4}$ pages & a large cut are too much to give to one third-rater—especially after the same third-rater has just had a whole issue dedicated to him! In that case you could easily prune the article down to almost any desired length. The anecdotes—about "Cassius"[2] & the "Horror"—could go; & you could also remove the other less essential touches . . . . about food preferences, &c. . . . . which have only a limited bearing on the subject's writing. I don't see that there's anything which needs to be added—& of course you might well try it on Hornig before you subtract anything. It is really a splendid writeup—covering all the essential points & selecting the most significant details. I hope you'll tackle other subjects in the same way—Smith, Long, Howard, Derleth, Wandrei, & so on. A series of biographies like that would certainly be warmly welcomed by the F F's clientele. Indeed—*Fantasy Magazine* has been doing something of that sort.

And now let me express my vast appreciation of Rimel's cut. Truly, it is a remarkable piece of work—capturing the essentials of the Barlow photograph with surprising skill. I had no idea, despite his extremely clever heading for "Dreams of Yith",[3] that Rhi-Mhel could turn out anything as accomplished as this! The likeness is certainly unmistakable, even though the limitations of the medium—with its uncompromising blacks & whites—cause it to be somewhat flattering . . . . suggesting a rather younger subject than the venerable E'ch-Pi-El. Certainly, I'll be glad to see it used if Hornig is willing to spare it space. It's all up to him. For my part, I think both you & Rhi-Mhel have done nobly—creating a synthesis of text & picture which may well serve as the pattern for a series. Congratulations all around!

Enclosed are the story-beginnings, suitably signed. Surely it isn't much trouble to repeat such familiar pen-strokes a few times! Glad Price is in touch with you. He is surely one of the pleasantest & most helpful persons alive. I am herewith sending the two old issues of the F F which you need. No charge—for these don't encroach on the three extra sets I'm keeping on account of my article. Hornig usually supplies me very generously—indeed, he sent me a prodigious bale of copies of the issue dedicated to me.

Thanks very much for the cutting about Pierce. Certainly roaring atmosphere of the old border towns isn't quite dead yet! Glad the Nantucket & Boston stuff came through safely. Yes—I'm always glad to see views of your part of the world, & thank you in advance for those you speak of.

I must thank you again, too, for "The Spot of Life" & "The Barbarian". Judging from the nature of the former, I am inclined to agree that the late Mr. Flint was the chief author of "The Blind Spot." "The Barbarian" was surely vivid—even if it did use the name "Iskander" (an Arabic corruption of *Alexander*, coined in mediaeval times) in the Punic period. Yes—I recall your interest in North Africa. I've forgotten the title of that Prorok book C A S lent me, but he'll know what you mean if you simply ask him for the book on Carthaginian excavations by Comte De Prorok which he lent me a year ago. I regret that I have no books on Carthage except Flaubert's "Salammbo." If you haven't read that, & would care to, I'll be delighted to lend you my tattered, paper-covered copy!

I read Merritt's "The Drone" in *Fantasy Magazine* (to which I subscribe), & was rather disappointed in it. It was surely kind of you to suggest lending it if I hadn't seen it. Wandrei's "Chuckler" was suggested by my "Randolph Carter". He called it a "sequel", but I'd scarcely consider it such. It is simply a tale with the same background. Thanks for the offer of lending "Portrait of A Man With Red Hair". I think I'll take you up on that before long. About "The Moon Pool"—when the original novelette was fused with the sequel to form the book (of which the *Amazing* text is a verbatim reprint), certain touches were left out. The result was distinctly weakening—& indeed, the whole process of tacking on a conventional cheap adventure sequel was barbarous & ruinous. I don't know where the original magazine texts could be obtained—though Barlow might. However—I'm enclosing a tattered fragment of the original novelette which you may enjoy. This is all that remains of my original copy—bought in June 1918 when first issued. Last spring I got a defective copy from Barlow in better condition—but with the first two sheets missing. Accordingly I took the first 2 sheets from this old copy, & patched up the edges with gummed transparent tape. The residue—all but 2 sheets—is what I am sending you. Don't bother to return it—keep it till it falls to pieces or until you can find a better copy. I regret to say that I don't know the date of the original *Argosy* publication of "The People of the Pit." Barlow could probably tell you, though. Your idea of giving me a copy of "Creep, Shadows" [*sic*] in one of your inimitably clever bindings quite overwhelms me! Thanks a thousand times in advance!! I have not seen the tale, & certainly shall not read it till your gift-copy arrives. Words cannot express my appreciation!

My indigestion is all over now—though something like writers' cramp in my right hand bothers me off & on. Coldish weather is indeed setting in—the days averaging around 45° or 48°. My trips are probably at an end, though I had some good excursions a fortnight ago in a friend's heated car. No—I never had any yearning for the late World's Fair.[4] I am not interested in mechanical "progress", & the futuristic architecture of the exposition buildings would have made me gnash my teeth. However—I would undoubtedly have enjoyed many individual exhibits—especially the reproduction of old-time villages.

The Nantucket trip certainly was great. The island lies 30 miles from the nearest mainland point, & is an elder world in itself. The town is on the north shore, & there are villages scattered along other parts of the coast. The surface consists of low, rolling moors almost treeless—except for the town. The town, rising on hills above the harbour, is precisely like the old Yankee seaports of 100 or 150 years ago. Cobblestoned streets with ancient houses—a 1746 windmill—curious lanes & wharves—everything of the past unchanged, despite the presence of summer visitors & artists. The island was settled from Massachusetts in 1660, but belonged to New York till its transfer to Mass. in 1691. The town was founded about 1720. I was there a week, & explored the whole island very thoroughly. Whaling was the life of old Nantucket, & when that failed in 1870 the place became largely a summer resort. The general lack of prosperity after 1850 is what kept the town so ancient-looking—no new houses being built.[5]

Barlow hasn't had any definite verdict on his eyes as yet, but the observation & treatment continue. He is taking an art course at the Corcoran gallery—a light one, since his oculist will not permit more.

As for old de Castro—he hasn't been away from New York, but had somewhat dropped out of sight until this autumn. He never succeeds with his various financial ventures, & is now really badly off. What is more, his eyes are in dangerous shape, & his wife is an advanced tuberculosis sufferer. Now he wants Long & me to collaborate with him on various projects—to take half the profits if they succeed. Neither of us can do so just now, though we'd like to help the old boy. He s a curious character—a bit of a poseur & charlatan, though perfectly honest financially. In his life of Bierce he drags himself in rather egotistically, & perpetuates several unmistakable myths. But he is really a profound scholar—graduate of Bonn & master of 7 languages—& has had published work of undoubted importance. Some of his unpublished books are probably of real value—& I surely hope he can get a collaborator even if I can't tackle the job. He is 74 years old. In the matter of Bierce's disappearance—de Castro lived in Mexico from 1922 to 1925, & had interviews with Villa & his generals in 1923. He claims to have received an account of Bierce's end from those revolutionists—but there is no reason to think this account any more correct than the other two accounts now current. In a way, all three reports are alike—so that it is pretty likely that Bierce was somehow shot by the Villistas in 1914. Bierce was 72 years old, & bored with everything. He wanted to get into some military excitement, so went to Mexico where revolution was raging. His plan, as stated to friends, was to mix in the row a bit & then go on a trip to South America. The last letters ever received from Bierce came from Chihuahua City late in 1913. My friend Samuel Loveman last heard from him in September—from Washington, D.C., where he lived. He wrote: "I am going away to South America in a few weeks, & have not the faintest notion when I shall return."[6] As for the end—Villa told old de Castro that Bierce did *not* join any army, but that he was in Chihuahua when the rebels took it. He got drunk & criticised Villa very harshly—praising Carranza in contrast. Villa didn't like this, & ordered Bierce to leave town. As he expressed it to de Castro—*'Lo hemos hecho fuera.'*[7] Later an officer told de C. that Villa really arranged to have him shot outside the village—leaving his body to the vultures. This account is believed by the well-known editor R. H. Davis.

Another account is that of a newspaper man named George F. Weeks. He met a Mexican in 1918—a Dr. Melero—who claimed to have known Bierce. According to Melero Bierce joined Villa's army but got disgusted & went over to Carranza. Later he was captured near Icamole by one of Villa's generals—Urbina—& was shot after his refusal to answer questions. This is the account accepted by the late George Sterling. The third account is given by a roving character named O'Reilly. He says that Bierce was treacherously murdered by some Mexican associates & buried at Sierra Mojada. And so it goes. Wildcat legends about Bierce have persisted to this day—including accounts of his participation in the World War. It is, however, almost certain that he was killed in Mexico before the middle of 1914. In September of that year the formal search for him began. I am inclined to favour the Weeks–Melero account. De Castro is an inveterate myth-maker & embroiderer, & had quarrelled with Bierce. It would be just like him to doctor an account subtly enough to place Bierce in a less favourable light. But there's no telling. It will take radically new evidence to settle the fate of Bierce. De Castro's original name is Gustav Adolf Danziger—he changed it during the World War because of the unpopularity of

German names . . . taking the name of a remote Spanish ancestor. He came to America in 1886 & was a dentist for a long period. He also dabbled in politics, & was American consul at Madrid for a time. The piece of work he did with Bierce was translating the German novel of Richard Voss—"The Monk & the Hangman's Daughter." He was German-speaking & (in 1889) could not write even passable English. Bierce, on the other hand, was a master of English but knew no German. De Castro—or Danziger—admired the Voss novel & made a very crude translation into such English as he knew. Then Bierce took that crude translation & made the present admirable English novelette of it. It is rather amusing to reflect that Bierce & de Castro always quarrelled over the chief credit for this production—both forgetting that the real author was neither of them! Undoubtedly, the *real* power in the poignant drama & stirring descriptions is that of Herr Voss of Heidelberg—neither Bierce nor de Castro being anything more than an adapter. Certainly, the book as it stands is a curious three-man job! It is not a weird tale, but if you'd like to read it I'd be glad to lend it to you. Old de Castro gave me a copy 5 or 6 years ago.

Regarding the end of Homer Eon Flint—my memory is hazy about it, but I don't think he *disappeared.* My vague impression is that he was *found dead* under mysterious circumstances—in an automobile full of machine-guns or other bandit paraphernalia in a lonely cañon somewhere in the Southwest. When I read the account I had never heard of Flint before, & thought it was fiction—hence didn't particularly recall it later. But Barlow says it seems to be fact. Since my recollection is so dim, I won't even pretend to be right. I may have mixed this incident with another. Barlow is the boy who can set you right—for he has the account as published in a note in *The Argosy*.[8] Hall, so far as I know, is still living & very far from the disappeared state. However— I fancy Flint's death (or disappearance, if it *was* that . . . . . I can't be certain . . . . maybe it was his *car* & not his *body* that was found) is amply picturesque enough to form the basis of interesting speculation—either independently or in conjunction with Bierce. But first get your facts—from Barlow or any other *Argosy* devotee likely to know.

I trust that you & Rhi-Mhel will find the Science Fiction League of some interest. Since the weird & scientifictional files overlap in so many places, I'd probably join the organisation myself if there were a local chapter here. Curious that the Lewiston chapter has the second-oldest charter! It is interesting to hear that this group is considering the purchase of a new press on which the "Colour" might some day be printed. Hope the matter will eventually turn out favourably. Barlow seems to be quite anxious to do an illustration or two for this venture, & considering his ability I believe it would be well to let him—if there are to be *any* illustrations. Rimel will shew you a title-page border which he tentatively prepared, & which is really eminently satisfactory. But there's no hurry about any of this.

About George Allan England's "Golden Blight"[9]—I don't think I've read it, but can't be sure. It must have been years ago, & at that distance I recall only very remarkable stories—& even then, I recall *plots* better than *titles*. Hope you can get the issues wanted. About Whitehead's "Black Beast"—it appeared in July, 1931, in the *last* issue of *Adventure* before the lowering of the price. I can't recall the exact date, & there's nothing in the sheets I have to fix it. But I think it was late in the month—perhaps July 25.

You have surely seen some unusual things during your current orchestral experiences. The "skin game" at the carnival[10] must have given you quite a bit of insight into human nature—especially the eternal gullibility of mankind. I never could understand the lure of games of chance, since the opportunities for losing are so much greater than the opportunities for winning—but I realise that the majority are fascinated by them. Sorry you acquired a discoloured optic at such an awkward time—but trust that no permanent effects remain. I suppose Robert E. Howard would think such a thing only a mild preliminary to a *real* fight. When the blood begins to be ankle-deep, & severed ears & hands are floating around in it, he considers a combat well started—& perhaps likely to get really rough later on!

There has just been an interesting exhibit at the John Hay Library next door—books & papers & other reliques of Dr. Thomas Holley Chivers of Georgia, the contemporary of Poe who influenced & was influenced by the latter so considerably. Chivers is almost unknown today, but his poetry represents the same school as that of Poe. It is, however, much inferior—even tawdry & childish in spots. Chivers was born in the same year as Poe—1809—& survived Poe by 9 years, dying in 1858. He was a physician, & a rather odd character generally. His mystical, fantastic work earned him the sobriquet of "The Wild Mazeppa of Letters."[11] My friend Loveman has been interested in him for years—& Prof. S. Foster Damon of Providence has written the only biography of him. The best existing collection of his works is that in the John Hay Library here—next door to 66 College St. Of these works one is the **only** existing copy. All Chivers students have to come to Providence for material.

Another local event which would have interested you was a lecture on the evolution of American music by the well-known composer John Tasker Howard.[12] He doubts very much whether folk music of negroid origin can ever express the emotions of the real American people of European origin. He also doubts—& rightly, I think,—whether any laboured, conscious efforts at expressing the American scene can ever succeed in doing that. True art & expression, he maintains, must be purely *unconscious*. The thing for composers to do is to write *just what they feel like writing*—without paying any attention to its resemblance or non-resemblance to European or other types of music. Only in that way will the American people find genuine musical expression. And that expression, because of European sources, must bear more or less kinship to the European main stream.

Last night I saw something which might mildly interest some of the forward-looking science-fiction fans—a modern streamlined aluminum train of the Union Pacific Railway, on exhibition in the railway yards behind the station. It surely is a queer-looking mess—but it is supposed to make 110 miles per hour. I walked all through it. It is full of odd conveniences, but on the whole is not very radical in its interior aspect. The engine & the rear car, as seen on the outside, are the queerest things about it. The locomotive has a Diesel oil engine which runs an electric generator—& this, in turn, operates the electric motors which drive the train.

It's getting very cold—under 40° last night. I'm certainly glad of the steam heat here!

Again congratulating you on your article, & Rhi-Mhel on his cut, I remain

Yrs most cordially—

E'ch-Pi-El

P.S. I've just lent Rimel a couple of books on astronomy. Read them if you like. They ought to help you appreciate interplanetary fiction.

Notes

1. F. Lee Baldwin, "H. P. Lovecraft: A Biographical Sketch"; originally intended for *FF*.

2. See DWR 18.

3. DWR modeled the heading he cut for his poem "Dreams of Yith" (*FF*, July and September 1934) on Hugh Rankin's headings of Donald Wandrei's "Sonnets of the Midnight Hours" and HPL's *Fungi from Yuggoth* in *WT*.

4. The Century of Progress Exposition opened at Chicago world's fair on 27 May 1933. It had a second season from 26 May to 31 October 1934, so had just closed when HPL wrote to FLB.

5. See HPL, "The Unknown City in the Ocean."

6. 10 September 1913. See Ambrose Bierce (1842–1914?), *Twenty-one Letters of Ambrose Bierce*, ed. Samuel Loveman (Cleveland: George Kirk, 1922 [*LL* 89]; rpt. West Warwick, RI: Necronomicon Press, 1991), 19.

7. "We have done away."

8. Homer Eon Flint (c. 1892–1924). His body was found at the foot of a canyon. See Mike Ashley, "The Galactic Emancipator: Remembering Homer Eon Flint," *Fantasy Commentator* 8, Nos. 3 & 4 (Fall 1995): 258–67.

9. George Allan England, "The Golden Blight," *Cavalier* (18 May–22 June 1912; rpt. 1916).

10. A rigged gambling game.

11. The title presumably derives from *Mazeppa* (1819), a narrative poem by Lord Byron about a wild, histrionic Ukrainian gentleman who becomes the leader of the Ukrainian Cossacks.

12. John Tasker Howard (1890–1964), music historian, composer, radio host, and writer. His *Our American Music* (1931) was an early history of music in the United States.

[19]   [ALS]

66 College St.,
Providence, R.I.,
Decr. 7, 1934.

Dear Eph-Li:—

   I'm glad to hear that Hornig took kindly to the biographical sketch, & hope that Rhi´-Mhel's cut will reproduce well in the press. The illustrated article is surely creditable all around—& I can fully appreciate what you say of the artist's skill. As I believe I mentioned to Rhi-Mel himself, I never before saw linoleum block work used for portraiture, & never suspected that anything so detailed & exact could be achieved. I had thought of the process as being largely confined to simple decoration conceptions—& indeed marvelled at the cleverness of the "Yith" heading. The skill of the present portrait is all the more remarkable in view of the engraver's comparative lack of experience. It surprises me to learn that he is not an old hand at the process! Assuredly, he ought to illustrate some of his tales & poems. I feel certain that both Hornig & Crawford would welcome block prints of such excellence. And, as I said before, I hope that both of you will continue the series of illustrated biographies. Long, Smith, Price, Howard, & Derleth would be ideal subjects—though as you say, the F M writeup of Wandrei rather rules the latter out for the present. F F & F M have a common circulation to a large extent. Not long ago Schwartz wanted to do an account of me, but he agreed that such would be redundant after I told him of the one you were planning. You are right, I imagine, in believing that a spell of correspondence gives one a better perspective of a biographical subject. Discussion of varied topics does bring out aspects of personality which would otherwise remain hidden. Price—who has knocked about the world & done a little of everything—will make splendid material. So will Howard with his picturesque views & sanguinary southwestern background. Smith's life has been very stationary & uneventful, but the history of his artistic development ought to be fascinating indeed. The same is true of Long & Derleth.

   Yes—Two-Gun Bob's work certainly averages vastly higher than the recent output of Sultan Malik. The latter has frankly sold himself to the powers of pulpdom, & simply grinds out an endless stream of mechanical stuff of the sort that editors want. Which is tragic in view of what he could do in his own field—the Orientale. When shall we ever see another "Stranger from Kurdistan" or "Dreamer of Atlanaat"?[1] Howard, on the other hand, manages to put a lot of himself into even his cheapest work—so that his stories have a distinct personality & vitality despite their commercial cast. He is, however, obviously veering away from the weird toward the field of sheer adventure. In his latest yarn there is nothing of the supernatural save the rather casually dragged-in monster toward the end.[2]

   Enclosed are the signed sheets. No trouble at all to fix them up—though

I fear they aren't worth any too much either before or after the signing! Glad you found the original "Moon Pool" interesting, & hope you can get a complete copy in better condition. As for the gummed transparent paper tape—I fancy it is obtainable in any stationery store . . . . . or any Woolworth's, where I get mine nowadays. If for any reason the shops up your way don't keep this commodity, let me know & I'll get you several packages at the local Woolworth's. I find it almost indispensable for book-mending & dozens of other assorted purposes. About your belief that dampness & abundant steam heat affect paper sooner than do other climatic & thermal conditions—I rather fancy you're right. Not that *steam* heat in particular has any deteriorating effect, since there is no special chemical quality about the radiations from hot iron—which such a system amounts to. But the abundant & constant warmth which my physique requires, probably does play the devil more or less with paper, leather, glue, & nearly everything which goes to make up a book. At least, my library as a whole is getting into a deplorable condition. If I had the cash, I'd have an enormous amount of re-binding done—since many of my books are sans covers & literally falling to pieces. As for the *climate*—humidity & all that—I suppose coastal New England may be a bit disadvantageous for books. Some localities are notoriously so—especially the west coast of Florida, where the public libraries treat all their books with a special kind of shellac. Inland Florida is rather unfavourable, too—with insects that attack books. Barlow keeps his library in a dark, windowless closet—& wraps his most precious unbound magazines in cellophane. I'm tremendously sorry that "The Barbarian" & "The Spot of Life" suffered even slightly through their eastward visit. Climatically, your region seems to be very much in luck!

Let me thank you extremely for the postcards of the Snake River region. It delighted me to get a glimpse of modern Boise City—what a splendid State House Idaho has! The edifice reminds me of Rhode Island's rather famous marble capitol. I don't recall my grandfather's ever mentioning it, hence imagine it must be a 20th century addition since his time. The railway station is a striking & unusual building, & seems to be most picturesquely situated. Of the hotels, the Idau-ha looks as if my grandfather might have seen it—although The Owyhee is evidently more modern. Walla Walla certainly has an imposing hostelry in the Marcus Whitman. Yes—I'd be delighted to see other views of the region, & would safely return any which you might wish back. Thanks for the suggestion! This reminds me to thank your mother for giving my name to the Phoenix Chamber of Commerce. I did indeed receive some alluring material from them, which made me wish I could sojourn indefinitely in the Arizona sunshine. It certainly is a healthful climate—you are perhaps aware that the dryness & mildness of Tucson are about all that keep the weird writer Francis Flagg alive. Hope you can arrange to live there some time. Besides being climatically agreeable, Phoenix has quite a bit of literary life—so has Tucson, for that matter.

Yes—Rhode Island had a fortunately mild Thanksgiving, so that my aunt

& I were able to take a quite enjoyable stroll among the byways of Providence's ancient hill. The week-end before that I was in Boston—to see W. Paul Cook, who came down from New Hampshire for a week. We had quite a good time, although the outdoor phases were cut down by a cold spell then prevailing. Our one side-trip was to ancient Medford, where we saw the Royale mansion—built in 1737 & one of the finest specimens of its period in New England. I had been over it twice before, but Cook hadn't—so I took him through. It is owned by the Colonial Dames & D.A.R., & is furnished in the manner of its day. The exterior & the panelled interior are both imposing, & I wish there had been some postcards on sale.

This week I have been attending an unusual number of lectures on different phases of art—a programme fostered by the League of Professional artists.[*sic*] Wednesday evening the lecture was particularly interesting because it involved the simultaneous painting of pictures, in full view of the audience, by two of Providence's leading artists—H. Anthony Dyer (landscapist) & John Frazier (portrait painter).[3] It was tremendously fascinating to watch the pictures take form beneath the hands of the two artists. Dyer was the more rapid workman, & finished two pictures while Frazier was doing one.

Barlow seems to be getting along in Washington all right—did I tell you that he had shifted his temporary address to 1218 Sixteenth St., N.W.? His eyes seem to be somewhat better, & he is apparently deriving considerable good from his art course at the Corcoran Gallery. He was delighted to learn of your liking for his title-page design, & will probably send you some sort of frontispiece &c in due course of time. I don't know when he intends to issue "The Shunned House."

Regarding old de Castro—I hope your writeup didn't include anything that placed him in an ignominious light, or that mentions his unfortunate plight to-day. It would hurt him deeply if anything of that kind were to appear, & he would doubtless suspect that I served as a transmitter of the data. As I said, he's really a good & likeable old soul despite his many ventures into charlatanry. If you use the three stories about Bierce's disappearance, don't say anything to discredit old 'Dolph's in favour of the others—& don't repeat what I said about his animus regarding Bierce. Under separate cover I have sent you "The Monk & the Hangman's Daughter" with de Castro's inserted explanation regarding authorship. Also a cutting regarding one of the old boy's little scrapes . . . . out of which he seems to have wriggled without disastrous consequences! In the same bundle is also Flaubert's "Salammbo"—the novel of ancient Carthage about which I told you. Keep both of these as long as you like, & let Rhi´-Mhel also read them. Thanks for the future loan of the Walpole book—about which, in view of my frantically crowded programme, there is certainly not the least hurry!

Glad the orchestra is getting some new engagements, & hope you'll find the new circuit an interesting field. Congratulations, too, on your plan for a lucrative song-writing venture. It surely seems as if a Science Fiction League song dedicated to Brother Hornig ought to sell splendidly among the members—especially if mimeographed at low cost & advertised in F F, F M, & kindred publications. No—I won't mention the plan—& I certainly wish you & Rhi´-Mhel all success with it! You two ought to be able to handle such a proposition adequately if anybody could!

You are certainly lucky to pick up parts of the "Darkness & Dawn" cycle. I read the whole business when it originally appeared, & was considerably impressed by it. Afterward, as you doubtless know, the three separate novels were published together under the single title "Darkness & Dawn." This book version is now out of print & very hard to obtain—though Barlow has a zealously guarded copy. The plates are still in existence—in England's possession—& some years ago W. Paul Cook & H. Warner Munn had a plan for publishing a new edition at popular prices. They visited England in New Hampshire & had quite a bit of discussion. He was enthusiastically in favour—but the plan fell through for lack of capital.

Haven't progressed beyond p. 34 of "The Shadow Out of Time"—imperative matters interrupted it, & no good chance for resumption has appeared. I can't work on a story unless I have unlimited leisure for it. Hope to finish the thing within the next month—& then I'll see whether it seems good enough to type & shew around. I feel pretty certain that it will *not* suit any professional editor . . . . . & I can't say that it suits *me* overly well so far! About the MS.—alas! that is promised to the insatiable Barlow . . . . but if you want anything as worthless as a MS. of mine, you're welcome to "The Thing On the Doorstep" as soon as the text is printed somewhere.[4] Since lending copies are apt to get lost, I make it a rule always to keep some sort of a copy of my stuff in my files. When the text is unpublished, my original longhand draught usually fulfils that function—but after publication, I let the printed version form my file copy & throw (or *give,* since you & Barlow have so flatteringly set a value upon such junk!) away the old original scrawl. So remind me to shoot you the MS. if ever the "Thing" achieves publication.

Glad you have acquired a complete Tolstoi—good solid stuff, although my own personal taste for it is somewhat limited. I have a few scattering volumes—which include "War & Peace." Of de Maupassant I have a set—though not a complete one. No one, I think, ever excelled him in the field of the short story. He set a new standard, & all subsequent writers are indebted to him.

No—I haven't entered anything in the F M cover contest. Let me wish you luck with your entry—I hope to see it in course of time, either in print or in MS.[5] I'll be interested to examine a sample of your fictional style. Why don't you try more stories?

I received the new M T, & deem Keller's "Golden Bough" the best story by a long shot. The volume with the "White Sibyl" & "Men of Avalon" also came—but here Keller is not so successful. Klarkash-Ton's piece is splendid. Crawford has a sadly crude taste, & holds the most grotesque opinions about literature. Just now I'm trying to convince him of the excellence of Keller's "Dead Woman"—which he considers ridiculous, & which he turned down when it was offered to him![6]

The December W T is strikingly better than its mediocre predecessor. Klarkash-Ton's fascinating "Xeethra" easily leads, with "The Black God's Shadow" as a fair second. The Derleth–Schorer & Byrne stories are both good of their kind, while "The Graveyard Duchess" is really excellent. "Vengeance of Ti Fong" is well-written, though Morgan's endless repetition of his *one* basic plot-idea gets to be monotonous & exasperating. Howard's novelette is good, though the weird element is very slight. The reprint is nothing to get excited over. Owen surely does overdo the exotic Chinese stuff— though I haven't the late Dr. Whitehead's all-inclusive contempt for his work.

Well—now to get to work. Hope you'll find the books of interest—& congratulations again upon your article. And thanks again for the views.

With best wishes for all your ventures—
Yrs most sincerely—
E'ch-Pi-El

P.S. Wandrei has paid Klarkash-Ton a highly interesting visit in Auburn—or perhaps C A S has told you about it.

Notes

1. "The Stranger from Kurdistan" (*WT,* July 1925; rpt. September 1929); "The Dreamer of Atlanaat" (*WT,* July 1926).
2. "A Witch Shall Be Born" (*WT,* December 1934)
3. Hezekiah Anthony Dyer (1872–1943); John Robinson Frazier (1889–1966).
4. The ms. was given instead to DWR in December 1936.
5. Presumably not published.
6. David H. Keller, "The Golden Bough," *Marvel Tales* 1, No. 3 (Winter 1934): 92–111; "The Dead Woman," *Fantasy Magazine* 3, No. 2 (April 1934): 1–5.

[20]   [ALS]

66 College St.,
Providence, R.I.,
Decr. 23, 1934.

Dear Eph-Li:—

Your gorgeous card with letter & enclosures arrived yesterday, & I hasten to acknowledge the message—albeit inadequately. Tasks have piled up bewilderingly during recent weeks, so that all my epistolary jottings tend to be more or less illegible, incoherent, & fragmentary.

Glad you are in touch with Price. Has he told you of his plan to buy a lot & build a house at San Carlos? Here is a card in which he outlines his idea.

He is surely grinding out salable copy at an amazing rate, though of course his literary quality suffers thereby. Yes—the "Gates of the S.K." suffered rejection prior to acceptance. Wright is very capricious in this way. At first submission he turned it down; but scarcely had he returned it than he asked to see it again . . . this time accepting it at $140.00. There's no telling at any time what the fellow will do next! As for my new story—amidst the feverish pressure of other tasks I haven't been able to go on with it. It still remains stalled on p. 34. Sooner or later I mean to finish it, but I have to have leisure when I tackle original fiction. Whether it will be worth typing & shewing to anybody—or whether it will have to be destroyed & started anew—yet remains to be seen.

I am extremely glad to hear that you find Dunsany enjoyable & imaginatively stimulating. There is something utterly distinctive about him—a potent magic evoking a peculiar sense of the actual nearness of strange worlds of wonder, & of hidden gates leading into them. I recall "Carcasson[n]e"—it surely is exquisite.[1] Indeed, with the exception of Poe, I don't know of any author who has enchanted me as powerfully & as persistently. As you know, all my writing during the 1920–22 period bore strong marks of his influence. Yes—I recall "The Land of Lur"[2]—which is either a broad parody of this style or a very crude & ignorant attempt to employ it. I rather fancy it is a parody, since I've heard that the author has produced other work quite free from the extremes of crudeness.

Enclosed is an envelope full of Ar-E'ch-Bei's weird sketches,[3] which I think you'll greatly enjoy. The kid undeniably has a rich & resourceful talent in the realm of fantasy, & will go far if his eyes hold out. No hurry about returning these drawings. Let Rhí-Mhel see them, & be as leisurely as you like.

Climate certainly has a good deal to do with the survival of books & papers. So has *light*. Things keep twice as well in the dark as in a brilliantly sunlit room. When I lived in Barnes St. I had no sunlight, & my things stayed white a long while. Now I have a sunny southwestern room for a study, with two windows on each side—& papers get yellow in half the time. Barlow keeps his collection in a large windowless closet—jet-black—which he has nicknamed (from Klarkash-Ton's story) "The Vaults of Yoh-Vombis."[4] Why not get some salient facts from Ar-E'ch-Bei & write up his collection? I'm sure he would be willing. His use of cellophane wrappers is indeed worth mentioning. I don't think he takes F M regularly, but now & then he buys back numbers—stipulating that they be sent *flat*. He is a fanatic about the condition of his magazines, & will try a dozen news stands sometimes before he finds a copy perfect enough to suit him. Often he can't find anything in the condition he wants—& then he sends to the publishers for a flat, specially wrapped copy.

Thanks infinitely for your suggestion of salvaging my disintegrating copy of "Salammbo". Its decrepitude had seemed hopeless to me—so that I've been on the lookout for another copy for some time. I would surely be endlessly grateful for anything your skill could do toward arresting its further decay—though it seems a shame to put you to so much trouble. Most certainly you have my "permission"—& my profound appreciation as well—in the matter of the restoration!

Regarding the matter about de Castro—thanks exceedingly for sending the rough draught of your notes. I am returning this with certain slight alterations which I really think would be advisable. If you could get these changes embodied in the printed version it would probably be advantageous all around. Old de Castro is in severe straits now, & almost paralysed with grief over the probably fatal illness of his wife—an advanced consumptive who lately went to the hospital, perhaps never to return. The poor old codger has been treated tough enough by the press—so that I fancy he's had sufficient punishment for all his petty charlatanries. And he is good-hearted & likeable in his way.

About my current revisory work—I assume it is of the de Castro job which you wish to hear, since other odds & ends are of no distinctiveness at all—a novel to be put in shape for a Kansas City lady[5] (confused threads of plot to be harmonised, language to be made clear, time-schedule to be rectified, &c), some crude verse from a Vermonter to be made sensible, correct, & fluent, an article on Roman architecture to be prepared to order, &c. &c.[6] Well—to begin with, I think I'll have to refuse Old Dolph's assignment— since he can't pay in advance & since it's so great a mess as to be virtually hopeless. What I will do—to cheer the old boy up amidst his present misery— is to touch up the phraseology a bit, & point out the more easily recognisable historical & scientific errors, & give some general critical advice. That will make it easier to revise later on if he ever finds anybody to do it. The MS. is a full-length book of miscellaneous social, political, & historical essays rather vaguely entitled "The New Way", & has very little internal coherence. It appears to endorse the philosophy of Lenin & the bolsheviks, & in certain parts tries to give new & sensational interpretations of accepted history. In this latter field de Castro's inescapable passion for charlatanry comes to the fore, & leads him into statements, theories, & alleged "discoveries" of every sort.[7]

His climactic essay is a claim of having discovered the real facts concerning that most baffling of historico-mythical figures, Jesus Christ, including his true parentage on both sides. One can realise how important such a discovery would be, if it were true. Actually, we have so little *reliable* information about Christ that there is much doubt as to whether such a person really existed. Many of the stories told in the Gospels are old myths which have been told about others before. Probably there was some prophet or leader like Gandhi or Buddha at large in Judaea around the time of Tiberius, about whom a vast body of fabulous & ethical lore clustered, & whose legendry eventually became condensed into what we know as the New Testament. More than that it is unlikely that we shall ever know, since records are next to non-existent.

But old de Castro says he has all the unknown inside facts—which he claims he has discovered in "Germanic & Semitic sources." According to him, Jesus was the illegitimate son of the imperial procrator Pontius Pilatus (who later tried him) by a Galilean gentlewoman named Mary, who later married the carpenter Joseph. Pilatus himself, continues Old Dolph, was likewise illegitimate—the offspring of a Roman named Tyrus & a German princess of Mainz, on the Rhine. As the story goes, Tyrus was a "king" or governor of Germany sent out by Augustus. At the capital Mainz he met & wooed the princess, but was forbidden to wed her by the Roman rule against the presence of wives abroad with proconsular officials. The result was Pilatus' unsanctioned birth. Later the youth Pilatus went to Rome, killed a man in a duel, & was given a choice of two penalties by Augustus—to fight in the arena, or join a forlorn-hope expedition against a city called Pontus, where the Etruscans were in revolt. Choosing the latter, he behaved so bravely that Augustus gave him the complimentary name of *Pontius* & appointed him a tax-collector in Syria. There at the age of 20 he met & courted the fair Galilean—who refused to wed him because he was a pagan idolater. Her delicate Judaic scruples did not, however, prevent her from giving rise to the anniversary now about to be celebrated for the 1934th (or so) time. Pilatus, recalled to Rome, never knew that there had been a chee-ild until years later when—back in Iudaea as procurator—he condemned Jesus to death & learned only too late that he was his father! Such is de Castro's dramatic story—offered as a true historic discovery. He isn't very specific about his "sources"—& overlooks the fact that the German tribes had no written speech in Tiberius' time, so that "Germanic sources" couldn't be very first-handed at best. Also—who supposes that the Germans of that age gave a damn about what was happening in Syria? I can't criticise his "Semitic sources" (the Jewish Talmud &c) because I don't know anything about them. But on the other hand, the yarn touches *Roman* history at several points—& there I *have* something to say. See how the "true historic discovery" stands up under the following undoubted facts:

1.   *Tyrus* is not a Roman name.

2.   *Maguntiacum* (mod. Mainz) was *not* the capital of any part of Roman Germany till later in the imperial age. It was an originally Celtic village, & was merely the tribal capital of the (probably Germanic) Vangiones in the Augustan period. It became the site of a fortified Roman post in B.C. 12.

3.   Augustus appointed no civil governors of Germany till A.D. 17. The rule against having wives with them *did not apply* to the military commanders who ruled Germany before it was a civil province—or pair of provinces. Thus Germanicus Caesar was accompanied by his wife, & their daughter Agrippina the younger was born in camp at Oppidum Ubiorum—later named Colonia Agrippinensis (Cologne) after her.

4. Allowing for certain corrections in chronology, the date of the birth of Christ is traditionally set at what we now call B.C. 4. That would make it necessary for his father, if he begot him at the age of 20, to have been begotten at Mainz in *B.C. 26. But there was no Roman occupation of Rhineland Germany till the expedition of Claudius Drusus Nero in B.C. 12.* Prior to that date, all the fresh western conquests were below the Danube—Noricum, Rhaetia, & Pannonia (Tyrol, Austria, Hungary). In B.C. 26 the Rhineland was not subject to Roman rule—Caesar's raids in B.C. 55 & 53 having come to nothing. Therefore Augustus could have appointed no governor there. As a matter of fact, there was never any Roman commander in Germany with any such name as "Tyrus". The following are the *only* commanders appointed to Germany prior to the organisation of the civil provinces of Germania Superior & Inferior in A.D. 17:

B.C. 12—   Claudius Drusus Nero stepson of Augustus, brother of Tiberius, & father of the Emperor Claudius. He first brought the Roman power to the Rhine, & formed the string of forts now surviving as the cities of Coblenz, Bonn, Bingen, Mainz, &c.

B.C. 9—   Tiberius Caesar

A.D. 9—   Quintilius Varus massacred with all his army in the Saltus Teutobergiensis by the German leader Arminius or Hermann

A.D. 14—   Germanicus Caesar

There were no others. "Tyrus" is obviously a myth.

5. The *duel* did not exist in classical times.

6. There is no *town or city* in Italy or elsewhere called *Pontus*. Pontus was a *nation* in Asia Minor on the Black Sea—famed for its Mithridatic kings.

7. The *Etruscans* were never in revolt as late as the Augustan age. By that time they were cordially assimilated into the Roman people, so that Romans affected Etruscan fashions & boasted of Etruscan ancestry. C. Cilnius Maecenas was of Etruscan descent.

8. The honorary surname bestowed for conquering a place called *Pontus* would never be *Pontius*. According to Roman usage, it would be PONTICUS. On the other hand, *Pontius* was a very common gens-name of Samnite origin. (cf. C. Pontius, who sent a Roman army under the yoke in B.C. 321, & Pontius Telesinus, who fell in the wars of Marius & Sulla B.C. 82.) The name *Pilatus* probably came from the word *pileatus* (from *pileus*, a freedman's cap), signifying a freedman. Probably Pontius Pilatus,

though himself an eques, was descended from some freed slave of a Samnite named Pontius.

9.   There is no record of Pilatus' ever having been in Syria before his appointment by Tiberius (through the pull of the infamous Aelius Sejanus) as procurator of Judea in A.D. 26. Very little is known of P.—all the accounts of his later life & suicide being definitely apocryphal. There is nothing of this sort of thing antedating the biassed Christian writer Eusebius (A.D. 324).[8]

In view of these things, you can judge for yourself what Old Dolph's "historical discovery" really amounts to. It is, in truth, so crude that I have had to warn the old geezer that he can't possibly get away with it. How a scholar of his calibre could be so ignorant of Roman history—or imagine others to be so—is quite beyond me. Whether he made the whole thing up himself, or found some crude German myth to base it on, I really haven't the slightest idea. Of course, in discussing the matter with him I've had to be tactful & imply *that his Germanic sources are unreliable*. I can't tell him to his face that he's an old faker! But I've warned him that the legend has fatal flaws.

Here's the "Erich Zann" sheet, duly signed. I am surely glad to hear your high opinion of the story, since it is—as you know—one of my own favourites among my efforts. That effect of a hinted dream-world of which only shadows & reflections are perceptible is what all weird stories should suggest—but how pitifully few of them succeed in doing it! To be told that any of my own things possess a trace of this effect cannot but please & encourage me immensely. I can well understand that occasion when you virtually entered a finely-described scene & became a direct, integral part of it to the exclusion of the actual objective world. Such an experience has more than once been my lot—though there are not many authors who can weave such a spell as potent as that. You describe your emergence from the enchantment very graphically—I can picture the process!

And now let me thank you most sincerely & profoundly for the postcard views—two of which I am herewith returning as per request. They certainly bring the Snake River country to one's very hearthside, & I have gained from them a clearer idea of many geographical features than I ever had before. The Lewiston Spiral Highway must be a marvellous thing—I had not previously appreciated its scope. Nor are any of those scenes other than impressive. The dam at Boise City has a keen & almost melancholy personal interest in view of the unsuccessful dams constructed under my grandfather's auspices. My aunt was likewise much impressed—& the reminder of old events took her back in fancy to that trying period in the earlier 1890's when the first dam broke. The telegram to my grandfather announcing the bad news came at midnight, & she was the only person in the house who was wakened by the doorbell. She signed for the message & waked my grandfather—& he did not get much sleep during the rest of the night!

Your description of Whitebird, & the dizzying route leading to it, interests me immensely. Many trips over that road during icy weather would certainly wear badly on the nervous system! It reminds me of the experience of a friend on slippery roads in the Green Mts. of Vermont. The town itself must be distinctly picturesque in its way, with its vestiges of old western life. Evidently it is salubrious enough—if little old men there can tear up husky opponents & still be alive, hale, & hearty 20 years later! It would take Conan the Cimmerian to equal that record! Curious that you've never seen that formidable grade by daylight—but then, that is also true of myself & central Vermont. I have never been north of Bellows Falls in ordinary Vermont travel, but have of course whizzed all the way up & beyond in trips to Montreal & Quebec. In each of these trips, however, the central part of the state has been traversed at night. I've seen the dawn in extreme northern Vermont, but know such places as Wells River, White River Junction, & St. Johnsbury only by electric light! That abandoned Chinese copper mine must be interesting . . . . & the mystery of the heavy tools surely provokes speculation! That slipping & crack in the mountain must have been alarming—though I never heard of it before. Geological freaks have caused terror more than once. Did you ever hear of the "Moodus Noises" in Connecticut about 200 years ago? These noises consisted of alarming rumblings in the earth near some lonely hills, & the colonists swore they were either devices of the Devil or indications of the wrath of God. Later geologists decided that they were caused by certain harmless but unusual settlings in connexion with "faults" in the rock strata. They have had a tendency to return at long intervals—decades apart—& only a few weeks ago a fresh example of them was reported. This time, however, there were no fears, & no speculations as to the "work o' the Devil" or the "wrath o' Jehovy".[9]

Phoenix must have a delightful climate, & I surely hope you can get out there some day. As to the reason I don't move to a more congenial climate— it is sheer attachment to familiar scenes. I am very sensitive to landscape, architectural, and atmospheric impressions, & would miss the typical scenery of my native region most acutely if I were permanently exiled from it. The landscape of New England is perhaps the most mellowly beautiful & subtly distinctive in North America, & it is virtually the only one this side of Europe where the architecture is perfectly adapted to the geography. Adaptations like that occur only when the same people have inhabited a region for hundreds of years & have worked out a perfect harmonisation with the soil . . . . following an unbroken tradition & handing down certain customs & fashions from father to son. New England was thickly settled from the start, hence has had 300 years of orderly life much like that of Europe. The result is something peculiarly characteristic & old-world-like—an effort enhanced by the close resemblance of the salient scenery to that of northwestern Europe. It would be hard for me to feel at home anywhere else—hence my apparently foolish clinging to a climate obviously too cold for me.

I trust that before long you & Rhi´-Mel may hit upon some joint idea suitable for the Science Fiction League song. You will undoubtedly produce something good in the end. Hope also you can get the whole of the "Darkness & Dawn" cycle. It is certainly a grievous pity that the plates of the complete book are lying neglected!

Haven't sent out "The Thing on the Doorstep" yet, but if it ever gets into print you shall surely have the rough draught. Am enclosing some odds & ends of possible interest—cutting about Carthage, letter from Bloch for your news column, & two verses which R. F. Searight asked me to forward to you.

Having a pretty good Christmas hereabouts. We have a *tree* for the first time in over 25 years, & the pleasing task of decorating it quite brings back my childhood. There is a possibility of my visiting Long in N Y around New Year's, though it is by no means settled. About that time Barlow expects to be in New York—which would make quite a "family party" if the visits coincided. Wandrei may also pass through N Y on his way—by boat through the canal, I believe—from California. How long he intends to stay I don't know. Hornig expects a visit from Barlow, & on Dec. 31 will make a hurried trip to Florida—Miami & perhaps Key West—with a few stops along the route. If he were going to stay longer, I'd envy him—but a plunge of only a few days would be merely a tantalisation for me . . . . worse than staying home. To go to a warm climate & then suddenly plunge back into January cold would be, for me, a horrible experience.

I must thank you for your Christmas card—the largest & most impressive I ever received!* I shall keep it permanently—indeed, it is really worth framing. Our neighbour downstairs[10]—a high-school teacher of German who spends a good part of every summer in the ancient town depicted—was especially enthusiastic about it. Ar-Ech-Bei's card was a linoleum block print—evidently his own work.

Correspondents tell me that two of the newly-founded weird magazines—*Mystery Novels* & *Horror Stories*—are out, but that neither is any good. I knew they wouldn't be, so didn't even bother to see them. Koenig has just lent me a translation of the famous old "Malleus Malificarum"—book of 14th century German witchcraft trials—which promises to be highly interesting & informative. Haven't had a chance to read it yet.

Well—I trust your Christmas & New Year may be festive, & that 1935 may bring happiness & prosperity all along the line. ¶ Yrs most sincerely—E'ch-Pi-El

---

*That is, if you count out the crayon drawings of monsters—one 22 × 14 inches & another 20½ × 11½—which young Bloch sends as Yuletide greetings!

Notes

1. "Carcassonne," in Dunsany's *A Dreamer's Tales.*
2. Earl Leaston Bell, "The Land of Lur" (*WT,* May 1930).
3. Probably parts of "Annals of the Djinns."
4. CAS, "The Vaults of Yoh-Vombis" (*WT,* May 1932).
5. Zealia Brown Reed Bishop. The item in question is unidentified.
6. The revision projects have not been identified. HPL's article was "A Living Heritage: Roman Architecture in Today's America."
7. The work in question was never published. See HPL to Adolphe de Castro, 14 October, 6 November, and 14 November 1934, and 26 January 1935 (mss., JHL).
8. Eusebius (260/265–339/340), bishop of Caesarea, wrote *Historia Ecclesiastica,* the first surviving history of the Christian Church based on earlier sources, complete from the period of the Apostles to his own epoch.
9. HPL used such sounds in "The Dunwich Horror."
10. See FLB 33n5.

[21]   [ANS][1]

[Postmarked Providence, R.I.,
10 January 1935]

Just home from a visit to Long in N.Y., & found your package awaiting me. Many thanks for the Walpole item—which looks very promising & alluring. I shall read it with great appreciation at the very first opportunity. ¶ Had a very pleasant sojourn in the metropolis—seeing all the old group . . . Morton, Long, Loveman, Kleiner, Kirk, &c . . . as well as newer acquaintances. Young Barlow was up from Washington, so that our sessions had something of the aspect of a convention. Koenig shewed us all over his Electrical Testing Laboratory, & we duly absorbed museums, &c. Barlow laid in several book bargains, as well as a valuable etching & a set of apparatus for dry-point copper-plate engraving. I purchased a copy of Lewis's "Monk" for a dollar. ¶ All good wishes—E'ch-Pi-El.

Notes

1. *Front:* The Carrie Tower, Hope, Manning and University Halls at Left. Brown University, Proidence, R.I.

[22]   [ANS][1]

[Postmarked Providence, R.I.,
13 February 1935]

Thanks a thousand times for "Creep, Shadow", which arrived this morning in the best of condition. And give my thanks to Rhi-Mhel for his share in the

generous & ingenious enterprise! It is truly a triumph of neatness & art—as firm & harmonious as if a professional bindery had turned it out. I can't begin to express how grateful I am—& I am eagerly looking forward to reading the text. ¶ Meanwhile I've at last found the six instalments of that wretched magazine *Home Brew,* which contain my equally wretched "Herbert West". I've done them up, & will mail them to you as soon as I can get down to the P.O. (possibly tonight, possibly later) Don't expect anything of any value—for the stuff is simply lousy. No hurry about return—let D W R see them. ¶ Read Dunsany's new collection—"Jorkens Remembers Africa"—last Saturday. A few of the tales aren't half bad. ¶ Saw a fine exhibition of Hokusai's prints—with explanatory lecture—at the museum yesterday. ¶ Had another snowfall—but only a light one. Fairly warm again. ¶ Again thanks to you & Rhi-Mel for the book. I can see the lumber marks (or what I take to be such) on the leather.
All good wishes —
    E'ch-Pi-El.

Notes

1. *Front:* Benedict Temple of Music, Roger Williams Park, Providence, R. I.

[23]   [ALS]

#66
—Feby. 16, 1935

Dear Eph-Li:—
        Glad you enjoyed the Barlow sketches. Upon receipt of your letter I sent along an envelope of larger specimens—plus a particularly good photograph of Ar-E'ch-Bei. Keep these as long as you like & shew them to Rhī-Mhel—so long as they come back safely in the end. Too bad the big Bloch drawings are so hard to send. Later I'll get together some of the smaller Blochiana & let you see it. Much of it is hastily scrawled on the margins of letters.

Well—Price now has his country estate! Out of all alternatives he chose a colonially designed cottage on the top of a wooded, terraced hill near Emerald Lake & Redwood City, California—within sight of San Francisco Bay, & with a fine landscape vista on all sides. His new address is Route 2, Box 100-U-5, Redwood City, California. He finds the new place delightfully restful, & is now all moved in. Recently a huge white fighting tomcat—a cousin, perhaps, of Rhī-Mhel's Crom—ambled in & voluntarily took up his abode with Price. He has topaz eyes, & the hugest appetite of any quadruped short of a wolf that Price has ever seen. He is a mighty hunter, too—the other day he clawed a gopher out of its hole & brought it for his new master to see before devouring it. In recognition of his prowess in the chase, he has received the name of Nimrod.[1] So far as current news goes—E H P is still plugging away & raking in the dollars. The other day—Chinese New Year's—he made the distance to San Francisco (21 m.) in 26 minutes in his faithful Juggernaut—dining at an exotic restaurant in the Oriental quarter. As for his nickname—I generally call him Malik Taus, the Peacock Sultan.

Young Bloch's group certainly appears to use its brains! I myself have never been as much interested in actual abnormal psychology & its grotesque horrors, as in the wholly mythical & cosmically speculative branches of weirdness & shadow. But abnormality—either among primitive or among civilised groups—is certainly a profound & extensive subject, to which none but a specialist could do real justice. It is certainly a fact that savages & barbarians are fully as liable to repulsive perversions as civilised races—though this was not generally recognised till recently. Races seem to vary in their tendencies toward wholesale abnormalities—waves of such tendencies, & of an almost morbid interest in them, coming & going at long intervals. No—I'm not familiar with the book "Voodoo-Eros",[2] although I vaguely recall seeing it mentioned in some bookseller's circular a while ago. Within recent years a tremendous amount of writing on such anthropological arcana has appeared, but unfortunately I've had no time to become even reasonably conversant with it.

My New York trip surely was enjoyable. Here are two of those pictures (enlarged) that Talman took of the meeting. Sorry I have no others of anybody in the weird group. My own was so ridiculous that I tore it up.[3] Please return these snaps—also the additional small Barlow drawings which I'm enclosing. As for poor old de Castro—he couldn't have seen us if we had called, for I've since learned that he was laid up all through January with a nervous breakdown—through worry over his wife's illness. And to cap the climax, she died Jany. 23 at St. Joseph's Hospital. We certainly do feel sorry for the old cuss, for he is really an enormously likeable & generous chap aside from his incurable penchant for charlatanry. Hope he'll gradually recover from the strain & bereavement. His chapter on the ancestry of Christ surely was grotesque & vulnerable. Actually, the chances probably are about 60 against 40 that there was some one definite person behind the conventional figure of Jesus. The biblical accounts obviously fuse together anecdotes of many different preachers & fanatics, & add a good deal of legendry taken from earlier sources; but after all it seems rather more probable than not that some especial figure attracted to itself the various bits of floating folklore. Myths are just as often built up around actual persons as around abstract ideas—at the present moment a definite cycle of romantic & mystical myth-making is gradually accumulating around the figure of the late Pres. Lincoln . . . a man so recent that scores of people still living have seen him in person. Of course, any actual prototype of Christ was doubtless vastly different from the traditional conception. There is no reason to think that any such persons as Joseph & Mary ever existed—though there is equally little reason to think they didn't. It is not at all likely that the real Jesus (if such existed) ever claimed a virgin birth. That was one of the stock attributes of the various mythical hero-cults of antiquity—which naturally became fastened to Christ along with other well-recognised cult attributes.

Yes—I fancy Barlow would have a hard time getting accomodated [*sic*] [to] your water-drawing routine—although Klarkash-Ton wouldn't. C A S lives on Indian Hill, considerably out of the village of Auburn, & has to bring all the household's water from a well uncomfortably distant from the house.

You certainly had a strenuous New Year's trip—but as you say, it's lucky you did not have to go the following week when the snow was worse. New England was quite tied up with a 13-inch snowfall Jany. 23–4, but that is now gradually melting off. Interested to hear of the changes of personnel in your orchestra—including the trumpeter from Auburn. Wonder if he ever heard of the Smith family on Indian Hill? Your new saxophonist sounds very interesting, too. The Finns form a really remarkable strain—producing an unusual number of capable & gifted individuals in proportion to the size, population, & wealth of their native region. The original nucleus of them was undoubtedly *Mongol,* as their language & certain occasional physiognomical traces shew; but they have picked up so much Aryan blood during their long subjection to Sweden & Russia that the stock today is dominantly Caucasian. I fancy the aristocracy of Helsingfors is practically *all* Nordic—a good part of it being even Swedish-speaking instead of Finnish-speaking. A friend of mine is engaged to a young lady of Finnish descent (whose brother is American consul at Helsingfors), whose appearance is absolutely that of a purely Aryan Scandinavian. Incidentally—the best existing book on the English weird novel ("The Haunted Castle", by Eino Railo) is by a Finnish professor who has studied & taught in England.

As for "The Shadow Out of Time"—I managed to get to the beginning of *p. 55* when a fresh influx of other tasks stalled me again. It's near the end, though, now. I rather fear it won't be commercially acceptable anywhere--& I have many doubts to its actual intrinsic merit. I didn't intend to let it get so long—but it simply ran away from me! Yes—the final scene is laid in the Great Sandy Desert of Western Australia—& I suppose it is shot all through with geographical mistakes. Glad you recall the "Mts. of Madness" favourably—for as you know, that's my own favourite. A review of it by you would undoubtedly be capable & interesting—but it's rather unusual to review a thing which hasn't been published anywhere. As for "Yule-Horror"—I'd forgotten all about that myself! I wrote dozens of weird verses in the old days—some of which got published here & there while others didn't. Now that you remind me—I remember that "Yule-Horror" was a trifle which I wrote almost for fun—not for publication at all—& sent on a Christmas card to Wright in 1925. He seemed to like it, so cut out the last stanza with its personal allusions & comic touches & decided to publish it in the magazine.[4] The Poe home article was rather a routine piece of work—prompted by my visit to the recently-opened Poe House in Philadelphia.[5]

Hope you'll soon get a letter from Ar-Ech-Bei. In his latest to me he says: "It grows, for some unknown reason, increasingly difficult for me to write letters. I shirk; I evade; in a word, I loathe the process. What shall I do, when I like so much to receive them? I seem to have practically everybody angry at me, so I'm not getting any, anyway, at present." I've advised him to forget that there's any difference between *talking* (which he does freely enough) & setting words down on paper; & to ramble along on his typewriter without any thought of formality—just as if he were sitting in conversation with the one he's addressing. Incidentally, I've urged him to break the silence toward those whom he has owed letters so long. Sooner or later you'll hear from him. His eyes are better, & his art course seems to flourish—although now & then he gets bored by the task of continually drawing figures from plaster casts. Yes—I told him about the "Colour" illustration project, & he seemed quite enthusiastic.

By the way—the other day I had a letter form Loring & Mussey of N Y, the publishers of Derleth's books, asking to see some of my weird stuff with a view to bringing out a book. They named the tales they wanted to see, having heard about them from A W D. Among them was the "Colour"—& I sent it with the rest, trusting that such submission may not cause any complication or inconvenience at your end. Of course, the chances that anything will come of this matter are practically nil. This is the 5th time a publisher has asked to see my tales (first Wright, then Putnam's, then Vanguard, then Knopf, & now L & M!)—yet nothing has ever come of such invitations. In such cases I send the stuff along in a sheerly perfunctory spirit—just to leave no stone unturned. Then I can never say afterward that I *might* have had a book *if* I had sent my stuff in. By the way—L & M expect to have Derleth's new detective novel "Three Who Died" out on Feby. 21; issuing his serious novel "Place of Hawks" April 24.

Enclosed is the signed "Fungi" sheet. Sooner or later I presume Hornig will print all of the Fungi which have not been professionally published. I wouldn't mind his reprinting those in the Providence Journal, since they had a merely local circulation.[6] Eventually I'll send you "Herbert West"—though you will see that it is a very inferior piece of hack work. I have now wholly disavowed it. My file-cleaning is only partial as yet. In mid-January I picked up a pair of dark walnut chests of drawers to accomodate the excess of loose papers & pamphlets, but so far I haven't had a second in which to do the necessary classifying & eliminating. I have piled one of the chests on top of the other, so that they form a neat single cabinet. They have a plain, old-fashioned look which makes them harmonise very well with the atmosphere of my study. I have put them beside a tall bookcase—in such a way as to avoid disturbing any previous piece of furniture. No hurry about "Salammbo" or anything else. I haven't yet had a second in which to read "Portrait of a Man With Red Hair", but hope to get at it soon. As for the Salammbo cover—bless me, but anything is all right which can roughly keep the text from further harm! And I'm sure the "Creep Shadow" binding will be tremendously clever, despite your modest disclaimer. Yes—I'll let you know if it ever comes unglued. And again let me thank you most abundantly for your kindness in going to all this trouble on my account! The leather surely has abundantly historic associations— there is something quite poetic in your thought of the numberless fragments of forest monarchs which have slid across its surface!

Sorry your tale didn't win the F M cover contest—but what *first* story could be expected to do so? By all means let me see it some time. Not many of the weird crowd are ever likely to "crash" the highly-paying popular magazines, since (as you point out) these periodicals have a highly arbitrary set of formula-following demands. Most of the things they insist on are just the things which spoil a weird tale!

Hope you can get a good biography of Robert E. Howard. Wish I had time to delve into his voluminous letters & get some of the facts buried there, but at the moment can give only a few points from memory. R E H was born in Texas in 1907, of old Southwestern & Southern stock. The Howard line came from England to Georgia in 1735. The Ervin line has produced men of high standing & ability—Confederate officers, planters, Texas pioneers. A large part of R E H's blood is Irish, & he takes great pride in his knowledge of Celtic history & antiquities. He lives with his parents in a village from which pioneer violence has not yet fully departed. His father is a physician of high standing, & great courage & resourcefulness, who once fought a knife duel with one hand tied behind his back. R E H is a typical primitive throwback in emotions—idealising barbaric & pioneer life. He hated school—yet loved books so much that he used to force open a window of the school library in the summer, when it was closed, in order to take & return things he wanted to read. He is today a really profound authority on Southwestern history & folklore—as well as on ancient history. He began to write stories very young, but takes very little pride in them—saying he'd rather be a good prize-fighter than a good novelist! Being brought up in a rough town, he came to accept rough ways as a matter of course. He has been through dozens of fights, with & without weapons, & has served as an amateur boxer. I think he was once connected in some way with a travelling carnival. I judge he was rather a roving character in his teens—away from home a good deal. He says he feels most at home among rough workmen, & has passionately strong sympathies for the under-dog despite a personally aristocratic ancestry. He is very bitter & cynical in temperament—but kindly & sympathetic at the same time. Extremely brave & conscientious. At one time during his teens he worked at a drug store soda fountain. He has seen a good deal of the rough side of oil boom towns, & hotly resents the way large eastern corporations exploit Texas. When he says his life is 'tame & uneventful', he is thinking only of western standards. Actually, he sees a vast amount of violence. He sympathises greatly with outlaws, & is really a fanatic on the subject of alleged police persecu-

tions—unjust arrests, 3d degree, &c. His fetishes are strength, virility, justice, & freedom. Everything civilised, soft, effeminate, or orderly he hates with astonishing venom. In ancient history he detests Rome as strongly as I revere it. He travels occasionally in Texas & the S.W.—has seen the Carlsbad Caverns, & sometimes spends the winter in San Antonio. Has never been east of New Orleans. First stories published in W T in 1925 or 6.[7] A poet of savagely great power. So fond of his Celtic heritage that he has Gaelicised his middle name Ervin into EIARBIHN—as the fanatics in Ireland nowadays Gaelicise theirs. Tastes in literature somewhat uneven—despises all modern subtlety & likes books about simple characters & violent events. Would rather be a Celtic barbarian of 100 or 200 B.C. than a civilised modern. I'd shew you some of his letters if he hadn't asked me not to let anybody see them. I think I have shewn you his picture. ¶ Fred Anger & some other weird fans in the San Francisco region plan to make a mass pilgrimage to Auburn to see Clark Ashton Smith. Can't think of any other news at the moment. ¶ Sincerely yrs—
　　　　E'ch-Pi-El.

P.S. Glad the weather is moderating in your region. We've been snowbound here—though things are better now. I had to stay in the house for ages, but am now getting about more. Heard 2 good poetry readings at the college lately—one by Archibald MacLeish, author of "Conquistador."[8] ¶ Thanks immensely for the 2 pictures. That Whitebird grade surely is impressive! The Clearwater seems an attractive stream.

[P.P.S] Feb. W.T. very mediocre.

[P.P.P.S. on envelope] *Extra!* Tell Rhī-Mhel (since you don't share my partiality in this direction) that there are 4 new coal-black kittens at the boarding-house across the back garden—brothers of the late Sam Perkins. Born 2 days ago, but I've just heard the news.

Notes

1. According to the Book of Genesis and Books of Chronicles, Nimrod was the son of Cush, the great-grandson of Noah. He was "a mighty hunter before the Lord" (Gen. 10:9).
2. By Felix Bryk.
3. See cover of Kenneth W. Faig's *The Unknown Lovecraft*.
4. See Bibliography under "Festival."
5. "Homes and Shrines of Poe."
6. *FF* published only ten sonnets from *Fungi from Yuggoth*. The *Providence Journal* published five in the spring of 1930.
7. Howard's "Wolfshead" was his first story in *WT* (April 1926).
8. The other poet was Susanna Valentine Mitchell (Gammell) of Providence.

[24]   [ANS][1]

[Postmarked Providence, R.I.,
20 March 1935]

Barlow material safely arrived. Interested to hear of the Lewiston move—let me have the new address when it becomes effective. Rhi-Mhel will be sorry to have you at a greater distance. ¶ Glad you could endure Herbert West— but it really is a rotten hash. The trouble is that it was written to order— according to certain specifications as to length, gruesomeness, &c. I won't write that way any more. The magazine *Home Brew* was atrocious junk—of course the editor knew it, but it was what the rabble paid for in those days. It lasted through 1924—perhaps into 1925—after the change of its name to *High Life*. ¶ Death of the F F surely is a tragedy. I wish F M *would* print the rest of my article, but fear the editor[2]—as a specialist in scientifiction—might not care to. I don't think L. C. Smith's column[3] beats yours—but do as you like about specialising in biographies. ¶ New *Marvel Tales* is out—excellent format, but mediocre contents. ¶ Just finished Derleth's new detective nov- el—Three who Died. Very clever. ¶ A young science fiction fan named Ken- neth Sterling has just moved from N.Y. to Providence. Amazingly precocious kid—evidently Jewish, judging by his looks. ¶ Several springlike days lately— with temperature of 65° & 71°. Took a 12-mile rural walk March 6. ¶ Well— hope you get comfortable quarters in Lewiston. ¶ Best wishes—E'ch-Pi-El.

Notes

1. *Front:* Benedict Temple of Music, Roger Williams Park, Providence, R.I.
2. Julius Schwartz. The balance of "Supernatural Horror of Literature" was not pub- lished following the failure of *FF*.
3. Smith had a short-lived column in *FF* named "Gleanings."

[25]   [ANS][1]

[Postmarked Saint Augustine, FL,
20 August 1935]

On my slow & antiquarian way north after a visit of 2 months & 10 days with Barlow in De Land! It seems good to see ancient houses & gardens again af- ter so long a sojourn amidst rural modernity! Trust you find the new Lewis- ton environment enjoyable, & that Rhi-Mhel duly returned to you the copy of "Man with Red Hair" which I sent through him. Thanks again for the loan, which was tremendously enjoyable. ¶ Regards—Ech-Pi-El.

Notes

1. *Front:* The Roman Catholic Cathedral, St. Augustine, Fla.

[26]   [ALS]

66 College St.,
Providence, R.I.,
Jany. 18, 1936

Dear Eph-Li:—

Very glad to receive your card. I've been following your progress through bulletins from Rimel, & trust you find your present semimigratory career congenial. When you do settle down once more, you will doubtless find your perspective considerably broadened.

I spent last summer in De Land as Barlow's guest—duplicating my 1934 programme in that respect. We built a cabin across the lake from the Barlow home & installed a printing press—on which we issued an edition of Long's later poems (entitled "The Goblin Tower" after one of the verses) as a surprise for the author. On the way down & back I stopped at Charleston & other ancient & interesting towns—visiting Wandrei in N.Y. for 2 weeks on the return trip, & seeing most of the local group . . . Long, Morton, Koenig, &c. In the autumn I had several short trips around New England—to Marblehead, Cape Cod, New Haven, & the "Dunwich" country—& was outdoors a good deal because of the mildness of the season. At Christmas we had a tree—& around New Year's I visited Long for a week—seeing the gang & meeting several weird & science fiction figures whom I had not seen before—Arthur J. Burks, Otto (of "Eando") Binder, Donald Wollheim, &c. Saw Seabury Quinn for the first time since 1931. Long & the two Wandrei boys are going in heavily for pulp fiction, & are making surprising amounts of cash—something I'll never be able to do! Visited the new Hayden Planetarium of the Am. Museum—a highly impressive educational device, which makes clear nearly all the elementary points connected with the solar system & the starry heavens. When I visited my poet-friend Loveman he shewed me his new book—published by the Caxton Printers of *Idaho*. I read the proofs of this work last September, & one of the verses is dedicated to me.[1] Thus does *Idaho* continue to appear in my annals! I enclose a circular containing mention of the volume—Loveman gave me about 100 to distribute to correspondents. Reached home Jan. 7, & have since been lost in a limitless ocean of work. Programme so crowded that I've had to shift many matters to others. Nor has a severe cold helped any. It will take weeks to restore order to my schedule.

I surely was pleased to have the "Mts. of Madness" accepted. *Astounding* also took a newer novelette of mine, "The Shadow Out of Time." Saw the first instalment of "Mts." yesterday, & am generally pleased with cover design & illustrations. The chap who drew those monsters must certainly have read the text with care. The landing of this tale especially gratifies me because so many did not like it.[2] I've lately written a fairly short weird tale called "The Haunter of the Dark", based on the westward view from my dark window.

Barlow surprised me at Christmas by sending a little booklet containing my "Cats of Ulthar", of which he had printed 40 copies for private distribution. It was remarkably well done—without a single misprint so far as I can see. He is also going to print my "Fungi from Yuggoth" & Clark Ashton Smith's later poems—the latter in a volume entitled "Incantations." Barlow is also publishing an amateur paper—*The Dragon-Fly*.[3]

Speaking of Smith—his mother died Sept. 9, & he has been quite nervously exhausted by the blow. He has, however, taken up a new art—that of carving or miniature sculpture in the soft minerals of his region—& is succeeding phenomenally well at it. Most of his products are grotesque heads or figurines (he has given me two—"Cthulhu" & "The Outsider"), & a professional demand for them is growing in his locality. It would be curious indeed if Klarkash-Ton were to end up primarily as a *sculptor!*

Price went on a trip to Mexico in November, & had a great time. He stopped in Texas to see Robert E. Howard, & visited New Orleans—his old stamping-ground—on the return trip. In Mexico he saw an impressive array of Aztec ruins—temples, pyramids, &c.—& stocked his imagination with new images.

Well—I trust all is going prosperously with the orchestra, & that you find Grangeville a pleasant place. Rimel says the climate is severer than that of Asotin & Lewiston, but I presume you are able to stand it. Hope the winter isn't proving a severe one—it has been benevolently mild hereabouts so far.

Just had an interesting letter from Rimel enclosing his new story in *Progressive Youth*,[4] & the revised version of "The Blue Stone." He surely is coming on!

Today is snowy—our first in a long while. Hope it isn't the beginning of more typically arctic conditions!

Best wishes—& thanks for the Christmas card.

Yrs most sincerely—

H P L

Notes

1. *The Hermaphrodite and Other Poems*. "To Satan" was dedicated to HPL.

2. *At the Mountains of Madness* was illustrated by Howard V. Brown. The story was not, in general, well received by readers of *Astounding* either.

3. RHB published *The Cats of Ulthar* as his "'35 Christmas card" (HPL to W. F. Anger, 2 September 1936; *Letters to Robert Bloch and Others*, 246) in an edition of 42 copies, and two numbers of the *Dragon-Fly*. He did not, however, publish *Incantations* or *Fungi from Yuggoth*, although he printed some of the latter. CAS's *Incantations*, conceived as early as 1925, following the publication of *Sandalwood*, was never published as a separate book, but there is a section of that title in his *Selected Poems* (1971) that mostly follows the plan for the edition RHB had intended to publish.

4. Not located. DWR had at least two stories in this periodical.

Duane W. Rimel c. 1940 (courtesy Andrew Porter)

Letters to Duane W. Rimel

[1]   [ALS, JHL]

66 College St.,
Providence, R.I.,
Jany. 10, 1934

Dear Mr. Rimel:—

When your letter of Dec. 26 was finally forwarded to Providence I was away on a two weeks' visit, & for some reason it did not get re-forwarded with the rest of my mail. Hence the late date of this reply, which I trust you can excuse.

Regarding Ackerman—he is probably a bright enough youth, but somewhat given to excessive egotism & the shewing-off tendency. I had not intended to comment publicly on his outburst, but am not after all especially sorry that Hornig printed my personal opinion. It is needless to say that Ackerman's opinion of Clark Ashton Smith shews a complete lack of literary appreciation.[1]

It pleases me greatly to learn that you like my own fictional attempts, & I hope that future specimens will not disappoint you. If you would care to see more of my stuff, you have an excellent chance right now—since a large assortment of my old tales is at present in the hands of a fellow-townsman of yours—Mr. F. Lee Baldwin—as a loan. I will ask Mr. Baldwin to sub-lend the material to you if you like. There is no hurry about its return—either you or he can send it back at leisure after you are both wholly through with it.

As for autographing a copy of "The Dunwich Horror"—I would surely be very glad to do it if you think the signature of so mediocre a scribbler is of any value. You must realise, though, that the actual literary standing of the poor devils who write for cheap magazines is very slight. It is almost humorous to think of the signatures of such plodding hacks as worth anything—though I suppose they may well have a certain personal or associative interest for those who like the stories in question. At any rate, I'll be delighted to scrawl my name over anything you wish except cheques, death-warrants, or incriminating documents! There's no need of hesitating about asking any of the magazine contributors for autographs & kindred things—such a request is highly flattering, since it gives its recipient the momentary sensation of being a celebrity! Here are the names & addresses of some of the W T writers I know—all of whom would be glad to autograph anything sent them:

Robert E. Howard, Lock Box 313, Cross Plains, Texas.
Donald Wandrei, 84 Horatio St., Apt. 4B, New York, N.Y.
Wilfred B. Talman, Scotland Post Road, Spring Valley, N.Y.
Seabury Quinn, 34 Jefferson Ave., Brooklyn, N.Y.

August W. Derleth, Sauk City, Wisconsin.
Clark Ashton Smith, Box 385, Auburn, Calif.
H. Warner Munn, Route 1, Athol, Mass.
Frank B. Long, Jr., 230 W. 97th St., New York, N.Y.
A. Merritt, % American Weekly, 235 E. 45th St., New York, N.Y.
E. Hoffmann Price, 1416 Josephine St., New Orleans, La.
Hugh B. Cave, 94 Montgomery St., Pawtucket, R.I.

What you say of your tastes in weird fiction interests me greatly, since they seem to coincide to a large extent with my own. I, too, prefer stories with a strong touch of cosmic *outsideness,* & with hints of subterranean cults which have darkly survived & persisted down the centuries. Weird verse also appeals greatly to me—& I have written quite a bit of it. You may possibly recall my sonnets called "Fungi From Yuggoth" which ran in W T two or three years ago.[2] I have read your own specimen with much interest, & congratulate you on the excellently chosen image it contains. You certainly have a very genuine sense of the weird, & a distinct talent for selecting symbols with which to express this sense. The main defect of the poem is merely its technical form, which shews a need for studying the rules of metre in some detail. Later on I may be able to supply a few useful hints (just now, as a result of my fortnight's vacation, I am rushed to death!)—& meanwhile an excellent thing to study would be the extremely clear & easy pamphlet by George E. Teter entitled "An Introduction to Some Elements of Poetry"—which can be obtained by sending a quarter to the Kenyon Press, Wauwatosa, Wisconsin. By the way—in typing the present copy of "Midnight Fancy" didn't you make a mistake in writing *reverie* instead of *revelry?* But—as I said before—this verse is very good indeed save for the purely mechanical technique. Keep it up! Have you ever written weird stories? I imagine you ought to be able to concoct some pretty good specimens. Don't worry about your lack of years— that is something which time will automatically alter all too soon!

During the last two weeks I have been visiting Frank Belknap Long, Jr.— whose stories you undoubtedly know. I have also seen Talman, Wandrei, Merritt, T. Everett Harré (who edited the collection "Beware After Dark"), Desmond Hall, (editor of *Astounding* Stories [*sic*]) & the two youths (Conrad Ruppert & Julius Schwartz) who run the magazine *Fantasy* (formerly *Science Fiction Digest*). Ruppert is also the printer of *The Fantasy Fan.* From now on, I am told, *Fantasy* will include weird material as well as science fiction. This magazine, together with the F F & the soon-to-appear *Unusual Stories,* forms an excellent place for the beginner to try his hand. No pay—but great hospitality toward unknown & incipient writers.

Well, as I said, I shall be glad to sign any stories of mine which you may send. Meanwhile get in touch with your fellow-Asotinian Mr. Baldwin if you would like to see a wider array of my stuff.

With every good wish, & thanking you for the interesting & effective weird poem, I am

Yrs most cordially & sincerely,

H P Lovecraft

Notes

1. In the first installment of "The Boiling Point," *FF* 1, No. 1 (September 1933): 6–7, Forrest J Ackerman impudently took *Wonder Stories* (a science fiction magazine) to task for publishing Clark Ashton Smith's "Dweller in Martian Depths" (a horror story). Subsequent columns (October 1933–February 1934; now collected in *The Boiling Point* [West Warwick, RI: Necronomicon Press, 1985]) contained mostly rebuttals to his comments.
2. Ten sonnets from the sonnet-sequence *Fungi from Yuggoth* appeared in seven issues of *WT* between September 1930 and April–May 1931.

[2]   [ALS, JHL]

66 College St.,

Providence, R.I.,

Jany. 22, 1934.

Dear Mr. Rimel:—

Your ingeniously bound & decorated copy of "The Dunwich Horror" duly arrived, & I feel vastly honoured at having my lowly product preserved in such a form. A series like that is surely a convenient way of keeping stories. There's really no reason for keeping the magazines whole unless one has a complete file—as I have. You didn't tell me *where* to sign the story, but I used my judgment & drew my rooster-tracks at the end, where signatures are often printed. Hope this treatment fills the bill.

As to the status of the writers who contribute to W.T. & its equivalents— of course, one can't generalise too closely. Once in a while an author of real standing—like E. F. Benson—is represented in these rags;[1] while in other cases a more regular contributor may achieve one or two stories which approach the level of literature. The level of merit is tremendously uneven—a thing of peaks & valleys. But in the main we have to admit that the regular weird & science-fiction writers featured in these cheap magazines are in a class miles below that of real authors like Poe, Machen, James, Dunsany, Blackwood, de la Mare, Bierce, & so on. I'm not unduly prejudiced by the form of the magazine—but I can see by comparison & analysis that none of the cheap standbys produce any work like Machen's "White People" or Shiel's "House of Sounds" or James's "Count Magnus" or Blackwood's "Willows." We are dealing with a realm wholly below that of real literature, though of course many of the writers in question may some day work up to the level of literature.

You can easily see that fully ¾ of the yarns in these pulp rags are "formula stories"—that is, mechanical concoctions designed to tickle simple & uncritical readers, & having cut-&-dried stock characters (brave young hero, beauteous heroine, mad scientist, &c. &c.) & absurdly artificial "action" plots. Only a very small minority of the tales have any serious merit or literary intent. A really artistic weird tale must be simply an attempt to capture a certain mood or reproduce a certain atmosphere—swift "action" is ridiculous & out of place, while wooden romantic characters & hackneyed situations dilute & destroy whatever value it might otherwise have. I've always tried to escape the cheap magazine formula, though unconsciously & against my will I have probably been tainted by it.

I hope you've been able to see some of the tales I lent to Mr. Baldwin. One batch came back a few days ago—so I am sending it on under separate cover—3d class—for you to see. Hope it won't disappoint you. No hurry about its return. Hope nothing will be lost—one item last month failed to reach Mr. Baldwin, though other things in the same envelope did. If you don't catch the other items before they come back I'll send them to you later. Still later—when they come back from a long-term loan—I'm going to send my two long MSS. of 1931 to Asotin for both you & Mr. B. to see.[2]

Glad my remarks on your verse proved of some use, & hope the Teter booklet will be a substantial help in further composition. I can sympathise with you regarding composition on a typewriter. I hate the damned things, & could no more write a story or piece of verse on one than I could fly with a submarine boat. I never touch a machine except when absolutely compelled to. Not only does it dry up all the founts of thought & imagination, but it makes me acutely nervous & gives me a headache if I keep on too long (whereas I can write on by hand for any length of time). The only typing I ever do is when I copy MSS. for professional publication—& I don't do even that when I can persuade anybody else to do it for me. Incidentally—I have a devilish time getting a fountain pen to suit me. I need something that will race along at mile-a-minute speed with virtually no pressure—which means a very smooth & flexible point, plus a feed of incredible copiousness . . . . about as free a feed as can be had without the actual seepage of ink-drops. Only once in a while can I seem to get the right combination—& whenever I do, something usually happens to spoil it. I try to keep *two* pens in fair shape, so that I'll have something decent to write with in case one gives out & requires weeks of repeated experiment & exchanging. Just now I've secured a fine specimen—the result of pestering the life out of the central Waterman office in N.Y. during a fortnight's visit to the metropolis.

About my "Fungi from Yuggoth"—here is the entire lot in MS. form—to be read & returned at your leisure. There are more here than were used in W.T.—some published elsewhere & some not published at all.[3] Glad you liked "The Whisperer in Darkness"—whose Vermont local colour was obtained at first hand.[4]

I am interested to hear of your own weird work, & trust you'll let me see specimens some time. What you say of "The Ladder of Thought" sounds highly promising—I imagine it ought to be acceptable to "scientifiction" as well as weird periodicals. "The Spell of the Blue Stone" also sounds alluring—I always did have a partiality for tales of secret cults surviving from primal aeons. As for placing your tales—I think there is no question but that they would be well received by all three of the non-paying magazines—F F, *Fantasy*, & the still unborn *Unusual*. There is always benefit in having things published, even without pay. The printed copies are useful, & you are brought before a wide circle of interested readers, many of whom will have valuable criticisms & suggestions to offer.

By the way—your quasi-bookplate design on the back of the bound "Dunwich" interested me greatly. Here's a specimen of my own bookplate—depicting one of the typical Colonial doorways of ancient Providence.[5] I am an enthusiastic amateur antiquarian, especially fond of the 18th century & devoted to old houses in particular. My native town is full of them (in fact, I now live in one), & my principal recreation is visiting other old towns where different varieties of them abound. In the course of the last decade I've seen most of the old towns & cities from Quebec to Key West & New Orleans.

All good wishes—

Yrs most cordially & sincerely—

H P Lovecraft

Notes

1. Seven stories by E. F. Benson (1867–1940) were reprinted in *WT* between July 1929 and December 1933.
2. *At the Mountains of Madness* and "The Shadow over Innsmouth," both unpublished at the time.
3. The typescript lent to Rimel consisted of 33 sonnets. Some had been published in the *Providence Journal*, *WT*, *Driftwind*, and a few other scattered journals.
4. HPL lifted text from his "Vermont: A First Impression" (written 29 September 1927) to incorporate into the story.
5. Designed by Wilfred B. Talman.

[3]   [ALS, JHL]

66 College St.,
Providence, R.I.,
Feby. 2, 1934.

Dear Mr. Rimel:—

Glad the signature was in the right place. By this time you will have received the batch of stories Mr. Baldwin returned, & I hope you will not be disappointed in them. I have since then sent Mr. B. another tale—"The Shunned House"—in the form of loose printed sheets, & have asked him to let you see it. Glad you like "The Picture in the House" & "Cool Air."

Old deserted houses are fascinating wherever one finds them—& they have much the same atmosphere whether they are 50 or 75 years old, as in your part of the world, 200 or 250 years old, as in my locality, or 500 or 1000 years old, as often in the Old World. I'd like to see that desolate shanty up the Snake! The house described in "Cool Air" is an actual one—in which a friend of mine once had quarters.[1] I shall later send on the long MSS. for you & Mr. Baldwin to read.

I am glad to hear that you are in revolt against the cut-&-dried formula stories so preponderant in the cheap magazines. I believe that many of the readers would be glad to get really original & distinctive material—but editors are afraid to try experiments. I hope, as you do, that the F F & *Unusual Stories* will arouse a taste for truly unique & unhackneyed fiction. In the end, it might become popular enough to make the more conservative editors willing to risk it.

Hope you'll like "Fungi from Yuggoth". I've read your new poem with much interest, & am returning it in slightly amended & annotated form. It has a delightfully tense & macabre atmosphere, & certainly indicates that your poetic powers are worth developing. Such faults as there are, are purely technical—indicating only a need for continued practice & study of the rules. Hope my pencil notations are legible. Some of the corrections concern small points which a very thorough & attentive review of books on grammar & correct usage would help to clear up. For instance—"wither naught" cannot be used in place of "wither *to* naught", while "come not to their harken" is also quite inadmissible. Be careful, too, about *rhyme*. *Slime* & *shine* don't make a rhyme. Increased practice will make your verses more fluent & idiomatic, & will cause the meaning of each stanza to be clearer. This piece, though, is really amply good enough for publication—why not send it to F F in its corrected form? I'll be very glad to read "The Spell of the Blue Stone" when you have it ready, & will make all due allowances for the W.T. influence. Don't worry about your lack of special training—gradual good reading plus a slow study of some good books on writing will give you what you need. You ought to read some of the actual weird classics—Machen, Blackwood, Dunsany, James, & so on. I am lending Mr. Baldwin two of Machen's best items, & advise you to borrow & read them before he returns them. These will give you a splendid idea of what really sincere & original weird literature is like.

Your linoleum cut struck me as really splendid, & I sincerely congratulate you on your skill. Mr. Baldwin says that you intend to do some illustrations for the publications you & he are planning, & I'm sure they'll be thoroughly creditable. You can probably discover some good paper of rough—& perhaps slightly absorbent—finish which will take the impressions as well as cheap paper.

My trip of last month was indeed very pleasant, though it didn't cover a vast deal of ground. The part of N.J. which I visited was rather close to New York City—which in turn is only 190 miles from Providence. When I am able, I take longer trips—largely to explore old & quaint places—& have at various times been as far north as Quebec & as far south as New Orleans & Key West. I have never, however, been to Europe or out West. You have certainly been fortunate in your weather. Here we are just pulling out of a second cold spell during which the mercury was down to zero. I couldn't go out of the house for three days.

"Buffalo Rock" must be a tremendously interesting landmark. Unknown reliques of forgotten races are always fascinating, & this would seem to be quite a notable specimen. The early history of America is a baffling mystery which archaeology may or may not partly solve. Who were the first inhabitants? When did they appear? What were they like? How much development did they attain? Recent discoveries seem to indicate the presence of human beings at a very primitive period—something previously denied. There are many rather mysterious-looking carved rocks in the East, though experts generally attribute the inscriptions either to Indians or to the first white colonists.

What you say of Asotin & the Snake Valley & the prevailing landscape is of great interest to me, since in the 1890's my grandfather was very familiar with Idaho. He was head of a company interested in land & irrigation, & tried to build a dam in the Snake River. During that period he was in Idaho a great deal, & I heard all about the region from him. In the end his attempt to build a dam was a failure—the structure being twice washed away—but Mr. Baldwin tells me that two years ago the trick was successfully turned. When I was very small I used to get letters postmarked "Boise City", "Bruneau", "Mountain Home" & "Grand View"—this latter place having been named by my grandfather. His name was Whipple V. Phillips, & his corporation was called the Owyhee Land & Irrigation Co. I still have some of the records & booklets of the company, & remember the many specimens of Idaho products at the offices downtown. So I have always felt a strong interest in Idaho & the Snake River, which makes descriptions of any sort welcome. Speaking of localities—I enclose a postcard shewing my next-door neighbour, the John Hay Library. My home is at the back of a rather quaint grassy court which opens off College St. just below the library wall. ¶ With every good wish—

Yrs most cordially & sincerely—
H P Lovecraft

[Postcard enclosure (John Hay Memorial Library, Brown University, Providence. R.I.)] entrance to 66 College St.

Notes

1. George Kirk's residence and business, the Chelsea Book Shop, were at 317 West 14th Street, between Eighth and Ninth Avenues in Manhattan.

[4]   [ALS, JHL]

66 College St.,
Providence, R.I.,
Feby. 14, 1934.

My dear Rimel:—

I am glad to hear that the MSS. safely arrived, & that you have not found them disappointing. The geographical colour in these tales is taken from actual fact—"Arkham" being a sort of exaggerated version of Salem, Mass., & "Kingsport" of Marblehead. "Pickman's Model" describes the Boston North End as it was until a few years ago, though many of those old tangled alleys have now been swept away by civic change—the ancient houses demolished, & warehouses erected on their site. I remember when the precise location of the artist's house in the story was hit by the razing process. It was in 1927, & Donald Wandrei (whose stories you probably know, & who was then living in his home town of St. Paul, Minn., though he is now in N.Y.) was visiting the east for the first time. He wanted to see the site of the story, & I was very glad to take him to it—thinking that its sinister quaintness would even surpass his expectations. Imagine my dismay, then, at finding nothing but a blank open space where the tottering old houses & zigzag alley-windings had been! It took me all the more aback because they were still there as late as the preceding summer. Well—Wandrei had to accept my word about what had been there, although we could still trace the course of the principal cobblestoned lane among the gaping foundation walls. A year later the whole thing was covered up with a great brick building. In Brooklyn, the Red Hook section described in my story is probably about the same as it was. I haven't been there in years, but doubt if any demolition or development process has been inaugurated. When you come to read "The Shunned House" you'll see a description of an old Providence district not far from where I live—a Benefit St. neighbourhood half way down the hill & several blocks north of here. Glad you like "The Nameless City"—which all the paying editors rejected, & which I've now sent to the F F.[1] "The Picture in the House" received a 2-star mention in O'Brien's 1924 annual. The graveyard in "The Unnamable" is really the old Charter St. Burying Ground in Salem. There *is* an old house abutting on it (also mentioned by Hawthorne in "Dr. Grimshawe's Secret"), with a cracked tomb nearby; & there is also a huge willow engulfing a illegible slab near the centre of the cemetery. "From Beyond", like "The Nameless City", was rejected by all the paying magazines. Hope the rest of the Yuggothian Fungi won't disappoint you. By the way—as to those artificial names of unearthly places & gods & persons & entities—there are different ways of coining them. To a large extent they are designed to suggest—either closely or remotely—certain names in actual history or folklore which have weird or sinister associations connected with them. Thus "Yuggoth" has a sort of Arabic or Hebraic cast, to suggest certain words passed down from antiquity in the magical formulae contained in Moorish & Jewish manuscripts. Other synthetic names like "Nug" & Yeb" suggest the dark & mysterious tone of Tartar or Thibetan folklore. Dunsany is the greatest of all name-coiners, & he seems to have three distinct models—the Oriental (either Assyrian or Babylonian, or Hebrew from the Bible), the classical (from Homer mostly), & the Celtic (from the Arthurian cycle, &c). Thus he invents Eastern-sounding words like "Gyshow", "Sardathrion", "Bethmoora", &c., Hellenistic names like "Argimenes", "Poltarnees", &c., & pseudo-Celtic names like "Arleon" & "Camorak". I myself sometimes follow Dunsany's plan, but I also have a way strictly my own—which I use for devising *non-human* names, as of the localities & inhabitants of other planets. It is clear (though most writers fail to realise it) that the language supposed to be used by non-earthly beings—without human vocal organs & with no knowledge of terrestrial traditions—*ought not to resemble human speech in any way*. The sounds ought not to follow any human language-pattern, & ought not to be derived from—or adapted to—the human speech-equipment at all. In other words, the whole design ought to be alien to both the ideas & tongue of mankind—a series of sounds of altogether different origins & associations, & capable only in part of reproduction by the human throat & palate & mouth. Just how far, & in what direction, such a sound-system ought to differ from human speech, must of course depend on how far & in what direction the imaginary users are represented as differing. In representing such sounds on paper, it is of course understood that our Roman alphabet can do it only imperfectly— since that alphabet was designed for a human language. Usually my stories assume that the non-human sounds were known to certain human scholars in elder days, & recorded in secret manuscripts like the "Necronomicon", the "Pnakotic Manuscripts", &c. In that case I likewise assume that the prehistoric or ancient authors of these MSS. gave the non-human names an unconscious twist in the direction of their own respective languages—as always occurs when scholars & writers encounter an utterly alien nomenclature & try to represent it to their own people. Thus when I cite the name of some wholly non-human thing *supposed to be mentioned in the Necronomicon,* I try to have the *foundation* of the word absolutely unearthly & alien, yet give it an outwardly *Arabic* aspect to account for the transmitting influence of the mad Arab Abdul Alhazred. Typical Necronomicon names are *Azathoth, Yog-Sothoth, Shub-Niggurath,* &c. Often Clark Ashton Smith (who is almost as fertile a name-creator as Dunsany!) & I try to give different *variants* of the same unearthly or prehistoric name to represent the different variants under which different races refer to the same thing as remembered from primitive times . . . . . . as, for instance, some Nordic races spoke of *Odin* & *Freya* while others spoke of *Woden* & *Frigga,* or as the Hindoo *Dyaus-Pitar* became the Roman *Iuppiter.* Thus I have had *Yog-Sothoth* occur (in a story I wrote for a client) as *Yocsototl* among the Aztecs, while Smith (borrowing it from me) has coined the mediaeval form *Iog-Sotôt* for his mythical "Averoigne."[2] And he has used his own *Tsathoggua* in various forms such as the pseudo-mediaeval *Sodaqui*, &c. Many Realists violently object to the practice of using these coined names, averring that it gives a childish effect to the stories concerned. I can see their point, but do not think their objection can be applied indiscriminately. Carelessly, injudiciously coined, or excessively used artificial names do rather cheapen a tale; but it is certainly advantageous now & then to introduce a coined word which has been shaped with great care from just the right associational sources. At times I have *dreamt* certainly utterly alien names such as *Kuranes, Nasht*, & *Kaman-Thah*[3]—all of course having vague linguistic sources in things I have read. As for writing out the hellish & forbidden Necronomicon—that would be quite an order, though I might manage to produce an isolated chapter now & then. Incidentally, as a sort of a joke anent the synthetic names we use so much, Clark Ashton Smith & I call each other *Klarkash-Ton* & *E'ch-Pi-El*. I once built up a whole cycle of legend around Smith's *Tsathoggua* & used it in a story I wrote for a revision-client, but unfortunately the story was rejected.[4]

Yes—*Unusual Stories* is having a very hard time, & I hope Crawford can find a good way out. Like you, he is thinking of doing his own printing, & is now trying to hire a press of suitable size. He has also considered getting out one or two issues on a mimeograph, but hesitates for fear of the impression it would produce on his subscribers. Another idea of his is to have another printer quickly issue the *first* regular number, & let the delayed copy now in the press come out as #2. But I don't envy him his situation! The story of mine in the contemplated first issue is a dream-phantasy in the Dunsanian manner called "Celephaïs" (the one, incidentally, in which I use the name "Kuranes", which I dreamed in 1920) In another issue my "Doom that Came to Sarnath" will appear. My use of that word "Sarnath" is rather odd. I *thought* I had coined it myself, but later discovered that it occurs rather obscurely in one of Dunsany's tales.[5] I must have read it & *unconsciously* remembered it. Things like that often cause perfectly innocent people to give the appearance of plagiarism.

Glad my remarks on your verse proved helpful, & hope the result will land in the F F. Practice is what makes perfect, & one can't expect to turn out a wholly finished product at first. We learn gradually just what is expected of good verse. You have a really good sense of rhythm, & an excellent conception of weird atmosphere—& time & diligence will take care of the rest. Practice, study of textbooks, & reading of the best (not necessarily weird) poets form the corner-stone of progress—which reminds me, do you know of the "Little Blue Books" sold for a nickel apiece by the Haldeman-Julius Co. of Girard, Kansas? These are small paper-bound pamphlets which cover a vast range of subjects (over 1000 titles) & include both excellent manuals of instruction & reprints of prose & verse classics. There are some fine booklets on poetic technique & general English usage on the list. Take my advice— especially since local library facilities are so poor—& send for a catalogue.

You'll find scores of items worth getting—& at a nickel each you can afford to plunge a bit! Don't miss #514—"Hints on Writing Poetry", by the very capable poet Clement Wood. As I said, I'll be very glad to see "The Spell of the Blue Stone" when it comes, & will make all due allowances for the corrections you mention. And I shall certainly lend you some of the weird classics from time to time, although my collection of course has only a fraction of what ought to be read. When you're through with the volumes that Mr. Baldwin now has, I'll lend you more of Machen & some of Blackwood—& also M. R. James. There will be no hurry about the return of any of these, & I think it would be a good idea to let Mr. Baldwin look over each shipment—so that he can read any he hasn't read & thinks he'd like to. It's certainly too bad that your public library is so limited. In time it would be a good idea to build up a collection of your own—one can get things surprisingly cheap at the second-hand book shops in large cities. I don't know whether such shops are as plentiful in the west as in the east, but fancy a place the size of Spokane ought to have one or two. Of course, New England, New York City, & other thickly-settled districts as far down the Atlantic Coast as Richmond have unusually good facilities both in the library & in the second-hand bookshop line. I imagine this is also true of Chicago—& I know it is of Cleveland & New Orleans. In some places, however—such as Florida, & certain parts of New Mexico & Texas where friends of mine live—it is very difficult either to buy or to borrow the various books one generally wants. For example—a man I know in Clovis, N.M.[6] has only the high-school library at his disposal. There is no public library. This seems unusual in New England, where even the smallest village usually has a public library of some sort—though in many cases only a very modest one with nothing but the best-known standard English classics. Florida is improving in the library line—Clearwater (near Dunedin, where Whitehead lived) now having a fast-growing one. St. Augustine's library—housed in an old Spanish mansion built in 1755—is also on the up-grade. But Key West's is still pitifully meagre. The largest city I ever saw without a public library is Quebec—where one has to depend on the various colleges. French being the main language, it is doubly hard to get just the English books one wants.

Don't hurry with the "Colour Out of Space" venture. What you say of the contemplated format sounds very promising. As I said to Mr. Baldwin, a small page-size is really preferable when so short a tale is published separately as a booklet. Otherwise the extreme thinness makes for awkwardness, as in Smith's "Double Shadow". Glad you are picking up some useful hints from a professional printer. W. Paul Cook—who issued so many items, including "The Shunned House"—had the advantage of being in charge of the printing department of a newspaper—so that he had all the type & machinery at his free disposal, plus the professional skill.

Providence is coping with a devilish cold spell just now. Last week all low temperature records were broken by a minimum of *17 below*, & now—after a brief respite—the mercury seems to be sinking again. I have to stay indoors in such weather—my health making it unsafe for me to be out in temperatures under +20°—but fortunately the house heats excellently. You in the northwest probably don't get extremes as bad as this.

Well—I hope you'll enjoy the other stories, & the books which Mr. Baldwin will pass on. No hurry—& let me know when to send some Blackwood, James, &c. specimens.

All good wishes—

Yrs most cordially & sincerely,
H P Lovecraft

[Postcard enclosure (John Hay Memorial Library, Brown University, Providence, R.I.):] entrance to College St.

Notes

1. *FF* accepted the story but folded before it could be published.

2. Adolphe de Castro, "The Electric Executioner" (as Yog-Sototl; no published story refers to *Yocsototh*); CAS mentions "Yok-Zothoth" in "Ubbo-Sathla."

3. *CB* 63: "Sinister names—Nasht—Kaman-Thah." HPL used Kuranes in "Celephaïs" and Nasht and Kaman-Thah in *The Dream-Quest of Unknown Kadath*.

4. Zealia Brown Reed Bishop, "The Mound." The story appeared after HPL's death.

5. HPL is mistaken; "Sarnath" does not appear in Lord Dunsany's work. Perhaps HPL was thinking of "The Fortress Unvanquishable, Save for Sacnoth," in *The Sword of Welleran and Other Stories* (1908).

6. Eugene B. Kuntz, an amateur poet.

[5]   [ALS, JHL]

Feby. 15[, 1934]

My dear Rimel:—

My letter of yesterday had scarcely left the house when your package safely arrived—with my old MSS. & your "Spell of the Blue Stone". I was able, by a lucky chance, to give the tale an immediate reading—hence am returning it with a promptness I might not always be able to achieve. My comments & emendations, I hope, may prove helpful rather than confusing.

Well—let me congratulate you on the excellence of the tale. Actually, it is very remarkable for a beginner's work—vastly better than the best attempts of some of my professional clients who have been plugging away for years. You obviously have certain natural qualifications which many aspirants lack—notably, a sensitiveness to *atmosphere* & a knowledge of how to build it up with words, & a keen instinct for narrative values & dramatic situations. I have marked certain parts of the tale which I like especially. You begin finely—striking just the right note of mystery & tension. Of course the influence of the popular tale is here & there discernible—but this will diminish as you read Machen & other standard fantaisistes.

The slight corrections I have made have very little to do with the story *as a story*. Rather do they cover certain minor points of *language*—about which one must be very careful in order to produce the desired effect. I don't believe any of these really needs explaining—the changes speak for themselves, & a study of them in the MS. will help you more than anything I could specifically say. If the reason for any of them seems obscure, let me know about it & I'll try to make the matter more comprehensible. In most cases mere *good usage*—not actual grammar—is concerned.

This is such a good story that you'd better try it around a bit. Begin with Wright—though of course the chances for acceptance in that quarter are not bright. Then—if rejected—tackle the non-remunerative magazines . . . . F F, *Fantasy Magazine* (255 E. 188th St., New York City), & *Unusual*. One or the other of these will certainly want to accept it.

As for possible improvement-suggestions—in another story of the same nature you might want to make the presence of the strange cult in the given locality more thoroughly & specifically motivated. Also—you might want to explain the presence of the learned solver more plausibly. As you can see, it is stretching coincidence a bit to have the unusual phenomena happen just where there is an expert with the rare knowledge needed for solution & defeat. It would be more natural to have to send for a special expert from a distance. But these form only minor points in the story. It's an excellent—highly promising—piece of work; & there's really no need of making any further changes. If you type it again as it now stands, I feel sure that it will find a welcome with some editor—even though a non-paying editor.

That threatened relapse of the cold spell didn't quite materialise—though today is by no means springlike! Looks like snow.

Again congratulating you upon the story—I remain

           Yrs most sincerely,

              H. P. Lovecraft

[6]   [ALS, JHL]

           66 College St.,

             Providence, R.I.,

               March 4, 1934.

My dear Mr. Rimel:—

           The printed stories duly came back, & I am very glad to hear that you found them enjoyable. It pleases me especially to learn that you liked "The Shunned House", since that was so summarily rejected by W.T. Some day I'll try to get a snapshot of the edifice I used as a model for that tale[1]—though the situation of the place will make it rather difficult. You can get a rough sort of idea from the accompanying crude sketch—which shews the two different levels of the house. Our steep hill gives rise to all sorts of odd building effects—for example, structures whose front doors are at the foot of the hill in North or South Main St., often have back doors opening out of the *fifth story* directly on Benefit St.—& so on.

Glad the Yuggothian fungi proved pleasing—& that the account of my synthetic nomenclature interested you. You must read Dunsany sooner or later—I can lend the principal volumes. I shall probably write a "Necronomicon" chapter some day to match Smith's extract from the "Book of Eibon".[2] Yes—I spent quite a bit of time on that paragraph attached to "The Festival". This kind of writing ought to *hint* a good deal more than it *says*.

I still hopefully await *Unusual Stories*. Crawford's latest report was that he had succeeded in getting a press, though accessories are still to be added. He's having a hard time—& incidentally learning a lot about the practical end of publishing! Glad to hear that you're beginning to place things in the F F, & hope you'll keep it up. These small magazines are really very valuable in helping one get a start—they encourage production, & place you in touch with appreciative readers & constructive critics. I've just read the latest W.T., & noted your Eyrie letter with interest. This number is of about the average quality—& I was glad to see Klarkash-Ton's subtly haunting drawing.

Glad you're already in touch with a Blue Book catalogue. You'll find some of the brochures infinitely helpful. Hope the poetry booklet will arrive soon. Yes—Shakespeare really ought to be read by everyone as a bit of general literary training. Careful study of the best plays gives a keen insight into the use of imaginative language at its best. Fortunately this material is easy to get at libraries. Hope you'll like the Machen items when you get at them. Before long I'll make up a bundle of James & Blackwood & send it along for you to read & pass on to Mr. Baldwin for ultimate return to me. Later still I'll send other items. Unfortunately I haven't much Blackwood stuff—but I have virtually all of James. I also have the best of Dunsany. Before long I shall also be sending to Mr. Baldwin a book containing Blackwood's "The Willows", plus another with the famous "Turn of the Screw" by *Henry* (not M. R.) James. He'll pass them on to you—& you can return them to me at your leisure.

Glad my remarks on "The Blue Stone" seemed helpful, & hope the present version will eventually find its way into print—in one of the small magazines if not in W.T. You have an excellent atmospheric touch, & I feel sure you can effectively go ahead in weird fiction. I hope to see "The Tree on the Hill" in the course of time.[3]

Thanks extremely for the graphic though miniature view of Asotin—which has a double interest in view of its relation to "The Blue Stone". Your house seems to be very pleasantly situated, & I can picture the invisible left-ward parts of the town containing Asotin Creek & the Baldwin home. I imagine, from its resident's description, that the latter must have a quite delightful setting. You are both very fortunate to be in the same town—for it is not often that more than one person with such unusual tastes happen to be found in so relatively small a community. I've never discovered another thorough weird tale fan in Providence, though it is a largish city in which I've lived all my life! You & Mr. Baldwin must also find each other good company because of your shared musical tastes. Music is my own weak point. I took violin lessons in early childhood, but the practicing got on my nerves & turned me against music as a whole. Now I have no real taste at all, but like to hear light stuff of the Victor Herbert grade. I note the various Asotin landscape features with interest. The whole terrain must be very attractive. Do you wish the view returned? It is safely filed in case you do. When I can find some good Providence views I'll send them along. One booklet I may be able to get has a frontispiece shewing the city's steep hill on which *this house* is distinctly visible. I think I sent a card shewing the library next door to this house. Here's a church calendar with something about a very historic edifice. The background of the picture shews the ancient hill at a point about half way betwixt "The Shunned House" & my present residence. On the back of the leaflet is an interesting history of the church—which my aunt attends.

The pictures of "the gang" came back soon after receipt of your letter, but I trust they were shewn to you (as I requested) before transmission. Some of the faces may be surprises, while others may bear out previous concepts. Some time when it's convenient I'd like to see pictures of you & Baldwin.

I've done quite a bit of reading lately—Dunsany's "Curse of the Wise Woman", A. Merritt's "Metal Monster" (magnificent!), & the long novel "Anthony Adverse",[4] which took me 5 days to get through. I am now about to read Count de Prorok's book about his excavations on the site of ancient Carthage—which Klarkash-Ton has lent me. Don't hurry with the Machen books—re-read & digest them if you can derive any additional benefits thereby. They ought to have quite an influence on your style. I shan't wait for their return before sending the Blackwood–James packet—& there won't be any hurry about that, either. ¶ Some warmish weather at last. May be able to take an enjoyable rural walk before long. Had a terrific snowfall Feb. 26, but it's about melted off now. Glad you've had springlike conditions.

Every good wish—
Yrs most cordially—
H P Lovecraft

[Enclosure: Bulletin for the First Baptist Church] "Shunned House" about here in relation to picture. [/] my house about here

Notes

1. See FLB 8n4.
2. "The Coming of the White Worm" (written on 15 September 1933) purports to be Chapter IX of the *Book of Eibon*.
3. For discussion of HPL's hand in revising this story see "A New Lovecraft Tale," *Crypt of Cthulhu* No. 17 (Hallowmass 1983): 3–21.
4. By Hervey Allen.

[7]   [ALS, JHL]

66 College St.,
Providence, R.I.,
March 16, 1934.

My dear Rimel:—

Glad the crude "Shunned House" sketch seemed to bear out the text. As for a peaked corner room—I'd say that the easternmost attic chamber of the wing ought to correspond go that description fairly well . . . . or the corresponding room of the main edifice might do so likewise. Here is a sketch of the ap-proximate way the place looks from the rear—that is, from the higher parts of the hill to the east. The rural grounds still run back to the next higher street—these bits of overtaken countryside forming one of the most fascinating features of Providence. I may call there before long; for after a long period of court litigation it has been bought back by members of the original family—friends of ours—whose claims were disputed by other heirs. In 1919 & 1920 my elder aunt—now deceased—lived in the Shunned House;[1] hence my familiarity with it. The other buildings near by are probably about 30 or 40 years later in date . . . . built around 1800. It was about 1800 that the solidly built part of the town approached the top of the hill—the house I now live in (near the top) being of that date. As for the booklet—I'll see that you get a copy when it's out. Cook & Coates will not be able to handle it; but the edition is being shipped to young Barlow in Florida, & he hopes to bind & issue the sheets gradually.[2]

As for books—you'll see "The Willows" before long, & I'll ask Barlow to send you the copy of Dunsany's "Dreamer's Tales" now lent to him. Others later. Glad you find Machen congenial. His prefaces are fascinating, although they include some rather extravagant lies about wonderful things he claims to have experienced. Work like that of Machen, James, Blackwood, & Dunsany represents really serious & artistic weird writing, & belongs to a category entirely above that of the junk in W.T. & other popular magazines. It is this kind of writing which I—however imperfectly—have tried to achieve myself—hence my great percentage of rejections by Wright. As you say, this serious material is not wanted by weird editors—but I had rather succeed even to a slight extent in producing it, than aim lower & have my stuff more widely accepted. My great fear—confirmed by certain criticisms—is that an habitual reading of W.T. has to some extent unconsciously tainted my style.

Regarding *Unusual Stories*—there will be no mimeographed issues, since Crawford has just secured a printing press. He still lacks rollers & type, however. I am not greatly prejudiced against duplicated papers—indeed, I used to issue a hand-printed, hectographed astronomical paper when I was between the ages of 12 & 17.[3] In the National Amateur Press Association, to which I still belong, there have been many typewritten & duplicated papers of great neatness—even with "justified" right-hand margins. Generally speaking, I am so much more interested in *writing* than in *publishing* that I don't care what form a given piece of work comes in. So long as the correct text gets distributed, I'll put up with any sort of a transmitting medium. Not, however, that I don't appreciate tasteful printing when such is practicable. I merely prefer a badly-printed or duplicated text to no text at all.

If you like, I'll lend you both of Bierce's books of tales—"In the Midst of Life" & "Can Such Things Be." Later, if you're interested, I can lend you C. Hartley Grattan's life of Bierce. Bierce was born in 1842, & disappeared in 1913. He was a Civil War veteran, & a journalist of great prominence in San Francisco—a fearless political satirist who had many enemies. Altogether, he was something of a fiery eccentric. My friend Samuel Loveman knew him personally. As to the disappearance—it is likely that he mixed into the Mexican revolution under an assumed name & was killed by one of Villa's firing-squads. Several separate reports point in that direction, though nothing is conclusive. He had expressed a yearning for military action—looking back wistfully to his Civil War days. Though over 70 when he vanished, he had the strength & appearance of a much younger man. Bierce's tales have a peculiar kind of sardonic gruesomeness—& certainly come within the boundaries of real literature.

Sorry "The Blue Stone" didn't land—but I don't think much of Wright's comments. They sound like the showy & would-be-impressive routine stuff which he reels off thoughtlessly by the yard in order to sound like a discriminating connoisseur. Sometimes, in dealing out this pontifical hokum, he gets forgetful & contradicts himself. What really prompts his rather capricious rejections is his belief that the tales in question don't follow the conventional popular formula. In flaw-picking Wright sometimes becomes so pedantic &

carping that his dicta lose all common sense. Thus in the matter of the phrase "cosmic ecstasy". It ought to be plain to any person of reasonably developed imagination that *cosmic ecstasy* signifies a hypothetical state of intense emotional excitement or exaltation caused by the impingement on the senses & consciousness of utterly non-human & non-terrestrial impressions from ultimate outer space. That is, *cosmic ecstasy* is what would occur if any normal human being were faced with even a moment's perception or suggestion of the seething forces or manifestations of the universe's ultimate being. Naturally there isn't any such thing in daily life—any more than there are space-ships or ghouls or vampires or time-machines in real life—but anybody must be a damned fool if he can't see what the descriptive phrase is driving at. The trouble with Wright is that he didn't stop to give the matter a moment's real thought. He fancied that the phrase sounded like some of the meaningless grandiloquence of certain extravagant writers, & shot off his mouth before actually analysing it. That's all too common among the cheap editors who constantly handle thin, unimaginative "action" stuff, & seldom encounter anything with larger implications & overtones. As for the tale's opening—don't pay any attention to Wright's objection. I know him of old on this subject—just fancy what he would do to a leisurely opening tale like "The White People" or "The Great God Pan"! Your opening is splendid, as I remarked when I read it. The kind of action-plunge which Wright demands is the ruination of any weird story. This sort of fiction, depending as it does on the presentation of phenomena contrary to reality, requires the subtlest & most gradual emotional preparation in order to make the reader ready to accept the marvels portrayed. If this slow preparation is lacking, the story is thin-blooded, mechanical, & unconvincing. I would not call "The Blue Stone" chaotic in any way. In the opening section the stage is set & the atmosphere worked up. Then—& only then—we are ready for a rapid succession of developments. The matter after p. 4 would be forced & unmotivated except for the preparation which comes before. As to the general English—of course any beginner's prose is not as smooth as it will be after months & years of practice. I have myself indicated a need for certain added graces & exactitudes of phraseology. But I'll be hanged if the prose of the B.S. is any more "muddy" than that of the average youthful product—or of a large part of the matter Wright himself accepts & prints! Wright is, I think, a little caustic—all editors tend to become so. They are an arbitrary lot, & it certainly takes time & repeated attempts to get anything accepted by them. Many acquaintances of mine whose work is excellent have so far failed to land anything—or at least more than one or two things—in W T & its analogues. But there's no harm trying—& your material seems to have a vitality greatly in its favour. You'll probably find sheets of the F F type greatly encouraging . . . . . which reminds me to enclose a circular & blank of the National Amateur Press Association, the leading present exponent of "amateur journalism", which I found such a stimulus. I fancy you might greatly enjoy membership in the N.A.P.A. I'll send you some of its papers if you're interested. About "The Tree on the Hill"—if you're becoming dissatisfied with it, I'd advise revision or re-writing rather than complete destruction. Certain old tales of mine have begun to impress me as rather poor, but I am keeping them as possible material to work over.

As to the presence or absence of weird devotees in Providence—I dare say there must be several amongst the approximate 500,000 (city plus suburbs) of the metropolitan area, but I haven't succeeded in encountering any. The nearest thing to it was the writer C. M. Eddy Jr., whose work you may have seen in old copies of W T; but fantasy was only a side-line with him, & he has now drifted entirely away from it. Another weird-writing neighbour is Hugh B. Cave, who lives in the adjacent city of Pawtucket (continuous with Providence); but he also takes this side of literature very lightly. I've never met Cave, but have exchanged letters with him. He once spoke of calling on me, but I'm afraid that some of my remarks anent commercial writing may have offended him. I have found weird fans to be pretty well scattered, & don't believe I know of any two in the same town except you & Baldwin, & the small group now assembled in New York. And of the latter group, only Long is a native. Wandrei used to live in St. Paul, Minn., Leeds in Chicago, &c.; while Talman, though a native of neighbouring Spring Valley, never came near N.Y. City until he had a job there. For a while, though, Wandrei & Derleth were co-residents of the Twin Cities. Derleth has always regularly lived in Sauk City, but was in Minneapolis a year as sub-editor of one of the Fawcett Magazines. His colleague in collaboration—Schorer—lives in Sauk City, but never concerns himself with the weird unless prodded by Derleth. Oh, yes, though—some more exceptions. Price & Mashburn did live in New Orleans at the same time for a brief moment, while I believe Hamilton & Kline are both Chicagoans. Quinn lives in Brooklyn, but is not personally acquainted with any of our group save Talman. Despite all exceptions, the general rule of isolatedness for "fantasy fans" undoubtedly holds good. Smith, Howard, Barlow, & others have never even seen a genuine fellow-enthusiast. Which reminds me—I may (barely possibly) be in on quite a little gathering of weirdists in Florida next May. Edmond Hamilton & Jack Williamson are wintering at Key West, & intend to call on Barlow in De Land when they move northward in May. Barlow, moreover, has invited me down for May 1st. Now if all turns out well, my visit may coincide with Hamilton's & Williamson's—thus bringing four inveterate weirdists together[4]—but I don't yet know whether I can finance the trip. I've never seen any of the others in question—nor has Barlow seen any save the one his mirror reflects. Hamilton is very brilliant, but has allowed popular magazine taste to injure his writing. Williamson is young & very promising—& I hope the popular ideal won't 'get' him. Barlow is just a kid, but is progressing rapidly. When I visited Whitehead in Florida in 1931, Barlow was in western Georgia. He didn't strike Florida till after Whitehead's death, but even that nebulous amount of pseudo-contact has impelled him to attempt an edition of Whitehead's letters .... which he is printing on a newly-acquired press. Whitehead was an Episcopal clergyman, & very learned & brilliant. He was a Ph.D[.]—& a classmate of President Roosevelt's ('04) at Harvard.

Glad you saw & were interested in the pictures. Yes—Howard certainly looks the part of his sword-slashing heroes, & has a psychology very comparable to Conan's & King Kull's. He hates civilisation, & wishes he could go back either to the wild days of the West, or to the days of the primitive tribal Gauls, Northmen, & Britons. He has led a very active & adventurous life in his brief 27 years. I'll later let you see a recent snap of Wandrei—when the present long-term borrower returns it. He is 26 now. Smith is 40, but some recent pictures look younger than the one I sent. You had my years spotted fairly well—I shall be 44 next August. Long will turn 32 next month, but he doesn't look even nearly that. I hope to see snaps of you & Baldwin in the course of time—& meanwhile let me thank you for permission to retain the view of Asotin. As I believe I mentioned, my grandfather's business connexion with the Snake River Country in the 1890's gives me an unusual interest in it.

Regarding music—I am not enough of an authority to make any real predictions regarding its future in America. The whole question is too complex for a layman to deal with—& is mixed up with the larger question of continuity versus innovation in the general field of aesthetic expression. I don't think that freakish extremes & experiments can do the main stream of art much good, although they may contribute certain freshening tendencies now & then. Whether negroid syncopation can ever form a dominant element in the music of a nation of European descent seems to me rather debatable. It may contribute, but I hardly think the instinctive rhythms of a primitive stock can form a typical expression of the feelings of an advanced Aryan people. I confess that I *like* the coon-songs & cake-walks forming the cheap popular melodies of my youthful days, but I'd hesitate greatly before assigning their type any major role in the serious musical tradition. However, I may be all wrong—since my ignorance of music is virtually complete. I don't think it's likely that music will ever be a leading form of expression in America, since the people have not a lyrical temper & heritage. Literature & architecture will probably express the feelings of the population more perfectly. Of all modern civilisations only two—the German & the Italian—are preëminently musical.

I'll lend you "Beware After Dark" as soon as my copy is returned by another recipient. The tale of mine in it is "Cthulhu"—which I'm sure is among the specimens you've seen. The general run of selections is very good, & I was pleased to meet the editor—T. Everett Harré—a couple of months ago. Machen will undoubtedly have a very good effect on your style—he & Dunsany are well worth studying as models. The bulk of Blackwood's prose is not so good—it tends to be careless & journalistic in places—though the sheer imaginative power of the author makes his best work supremely powerful in spite of it. Certainly, everything of Machen's deserves a re-reading. Keep these volumes any length of time—no hurry so long as they come safely back in the end.

Glad you have the Teter book & find it helpful. Your new verse specimen certainly shews a marked metrical improvement—in addition to genuine imaginative power & cleverness of conception. I am returning it herewith—with a few changes & annotations which you may possibly find helpful. Hope it can eventually be printed advantageously. Searight & Lumley are both correspondents of mine, & the latter's verse in the F F embodies some of my emendations. Lumley has an occasionally rich imagination, but tends to be crude technically. He is an oldish man—quite a quaint & interesting character who has been at sea & seen odd parts of the earth—now living in Buffalo, N.Y. Some of his occult beliefs are rather naive & amusing.

I can understand what you say about the hatred of literature commonly imparted by high school. It is unfortunate, & is certainly the result of careless, incompetent, or over-conventionalised teaching. Too many courses centre around types of expression essentially dead, & present great works as dry specimens for analysis instead of as vital utterances to be enjoyed. This is especially true of classical Graeco-Roman literature—it is really tragic to see how students are systematically alienated from great living forces like Virgil. Poe & Longfellow are both good to read, though the latter is more of a polished, urbane copyist than a really vital poet. His insipidity & didacticism are inescapable. There is no limit to the amount of good poetry one ought to read. The shorter things of Milton—Coleridge—Byron, Shelley, & Keats—Swinburne—there is no end. It is also useful to get hold of a good anthology like Palgrave's Golden Treasury. That was recently brought out in a *15¢* paper-bound edition by the Jacket Library (National Home Library Foundation, Washington, D.C.). You might send for one if it can't be picked up locally. I have several of these marvellous 15¢ volumes, which are commonly on sale in drug & department stores. Poe is a great & living force in poetry. You might also try his French admirer Baudelaire—preferably the translation in the Modern Library.

Now about the technical questions—I'm afraid one ought *not* to use thin, postage-saving paper of the "Fungi" type in approaching the average editor. I have used it myself, since the only editors I bombard know me well; but the common impression is that magazines are prejudiced against it. This was brought home to me by some of my revision clients, who complained when I typed their work on such paper. However, there is no need of using expensive stationery. Any ordinary-weight* white 8½ × 11 paper will do. I often get mine

---

*If you look widely around, you can find many sorts of paper which are fairly light, yet which are not as frankly flimsy as that old stuff of mine. Never get a *heavy* paper—try to get as light a thing as you can without having it fragile. This present paper of mine is thicker than I'd like.

at Woolworth's, & this batch I'm now using is a still cheaper bargain—35¢ a ream—from a local shop. No—nothing need be sent to an editor save the MS. itself, a return-addressed envelope with full postage, & the very briefest of notes. Put your name & address in the upper left hand corner of your manuscript's first page, & in the upper right add the inscription First North American Serial Rights Only to protect your interests in case of reprinting. Do not put the title of the story in quotation marks. To save your MSS. it is well to add blank front & back pages—or you might write the title on the front sheet. These can be changed when the MS. begins to shew signs of wear. Editors are said to be prejudiced against obviously worn MSS., since such a condition argues repeated rejections. When Wright sends back a MS., be sure that you erase all his little red-pencil notations before submitting it to another editor. Everyone knows his practice, hence his marks advertise the fact that he has rejected such MSS. as bear them. Now as to whether a MS. must be sent first class—so far as anything of average short story length is concerned, I am forced to reply sadly that it must indeed. In Canada there is a special MS. rate—envelopes to be marked "Printer's Copy Only"—but our more southerly provinces have not yet attained that degree of civilisation. As to longer & heavier MSS.—up to last Sunday I'd have told you that the same savage rule applies—but look at what I found in the N.Y. Times on that date! It seems almost incredible that this ruling has existed without the knowledge of anyone I know—you'd better ask some postmaster about it, for there may be a mistake. I simply send along the cutting for what it is worth. If it is true that MSS. of parcel-post weight can go at parcel-post rates, some amusing & amazing paradoxes are involved. The under limit of parcel post is 8 ounces—hence a MS. weighing *more* than that can go for a dime or so to distant points, whereas one weighing an ounce *less* must pay *21¢*, the first class rate! It would seemingly pay to stuff a small MS. package with blank paper to make it weigh half a pound! But all this may be wrong. Look it up.

Local weather certainly has been shifting about. Blizzard Feby. 26—but just a week later a summerlike day—almost 70°—which beckoned me forth to the woods & fields. It was fascinating to slosh about over the awakening hills amidst the melting snow. I never saw the ponds & brooks higher, & when I crossed the broad gorge of the Blackstone I found all the lower banks flooded, so that great trees & cottage roofs rose above the water like remnants of lost Atlantis. The papers express a fear of floods, though nothing as violent as those of 1927 is anticipated. Since that warm day there has been more snow—& last Sunday the steep hill of College St. was so slippery that crowds of college students were lined up to watch & spoof the skidding motors . . . some of which became completely turned around. At last my aunt, in a burst of civic spirit, telephoned the police station & had barriers placed at the top & bottom of the hill till the roadway could be sanded. When I went downtown a skidded car blocked the sidewalk—forcing me out into the slippery street, where I took three tumbles in succession! But now the snow is about melted off, with considerable promise of spring in the air. Up in Vermont Cook tells me that the weather is getting much warmer—often up to ten below zero or zero!

March W.T. seems rather an average issue—Smith's tale & illustration being the leading feature . . . . . come to think of it, though, I mentioned that in my last letter. Glad you share my predilection for cats. There's a fine specimen named Oswald at the Pawhuska garage where Price has cast his immediate destinies. The kittens across the back garden here are fast growing—getting playful now!

I've just finished Count de Prorock's book about his North African archaeological excavations—lent me by Clark Ashton Smith. I fancy it would interest our friend Baldwin, who has spoken of his wish to get in on some sort of exploring expedition. Though I always knew that North Africa was one of the world's most populous & prosperous spots in Roman imperial times, I had not realised how much ancient material still exists there. Roman ruins are abundant, & more & more of the older Punic & prehistoric Libyan material is found nowadays. Certainly, the systematic & scientific archaeology of the past 30 years has brought up a surprising amount of material in every spot where civilisation anciently existed. Today we are closer to the ancient world than we were a generation ago—as if time had moved backward a bit.

With every good wish, & hoping that the books I sent reached you safely, I remain

Yrs most cordially & sincerely,
H P L

[Enclosure: HPL's revision of DWR's "Its Prayer."]

Notes

1. Lillian D. Clark. The 1920 census has her listed as a companion for the owner of the house (135 Benefit Street), Mrs. C. H. Babbit.
2. W. Paul Cook of the Recluse Press set in type and printed *The Shunned House* in 1928, but the sheets were not bound. In 1933, Walter J. Coates of the Driftwind Press planned to bind the sheets but never did so. RHB acquired 115 copies in 1934 and 150 more in 1935, but bound only a few copies. The sheets RHB obtained were eventually bound and distributed by Arkham House in 1959–61.
3. *The Rhode Island Journal of Astronomy.*
4. This did not come to pass.

[8]　　　[ANS, JHL]

[Postmarked Providence, RI,
19 March 1934]

[Printed letter from *New York Times* affixed to postcard:

Manuscript Postage.

In last Sunday's edition you published part of a letter of mine in which I quoted my postmaster as giving the information that typewritten manuscripts are legally mailed as parcel post. I have since found this to be erroneous. May I be forgiven when I add that I sought and received my information by proxy and am assured that the postmaster did not so fail in his duty. This matter simply proves how thoroughly THE NEW YORK TIMES is read, and what an excellent threshing floor it makes for our more liberal education.
MARY PELHAM GIBBS, Springdale, Conn.]

P.S. That letter of mine in the new F F is all hashed up. The phrase "AN especial morbidity" should read "NO especial morbidity". This slip spoils the whole meaning. Also—PERSPECTIVE is misprinted.[1]

　　　Regards—H P L

Notes

1. The passage as printed in *FF* 1, No. 7 (March 1934), 105 reads: "It can be said that anything which vividly embodies a basic human emotion or captures a definite and typical human mood is genuine art. The subject matter is immaterial. It requires an especial morbidity to enjoy any authentic word-depiction, whether it is conventionally 'pleasant' or not. Indeed, it argues a somewhat immature and narrow prospection when our judgment is by the mere conventional appeal of its subject-matter or its supposed social effects. The question to ask is not whether it is 'healthy' or 'pleasant,' but whether it is *genuine* and *powerful.*"

[9]　　[AHT]

66 College St.,
Providence, R.I.,
March 29, 1934

My dear Rimel:—

　　　　　Yes—there is certainly a vast difference between different grades of mimeographing. I wish I had one of the old amateur papers I told you about to send—the recent specimen in the accompanying package is by no means as neat and effective as Horace L. Lawson's *Wolverine*, which appeared in the early 1920's. As for my old hectographed astronomical paper—I'm afraid it would only increase your prejudice against duplicating devices, since I was wretchedly clumsy in managing such things. However—for the fun of it I'll enclose a couple of issues, published when I was fifteen. You'll note that about that period I changed it from a quasi-newspaper to a quasi-magazine form. Pretty crude and kiddish—but good for a laugh, anyhow. Astronomy was a great interest of mine in youth—indeed, at one time I hoped to become professional astronomer. That was before I realised how far beyond me the intellectual demands of a genuine astronomer's career are. I always took a mystical interest in the sky, but did not systematically study astronomy till I was eleven or twelve. Geography, chemistry, and mythology were my great interests in early childhood. It was in 1902 that I began to buckle down to astronomy—with the aid of an old textbook (Burritt's "Geography of the Heavens"—famous a century ago) and star atlas[1] which my grandmother had used when studying in the old Smithville Seminary (in western Rhode Island) about 1845. Of course I realised that this book was out of date, and soon obtained Young's "Lessons in Astronomy", which brought me more in touch with the current state of the science. From then on I slowly picked up more and more astronomical books, till at one time I had over sixty on that subject. In later years I eliminated about half of these, but among those retained are the old Burritt and Young books. I obtained a telescope with $2^1/_6''$ object glass in 1903, and in 1906 bought the 3″ instrument which I still have. At different times I have had other astronomical instruments, though I no longer specialise in the subject. From 1906 to 1918 I contributed monthly articles on astronomical phenomena to one of the lesser Providence dailies. One thing that helped me greatly was the free access which I had to the Ladd Observatory of Brown University—an unusual privilege for a kid, but made possible because Prof. Upton—head of the college astronomical department and director of the observatory—was a friend of the family. I suppose I pestered the people at the observatory half to death, but they were very kind about it. I had a chance to see all the standard modern equipment of an observatory (including a 12″ telescope) in action, and read endlessly in the observatory library. The professors and their humbler assistant—an affable little cockney from England named John Edwards—often helped me pick up equipment, and Edwards made me some magnificent photographic lantern-slides (from illustrations in books) which I used in giving illustrated astronomical lectures before clubs. I still have my old lantern, and until recently thought I had the slides as well—but a survey of my stored effects the other day failed to bring the latter to light, hence I fear they may have become lost in one or another of the removals I have undergone since last using them.

By the way—let me hasten to correct your all-too-kind suspicion that I am the artist behind my own bookplate. Alas, I am most emphatically *not*, nor could I do a sketch as neat and delightful as that if I tried all my life! The artist in question—as I thought I had mentioned before—is my young friend *Wilfred B. Talman*, whose stories and verse you must have seen occasionally in *Weird Tales*. Talman is not a *fantastic* artist, but excels in everything pertaining to *formal design*. He has studied at the Rhode Island School of Design, and has won several prizes for work of a decorative sort—being especially skilled in heraldic blazonry. He made a splendid sketch of my coat-of-arms and wanted to use it on my bookplate, but I preferred something more closely connected with Old Providence—hence the typical eighteenth century Providence doorway. Talman has done bookplates for several of our group—including himself. He is a pleasant chap of twenty-eight—of an old Dutch family of Spring Valley, N.Y., where he was born and where his ancestors have lived for two hundred fifty years. I encountered him through the amateur journalistic circle—it being pure coincidence that he attended Brown University and the School of Design in my town. His chief interests are genealogy, design, heraldry, history, and New-Netherland Dutch folklore—weirdness being a subsidiary interest connected with his folklore tastes. He is an authority on the history and colonial architecture of his region—this antiquarianism being quite a tie between us. Despite his youth he is prominent in the famous and exclusive Holland Society of New York, and is editor of its quarterly publication *De Halve Maen*. I'll enclose a copy of the latter (please return) with an article of mine on Dutch influences in colonial New England.[2] Talman was once a reporter on the *N.Y. Times*, but is now associate editor of the four trade papers published by the Texas Oil Co. His offices are in New York, on the eighteenth floor of the Chrysler Building (second-tallest building in the world), but he hates the metropolis so bitterly that he will not live there. Instead, he has fitted up as a home for himself, wife, and infant son, a disused stable on his father's estate—the land where he and all his direct paternal forbears since the 1600's were born. He commutes from Spring Valley to New York every day, despite the two-hour trip. Incidentally—the mother of Talman's wife is an own cousin of the prominent German statesman Dr. Hjalmar Schacht, President of the Reichsbank. As a *weird* writer Talman will never be in a class with Smith and Howard and Wandrei and Long and Price. He is too much of an intellectual as opposed to a dreamer to shine in bizarre and fantastic conceptions. Yet his ideas are often tremendously clever, and occasionally tales of his are really splendid.

About Old Providence views—I can do better than sketch places myself, since my files recently yielded forth quite a number of typical specimens. A good many have been sent to Baldwin with the request that he shew them to you—among this batch being a booklet whose frontispiece, a view of Providence's ancient hill, actually shews *this house*. I think I shewed you and F. L. B. a snapshot of #66, did I not? Enclosed is something which I dug up after writing Baldwin, and which I'll ask you to return some time—after shewing it to him . . . . . a folder of a "rubberneck wagon" service. You will here see illustrated the same church (1775) whose illustrated calendar I sent you, together with the Betsey Williams cottage (a typical gambrel-roofed Providence house of the 1740–50 period) and the Stephen Hopkins house (1742), now probably the oldest edifice in the heart of the city. Stephen Hopkins was a colonial governor of Rhode Island and a very prominent statesman in every way—in his old age a signer of the "Declaration of Independence". He did much to promote the cultural welfare of Providence in the busy 1750–60 period, when the town began to grow at an increased rate and surpass Newport as the leading place in the colony. It is through his efforts that the first public library in Providence was founded.

For other old-Providence views I *will* have to fall back on my own inept Waterman pen. Here is the famous old Court and Colony House of 1761[3]— at the head of a long grassy parade between N. Main and Benefit sts., and still in good condition, now housing the Sixth District Court. This place is mentioned in "The Shunned House"—that hellish abode lying directly behind it. N. Court St.—the old doctor's residence—lies just to the left of the view. Some day this building may be used as an historical museum—when the district court finds a home elsewhere.

Another place that might interest you is the home of Sarah Helen Whitman—the poetess to whom Poe was for a time engaged. The rear of this house overlooks the hidden courtyard of St. John's, where Poe used to wander on moonlight nights.[4] The engagement was finally broken off through the influence of Mrs. Whitman's mother—old Mrs. Power—who objected to Poe's drinking habits. Many of the older Providence people remembered Poe, and refused to appreciate his work because of his frequent drunken appearances on our streets. The mother of my elder aunt's husband[5] knew Mrs. Whitman, and so prejudiced her son against Poe that he always argued with me when I defended him. Mrs. Whitman herself was a very passable poetess—smooth and pleasing, though in no way original or distinguished. Her house in Benefit St. at the corner of the steeply-descending Church St. is a very typical sample of the ordinary Providence houses built from about 1750 to about 1800. It is still in excellent condition—owned by the Episcopal diocese of Providence and used as an adjunct of St. Dunstan's choral school.[6] Poe and Mrs. Whitman, in the days of their engagement, used to stroll frequently in the alcoves of the venerable Providence Athenaeum—also in old Benefit St., and still in unchanged active use as a select proprietary library. On one occasion Mrs. Whitman called Poe's attention to a poem in the *American Whig Review* which she thought especially notable and splendid. It was unsigned, and she asked Poe if he could possibly guess who the author was. With vast pride Poe responded that the poem was *his own* . . . . the item in question being none other than "Ulalume". Upon recovering from her surprise, Mrs. Whitman expressed regret that he had not signed it—whereupon he pulled forth a pencil and affixed his delicate, well-known signature to the lines as they stood in the magazine. Such was the anecdote orally current in Providence for sixty years without being printed in any biography of Poe. In 1909, when Poe's centennial revived interest in the subject, Prof. H. L. Koopman, Librarian of Brown University, resolved to see if the tale could be verified. Accordingly he explored the Athenaeum's files of old bound magazines—and there, surely enough, he found "Ulalume" in the Dec. 1847 issue of the *American Whig Review*—with Poe's pencil signature below the printed text! Ever since this rediscovery the volume containing the poem and signature has been kept easily accessible for display—and I always take visitors from out of town to see it. I shewed it to Price last summer. Well—this is what the old Athenaeum looks like—unchanged since Poe was there. Even the adjacent house in the foreground is just the same. It was built in 1837, and follows the revived Greek architecture common at that time—a style of which Providence has many notable examples. Set back from Benefit St. at the corner of College (only a stone's throw from the mouth of the court where I live) on a high terrace, it is one of the notable landmarks of the ancient hill. It is worthy of remark that the text of "Ulalume" in the 1847 magazine contains one stanza more than the final version approved by Poe and now printed in standard editions of his works. This deletion was performed at the advice of Mrs. Whitman—whose taste was very good, and whose judgment in this matter has been confirmed by posterity. Thus did old Benefit St. see a classic remodelled! Oh—but I must not forget the ancient Golden Ball Inn—likewise in Benefit St.—which has sheltered Washington, Lafayette, Jefferson, Adams, Monroe, James Russell Lowell, and Poe . . . . and where, in later years, my younger aunt's husband[7] roomed when he attended Brown. Yes—and where, even unto this day, I get my suits pressed and mended by the Jew tailor whose shop occupies the north front corner! This edifice was built in 1783, and is still in good condition. It has borne several names—having been called the Mansion House for the last eighty or ninety years. As here shewn, the main frontage is in Benefit st., while the northern side abuts on South Court St.—a precipitous hill winding up to Wheaton and Congdon Sts. in the rear. On the southern end—not shewn because it involves a Victorian addition—is Meeting St.—formerly Gaol Lane. This is so steep that it breaks into a flight of steps in order to reach Congdon St.—a quaint, old-world effect eminently deserving pictorial representation. Also in ancient Gaol-Lane is the now-crumbling house where in 1763 John Carter had his printing-office at the Sign of Shakespear's Head, and published the *Providence Gazette and Country-Journal,* containing the Freshest Advices, Both Foreign and Domestick.[8] This structure is now in a perilously bad condition, and heaven only knows what will become of it. It was recently one of the historic buildings to be surveyed and diagrammed by the architectural division of the C.W.A.[9] Let us see what it looks like in its old age . . . . . Not very impressive, as a matter of fact. Note the double flight of steps at the front door—a typical Providence feature made very common because so many of our houses are on steep hillsisdes. In the old days the sign bearing Shakespeare's head stood on a post in the street in front of the house. Another and more curious-looking old house of the colonial age is to be found a mile farther south on the ancient hill—in Transit St. This thoroughfare was named because it marked the spot from which Joseph Brown, Stephen Hopkins, and Benjamin West watched the transit of Venus in 1769,[10] with a reflecting telescope recently imported from London. This telescope—still in good condition—is preserved at the Ladd Observatory, where I have frequently seen it since youth. The house I refer to was undoubtedly on the spot in 1769, when the periwigged astronomical party brought up their telescope, took off their three-cornered hats, and started in to watch the black planetary dot creep across the flaming solar disc. (One may hope that they had a suitable piece of smoked glass to put before the eyepiece!) Its type was never a *common* one, but for some reason or other (perhaps to allow people to build on very narrow strips of street frontage) several existed in Rhode Island. I have seen another one in a nearby village, but this—so far as I know—is the only one left in Providence. Houses like this used to be called "Lightning-Splitters"—a perfectly self-explanatory term.[11] This house is now inhabited by negroes, but when last I saw it—a few months ago—it was in fairly good physical shape.

Glad you found the remarks on various weird authors interesting. Yes—Price is a thoroughly delightful chap. Born July 3, 1898, in California, and enlisted in the cavalry at the outbreak of the war. Saw service in various parts of France, and stationed a long time in Bayonne, in the South; an ancient and mysterious city which produced a great impression on him. Home in 1919, and won an appointment to West Point, from which he graduated with high standing in 1923. Lieutenant and Captain of Cavalry—but soon fed up on peace-time soldiering, so resigned from the service and entered business. Used his engineering knowledge in the acetylene gas machinery industry. Some time in Chicago, when he became a close friend of Farnsworth Wright, and later in New Orleans—where he managed the local plant of the Prestolite Co. Lost his job with the depression—May 1st, 1932—and went into commercial writing on a large scale. Placed a sensational number of manuscripts, but quality fell. Has now gone to Pawhuska, Okla.—in the oil and Osage country—to utilise his mechanical skill [&] executive ability as partner in a garage business. Can now write more at leisure, as he used to, and cultivate quality. Special interests centre in Mohammedan civilisation—has a fair working knowledge of Arabic. Authority on all Moslem customs. Connoisseur of Persian rugs, of which he has a choice collection. Extremely versatile—amateur fencing-master, wrought-iron and hammered-brass worker, mathematician, chef, fictional technician, and about everything else. Fascinating and friendly personality—highly strung, and a rapid and incessant talker on every subject under the sun. Daring and reckless motorist since last year, when he learned to drive a car (a second-hand Ford[12] which—mirabile dictu—is still in existence and in fair shape!) by climbing trees and dodging trucks at sixty miles an hour. You have Wandrei seized up quite correctly. A genial and likeable youth, but with a distinct strain of pessimism and melancholy. He used to like to withdraw suddenly from company to meditate alone, and expressed a hatred of mankind as a whole—seeking scenery which shewed no trace of man's existence. Not so markedly gloomy now, though still inclined to get off cynical epigrams when a good opportunity appears. Has a habit of getting bored with prosaic jobs and suddenly resigning them. A native of St. Paul, and a graduate of the University of Minnesota—where he has also done post-graduate work and acted as English instructor. Born 1908. Dark. Six feet two inches tall. Now lives in the Greenwich-Village section of N.Y. City. Very cosmic-minded and a worshipper of Klarkash-Ton—but latterly, under Derleth's influence, experimenting in serious realism. Is now thinking of attempting a drama.

Yrs most sincerely
H P Lovecraft.

Notes

1. By Winslow Upton of Brown University.

2. "Some Dutch Footprints in New England."

3. The Old State House (1762), 150 Benefit Street. Rhode Island declared its independence from England in the Providence Colony House two months before the Declaration of Independence. The AHT of this letter does not include any copy of HPL's drawings.

4. Sarah Whitman's house is at 88 Benefit Street, just down the street from "The Shunned House" of HPL's story. St. John's Episcopal Church at 271 North Main Street, founded in 1722 as King's Church, closed in April 2012.

5. Mary Ann (Chase) Clark (1814–1906) was the mother of Franklin Chase Clark (1847–1915), husband of HPL's aunt Lillian.

6. St. Dunstan's Choir School was at 84 Benefit Street.

7. Annie E. P. Gamwell's husband was Edward F. Gamwell (1869–1936). They separated in 1916 and divorced sometime thereafter.

8. The John Carter House (1772), 21 Meeting Street. The *Providence Gazette and Country Journal* (est. 1762) was published by William Goddard in a shop marked by the sign of Shakespear's Head on North Main Street. Carter joined the paper in 1767 and by 1768 was sole proprietor. He and his wife moved the business into the house they built on Meeting Street.

9. The Civil Works Administration, a short-lived New Deal job creation program.

10. They observed the transit of Venus at the crest of College Hill, 100 feet east of Benefit Street near the southern end of Thayer Street, not far from what is now Transit Street.

11. The Daniel Pearce house (c. 1781) at 53 Transit Street in Providence is noteworthy for its very steep "lightning splitter" roof.

12. HPL referred to Price's 1928 Ford as "Juggernaut"—a force or object regarded as unstoppable that can crush all in its path; or chiefly British: a large heavy truck. H. G. Wells refers to such a forceful vehicle in *The Wheels of Chance* (ch. 12).

[10]   [ALS, JHL]

66 College St.,
Providence, R.I.,
April 13, 1934.

My dear Rimel:—

Glad you're enjoying M. R. James, & hope that Blackwood & the others will appeal equally to you. Not the slightest shadow of haste about the return of anything—all the less because I'm on the point of hopping off for Florida (in slowish stages) to visit Barlow. My aunt will safely receive anything which comes to the house during my absence. Incidentally—if Barlow doesn't forward my Dunsany soon, I'll send it along myself when I get down there!

I've always sent heavy MSS. by express, though relatively few of my own have been heavy enough to make that method pay—except according to Price's scheme. Glad my card reached you in time to forestall any injudicious purchases. I thought that pipe-dream of parcel post was too good to be true!

Hope the N.A.P.A. journals reached you safely, & that you were not disappointed in them. I think you'll like the organisation—& as I said, there'll be no trouble at all about a credential. Hope you'll win a laureateship after you join—I like to see my recruits distinguish themselves, & was pleased when Barlow pulled down the story title immediately upon joining.[1] Hope you can get a press soon. Amateurs with a mechanical twist seem to succeed from the start—Barlow does well, & Crawford has just surprised me with some excellent home-printed sheets of his long-delayed magazine. Incidentally, my story "Celephaïs" has about a dozen misprints, including two or three which make me appear illiterate. I wish something could be done to inculcate youthful editors with the habit of typographical accuracy. Even the non-printers are slipshod with their proofreading. But I'm glad to see that Crawford's sheet *is* coming along. I had about given up hope!

By all means let me see "The Tree On the Hill." Perhaps Theunis & Singleton will some day be as famous as the immortal Jules & Friend Trowbridge![2] The old house story sounds interesting—& you surely don't need to wait to see one before using the theme. I've never seen a mediaeval castle, but I wrote the "Rats" just the same. Your title—"The Tenth Brick"—sounds to me like a winner. Indeed, all that you cite of the tale seems prepossessing.

No hurry about the *R.I. Journal.* I fear that my knowledge of astronomy has never gone beyond the simplest elements, yet I have surely enjoyed those elements in my day. I know how odd it is to see an amateur journal antedating one's birth—that's the way the old N.A.P.A. papers of the 1870's & 1880's strike me. And yet the similarity of all these things is remarkable. Boys' papers of 1870 & those of 1934 all have a profound note of community. Childhood is a pretty fixed type at bottom—the same basic impulses & reactions from generation to generation, let manners & customs change as they will.

On behalf of one of the amateurs I'm looking up a boy's paper of *1828*, & will wager it will not differ extensively from the average amateur product of the soberer type today. Statelier language, perhaps—but the same essential spirit.

I think you'd find the simpler elements of astronomy highly fascinating; & if you wish, I'll lend you some beginners' manuals that I like rather well. I can't say that the skies arouse any pious reflections in me; for the more I learn of the structure & motions of the galaxy & the larger units beyond it, the more impressed I am by the impersonal, unconscious, accidental, automatic mechanism of the whole thing. I don't see the slightest reason for assuming the existence of any vast governing consciousness in the cosmos. We have strong evidence that all consciousness is confined to the cerebral tissue of highly evolved material organisms, so that an universal governing brain would postulate the existence of what Haeckel ironically called a "gaseous vertebrate."[3] There's no evidence for such a thing, and we can understand very clearly the psychological processes—poetic attempts to explain the unknown through personification—which caused our primitive ancestors to invent the conception.

Glad you think kindly of the crude pictorial efforts, & hope some miracle will enable me to hit on a farmhouse design worthy of working into the "Colour" booklet somehow, even if not as a frontispiece. The next time I sketch something out for a story I'll let you see it—although such sketches are usually in pencil . . . . very crude, & generally destroyed as soon as the picture in words is complete. As for Klarkash-Ton's drawings—my set is now in Koenig's custody with instructions to pass on to Searight. I'll tell the latter to place you on the list. When you get them, of course, you must let Baldwin see them—& he can return them to me. Enclosed are the snaps of Howard Wandrei's drawings. These, very plainly, are miles above the amateur class—miles above even Smith & Rankin. H W is really breaking into the ranks of the real artists, & it would take only one or two lucky illustrating jobs to win him wide & discriminating recognition. Inferior as these prints are to the originals, I think you can catch enough of the artist's genius to see what an important figure he's getting to be. He is 24 years old—Donald is 26. Both are lean & over six feet tall. Donald is dark & clean-shaven; Howard is blond, spectacled, & possessed of a faint moustache. Yes—I know a simple drawing with a few significant lines or masses of black is often more effective than an elaborate conception . . . . but it takes skill to achieve such a thing. One has to have a keen artistic selectiveness to pick out the intensely relevant lines on which a sketchy design is based. Smith confesses he can't do it—& I couldn't if I tried all the rest of my life! Talman is the best draughtsman of all the gang (Howard Wandrei, of course, is counted out—being in a wholly superior class)—the logical designer for a bookplate or heraldic shield. I can understand his hatred for cities, although I like small towns more than he does. Most weird devotees, I fancy, enjoy wild & lonely places. Long, however, is perfectly at home in the metropolis—where he was born. I can see what you mean about the prosaic nature of machinery, though weird effects have been woven around it. In "Cool Air" I tried to see whether I could conjure up an air of horror in a sunlit room with street cars clanging outside . . . . but doubt whether I succeeded. Some of these tales of telephone listening, though, (cf. new F F)[4] catch at real horror.

Glad the antiquarian material proved of interest. Keep anything permanently that seems of real interest—I have several copies of that *Halve Maen*. As to the pen sketches—that old colony house does not *face* the Shunned House. It is its *rear* which touches Benefit St. across from the accursed brooding edifice. The facade faces North Main St. at the foot of the hill, down to which that narrow railed park or parade (with original iron fence & stone embankment of 1761) runs. About Poe—it was only the older people who retained that prejudice against him hereabouts. Today it would be hard to dig up a trace. The uncle in whom I encountered it was born in 1848. So you don't have shutters in the Northwest! Many houses built around 1900 here lack them, & they have been removed from some old houses (including, alas, *this* one!); but most of the very new ones—built in the old style—have them again. Most New England shutters are of the slatted sort, while those of the Central & Southern states tend to be solid. About "Ulalume"—I must have told that anecdote wrong, for what Mrs. Whitman advised was *not* the *addition* of another stanza, but the *removal* of one *which was there before*. You won't find it in modern standard editions of Poe, & I dare say a good many casual readers of the younger generations don't know it at all. Do you? Here it is—see if you recall ever encountering it. It was the last stanza—& really subtracted from the strength of the poem, just as Mrs. Whitman said:

> "Said *we*, then—the two, then—'Ah, can it
>   Have been that the woodlandish ghouls—
>   The pitiful, the merciful ghouls—
> To bar up our way & to bar it
>   From the secret that lies in these wolds—
>   From the thing that lies hidden in these wolds—
> Had drawn up the spectre of a planet
>   From the limbs of lunary souls—
>   This sinfully scintillant planet
> From the Hell of the planetary souls'?"

Whenever you get to Providence I'll be delighted to shew you the Poe signature in the Athenaeum—but you can see many more of them, as well as genuine letters & MS. sheets, in the small cottage in Fordham, N.Y. (now part of New York City, in a densely settled district with a subway station close by) where he lived his last years. It is now a public museum. Yes—Benefit is a great old street. Somewhere around here there is an illustrated article on B. St. that I want to send you, but I can't seem to locate it at the moment.[5] By the way—those street steps don't lead up from South Court St. but from *Meeting St.* (the street that has the old colonial printing office) . . . & the street they lead to is not Gordon (pardon my wretched handwriting!) but CONGDON. The reason I take pains to correct the details is that the errors would mislead you in trying to locate points on a city map. If you'll study the map closely you'll find some interesting street names—especially along the old waterfront. Maritime days are reflected in India, Doubloon, Bullion, Guilder, Coin, Dollar, &c. streets.

Price is indeed an interesting chap. To his history must now be added another page . . . . . The Pawhuska garage didn't pay, so he's now hitting the road again in his faithful Juggernaut—planning to call on Robert E. Howard, to dip into Mexico, to glimpse Clark Ashton Smith, & finally to wind up for a while in San Francisco. Happy go lucky! His beloved rugs are with him in the car.

I've read several things in magazines by Ray Cummings—who is an originally clever writer run all to seed artistically through commercialism. His earliest & most famous work—"The Girl in the Golden Atom"—was published over a decade ago. Bright, but full of stock characters & artificial romance. Later stuff is positively puerile. I hate to say so, though, for he once praised me generously in the Eyrie.[6] It is just possible that I may meet him next month, for he is now in Ft Lauderdale, Fla., & may pause in De Land as he comes north.

Derleth's novel[7] is detective—not weird—but I mean to read it just the same. It's quite a problem whether any others of the crowd will follow him to substantial achievement & general recognition. Wandrei may do it with realism (his fantastic stuff is going commercial), but he's far behind as yet—& still unsettled as to his true metier . . . . whether novels or plays. Klarkash-Ton might with a stroke of luck. But about the others I'm doubtful. Bob Howard, though, may cut a commercial swath. There is more to his pulp stuff—more real zest & vividness—than to Price's or Quinn's or Hamilton's. He really enters into what he writes as they don't. Glad you've heard from Klarkash-Ton. I think the majority of the W T group would be pleased to hear from you, though Long & Munn grow worse & worse as letter-answerers. C A S would be admirably pleasant & helpful as a correspondent. Why not ask his opinion of "The Blue Stone" & see how it tallies with mine? A variety of opinions is always broadening. I think, as I said before, that any weird author would be willing to autograph whatever you might send him. Remember that these birds aren't real authors like Machen & Blackwood & James. For the most part they're merely unknown strugglers who feel flattered if anybody thinks their non-financial signatures worth anything. As for this Ackerman person—he's simply a pompous little joke, though doubtless a nice enough kid personally. He's no writer, but simply a sort of enthusiastic relique-chaser. His making a paying institution of himself is certainly a bit of rare comedy—which you wouldn't be apt to find duplicated in any real writer. Baldwin told me of his photograph business, & let me see the specimens in question.

Yes—a number of tales nominally by others have had my hand behind them. "The Curse of Yig" was reprinted in the S & B (London) "Not at Night" anthology some years ago, & "The Horror in the Museum" is scheduled for such reprinting this year. "The Hound" is rather poor. Horror laid on rather indiscriminately, as with a trowel. Have had no time to do the Arkham tale, but will take my notes & map along & perhaps write it in Charleston or De Land.

I vastly enjoyed your descriptions of Asotin, & the pictures accompanying them. Yes—I fancy a region without hills would seem as strange to you as to me. You'd probably like Charleston, though—the live-oaks & palmettos are highly distinctive. That's the farthest south Poe ever went, & the touch of subtropical exoticism impressed itself permanently on his work. Not so much trailing Spanish moss in Charleston, but just south of there it begins in earnest. Savannah looks much more tropical—with profuse moss & taller palmettos. Northern Florida is luxuriant, but toward the south it begins to get barren—meagre pines & scrub palmettos. Key West is wholly different—real tropical flora like the West Indies. Only 90 miles from Havana—but I didn't have the cash to get across when I was there. As for travel range—I didn't get more than 100 miles from my home till I was 31 years old. My first burst of travel was in 1922, & I have been enlarging my radius ever since. This trip, though, will involve no new territory—unless some sudden windfall lets me keep on to Havana, which is not in the least likely. The scenery of your region was first made familiar to me by my grandfather when I was very young. Cherry-blossoms in March surely are notable! Thanks immensely for the offer of some of your giant cherries, for this fruit is one of my favourites! If I'm not home to receive them at the proper season, I may let you forward them to where I am—for cards will keep you informed as to the essential points of my course. The primary destination, of course, is ℅ R. H. Barlow, Box 88, De Land, Florida. I'll be glad to see a snap of you when you have one, but don't hurry or go to any trouble. Sorry you've had so much illness—I believe I mentioned that my own youth was virtually a continuous chronicle of semi-invalidism. I've also suffered from a lack of facial presentability—having had a highly troublesome tendency to ingrowing beard-hairs since the early days of my shaving . . . . on a scale which necessitated widespread needle-&-tweezer probing of a very scarring sort. In latter years, however, this is not so bad—for some of the worst hirstute [*sic*] offenders have come out for good. The worst trouble now is under the jaw, where the visibility of the amateur surgery is not so disconcertingly high. I think I mentioned that I've also paralleled you in losing much school time through illness. You've surely had some fluctuations in weight! I average around 145 or 150. A little over a decade ago I grew uncomfortably fat through the overeating habits urged on me by a solicitous family who sought to combat my lack of ravenous appetite—but in 1925 I inaugurated a record-breaking reducing campaign & knocked off 50 lbs. in five months. Now I keep track of my diet & have no tendency to pile on the suet again. I must have shot above 200 in 1924 . . . I stopped getting weighed when I went over 188. My collar size, now 14¼, shot up to 16¼! Thanks for the snap of your father—who has exactly the type of physiognomy I most admire. Some day I'll dig up a picture of my father small enough to send. Long—who has seen a good many of his pictures—insists that he looked like the novelist Gustave Flaubert. I can barely remember him. My mother survived till I was 30. My study (as well as other parts of the house) is covered with paintings by my mother & my elder aunt who died only 2 years ago. I have also an interesting view by my grandmother. At the old home we had many more, as well as other paintings, but these had to be disposed of when we sought smaller quarters. My grandfather was quite an art connoisseur, & travelled in Italy twice—picking up paintings, statuary, vases, mosaics, & the like. We still have a few remaining—some of which were in storage for years, but are now resurrected in our cheap but fairly commodious quarters. These things make the place seem startlingly like a miniature version of the old home. I was interested in the picture of your birthplace, which is very trim & prepossessing, & which certainly has a hauntingly weird southward view—with those curiously rounded hills bare of vegetation. Little brother & the tiger also interested me greatly. Both, I'll wager, have grown some by now! I don't wonder that you still dream about the old birthplace—I've been away from mine nearly thirty years, yet still dream of it more than of any other spot on earth. I have very strong geographical attachments, & quitting my old home was a kind of death—but it could not be avoided, since at my grandfather's death in 1904 his estate was virtually wiped out by the calamities of his business . . . . . the same land & irrigation business which took him to your region at times, & which went to smash with the bursting of a new dam on the Snake River. I'll enclose a sketch of the old home as it used to be—later I may find a snap small enough to send. I was still there when I had my first kodak.

I envy your father his ability to paint, & hope I can see his work some time. Sooner or later I must try to make a trip to the west coast, seeing you & Baldwin & Klarkash-Ton, & pausing midway to glimpse my many friends & correspondents in the Chicago–Wisconsin region. The boat sounds interesting—I used to row considerably on the Seekonk, which you'll find on your city map . . . & also on general maps of R.I. Often I would land on one or both of the Twin Islands—for islands (associated with remote secrets, pirate treasure, & all that) always fascinated me. I have occasionally found arrowheads—for R.I. was the core of the old Narragansett County—but for petrified wood I had to depend on my grandfather's collection. You & your father & Baldwin must have some delightful musical sessions together—I'd enjoy hearing them even though unqualified to participate. Congratulations on the timely Easter rabbits! The Kappa Alpha Tau[8] is stirring to new life under April suns—old Pres. Randall is a visible fixture once more—but the two grey kittens across the garden have gone to their new home. Your family is surely gratifyingly ample—mine has narrowed down to one aunt now. I've heard before how difficult the human hand is to draw—my book is full of precepts & illustrations, but on account of my dominant interest in landscapes & buildings I haven't studied them very closely. Hope your poems land with the *Spokesman-Review*[9]—I must see them eventually, whether they do or not. I once used ottava rima.[10] The Yuggothian fungi vary in precise rhyme-scheme. Some are true sonnets, others are not. I'd like to see your early writings some time. Later I'll shew you a story I did at 14—a record compilation of pompous words & phrases . . . "The Beast in the Cave". It took a lot of study, though—the scene is the Mammoth Cave in Kentucky. I had then never seen a cave—though now I've explored two—Endless Caverns in Va. & Lookout Mt. caves in Chattanooga, Tenn.—where there's a spectral underground waterfall 150 feet high . . . thundering in eternal night! I must get some snaps of myself soon—or have the owners of older negatives make some prints. When I do, I'll supply both you & Baldwin with permanent copies—free of charge, unlike young Effjay Akkamin![11] ¶ April F F just came, & has a very good story.[12] April W T is above the average. "Black Thirst" & "Bells of Oceana" magnificent, "Malygris" & "Shadow in the Moonlight" excellent. C A S's drawing, though, is a bit stiff. ¶ Well—I hop off tomorrow at midnight. A week in N Y with Long, then Charleston, & finally De Land. You'll hear from me—as will F L B—en route. All good wishes—

Yrs most sincerely—

E'ch-Pi-El

Notes

1. "Eyes of the God" (*Sea Gull*, May 1933) won the story laureateship of the National Amateur Press Association.

2. HPL compares DWR's characters to stock characters in Seabury Quinn's stories about the psychic detective Jules de Grandin.

3. German biologist and philosopher Ernst Haeckel (1834–1919) used the term "gaseous vertebrate" to ridicule the paradoxical qualities of the standard conception of godhead. See *The Riddle of the Universe,* tr. Joseph McCabe (New York: Harper & Brothers, 1900), 288.

4. Eando Binder, "The Ancient Voice," *FF* 1, No. 8 (April 1934): 117–23.

5. *Netopian* 10, No. 7 (January 1930) contained "Looking Backward through the Years on Benefit Street" (7, 10–11) and "On Benefit Street, Providence, May Be Found Some of Rhode Island's Most Characteristic Colonial Architecture" (8–9).

6. Ray Cummings, letter to "The Eyrie," *WT* 7, No. 6 (June 1926): 858; rpt S. T. Joshi, *A Weird Writer in Our Midst* (New York: Hippocampus Press, 2010), 66.

7. I.e., *Murder Stalks the Wakely Family.*

8. This appears to be HPL's first mention of K.A.T., but he assumes DWR is familiar with the group. Because 66 College Street was on Brown University's fraternity row,

HPL devised the Greek name K.A.T. (standing for Kompsōn Ailurōn Taxis, or "band of elegant [or well-dressed] cats") for the array of cats at the boarding house.

9. The daily newspaper based in Spokane, WA.

10. See HPL's "Earth and Sky."

11. I.e., Forrest J Ackerman. See FLB 4n2. HPL lampooned him similarly in "In the Walls of Eryx," referring to slimy and wriggling "ackmans."

12. See n. 4.

[11]   [ALS, JHL]

Box 88,
De Land, Fla.,
May 13, 1934

My dear Rimel:—

Your very interesting letter duly arrived—together with the story, poem, postcard, & Wandrei pictures. Thanks! This acknowledgment must necessarily be very sketchy & inadequate, since my genial hosts keep me so busy with pleasant conversation & occupations that I have not a moment to write except late at night or in the morning before I make my appearance.

Glad you received & enjoyed the Charleston material. A great old town! While there I received & answered a letter from Baldwin, & in my reply to him you'll find quite a few descriptive touches. You are right in citing the old gateways & the Pringle or Brewton house as typical high spots. On my way south I spent 8½ hrs. in Savannah—a fascinating old town, though not as quaint as Charleston. Hope you duly received the pictorial material I sent from there. I did the place rather thoroughly, & went through the art museum—which is housed in a mansion built in 1819.

That was May 1st. In the evening I rode on to Jacksonville, Fla. & put up for the night. The next morning I proceeded onward to De Land, where my brilliant young host met the 'bus.[1] I was now in the real subtropics, as the enclosed pictures will graphically hint. Through some chance incident of highway repair the coach did not proceed on its usual route, but detoured to ancient *St. Augustine*—that fascinating relique of 16th century Spain which I intend to visit for a week on my way back, & from which I'll send you some antiquarian material. On this occasion the 'bus did not stop or even enter the venerable town—but merely raced tantalisingly by the crumbling city gates . . . . those striking pillars of coquina-stone (stone formed by the coagulation of tiny shells & bits of shells by sea-water, & common on the east coast of northern Florida . . . different from the tapia or "tabby" stone formed of coral & common in Charleston) erected in 1730 or thereabouts. I had just a glimpse of old Fort San Marcos (or Marion) & the ancient Tolometo Cemetery with its strange slabs & spectral live-oaks. Of these you'll hear more when I stop there on my return.

As for De Land—it is a delightful town scenically, as you can see from the views; though just as modern as anything in your own state. The only *old* things are ruins which one sees on side-trips—such as old Spanish sugar mills antedating 1763, the old Turnbull plantation of 1768 at New Smyrna, & the ruins (great arches of coquina stone amidst great oaks & tangled vines—very picturesque) of a Franciscan mission of 1696. You would have been interested in the open sea as seen from Daytona Beach—with no land between the spectator & the coast of North Africa far to the east! De Land was founded in 1876, contains a small college, & is an attractive though scarcely picturesque place.

The Barlow home is out in the open country 14 miles west of the village—in a region where the live-oaks give place to tall Australian pines which stand out against the sky like the trees of a Japanese print. The house is of 2 stories & log exterior—a rustic type—& is not yet quite finished. The grounds are still in the process of landscaping—pool, walks, rustic bridge, &c. Behind the house is a delightful lake on which we row, & across which is an impressive oak grove where we sometimes take our current reading & writing. Bits of typical subtropical jungle can be found here & there, & all sorts of snakes abound—Barlow shoots them for the sake of their skins, which he uses in bookbinding. The climate is absolutely ideal for me—temperatures of 85° or so every day—& I feel three or four times as well & active as I ever feel in the north. I habitually go hatless & coatless, & am preserving & augmenting the coat of tan I began to acquire in Charleston. A few points on the predicted programme have fallen through—for example, I shall not see Cummings, Hamilton, or Williamson, & shall probably not be able to get down to Dunedin.

My young host—Robert Hayward Barlow—is a really brilliant boy prodigy only 16 years old but immensely mature for his age. He is the son of a retired army colonel now in poor health & on a visit in the north. An elder brother, also absent, is an active army officer. Young Barlow is extremely versatile—a writer, painter, sculptor in clay, pianist, landscape gardener, book collector, & scores of other things despite the handicap of desperately bad eyesight. In the autumn he is going north for a session with expert oculists who have promised him some relief. He is small, dark, & active in his mannerisms. I enclose a picture of him which you might return after shewing it to Baldwin. The present household consists of Barlow & his mother; & of a mother & son named Johnston, from Virginia, who keep house & attend to various duties. The son, Charles Blackburn Johnston, is a lean, tall, dark chap of 37 who possesses considerable talent in painting & in other directions. Somewhere amidst the current enclosures you'll find a crude sketch of the place—I've had no time to study out a good one. Later I hope to get a snap shot to send. There are four cats—all delightful. A veteran white Tom named Doodle-Bug, & three little tigers named "High["], "Low", & "Jack". My especial favourite is High—the darkest of the three—who trots like a little dog with Barlow & me when we take our evening walks. Also in the household are four infant opossums—tiny creatures that have to be fed with a medicine dropper as yet. Their mother was slain by a passing motor. Barlow's collection of weird books & magazines would make you turn green with envy. He keeps it in a deep closet off his room, which he has christened—after Klarkash-Ton's story—"The Vaults of Yoh-Vombis."[2] Since my arrival he has demonstrated his sculptural skill by making a marvellous clay bas-relief of Cthulhu & a fine statuette of the Hindoo elephant god Ganesa (probably the prototype of Long's "Chaugnar")—the first for me, & the second for our amiable & eccentric correspondent, old Bill Lumley of Buffalo, N.Y. I'll try to get good snaps of both to send you.

Another event since my arrival is the coming—at last—of the loose sheets of "The Shunned House" from Cook. There are only 115 copies left (some being lost or spoiled), but Barlow plans to bind & issue them eventually. He also has a plan for circulating photographic copies of one or two of Howard Wandrei's best drawings—getting 11 × 14 prints made by an expert professional photographer.[3] The execution of this scheme now awaits Wandrei's consent. Barlow is certainly one of the most enterprising youths on record! And by the way—before long you'll be receiving a sizeable bundle of loans from these parts—my Dunsany's "Dreamer's Tales", & two things which Barlow thinks you & Baldwin might like to read . . . . . . Merritt's "Metal Monster" & the old serial "The Blind Spot" by Austin Hall & the late Homer Eon Flint. When you & F. Lee are through with them (not the least hurry!) you can return the Dunsany to 66 College st. & send the other two to Klarkash-Ton. About the new Dunsany book—"The Curse of the Wise Woman"—it is very good, but not overtly weird. I've read it. Weirdness just hovers in the background in the form of allusions to Tir'nan'og, the fabled land of heart's desire & eternal youth beyond the western sea—the bulk of the book being a delicate & imaginative study of boyhood in Ireland.

Well—I'm glad that James & John Silence are proving interesting. Keep a record of the volumes you've read, so that I can avoid duplication in future loans. I'm interested in what you've learned about MS. postage, & hope it doesn't turn out to be an error—as the similar ruling mentioned in the newspaper cutting did. At any rate, your story came through all right without any "postage due" notice.

Glad you got the N A P A stuff, & hope you'll join in the course of time. I'll send you Barlow's tale in Hanson's paper when I get it—although the author modestly assures me that it isn't much good.[4] It would certainly be pleasant if you could secure a press & issue a paper. *The Muse* would make quite an apt title! I saw *Marvel Tales* only the other day, & believe that Crawford did a very fair job considering his inexperience. My young host's "Caneviniana" promises to be a much better job, but is temporarily held up owing to his eyesight. He may postpone completion till he returns from his ocular repair siege in Washington & N.Y.[5]

I read your "Tree on the Hill" with great interest, & believe it truly captures the essence of the weird. I like it exceedingly despite a certain cumbrousness & tendency toward anticlimax in the later parts. I've made a few emendations which you may find helpful, & have tried a bit of strengthening toward the end. Hope you'll like what I've done. If any point seems obscure, let me know, & I'll try to explain it. Barlow also liked your tale, & based a crude sketch upon it—which he is enclosing with his compliments. Let me see "The Tenth Brick" when it's ready—it surely sounds promising. Sorry "The Blue Stone" hasn't yet landed, but feel certain it will in the course of time.

I'll send a volume or two on astronomy when I get home. Down here the skies are superb—it's too bad Barlow isn't an amateur astronomer! I'll have to try to interest him! I share your distaste for mathematics, with which I've always had a hard time. Irregular education has its advantages & disadvantages. Barlow's school experience (largely in military schools) has been as fragmentary as mine, but he does not shew any lack of general education.

A misunderstanding of Searight's will somewhat delay the Klarkash-Ton drawings, but you'll see them in the end. Glad you appreciated the Howard Wandrei material. It certainly is tremendous stuff, & I fervently hope that Barlow's plan for photographic reproduction can be put through. Glad Baldwin & your father likewise enjoyed the views. I'll be delighted to see some photographs of the paternal paintings when you get some. Thanks in advance!

College Street runs due east up the steep hill, & is the street shewn in the foreground of that booklet's frontispiece. #66 stands back from the highway, at the rear end of a grassy court which runs due north from College St. proper, & which (though no longer a named public highway) used to be called "Ely's Lane".[6] The college grounds are at the head of College St. at the top of the hill—old University Hall with its white belfry (built 1770) being at the end of the vista as one looks up the street.

Price & Howard had a congenial meeting, without pugilistic or gladiatorial casualties of any sort . . . . after which the Peacock Sultan proceeded west & north to his family homestead, 5314 E. 12th St., Oakland, California, where he can be addressed from now on. He has just made a shorter trip to Auburn, where he has met Klarkash-Ton for the first time. Judging from their enthusiastic joint postcard, the event was a highly pleasant one. Price forms the first fellow-weirdist that either Two-Gun Bob or Klarkash-Ton has ever seen.

No—Derleth won't by any means stop writing for W.T. Many fairly "arrived" writers keep on with the pulp magazines for the sake of the cash they can pick up, & Little Augie is no exception. You are right in deeming England more appreciative of weird material than the U.S. Let us hope that commercialism won't "get" all the gang. Many of the lapsing ones are still young enough to stage a comeback!

You'll hear from C A S, if indeed you haven't done so already. I am sure he'd be very glad to give a verdict on any piece of work—prose or verse—which you might send him. He usually has some very helpful suggestions to offer.

Your new series of verses sounds highly interesting, & both Barlow & I went over the enclosed specimen with minute attention & sincere appreciation. It has a true sense of the weird—manifest in the unusual images & conceptions—though occasional points need a certain amount of alteration. At the moment I can't get time to give a detailed exposition of this matter, but I'll enclose the rough draught with notes, plus a finished version . . . . all of which combined ought to serve as a help of some sort. Since "Yid" has a slang connotation, I'm suggesting that "Yith" be used as a generic title. I'll be glad to see the first five when they're available.[7]

About reprints in anthologies—several of mine have been used in Great Britain. I've never had a tale *directly* in a British magazine, but "Erich Zann" was reprinted in the *London Evening Standard*. No—I've never written Machen or Blackwood, since I hate to intrude my own mediocre personality on men of real prominence. These celebrities are, however, very easy to approach. Derleth has had cordial correspondence with both Machen & Blackwood, & with the late A. Conan Doyle.

Yes—a hundred-mile circle with Providence as a centre certainly includes a lot of highly interesting & historical material—Salem, Marblehead, Plymouth, Concord, Lexington, New Bedford, Newport, & dozens of other ancient towns. Florida, on the other hand, is more like Washington in its undifferentiated distances. All your descriptions of the local terrain proved extremely interesting—& I shall certainly appreciate the cherries. It is, indeed, odd how a region's relationship to the source of supply determines whether a given product is a rare delicacy or an every-day matter of course. Thanks for the view of your house, which I return herewith. As you said, the same one came from Baldwin. I hope you can some day get back your earliest home— & wish I had a chance of getting back mine!

Asotin views are always interesting, & I was especially glad to see the singular eastward hill enclosed. The scene is certainly unusual & almost weird, & I can well imagine the locale of "The Tree on the Hill" as being not far away. The lane is fascinating, & I can imagine how much you must have enjoyed it. Some day I hope to see a photograph of the picture of the hill which your father intends to paint—what a pity his first one perished in the municipal conflagration!

Sorry that cat of the photograph disappeared. I think I told you that disappearance was also the fate of my beloved old Nigger-Man.[8] The felidae here are delightful . . . . . Doodle-Bug must be very like your own white tom. Hope the coming kittens all turn out well, & look like their parents!

It will be a good thing if the *Spokesman-Review* establishes a poetry column. The *Providence Journal* used to have a literary column or page open to readers, in which some of my "Fungi from Yuggoth" were first printed; but it has no longer.[9] Glad Baldwin has placed some free verse in the F F,[10] & hope his other literary ventures may turn out well. I'll be interested to see your early specimens, & may some day send along a juvenile thing or two of my own good for several laughs.

This epistle has had several interruptions, during one of which I've secured four local snaps which may prove of interest. In the one of me with my eyes accidentally closed you will see two of the local felidae, as well as the westerly end of the house. Another shews my young host in the same spot. You might return these to me after shewing them to Baldwin. Later on I may find some more good items to send.

Duration of my visit here still uncertain—my cordial hosts urge me to stay on indefinitely. I'll drop you cards whenever I make a shift of base. St. Augustine will probably be my next stop. A chap in Macon, Ga.[11] wants me to visit him, but I'm not certain about it. Shan't be back north for quite some time!

¶ And so it goes. All good wishes—

H P L

[*Enclosures:* Drawing by RHB "derived from The Tree on the Hill." Dried flower mounted on card with note by RHB: "De Leon Springs / May 3, 1934.] [HPL's sketch of the Barlow estate: Reverse:]

Drawn by R. H. Barlow,
Box 88, De Land, Florida

— derived from The Tree on the Hill

Shadows[12]

Amid dim hills that poison mosses blast,
    Far from the lands & seas of our clean earth,
Dread nightmare shadows dance—obscenely cast
    By twisted tales of archaean birth
On rows of slimy pillars stretching past
    A daemon-fane that echoes with mad mirth.
And in that realm sane eyes may never see—
Far black light streams from skies of ebony.
             —Duane W. Rimel [in HPL's hand]

[P.S.] Barlow & I both congratulate you on the sketches you enclosed. They certainly shew a genuine and promising power. Thanks exceedingly for permission to retain.

Notes

1. RHB's account of the meeting is given in "The Wind That Is in the Grass," *OFF* xxix.
2. CAS, "The Vaults of Yoh-Vombis" (*WT*, May 1932.)
3. This was Lucius B. Truesdell (1873–1974) of DeLand, who took the well-known portraits of HPL from late in life.

4. Edgar M. Hanson of West Concord, NH, was publisher of the *Granite State News* and the *New England Amateur,* official organ of the New England Amateur Press Club. RHB's story is unidentified.

5. See FLB 4n3.

6. Regarding Ely's Court, see and Kenneth W. Faig, Jr., "Can You Direct Me to Ely Court?: Some Notes on 66 College Street" (54–69), and David E. Schultz, "66 College Street" (70–81) in *Lovecraft Annual* No. 9 (2015).

7. DWR's "Dreams of Yith" appeared in *FF* in two installments. Both had a headpiece designed by DWR along the lines of those made by Hugh Rankin for Donald Wandrei's *Sonnets of the Midnight Hours* and HPL's *Fungi from Yuggoth.* Curiously, sonnets I–III of *Fungi* appeared in *FF after* Rimel's numbered poem sequence appeared in a fashion resembling the appearance of latter poems in the *Fungi* sequence in *WT.* HPL mentions Yith only once, in "The Shadow out of Time": "Thus it was when the minds of the Great Race sped across the void from that obscure trans-galactic world known in the disturbing and debatable Eltdown Shards as Yith" (*CF* 3.406–7).

8. Also the name of Delapore's cat in "The Rats in the Walls."

9. "The East India Brick Row" and five sonnets of *Fungi from Yuggoth* appeared in "These Plantations," edited by W. Chesley Worthington.

10. Apparently not published.

11. John Milton Samples, editor of the *Silver Clarion.*

12. Alternate version of "Black Sacrifice" (p. 377), and sonnet VI of "Dreams of Yith."

[12]   [ALS, JHL]

% Barlow, Box 88,

De Land, Fla.,

June 1, 1934.

My dear Rimel:—

My genial young host keeps me so busy that I shan't be able to do full justice to your generous array of material, but here goes for a brief & appreciative acknowledgment anyhow. I have tarried on beyond all my expectations, but will have to be getting in motion before long. I'll send you plenty of views of ancient St. Augustine—including the city gates which I mentioned seeing as the coach flew tantalisingly by. I was there three weeks in 1931, & shall be glad to get back & reëxplore its historic byways.

Glad you enjoyed the snaps of the Barlow place. No—it would be hard to get snakes enough for full book bindings, but Barlow uses them only for back strips. He appreciates your offer to send him the skins of some of your northwestern ophidians some time. Rhode Island has rattlers, too, though they are not (except in special localities) as numerous as in the south. Texas is a great place for them—Robert E. Howard has sent me several impressive sets of rattles.

The climate continues to brace me up, although there was one disconcertingly cold day recently (which would not, however, have been considered cold in the north). So you are one of the perennially hatless clan? I know that many young fellows dispense wholly with lids—although men of my age in the north stick to the traditional headgear.

Barlow certainly is a great boy, & I hope the oculists can straighten out his vision next autumn. As for his musical tastes—he seems to be very old-fashioned & classical, with but little interest in syncopation or innovations of any sort. You & Baldwin & he could undoubtedly have some highly interesting debates on musical matters.

In the view of "High" & myself I didn't notice that the former had also closed his eyes till you pointed it out. So old Doodle looks like your white cat? He is about three years old, but looks rather older & tougher than his age. He hunts a good deal, & goes off on long wilderness expeditions alone. I'll wager your cat is fascinating! The other day Jack (the larger tiger kitten) received a mysterious injury of some sort, & was lost for 36 hours. When he returned he shewed a tendency to stagger & lurch, & generally to lack muscular control. It is thought that a snake bit him. He is now growing stronger, & will probably pull through all right. Of the infant opossums, only one has survived; but it looks as if he would pull through & flourish. He is called "Henry", & now eats milk & crushed banana all by himself. Even now he is scarcely larger than a good-sized mouse.

About the local white sand—that is very typical of central Florida. It is calcareous—composed of minute pulverised shells attesting the former submerged state of the terrain. Now & then little shells will be found intact in it. This is not the clay which Barlow uses in modelling—the latter occurs only in small special localities. About the coach-whip snake—it is over 7 feet long, but not deadly or harmful in any way.

Later on I'll try to enclose photographs of Barlow's sculpture—we're going to see if we can get clear pictures of it taken at a local 4-for-a-dime gallery like the one I patronised in Charleston. I'm glad, by the way, to hear that you like that Charleston snap. Yes—it is for your permanent retention. I fancy that both this & the one I sent Baldwin are equally representative. They shew different angles, & one looks as much like me as the other.

About "The Shunned House"—it appears that the other half of the edition is *not* lost after all, but merely sidetracked in the cellar of Cook's sister. Therefore there are about 225 copies instead of 115. I doubt if the sale will be rapid. Naturally, you'll get one . . . . though probably there will be nothing done toward distribution till autumn. By the way—I hope the package with Dunsany & the Metal Monster & the Blind Spot arrived safely. When I get home I'll send you some volumes on elementary astronomy. Keep a record for me of everything you've read, so that I won't duplicate previous loans in sending additional material. I lend so many books to various persons that I really can't keep track of what I've lent each one.

Barlow's collection is surely a notable one. About that mis-labelling in the 19th volume of W T.—he says that the error exists on the contents page (both March & April 1932 marked #3), but *not* on the back strip. April is there properly labelled #4.

Thanks for the graduation announcement, & congratulations on being class poet! Writing the poem must surely have been some job! It interests me to know that you have composed a song.

Sorry "The Blue Stone" didn't land with *Fantasy*—but I feel sure it will be printed sooner or later. Glad you liked the amateur journals, & hope you'll eventually join the N.A.P.A. I'll send some more papers later on. Hope "The Tree On the Hill" will eventually land somewhere. As for a tale with an Egyptian theme—it surely might be splendid, though of course the field is rather well worked. In any case, research on Egyptian antiquities will help you greatly in building up a convincing weird background. I was glad to see "The Tenth Brick", & am returning it with certain comments & emendations which I hope you may find legible. Both Barlow & I think it is considerably more powerful than "The Tree on the Hill". There is subtlety, atmosphere, & restraint—& no attempt to over-explain or reduce the whole horror to definite concreteness. I hope that all my notations will prove helpful. If not, let me know—& this goes also for the "Tree on the Hill." Yes—I think the Tree ought to have a chance of landing in print. You might try it on Wright, Hornig, Crawford, & Schwartz, in the order named.

I trust that by this time the Klarkash-Ton drawings have duly arrived from Searight, & that you & Baldwin have been duly impressed. Remember, of course, that this is not Smith's best work. Barlow has just bought one of his better water-colours for $4.00. The plan for issuing Howard Wandrei's drawings meets with the artist's favour, although his brother Donald (who plans to issue a booklet of reproductions himself later on) is not especially enthusiastic.

Let me thank you & your father tremendously for the pleasing assortment of his sketches & water-colours. He certainly has an enviable talent, & I wish I could approximate such skill! All are delightful, & the large views are refreshing in their grace & brilliancy. I am exceedingly grateful for the privilege of retaining the Providence sketches—all of which vividly & accurately reflect the quaintness & beauty of the ancient town. Your own cartoon is decidedly clever—away beyond anything I could ever do! As requested, I return the Asotin views & the cartoon. Another vastly artistic thing is the block print heading for "Dreams of Yith"—thanks enormously for the specimens.

Glad to see the poems. And by the way—you can change things in copy which editors have accepted. Why not send to Hornig & substitute revised verses for those he has? You could also have the heading changed from Yid to Yith. I like these poems exceedingly, & think C A S's corrections were all in the right direction. I enclose a copy with a few added suggestions for possible change. "The Snake" is extremely good—I enclose it with a few revisions & observations which I hope you will like.

Glad you're in touch with C A S—I know you'll find him interesting & helpful. Hope he'll have useful suggestions to make regarding "The Blue Stone".

About College St.—no, it is *not* this thoroughfare, but the little court or alley opening off it & having #66 at its rear, which was once called "Ely's Lane". I enclose an illustrative diagram. The old names of College St. are Presbyterian Lane, Rosemary Lane, & Hanover St. Ely's Lane was so-called because it abutted on the property of the Ely family.

The May W T was much above the average, with "Scarlet Dream", "Queen of the Black Coast" & "The Tomb Spawn". Havent [*sic*] read the June one yet—but I know "The Colossus of Ylourgne" is good unless the MS. has been changed. By the way—Wright expects to reprint my "Arthur Jermyn" before long.

Hope Hornig can use your linoleum heading. Couldn't you change *Yid* to *Yith* by shaving down the *D* & glueing on a *TH* cut separately? And by the way—about returning MSS.—why not have express envelopes prepared for the text, & send stamped postal envelopes for the editor's letter—so that each can be sent separately, without 1st class rates on the MS? I think that's what Price does.

Am interested in the references to Asotin, & glad that a rich cherry harvest is promised. Will be glad to see a sketch or snapshot of the lone tree. What you say of the park sounds highly alluring.

Glad you've been able to pick up a bit of cash from piano-playing, even though it takes you into rather incongruous surroundings. I envy anybody who can find a source of revenue apart from hack writing & revision. Baldwin tells me that his orchestra has had quite an upheaval, but that he & other members have found berths in another organisation of the sort. Barlow's musicianship has not yet reached the professional stage.

New anecdote of the returned Jack since I began this letter. He is stronger now, & upon being let out of the house made a bee line (despite his staggering) for a clump of palmettos near the lake. There he paused abruptly, raised his head, & began to purr loudly. Upon examining the clump we found a small dead snake with the head chewed up. This, without doubt, is the source of Jack's trouble. He must have caught & tried to eat the thing, & have been poisoned thereby. But what an ardent hunter to *remember* his prize & want to shew it off to the family! There's no question now but that he'll recover safely.

Well—thanks again for all the matter sent. Give your father my regards & congratulations anent his paintings, & thank him especially for the Providence views—all of which go into my permanent files. Trust my comments on "The Tenth Brick" & the poems may prove of interest. Must close now & get this in the mail. There is no rural delivery here, so mail comes & goes only when the family goes into De Land in the car.

All good wishes, & regards to Baldwin.
                    Yrs most cordially & sincerely,
                              H P L

[Enclosure: HPL's hand-drawn street map of area around 66 College]

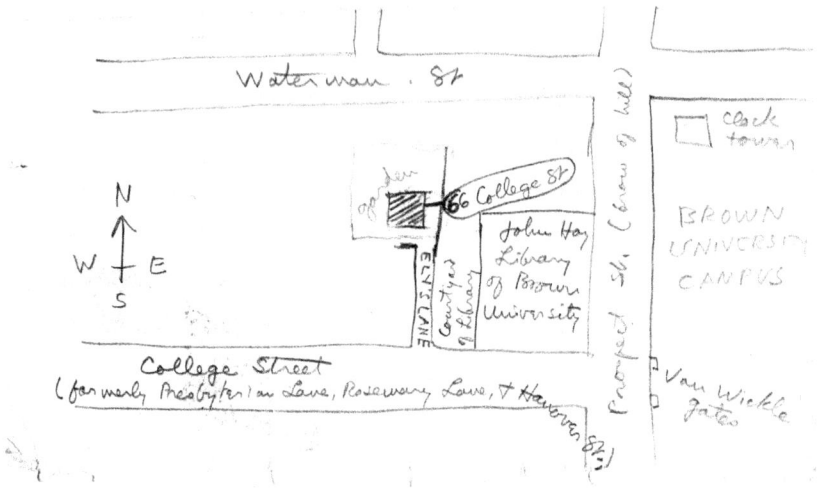

[13]   [ALS, JHL]

De Land—
June 17, 1934

My dear Rimel:—

Glad to hear from you & to receive the interesting verses. Once more my reply will have to be inadequate, though I'll see what ground I can cover in the time at my disposal. Thanks in advance for the cherries, which I know I shall enjoy. What a shame the prices on them are so low this season!

Owing to the super-hospitality of the Barlows I seem to have become a sort of De Land fixture, though I fancy I shall begin moving along pretty soon. You'll hear from me when I get to St. Augustine. The rainy season is now on, & some days afford veritable floods—though with certain exceptions the rainfall is not of long duration. I think it was rather less rainy in Florida at the same time in 1931.

You & Barlow could surely exchange many ideas in the music line. He, however, is only a beginner at the piano—having taken no lessons prior to last October. Even now he has no professional teacher—being instructed on-ly by his mother & by the exceptionally gifted & versatile son of the house-keeper—Charles Johnston. About the Fungi which Harold Farnese set to music—they are "The Elder Pharos" & "Mirage". I hope we can both see the script some time—though I suppose Farnese would have to have photostatic copies made. He tells me that the melody is of a distinctly weird character.

You'll see Barlow's story in the amateur journal in course of time—though of course it is merely a beginner's work, & nothing to take as a model. I'm sure your brief story "The Kiss of Zak" would form a good N.A.P.A. credential—the plot outline sounds unusual & highly promising. Under separate cover I'm sending along some new N.A.P.A. material which you may find of interest—& which you can keep.

Glad the cat is coming along well—I'll be delighted to see a snap of him. By the way—my aunt tells me that there are more new kittens at the boarding-house across the back garden—which makes me rather anxious to get home. They'll probably be at a rather playful & interesting age when I arrive. Jack—down here—is almost well again, though he still has an odd tendency to carry his head on one side. He has taken to walking with us in the road like his brother High . . . . which Barlow discourages, for fear of accident from passing motors. Henry the 'Possum, alas, did not survive after all; but departed this life on June 10th from no apparent cause. Probably he & his brothers were too young to be weaned—though the Barlows certainly took marvellous pains to feed & lodge them!

Yes—of course it was all right to copy the list of my fictional junk. You'll surely get a signed copy of "The Shunned House" in time, though it may be quite a spell before Barlow issues the thing. His eyesight retards him badly, & he has so many irons in the fire. Glad the "Blind Spot" &c safely arrived . . . & that Barlow's binding methods have given you & Baldwin some hints. Your illustrations & block prints would surely be assets. Glad you've made a list of the books I've sent to you & Baldwin. Let me have a copy of it when I get home, & I'll send other good items, thus avoiding duplication. I'll surely include some elementary volumes on astronomy. Don't get up any high expectations over the coming Silver Key sequel in W.T. I don't do very well in collaboration, & this thing in many ways fails to satisfy me. Yes—I surely hope that the illustration is by Rankin. It does *not* get the cover design. As for the covers in general—I don't really give a damn what they are, though of course the existing parade of undraped females is amusingly irrelevant. From the standpoint of the weird they are simply excess baggage—though Wright has a silly idea that they help to sell copies of the magazine to sporty gents who might not otherwise buy it. It actually is too bad to waste the space when there might be really weird drawings such as Utpatel or Rankin or Howard Wandrei or St. John[1] could produce. Yes—the last-named artist certainly has done some excellent cover work.

Trust you'll eventually have many things printed in the small magazines—as well as W T. Crawford hasn't much taste—he's having a controversy with Derleth which shews up his limitations rather vividly. He really doesn't like weird fiction, as distinguished from science fiction, at all. Hope you'll have no difficulty assembling material for the Egyptian tale. Glad the notes on "Tenth Brick" & "Tree on the Hill" proved helpful, & trust both tales may find an appropriate typographical haven somewhere. As for modes of writing tales—there really are no general rules applicable to everybody. Each person must discover for himself what methods fit him best, individually. Thus some people find it best to develop several ideas at a time—having two or more stories under way at once—while others (like myself) prefer to tackle only one thing at a time. Same way about developing a story from a "plot germ". Many people prefer to spin the yarn as they go, not knowing what the end will be, while others do best when a synopsis of the whole thing is prepared. I myself use both methods—according to the effect the subject matter has on me. Sometimes I shoot ahead of any previously planned idea, yet at other times I am guided by an outline. Several years ago I drew up a set of suggestions for writing a story—though I've never literally followed them myself. In case they'd be useful to you (& I feel sure they are sound in principle), I'll try to give the substance of them here:[2]

Suggestions for Writing a Story
(The *idea* & plot being tentatively decided on)

1. Prepare a synopsis or scenario of events in order of *occurrence*—not order of narration. Describe with enough fulness to cover all vital points & motivate all incidents planned. Details, comments, & estimates of consequences sometimes desirable.

2. Prepare a synopsis or scenario of events in order of *narration*, with ample fulness & detail, & with notes as to changing perspective, stresses, & climax. Change original synopsis to fit this outline if such a change will increase the dramatic force or general effectiveness of the story. Interpolate or delete incidents at will—never being bound by the original conception, even if the ultimate result is a tale wholly different from that first planned. Let additions & alterations be made whenever suggested by anything in the formulating process.

3. Write out the story, rapidly, fluently, & not too critically; following Synopsis 2. Change incidents & plot whenever the developing process seems to suggest such change, never being bound by any previous design. If development suddenly reveals new opportunities for dramatic effect or vivid storytelling, add whatever is thought advantageous—going back & reconciling early parts to the new plan. Insert or delete whole sections if necessary or desirable, trying different beginnings & endings till the best is found. But be sure that all references throughout story are thoroughly reconciled with the final design. Cut out all possible superfluities—words, sections, paragraphs, or whole episodes or elements—observing the usual precautions about the reconciliation of references.

4. Revise the entire text, paying attention to vocabulary, syntax, rhythm of prose, proportioning of parts, niceties of tone, grace & convincingness of transitions (scene to scene, slow & detailed action to rapid & sketchy time-covering action & vice versa, &c. &c.), effectiveness of beginning, ending, climaxes, &c., dramatic suspense & interest, plausibility & atmosphere, & various other elements.

5. Prepare a neatly typed final copy, never hesitating to make last-moment corrections.

———————

Yes—it's a good thing to take pains when writing, & to take care of the chronology when the tale extends over long time-periods.

The Klarkash-Ton drawings arrived safely—glad you & Baldwin liked them. The "Lurking Fear" drawings accompanied the original appearance of the tale as a 4-part serial in the wretched little magazine *Home Brew* in 1923. The version in W T in 1928 was a reprint—though the text is unchanged. C A S has done larger work than the samples you've seen, though he probably inclines toward a small scale. Yes—I know work designed for reproduction ought to be drawn far above the intended final size. I'll be interested to see your bookplate when you get it done. C A S excels in hellish heads & strange vegetation—his story illustrations (especially when the human figure is introduced) tending to be a trifle stiff. The water-colour bought by Barlow—"Beyond Cathay"—is a splendid specimen of bizarre floral growths.

About Howard Wandrei—what Barlow wants to publish are his *drawings*, not his *stories*. Don't know yet what will come of the plan. H W will have a story in W T shortly, though Wright rejected the illustration he drew to go with it. Incidentally—don't overrate Barlow's "Flower God". Actually, the ending is abominably flat, & R H B is disgusted with the whole thing.

I would indeed be delighted to see your father's picture of the northeastern hills, & hope he'll send it along when it is finished. If he is in no hurry about its return, 66 College may be the best destination—since I don't know how long I'll be lingering in De Land. I certainly did appreciate his views of Providence. I'll also be glad to see the local snapshots you mention . . . . . as well as the new linoleum cut for "Dreams of Yith". You surely do excel in this block printing work.

Thanks very much for the poems, which are all really excellent. I enclose them with certain slight emendations—the reasons for which I have tried to give on the margins. Hope the changes will be of some help. You certainly put a very genuine weirdness into the verses.

Yes—C. L. Moore is certainly the most powerful & genuinely weird new writer secured by W.T. in many years. She is indeed of the feminine gender, the C. standing for Catherine. It is her wish, however, not to have this widely known—since she hopes to conceal the fact of her writing from her regular employers. She has a secretarial job with some corporation in Indianapolis, &

fears she will be fired if it is known that she has another source of income. Miss Moore is also an artist of ability—last month she sent Barlow a drawing of Shambleau which displays phenomenal power. Some of her later W T work will be illustrated by herself—Wright having accepted several sketches.

About sending things—never bother about 1st class unless you have to. Shoot back all my stuff by express or parcel post or whatever is cheapest. Which reminds me that before long you or Baldwin ought to be getting my "Mountains of Madness" & "Shadow Over Innsmouth", both of which are circulating in your direction. Keep them as long as you like, & send them to 66 College in the end. Later you will receive my "Thing on the Doorstep"— to be sent on to someone else in Pittsburgh. Thanks—I've seen most issues of *The Magic Carpet,* which Price, Howard, & other contributors have sent me. It was quite a thing while it lasted.

I agree about the intelligence, fine coördination, & independence of the cat—a great species! That tale of Blackwood's was fascinating—& Carl Van Vechten reprinted it in his anthology of cat stories—"Lords of the House-tops."[3] The apparent sensitiveness of your cat to intensive staring surely seems unusual, though I doubt if any messages can be transmitted save by the usual apparatus of the five senses. Coincidence is responsible for the average case of apparent telepathy.

Your recent recurrent dream of vast wheels & spheres is certainly ex-traordinary, & I hope you can eventually make literary use of it. The extended cup is surely a tantalising phenomenon. No—I never had any of the fever-dreams (of the turning & rolling of vast bulks) which you mention, though I often dream things of the most bizarre & vivid sort—some of which I have already incorporated into tales or verses. The only well-defined delirium I ev-er had was in 1903, when I was 12 years old & suffering from an exaggerated cold. I then (my mother said afterward) mumbled things about flying to Mars & Saturn. As for the nature of dreams—I think there is no question but that they consist of dissociated scraps of previous impressions (some utterly for-gotten & ordinarily deeply buried in the subconscious) re-grouped by the un-disciplined sleeping fancy into new & sometimes utterly unfamiliar forms. Their surface aspect is strange, yet every basic ingredient is something the mind has picked up at one time or another . . . . from books, pictures, experi-ences, &c. I don't believe in hereditary memory at all. Acquired characteristics are not ordinarily inherited; & even if they were, they would be merely general tendencies—certainly not the special, individualised impressions involved in that curious sense of unaccountable familiarity which some scenes or dreams awake in us. Yes—I have often had that sense of previous knowledge of things absolutely new to me,[4] but in most cases I have been able to trace it to very early & largely forgotten impressions. For example—a certain village land-scape at sunset looked familiar when I first saw it, & I eventually traced it to a picture I had seen in virtual infancy. Vaguer dreams of pseudo-memory—the sort involving strange cyclopean cities—usually refer back to forgotten bits of reading or pictures, more or less combined in a new way. However—for *fictional* purposes it is quite all right to adopt such false but attractive explanations as reincarnations, hereditary memory, & so on. I do myself!

I'll send you photographs of Barlow's Cthulhu & Ganesa statuary when I get some good ones. They are certainly tremendously impressive. Barlow has just secured a 5 × 7 camera, with which he expects to do some rather unusual work. So far, he has no films to fit it—supplies of that size being unobtainable in a place as small as De Land. The nearest large city, where everything can be bought, is Jacksonville.

Last week I visited a marvellously impressive place—Silver Springs, about 60 miles from here. There is a chain of placid lagoons whose floor is riddled with great pits 30 to 80 feet deep—covered with curious growths & studied by means of a glass-bottomed boat. In some of these submarine chasms the bones of prehistoric monsters are found, & in one is the weed-grown outline of an ancient sunken boat. Out of this series of basins flows the Silver River—as typical a tropic stream as the Congo or Amazon. It winds through miles of lush, impenetrable jungle, with palms, cypresses, festoons of moss, & tangles of vines leaning into the water. Alligators, turtles, snakes, & strange birds abound throughout its length. It was here that all the jungle scenes in the Tarzan films featuring Johnny Weismuller were taken.[5] I traversed this river for 10 miles in a launch, & could easily believe I was in the heart of Africa. At one landing a group of natives hailed the boat & exhibited a huge cotton-mouth moccasin snake that they had caught alive—& one of them got aboard with the quarry to bring it alive to the snake-house at Silver Springs. Quite a bizarre fellow-passenger! During this trip I saw, for the first time, alligators *in their native habitat.* Previously I had seen them only in zoos, or at the alligator farm on Anastasia Island opposite St. Augustine. At this latter place, though, the surroundings are made to look like a bit of real jungle. There's an alligator in the lake behind the house here—but I've never seen him, although Mrs. Barlow & Charles Johnston have.

Well—I must ring off & get this in the mail. Hope the amateur papers will come all right, & thanks abundantly for the cherries. By the way—we pick lots of blueberries here.[6] You'll hear from me again when I'm in St. Augustine. All good wishes to you & Baldwin.

——Yours most cordially,

H P L

Notes

1. Frank Utpatel (1905–1980), Hugh Rankin (1878–1956), Howard Wandrei (1909–1956), James Allen St. John (1872–1957).

2. The following is a variant of "Notes on Writing Weird Fiction" (1933; *CE* 2.175–78).

3. The book contains Blackwood's "A Psychical Invasion." Van Vechten himself wrote *The Tiger in the House: A Cultural History of the Cat* (1924).

4. The phenomenon known as déjà vu.

5. Six of the original Tarzan movies, starring Johnny Weissmuller, were filmed on location at Silver Springs between 1932 and 1942, including *Tarzan the Ape Man* (1932) and *Tarzan and His Mate* (1934).

6. See RHB's anecdote about HPL picking blueberries in "[Memories of Lovecraft (1934)]," *OFF* 406–7.

[14]   [ANS, JHL (enclosure with preceding letter?)][1]

[No postmark;
c. 18 June 1934]

Later—the cherries have arrived in fine condition. Thanks a thousand times! They have a magnificent flavour, & both Barlow & I appreciate them enormously. We've treated everybody around the place. It certainly gives me a kick to partake of the fruits of a region my grandfather knew so well—he used to have sample bottles of preserved Snake River apricots &c. around his office. Glad to know the names of the two varieties.

¶ Glad the revised "Yith" has gone to Hornig. Shall be interested to see the results of the new linoleum block when it's done.

¶ Part of the road washed out by floods, & being repaired by a negro convict gang. This is the rainy season in earnest!

Regards——H P L

Notes

1. Front: Entrance to Grounds at Silver Springs, Fla.

[15]   [ALS, JHL]

66 College St.,
Providence, R.I.,
July 23, 1934.

My dear Rimel:—

I found your interesting letter of last month, with enclosures, when I reached home on July 10th; but so desperately busy have I been—with piled-up work & papers—that I could not get around to replying until now. Meanwhile I trust you duly received the St. Augustine material. I left De Land June 21st.—the Barlows driving me up to St. Augustine, where I secured a room at the same place I stopped in 1931—overlooking the harbour. I spent a week in the ancient town, & certainly enjoyed it to the limit. You can imagine the fascination of roaming about a place abounding in houses which were 50 years old when the first pilgrim landed at Plymouth Rock. Some time I'll try to sketch a few typical St. Augustine places for you—but meanwhile I fancy the folder I sent—plus the booklet sent to Baldwin—will give a very fair idea of the place. The typical old Spanish houses built around 1570 to 1600 are of coquina stone—a stone formed by the compression of tiny sea-shells under the action of water, & quarried extensively on Anastasia Island, which lies just across the harbour from St. Augustine. It is the only stone found in Florida. Sometimes the upper parts of the houses are of wood. The architecture is very plain, & the houses are flush with the street—with exquisite gardens in the rear. Walls are very thick, so that all the windows & doors have deep embrasures. Small wooden balconies generally overhang the street. The roofs of these old-timers were originally flat, but during the British period—1763–1783—pointed roofs of the West Indian type were generally substituted in order to keep the top story cooler. From about 1590 onward, large mansions with patios & arcades & outside courtyard staircases (resembling the houses of New Orleans) began to be built; & several of these survive. The Post Office occupies one of them (the Spanish governor's palace, built 1591), while the Public Library is in a later specimen erected 1755. Many of the ancient houses are open as museums, & I have explored all of these. The streets are narrow & picturesque, & in the centre of the town there is a large square—La Plaza de la Constituciíon—shaded by great live-oaks & dominated by the old Spanish cathedral. Here also is the old slave-market, where today idlers sit & play chequers. The great walled gardens are very beautiful, & often contain huge circular wells or fountains of the Spanish type. The prevalence of high walls bordering the street gives the town a very Spanish aspect. The great stone city gates are still standing, though the walls (which were of wood & earth) are gone. The ancient fort with its corner turrets (a typical Spanish fortification) is still in fine condition & open as a museum. A great modern bridge spans the harbour & leads to narrow Anastasia Island, on whose farther side is a picturesque deserted beach where one can be alone with sand & sea & sky. The vegetation is subtropical & picturesque, with great palms, abundant vines, & luxuriant, moss-draped live-oaks. North of the town is a great orange-grove, leading to which is the finest avenue of live-oaks that I have ever seen—giant gnarled trees whose lower branches double back & touch the ground in banyan-fashion on the other side of the road. The old cemeteries are ineffably picturesque, with curious forms of gravestones & tombs. Most are in varying conditions of neglect; & they look like ideal spots for Pickman's Model & his brethren. On the whole, it is easy to imagine St. Augustine as a lone Spanish outpost long before our ancestors settled the regions to the north. There are modern houses, but the eye can easily be trained to overlook them. Some of the elaborate hotels affect a Moorish style of architecture, & loom up with almost magical glamour against the skyline from a distance, especially at sunset. I spent all my time outdoors; reading & writing in various picturesque spots, & assimilating the antique colour of the place. The terreplain of the old fort, & the arch of the great bridge, were favourite spots of mine. Weather favoured me—in contrast with the rainy season I had endured at De Land. *Every* day was fair & sunny. The climate is rather better than De Land's—nearly as warm, but dryer. No wonder the town is famous for its centenarians! The inhabitants—aside from Northerners who have drifted down—are of mixed Spanish & English descent. Spanish has not been spoken for nearly a century by the old stock, although immigrants from Cuba are bringing it back in certain sections. The old Spanish names—Sanchez, Segui, Ponce, Genovar, &c—still survive, & the dominant religion is still Catholic. Another Spanish element is provided by the descendants of the Minorcans who were brought as indentured settlers to New Smyrna, down the coast, but who were freed & established in St. Augustine in 1774. People of other stocks affect to look down a trifle on the Minorcans, though they now occupy many positions of influence. The Spanish type of physiognomy is still frequent among the old St. Augustinians, so that it is hard sometimes to tell a recent Cuban immigrant from one of the ancient stock until he begins to speak. Negroes are numerous, but they know their place & keep to it. Aside from the Cubans, the only foreigners are a sprinkling of Jews. The regular year-round population—counting out the winter visitors—is about 12,000. One unusual thing I saw was a newly-discovered Indian graveyard in the northern part of the city. It had been found only a few weeks before—while I was in De Land—by gardeners who were setting out an orange grove. The skeletons lay with their hands folded & feet toward the east, indicating that they were Christianised allies of the Spaniards & had been buried by the Franciscan friars. The probable date of interment was around 1600. Today they can be seen lying side by side, just as found—with the earth around each skeleton protected by a low cement rim. The whole excavated area is covered with a huge tent, & eventually a large building will replace it—forming a permanent museum where, for the first time, exhumed skeletons can be seen reposing on their original site.

I hated to leave St. Augustine, but a 2-day pause in old Charleston made the break endurable. After Florida, Charleston seemed curiously northern—fewer & smaller palmettoes, & only a trace of Spanish moss—yet on the other hand its Georgian doorways & steeples gave a welcome homelike touch. Altogether, it is the most fascinating place I know. Then came the hop to Richmond—wholly out of the zone of subtropical scenery, & back to the familiar northern landscape I have always known. The scene looked very strange—almost bleak—at first, but I soon became attuned to its subtler beauty. In Richmond I spent much time in the exquisite landscape gardens—Italian & Japanese—of Maymont Park, & revisited most of the scenes of Poe's boyhood. Incidentally, I stopped at a cheap hotel only 2 doors from the site of the house where Poe grew up! The next jump was to old Fredericksburg—Gen. Washington's home town, which has changed very little since

Washington was a boy at Ferry Farm across the river. Here I went the usual rounds—seeing among other things the house where Washington's mother spent her last days (1775–1789), the manor-house of Washington's brother-in-law & sister, & the grave of old Mrs. Washington beside Meditation Rock—a lofty outcrop shaded by a giant oak & overlooking a beautiful valley—where she used to sit & read the bible. After that came Washington, D.C.—where I did several things I had never done before—visited Rock Creek Park, explored the interiors of the capitol & the Pan-American Union, ascended the Washington Monument (what a view!), & inspected the restored & appropriately furnished interior of the old Custis–Lee mansion—Arlington—on the heights across the river. This latter is the finest specimen of a Virginia plantation-house that I have ever seen. Next came old Philadelphia; where I surveyed many of my favourite antiquities, wandered among the old stone houses of Germantown (settled by German Quakers, Mennonites, & Dunkards in the late 1600's—now a suburb of Philadelphia), dipped into the awesome wooded valley of the Wissahickon, & visited the newly opened Poe cottage at N. 7th & Spring Garden Sts., where the poet lived from 1842 to 1844. This cottage is a pleasant brick structure of 3 stories in the rear of a larger house. Around it is a small & tasteful garden, now restored as in Poe's time. The cottage has lasted well—its small-paned windows, harmonious mantels, & panelled doors all bespeaking the quiet grace of Georgian architecture. There are only 2 rooms to a floor, & all are furnished just as during Poe's tenancy, though only a desk & a chair were actually his. Eastward on the ground floor is a parlour with its attractive fireplace, pianoforte, sofa, & book-closet. Across a narrow hall is the kitchen, where the family also ate. On the second floor is Poe's bedroom, with a neat black slate mantel; while just across the hall is a smaller study—with his desk. On the low-ceiled third floor are the rooms of Poe's invalid wife & aunt, with modest fireplaces & small casement windows. Everything is neatly kept—curtains, flowers, plants, pictures, china, & linen—just as in Poe's time. In the large adjoining house is a notable collection of Poe material, including magazines with the first printing of most of the tales & poems. The dedication of this cottage as a memorial museum occurred last winter, & I heard the exercises over the radio. I had seen the place many times before, but had never been inside until now.

When I reached New York I found Long & his parents about to leave for a week-end at Asbury Park & Ocean Grove, N.J., & at their cordial invitation went along with them. Shore resorts rather bore me, but literary & philosophical discussion with Belknap is always interesting. I didn't have cash enough to stay long in N.Y., so couldn't look up any of the group except Loveman—who quite overwhelmed me by presenting me with an object from his private museum which I had always admired—a slim, conventionalised bird of carved & black-lacquered horn. It is a typical specimen of the carving of Yankee sailors in the India trade a century ago—made under the influence of Sino-Japanese craftsmanship traditions. It stands as if poised for flight through gulfs beyond the galaxy—so that I have always called it "The Bird of Space". It is needless to say how glad I am to be its possessor!

I came home on the midnight coach July 9–10th. Dawn broke near the Rhode Island line, & it was surely good to see once more the rolling hills, stone walls, & white village steeples of my native realm! Then there loomed up before me a distant prospect of the spires & domes of ancient Providence, all golden in the morning light. Home at last! I found my aunt in excellent health—going everywhere without a cane. And at the boarding-house across the back garden I found something else of infinite interest & grace—the tiny, coal-black survivor of that last month's crop of kittens of which I spoke in my preceding letter. He was then just a wobbly-legged handful, but every day sees him growing stronger & prettier & more playful. I borrow him continually, & shall try to snap a picture of him before long. He looks like a bear-cub of paperweight size. Doesn't purr yet, but probably will before long. He's so venturesome in his explorations of walls & steps that he keeps his mother rather worried! I call him Samuel Perkins—& when he grows up he'll doubtless join the Kappa Alpha Tau & sprawl in state amongst the furry dignitaries of the neighbouring shed roof. Meanwhile the remaining February kitten—Betsey Perkins—has grown to be so big that one can scarcely distinguish her from her black-&-white mother . . . . though she still condescends to seek nourishment from the maternal bosom along with little brother Sam. I found my desk piled mountain-high with work—so that I haven't had time even to finish the unpacking of my valise! As usual, I do most of my reading & writing in parks & rural places. The weather has so far been uniformly fair & sunny—this phenomenon indeed assuming something of the proportions of a drought.

Turning to your letter—the cherries surely were appreciated, & I am greatly interested in what you say of the various species. So you appreciate the plentiful apricots of your region. I am likewise very fond of them, & nearly always have a supply of dried or canned ones on hand. Their pleasant tartness is a distinctive & welcome flavour. Sorry the mosquitoes have been bothering. Yes—Florida is a great place for all forms of insect life, including both giant roaches & gnats so small that they can sift through the finest screen. There used always to be a flock of the latter around my lamp in De Land. In general, though, mosquitoes don't bother me extensively. Perhaps I'm too tough a morsel for them to enjoy as a steady diet! Hope you'll have plenty of swimming opportunities. I don't swim, since the chill of northern waters, even in midsummer, almost paralyses me. I'd probably adopt the sport if I lived in the far south. As for music—you certainly have made a very little instruction go a long way, indicating that you must have marked natural talent. I really regret that I am so completely ignorant of music. Sorry to hear of your recent indisposition, & hope that the warm weather has thoroughly baked all febrile & rheumatic tendencies out of you. I still feel splendid as a result of my long subtropical sojourn.

Little Henry's untimely end confirms what is generally said of the difficulty of raising wild living things in captivity when they are too young. We don't know their dietetic needs well enough to supply them exactly. You certainly had good luck with the magpies—& what a beastly shame that the last pet one had to be eliminated! Neighbours once complained of some bantam roosters I had, but I was able to find a congenial & permanent home for them in the country. Latest news from De Land indicates that Jack shews almost no effects of his recent painful experience. He & High are uncles now, since Low has just presented the household with two likely-looking kittens.

Glad the stories lent by Barlow proved interesting. "The Metal Monster" has great stuff in it, but needs extensive revision. I think I told you that Merritt calls this his "best & worst" story. The June W.T. was very poor except for Klarkash-Ton's "Ylourgne". That tale "They Call him Ghost" had a fine idea, but was probably the *worst-written* piece of prose that Wright has ever printed. Hope you'll like Dunsany—I'll lend you more if you do. When I get that list of what I have sent, I'll know what to send next. The July W.T. is even worse than the June—C A S again being the author of the only acceptable item. I disliked my collaborated tale in print even more than in MS. Before long I hope my newer & longer tales will be reaching you in the course of circulation. Perhaps, indeed, you have them by this time. Hope you won't dislike them too violently. As for "Polaris" & "From Beyond"—I trust you will make all due allowances for their misprinted condition. It is apparently impossible for these little papers to print text correctly.

Glad my hints on story-writing seem likely to prove helpful. As for the doubtful point—when I speak of writing down a synopsis of events *in order of occurrence,* I mean that the events are to be recorded one after the other, in chronological sequence, *just as they are supposed to happen, regardless of how they will be told or presented to the reader.* Thus we may be writing a story which will begin with a certain incident, & then go back & tell about things which happened a long time before—*but in this first synopsis we don't pay any attention to that.* Instead, we begin to jot down the *things which happen first in point of time,* no matter how late the telling of these things may be postponed in the final version of the story. That is what we mean by the order of *occurrence.* Now the *order of narration* means simply *the order in which things are told.* The word "narration" means simply "telling". In this connexion it has nothing to do with any "narrator" of the story, but means simply the *way the events are presented to the reader.* When we prepare a synopsis of events *in order of narration,* we first set down *not* the thing which *happens* earliest, but the thing *which will be told to the reader first.* And so on all through the plot, each event being entered *in the order in which it will be presented to the reader.* That is what the *order of narration* means. Naturally, this forms the *second* stage in plot construction. First we mapped out *just what was supposed to happen,* regardless of the telling; & next we map out *just the way we will present these happenings to the reader.* To give a concrete example—here is the way one would prepare synopses for "Randolph Carter":

Order of Occurrence	*Order of Narration*
1. Ghouls exist in a certain cemetery	1. A man whose friend has disappeared is questioned by the police & tells a terrible & incredible tale of a graveyard tragedy.
2. A profound student hears about them from a strange book.	
3. With a friend he starts out to investigate them.	2. He tells of his friend's strange studies of ghouls & vampires, & mentions a terrible book he received from abroad.
4. Descending into a tomb, he telephones up certain fears.	3. He tells of an expedition into a graveyard for an unknown purpose.
5. He is seized by a throng of ghouls, & one of them telephones up a mocking message after he is killed.	4. He tells of his friend's descent into a tomb, & of the messages he telephoned back.
6. The friend, unable to explain the disappearance of the student, is questioned by the police & thus tells his gruesome story.	5. He tells of the cessation of the messages & of a strange, hideous voice which telephoned up that his friend was dead.

Do you get the idea now? *Order of narration* means simply the order in which the author presents the incidents of the story to the reader, & has nothing to do with any fictional "narrator" in the story. Indeed, a good half of the short stories written are in the 3d person & have no fictional "narrator". As for what I mean when I say "be sure that all references are reconciled with the final design"—that is just *a caution against changing an unfinished story incompletely, so that certain things in the new plot will conflict with & contradict certain accidentally left-over things in the old plot.* For example—if you originally name a character *John* & then decide later to call him *James,* be sure that you change *every* part of the story to match the new thing you have decided on. Go back & cross out the name *John* & substitute *James* wherever the character is named. Or if you've had a character killed in the original version, & then make a second version in which you let that character stay alive, be sure that you go back & cut out of the manuscript any passage in which it is implied that the character is killed. That is what is meant by *reconciling references.* Do you get it now? This caution had nothing to do with the exclusion of merely *irrelevant* (as distinguished from actually *contradictory*) material, although it *is* important to cut out anything which is really irrelevant.

About "The Lurking Fear" & its original printing—it was *not* an amateur journal, although the editor of the professional magazine *Home Brew* was an old-time amateur journalist. However, I did have lots of stories in the amateur journals—including "Dagon", "Randolph Carter", "Nameless City", "Polaris", & others. Yes—the quality of amateurdom was considerably higher then than now, although this year's N.A.P.A. administration (Babcock Pres; Bradley Off. Ed.)[1] is going to try its best to bring back the old standards. In the old days my association was neither the National nor the society which now calls itself the "United", but another branch of the United which unfortunately became abeyant in 1927. Regarding laureateships—I never landed a poetry one, but captured each of the others three times,[2] so that further entries on my part were (according to the U.A.P.A. rule) debarred.

That anecdote in the Wandrei interview about Cthulhu is largely fictitious. I don't recall anything of the kind, although I probably explained to Wandrei as I have to others that the word is supposed to represent a fumbling human attempt to catch the phonetics of an *absolutely non-human* word.[3] The name of the hellish entity was invented by beings whose vocal organs were not like man's, hence it has no relation to the human speech equipment. The syllables were determined by a physiological equipment wholly unlike ours, *hence could never be uttered perfectly by human throats.* In the story, we have human beings who habitually use the word as best they can; but all they can do is to *approximate* it. This they accomplish by using their throats in a queer way to *imitate* the original sound as their ancestors heard it from non-human throats. This queer use of the human throat makes a sound something like the original non-human sound, *but it is not like any human speech or sounds that we commonly hear.* It is an alien, unfamiliar sound that human beings can make only with an effort, & that they would not ever think of making if they were not imitating something non-human. The kind of effect or noise made in this way is *not really like speaking,* but is more like the sound a man makes when he tries to imitate a steam-whistle or crowing rooster or howling wind or neighing horse with his mouth. Up to the time of the story, when Prof. Angell became interested in the matter, there had never been any attempt to render the name of the hellish R'lyeh monster in our alphabet—although Abdul Alhazred made an attempt in Arabic letters, which was repeated in Greek by the Byzantine translator. The Latin translator merely copied the Greek. The letters CTHULHU were merely what Prof. Angell hastily devised to represent (roughly & imperfectly, of course) the dream-name orally mouthed to him by the young artist Wilcox. The actual sound—as nearly as human organs could imitate it or human letters record it—may be taken as something like *khlûl'-hloo,* with the first syllable pronounced gutturally & very thickly. The *u* is about like that in *full;* & the first syllable is not unlike *klul* in sound, since the *h* represents the guttural thickness. The second syllable is not very well rendered—the *l* sound being unrepresented. My rather careful devising of this name was a sort of protest against the silly & childish habit of most weird & science-fiction writers, of having *utterly non-human entities* use a nomenclature *of thoroughly human character;* as if alien-organed beings could possibly have languages based on *human* vocal organs. Actually, every name supposed to be originated by non-humans should be painstakingly shaped in such a way as *not* to conform to the principles of human vocalism & language.

Yes—I read "The Magic Island"[4] in 1931, when I was visiting Whitehead in Dunedin. He thought very highly of it, & considered it as quite authentic, though overdone & romanticised in spots. It is certainly a marvellous source-book of voodoo material, & one can trace its influence in most of the Haytian & other voodoo fiction written since its appearance. If you haven't seen Whitehead's "Black Beast"—which is based on a passage in "The Magic Island"—I think I can find a copy to lend you somewhere around the house.

I shall certainly be grateful for a glimpse of your father's sketch of the northeast hills when it is done. Meanwhile I rejoice to hear that his painting of "The 25" is not, after all, a victim of the flames! Hope you'll have it at home soon—& I shall surely be glad to see a photograph of it if such can easily be taken . . . . . which goes for the other large canvases as well. I don't know Moran's[5] work—wish I'd had your letter in time to look it up at the Congressional Library as I passed through Washington. Congratulations on the excellence of the new "Yith" block! It is certainly an improvement—in addition to embodying the amended name. Hope it can be used in the F F in connexion with your verses. Which reminds me that I like the new "Yith" verses very much. I reënclose them with a few comments & possible emendations. Thanks exceedingly for the sketch of Pickman's Model, which is tremendously clever & powerful—far better than anything I could do. The location is all right—for of course the thing roamed widely afield in its quest for nourishment. In response to your request I am enclosing a crude diagram giving my idea of the Model. Barlow & I had quite an argument on this theme. He has always drawn ghouls as long-eared things with incredibly broad shoulders; but I tell him that they ought to be thin, slippery, & streamlined—with no large projections—because of their *burrowing* habits. As to Miss Moore's drawings—"Shambleau" is extremely well done, though not as subtly horrible & richly potent as Howard Wandrei would have made it. It is in pen & ink, & so far as I know all her other drawings are. She most certainly has great & enviable talents.

Regarding telepathy—while the transmission of specific thoughts & messages is probably wholly mythical, it would be going too far to say that some vague sort of apparently intangible signalling is conclusively impossible. All active transformations of energy—such as combustion, light, heat, radio-activity, &c—are accompanied by radiation of some sort; & the form of oxidation called life is not necessarily any exception. Conceivably, the process of cerebration might give rise to some form of wave-energy or etheric bombardment—or simpler still, to the emission of some very subtle odour or other sensory impression-producer—which another person might pick up at a moderate distance. All we can say is that, up to the present time, the evidence in favour of such communication is suspiciously slight. What very slight evidence there is on the side of telepathy is extremely recent & still undigested.

For example—some experiments conducted a few months ago at a southern college have been interpreted as slightly favouring intangible communication. In his latest book Dr. Freud inclines toward belief in something of the sort[6]—a faculty which he considers common in certain lower forms of life (especially insects), & which he thinks exists vestigially in some human beings. But aside from these exceptions, it may be said that the mass of conservative scientific opinion does not credit any telepathic force. Personally, I have never encountered any phenomenon suggesting telepathy. I have never suddenly turned to find anybody staring at me, nor have I ever made any others turn by staring at them. I have never had a premonition verified, & have never foreseen any event. [Passage crossed out] As for dreams—of course they go beyond human experience, since they represent wholly undisciplined wishes & imaginings. Naturally it is impossible to trace many of them to their sources, since those sources are often so infinitely complex, varied, & remote.

Here is a photograph of Barlow's Chaugnar statuette—which went to old William Lumley of Buffalo. I think you'll agree that it is a darned fine job. The picture was taken by a professional in De Land before Barlow got his new camera. In my next letter I'll send you a picture of the Cthulhu bas-relief which Barlow took himself. I'll have to ask the return of this elephant-god, since the print is the only one I have. Sorry to hear that photographic supplies, magazines, & other common essentials are so hard to get in Asotin. De Land has every kind of shop—including probably more than a dozen news stands. I should think at least one news stand could do a thriving business in any sizeable village. Or does everybody in that section *subscribe* to magazines?

Very glad to see the new tale[7]—which reminds me somewhat of Dunsany. I'm returning it with a few changes which I think would help somewhat. It is really extremely clever, & I believe it would be welcomed either by the N.A.P.A. or by the little weird magazines. I've taken the liberty of changing the name of the hero—since the common English name of *Alfred* hardly fits in with the fabulous setting—the city of Bel-hoz-en, the river Oll, & the mountains of Azlakka! Hope you'll find *Aphlar* suitable as a successor. I'm greatly interested in what Klarkash-Ton says about "The Blue Stone", & advise you to act on his suggestions. It is certainly a good story, & it stands up well beside the best of your other work. As for the point about the non-recognition of friends & neighbours at the Sabbat—I can see what C A S means, though I'd scarcely have brought it up myself. I assumed that the light was faint & weird, that the watcher was at a considerable distance, & that the dancers were in postures so grotesque that recognition would not be likely. Concerning the conversation—I guess much of that could be advantageously cut down. But leave the beginning as it is—the gradual atmospheric preparation for the marvel about to be unfolded. Regarding the recognition—it might be well to follow Klarkash-Ton's advice & let it occur gradually. Certainly, this tale is worth experimenting with; & in my opinion it ought to land somewhere in the end. Which reminds me—my youthful friend Robert Bloch of Milwaukee has just sold his first story to W.T.—a ghoulish thing called "The Secret of the Tomb." Yes—C A S ought to know quite a bit about mining, since his uncle owns a mine. Auburn is one of the oldest gold camps in California, having started in 1848 under the name of "Woods' Dry Diggings."

Silver Springs certainly was impressive. I had seen live alligators before in zoölogical gardens & alligator farms, but this was the first time I ever saw one in his native setting. There were some in the ponds near Barlow's—Charles Johnston saw & tried to shoot one during my visit—but I couldn't catch a glimpse of these. As for my ophidian fellow-passenger in the launch—it was all right in view of the firm grasp his captor had on his neck, but I'd have hated to see that grasp relax for any reason!

I'd be delighted to see scenic cards of the Lewiston region. Your description of the launch trip up the Snake is most fascinating, & makes me wish I could take it some time. That place where the hills rise directly above the river must be something like the famed Saguenay in Quebec, where the dark stream flows almost spectrally betwixt great overshadowing cliffs. I've never sailed up that stream, but sometimes see the boats at the wharf in Quebec. Hope I can afford to make the trip some time.

Those nigger convict gangs on the Florida roads are certainly well guarded—two or more deputy sheriffs with loaded rifles always being present. The blacks are a mean lot, & once in a while need rough measures. On my return trip north I saw quite a snatch of drama from the 'bus window—a big buck nigger trying to attack his boss, but getting a sledge-hammer blow on the chin every time he charged. The rifles are never used except in emergencies or cases of attempted escape. There are some road gangs of white convicts, but I've never seen one. Prison reformers disapprove of these groups, & believe that the convicts are sometimes brutally treated; but I guess most of them are tough enough to deserve all they get. This system does not seem to exist north of Georgia.

Glad the amateur papers duly arrived. I'll send another batch later—though parts of it may duplicate what you have, since I've forgotten just what I sent. The Chicago convention was a great success, many old-timers & prominent contemporary amateurs being present. Babcock was elected President, & Bradley editor—very good choices. The next convention goes to Oakland, California. I don't think Barlow is entering anything for laureateship—indeed, he didn't last year. Someone else made the entry for him without his knowledge.[8] Good stories are scarce in amateurdom because the papers haven't space to print them. There may be an improvement this year. Bradofsky recently asked me for an article of 2000 words for *The Californian*—which is quite a generous length as compared with most of the contemporary thumbnail stuff. I hadn't anything to send, but finally cooked up a hasty thing about the Poe cottage in Philadelphia—together with other homes of Poe.[9] By the way—one good thing about contemporary amateurdom is the way the old-timer Maurice W. Moe is getting re-interested. He attended the convention, & may help some of the young editors in an advisory capacity. Moe is the high-school teacher whom I once mentioned to you as an authority on poetical technique & the author of a splendid unpublished manual called "Doorways to Poetry." There is a possibility that "Doorways" may get published within a year—albeit in somewhat humble form.[10] If so, I shall see that you get a copy. As I told you, it is a vastly better & fuller treatise than the Teter one; though the latter is the best cheap aid now available.

Well—I fear I must close & tackle some more of the piled-up work. Regards to Baldwin & best wishes all around.

Yrs most sincerely,
H P L

[P.S. on envelope:] Well—talking of telepathy! Just recd. your card. Glad you like Mts. of Madness. In the same mail came the new F F with your Yith poems & an excellent impression of the block. Also Marvel Tales.

Notes

1. HPL refers to Ralph E. Babcock and Chester P. Bradley, respectively president and official editor of the NAPA for 1934–35.

2. For the 1919–20 term, HPL won the Story, Essay, and Editorial laureateships for the year (for "The White Ship," "Americanism," and "The Pseudo-United," respectively). HPL also won the Editorial Laureateship for "A Matter of Uniteds" (1927).

3. See "Donald Wandrei," interviewed by Julius Schwartz and Mortimer Weisinger, *Fantasy Magazine* 3, No. 3 (May 1934): 10–11, 32 (quotation from p. 11): "When I met Lovecraft I chanced to comment on his excellent story, 'Call of Cthulhu,' and I pronounced the word as it was spelt. Lovecraft enlightened me on its correct pronunciation, which sounds like a series of witches' whistles. I asked Lovecraft how he could possibly pronounce the name different from my version of it, which was correct phonetically. He then said to me, 'Look here, I ought to know how to say it, don't you think?'" Cf. Wandrei to HPL, 21 May 1934: "P.P.S. Copy of 'Fantasy Magazine' arrived, containing interview with me. Schwartz & Weisinger garbled a remark I made about 'The Call of Cthulhu' into an anecdote that is discreditable to both you and me. I have already taken them to task, and I herewith extend apologies for my unfortunate part in the incident. I knew nothing of their action until the interview appeared, and the quotations are flatly not mine" (*Mysteries of Time and Spirit* 345).

4. By William B. Seabrook.

5. Probably Thomas Moran (1837–1926), American painter and printmaker whose work often featured the Rocky Mountains.

6. See *New Introductory Lectures on Psycho-Analysis*, tr. James Strachey et al. (London: Hogarth Press, 1933), esp. Lecture XXX ("Dreams and Occultism").

7. HPL refers to the story published as "The Sorcery of Aphlar."

8. See DWR 15n10.

9. "Homes and Shrines of Poe."

10. HPL had assisted Moe in preparing the book in 1929. It was never published.

[16]   [ALS, JHL]

Out in Roger Williams Park
—August 10, 1934.

My dear Rimel:—

I enjoyed very much your interesting letter of the 30th, the excellent snap-shots, & the Lewiston cards & drawing by your father which have just arrived. I am herewith returning the latter in the envelope provided for that purpose. Please congratulate the artist for me on the marvellously vivid way he has captured the rugged mountain scenery. I envy him his talent—which shines also in the magnificent paintings of which you enclosed photographs.

You certainly have had some weather—though nothing approaching it has been noted hereabouts. I doubt if it has been over 90° since my return home, & nearly all the evenings get too cool for my comfort. Coastal regions seldom get the extremes common to inland places. The Middle West seems to have suffered most—with the drought as a complicating factor. The latter has existed here, so that most of our lawns—unless artificially watered—are burned to a dull grey or brown. I haven't seen a real rain since the deluge season in De Land, which ended around the middle of June.

As for that recent spoof in weird & science fiction circles—I was amused to note how many have attributed it to me . . . . despite the fact that it is scarcely the sort of thing a staid old-timer would be likely to start.[1] Especially since the Eastern recipients say it came long before I passed through Washington. I found a copy when I got home, & was considerably amused by it. If you'll look more closely, you'll see that I was *not* left out—since "Horse-Power Hateart" can scarcely refer to anyone but myself. Oddly, the only name given without a comic twist is that of Otis Adelbert Kline. I don't know why they left him as he was—it would have been easy to think up something like Oatmeal Addlepate Crime. The fling at Little Effjay was rather apt—though many of the others were so personal that they can only be guessed at by those not 'in the know'. Curious that one of the corrections looked like my script—I didn't notice it, but will take another glance if I can find the thing.

Yes—Hornig told me that the old Scott house in Elizabethtown was gone, & I mo[u]rned very deeply when I heard the news. It was built in 1760 or so, & once had extensive landscaped grounds—though these had disappeared when I knew it in 1924 & 1925. The whole town is very attractive & full of vestiges of the past, though it has changed a lot since 1925. I almost took a room there a decade ago, but found prices so high that I stuck it out in Brooklyn till I finally returned to Providence. The oldest house dates back to 1664, & there are many pre-revolutionary structures left.

Well—I had a great trip, but was glad to get home. I used to be extremely homesick even on short trips, but do not become so now if I know that everything is ready for me—books, pictures, & all familiar objects—when I do get home. But I *would* be homesick if all my roots in Providence were pulled up. I was in 1924 & 1925, when I had moved completely to Brooklyn.

Your musical engagement on the Oregon state line must have had its interesting aspects, even though the celebration as a whole was garish & boresome. The scenery you describe was surely marvellously impressive—& the trip & camping sound like highly pleasant experiences. I can understand the delight of exceptional drinking-water—especially after a trip to Florida, where the water is often relatively poor. (in St Augustine it is infused with some unpleasant sulphur compound—very healthful but annoying) Once in a while one stumbles on a rare well or spring that one always remembers. The best I've ever struck are a well on an abandoned farm amidst the sandy heights of northern Rhode Island, & a spring in a wooded ravine in Westover Hills, across the James from Richmond. Close rivals are the so-called "Gunnery Spring" in Fredericksburg, & an unnamed spring in the Wissahickon gorge near Philadelphia. Just what makes these particular springs so bracing (aside from their ice-coldness), it would take a geologist to figure out.

Little Sam Perkins continues to be an important figure in the neighbourhood of 66 College. He was ill a week ago—languid & drooping—but is now quite his dynamic little self again. He purrs off & on, but not very steadily. His eyes are turning out to be yellow, & his face is one of the prettiest I have ever seen. Altogether, he is an unimaginably graceful little piece of the night! I've tried to snap him twice, but shan't know how well or ill I've succeeded till the film is developed. You'll be sorry to hear that his big sister Betsey has suddenly disappeared—a very singular thing, since she never went out of the garden & on the streets where she might be run over. The people at the boarding house are quite disconsolate. As for the name—an old lady at the boarding house[2] started the *Perkins* business last February when Betsey & her 2 brothers were born. For some reason or other—perhaps because "Perkins" has a kind of quaint, old-fashioned sound—she named the black & white kitten "Betsey Perkins", though leaving the others (slated for presentation to a family across the city) undesignated. I, however, called the little fellows "Newman Perkins" & "Ebenezer Perkins" after ancestors of my own—for I have a Perkins line. When the black kitten appeared, I went back along my Perkins ancestry & called him Samuel, after a forbear who fought in King Philip's War in 1676. If there are any more kittens later on, I shall probably keep going back along my Perkins line (which is traceable to 1380 in Shropshire & Warwickshire) for names—*John* being the next in order. But I seldom call a cat by any *one* name. When I speak to little Sam I call him all sorts of things—"Little Black Devil", "Old Nigger Man", "Spawn of the Shadows", "Little Piece of the Night", "Old Black Panther", "Little Onyx Sphinx",

"Child of Bast", & so on, & so on . . . . . not excluding the succinct & universal "kittie"! Regarding a name for your splendid snow-white beast, I fancy the Arctic suggestions of his colour might serve as a guide. He could be one of the frosty gods of our old Northern ancestors—Odin, Thor, Freyr, Ymir, Loki, & so on . . . . or you could name him *Crom,* after the icy deity of Bob Howard's mythical "Cimmeria". "Polaris" wouldn't be a bad monicker—& if you wanted to go to the *antarctic* for your snowy whiteness, you could call him "Tekeli-li" after the cry of the bird in the white polar world of Poe's "Arthur Gordon Pym". Thanks immensely for the picture of yourself & the furry gentleman—which shews up splendidly under a magnifying glass. Very glad to see the other pictures, too—now I have a good idea of what you & Baldwin really look like! Incidentally, I'm enclosing a picture of myself which Barlow took when trying out his new camera,[3] & which turned out to be the best likeness I've had in 30 years or more. Though only an experimental job— you'll note the spots due to careless developing—it somehow caught my typical expression as no formally posed picture ever could have done except by chance; & my aunt likes it so well that she has framed her copy! A damn poor subject—but it certainly looks like what the camera was aimed at! You can keep this print if you like. I also enclose—subject to return—a print of Barlow's Cthulhu bas-relief taken with the same camera. The original clay plaque now hangs on my walls. I think you'll agree that Barlow did marvellously well.

Glad the mosquitoes aren't thick—they're rather pestiferous here. For the last decade or so Providence has been remarkably mosquitoless because of the chemical treatment of the ponds; but finances for this work are now lacking, so that the winged pests are staging a gradual comeback. If the drought has exterminated them in your region, it will have given at least a little pay to compensate for its devastations! Glad the rheumatism is gone, & hope it will stay gone permanently.

I liked "The Blind Spot" myself, & must read the sequel sooner or later. No hurry about passing things on—get your fill of each story while it's with you. I am literally swamped with reading matter—haven't read the latest W.T. or the new *Terror Tales,* & a book given me by Derleth & 3 lent by Koenig remain equally untouched. Glad you like Dunsany. The "Nuflo" tale wasn't bad—obviously a Seabrook derivative.[4] I also liked Klarkash-Ton's "Epiphany of Death". And as I guess I said before, I am immensely pleased & encouraged by the way both you & Baldwin react to the "Mts. of Madness". Too bad the F F pulled such a boner in printing "Yith"[5]—but that's what they do to all MSS.

Glad my notes on story-composition seem clearer & more helpful now. It astonishes me to learn that you've never read "Randolph Carter", since I thought I had lent you & Baldwin every tale I ever wrote—or rather, every tale I have not definitely repudiated & withdrawn from circulation. Let me hasten to repair the omission by enclosing herewith the MS. in question. If Baldwin hasn't read it, let him. This tale is an almost literal transcript of a dream I had in December 1919—with myself in the role of "Carter" & my friend Samuel Loveman in that of "Warren." The dream was incredibly vivid & horrible, & when I awaked I hastened to write it down in the form of notes. Less than a week later I prepared the story version. Your plot about the tomb-gems, the hellish book, the ghoul, & the footprints sounds excellent to me, & I hope you will go ahead & develop it.

Glad you like "The Nameless City". Yes—it will appear in the F F. C A S did not get in touch with amateur journalism till the beginning of the great decline which almost put an end to it prior to 1930, hence had very little—only a few poems—in the amateur papers. He has had many poems in the small poetry magazines, & in his local paper, *The Auburn Journal.*

Whitehead's "Black Beast"—the "Magic Island" derivative—is a great story, & I am sending you a copy under separate cover. Please return it some time, though there is no hurry. Better give Baldwin a chance to read it.

Regarding ink—what I now use is Sheaffer's Skrip, *permanent jet black*. Be sure to specify the *permanent*, for they have another kind that washes out, which some people use to avoid hopeless ink spots. It is more expensive than the Waterman's & Carter's which I used to use, but is so much better that it's worth the difference. I guess I've told you of the trouble I always have with fountain pens. Sheaffer's is the only ink I've ever struck which is *thin* enough to afford the free flow I need. My aunt introduced me to it a year or two ago. Better inks, though, may exist. Wandrei uses *Higgins'*—still more expensive—& Morton thinks there is nothing equal to *Parker's "Quink"*—whose quick-drying feature appeals to him. That, I believe, costs about the same as Sheaffer's. I get Sheaffer's in 25¢ bottles—which now have a patent filling device.

As I said before, I'm immensely grateful for the pictures. The snap of the northeastern hills is doubly interesting now that I've seen your father's crayon rendering of the same region. The drawing brings out the significant essence & latent beauty of the scene in magnificent fashion. Glad to see the exact locale of "The Tree on the Hill." About the painting of the "25"—if the library display it well, that would really be a good place to leave it—where the public can enjoy it. On the other hand, if it is tucked away in some corner of doubtful accessibility, I'd advise your father to reclaim it for personal possession & household display. Your photographs of his other paintings are splendid—as are the paintings themselves—& I think you have coped nobly with the colour difficulties. That is what Donald Wandrei was up against when he took those photographs of his brother's drawings—some very highly coloured—which you saw. I have studied the pictures with a magnifying glass, & hardly have words with which to express my appreciation of their glamour & charm. I agree with you that the Grand Canyon one is probably the greatest . . . . & the limitations you mention do not obscure its merit in any way. Most certainly, your father is a real artist of the first water—& if he were to devote himself wholly to painting I don't doubt but that he would quickly gain recognition in the most serious professional circles.

I was very glad to see the excellent panoramic view of Asotin's main business street—a finely planned shot with its picturesque scope & its mountainous background with the omnipresent "25". What you explain of various buildings, ruins, & other features adds immensely to its interest. The town is certainly an attractive & impressively situated one, whatever its limitations as a buying centre may be!

Interested to hear of the changes in the new "Yith" verse, & hope it won't get too badly mangled when printed. Glad "The Snake" appeared in the Lewiston paper—it certainly deserved recognition. Hope you'll follow it up. As for what newspapers & magazines do with the return envelopes when they accept contributions—it seems to be the custom for them to retain these items. Whether they soak off & use the stamps I really couldn't say—I must ask Wright some time. But anyhow, the tactics of the Lewiston editor were only the usual ones everywhere met with. Glad you'll have some verses in *Marvel Tales*. #2 of this venture seems to me a vast improvement both literarily & mechanically. #3 will be cruder in outward aspect, since a recent accident to the press has caused the impression to be relatively poor. The booklet idea strikes me as excellent. I've never seen "The White Sibyl", but believe Klarkash-Ton thinks quite highly of it. As for Long's story[6]—it's curious how differently different people react to it. I thought it excellent—one of his best *recent* efforts—because of the restrained, brooding atmosphere of menace, & because of the absence of the pseudo-sophisticated snickering irony with which Belknap spoils so many of his tales. The one great fault was the excessive amount of soliloquy attributed to the idiot boy. It was a clumsy, amateurish device to have so much of the explanation of preceding events concentrated in this soliloquy. All this explanatory preparation ought to have been introduced imperceptibly in other places—for no soliloquiser—idiot or not—would ever recapitulate a whole chain of events like that. Also—the *poetic* reflections toward the end of the idiot's soliloquy are wholly out of keeping with the character of a rural nitwit. But in spite of these obvious defects I thought the story a good one. Others—notably Robert Bloch & Farnsworth Wright—agree with you.

As for communication at a distance, & whether or not unrecognised senses exist—that is for psychologists & biologists of the future to settle. Fortune-telling, of course, is absolute charlatanry—whether through palmistry, astrology, or any other fake.

Yes—Long has seen the picture of Barlow's statuette. The elephant-god in question is probably a form of the Hindoo Ganesa, & the prototypical statuette is in the Louvre in Paris. Long has a reproduction of this statuette—about a foot tall & of the same greenish colour as the original—which his aunt bought him when in Paris . . . they sell these fac-similes at the Louvre. It was from a discussion of this statue which he & I had several years ago, that the idea of the Chaugnar story was born. I said it would be interesting to have a Chinaman fall down in fear before the statue in the Louvre, & scream something about "those who tramp on the mountains"—& Belknap did the rest . . . . . except for the Roman dream incident, which I wrote as a literal transcript of an actual dream I had in October 1927.[7] Belknap's statue has a headdress, & differs in other slight details from Barlow's.

The difficulty of securing magazines in Asotin is surely annoying, & I really wonder whether one couldn't profitably establish a news stand there. Even if most of the residents do subscribe to things, they might buy from a stand if one were available. But of course it would take a regular business man to found such a thing—& I fancy you don't relish commercial tactics much better than I do! The really best thing would be for a druggist or someone like that—already established in business—to put in some magazines as a side line. I wonder just what the population of Asotin is—that is, the number of people depending largely on its business section for their every-day purchases?

Yes—I like your brief fantastic tale, & hope it may win advantageous placement. Hope the Blue Stone, too, will turn out well. About Bloch—he must be just about 17 now, a year older than Barlow. He's not quite as far advanced as Derleth was at his age, but is coming ahead steadily. His present fault is overcolouring—he lays horror on too thickly—too many adjectives & theatrical flourishes.

Sorry the Tree didn't land with Wright, but its long tarrying in the office was a good sign. Better send along the Brick—you never can tell just when a yarn will strike Wright's fancy.

As I said, I am very grateful for the Lewiston cards—& shall likewise welcome those of the once-familiar OWYHEE region. That name, by the way, is the old-fashioned way of rendering the native designation of the Sandwich Islands—now rendered HAWAII. I've often wondered just how it came to be fastened to an Idaho county—but I know that in the old days people liked to apply exotic geographical names. It would be interesting to have a view of the successor of the ill-fated dam about which I used to hear so much in the late '90s & early 1900's. But don't take too much trouble about the matter—sooner or later you'll probably find some views easily accessible.

Glad you enjoyed the N.A.P.A. items. Since then I've sent along a fresh lot, which I hope will prove equally interesting. When you join you'll be no raw recruit—since you'll have quite a familiarity with the amateur press. I'll see that you get a copy of that article on Poe houses. Just now I've prepared a hasty critical report for the Natl. Amateur, although I'm no longer officially a critic.[8] I shall accept reappointment only if no other qualified victim can be found.

Yes—I read "Burn, Witch, Burn!" at Barlow's—in fact, I completed a 100% reading of all of Merritt's work while there. This novel has possibilities, but is a little too much on the popular-adventure-detective order to be really artistic. Unfortunately Merritt can't quite shake off the artificial popular tradition. The sequel to this—"Creep, Shadow, Creep"—will appear in the *Argosy* during September.

Had an interesting guest Aug. 2–3–4, in the person of James F. Morton, curator of the Paterson N.J. municipal museum. We took in most of the local sights, & also made a trip to ancient Newport, 30 miles down the bay. Newport is a very quaint colonial town which has changed but little since the revolution. The skyline—dominated by the steeple of Trinity Church, built in 1726—is still typical of an old New England seaport. Houses of the 1600's & 1700's are common—including several public buildings of importance. In short, it is a place like Charleston or Salem. We went by boat, & saw the assembled U.S. fleet in the harbour—also exploring the venerable streets & walking on the famous ocean cliffs. The enclosed card shews old Trinity, with a churchyard full of material for Pickman's Model.

On Aug. 23 I expect to visit the old-time amateur Edward H. Cole for a few days—in Wollaston, just south of Boston. W. Paul Cook will also be on hand—for he is leaving Vermont & on the lookout for professional openings in Boston & N.Y. We shall all have a pretty good time if I can get my work in any kind of shape by then.

Price has paid Klarkash-Ton a second visit, & both report the occasion as highly pleasant. Bob Howard lately visited the vast Carlsbad Caverns & was almost stupefied by their colossal nightmare magnificence. R. F. Searight has been travelling enjoyably in Michigan's northern peninsula. Donald Wandrei is making an extensive canoe trip with friends in Minnesota. Barlow expects to go to Daytona Beach for a while soon, & will come north to Washington in September for optical treatment. Long & his parents spent a weekend recently at Atlantic City.

Well—night creeps on apace, & I'd better quit. Again thanks for all the various pictures—& I hope your father's crayon drawings will get back safely. Regards to Baldwin, & good luck with all your ventures. Haven't seen little Sam Perkins today, but had a long & pleasant conversation with Pres. Randall of the Kappa Alpha Tau as I left #66. Mr. Randall is black & white, largely, elderly, & dignified—hard to get acquainted with, but very cordial when once you know him. Once in a while—with old friends—he rolls over & plays like a kitten! ¶ Best wishes—

Yrs most sincerely—
H P L

Notes

1 "The Battle That Ended the Century." HPL did in fact have a hand in it, collaborating on it with RHB.

2. I.e., Marian F. Bonner residing at The Arsdale at 55 Waterman Street, just behind HPL's residence.

3. See frontispiece, *Selected Letters* 5.

4. Nuflo is a character in *Green Mansions: A Romance of the Tropical Forest* (1904), but HPL refers to the story "The Thunderstones of Nuflo" by Ralph Allen Lang (*WT*, July 1934) as being derivative not of that but of Seagrave's *The Magic Island.*

5. HPL probably refers to a typographical error in Sonnet I, line 2 of "Dreams of Yith" (*FF*, July 1934). The printed line reads "On far-flung islands lost to worldly years," but the final word must in reality be "eyes" (to rhyme with "cries" in line 4).

6. "The Dark Beasts," *Marvel Tales* 1, No. 2 (July–August 1934).

7. Frank Belknap Long, *The Horror from the Hills.* HPL's Roman dream, as described in a letter to Donald Wandrei, was published as "The Very Old Folk."

8. "Chairman of the Bureau of Critics Reports on Poetry."

[17]   [ALS, JHL]

August 23[, 1934]

My dear Rimel:—

This is going to be a very poor reply to your interesting letter of the 17th, but I want to hustle it off before I start on the trip which will form my last of the 1934 season. As I've just written Baldwin, I'm going to spend the week end with Edward H. Cole in Boston—incidentally seeing W. Paul Cook—& then I'm going to try to get to ancient Nantucket—an island town which I've never seen, but which everyone tells me is the most unchanged bit of early Americana in existence. According to some, it will reduce to insignificance all the other ancient towns I've ever seen. Well—time will tell. Hope I'll have good weather—it has been beastly cold here. I'll probably be back in a week or a little more. Am having a hades of a time getting my work cleaned up—a rush verse-revision job arrived at the last moment & has forced me to cut out 2 nights' sleep . . . . but I'll make it up on the trip.

Under separate cover I've sent you "The Hill of Dreams"—an exquisite portrait of a sensitive young author which I hope you'll enjoy. The actual supernatural does not figure in it, but there is so much about dream life & weird scenery that it almost comes into the bizarre category. It is probably the greatest thing that Machen ever wrote—the prose is exquisite. Don't hurry about returning it, and let Baldwin read it. Glad the other books aren't disappointing. Like a fool I seem to have lost the list of books I've lent you—which you sent recently—but I hope to find it when I get home & thus avoid asking you to supply another. About "The Willows"—I consider its "outsideness" much *better* than that in any of my own tales. It is subtler & cleverer in every way. I wish I could write like that! Yes—the August W T beats the July. The Moore tale (which I read in MS. in De Land) is excellent; but as you say, not up to the author's previous work. Howard's yarn is the next best, & Flagg's deserves honourable mention. Cave's, too, is not bad for commercial stuff.

Little Sam Perkins gets bigger & more playful all the time. No—Betsey never turned up. She must have been either run over by a motor or stolen. I'd surely like to see old white Crom—who I take to be rather more amiable than his chromatic counterpart Doodle Bug of De Land. Interested to hear of the changes through which the name *Rimel* has passed. How is it pronounced? Barlow, Long, & I have been calling you Rî-*Mel* . . . . but from what you say I judge that the correct version is *Rye'*-mel—with a long ī. My friend Talman also stems from Holland in the male line, his ancestor (whose name was spelled *Taelman*) coming to Nieuw Nederland in 1630 or so. Did I send you a copy of the quarterly he edits for the Holland Society of N.Y.—with my article on Dutch influences in New England?[1] Glad you liked the portrait. I usually photograph rottenly—my pictures tend to look fierce & savage, though I'm the mildest old gentleman that ever stroked a kitten! Barlow knows how to pose subjects & arrange lighting.

I bought & read *Terror Tales,* I found it cheap & wretched. Don't waste your cash on it. I liked "The Blind Spot", & am going to borrow the sequel from Baldwin. One of the authors of the original—Flint—is now dead. About those things of mine you haven't read—I've virtually disavowed "The Tree", "Herbert West", & "Hypnos". I have no loose copies of these, but will try to lend you "Hypnos" (the least rotten of the three) in the big Summer 1924 W T some day.[2] Glad you like "Randolph Carter". That's the second time a friend of Loveman's has killed him off in fiction[3]—he seems to be a popular victim!

Well—I've read "The Jewels of Sharlotte" (is that name an actual variant of Charlotte?) & believe it marks a vast amount of progress on your part. Good work! The reading you're doing is taking effect! Some might say that not enough is revealed—but to me this artistic reticence is one of the most effective points. Your prose style & sense of structure are improving by leaps & bounds, & I honestly don't think it will be long before you make W T. In the present tale, as you may see, I haven't made a single *major* change. Just a few rearrangements & substitutions, & it stands as originally written. Congratulations! You work up a magnificent atmosphere of menace—through hints & details—nor is there any letdown anywhere. A darned good job! Send it around, beginning with W T. And incidentally, by all means try "The Tree on the Hill" on Crawford. Glad "The Ship" is to appear—& that "Aphlar" has landed with Hornig. Hope Wright takes "The Tenth Brick"—if he doesn't, there are always the small magazines. I've just renewed my F F subscription. Yes—Derleth started contributing at 15, although his style was very slow in maturing. Wandrei started at 17 & matured very quickly. It takes time to get into a professional magazine. None of the stuff I wrote before the age of 25—fiction, that is—could possibly have made a periodical of the W T grade. Glad C A S continues helpful.

No—Klarkash-Ton never had anything in *Driftwind.* Whitehead's "Black Beast" was in *Adventure*—you'll like it. I gave H S W the idea for "Cassius"— at first he wanted me to collaborate, but our styles & approaches were so different that I couldn't. It all came from a freak I saw in a dime museum—an Italian with a rudimentary twin growing out of his abdomen.[4] Some time I'll tell you how I had meant to develop the theme—I may do it yet. About the puppets in "Burn Witch Burn"—Merritt didn't necessarily get the idea from "The White People", since this form of magic is very well known & widely exploited. Some day I'll lend you the 2 issues of W T containing Long's elephant-god story. As for books on witchcraft, vampires, magic, &c aside from fiction—I regret that I don't possess any notable specimens, but you might try the libraries for Arthur Edward Waite's "History of Magic"[5] & other works, for a popular treatise of the sort (I forget the name—possibly "The Romance of Sorcery") by Sax Rohmer, for any of the curious works of "Eliphas Levi", & for the monumental anthropological studies ("The Vampire, his Kith & Kin", "The Vampire in Europe", "The Geography of Witchcraft", &c. &c.) of the Rev. Montague Summers (C A S owns one, Koenig others). Also read the old witch trial reports—Kremer & Sprenger's "Malleus Maleficarum", "The Examen of Witches,"[6] &c. And any & all books on the Salem Witchcraft. I could lend you Sir Walter Scott's rather tame & unscientific "Demonology & Witchcraft", & you might find (in some large city library— say Spokane) a copy of the standard treatise on the actual secret organisation of mediaeval "witches"—"The Witch-Cult in Western Europe", by Margaret Alice Murray. Anthropological works like Frazer's "Golden Bough" have much witch material, & the books on savage folklore embodying bits of the subject are almost limitless. Koenig can help you out better than I on loans. Drop him a line on the subject—540 E. 80th St., N.Y. City.

Glad the N.A.P.A. journals came. About the Recluse Press—except for my still unbound "Shunned House", & for the contributions in the one issue of *The Recluse*, it printed nothing by either C A S or myself. Cook, however, used some of my stuff in his earlier amateur magazine, *The Vagrant*.

About inks—I think Skrip is about as good as there is. I like black best, but used blue-black for years because I could never get a black that worked decently in any pen I had. Then my aunt tipped me off to Sheaffer's—& you see the result. I never used the Washable.

I'm certainly indebted both to you & to your father for pictorial glimpses. Glad he's embarking on another productive period & planning another canvas of "The 25". His work is splendid indeed. You might do better in black & white—individual aptitudes vary enormously. That "Yith" heading certainly displays vast talent. Interested to hear that your father is a Justice of the Peace—marrying couples of various types must surely give him quite an insight into human nature. That incident of the English bride was surely tragic enough!

You'll find plenty of *Tribune* subjects in time. Something about a "Ghost City" would be splendid. Interested to see views of Asotin & to learn of its population & relation to Lewiston. You are only half as far from Lewiston as the Barlows are from De Land village! Hope Asotin will ultimately get a news stand somehow.

About a list of Merritt's works—I included one in my recent letter to F. Lee, & fancy you'll see that shortly. ¶ Barlow is spending a fortnight at Daytona Beach, & on Sept. 2 will start for his ocular siege in Washington. ¶ Well—I must be hustling for the Boston 'bus. I'll send you cards of any interesting antiquities I see. Nantucket will probably be great! ¶ Apologies for brevity & omissions. ¶ All good wishes, & regards to your father. And renewed congratulations on the new story!

Yrs most cordially—
H P L

P.S. No—magazines almost never return the MSS. of stories they accept. Most of them, though, would probably be willing to do so on request.

Notes

1. "Some Dutch Footprints in New England."
2. The issue, which contained three pieces by HPL (only one with his own byline), was in a very large format.
3. The other instance is unidentified.
4. HPL made the following entry (no. 133) in his commonplace book: "Man has miniature shapeless Siamese twin—exhib. in circus—twin surgically detached—disappears—does hideous things with malign life of his own. [HSW—Cassius]" The concluding note was written for the edification of RHB years after the entry had been made.
5. Waite's "history" was his translation of *Histoire de la magie, avec une exposition claire et précise de ses procedes, de ses rites et de ses mysteres* (1860) by Eliphas Lévi (pseud. of Alphonse Louis Constant).
6. By Henri Boguet.

[18]   [ALS, JHL]

66 College St.,
Providence, R.I.,
Septr. 12, 1934.

My dear Ryé´-mel:—[I'll get that straight in my instinctive consciousness if it kills me! Hope Barlow, the sharer of my error, will do the same.]

I was very glad indeed to receive yours of the 30th, & trust you have meanwhile received the folder of Nantucket views. I also sent some cards to Baldwin, so that by comparing notes the two of you can form quite an idea of the ancient scenes I have been enjoying. Here are two or three more cards for good measure.

I certainly had a great time. Nantucket is, without question, the most perfectly preserved bit of the elder America that I have ever seen—& it is really almost comical that I should discover it only at this late date, after pursuing antiquities all the way from Quebec to Key West & New Orleans. Here, just 90 miles from my own doorstep, is a Yankee whaling port of a century or more ago which has not changed in the slightest detail since the old days. Cobblestoned streets with nothing but colonial houses on either side—horse-blocks, hitching-posts, & silver doorplates—picturesque alleys & wharves—a 1746 windmill on a hilltop—old churches with box pews & galleries—everything that the antiquarian could ask for! I stayed a week, having a room at The Overlook—an hotel made over from a large house 150 or more years old, with small-paned windows, wide floor-boards, six-panel doors, & all the rest. I was on the 3d floor, with a splendid view of town, harbour, & sea. During my stay I saw about everything there was to see—exploring all the ancient streets & lanes, entering all the old churches & public buildings & museums, & studying the mechanism (still effective) of the 188-year-old windmill. I also observed Saturn & its ring through the 5″ reflecting telescope of the Maria Mitchell Observatory—an adjunct of the birthplace of Maria Mitchell, the famous female astronomer. The outlying districts I studied by means of a hired bicycle—this being the first time in 20 years that I had been on a wheel. Riding was just as easy & familiar as if I had last dismounted only the day before—this evidently being a thing one does not easily forget. It was a most exhilarating & rejuvenating experience—bringing back so many memories of youth that I half felt as if I ought to hurry home for the opening of Hope St. High School! I wish it weren't conspicuous for a man of my age to ride a wheel in Providence. In my youth I was scarcely ever off one! Well—I also took a motor sightseeing trip around the entire island, seeing among other things the quaint old fishing village of Siasconset (locally pronounced *Sconset*) with its tiny shingled cottages & rambling, garden-bordered lanes. This is now a thriving summer-resort. The island as a whole is roughly 15 miles long & 7 wide, mostly a rolling expanse of treeless moors. There are a few scrub pine groves—while the town has magnificent trees. The town (called *Sherburne* until 1795, but thereafter *Nantucket* after the entire island) is on the north shore of the island, on a fine land locked harbour. It dates only from about 1722, the bulk of the houses having previously been farther west—on a small harbour which in 1720 was closed by a sand bar. Nantucket was first noticed by Gosnold in 1605,[1] & was settled about 1660 by Massachusetts people—a great part of whom became Quakers a little later. In 1664 it was made part of the Province of New York, & in 1692 it was transferred to Massachusetts. Its great prosperity came from the whaling industry, which began about 1670. Whales were first sighted from observation towers & killed off shore from small boats; but when they grew scarce in New England waters the Nantucketers began to fit out whaling ships & pursue them. By 1730 Nantucket whalers covered the whole Atlantic, & after 1791 they rounded Cape Horn & invaded the Pacific. The revolution & war of 1812 were great setbacks, but in spite of everything the industry rose to a climax in 1842, when the town was immensely wealthy & the island had a population of about 10,000. After that there was a steady decline. The demand for whale oil fell off, & sperm whales grew scarce. The last Nantucket whaler came home in 1870, & after that the town almost fell to ruin. Oddly enough, the Nantucketers never cared to go after the so-called "right whale" (the kind with whalebone in its jaws), which remained more plentiful. This kind of whaling was left to New Bedford, which kept the industry going half a century more. Few realise that the greater part of New Bedford's famous whaling career lay during the decline of the industry. The last whaler went out of New Bedford in 1922—during your own lifetime—which shews how closely this grand old industry is linked with the present. The only whalers today are Norwegians, who use large steam vessels & shoot their harpoons from guns. Whaling apparatus, however, is still manufactured in New England; & a few Yankees still ship on the Norwegian vessels.

Since 1870 the summer-resort traffic alone has kept Nantucket alive. The depth of the mid-century depression was such that in 1870 one could buy a fine Nantucket house & lot for $200—or hire one for $5.00 per month! Providentially enough, this kept people from building new houses—so that we still have the ancient town just as it used to be. The summer visitors—who have been coming ever since '72 or '73—have taken pride in preserving & restoring everything just as it was. In appearance, Nantucket town is something like Salem—except that it lacks the 17th century gabled type of house. Or rather, it looks as Salem did 100 years ago. There are some fine old Georgian mansions, many pillared classical edifices, churches with quaint belfry or steeple, & any number of simple colonial cottages. The favourite type of house before 1780 or 1790 was the so-called "Salt Box" style, well illustrated by the oldest house on the island (1686) as portrayed in the folder. This type—also common on the Massachusetts mainland—was of 2 stories in front, but with a roof sloping to the ground on the rear side (always the north). A typical feature of the town houses is a railed platform on the roof, from which in the old days the shipping was assiduously watched. Other New England seaports have corresponding architectural features—cupolas or promenades along the edge of the roof—but nowhere else is the "walk" so commonly found, or of exactly the same pattern. The platform tends to be small—usually surrounding a great central chimney. Nantucket's year-round population is now reduced to about 3800—all descendants of the ancient stock . . . . Macys, Coffins, Starbucks, Folgers, Husseys, Pinkhams, Gardners, Rays, &c. Benjamin Franklin's mother was a Nantucket Folger. The chief industry is summer-resort real estate, but a small amount of fishing persists—largely for flounders & deep-sea molluscs. Despite the plethora of vacationists, I don't know of any place where the early-American atmosphere survives so well. It is like another world—& yet it lies only a 6-hour trip (1 hour by motor-coach to New Bedford, plus a 5-hour sail) from Providence. I hated to leave, & certainly hope to get there again next summer. The only flaw in the trip was the cold weather which prevailed during the middle days of my sojourn—that, & the high (for my perilously lean purse) prices which prevail for food & lodgings. The climate of Nantucket—being tempered by the sea—is more equable than that of mainland New England. The summers are cooler, & the winters warmer. Owing to this last circumstance the vegetation is gratifyingly rich—including shrubs & creepers not usually found north of Virginia. During the last terrible winter the hedges of Nantucket were not killed by the cold as were those on the mainland.

The antiquarian charm of Nantucket almost overshadowed the earlier half of my outing; & yet that was highly enjoyable, too. Boston has a distinct old-world charm, & is generally considered to resemble a typical European city—notably London—more than any other place in America. It has very few tall buildings, & the traditional skyline of chimneys, spires, & domes is from certain vantage-points very striking. The most fascinating section is Beacon Hill, where the old brick mansions of the late 18th & early 19th centuries remain unchanged. This section—especially Louisburg square—is often sought by cinema companies wishing to film old London scenes. For sheer beauty, though, I prefer Providence. My visit was in one of the southern suburbs—Wollaston—but I saw Boston proper every day. Cook stopped at his old rooming-house on the north slope of Beacon Hill. We took side-trips to Salem, Marblehead, Nahant, & Haverhill—visiting good old "Tryout" Smith (82 next month) at the latter place. You surely must see this region some time—allowing plenty of time to do it, since the points of scenic, historic, & antiquarian interest are virtually inexhaustible. On this occasion Cole & his family brought me home in their car—& my aunt & I shewed them around Providence a bit. I merely stopped over night in my own home—not even unpacking my valise—& set out for Nantucket the next morning.

I returned from Nantucket on the evening of Sept. 3d, & have since been immersed in a maelstrom of accumulated work. Just now I am the sole lord of all I survey—since my aunt is in Ogunquit, Maine, for a fortnight. It is impossible, however, to be lonely with little Sam Perkins as a guest! How that tiny devil has grown! After offering fight to all the huge Toms of the Kappa Alpha Tau he has now made his peace with them, & is often to be seen curled up on the clubhouse roof—a duly initiated member! He is more wildly playful than ever—if such a thing be possible—& now purrs like a young steam engine. He sends his most cordial regards to Crom—a being so much his opposite in a chromatic way!

I still do a good deal of my reading & writing outdoors, but can easily see that autumn is close at hand. Some elm leaves are prematurely falling, & occasional bonfires attest the advent of harvest-time & the birth of the melancholy season. I notice the shorter days—though daylight-saving time gives this section longer evenings than other parts of the country enjoy. Around the 22nd will come the harvest moon (the one nearest the equinox, not the August full, bears this title), rising at nearly the same time night after night & flooding the fields of sheaves . . . . an ancient magic on an ancient land. We have gorgeous sunsets, too—though perhaps your western ones have certain qualities lacked by ours. Wandrei tells me that in St. Paul a certain kind of dust from the prairies gives the sky a set of bizarre effects absolutely unknown elsewhere.[2] However, I know the sort of sunset caused by a smoky atmosphere—since, alas, forest fires are by no means a purely western phenomenon. It may surprise you to know that—despite the oft-repeated fact that Rhode Island is the most densely-populated political unit in the world except Belgium—this state *has the largest proportion of woodland of any state in the union.* The secret of this paradox is that our population is all packed into the urban population centres & along the factory-lined river valleys. Beyond these areas there are miles & miles of utterly deserted countryside & deep woods. Some westerners think of the east as completely filled up & without open spaces—yet there is not a New England state in which a person couldn't wander all day without meeting any evidence of human habitation if he chose the right areas. This was less so in 1790 than today, for during the 18th century the farming population covered a good deal of ground. As soon as the factories, [*sic*] appeared, however, the people began to drift toward the towns & river-valleys; leaving the back country in an increasing state of desertion. Today some of the wild animals are coming back—snakes are more abundant, & deer are frequently seen. Now & then vague rumours of a bear or wolf appear, though there is no real evidence that any of these formidable old-timers are on deck again. But bobcats certainly are on the increase. It is curious how an age of intensive urbanisation also promotes the return of the primitive wilderness! That green moon-effect you mention must have been very striking indeed—& obviously sprang from the smoke in the atmosphere. It is curious how certain substances act as ray-filters—giving us red suns, green moons, yellow days (such as New England had in 1880), & the like. The yellow day of half a century ago[3] was traced to the smoke of a volcanic eruption in the East Indies. By the way—the "green-cheese" moon theory wouldn't really involve the *colour* green at all, since "green" cheese means simply *new* & *unseasoned* cheese fresh from the press . . . . . what we ordinarily call *mild* cheese. This, of course, is whitish-yellow in hue—exactly as the moon appears in ordinary northern latitudes. In the tropics the moon has a striking *white* lustre not elsewhere seen. It was quite apparent in Dunedin in 1931, though not so marked this spring in De Land.

Glad "The Hill of Dreams" reached you safely—which reminds me that the other books have come back in good order. I know you'll like the "Hill"—which amply deserves its high reputation. Take your time about reading it—I also like to read important or congenial books very slowly, in order to assimilate all the overtones. Bought the Sept. W.T., but haven't had a moment to read it as yet. Those who have read it say it is rather poor. I also wait till a serial is done before I read it—since I can never appreciate a thing when a whole month elapses between fragments. Most of the W.T. serials are impossible junk, though anything by Bob Howard must be good. I read only a few—I didn't read "Golden Blood"[4] till a year after its publication, when Price told me how good it was. Williamson started out well, but his close friendship with Hamilton has caused him to adopt cheap pulp standards & fall into the usual trivial rut. His last alleged story was atrocious! The only good in *Terror Tales* is its ability to make us appreciate W.T.! At one time—before 1926—I thought W.T. was about as poor as a magazine could be. I had never read a Macfadden publication then. In that year I first saw *Ghost Stories* (now defunct), & began to see how much *worse* than W.T. a magazine in the same field could be! The account of Flint's death as usually given sounds so mysterious & melodramatic that one is inclined to suspect a certain touching-up in reporting. It would be interesting to get hold of newspapers giving the precise facts, so far as known, from an impersonal angle. In a way, this case parallels Ambrose Bierce's still mysterious withdrawal from human ken.

Your correspondent Dilbeck[5] surely must enjoy letter-writing if he wants to establish a regular weekly schedule! He couldn't do it if he had a correspondence the size of mine—I have some 51 or 52 regular correspondents, & perhaps 75 counting long-term occasionals. The list keeps growing, & only a very few drop off. Some are of 20 years' standing. If I ever adopt a more intensive working programme—as I may have to do—I shall have to train myself to write more briefly . . . . . although there is scarcely any correspondent whom I'd wish to drop. With me correspondence largely takes the place of conversation. I've found very few congenial persons in my own town, hence seldom do much conversing except when on visits. No—I never before heard of a weekly letter as a regular institution.

About "Hypnos"—some day when I have an unusual burst of time & energy I'll see if I can devise a way to send the large flat (& ill-conditioned) magazine containing it safely through the mails. I have no detached copy, & can't even think of typing one. But it's a very poor yarn—which I've virtually repudiated. I can't see yet why Loveman overvalues it so.

Glad that my verdict on your new story seemed encouraging. You're certainly getting there—& it probably won't be long before something of yours lands professionally. Your reading is certainly taking effect—& much more rapidly than in most cases. Yes—it is all right to send MSS. to an editor even when he is holding a previous one for decision. Each will be considered in its turn. Wright, by the way, is now in Seattle in your own state unless my informants err—so that anything sent to Chicago will have to wait a bit for consideration. As to notifications in case of acceptance—Wright always notifies, though a few others (including Bates when he edited *Strange* & *Astounding*) don't. If the "Brick" is accepted, you will be told of it. Delays of a month or two before the rendering of a decision are not uncommon when a story is good enough to pass the first reading. Crawford will probably take the "Tree" in the end, although his taste is frightfully undeveloped. He is utterly ignorant of real literary values, & holds some positively childish & laughable ideas on the merits of cheap pulp writers as compared with real authors. What is more, he is egotistically stubborn in his crude defence of cheapness & superficiality. When Derleth tried to set him right on literary values he became almost insulting, & precipitated a really bitter quarrel—although I fancy the youthful Comte August-Guillaume may have been a bit provocative in his conscious superiority! I've avoided bitter words so far—perhaps through the milder methods of elder years—though telling him practically the same things that Derleth told him. As a matter of fact, none of these semi-amateur editors—Crawford, Hornig, or Schwartz— has a very mature taste or a very thorough knowledge of literature. Schwartz is probably the most scholarly—he's a junior or senior at CCNY—& Hornig probably has the most natural taste. But all of them are earnest & devoted disciples of bizarre fiction, & they all deserve encouragement. Hornig may pay me a visit during the coming autumn or winter. He tells me that he's dedicating his October issue to me. He likes your "Yith" poems very much, & would welcome more . . . . . but don't *force* yourself to compose any. Wait till the ideas spontaneously come. That's the way I always do. I wrote 35 "Fungi from Yuggoth" in 1929–30, & haven't written any since! Which reminds me that Hornig is going to print some of those which W T didn't take.

Yes—Wandrei was 16 when he wrote "The Red Brain" . . . . which is one of a long cosmic series, most of which is still unpublished. I am urging him to let Hornig, Crawford, & Schwartz print the other items. Klarkash-Ton's first *story* in W.T.* was "The Ninth Skeleton" (Sept. 1928), although he had had *verse* appearing off & on since the early days of the magazine. He wrote fiction—of a more realistic cast than his present work—as early as 1910 or 1911; some of it appearing in the long-defunct *Black Cat*. He was then 17 or 18. Afterward he dropped prose entirely, not writing any stories again till 1925, when he produced "The Abominations of Yondo" (rejected by W T, published in the *Overland Monthly*) & "Sadastor" (also rejected by Wright, but accepted by him a few years later & printed in W T). "The Ninth Skeleton" was written long after "Yondo" & "Sadastor"—its early appearance being merely a matter of chance. Whitehead was one of the best & maturest writers ever connected with W T—there was a maximum of scholarship behind his work. About the twin story—I was divided between two plans of development. One would have had the monster escape as Whitehead had it—but would have had it much more terrible & much less human. I would have had it grow in size, & frighten people much more terribly than "Cassius" did. Indeed, I would have tried to convey the implication that some *Outside* force or

---

*the *second* (after which they came rapidly) was "The End of the Story"—May 1930.

daemon had taken possession of the brainless, twisted body—impelling it to strange acts of *apparently deliberate but plainly non-human motivation.* The climax would have consisted of some dramatic & unmistakable revelation of this Outside tenancy—probably connected with the spectacular destruction of the thing in one way or another. My story would have had none of the lightness, suavity, & humour of Whitehead's, but would have been grim & terrible all through. So much for *one* plot. The other plot I had in mind was much more human—not supernatural at all, in fact. This idea was to have the connexion of the man & his miniature twin *much more complex & obscure* than any doctor had suspected. The operation of separation is performed—but lo! An unforeseen horror & tragedy results. *For it seems that the brain of the twin-burdened man lay in the miniature twin alone . . . .* so that the operation has produced *a hideous monster only a foot tall, with the keen brain of a man,* & *a handsome manlike shell with the undeveloped brain of a total idiot.* From this situation I planned to develop an appropriate plot, although—from the magnitude of the task—I had not progressed very far. I had an idea of having the midget monster assume the guardianship of his handsome, brainless twin & endeavour to hypnotise it in such a way that it could do his talking for him & act as his substitute in the outside world. I meant to have him succeed, so that after about a year there appears in society a handsome, brilliant man *who always carries a satchel, & who displays vast alarm when there is any danger of his being separated from it.* This, of course, is the brainless twin—who now serves as the mouthpiece & exterior facade of the intelligent monster, who rules him by hypnotism from the shelter of the satchel. From then on I had decided nothing. One idea was to have an accident destroy the satchel, causing the idiot to collapse helplessly & perhaps die. Another was to have the man gain fame—but finally to have the idiot body die in such a way that the death can hardly be concealed. The intelligent twin still lives—but how can he now keep his secret? He may be able to hide bodily, but how can he continue the work which brought him fame (say as a writer or painter or scholar) when the famous man is supposed to be dead? I had not progressed to the point of solving that problem—or even deciding whether I'd have such a problem—when Whitehead began urging the collaboration & I finally gave him the plot to develop in his own way. Hence "Cassius". Now—after years—*another* alternative occurs to me. I might have the death of the handsome idiot-body concealed, & have the intelligent monster embalm it & display it seated in a chair—ostensibly still alive but paralysed. He would have it appear to speak—in a feeble, alien voice supposedly due to the paralysis—through the clever practice of ventriloquism. Then some awful climax of revelation could occur—any one of a dozen hideous sorts. The embalming could be *imperfect,* so that the supposedly living man would display signs of decomposition. Or notice could be attracted by its failure to age through the passing years. In writing such a story, I'd probably *begin near the end*—that is, have the bulk of the action concern the final phase, when the supposed paralytic begins to arouse suspicion. The antecedent history—the operation &c—would be subtly worked in as backflashes. I would make the revelation very gradual & suspense-filled—& at the last might leave the reader in some doubt of what the truth really was. Whether I shall ever do this or not remains to be seen. It certainly wouldn't be duplicating "Cassius"—for the whole spirit & emphasis of my conception is antipodally alien to Whitehead's. Whitehead urged me to go ahead & try—but I thought some time had better elapse in any case. I believe I mentioned that my idea came from seeing an actual case of the undeveloped-twin anomaly in a freak shew (Hubert's Museum in W. 42nd St.) in New York. The man in question—an intelligent Italian who for some reason billed himself under the French name of "Jean Libera"—had a little anthropoid excrescence growing out of his abdomen which looked hellishly gruesome when uncovered.[6] Clothed, he looked merely like a somewhat "pot-bellied" individual. So far as I know, he is still living & on exhibition. He looked so essentially refined & high-grade that I wondered at his willingness to be exploited as a freak, & speculated as to what he would do if a stroke of luck removed him from the need of such an ignominious occupation. The first thing he would do, I argued, would be to have the excrescence cut off—& then & there the idea of the story came. This was in 1924 or 1925. Now the odd & amusing thing is this. Years afterward—after I had given the idea to Whitehead & was awaiting the appearance of "Cassius"—I chanced to mention the matter to my old friend Arthur Leeds of New York, who has had extensive dealings with freaks & other amusement enterprises. Fancy my surprise when he told me that he knows Libera well—that the man's real name is *Giovanni* Libera, that he is an Italian of great intelligence, that he is interested in everything *weird,* & that (believe this or not—it's actual truth!) he is especially fond of *my* work in W.T.!!!! Talk about coincidence! Leeds was going to tell him about "Cassius", but I told him not to, since he might feel some delicacy (despite his occupation) about being used in that way. At the time (1930) Leeds was going to introduce me to Libera; but something prevented, so the meeting never came off. It certainly would have seemed odd to meet one of my plot-germs in the flesh . . . . the flesh of *two* bodies, or a body & a half, at that!

I hope you'll enjoy "The Horror from the Hills." The works on magic *will* be hard to find in your part of the country (as indeed they are here), so I fancy you will eventually have to get in touch with Koenig. Indeed—I'm in a way putting you in touch with him right now by placing your name (with his permission) on the borrowing-list of the three William Hope Hodgson books I lately mentioned. You can't afford to miss these—they have a peculiar & authentic weirdness all their own. They will come to you from Derleth—& with them will probably come a paper-covered volume of tales by Barry Pain—one of which, "The Undying Thing", is positively tremendous. This also belongs to Koenig. Keep all of these as long as you like—& let Baldwin read them, too.

Then either return to Koenig or pass on to some other borrower whose name will be supplied. I've suggested to Crawford that he write you in case he wishes to read these books. Koenig is incredibly generous about lending his rare first editions. Not many would wish to subject such valuable books to wear & tear—but he cares more for the diffusion of weird literature than for anything else. Which reminds me that his article on Charles Williams in the new F F piques my curiosity considerably. I never even heard of Williams before.

I missed the opening of Merritt's new tale—your letter being my first inkling that it had appeared. Now I think I'll let it go for the time being, since there will be plenty of friends who can lend the magazines to me when the thing is finished. I believe Merritt intends to make some radical changes when he reissues it in book form. By the way—your own proposed story, about a subtle & indirect manifestation of hereditary memory, ought to be good. I hope to see it in the course of time.

Barlow got home from Daytona, & in two days set out for Washington. Naturally he hasn't been having much time for letter-writing. His present address is 7019 Georgia Ave., N.W., Washington, D.C.

I guess Sheaffer's permanent jet black is as good a black ink as you can get for a fountain pen. There are some who insist that *all* black inks are unadapted to fountain use—that they tend to clog the feed—but I find that Sheaffer's does this far less than the blue-black Waterman ink I used to use. Of course, it is possible that some of the higher-grade coloured inks would be even less clogging—but I like black & will stick to it for a while anyhow. It reminds me of my youth, before I had a fountain pen, when Carter's or Stafford's black ink was the only kind in common use anywhere. Even after that I used to use a steel pen & black ink constantly at home, employing a fountain (with blue-black ink) only when away. Gradually the added convenience of non-dipping came to appeal to me, so that I used a fountain altogether—at home or abroad. It was then that I got out of touch with black ink. Then— only 2 years ago—my aunt got me back to black again by using it successfully in her own pen. She found Sheaffer's the best—& I surely have no fault to find with it. But my friend Morton is all for Parker's "Quink"—which claims to be especially quick-drying & non-clogging. They even advertise "Quink" as a *cleaning-agent* to dispel the clogging caused by other inks. I don't know whether there's a black "Quink" (Morton uses blue), but if there is, I might try it some time. Am having some more pen trouble—I always am!

All good wishes—& regards to your father, Baldwin, & Crom.

Yrs most sincerely—

H P L

Notes

1. Bartholomew Gosnold (1571–1607) was instrumental in founding Jamestown in co-

lonial America. He led the first recorded European expedition to, and named, Cape Cod.

2. See Wandrei to HPL, 6 April 1927 (*Mysteries of Time and Spirit* 72)

3. The *Providence Daily Journal* (7 September 1881): 1 reported that the previous day, the atmosphere throughout New England was "pervaded with a yellowish light, which lends a strange appearance" to the landscape. The cause of the atmospheric effect was attributable to smoke that had travelled eastward from the "Thumb Fire" that had burnt more than a million acres of woodlands in Michigan's Thumb Area. Note that this event antedates the eruption of Krakatoa in the Dutch East Indies on 26 August 1883.

4. A six-part serial in *WT* by Jack Williamson from April to September 1933.

5. Lionel E[dgar] Dilbeck (1917–1977), a member of the Wichita Science Fiction League whose poetry appeared in *FF* and *Supramundane Stories*.

6. Giovanni Libbera (1884–1936) was born in Rome. The miniature twin growing from his body was well formed, not "shapeless." Its rudimentary head was embedded in Libbera's torso, and since it had its own nervous system, Libbera could tell when it was touched. Arthur Leeds, HPL's writer friend and member of the Kalem Club, knew Libbera and wanted to introduce HPL to him because Libbera enjoyed HPL's fiction. Leeds himself had written but not sold a story about Libbera (Frank Belknap Long, *Howard Phillips Lovecraft: Dreamer on the Nightside* [Sauk City, WI: Arkham House, 1975], 62). Hubert's Museum at 234 West 42nd Street in Times Square opened in 1925 and went out of business in 1965, although some exhibits remained until c. 1969.

[19]   [ANS, JHL][1]

[Postmarked Providence, RI,
14 September 1934]

P.S. to my letter. When the Koenig books come—& when you're through with them—please send them to

        Bernard Austin Dwyer,
            Box 43,
                West Shokan,
                    Ulster Co., N.Y.

I think I suggested Crawford as the next recipient, but Dwyer ought to come first. ¶ Tell Baldwin that I safely received the returned magazine—with "The Face in the Abyss"—this morning.
                Regards—H P L

[P.P.S.] Innsmouth & M of M just came, & the damned P.O. made me pay 43¢ on 'em! MS. & writing!

Notes

1. *Front:* Boston Common and State House, Boston, Mass.

[20]   [ALS, JHL]

66 College St.,
Providence, R.I.,
Octr. 8, 1934.

My dear Rhi´-Mhel:—

If this proves a sorely inadequate reply to yours of Sept. 19, the reason will not be hard to find—for I am just pulling around from a bad siege of indigestion which got me about the time I last wrote. I was in bed—or dragging betwixt there & the kitchen & bathroom—a week, & have thereafter been distinctly flabby & shaky. But the pain is over, & with suitable dietary care I ought to be able to avert any relapse. The worst thing is the congestion caused in my programme by the long hiatus. I've had to cancel one job outright, & postpone another in [a] way which may result in cancellation. However, it'll be all the same in a hundred years!

But the worst news is yet to come. A melancholy shadow has fallen upon the Kappa Alpha Tau, & the autumn flowers of the garden droop in sorrow. For—just as I was most garrulously proclaiming his graces & virtues—Little Sam Perkins is no more! He was found lifeless one morning amidst his favourite shrubbery, & now he sleeps beneath the grasses with which he loved to play in life. No cause for his early passing could be discovered—but it was probably a recurrence of a trouble which he had early in August, when he was inexplicably ill for three days. Blessed little Piece of the Night! He lived but from June to September, & will never know what the savage rigours of winter are like. The grave elders stare wistfully from the clubhouse roof, & mew in elegiac numbers:

The ancient garden seems tonight
    A deeper gloom to bear,
As if some silent shadow's blight
    Were hov'ring in the air.
With hidden griefs the grasses sway,
    Unable quite to word them—
Remembering from yesterday
    The little paws that stirr'd them.[1]

Crom, I know, will sympathise sincerely with us. I learn with pleasure of his growth & prosperity, & am interested in your account of his diet & habits. A fine boy, & with a distinct individuality of his own! I shall indeed be glad to see a more recent picture of him—& will shew it to President Randall (black & white) & Vice-President Osterberg (tiger) of the K.A.T. I feel confident that they will ensure his election as an honorary member!

I guess I have *Rye´mel* down pat now, & I always pronounced *Duane* right . . . if *Dwain* is such. Proper names often present unexpected pitfalls when one has known them only on paper. Take *Koenig* for example. I called this *Coin´-ig* & Belknap [whose name, incidentally, sounds like *Bel´-nap*—with silent k] called it *Cō-nig*. Then somebody supposed to be a German scholar corrected us & said it ought to be *Ker´-nig*. At this point I first had occasion to get in touch with Koenig himself by telephone. Calling up his office—& keeping the latest tip in mind—I asked the clerk for Mr. "Kêr´-nig", & met only with the telephonic equivalent of a blank stare. Then light dawned at the other end. "Oh! You mean Mr. *Kay´-nig!!*" Well, that was that. When the gentleman came to the instrument I hailed him as *Kay´nig* & received no correction, nor did he demur on a later evening when I met him face to face. So Kay´-nig I suppose it is—though I was long enough in getting it. Belknap—who is slow to learn new ways—still says *Cō´nig* quite unashamedly! Wandrei´s name is pronounced *Wan´-drȳ* (rhyming with *eye* & *pie*), though several (including myself) called it *Wan´-dray* (rhyming with *pay* & *day*) until instructed. There are many names in my own ancestry which—knowing them only from genealogical charts—I probably pronounce all cockeyed. Only lately did I learn that *Rhys* (on my Welsh side) is *Reez*. I had called it *Riss*. Local usage often varies the pronunciation of both personal & place names. Rhode Island is very conservative, & sticks to old British pronunciations obsolescent elsewhere in the U.S. We pronounce *Greenwich* as *GRINN´IDGE* (in N.Y. & Conn. they call it *GREN´-ITCH*), *Norwich* as *NORRIDGE*, *Thames* as *TEMS* (in Conn. *Tames*), *Berkeley* as *BARK´LEY*, *Warwick* as *WAR´ICK*, *Olney* as *Ō´NEY*, & so on. I was utterly astonished to learn about a decade ago that the statesman Richard Olney (of Mass.) pronounced his name *ŎL´-NEY* instead of *Ō´-NEY*. Such a thing would be unheard-of in Rhode Island, where the Olney (*Ō´-ney*) family has flourished for 300 years, giving its name to Olneyville (*Ō´-NEY-VILLE*), now a part of Providence. Charleston S.C. has some very odd name pronunciations, especially among the Huguenot descendants. Offhand, how would you pronounce *Huger, Legare, Hassell,* & *Manigault?* Well, in Charleston the respective sounds are *YOU-JEE´, LE-GREE´, HÁ´ZEL,* & *MAN´-I-GO*. And the Dutch name *van der Horst,* early naturalised in Charleston & repeatedly appearing in the local geography (creek, street, row, block, &c) is rendered as a dissylable, *VAN-DRORST* or *VAN-DRAWST*, with the syllables about evenly accented. Dialect & accent certainly vary widely in America, though not so much as in the different parts of England. Have you heard of the scientific survey of local dialects now being made by Prof. Hans Kurath of Brown University—to be incorporated into a "Linguistic Atlas of North America"? All of the U.S. & Canada will be covered eventually, & even now some surprising differences within small areas have been found. Rhode Island alone has 7 or 8 local speeches, varying in intonation & exact verbal usage—all these hereditary, & not including any foreign dialects. East of the bay, Block Island, South County, North of Providence, near Connecticut line, &c. &c.—all these regions shew variations. Such are, of course, most marked among the old rustics. Uniform compulsory education, radio, &c. are fast ironing out these individualities, so that the large linguistic survey has been undertaken none too soon. In another generation many historic idiosyncrasies will have disappeared. All *islands* have strong local peculiarities. Nantucket, for example, provides a whole glossary of unique words & word-usages & pronunciations. As a whole, the speech of southern New England is closer to the ordinary cultivated speech of Great Britain (*not* the Oxford drawl & clipped speech fashionable in London for the last 2 or 3 generations) than is any other native American speech. We do not sound the *r* in words like *farm* (= FÄM or FAHM), *water* (= WATTA), *course* (= COAHSE), *car* (= CÄÄ or CAH), &c., any more than it is sounded in London & the south of England generally. This is also true all the way down the Atlantic coast (except for Pennsylvania) throughout the South (E. of the Mississippi). The *r* in these words *is* sounded in *inland* northern New England (Vermont, inner part of New Hampshire) & in northern & central N.Y. state. Also Pennsylvania, Ohio, & the west generally. The typical drawl of the South begins in southern Maryland & extends down to Florida, although it does not appear in the newer & Yankee-settled Florida towns. In Georgia it has a curious thickness not found elsewhere, & west of the Mississippi it acquires Western characteristics. It has never existed in Charleston, S.C. because of the close relations of that city with England, together with its isolation from the rural hinterland. Charleston speech is much like that of Providence. Another city with a recognizable local dialect different from the surrounding country is Boston, with its broad vowels. New York city has an atrociously ugly patois of its own, with blunted vowels & an interchange of the *-er* & *-oi* sounds. (thus—"The *Oi*l of J*oi*sey bought Standard E*rl* stock" .... or "the critic Oinest Bird [Ernest Boyd] & the explorer Boid [Byrd]") It is comical to hear a New Yorker say *coil* when he means *curl*, & *curl* when he means *coil!* They also have difficulty with the *-ph* sound after the *s*— saying *spinx* for *sphinx* & *spear* for *sphere*. In my opinion the harshest & least likeable American dialects are those of New York, Pennsylvania, & the Middle West. In California (& I suppose in Oregon & Washington also) there is less of the *grating* quality than there is in Ohio or Michigan or Iowa. In Illinois there are regions where New England dialect exists untainted—little linguistic islands marking places where Yankees migrated en masse around 1830. One of these is the small city of Delavan in Tazewell County—settled largely by my Phillips relatives [two of my great-grand-uncles, James & Benoni Phillips, went there with large families a century ago] & other Rhode Islanders. [Greene, Lawton, &c] After more than 3 generations the speech of Delavan is still indistinguishable from that of Providence & Newport. Decadent idioms & corrupt pronunciations usually begin in the West or South & work east, or else in New York city, spreading in all directions. Thus the use of *like* where *as* or *as if* ought to be was first southern only. Then the west got it—& only in the last five years have the less careful people in New England picked it up. A decade ago the corrupt pronunciation *cär´mel* (like *Mt. Carmel*) for the candy *câr´-a-mel* was never heard east of the Mississippi. It is now heard in N.Y., but never in New England. In another decade our slipshod elements will get it. On the other hand the atrocious barbarism *kew´pon* for *coupon* probably originated in New York, as did *add´ress* for *address´*. I don't know where the very recent barbarism *coop* for *coupé* arose, but it has reached New England.

Nantucket certainly was great, & I surely hope you can get there some time. It will shew you more of the atmosphere of old-time America in an hour, than you could get from a lifetime of reading. I am still dreaming about it!

Glad the *Tryout* duly reached you. The mistake in your name is typical of good old Smithy![2] I shudder to think of what he will do, typographically, to the elegy on the late Mrs. Miniter which he persuaded me to write! Enclosed is a new amateur paper shewing something of the qualitative upturn for which the present administration is striving. I surely hope you'll be able to join in the near future!

So autumn's advent is also manifest in Asotin? That second cherry blooming is surely phenomenal! By the way, those vivid dust sunsets Wandrei spoke of were *not* in Milwaukee, but in *St. Paul, Minnesota*, his home town. I don't think Milwaukee is close enough to the prairies to get the dust that St. Paul & Minneapolis get. There is the whole width of Wisconsin between. Our leaves have now begun to turn, though the landscape is still predominantly aestival. A few warm days persist, & only recently I spent a long afternoon in my favourite country north of Providence—taking my reading & writing & sitting first on a stone wall overlooking a magnificent expanse of valley & distant hillside, & afterward on a high rock cliff above a silent tarn in the midst of deep woods. I shan't have many more chances to sit around outdoors this season, but I can take brisk woodland walks all through October. The autumn landscape in New England is very beautiful—full of a strange weirdness & melancholy. Now & then one comes upon a farm conducted just as it was a century or two ago—gnarled orchard & well-sweep, sheaves of corn in the rocky meadows, & barn bursting with pumpkins & other fruits of the harvest.

About *astronomy*—was it to *you* that I promised to lend an elementary textbook when in Florida & then forgot all about it? If so remind me, & I'll shoot one or two good ones along. I have a small telescope which shews such things as Saturn's rings. Yes—the moon would appear upside down in the southern hemisphere, & like the sun would cross the northern instead of the southern sky. The position of the constellations in relation to the horizon also varies. Our *circumpolar* constellations—those that never set here—(Great Bear, Lesser Bear, Draco, Cassiopeia, Cepheus, &c) are *never visible* in Argentina, Australia, or South Africa, while all the other constellations we see would be shifted radically northward. They also see a whole region of *southern circumpolar* constellations which we *never* see here (Southern Cross, Centaur, &c)—& which to them never set but just revolve around a fixed pole as our northern circumpolars do. All this is very thoroughly explained in any good textbook.

I know you'll like "The Hill of Dreams". Dunsany, too, is a revelation. He influenced me tremendously in 1919 & 1920. Some of the old W T things are very fair—anything of Whitehead's, of course, is good. Have you read his "Passing of a God"? Glad the new Howard serial is going to be good. I shall read it all at once later. Hamilton's best was "The Monster God of Mamurth". My first hint of the existence of Winford Publications came from Leeds about 2 days before your letter arrived. The new magazine, he tells me, is likely to be rather low-grade. Bierce was born in 1842—& was therefore 71 (though looking much younger) when he vanished in 1913. He probably joined some Mexican rebel army & was shot. His old associate Adolphe de Castro has just turned up again in rather distressed circumstances & wants Long & me to help him with some fiction—but it is very doubtful whether we can do so.

Yes—my stamp bill is certainly rather formidable! It can't be helped, though. When anyone has as peculiar tastes as mine, it would be extraordinary if he could find any considerable number of congenial minds in as narrow a compass as the same city. To build up a really sizeable circle one must have the whole area of the country to draw upon—& naturally, with so expansive an area, correspondence has to replace conversation to a great extent. I'll try to find a way to send "Hypnos" soon. Don't bother to tell Baldwin about that extra postage. The package was 3d class; but being a typed MS, came under a 1st class ruling when examined. I duly received "The Thing On the Doorstep"—though in a badly damaged stage on account of *rolling*. Such MSS. have to go flat or folded, else they suffer badly. However, gummed tape has patched up the worst places.

Sorry the new tale came back from Wright. That objection about the ending is just what was said against my Randolph Carter. I wouldn't pay too much attention to it. But of course the best thing to do with any story is to keep it always open for revision—meanwhile collecting as many opinions as possible from really qualified critics. Let us hope the inherited-characteristic story will come out well. The suggested title—"The Room of Pictures"—sounds excellent to me. Glad C A S is furnishing useful hints. As for Wright's red dots—I really don't believe I ever noticed them! Price or Howard or C A S might be able to shed light. Could they mean words too frequently repeated? I give it up. But Wright always was an inveterate marker! Glad "The Tree" landed—& don't mind Crawford's suggestions. He really puzzles me with his curious lack of assimilative power—in his last argument he seemed unable to follow a simple chain of reasoning which I had brought forward. I don't really know the ages of these semi-amateur editors, except that Schwartz (a college student whom I've met in person) must be about 20. I have thought that Hornig & Crawford were about the same, as the printer Ruppert (whom I saw with Schwartz last winter) obviously is . . . . but they may be older for all I know. Hornig is really doing finely with the F F—I'd like to see him some time. Schwartz's next *Fantasy* will be rather interesting—with a story by A. Merritt & a sequel to my "Randolph Carter" by Wandrei. Partly emulating Hornig, Schwartz is going to dedicate each issue of F M to some established weird or science-fiction *magazine*. The old *Black Cat* was good in its day—not all weird, but carrying about as high a percentage of weird stuff as the old *All Story*. Perhaps a bit higher. Some day I may try that twin plot, though many other propositions loom ahead. Glad you saw Belknap's Chaugnar tale with my Roman dream in it. Yes—the Chaugnar poem[3] was good.

The Hodgson books will come your way in due time—& I feel certain that you & Eph-Li will enjoy them vastly. They have a certain intangible atmosphere which nobody else but Blackwood can achieve. Hodgson, Koenig tells me, was killed in the war. What a pity to cut short such a writing career! Haven't yet read the Williams books which Koenig sent—but will do so shortly & send them along to Klarkash-Ton as instructed.[4] If they're any good I'll see that they come your way. Thanks prodigiously for the offer to lend the Merritt story when it's done—an offer I accept with appreciative alacrity. Yes—I hope you'll be able to work the febrile dream-vision of reeling worlds into one or another of your new tales.

Don't take too much trouble in compensation for having overlooked my birthday—for I never remember the birthday of anybody under 80! It wasn't till two or three years ago that I started sending birthday cards to Tryout Smith—& even he is a youngster compared with my good old friend Mr. Hoag of Greenwich, N.Y., who lived to be 96 & even then died of an accident. I used to write birthday verses for him—sending them for publication in his local paper. But ordinarily, birthdays slip my mind like the winds of summer. Probably I've been told the birthday of every member of the gang—but I don't believe I recall a single one! When Smithy commissioned me to write Mrs. Miniter's elegy he wanted the dates of birth & death prefixed, but neither of us could remember the birthday. I left it blank . . . . May _____ 1869 . . . . but Tryout conceived the idea of faking a date to make the text look smooth & stuck in the figure 5 at random . . . May "5", 1869. Thus it now stands in the proofs, but I'm trying to get the real date from some of the deceased's close friends in order to avoid what seems to me a rather absurd inaccuracy.[5]

I think Sheaffer's is a pretty good ink to tie to, though its cost mounts up when one uses as much as I do. This very free-flowing Waterman *might* take a cheaper ink now that the feed has been so carefully adjusted—but I haven't done any experimenting in that line so far. I may try some "Quink"—for I really like the thinnest & freest-flowing ink obtainable. As for the pen trouble—it's only one of my two instruments that is affected, so the handicap is not an immediate one. But I prefer to have 2 pens in good shape, since I never can tell when the dominant one will give out. When it does, I like another ready to take its place—for it sometimes takes months to get a pen properly repaired or exchanged. With my special requirements, I never get any satisfaction except at central Waterman offices in Boston & New York, where there are adjusting experts & an unlimited supply of points to choose from. The spare pen is a Parker, hence cannot benefit from Waterman service. But I shall keep trying at different places to get the point smoothed out, & hope it will be in shape before anything happens to this present goose-quill. Within the last year or so I've seen advertisements of new feather-touch pens that sound just like what I need. Possibly some of them will be worth investigating in the course of time. All new pens seem to have a greater ink capacity than mine. Sheaffer's undoubtedly forms one of the very best of the newer makes.

You'll hear from Barlow before long, if you haven't already—he told me to tell you & others that he'd write soon. He will be in Washington a considerable period, for the oculist wants to study his eyes thoroughly & test the results of different types of treatment. Before he goes south again Barlow will probably visit New York & look up Long & any others who may be in town. He may even get as far as Providence—though this is by no means certain. The new *Perspective Review* (N.A.P.A.) contains a tale of Barlow's—one of the Garoth series.[6]

Foliage looks tempting from my window today, but I fear it isn't warm enough to encourage outdoor writing. Steam is singing in the radiators—a very welcome element, which saves me the bother & expense of running the oil heater. We get heat piped in from the engineering building of Brown University, & the college is very generous with it. It begins early in autumn & lasts late in the spring, is ample in quantity, & keeps up all night. I can appreciate this acutely after having dwelt in houses where the opposite extreme of heating holds sway! As I glance out I see President Randall on the clubhouse roof, & he nods a greeting to you & Crom. It can't be very cold after all, or he wouldn't be out—for he is like me in his reaction to temperatures. Mr. Osterberg, on the other hand, appears off & on throughout the winter. Alas that Little Sam Perkins could not have lived to share the fortunes of this select brotherhood!

Well—I'll conclude at last. Best regards to yourself, your father, E'ph-Lee, & Crom.

Wishing you good luck with the new story

—Yrs most cordially,

E'ch-Pi-El.

P.S. Just finished critical report for N.A.P.A.,[7] so will send along the papers I've gone through. Hope you'll enjoy them.

Notes

1. HPL did not give the lines a title, but they are now reprinted under the name "Little Sam Perkins" following the first printing in the *Olympian*.

2. No works by DWR are known to have been published in *Tryout*. HPL may be referring to a misspelling of DWR's name on an envelope in which the issue was sent.

3. Frank Belknap Long, "When Chaugnar Wakes" (*WT*, September 1932).

4. Koenig had written of five books by British fantaisiste Charles Williams (1886–1945): *War in Heaven* (1930), *Many Dimensions* (1931), *Greater Trumps* (1932), *Place of Lions* (1932), and *Shadows of Ecstasy* (1933). It is unknown which three he lent to HPL.

5. Miniter was born 19 May 1869.

6. "The Inhospitable Tavern." *Perspective Review* (Autumn 1934): 3, 12.

7. "Report of the Bureau of Critics—Verse Department" for December 1934.

[21]   [ALS, JHL]

66 College St.,

Providence, R.I.,

Octr. 30, 1934.

Dear Rhi-Mhel:—

I greatly enjoyed yours of Oct. 15 with the enclosed story. The latter is excellent, & proves that your progress in fiction-writing is solid & genuine—no mere matter of accident.[1] In this tale there is genuine atmosphere & suspense, & I do not think anything about the ending could be called disappointing. The final touch about waiting for the child to come back is especially good. Some, as in other cases, might ask for greater definiteness—but I no longer pay attention to this sort of demand. It might, just possibly, help to suggest a bit more concretely exactly what the Hulls tended to become after death . . . . whether vampires, ghouls, or something less conventional. Evidently they liked to exert an influence on some one of their posterity—for I assume that Howard Hull's so-called "grave robbing" was really a response to some summons from an earlier ancestor comparable to that which he later—through his picture—sent his own daughter. A sort of general clarification *in your own mind* (not necessarily to be revealed in toto to the reader) of what is supposed to happen, & why each thing happens as it does, would produce a certain added convincingness worth securing. That is, all the happenings would hang harmoniously together—no one of them seeming irrelevant or unjustified in the light of the others. One tends to ask (a) just what the trouble with the Hulls is, (b) what relation the sinister-looking picture of Howard Hull has to the general trouble, & to the procedure of other Hulls involved in that trouble, (c) just what each of the dead Hulls wants with some living Hull, (d) how closely Loretta's fate at the hands of her dead father corresponds with *his* previous fate at the hands of some earlier dead ancestor, (e) just what Loretta will be wanting after she becomes a vampire or ghoul or whatever it is, (f) just what the secret staircase was first made for, &c. &c. Now all these questions don't need to be answered in the visible text, but they ought to be answered in the preliminary synopsis which you have presumably prepared for your own guidance—the synopsis of *events in order of their occurrence* which I recommended to you as the best device for getting the background of a story started. If you have all these points settled in advance, you'll be able to write with an easy consistency & assurance which will make everything seem (for the moment) real & probable. All the veiled, subtle allusions will ring true because they will be referring to a consistent background perfectly known to you. Of course, I dare say you *have* largely adhered to this plan in writing "The Room of Pictures"—for the story is excellent as it is. I was merely suggesting that this precision might be enforced a little more strictly. As for the externals—as you surely realise yourself, your *style* has improved marvellously. No longer do any radical changes have to be made. If there remains anything to suggest, it is that the *conversation of characters* tends to become at times the formal, literary English suited only to the author when he narrates in the 3d person. This is a common fault of pulp writers—using the speech of a character to carry on the story, & having it merely the literary language of the author without reference to what the actual speech of a person like the represented character would be. A little care ought to obviate this. Actually, in good fiction no character ought to be represented as using any style of language except the one he would naturally employ under the given conditions. The only other point I'd tend to bring up is one concerning the lawyer's letter. Is the *amount* of revelation quite natural? Would the attorney be apt to say that Hull had been a grave robber without at least hinting at the circumstances attending this terrible fact? But of course these matters are trifles. The story is, fundamentally, a splendid one; & is certainly worth trying on editors just as it is. It surely forms eloquent evidence of your progress! I shall be interested to hear what Klarkash-Ton has to say of "Charlotte". It seems to me it would be a good idea to try it on Hornig & Crawford. I don't recall its exact length, but doubt whether either F F or M T has rigid space regulations. The tale about the pirate in Hampden sounds promising. Of course the general theme is not new—Bierce has something, I believe, of the same approximate cast—but it is always capable of fresh treatment. Shall be glad to see the new poem, too. Hope C A S can clear up the mystery of Wright's red marks. It certainly puzzles me! Your material will appear in M T in time, but Crawford is very slipshod & can't even approach a regular schedule. Hope he'll accept your linoleum block illustration for "The Tree". Which reminds me—Barlow was very interested last spring in Eph-Li's idea of having an illustration for that possible "Colour out of Space" booklet in case its publication were ever possible. He thought he could fill the bill a good deal better than I—which is most assuredly true!—& has hung on to the notion more or less. The other day he sent the enclosed tree drawing for a decorative title page—& it strikes me as so thoroughly excellent & appropriate that I'm sending it on for you & F L B to use. While not directly related to the story, it could easily represent one of the grotesque trees of the deep woods west of Arkham. Better put it on file with the MS., & have it open for consideration if the venture ever proves practicable. It would surely add to the appearance of any brochure in which it might be used. The Oct F F is now out, & presents a very fair appearance despite misprints. I feel unduly flattered by the dedication. About "The Chuckler"—on reading it, I'd tend to say that it is not so much a *sequel* to "Randolph Carter" as something *suggested* by that yarn. It disappointed me just a trifle—as did the Merritt yarn in the same magazine. Yes—I noticed the twin matter in the Oct. Eyrie[2] after you pointed it out. Evidently this general idea bids fair to become common property!

Derleth's programme is very crowded, but the Hodgson books will be along in due season. I feel sure you'll like them. When you & Eph-Li are through with them, shoot them on to Dwyer—but use a new address for him: *C.C.C. Camp 25, Peekskill, N.Y.* He joined the C.C.C. about a month ago—a highly unusual thing for a man of 38—& is enjoying it immensely. He has been made editor of the camp paper,[3] & seems to be on his way toward receipt of a leader's chevrons. I'll notify you of any change in his address.

My indigestion is all gone now—though my right hand suffers from a sort of writer's cramp. I may yet be driven to the hated typewriter . . . or to a pencil. Glad you're feeling better, & hope the occasional rheumatic touches will become fewer & fewer.

Many thanks for the appealing elegy—which is tremendously graceful & clever—& sympathetic words anent the passing of little Sam Perkins! They are surely appreciated . . . . & when I next go through the Seventh Gate of Dream I shall certainly endeavour to visit Aklakar's thousand-minaretted palace beside the milk-white fountain! This is a bad season for the Kappa Alpha Tau's novices & correspondents, for melancholy tales of disappearance pour in from two widely separated sources. From De Land Charles Johnston writes that old white Doodlebug (surely a distant elder cousin of Crom) vanished three weeks ago—hope being virtually abandoned now, in view of the ophidian perils of the region. And from Auburn Klarkash-Ton reports the disappearance of staunch old General Tabasco, who has battled around the fane of Tsathoggua for many a long year. But the main official board of the K.A.T. still carries on . . . . & yesterday Pres. Randall informed me of the unanimous election of snow-hued Crom as a full-fledged member. He is, indeed, authorised to act as President in forming an Asotin chapter of the fraternity. Now that Pres. Doodlebug of the De Land chapter is absent from the scene, I suppose they'll have to hold an election down there—High & Jack being the obvious candidates.

About pronunciation—here's something I overlooked last time. How do you pronounce the name of your town? I had taken *A-sō´-tin* for granted, but the other day someone looking at an envelope on my desk pronounced it *Ass´-o-tin*. Neither side could shew any real authority, so I pass the question along to one qualified to answer it. Many place-names are very hard to pronounce. I don't know yet the really proper way (as recognised by natives) to pronounce *Los Angeles*. In New Orleans the education classes say *New Aw´l'yunz*, while the ignorant say *New Or-lēēnz´*. A similar class difference exists in Cincinnati—where the educated say *Sin-si-nah´ti* while the ignorant say *Sin-si-nâ´tty*. In St. Louis there seems to be a tendency of natives to sound the final *s*, while educated non-residents hesitate to do this. In *Chattanooga* the *ch* should be given the sound it has in *chat* or *chew* or *cheese;* not the French *sh* sound. The word is Indian. Certain state names present odd paradoxes. *Iowa* is called *I´-o-wah* by the educated & *I´o-way* by the uncultivated—& yet there is reason to believe that the latter may actually represent the real name of the Indian tribe from which the name was derived. In the pioneering age crude Yankees always rendered an *-a* termination as either *-y* (Ameriky) or *-ā* (Floriday); hence when they encountered an Indian name never before put into English letters, they naturally followed this plan. Probably the Iowa Indians had a name that sounded like *I-o-way*. The pioneers spelled this *Iowā* because they thought this form conveyed the sound. But it *didn't* convey the sound to educated people, hence the common educated pronunciation *I-o-wah*. This theory has been disputed, but it has much in its favour—notably the analogy of the name *O-jib-way* . . . . thus spelled & pronounced. *Arkansas* should be *Ar´-kan-sah* (or -saw)—the name being a French transliteration of the Indian sounds, hence subject to French rules of pronunciation. (cf. Dumas, Degas, &c.) Curious about *Koenig*—evidently my academic informant (who said *Ker´-nig*) was really right from a linguistic standpoint—the trouble being a gradual though partial Anglicisation on the part of H.C.K. I fancy he represents the 2nd or 3d generation of American birth—he had to study German in high school, & doesn't read it readily. That linguistic atlas will certainly bring out some curious facts. I don't think it will cover any but *English* dialects, hence will have to omit the interesting variants of French in Canada or of Spanish in the Southwest. In Canada it will have plenty of material, though, for local English accents vary greatly. Newfoundland has a curious brogue—probably of Scottish origin. In the maritime provinces a certain vocal quality derived from current British speech is manifest. In Montreal the speech approximates that of northern N.Y. state—& I believe that the western prairie provinces largely resemble the American western states above which they lie. Regarding the New York city patois—I don't think any slangy usage or playful interchange of sounds can be held responsible. That isn't the way dialects grow. The reasons are generally far subtler & deeper. This case is a particularly baffling one, but some day a plausible explanation may be devised by etymologists. "Youse" is evidently a variant of the "yeez" common among the ignorant in the British Isles—especially Ireland & the north of England. I think this especial variant did develop in the N.Y. slums. The basis of this & its parent form is evidently a reluctance of the ignorant to think of a *plural* without an *s*. When the forms *ye* & *you* supplanted *thee* & *thou* in the *singular,* simple people thought they'd have to tack on an *s* to get a *plural!* Later on, an opposite *corruption of the corruption* set in, whereby *yez* or *youse* came to be used as a *singular* pronoun! Your mention of "Chinook" reminds me of the large number of Northwestern Indian words which have entered the *colloquial* speech of Washington—or at least, of the Seattle region. One often finds them in the amateur journals of the United Amateur Press Assn. of America, whose chief local centre is Seattle. "Skookum", "tillicum", & "potlatch" are the examples which most readily occur to me. This, however, does not affect the standard literary language so far as I know.

Thanks for the list of books lent—I'll try not to lose this one! Take your time about those you have. Under separate cover I'm sending two books on astronomy. Read the small one by Bayne first—this is the most elementary I know of. Then browse at leisure among the ampler explanations of Todd. Unfortunately I have no *new* books on the subject—but these old fellows will do for all basic essentials. It is only in connexion with the larger structure of the universe that astronomy has been revolutionised since the date of these volumes. If you like, I'll lend you more items on the subject later on— including books with lore about the constellations. No hurry about any of these—& let Eph-Li see them as much as he wishes.

You certainly have had an unusual autumn—with second cherry bloom- ings & simultaneous apple-blossoms & apples! The apex of our autumnal fo- liage came around the week-end of Oct. 19–21—& I had an unusually fortunate chance to observe it under the best possible conditions. I spent the period visiting Edward H. Cole (my host of last August) in the Boston zone, & he took me to a number of ideal scenic spots in his car. On the 20th we ex- plored a section of north central Massachusetts that I had never seen be- fore—& in which I beheld some of the finest autumn foliage & landscape vistas in all my experience. The focus of the trip was West Townsend, where we lunched at a rambling old tavern built in 1774, & patronised the quaintest old general store that I've seen in 30 years. Nearby is the Wallis Brook State Forest, where we revelled in wooded hills, rock waterfalls, & leafy gorges of indescribable picturesqueness. From nearly every point the distant bulk of Mt. Wachusett loomed up, & once we had a splendid view of a steepled vil- lage in a valley. On the 21st Cole & his wife brought me back to Provi- dence—picking up my aunt at #66 & setting out for the ancient Narragansett Country which Price & I explored last year. We visited venerable Wickford with its drowsing wharves & elm-shaded main street, & later struck inland to the gorgeously lovely spot where Gilbert Stuart's birthplace—a snuff-mill built in 1750—broods beside the Narrow River. This ancient structure has been fully restored—wheel & all—so that it can grind snuff as well as it did when Stuart's father ran it 180 years ago. The surrounding landscape is dou- bly beautiful in autumn, & Cole insisted on some adventurous explorations which resulted in our getting partly lost. A heated Chevrolet is a very useful aid to exploration in weather like this!

No—I never heard of "Winford Publications" except in connexion with the proposed weird magazine. As for Bierce's end—old de Castro went down to Mexico about 1920 & interviewed Villa & other rebel leaders, but doesn't shed any more definite light than any other biographers. Of the numerous lives of Bierce, that by Carey McWilliams is generally regarded as the best. No—I haven't submitted "The Thing on the Doorstep" to Wright as yet, but will do so after I've collected a few more opinions. There's no telling how he'd receive it.

Barlow seems to be enjoying Washington—& I don't know how his future travel plans stand. He is taking an art course at the Corcoran Gallery—a rather light one, since the oculist won't sanction more. Wandrei seems to be still on the move. He hasn't been here yet—but Klarkash-Ton says he hopes to get out to California later in the autumn.

I'll have to try a Sheaffer "Feathertouch" some time—unless I fall back on a pencil! My script is getting worse & worse! Yes—I surely do manage to sling gallons of ink around!

Regards to Crom from myself & the entire K.A.T. Since he prefers cold to heat, I won't have to commiserate him on the changing season. ¶ And again let me congratulate you on "The Room of Pictures", & on the solid progress in style which it reveals.

Yrs most sincerely—
E'ch-Pi-El

P.S. Eph-Li has just sent the biography, & 2 prints of your linoleum block print of my likeness. Really, it's a splendid reproduction! Congratulations! The writeup, too, is fine.

Notes

1. HPL is discussing a nonextant story entitled "The Room of Pictures."

2. Charles Minarcik of Brooklyn wrote to "The Eyrie": "In the August issue you reprinted a story called The Parasitic Hand, by R. Anthony. The story seemed to me at the time to be rather far-fetched. Imagine my surprize [*sic*] upon finding a similar case in real life! Feeling that it would prove interesting to you also, I am taking the liberty of enclosing herewith the newspaper clipping which brought the real life case to my attention." The clipping read: "Richmond, Virginia, Aug. 15.—One of the strangest operations yet attempted by surgeons will be performed soon on Miss Daisy Violet Powell, in an attempt to remove what they believe to be the body of a twin sister from her body. The girl was born in Calcutta 24 years ago. The strange growth was first discovered when she was ten. An operation for what was believed to be a tumor in her side revealed another body with hair, tissue and bone. The surgeon called in to make a study of her case died and other doctors refused to attempt the operation, fearing it would endanger her life. The Powell family recently came to this country and Richmond surgeons, hearing of the case, studied it, and have finally decided to operate." *WT* 24, No. 4 (October 1934): 524–25.

3. The camp paper of the Peekskill Civilian Conservation Corps camp was the *Blue Mountain Survey*. Dwyer's story "The Old Dark House" appeared in it.

[22]   [ALS, JHL]

66 College St.,
Providence, R.I.,
Novr. 19, 1934

Dear Rhi´-Mhel:—

Glad to hear that my observations on the story proved useful & encouraging. The added material—in the attorney's letter & toward the end—seems to solve the major problem very well, & I trust that the completed product may have a favourable reception. Regarding the question of a preliminary synopsis—I have found that in most cases a very clear idea of what is going to happen pays extremely well; since after all, every part of a story ought to be in harmony with every other part. The secret of perfect effectiveness is an atmosphere so thoroughly coördinated that every sentence has some subtle bearing on the whole plan & outcome. It always helps to jot down the main points of a future story, although of course it would be just as good theoretically if every point were clear in one's head, even without being written. In practice, we are always apt to overlook some little point if it isn't written down. Common sense is the best guide as to what to do in each individual instance. Sometimes one has planned out a plot so thoroughly in one's head—changing & re-changing as days & weeks go by—that the story virtually exists in complete form before a word is actually written. In such a case, a formal synopsis can sometimes be dispensed with—but those cases are relatively rare, & not to be expected among beginners. And even then it is well to have a set of notes on the details, in order to avoid vaguenesses & contradictions. I have found that one extremely valuable thing is a perfect *time-schedule* assigning a definite date for every event & a definite age for every character. Indeed, it is sometimes useful to have a brief biography—& even a partial genealogy—of every character drawn up in order to make all casual allusions consistent. Beginners usually bungle frightfully in handling the *time* element. For example—a revision-client of mine wrote a story about a boy, describing the events of his life before the age of 9. When all the indicated time-lapses in the action were added up, I found that they consumed *eleven* years! All this had to be straightened out—& it could have been avoided altogether if the author had prepared a synopsis of dates. Anyhow—the general principle is that one ought to know *all about* the imaginary events he has chosen to describe, before he begins describing them. In weird stories involving bizarre monsters & forms of architecture & scenery, it is best to make an explicit (even though crude) sketch of the strange shapes, with a list of all their dimensions, aspects, & properties. Thus as I told you once, I had Cthulhu all down on paper before I tried to write about him—& likewise the curious entities of "At the Mountains of Madness." That's really the only way to be *sure* of avoiding vagueness & self-contradiction.

I was very glad to see the pirate treasure story, & found it delightful in every way. Congratulations! You surely are progressing at a great rate! This piece is extremely vivid, & full of macabre suggestion. The style is excellent—& so far as I can see, no major alteration is necessary. I've touched up a word or phrase or two, but that is all. Hope it meets with good luck editorially. As for titles—I really doubt if "The Forbidden Room" could be bettered. That covers the ground adequately—& I haven't much use for fancy trick titles. The Bierce story about an old pirate is one of the short sketches in the back of "Can Such Things Be?", & is called "The Isle of Pines". It is about an old pirate whose ghost was seen & heard in the decrepit house where he had lived during his latter years. Later two men search the house, & one of them thinks he is on the trail of treasure. The candle—carried by the other man—blows out, & when it is lighted again the treasure-hunter is found dead with a bag of old Spanish gold in his hand—ripped from behind the panelling. Death is ascribed to excitement—but no one ever goes near the house again. The story is really more of a synopsis than a finished tale. Actually, yours is much better—for it has the added element of the *grave*. To my mind, this ought to prove a popular item—let's see whether I'm right! I'm sure Klarkash-Ton will be glad to see "Charlotte"—& quite certain it will land in one or another of the small fantasy magazines.

Glad to see the verses, too. They have a very potent atmosphere, & ought to be well received. I've given them a few revisory touches, with explanations on the margin when necessary. If anything still seems obscure, let me know & I'll endeavour to explain more fully.

I surely hope you'll solve the Mystery of the Red Dots. Perhaps, as you suggest, they indicate only a nervous habit of jabbing at the paper while the pencil is held in readiness for possible corrections—but one guess is as good as another. I must ask Derleth & Howard & Long & others if they've noticed anything of the sort on their rejected MSS.

Hope your "Tree" drawing will land—& also that you'll submit that weird decoration to the F F. Your skill in this field is unmistakable, & the small magazines ought to have the benefit of it! Which reminds me that that linoleum cut of myself certainly is a marvel! I know how hard it is to catch a genuine resemblance on *any* kind of drawing—& can well imagine how the limitations of linoleum work magnify the difficulty tenfold. The fact is, I didn't know that linoleum cuts could be used for such a purpose—I thought they were confined largely to decorative work of a very bold & impressionistic nature. You certainly have made the most of your medium! I hope Hornig will use the illustration—& that the press impression will be as good as the two hand ones sent. The whole illustrated article is a 100% product of the "gang"—text by Eph-Li, photograph by Ar-E'ch-Bei, & cut by Rhi´-Mhel!

That title-page decoration of Ar-E'ch-Bei's, it seems to me, would be all right to use as it is—for the cut-out space would accomodate the printed title.

But of course it would be best to ask him first whether he'd rather let it go in its present form, or draw something else. He could certainly turn out an impressive frontispiece. I'd advise him on any details where a knowledge of Massachusetts architecture is necessary.

I certainly hope the F F will be able to carry on as a monthly, for it occupies a genuinely important niche in the miniature world of weird-fiction devotees. Glad you're renewing your subscription—I renewed some time ago. I liked both October & November issues, & feel quite flattered by the dedication. Now I am looking forward to the number devoted to Poe. *Fantasy Magazine* is also good, though of course specialising less in the purely weird. No— I don't think "The Chuckler" is Wandrei at his best . . . & "The Drone" is certainly nothing to judge Merritt by. "Nightmare" was a good piece of parody on my 1920 fictional style—so grave a spoof that naive readers may not have caught the satire.[1] Really admirably clever.

About Dwyer—did I insert "Barrack 5" in his new address? Once or twice that detail has slipped my mind . . . though I fancy a letter without it would get to him all right, especially since his editorship. Before long you will probably receive from him Barry Pain's "Stories After Dark" & Hodgson's "Carnacki, the Ghost Finder" & "The Night Land". For Hodgson at his best, read the three books which Derleth will forward sooner or later. One of the worst weaknesses of "The Night Land" is the *atrocious* attempt to reproduce an archaic form of English . . . a weakness which you'll also find in "The Boats of the Glen Carrig". Hodgson is evidently wholly ignorant of the real speech of any past age, hence gives the reader a hash of Chaucerisms, Elizabethanisms, Latinisms, & god knows what—such as was never uttered by any mortal man since the world began! But despite all this, he has a marvellous occasional power to evoke weird images—hence I consider him eminently worth wading through. "The House on the Borderland" is his masterpiece by a wide margin.

Writers' cramp is much better. Also, I'm using the Parker pen again . . . which, though a trifle more scratchy than the Waterman, gives a slightly better stroke. I've had the flow increased a bit.

Thanks vastly for the specimen of "wind shake"[2]—of which, in my abysmal ignorance of botany (a year's course in high school 30 years ago has slipped sadly out of my aged head!), I had never before heard. It certainly is a curious substance, & I must see if I can learn anything about its scientific aspects. It seems quite tough & tenacious—if you had a large piece of it you might even use it in bookbinding, as Barlow uses the skins of his ophidian prizes! Its leathery whiteness is intrinsically attractive, while its rarity would case it to appeal to the collector. I am surely glad to have a bit to add to my modest array of curiosities! Which reminds me—I surely would be vastly interested to see a wrapper of that Boise City product—the Owyhee Idaho Spud!

I dream of cats very often—did I ever mention my curious dreams about the ancient black sage who used to greet me daily at the entrance of one of the quaint colonial archways on the hill? He died in 1928 at an age substantially over 20 yrs. Dwyer once had an idea of weaving a story around him. I've dreamed several times about little Sam Perkins, & was pleased to see his name in your new story![3] The Kappa Alpha Tau are still eloquent in expressing their appreciation of your verses. As for the ill-fortune attending the feline population this autumn—it is really getting to be quite uncanny! The latest victim is the faithful tiger companion of my revision-client Mrs. Heald—who ate some Paris green in the cellar, was seized with a sort of frenzy, & dashed out of the house, never to be seen again. No further reports concerning Doodlebug or Gen. Tabasco—alas! But the K.A.T.'s original elders are still flourishing. Owing to the lateness of the season Pres. Randall (whose climatic tastes are like mine) is visible only on exceptional days, but Vice-Pres. Osterberg is a fixture at all times. Of late I've seen a stranger about—grey, plump, & rather youngish—but don't know whether he'll be voted in or not. Another new friend of mine—who I think is connected with the University Club at Benefit & Waterman streets—is quite young, & all black except for a small white star on his chest. He follows me quite a way up the hill when I pass his presumable abode, & is the most effusive & amicable of ankle-rubbers. But I haven't lately seen my huge tiger friend John Quincy Adams at the grocery next the Art Club. He had an accident a year ago, but was supposed to be recovering very nicely from it. Glad to hear that Crom continues to prosper! May he have as long & peaceful a life as Messrs. Randall & Osterberg appear to be having!

I was much interested in your remarks on the name *Asotin.* So *both* versions are correct! Too bad the change occurred if the earlier version was truer to the Indian original. Glad to know the etymology. Rhode Island is full of Indian names derived from the three Algonquin tribes—Narragansetts, (S.W.) Nipmucs (N.), & Wampanoags (E. & S.E.) who dwelt hereabouts. Two largish cities—Pawtucket & Woonsocket—perpetuate the aboriginal nomenclature, & numberless hills & rivers & other topographical features are similarly named. The two rivers which empty into Narragansett Bay are the Moshassuck & the Woonasquatucket—& on the east side of the town the Seekonk makes a third. The principal river of the State's middle section is the Pawtuxet, & of the South County, the Pettaquamscutt. In the extreme southwest is the Pawcatuck. Other Indian names attached to regions are Pascoag, Chepachet, Wanskuck, Moosup, Poneganset, Quinsnicket, Quidnick, Natick, Moswansicut, Cowessett, Chepiwonoxet, Cocumcussoc, Escoheag, Usquepaug, Nannaquacket, Potowomut, Apponaug, Canonchet, Miantonomi, Conanicut, Seaconnet, Matunnuck, Watchaug, Quonochontaug, Niantic, Weekapaug, Misquamicut, Pawawget, &c. &c. One of Providence's principal business streets is named *Weybosset,* which (leading to the ancient ford at the head of the bay, now spanned by the great bridge) signifies "place of wading". I was very glad to see the samples of Washington place-names, with their oc-

casionally unpredictable pronunciations. I once heard that Spokane is pronounced *Spo-kân´* instead of *Spo-kain´*—is this a fact? I doubt if any two people pronounce *Los Angeles* alike. I fancy the original Spanish was *Lōce Ong´hay-
lāce,* or something more or less like that. Possibly there is some variation in
rendering *Cincinnati,* but I'm sure the preferred form is *Sin-si-näh´-ti.* If it isn't,
we consistently mispronounce it in New England! I'll have to get hold of an
announcement of W L W on my aunt's radio & check up. Speaking of dialects—I enclose a cutting which may be of some interest. My aunt, who lived
in Cambridge 20 years, represents this "Boston" or "Harvard" accent in all its
perfection—having picked up its particularly broad vowel-values unconsciously through daily conversation. I do not, since Providence has the less
idiosyncratic speech of southern New England in general. To a native of the
west or south—or even of upper New York state or *northern* New England—
Providence speech would be scarcely distinguishable from that of Boston; but
within the Boston & southern New England areas themselves, certain subtle-
ties are manifest which clearly separate the two dictions. It is not a matter of
idiom, for syntactical use seems virtually identical. Nor is it wholly a matter of
precise vowel sound. For example—while in Ohio they say pǎss, grǎss, hǎff
[half], &c., the speech of both Providence & Boston gives a sound which can
be written as päss (or pahss), gräss, (grahss), häf (hahf) &c. But, although the
difference cannot be expressed in *written* symbols, the Providence & Boston
sounds really *are* unmistakably different. In Boston they *linger* on the broad
vowel—rubbing it in, as it were, whereas we don't give it any more *time* value
than the westerners, with their flatter sound, do. Very roughly, the three
sounds might be depicted thus—using *half* as a sample:

Cleveland, O.	Providence	Boston
haff	häf [hahf]	hääf

If written on a musical ◦, ♩, ♪, ♫, staff, with time-values indicated by
devices like those of the various notes—&c—the Bostonian *ä* would get a
longer-valued note than the Rhode Island one. It is curious to observe that
natives of New York City (who, like us, do not roll the *r,* & whose vowel-
values are less flat than those of the west . . . & who, incidentally, are singular-
ly deaf to their own local peculiarities) can almost always spot a Bostonian,
whereas they do not notice any difference from their own speech in a Provi-
dentian. Clevelanders, Detroiters, & Chicagoans, however, call a Providen-
tian's speech "Bostonian" or "Harvardian"—probably because the radical
difference in r-sounds & basic vowel-values strikes them so sharply that they
don't investigate further. In late years some Harvard instructors have tried to
re-introduce a slight sounding of the *r* in such words as *farm,* &c., on the
ground that the presence of the latter demands it etymologically. In a few cases they have succeeded in colouring the speech of students, but such conscious

inculcation seldom works in the case of dyed-in-the-wool Yankees & Southern-ers. We have lost that r-sound so completely & inveterately that any attempt to recapture it sounds forced & artificial. If we try to say *carrr* or *farrrr* we always have the psychological sensation of "talking dialect"—just as we would if we tried to ape Oxford speech with its *hawf*, & *secretry*, & *g'yo* [or *gayo*] (for *go*), & so on. Thus in the long run I fancy Rhode Islanders will continue to pronounce *water* in a way that the Clevelander would have to write as *watta*, instead of mak-ing an effort to say what the Rhode Island ear would set down as *wat-tirrr*.

Dialect is surely a fascinating study, & leads to all sorts of research. A decade ago I was greatly interested in tracking down some of the curious idi-oms I encountered in New York. For example—the phrase *"store cheese"*—which my palate preferences caused me to run up against continually. In southern New England the expression is—or at least was in 1924—unknown. Our principal cheeses are the large traditional sort—about a foot thick & 2 feet in diameter—& the modern tinfoil package or process cheeses run sec-ond. Thus the word "cheese" without any trimmings suggests to our mind one of the large ordinary old-fashioned sort. When we allude to the new sort we usually say "process cheese"[,] "package cheese" or [in the case of the long tinfoiled loaf] "loaf cheese". Well—in New York it is just the other way around. The word "cheese" in itself suggests to New Yorkers the modern tin-foil brands, & if you ask for "a pound of mild white cheese" a Manhattan grocer will begin to chop you off a section of a Kraft tinfoiled loaf. These process cheeses [they are artificially cured & not aged] are the principal kinds used in the metropolis, & in many shops no others are obtainable. And where they *do* keep the standard old-fashioned sort, they call them "store cheeses". Thus when I was in Brooklyn I used to have to ask for "medium white *store* cheese" if I expected to get my usual kind. The usage rather puzzled me, so I tried to track it down. I had assumed that it was purely a New York City form, so began enquiring about its use in circles extending gradually outward from the metropolis. I found it common in Newark, Paterson, Yonkers, Stamford, Elizabeth, Perth Amboy, &c. But when I investigated beyond the immediate metropolitan penumbra I felt puzzled. While it gave out in New Jersey & Connecticut, it persisted steadily *up the Hudson*—in Poughkeepsie, Kingston, & even Albany, Troy, & Rensselaer & Washington counties. And to cap the climax, I found it in full blast in *Vermont*—of all places, the *least* likely to be influenced by New York City . . . . . & the least likely to be over-run by process cheese! Well—this wholly changed my theory. Obviously, the phrase was *not* a Manhattanism, but something from the north which, escap-ing southern New England, had reached the metropolis through the Hudson River trade route. And so it turned out to be. "Store cheese" originated some 100 to 150 years ago in the zone of colonisation embracing both Vermont & up-state New York. The phrase sprang from a local custom which arose even before central dairies began to supplant the home making of cheeses—that of making *small* cheeses for private domestic use, & *large* ones to export to shops in the cities & towns. Thus the standard *large* cheese was a *store* cheese; & if a farmer's home-made supply gave out, so that he had to buy a few pounds from a "gin'ral store" at Schuylerville, Perkins' Four Corners, Newfane, or West Brattleboro, he would know that his order would be cut from one of the great cheeses sold to stores. Therefore he would be apt to say to the rustic or village shopkeeper—"Wal, Zeke, I guess I'll hev to git a couple o' paounds o' yer best yaller *store* cheese, seein' as haow M'randy used up the lâst o' whet we had in th' haouse fer supper Thusdy." And so the expression "store cheese" arose; inextricably associated with the large 2 × 1 foot cheeses of retail commerce. Since Vermont & upper New York traded but little with southern New England, we never acquired the expression; but because of the Hudson River— along which trade & population flowed, & which brought many up-staters to New York City—the metropolis acquired it early . . . even before the age of tin-foil cheese. It was at first used to distinguish the *then* common large cheeses from the choice potted brands which came in glass or porcelain jars. And so the puzzle was solved. It may be added that the phrase is *very gradually* filtering into southern New England from New York City—aided by the growing prominence of tinfoil cheese, & the presence of chain store clerks transferred from shops in the areas where it flourishes. Where tinfoil cheese is securing the ascendancy, there is a trend toward giving (heretofore) common cheese some distinguishing name—& in areas untouched by New York influence I have heard such amusing forms as *"cut* cheese" (Haverhill, Mass.) & even *"cooking* cheese" (A & P store in Providence). I have given this small matter in detail as a typical sample of the way dialects are formed & diffused. The small-scale research which I applied to this case must be fairly similar to much of the large-scale research prosecuted by Kurath's continent-wide survey.

Glad the books on astronomy have arrived. Don't hurry with them—go through them gradually & let the facts sink in one by one. And later on, if you are interested, I can lend you others—both general works, & some treating of interesting by-paths. I can also send volumes covering other sciences—a very good assortment in chemistry & physics (not recent books, though), & less ample material in geology, zoölogy, &c. I have the entire series of Steele's old "14 Weeks" textbooks—astronomy, geology, chemistry, zoölogy, physics, physiology—which were wildly popular half a century ago, & which I still think are almost unsurpassed in giving beginners a good introduction to the sciences they cover. Some of them sound quaint in places today—but they certainly prepare the mind for more thorough studies.

Don't hurry about "Creep Shadow"—it certainly was thoughtful of you & Eph-Li to bind a copy for me. Glad the tale isn't disappointing. Most readers seem to assign it a sort of middle place among Merritt's tales. I can well imagine how large a booklet all the parts will make. The bindings of "The Barbarian" & "The Spot of Life" are tremendously clever, & if this job is of equal proficiency I shall feel grateful & fortunate indeed! Derleth recently gave me his latest detective story—"The Man On All Fours"—which is pretty clever for a pot-boiling novel written in a single week. I'll lend it to you some time if you like—of course it isn't weird.

I haven't submitted anything further to W T, but am still experimenting with fiction. Am about ¾ through the second writing of a tale called "The Shadow out of Time", which may come to 50 pages—I'm beginning p. 32 now. I tried to develop it in a shorter form, but couldn't do it. The climax was not sufficiently prepared for—i.e., there was not enough atmospheric building-up to give the final revelation the illusion of being significant. I shall complete the thing, but may never type it or shew it around. I am virtually certain there will be no professional market for it. It is plain that nowadays the long & gradual tale is the type I naturally incline to—though of course the subject matter has a great deal to do with it. I hope I can arrange for more time for fictional experiments.

I surely envy you your pleasant autumn—though for the past three days it has been unusually mild here. I took a walk Saturday, & may possibly to-day—the temperature being around 60°. The leaves are now all gone—a thing I mourn, although it has the one compensating advantage of giving me a clearer view of the distant horizon from my desk window. As it is, I am now gazing all across the city to the purple hills of the western countryside, with a picturesque steeple (on Federal Hill, some 2 miles away) shooting up half way between. Such is the pleasantness of this afternoon, that both Pres. Randall & Mr. Osterberg are out on the clubhouse roof. They both send you & Crom their regards. And Mrs. Spotty—mother of the late Sam Perkins—is racing around the back garden.

Next Friday I shall probably go to Boston to see W. Paul Cook, who is coming down for a week. Whether the weather will be fit for any Salem & Marblehead exploration remains to be seen. Doubtless I shall see Cole, Parker, & possibly one or two other amateurs.

The Wandrei expedition didn't get here after all, but turned back to St. Paul. Whether the wanderer will get out to see Klarkash-Ton remains to be seen—it would surely be a memorable meeting if it did eventuate! So far, of all the W T group C A S has met only Price in person.

Price, by the way, hopes to resume travelling in the spring—making Chicago his headquarters & taking subsidiary tours in the east. He may get to Providence—a development I shall surely welcome!

The new *Marvel Tales* came the other day, but of all its contents only the Keller story is of any weird merit. That tale indeed has a rather potent atmosphere of evil & gathering menace, & I'm surprised that the remunerative magazines turned it down. Bloch's little sketch[4]—a palpable Derleth imitation—isn't bad for quasi-juvenile work . . . which reminds me that he has had a *second* story—"The Feast in the Abbey"—accepted by W.T. Have just read the Nov. W T, & am rather unimpressed. There's nothing really first-rate in it—Price's novelette being a palpable pot-boiler. Derleth's story is from an idea furnished by the weird-tale fan Harry Brobst (now of Providence), who is a native of the ancient Pennsylvania-German region where "hexerei" flourishes. The plot is as Brobst gave it, except that in the original a *bowl of water* was used instead of a mirror. Brobst thinks that the change rather needlessly subtracts from the local colour. I've read up Howard's serial at last, & am a trifle disappointed. Not as much suggestion of brooding, unholy antiquity as in some of his stuff.

Well—I must get to work before long. Have just bought the 143[d] number of the good old Farmer's Almanack, a New England fixture since 1793. It has changed very little in aspect & type of contents since its foundation. My family has had it virtually since its beginning—my file being unbroken since 1834, & with other specimens going back to 1805. I wish I could complete it, but early numbers bring very high prices. I'd also like to get good copies to replace some of the tattered ones I have.

Again congratulating you on your new story & poem, & with best regards to you, Eph-Li, Crom, & everybody,

     I remain

          Yrs under the Black Seal—
            Ech-Pi-El.

[P.S. on envelope:] Did I forget to give you Barlow's new temporary address in Washington? It is *1218 Sixteenth St., N.W.*

Notes

1. J. Wasso, "Nightmare," *Fantasy Magazine* 4, No. 1 (September 1934): 10–14. Wasso (1906–1987) was an Austro-Hungarian-born fan and letter writer residing in Pen Argyl, PA. He published eight letters in *WT* (1930–39) and one in *Startling Stories* (November 1948); one of these was signed John Wasso, Jr.
2. Also called anemosis, a flaw in wood resulting in partial separation of the complete annual ring, caused by wind where no fire or bacteria is present.
3. "The Forbidden Room."
4. *Marvel Tales* 1, No. 3 (Winter 1934): "Lilies" (78–80) by Robert Bloch; "The Golden Bough" (92–111) by David H. Keller.

[23]   [ALS, JHL]

                    66 College St.,
                      Providence, R.I.,
                        Dec. 22, 1934.

Dear Rhi´-Mhel:—

         This is the first even partial let-up I have had for weeks in the vortex of tasks pressing in on me—& so fragmentary is the respite that I fear my epistle will be both badly scrawled & sadly inadequate as a reply to yours of the 1st. Meanwhile I hope you duly received the package—consisting largely of old amateur papers exhumed during a long-overdue file-cleaning—which I despatched some days ago.

Sorry to hear of Wright rejections—but as you know, I've had plenty of them myself! You'll land something sooner or later—& after that the acceptance percentage will increase. Glad there were some useful & applicable hints among those I gave in my previous letter. I've found the preparation of a *time-chart* almost indispensable—without it one gets abominably mixed up as to characters & events, & their ages & sequence. Your description of "The Waterfall" sounds immensely promising to me, & if I were you I'd go ahead with the story—making a fresh start if your present one seems inadequate. As for the sketches of the "Mts. of Madness" entities—I'll be glad to let you have these just as soon as I can make copies. I want to keep clear pictures & exact data regarding all my horrors, (even details which do not appear in the stories) so that I can if necessary use them consistently in future work.

Yes—"The Forbidden Room" certainly illustrates your steady progress, & ought certainly to be welcomed by the small magazines even if their bigger & more remunerative brothers turn it down. About writing to editors—it is certainly best *not* to write anything long. I don't think that any letter is actually needed—but it's all right to enclose a note briefly stating any facts or conditions which need to be stated (as, for instance, unwillingness to submit to deletions or alterations). I have several enquiries out regarding the red dots, & will let you know any answers I receive. Hope Crawford will use "Charlotte", but a rejection from him really means nothing. He hasn't the slightest glimmering of ability to recognise merit in fiction. For example—it develops that he turned down Keller's splendidly realistic story of insanity, "The Dead Woman", which Schwartz later used & which has been reprinted in the latest British "Not at Night". He could see nothing in it, but says it "gave him a laugh"! A hopeless case! Glad my comments on the verses proved intelligible & reasonably illuminating. I'm sure Hornig will relish the poem. Why don't you do a linoleum-block design for it?

Speaking of blocks—your portrait work is surely remarkable, & I'm anxious to see what you'll do with other physiognomies. There is plenty of biographical work to be done amongst the gang—enough to keep you & Eph-Li indefinitely busy. Not only authors but editors ought to be written up. Wright—Hall—Hornig himself—&c.

By this time, of course, you've received the coverless F F for December. I was glad to see "Aphlar" in print, & am sure it will be cordially received. Hornig writes that he has some plan in mind to make the venture self-supporting—& I surely hope it may successfully develop. I've just sent in another insert for my article—describing Hodgson's "Night Land."

About J. Wasso, Jr., author of "Nightmare"—I have a vague idea that he writes science fiction of some sort . . . . though I've never read anything of his, & may be wrong.

Before long you'll doubtless be getting some Hodgson material—from both Dwyer & Derleth. I don't think "The House on the Borderland" will disappoint you. Yes—I often have a preconception of a story, from the title, which the text itself shatters—but this isn't a case of that sort. This novel is just what you think it's going to be—it doesn't let you down. You'll find the endlessly long "Night Land" (538 pp) hardest to wade through—Derleth absolutely refused to finish it. But I advise you to stick it out. It's an awful hash; couched in a pathetically erroneous attempt at reproducing old-fashioned language, but all the same it's worth going through. The masterly depiction of a dead world of midnight horror—with frightful landscapes & monstrous, unknown entities—is enough to atone for all the defects . . . . verboseness, repetitiousness, sentimentality, & clumsy pseudo-archaism. Koenig's article on Hodgson in the new F F interested me greatly—& mentioned one story (the short in the anthology) which I haven't read.[1] Weird fandom owes a great debt to K. for bringing Hodgson out of his unmerited obscurity.

"Wind shake" certainly is curious stuff! The sample you sent would surely make good binding material as it stands—but possibly its later stiffening would be against it. Does it get brittle & crumbling? Thanks for the "Owyhee Idaho Spud" wrapper. It surely does bring up the atmosphere of old days, when references to Owyhee County & the Snake were frequent in this household! So Idaho is making a specialty of its potatoes? That 'spud' on the motor license plates must have been picturesque . . . rather like the codfish on the 1928 Massachusetts plates, & the pelican which occasionally figures on Louisiana plates. The cod—typifying the great fishers off the Massachusetts coast—has always been a kind of symbol of the Bay State, & a gilded wooden codfish always hangs in the senate chamber of the state house. It has been so from colonial times—the same carved & gilded fish being transferred from the ancient Province House to the Old State House, & from that to the present domed edifice in 1800. A few years ago some Harvard students stole it as a joke, but it was soon safely returned to its traditional place. It is humorously known as "The Sacred Cod".

So I *hadn't* spoken about "Old Man" & my dreams of him! Well—he was a great fellow. He belonged to a market at the foot of Thomas Street—the hill street mentioned in "Cthulhu" as the abode of the young artist—& could usually (in later life) be found asleep on the sill of a low window almost touching the ground. Occasionally he would stroll up the hill as far as the Art Club, seating himself at the entrance to one of those old-fashioned courtyard archways (formerly common everywhere) for which Providence is so noted. At night, when the electric lights made the street bright, the space within the archway would remain pitch-black, so that it looked like the mouth of an illimitable abyss, or the gateway of some nameless dimension. And there, as if stationed as a guardian of the unfathomed mysteries beyond, would crouch the sphinxlike, jet-black, yellow-eyed, & incredibly ancient form of Old Man. I first knew him as a youngish cat in 1906, when my elder aunt lived in Benefit St. nearby, & Thomas St. lay on my route downtown from her place. I used to pet him & remark what a fine boy he was. I was 16 then. The years went by, & I continued to see him off & on. He grew mature—then elderly—& finally cryptically ancient. After about 10 years—when I was grown up & had a grey hair or two myself—I began calling him "Old Man". He knew me well, & would always purr & rub around my ankles, & greet me with a kind of friendly conversational "e-ew" which finally became hoarse with age. I came to regard him as an indispensable acquaintance, & would often go considerably out of my way to pass his habitual territory, on the chance that I might find him visible. Good Old Man! In fancy I pictured him as an hierophant of the mysteries behind the black archway, & wondered if he would ever invite me *through* it some midnight . . . . wondered, too, if I could ever come back to earth alive after accepting such an invitation. Well—more years slipped away. My Brooklyn period came & went; & in 1926, a middle-aged relique of 36, with a goodly sprinkling of white in my thatch, I took up my abode in Barnes Street—whence my habitual downtown route led straight down Thomas St. hill. And there by the ancient archway Old Man still lingered! He was not very active now, & spent most of his time sleeping—but he still knew his fellow-elder, & never failed to give his hoarse, friendly "e-ew" when he chanced to be awake. About 1927 he took on a sort of final second youth & began to be awake more. He had been sticking rather close to the market, but now I met him farther & farther up the hill, & very often at the old archway. Good Old Man! In 1928 he seemed a trifle feeble, but his purring friendliness was unabated. Not long before my 38th birthday I saw him—him whom I had known at 16. Then in August I began to miss him. Always when turning the corner on to the hill I used to look down ahead & see if I could discern a familiar lump of black by the archway or at the market. Now I failed to see the graceful old furry lump. I feared the worst—but scarcely dared to enquire at the market. At last—in September—I did enquire & found that my fears were all too well founded. After more than two decades Old Man had gone through the archway at last, & dissolved into that eternal night of which he was a true fragment—that eternal night which had sent him up to earth as a tiny black atom of sportive kittenhood so long ago! Assuredly, I felt desolate enough without my old friend—without any black lump to look for on the ancient hill. I had dreamed of him—& the mysteries of the archway—before; but I now began to do so with redoubled vividness. He would greet me in sleep on a spectral Thomas Street hill, & gaze with aged yellow eyes that spoke secrets older than Ægyptus or Atlantis. And he would mew an invitation for me to follow him through the archway—beyond which lay (as saith Dunsany) "the unreverberate darkness of the abyss."[2] In no dream up to now have I actually followed him through—but I have often wondered what will happen if ever I do . . . . . whether, in such an event, I shall ever again awake in this tri-dimensional world? When I mentioned these dreams to Dwyer he wanted to make a story about Old Man, but he has not yet done so. If he doesn't, I may myself some day. Good Old Man! But I am sure that no world he would lead me to would be a world of horror. He is too old & true a friend for that! When little Sam Perkins appeared on the scene last summer I decided that he must be a great-great-great-great-great-grandson of Old Man—perhaps a messenger despatched from the Abyss by my old friend. As soon as his great violet eyes began to turn yellow, I occasionally addressed him as Old Man, & fancied I could sense a spark of recognition! Perhaps he was my friend him-self in a new body! But, alas, he did not remain long. He, too, returned to that eternal Night of which he & all his kind are inalienable fragments! Thanks, by the way, for immortalising little Sam in the name of your character. The Kap-pa Alpha Tau is investigating the hostile influence which seems to hover over the felidae this year; & as soon as we discover the daemon responsible for it, we shall call forth some very strange force through monstrous midnight in-cantations! All hands, by the way, send their sincerest regards to Crom, & ex-press the hope that his indisposed paw may soon regain its pristine vigour.

Enclosed are some cuttings on place-names which you may find of inter-est. Only the one so marked need be returned. Yes—the Indians would have a hard time recognising some of their names as we use them. The number of *widely different* versions of the same Indian original used in the early colonial pe-riod, before any settled convention of spelling existed, proved how carelessly & inexactly our alien tongues & palates rendered the complex aboriginal syllables. Thus our local Indians were at first called *Nahigansetts* as well as *Narragansetts.* *Weybosset* was also known as *Weypauset,* & *Moshassuck* & *Mooshausick* are variants of the same word. The longest authentic Indian place name in the world is that of a lake near Webster, Mass., not far from the N.W. corner of Rhode Island. There are several versions of it, but the most authentic is the following—

Chargog'agogmanchaug'igoggigun'gimaug.[3]

Twelve syllables! It is, of course, a compound term, with many descriptive or qualifying root words fused together. I forget the exact meaning, but it is something like "black round lake of clear water in the high land of pines" . . . . . that is, a whole phrase condensed (or rather, coalesced) into a single word. Popularly, the lake is known as *Chargog'agog* (4 syllables) or even *Chargog* (2 syll); but in recent years the full name has been somewhat exploited as a curiosity for the benefit of the tourist trade. The 'bus that goes there has the name printed along its side—& it reaches the whole length!

Turning to English pronunciation—no, there is *no authenticity whatever* for a "long" sound of foot (rhyming with *boot*). Any radio announcer using such a quantity is making a mistake. This pronunciation exists among the lower classes in the north of England & perhaps in Scotland, but it has no standing or justification. I never came across it in an American, or in any educated person, British or American. Variations in dialect—& the paradoxical lack of sensitiveness to them existing in many quarters—surely form a study in themselves. Enclosed are a few cuttings—which you needn't return—connected with the subject of localisms. I was full-grown before I realised that the word "tenement" has any humble significance. It does not in England—nor does it here. Rhode Island is certainly closer to original British usages than any other part of the United States.

It is interesting to hear that in the Northwest large round cheeses are becoming obsolete. Here in Providence they certainly hold their own despite the infinity of different package products displayed side by side with them. I've sometimes watched a cheese counter for 10 or 15 minutes, & always find that the sale of old-fashioned cheese vastly exceeds that of the tinfoil varieties. It is only in the small neighbourhood centres that package cheese predominates. In such places I fancy the dealers have not enough refrigerator space to keep a wide assortment of large cheeses. In time, New England may change like the rest of the country—& if it does, I fancy the term "store cheese" will get a foothold. "Cut cheese" & "cooking cheese" are probably only temporary forms. Regarding limburger—I've sampled it only once, at the late Henry S. Whitehead's. I had heard it doubtfully spoken of all my life, but had never come across it at first-hand. Whitehead had some, & dared me to try it. It was not nearly as bad as its odour—although there are other kinds I'd choose. The kind I tasted came in a glass jar—& gastronomic purists have since told me that such a product is not altogether like the real, knock-'em-down original limburger of song & story. Can it be that my boast of 'knowing limburger' is unwittingly a false one? It said 'limburger' on the label, & Whitehead—as one of the most travelled & cosmopolitan of beings—ought to know what's what!

Glad the astronomical books are proving enjoyable. Take your time with them, & share them with Eph-Li. They'll certainly give you an admirable perspective regarding the earth & its fellow-orbs, & increase your appreciation of *good* interplanetary fiction. They'll also cause you to see the flaws & absurdities of a good deal of the trashy celestial junk in the pulp magazines. No one can appreciate interplanetary fiction without a smattering of astronomical knowledge. I missed a good deal through reading Verne *before* I studied astronomy in 1902 & thereafter. The book alluding to Carthage which I'm lending Eph-Li is Flaubert's famous novel "Salammbo". It really gives a tremendously vivid picture of the old Punic civilisation, since Flaubert studied the subject deeply & wrote with the greatest historical accuracy. You'll enjoy the book as much as Eph-Li.

I know I shall enjoy "Creep, Shadow", even if it isn't up to Merritt's highest level. It is certainly generous of Eph-Li to bind that copy for me! I'll lend you Derleth's "Man on all Fours" as soon as my aunt has read it. As such things run, it isn't bad at all. Regarding the phrase "pot-boiling"—I am astonished to hear that it is unknown in the west! It has for generations been part of the common slang of England & the Eastern United States, & is to be found in Brewer's well-known Dictionary of Phrase & Fable. A *pot-boiler* is a listless, forced, commercial literary product concocted solely for money—the imputation being that the poor hack who produces it needs the cash to buy fuel & food so that he can keep the pot boiling above the kitchen fire. No— except for Derleth, no living members of the gang have published novels to their credit. Whitehead was the author of several books—one a novel for boys, dealing with school life. The late Everett McNeill (d. 1929), one of the crowd in New York, was a fairly well-known author of boys' books ("The Totem of Black Hawk," "Tonty of the Iron Hand", &c.) Wandrei has written two novels—one weird & one realistic—but neither one is published or likely to be.[4] As for my new story—pressure of other matters has forced me to postpone finishing it, so that it stands just where it did last month. I require unlimited leisure for serious fictional composition. Your idea for the fish-pedlar yarn is really splendid, & I hope you'll go ahead & develop it. A thing like that, if well-written, ought to have a chance with Wright.

I surely envy you your mild autumn with its raspberry & barley crops. I went to Boston as planned, & saw Cook, but the weather was too cold to permit of the explorations we wished to make. We discussed the coming Miniter memorial, had dinner with Cole, visited the old Royall mansion (1737) in Medford, & examined some unusually interesting family papers left by Mrs. Miniter. These latter included letters from the fronts at Chippewa during the War of 1812, letters from gold-seeking California '49ers, Civil War letters, & all sorts of documents between 1800 & 1870. I am now storing these until a suitably appreciative heir of Mrs. Miniter can be found. Wandrei had a splendid visit in Auburn, & is now on the move again. Price is giving up his Chicago plans, & hopes to buy a lot at San Carlos & build a very cheap house of Spanish-Moorish design. But he still intends to make the Eastern trip next summer.

Early this month my aunt & I attended an unusual number of lectures in connexion with the local "Art Week". I had to miss the later ones because of a cold spell which kept me indoors from Dec. 8 to 12th, inclusive. The mercury was down to +10°, day after day. It is milder now, & I've been out often—getting some Christmas surprises for my aunt & some trappings for the tree we mean to have. I haven't had a tree before in a quarter of a century. After Yule I may possibly visit Long in N.Y.

I like your "Ship" in *Marvel Tales*—it suggests all sorts of marvels & strange vistas, which is what a weird poem ought to do. Glad "Erich Zann" stands up well with you & your father on re-reading. Yes—"The Canal" is great stuff. I once cited it as one of the 6 best stories W T ever printed—the other 5 being "Beyond the Door", "The Floor Above", "In Amundsen's Tent", "The Night Wire", & "Bells of Oceana."[5] The author is a woman, & has written other stuff—some very poor ("Light Echoes") & some distinctly good ("The Bird of Space").[6] "The Black God's Kiss", despite overtones of conventional romance, is great stuff. The other-world descriptions & suggestions are stupendous. "Black God's Shadow" not quite up to it. The Dec. W T is vastly better than the Nov. one—Klarkash-Ton's "Xeethra" leading. Yes—I got the Crawford booklet. "White Sibyl" splendid, but "Men of Avalon" a bit mawkish, artificial, & mediocre. The antarctic cutting interested me vastly—thanks! I think, though, that a later flight of Byrd's cast doubt on the positiveness of his anti-strait conclusions.

Glad to hear that you had a pleasant Thanksgiving, with appropriate gorging. Mine was also pleasant. My aunt & I gorged at the boarding-house across the back garden (home of the late Samuel Perkins), & took a walk through the ancient hill streets to the south of us. The day was gratifyingly warm, though cloudy. In the evening Brobst called.

Well—I hope Christmas will be no less delightful all around! Regards to everybody—including Crom.

Yrs most sincerely—

—E'ch-Pi-El

[P.S.] Enclosed is an article (please return) on the old Farmer's Almanack. In the bundle of papers I have enclosed a copy of this year's issue for you—so that you can see how close to the past New England keeps. ¶ Yes—Eph-Li spoke of that contest story.[7] I'd like to see it! ¶ Your Arkham church drawing is captivating indeed. Wish I could compete in that line! ¶ Just had a call for some more biographical material—this time in amateurdom. Pres. Babcock of the N.A.P.A. is preparing a brochure of the ex-presidents of the last 15 years—to supplement an earlier book of the kind.[8]

Notes

1. The story was "The Voice in the Night."

2. The last line of Dunsany's "The Probable Adventure of the Three Literary Men"; quoted in HPL's "The Nameless City" (*CF* 1.237).

3. The name comes from Nipmuc, an Algonquian language, and means "Fishing Place at the Boundaries—Neutral Meeting Grounds." The lake usually is referred to simply as Lake Webster.

4. HPL refers to *Dead Titans, Waken!* and *Invisible Sun.* The former was published in altered form as *The Web of Easter Island* (Arkham House, 1948); the latter remained unpublished until it appeared in *Dead Titans, Waken! and Invisible Sun* (Lakewood, CO: Centipede Press, 2011).

5. Paul Suter, "Beyond the Door" (April 1923; rpt. September 1930); M. L. Humphries, "The Floor Above" (May 1923; rpt. June 1933); H. F. Arnold, "The Night Wire" (September 1926; rpt. January 1933); John Martin Leahy, "In Amundsen's Tent" (January 1928; rpt. August 1935); Everil Worrell, "The Canal" (December 1927; rpt. April 1935); Arthur J. Burks, "Bells of Oceana" (December 1927; rpt. April 1934). HPL cites

these 6 stories in a letter to Farnsworth Wright ([January? 1930]), not published in *WT*. See "Letters to Farnsworth Wright," *Lovecraft Annual* No. 8 (2014): 22.

6. "The Bird of Space" (*WT*, September 1926); "Light Echoes" (*WT*, May 1930).

7. See FLB 19.

8. William C. Ahlhauser, *Ex-Presidents of the National Amateur Press Association—Sketches* (1919). Babcock seems not to have issued the brochure HPL speaks of, but he did publish "A Voice from the Grave," which consists of an extract of a letter from HPL to Babcock discussing NAPA and amateur affairs.

[24]   [ANS, JHL]

[30 December 1934]

[Appended to letter by August Derleth to HPL, 27 December 1934:]

Happy New Year, O Rhi´-Mhel! Here is (a) an answer—or attempted answer—to your red dot question, & (b) a possible news item for Eph-Li . . . . about Derleth's illness & recovery. ¶ Had a delightful Christmas—with the first *tree* since my boyhood. ¶ Am just about to start on my visit to Long. Barlow is in N Y, & I shall see a good deal of him. Wandrei also hit the metropolis Thursday after a sea voyage from San Francisco. It surely will be quite a convention! Expect to see Koenig, old de Castro, & others of whom you know either directly or indirectly. Hope the weather will be decently tolerable—ice on the roads is now delaying some of the coaches. I shall take a 1 a.m. coach, getting to Belknap's about 8 a.m. Monday. Regards to Crom.
          —E'ch-Pi-El

[*Enclosure:* August Derleth to HPL, 27 December 1934, *Essential Solitude* 672]
[. . .]
As for those little red dots—yes, of course, I know all about them. Those dots are just used by W. to indicate something he wishes to recall to his attention—it may be a good descriptive phrase, it may be an error, it may be faulty punctuation, it may be the *u* in such a spelling as labour, it may be an error in time or place or a detail error. If the matter is small enough, it is sometimes possible to find another red dot above the actual point in question apart from the one at the edge of the line. I hope this clears up the matter. The dots indicate nothing more, nothing set and definite, unfortunately. It is interesting to speculate upon what W. sometimes sees, but it is impossible to find it all the time. The *our* endings usually merit them.
[. . .]

[25]   [ALS, JHL]

66 College St.,
Providence, R.I.,
Jany. 28, 1935.

Dear Rhīʻ Mhel:—

Very glad to hear the news—& to see the delightful samples of your recent work. Enclosed is your story, with such alterations in wording as seem more or less advisable. It certainly is a powerful & haunting piece of work—full of a vivid, convincing atmosphere of brooding outsideness—& I believe your father is right in considering it your best effort so far. It *suggests* so much—& gets it across without any prosy explanations. Nor does it peter out. Interest keeps up till the end, & the conclusion itself strikes just the right note. Following synopses undoubtedly helped greatly. As you see, I am making no structural changes whatsoever—merely technical alterations in sentence structure, &c. Most of these slight alterations will probably be self-explanatory—but if any seem peculiar or unjustified, I'll be glad to discuss them. It is well to cultivate—gradually & easily—a habit of precision in the use of words & the modelling of phrases. Simplicity & clearness form the joint goal—you'll notice that most of the "Silver Sail" changes are in the direction of simpler expression. Beware of tautology—the needless piling on of two or more words which mean the same thing. Notice that I've eliminated tautological phrases in several cases—"fear *& panic*", "raiment *& attire*", "wish *or desire*", &c. &c. But of course these are minor surface matters. It's a splendid yarn, & I congratulate you on it! Glad you're forming an accurate concept of *Vesper*—good idea, making a map. You can use this seaport repeatedly in various stories—indeed, Hampdon & Vesper make quite a western analogue of Arkham & Kingsport! Just as well not to use fantastic & exotic nomenclature in this story—the proximity of the wonders to the every-day world makes them seem all the more vivid. I trust this story may encounter a favourable editorial reception when it sallies forth at last—it surely deserves it!

I'll be glad to see the fish-peddler yarn when it's done—the idea surely is potent. And I trust the tomb idea may likewise prove fruitful. Your recent dream of the dying old man & his terrifying discourse with the museum ought also to make gorgeous material—though of course we are never able to reproduce dreams with quite the same force & vitality which they originally had for us. Meanwhile I trust you won't neglect the waterfall tale. Glad "The Forbidden Room" will appear in the F F, & that "Charlotte" is definitely scheduled for M T.[1] Keep it up—& sooner or later you'll be adding *Weird Tales* to your list of available media! Glad you're going to make a linoleum block for "The Worm". I can say without flattery that you absolutely do the best work in this medium of anyone I've yet encountered. Those designs for Eph-Li's column & Petaja's sonnets are really major triumphs of their kind. Their firm, assured strokes, selective taste, & instinctive quality of harmony & balance mark them out as the finest illustrative or decorative work which any of the semi-pro magazines have yet had. They make the pitiful alleged pictures in *Marvel Tales* look like juvenile caricatures. Good as the "Yith" heading is, I believe these new specimens mark something of an advance on it. Again I say, keep it up! Petaja, by the way, is a very clever artist himself, as attested by sketches he has sent me. He shewed me the sonnet dedicated jointly to C A S & me. His versatility is really unusual—violinist, artist, poet, & fiction writer.[2] "Syzygy" is good stuff, & I hope you'll do a cut for it. There was a coloured design of his own on the copy he gave me—which might well furnish suggestions. Glad he's dedicating a sonnet to you . . . I suppose it embodies Yith & Sotho & the Blue Stone . . . . But really, there's no need of your envying his poetic powers, since your own verse is coming right along in the proper direction. Hope you'll do that series in ottava rima like "The Ship". All these things will surely keep you busy—but I trust you'll have time for some collaborations with Eph-Li. Some of his story plots ought to come out well under your verbal handling. Incidentally—I surely wish him success in the F M cover contest. And then, of course, the biographical series offers an unlimited field for both—with you as illustrator. Hope the F F keeps going in order to handle this material! Hornig hinted at a financing plan which would at least let him break even—but so far he has not explained what it is. I doubt if he'll ever get rid of the misprints—those seem to be inseparable from any magazine cheaply & hastily printed. So an issue is going to be dedicated to W T? That's rather copying after F M—but I suppose it's all right. By the way—I see by a biographical note in F M that Hornig is only 18 years old. That's even younger than I thought he was.

I congratulate Eph-Li on the distinction of a Merritt telegram. A M hasn't even answered my letter of a year ago! About "The Picture in the House"—it appeared in *Weird Tales* for Jany. 1924, & later received a minor citation in E. J. O'Brien's annual. Glad Derleth could solve the red dot mystery—although of course his solution doesn't explain just why the capricious Brother Farnsworth dots each particular passage in any given MS. About "-our" endings . . . . the letter implies a suffix & not a pronoun! What Derleth means is the conservative custom, still universal in Great Britain & personally followed by many in the U.S. (including himself—& myself), of retaining the letter *u* in such words as *colour, labour, favour, honour,* &c.—which in America have had a tendency since 1840 or so to be abbreviated to "color"[,] "labor", "favor", &c. Wright follows the new American fashions in spelling (indeed, he goes much further in the direction of novelty than do the best American magazines), hence marks every "-our" ending of the sort for alteration into "-or". It is this to which Derleth refers. Regarding "L & M"—this refers to the New York publishing form of *Loring & Mussey,* who have brought out all his books so far. Incidentally, they consider his new "Sign of Fear" the best yet, & intend to bring it out in due course of time. Derleth's letter need not be returned.

Yes—I had a delightful Yuletide, & your very attractive & distinctive card did indeed arrive on time. Glad to hear that your own Christmas was festive . . . . & that my message to you & Crom arrived on New Year's! Glad also that the package arrived safely. Bless my soul—of course that Farmer's Almanack was for you to keep! Some of the information, of course, won't work for the longitude of Asotin—but the general plan of the thing is universally useful . . . & capable of assisting the study of astronomy quite a bit. Take your time, by the way, with the astronomical books. These things are to be assimilated slowly—not to be swallowed in a single gulp! I think you'll find them a great aid in appreciating some interplanetary fiction. Take your time also with the other material. I think you'll like "The Monk & the Hangman's Daughter." "The Turn of the Screw" is subtle & masterful, but I wouldn't emulate Henry James's style too closely. He was so over-anxious to convey exact shades of mood & meaning that he finally fell into an involved, mincing, old-maidish sort of style which defeated its own ends. You'll like Hodgson, I'm sure, in spite of all his defects. Wish Derleth & Dwyer would hurry up & pass along the volumes in their custody! It surely is unfortunate that Hodgson was prematurely cut off by the war, & that so little is known about him.

My visit to Long—as you've doubtless learned from a postcard of a fortnight ago to Eph-Li—was a highly enjoyable event. The whole business acquired something of the atmosphere of a convention through the presence of Barlow & the arrival of *both* the Wandrei boys—Howard unexpectedly coming on from St. Paul as Donald landed from San Francisco. The brothers have taken a very attractive 4-room flat in Greenwich Village—at 155 West 10th St., above a rather well-known 'bohemian' restaurant called Julius's. The building is about a century old, but made over into apartments with all conveniences. Well—Barlow reached the metropolis Christmas morning, & Belknap took him in charge & found him an hotel 6 blocks north of the Long place. Young Bobby is rather hard to suit, since he demands especially good neighbourhoods & will not consider anything without a private bath. I am not so exacting—so the Longs always get me a room in one of the flats over theirs. These rooms have running water—but unlike Barlow, I am willing to dodge around to the bathroom for my matutinal tub! This was Bob's first visit to New York since infancy, so Belknap was kept busy shewing him the various museums, galleries, art shops, & bookstalls. What fascinated him most was the great Metropolitan Museum with its priceless paintings, Egyptian & classical collections, & everything else under the sun. We all agree that if any sudden holocaust were to engulf Manhattan Island, & if the gods were to allow only *one* object or institution on it to be saved, the Metropolitan Museum is what we would choose for preservation. I reached Belknap's on the morning of Dec. 31, & from then on the events developed rapidly. On Jany. 2 the gang held a monster meeting at Long's with 15 present—Morton, Loveman, Barlow, Leeds, Kirk, Kleiner, Koenig, both Wandreis, Talman, &c. &c. It was

the most enjoyable event I've attended in years—even if Talman did take sur-
reptitious snapshots of the guests with a new German camera which works in
ordinary electric light . . . . catching me in an especially awkward pose, with
my mouth looking as if I were about to whistle a tune or expectorate! Two
evenings later a smaller gathering met at Loveman's Brooklyn apartment, our
host shewing us his magnificent collection of almost 400 Clark Ashton Smith
drawings . . . mostly in colour & all tremendously impressive. This is undoubtedly the finest array of Klarkash-Ton's work outside Auburn—&
Loveman has only recently brought it to N.Y. from his old home in Cleveland. I had seen it in 1922 in Cleveland, but it was wholly new to Belknap, Ar-
E'ch-Bei, & the two Wandreis. On another occasion Koenig shewed Barlow,
Belknap & me through the Electrical Testing Laboratories, in which he holds
an important executive & engineering position. This is a fascinating place,
with all sorts of bizarre devices (suggesting space-rockets, bathyspheres,
atomic projectors, & every kind of scientifictional standby) for gauging the
safety & durability of various household electrical appliances—lamps, cords,
plugs, refrigerators, flatirons, heaters, &c. &c. As a climax to this exhibition,
Koenig gave us a demonstration of *artificial lightning* caused by the passage
through the air—betwixt two metallic poles—of a current of tremendously
high voltage. A good deal of our time was taken up by the book stores, art
shops, & art department of the public library. During the course of the visit
Ar-E'ch-Bei bought a copper-plate & dry point stylus, & began experimenting with the engraver's art. In the bookstalls we encountered several attractive
bargains. Barlow—lucky little rascal—stumbled on a fine old copy of George
W. M. Reynolds's "Wagner the Wehr-Wolf" for only *15¢!* My own chief bargain was a good modern edition of Lewis's "Monk" for a dollar. I now have
all three of the most famous Gothic novels—Mrs. Radcliffe's "Udolpho"
(1785), "The Monk" (1795), & Maturin's "Melmoth" (1820) . . . all in modern
editions. Other sessions of the Gang were at the Wandrei brothers' flat. We
didn't get a chance to look up old de Castro although we half started out for
his place at least twice. There was so little time—& so darned many things to
do! The breakup began Jany. 7th, when Barlow set off for Washington at
10:30 a.m. He cannot stand night travelling as I can, hence had to forfeit a
day in N.Y. I stayed on till midnight, when the Wandreis saw me to the Providence coach. Home at dawn—& struggling with accumulated work ever
since. The weather in general favoured me—only 2 days being so cold as to
give me much inconvenience. On these occasions the protection of the subway helped me to get about. Ar-E'ch-Bei reached Washington in safety,
though his coach was vastly delayed on the road through fog.

About those "Mountains of Madness" entities—let's see what I can do
toward depicting one. I'm not much in the drawing line—but here's a copy of
the rough sketch in my files. I fear it won't convey much except in connexion
with the detailed description in the story—& probably not much even *with*

the description! I never did explicitly draw out the bas-relief designs supposed to exist on the buildings—& unfortunately I can't find the crude pencil suggestions which I did jot down. I'm certainly glad that you like & remember the "Mountains"—whose rejection by Wright did much to discourage me & abridge my subsequent output.

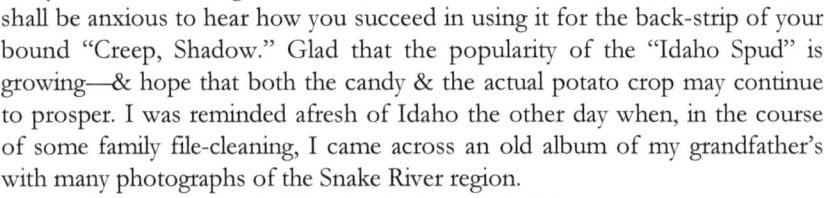

Many thanks for the thicker specimen of "Windshake". That certainly is a fascinating substance, & I shall be anxious to hear how you succeed in using it for the back-strip of your bound "Creep, Shadow." Glad that the popularity of the "Idaho Spud" is growing—& hope that both the candy & the actual potato crop may continue to prosper. I was reminded afresh of Idaho the other day when, in the course of some family file-cleaning, I came across an old album of my grandfather's with many photographs of the Snake River region.

So I *had* mentioned Old Man before! I shall have to write about him some day—& when I do, you can surely have the MS. No more feline disasters to date. Ar-E'ch-Bei has a dim, faint hope that Doodlebug may merely have gone native & taken temporarily to the jungle—but the odds are against anything so fortunate. However, the Villa Barlovia is still well stocked with felidae—a new crop of Low's offspring bringing the figure up to 9! Of Low's previous crop of three, one died & the other two are prospering—having received the respective names of San Marcos & San Sebastian. Congratulations to Crom on his recovery from the wounds of battle. By the time he's grown, he surely will be a young polar bear! Fortunate, in view of his colour, that he has the laundering habit strongly developed. Little Sam Perkins was a great washer too—though his sable coat made the results of the process less obvious.

Yes—place-names are sometimes peculiar things—growing up haphazardly & undergoing all sorts of accidental transmutations. His Satanic Majesty seems to be a very popular godfather for various topographical features—in Natchez, Miss., a deep & curious hollow is called "The Devil's Punch Bowl", while Rhode Island has its Devil's Foot Rock—a large boulder on the road toward Wickford, with a mark like the impression of a gigantic hoof. "Cape Horn" suggests quite a geographical imagination. In New England two rock chasms on the seashore are called respectively "Purgatory" & "The Churn".

Glad to hear that the honest, old-fashioned, man's size cheese is still making a valiant struggle for existence in the northwest! Here's hoping it gains ground & stages a comeback! There are certainly no signs of its decline in New England—for the downtown groceries continue to keep it in the most prominent front cases. Too bad the Asotin cheese was gone before you could get some . . . . better luck next time! But the quick sale was a good indication of popular demand . . . . if the grocer is wise, he'll handle ampler stocks of it! Limburger probably won't be as formidable as you anticipate—but you'd better get as small a package as possible. As I said, I didn't continue eating it for pleasure at Dunedin—although it was not in the least offensive or repellent.

Your report on that presentation copy of "Creep, Shadow" surely arouses my expectations—especially in regard to the 'surprise' you mention. Hope you & Eph-Li aren't putting too much time & energy into the generous project! I shall send along Comte d'Erlette's "Man on All Fours" as soon as I get hold of it again—which I trust will be reasonably soon. Haven't yet been able to finish "The Shadow out of Time" because of other duties—I need a lot of leisure for fiction. I'm really not sure whether I'll keep the thing in its present form, for many points are far from satisfactory to me.

Sorry the summer-like autumn didn't carry over into the winter season. I've been reading reports of very severe weather on the Pacific Coast, but hope you escaped the worst of this. Hereabouts the winter is distinctly not as bad as its predecessor. I've occasionally been kept a prisoner by temperatures under 20°, but spells of rain & fog intervene betwixt cold spells. On Jany. 23 there was a snowstorm of considerable depth & severity—the largest so far this season. Indeed, it had traffic wholly tied up for a while.

Klarkash-Ton & Wandrei certainly had a pleasant time together—it is too bad they didn't have some joint photographs taken. Regarding Sultan Malik's real estate venture—he didn't get the San Carlos lot, but instead purchased a hillcrest estate with house already built . . . also on the west shore of the bay, near Edward Lake & slightly beyond Redwood City. We shall doubtless hear more detailed descriptions when he moves out there. It will be a good thing for him to be settled in a congenial semi-rural environment.

Only just got around to reading the Jany. W.T. No—collectively it isn't nearly as good as the December—though Klarkash-Ton's "Dark Eidolon" is a notable masterpiece which in itself gives the issue distinction. Nothing as powerful as this has appeared before in months. I doubt if the Eadie serial is worth reading. The bit I skimmed through was merely cheap stock mystery junk. "The Canal" was certainly great stuff in its day—it deserves reprinting. ["]The Floor Above" *was* reprinted in the *June 1933* issue . . . . which I'll lend you if you can't find it in Asotin. I'll also lend you "In Amundsen's Tent" (January 1928) if Eph-Li hasn't it in his files. This latter will probably be reprinted in the course of time.

Yes—I was president of the N.A.P.A. in 1922–3. At that time my activity was mainly in the now-abeyant United branch, but Morton & others induced me to accept the National appointment after the newly-elected president— one William J. Dowdell—found it necessary to resign because of the pressure of outside affairs. The period was one of calm after a political storm, & I had a very smooth administration through the coöperation of such fellow-officers as Edward H. Cole, Harry E. Martin, & the late Mrs. Miniter. Babcock's request for an account of my term brings back those old days quite vividly.[3] Just now, by the way, the surface of amateurdom is badly convulsed by warfare. First the Fossils started their memorable row—still raging after a temporary truce—& then the U.A.P.A. of A (whose principal centre is in your own state in Seattle) flared up into spectacular hostilities. Now, to complete the picture, a fight has started in the National—based on Pres. Babcock's drastic removals of delinquent officers. A faction headed by Ex-Sec. Detrick[4] is out for Babcock's removal—but I think this can be averted. He may have been a trifle high-handed, but his general course is a sound one. If officers can't or won't deliver the goods, why retain them? He & young Bradley are certainly doing their best for the association. Meanwhile both factions are besieging Edward H. Cole (as Executive Judge) for legal opinions & interpretations of the constitution—& keeping him so rushed that he could scarcely find time to prepare his critical report. Hope you'll be able to join—the association, not the fighting!—in the course of time. Before long I'll send you another batch of current papers . . . . indeed, I'll enclose one (of which I have duplicates) now—*The Californian*, with an article of mine on the various homes of Poe.

Congratulations on the equipment & occupancy of your new study. It certainly sounds delightful, & I'm sure you'll find it a great help & inspiration in your literary work. Nothing has pleased me more in my present quarters than my ability to have a separate study & bedroom. Even when I've had to combine sleeping & working quarters, though, it has always been a case of sleeping in my library rather than working in a bedroom. When reduced to one room, I have always furnished it as a library & merely parked myself on a couch or folding bed. In one place I had a dressing alcove—& in another place had 2 alcoves to take care of clothes, &c. But the layout at #66 is ideal—a large study, a small connecting bedroom, a capacious clothespress, & deep cupboards on each side of the chimney. Even so, however, the storage & classification of my large files of papers, cuttings, MSS., &c form a titanic problem. Just this week I've tried to cope with the situation by purchasing two small five-drawer chests of dark walnut finish to serve as filing cabinets. By piling one atop the other I secure a tall, convenient cabinet which doesn't take up much floor space. This will help enormously in establishing order among my scattered papers—the arrangement isn't at all bad looking, since the pieces are plain & tasteful in design, almost suggesting the colonial. I got them very cheap at a department-store fire sale. Long has a single cabinet much like one of mine—though of a wood finish I don't particularly care for. I've been looking for such a thing for years, & this was the best bargain I had ever come across—$4.44 for each chest.

I keep getting bulletins from the American Fiction Guild (organisation of professional pulp writers) even though I've never joined. Price lately joined,

& has at once become a leading figure in the organisation. He is one of their board of consulting experts on the very diverse subjects of acetylene work, Oriental rugs, & New Orleans.

The list of persons wishing to borrow the Hodgson books is steadily increasing, but if everybody holds them up as the Two D's are now doing, they won't get around very quickly! Crawford comes after you & Eph-Li on the list for all the volumes—& I hope they help to educate his taste a bit!

And now to the task of clearing my files & getting them into the new cabinet arrangement.

All good wishes—
Yrs most sincerely—
E'ch-Pi-El

[P.S.] Will send "The Man on All Fours" very soon. Now let's see how early you can guess the correct solution of the mystery. I did on p. 32. Hope you'll enjoy it. Keep it as long as you like, & let Eph-Li read it.

[P.P.S.] Last Moment—Jan. F F just arrived. Glad to see "Late Revenge" in print. ¶ Have snatched some time & am doing a bit more on the "Shadow": I'm afraid it will have to be longer than I had originally planned. Am doing a bit of bluffing in describing the geography of Western Australia, but all this can be changed later when I get more detailed information about that region.

Notes

1. "The Forbidden Room" appeared not in *FF* but in *Fanciful Tales*. "The Jewels of Charlotte" appeared not in *Marvel Tales* but in *Unusual Stories*.

2. Petaja's poems are gathered in *As Dream and Shadow* (1972).

3. This appears to be "A Voice from the Grave," published posthumously in Babcock's *Scarlet Cockerel*.

4. Charles L. Detrick, secretary of the NAPA (1934–35).

[26]   [ALS, JHL]

Old 66
March 10, 1935

Dear Rhī-Mhel:—

Well—I'm certainly sorry to hear that you've been under the weather, & hope an early spring may help to bake the last traces of rheumatism out of your system. Glad the pain is over now.

"The Silver Sail" is surely a fine story, & I'm sorry Wright doesn't agree fully instead of partly with my opinion. His verdict is interesting—evidently he's slowly awaking to the merit of your work, & I wouldn't be surprised if he took something before long. As for the "abstruse" comment—that evidently stems from his incurable dislike of any subtlety in a story. He wants every-thing spoiled by a diagram—which of course prevents the best stories from landing at all. It was only by a hair's-breadth that my "Randolph Carter" squeezed in a decade ago. Wright thought my failure to explain *what* uttered those words at the last was well-nigh inexcusable! However—I guess he sometimes uses that pet word *abstruse* just on general principles. Another old standby of his is "unconvincing" . . . . & in the case of my MSS., "too long." No—I certainly wouldn't give in to his demand for a flat, explained ending. I'd rather not place a story than twist it to his mould. As for the red dots—of course some of them probably express mere personal preferences. Hope you can erase them readily without damaging the typed text. Glad the fish-peddler yarn is under way, & hope you'll hit on a fitting motivation in the second ver-sion. The other ideas are promising, too, & I hope you'll use them all one by one. Why don't you keep a note book of good story ideas, jotting each one down as soon as you think of it, so that none will be forgotten? That's the way I do. Glad to see "Reverie"—which is really excellent. The rhyme & me-tre have no flaws, & only the very slightest changes could be suggested. In the 3d line you might eliminate the split infinitive by saying *grimly to mock*. In the 5th line some might consider *old dark* a slightly more harmonious [*sic*] than *dark old*—though that is purely a matter of opinion. The whole thing is really very effective, & I hope it may find appropriate placement.

The death of the F F is surely tragic & regrettable, for nothing can quite take the place of that neat little forum for the exchange of ideas among the weirdists. Your letter formed my first hint of the calamity—though I soon received the new F M with its otherwise puzzling announcement of my biog-raphy. Many will mourn the F F's passing, for there is hardly any chance that F M will take over the bulk of its unpublished contributions & departments. F M is too largely slanted toward science fiction to give weird material a prominent place. And yet a certain amount of such material might well be transferred—in an effort to retain some of the F F's clientele who would oth-erwise drop off. I wonder, by the way, what Hornig will do about paid-up subscriptions? I had renewed, so stand to lose a dollar unless he refunds—or makes arrangements with Schwartz to transfer the subscription to F M. I hope your delectably clever cuts weren't made in vain, & shall urge Schwartz to use them if I have occasion to write him. But anyhow, I guess they'll keep—& there's no telling what fresh chances may turn up. The N.A.P.A. journals would welcome anything like that. By the way—your "Worm" heading is mag-nificent . . . . you certainly improve each time. Be sure to get back any blocks which Hornig may have. By the way—you ought not to have cancelled the dedication of Petaja's "Partings" to yourself. With your year of writing & art behind you, you deserve it just as much as the next man! He sent me a copy with a very clever coloured drawing of his own. Good stuff! As for biograph-ical material—I guess F M will be open to a certain amount of that. Perhaps

Schwartz will select other subjects than those you had in mind—since science-fiction has its own particular set of idols. Meanwhile poor Crawford is having all sorts of difficulties with M T. After having his right hand smashed in the press, he's up against the resignation of his colleague Eshbach. But he still seems set on getting out the magazine if he possibly can!

Glad you like "The Man on All Fours." No hurry—& let Eph-Li read it at leisure. I thought you'd guess the solution about the same time that I did. The tale is really very clever, & I enjoyed it despite a general satiation with detective fiction. The new Derleth detective tale will be out any day now—& on April 24 the serious "Place of Hawks" will appear. Oddly enough, I never read any of the van Dine tales, although the very first of them ran in *Scribners* years ago when my aunt took that magazine. Some day I may accept your kind offer to lend me the "Kennel Case"[1]—although at this moment I'm so swamped that I don't believe I'll have a chance to read it. Thanks for the offer. I haven't yet seen "Crows Fly High",[2] but mean to look it up at the library very shortly. Pleased to know that both you & your father are enjoying the astronomical books—about which there isn't the least hurry. I'll send along "The Monk" whenever you care to see it. Henry James's style is surely an irritating one, & any emulation of it is a mistake. By the way—I must prod Dwyer & Derleth about forwarding those Hodgson books. They surely are carrying delay to excess!

No doubt Eph-Li has mentioned that letter about my tales from Derleth's publishers—which came just before I wrote him. I don't think anything will come of it, but have sent along some junk just the same. Meanwhile I've finished "The Shadow Out of Time", but am so dissatisfied with it that I'm half-resolved to tear it up again & start afresh. About a desert of pure salt—I never recall hearing of anything precisely like that, though I know that in some places various saline & alkaline deposits strongly tincture the soil. The desert in my story is a very prosaic one of sand & rock. As for the MS.—I did promise Barlow that one, although I think I said you could have "The Thing on the Doorstep." Also the one about Old Man if I ever write it. But such things are really of no value. A writer has to amount to a lot more than I'll ever amount to in order to make his scripts of any actual worth.

The N Y trip surely did contain some interesting events. Too bad the non-existent visit to old de Castro will be mentioned! His wife finally died—on Jany. 23, as I guess I wrote Eph-Li. As for the artificial lightning—it really isn't so much of a visual spectacle, although it has a certain roaring impressiveness. The chief appeal is to the imagination—the idea of the stupendous power behind such a thing as a lightning bolt. About Ar-E'ch-Bei's bargain—no, "Wagner the Wehr-Wolf" is by a British author, George W. M. Reynolds, although its scene is laid in Germany. The same is true of its companion volume "Faust & the Demon."

Glad the sketch of the "Mts. of Madness" entity proved interesting. One of Wright's complaints about that story was that it can't be well divided into sections—but the real truth of the matter undoubtedly is that he simply doesn't like it. The same is true of "Innsmouth".

Well—though Doodlebug has not returned to the Villa Barlovia, something very like him has marched into Price's new home on a Redwood City hilltop. Crom has a rival for the pure white championship of the Pacific Coast, for this newcomer . . . an utterly strange, gigantic tom who appeared from nowhere . . . . is a mighty hunter & warrior indeed! His capacity for food exceeds all previously known bounds, while his belligerency is worthy of Conan the Reaver. The other day he clawed a gopher out of its hole & brought it for his master to see before devouring it . . . . . & more recently he attacked & routed a huge strange dog who had eyed his bowl of beans too calculatively. In view of his prowess in the chase, Sultan Malik has named him Nimrod, & he has been duly recognised as overlord of all the California chapters of the Kappa Alpha Tau . . . though of course General Tabasco might challenge his supremacy if he saw fit to return to the Temple of Tsathogua in Averoigne. So Crom is settling down in size! Glad he has such a fine, heavy coat—& hope he will soon recover his former industriousness in the matter of keeping it snowy. Turning to the other end of the chromatic scheme— there are 4 little niggers at the boarding-house across the garden from old 66—brothers or half-brothers of the late & unforgettable Sam Perkins. Frantic telephonic attempts are being made to find good homes for them, though I fervently hope at least one will be kept as a successor to little Sam.

Glad to hear that you got hold of a supply of real cheese, & hope you can replenish it when needed. Trust the limburger will not wholly knock you out!

Yes—"Creep, Shadow" duly arrived, & as I told Eph-Li, I am utterly delighted with its neatness & tastefulness. The two of you certainly did a splendid job—getting a trimness & continuity which I would not have thought possible with irregular magazine instalments including the endings & beginnings of other things. Beside this performance, Munn's amateur serial-bindings seem very primitive indeed! As yet I have not had a moment to read the story, but I am looking forward to that process with the keenest anticipation. Most who have read it speak of it favourably.

Glad your cold spell was brief. Since the long cold of January, R.I. has not been conspicuously troubled with severe weather—though we've had nothing to rival your springlike days. It sounds cheering to hear of vernal agricultural operations—which is more than this region could ever boast in February. Well—it's over the line in March now, & that sounds cheerful, anyhow. ☉ enters ♈³ on the 21st at 8:18 a.m. according to the Old Farmer's . . . . the most cheering event of the year in a psychological way, even though it does not bring the immediate genial warmth which I need for an outdoor programme.

I surely wish that Klarkash-Ton & young Melmoth had had some joint snapshots taken during the latter's sojourn in Averoigne. C A S has been greatly overworked & in very indifferent health during the past autumn &

winter, but he'll probably get around to correspondence before long. By the way—four young weird-fiction enthusiasts in the San Francisco region are planning to motor out & visit him en masse. Since Sultan Malik broke the ice, he has evidently become destined for more frequent contacts with the outside world. The Sultan himself is hammering out fiction as usual. He surely does like California, being a native thereof—born in San Jose & reared in Oakland. I think his work for the A.F.G.[4] will be more than nominal. These consultants are approached by other writers who want accurate information in the fields concerned. Thus if some guild member wants to describe an Oriental rug with minute accuracy, he'll write to Price for assistance. The magazine *Adventure* has long had a staff of experts of this kind.

No—I've never considered collaborating with Long. Collaboration is to me the most difficult & irksome of all work . . . five times harder than writing a story of my own, & with only half the possible reward. It has absolutely no advantages, & every possible disadvantage, so far as I am concerned! I've never done it except as a favour, or on a paid-in-advance non-speculative basis—& this winter I've resolved never to attempt it under *any* circumstances. It isn't worth the nerve-strain it causes.

Glad you found the amateur material of interest. I've now sent along another package which I hope will prove equally so. The political squabbling certainly is discouraging—but one does not have to get mixed up in it. This year it does not seem to have hurt the association as badly as was feared—at least, plans for literary improvement go right ahead. I hope you can join sooner or later—your stories would certainly be appreciated, as Barlow's have been.

Feby. W.T. was pretty mediocre except for the excellent Whitehead reprint. I always admired that tale—which I read long before I came into contact with the author. Glad you & your father share my opinion. The serials are nearly always tedious & puerile—although, as you say, "Golden Blood" was an exception. I didn't read that until a year after its appearance—when Price called my attention to its merits. Haven't yet had a chance to look at the March W T.

Your new study must be delightful, & I'm sure you'll find it an aid to composition. It sounds admirably convenient & well-situated. My files will be a great boon as soon as I get time to classify my overflow material & fill them.

Well—I must get in motion. Thanks & congratulations anent "Reverie". You surely have no need to feel discouraged about your writing, for what you have done in a year is really much above the average. Authorship is a slow process, & one must have infinite patience about it.

All good wishes to you & everybody—
Yrs most sincerely
—E'ch-Pi-El

[P.S.] Heard some good lectures recently—a reading by the poet Archibald MacLeish, a discourse on the Japanese artist Hokusai (1760–1849) in connexion with an exhibition of its prints at the art museum, & an account of contemporary Russian soviet art. It seems that the latter isn't quite so freakish & backward as one might expect.

Notes

1. By S. S. Van Dine.
2. By August Derleth
3. I.e., the sun enters Aries.
4. The American Fiction Guild, a writers' group.

[27]   [ALS, JHL]

April 16, 1935.

Dear Rhi-Mhel:—
            Glad to hear the news, & to learn that you have joined the N.A.P.A. Papers ought to begin to arrive before long—& if you don't receive the March official organ you'd better drop a line to Official Editor Bradley. I'll send you the next batch of papers after I've prepared my June report[1]— there may be some you will not have received. I think you'll find the National enjoyable in spite of all its limitations. Wish you could get down to Oakland to attend the convention in July. Many amateurs of prominence will be likely to be there. I'm sure there can be no dispute about the acceptability of your credential—& in the course of time both your tales & your linoleum block prints will undoubtedly be in great demand. You can send the amateur papers both new material & material which has appeared in the "fan" magazines— since there is scarcely any overlapping between the amateur & fantasy files. I think that you, Long, Talman, Barlow, Mrs. Wooley, Cook & myself are about the only persons interested in both fields . . . . although in the Feby. W.T. there was a tale by an old-time amateur—Fanny Kemble Johnson, who was active 40 to 45 years ago. Long became an amateur in 1919, but has not been active in recent years.
            And now I must congratulate you on your new story—"The Organ"— which I read with the keenest interest & admiration. It is truly splendid—full of a tense & menacing atmosphere, & with a genuinely effective surprise climax. The style, too, is smooth & excellent—you can see how little correction I have made. Of your improvement—steady & solid—in the fictional art there can be no question. By all means try this story on the professional press—first *Terror* & then Wright. I recommend this order because I have recently discovered that *Terror* (though of vastly lower grade literarily) pays virtually twice what *Weird* does. Regarding the title—if you wish a change, how would "At the Morning Service" do? The plain title "Diana" also wouldn't be bad. Of course the object of titling is to find something which expresses the

most important or dramatic element in the given story. This story is really great stuff—full of the elusive menace & disquieting doubt that Poe put into his work. I hope it will land professionally—but if it doesn't, Crawford ought to be glad enough to get it . . . provided his magazine lasts long enough. And of course F M will also probably handle at least a little weird material. Don't hurry with your other yarns—let them develop easily & spontaneously. No need of keeping the fish-peddler in the story which he originally dominated. I have often eliminated something from a story which was at first its central element. Glad you've begun to keep a note book. I can generally recall an idea pretty well, once the essential outlines are down on paper. I also save press cuttings bearing on weird topics—reports of monsters, lost races, excavated cities of antiquity, sunken islands, &c.—for possible future use in fiction. As for "abstruseness" in stories—all the pulp magazines seem to demand detailed & prosaic explanations for every unusual element. It ruins the story from a truly artistic standpoint—but editors don't care about that. They aim to please the very lowest grade of readers—probably because these constitute a large numerical majority. When you glance at the advertisements in these cheap magazines (& they wouldn't contintinue [*sic*] to be inserted if they weren't answered) you can see what a hopelessly vulgar & stupid rabble comprise the bulk of the clientele. These yaps & nitwits probably can't grasp anything even remotely approaching subtlety. *Suggestion*—the most artistic way to present any marvellous event—means absolutely nothing to them. One has to draw a full diagram & drive the idea into their heads with a hammer before they "get" it. Indeed—many persons of far greater literacy are surprisingly slow in grasping the fine points of a story. I know a really brilliant chap who didn't grasp the meaning (a very subtly concealed meaning) of Machen's "White People" until I carefully & detailedly explained it to him. But it doesn't pay to cater too extensively to this taste for diagrams & hammers. Many a writer has been ruined by so doing. I can see where the reiteration of this demand has injured my own work—in my more recent stories I undoubtedly explain too much. I don't *mean* to, for I despise the cheap ideal demanding it—but the constant objection to obscure endings has doubtless crept somehow into my subconsciousness. Speaking of Wright's demands—I fancy the *detective* tales he wants are those having a distinct atmosphere of *weirdness*. They will be no innovation, since Quinn's "de Grandin" junk belongs within this category. I fear there will also be an increase in the amount of science fiction used. Evidently it is becoming harder & harder to market a really good weird tale—certainly, they are scarcer & scarcer in the magazine! Hope "The Silver Sail" will achieve type somewhere, sooner or later. Of the amateur papers, you'll find *The Californian* most receptive just now. As for "The Room of Pictures"—Crawford will be a fool if he doesn't take it. He can't afford to let his childish & undeveloped "taste" guide him in choosing material, for he has no idea of what a good story is. I told you how he rejected Keller's excellent "Dead Woman" (later used in F M) because he thought it was '[']ridiculous" & didn't know what it was about! Yes—I saw the new M T—which has a prepossessing format despite very mediocre contents. Of the stories, John Beynon Harris's "The Cathedral Crypt" is probably the least poor.[2] Crawford is having very bad luck marketing this issue, & thinks seriously of giving up after an issue or two more unless his luck turns. I'm advising him to give up the crazy idea of trying to float *two* magazines when he can't properly issue even one. Certainly, M T needs all the energy he can command! Well—I hope he can get by somehow, since M T is capable of forming a valuable element in the weird world. It would make a fine place to use your linoleum blocks—which reminds me to thank you for the extremely excellent print enclosed. Really, I had no idea that linoleum was capable of such effective use in illustrating! I'm not flattering nor exaggerating when I say that your block prints seem to me the cleverest I've ever seen—& I've seen a good many in amateur journalism. You make the process cover fields—like illustrating & portraiture—which few others try to make it cover. This "Charlotte" cut is enormously vivid, & I don't see how it could well be bettered—except, perhaps, by making Theunis's *neck* just a bit less thin. Maybe I'm wrong—heaven knows I'm no anatomical expert—but see what you think of the cut (as reënclosed) with the proportions slightly altered as suggested. Ferguson, by the way, seems to be quite an artist in his line. He certainly forms a vast improvement over the unspeakable bungler Guy L. Huey! I'll be interested in seeing your illustration for "The Tree"—a job which will certainly give your imagination & ingenuity unlimited scope. As for pen & ink work—I'm sure you could excel in that as well as in linoleum cutting—though if Crawford is wise he'll stick to linoleum & avoid the cost of having metal cuts made. Hope none of the blocks made for the F F will be wasted. Possibly Eph-Li will resume his columning somewhere some day—in any case, don't let any of your cuts get lost.

The F F's death was surely a calamity. Yes—my last issue came, & I took out my subscription for the following year in back numbers—a full dollar's worth. Wish it could have been arranged to fill out F F subscriptions with F M—but actually it would scarcely have been possible. The enterprises were wholly separate, notwithstanding the fairly close rapport of Schwartz & Hornig & the fact that both employed the same printer—Conrad H. Ruppert. How much F M will bend its policy toward the weird to attract former F F readers remains to be seen. There will, I think, be some concessions in that direction. Hope "The Forbidden Room" & "Its Prayer" will be used. Doubt whether Schwartz will want anything as protracted as my serial article.

C A S also dropped me a line mentioning illness in his household. I fear his mother found the shock of her accident of last year (burns from an overturned tea kettle) hard to recover from. His own health has also been poor during the last few months. Hope the new Zothique tales get accepted.[3] I don't think that proposed Auburn visit of the San Franciscans has materialised as yet. Anger, L. C. Smith & Bernal[4] were among those going, but I don't know about Grand Duke Effjay. He affects a great contempt for all weird work in general, & Klarkash-Ton's in particular—though C A S is merely amused by the little louse. Hope you & Eph-Li can get down to Averoigne some day. Meanwhile Sultan Malik is transforming the slopes of Mt. Kaf to a veritable orchard—planting orange, fig, peach, nectarine, & other fruit trees around his new abode. Nimrod valiantly fights the gophers that nibble at their roots—& to aid in the battle the Sultan is going to get the dauntless warrior a harem of 3 or 4 furry ladies—who, together with the future Nimrodic heirs, will probably be able to exterminate the whole colony of burrowers. Nimrod's prowess—& appetite—continue unabated . . . & no rival is likely to stand much chance in the annual election of the California chapter of the K.A.T.! No word, alas, from Genl. Tabasco . . . . or from Doodlebug! Yes—I've heard from Robert Nelson several times. He seems to have a good deal of talent, though he suffers the handicap of a neurotic & hyper-sensitive temperament. His verses in the recent W T are exceedingly vivid—though much of his work has a faint suggestion of immaturity.

Sorry Eph-Li is discontinuing his column—but the biographies will probably keep him busy. His study of Two-Gun Bob promises to be highly interesting—& I know you'll handle the portrait magnificently. A silhouette effect ought to be just the thing for linoleum work.[5] The Terror of the Plains certainly is a vivid & unique character. His writing shews a prodigious zest, & reflects a good deal of his virile & bellicose nature. His "Jewels of Gwahlur" in the March W T is splendid.

Eph-Li dropped me a card telling of his Lewiston move, & I could well imagine that both you & he will miss the frequent visiting of the past. I presume, though, that the change was necessary & advisable—he spoke of his mother's coming departure for the southwest. Hope he finds more pupils & in general encounters increased prosperity. Since (as I believe you or he once mentioned) Lewiston is only 7 miles from Asotin, the good old team won't suffer any really radical breaking-up. Some time you & he & Petaja ought to arrange a general get-together.

Which reminds me—I wish indeed that you could get to the U. of Mont. while Petaja is there. Your joint musical as well as literary interests would make you doubly congenial. In any case you certainly ought to meet. Is the 'bus fare very great between your respective regions? The distance is only about that between Providence & New York—yet the fare for that trip never rises above $3.00. Possibly, though, the competition of different companies makes this an exceptional case. (The fare has been as low as $2.00!)

Glad everybody liked "The Man On All Fours". Would you care to borrow Derleth's new detective novel, "Three Who Died"? This is distinctly cleverer than its predecessor—being of a more probable & realistic cast. At the same time it is less of a *story* & more of a frankly abstract *problem in detec-*

tion. It kept me guessing longer than its predecessor—not till p. 145 (out of 252) did I fully grasp what was coming. You had an advantage over me in the matter of recognising "Minnie the Moocher".[6] I never heard this celebrated ditty—that is, I don't know it by name, although the tune may have floated to me many a time from distant radios. Say the word when you want to see "Three Who Died." Some day I'll take you up on that Van Dine offer. Yes— I know the Vance stories usually involve some field of curious erudition, & that the characters tend toward a sort of brilliant artificiality. These tales are getting to be almost as celebrated as the Sherlock Holmes stories were in my day. Which reminds me that I've never read the *newer* "Sherlock Holmes" material—i.e., that written after 1908.[7] Glad you & your father continue to enjoy the astronomical books—& that you have newspaper articles of current phenomena, with suitable charts. I used to write articles like that years ago. An excellent aid in learning the constellations is a revolving *planisphere,* which can be turned to shew the heavens as seen at any hour of any given day. So you've read "The Monk". No hurry about "Salammbo" or the other items. Yes—I've read—& own—W. H. Hudson's "Green Mansions". A peculiarly fascinating work. I'm trying to hustle Derleth & Dwyer about the Hodgson books, but both seem hard to get in motion. Rather an odd coincidence that the volumes should be divided between two such flagrant delayers at the same time!

No word from L & M—indeed, I'm almost certain that nothing will ever come of the book proposition. I really don't know what a publisher would wish to include in a collection. A book would comprise some 75,000 words— & the *number* of stories would depend on whether long or short ones were chosen. As to the question of whether letters to L & M would influence their decision—I'm hanged if I know! Tremendously kind of you & Eph-Li to think of it. What a firm generally wants is a guarantee of the sale of a certain number of copies—for example, Knopf approached W T in 1933 & asked whether Wright could manage to dispose of 1000 copies through the magazine. When Wright said he couldn't be sure, the proposition fell through. I'd be willing to bet quite a sum that no book of mine will ever be published.

Congratulations to Crom upon his children! Hope they'll all prosper & do their noble sire proper credit! Glad the snowy paterfamilias is prospering, & hope he'll continue to dominate the Washington chapter of the K.A.T. White seems to be a favourite colour with K.A.T. leaders—what with Crom, Nimrod, & the vanished Doodlebug! The Providence chapter is duly responding to the call of spring—& I had an excellent talk with Pres. Randall yesterday afternoon. Of the little niggers across the garden *one* remains—& oh, boy, what an one! Meet Mr. John Perkins, successor to & near-double of the late lamented Sam! Is he a little streak of playful black lightning? Just like little Sam—except that he has a tiny white shirt-stud visible on close inspection. His eyes still have the violet wideness of infancy, but he is strong & active—& has just begun to *purr*. I think he is larger & stronger than Sam at the same age—& I certainly hope he'll survive & flourish! He has visited me several times—& I play with him with a stick of which his late brother was especially fond. He is just beginning to assimilate other than maternal nourishment.

So the limburger experiment didn't come off? Well—I'm hanged if I blame you! I really fancy that the glass-jar brand I sampled at Whitehead's wasn't as riotously unrestrained as the average sort . . . . . indeed, someone suggested as much when I described it once. The smell was distinctly uninviting—though hardly as *extreme* as that which you describe. H S W said it wouldn't *taste* as bad as it *smelled,* & he was right. However—as I mentioned before—it wasn't anything I'd choose, or eat for pleasure. Some human tastes are hard to account for! *Roquefort* is another cheese I dislike.

Well—I've read "Creep, Shadow" at last, & must thank you & Eph-Li all over again! While of course the general style is of the popular sort, it has innumerable touches of the genuine Merritt magic—hints of dark backgrounds, shadows of cosmic outsideness, & an absolutely magnificent series of climactic tableaux at the end. I am infinitely grateful for the volume—& note with interest your allocation of credit for the binding. By the way—don't bother too hard with "Salammbo", for I may pick up another copy—or a set of Flaubert's complete works—some day.

Just read Gustave Meyrink's "The Golem", lent me by Ar-E'ch-Bei. The most impressive weird thing I've come across in aeons! The cinema of the same title which I saw in 1921 was a mere substitute using the same name—with nothing of the novel in it. What a study in subtle fear, brooding hints of magic, & driftings to & fro across the borderland betwixt dream & waking! There are no *overt* monsters or miracles—just symbols & suggestions. As a study in lurking, insidious *regional* horror it has no peer—doing for the ancient, crumbling Prague ghetto what I unsuccessfully tried to do for rotting Newburyport in "The Shadow over Innsmouth". I had never seen the novel before, but mentioned it in my article as a result of having seen the cinema. Would you care to borrow this semi-classic? I am instructed to send it along to Miss Moore, but a request to Ar-E'ch-Bei would undoubtedly win you a later place on the lending list. Let him know if you'd like to see it—his address is 1218 Sixteenth St., N.W., Washington, D.C.

Sorry your early spring has been punctuated with damp & chilly weather. The season seemed to be early here—there were early March days with temperatures of 65° & 71°, & I took several outings, including a 12-mile rural walk—but later on an unpleasantly coolish spell supervened. Just now there are encouraging-looking buds on some of the shrubs in the garden. Hope conditions in the N.W. will prove favourable for fruit-growing & all the various forms of agriculture.

Glad the new study continues to be helpful. I've lately acquired some **more** cabinets for my files—6 small ones which I picked up at a bargain sale for a dollar apiece. They are of papier-maché with wood frame, & with an imitation grained wood (brown) finish. On account of their size (22 × 13 × 9½") I can tuck them into odd corners without disturbing the general furnishing scheme. Each has 4 drawers (12 × 8¼ × 4¾"). I spent 48 hours transferring my material, & at last have my things in the best order they've been in for 25 years or so! Yet even now a lot of junk still remains in frail cardboard boxes or piled on open shelves.

Your task of writing a poem for the H.S. annual was surely an honour—a testimonial to your local literary fame! I'm sure you can do justice to the occasion, even if the H.S. spirit does seem a bit remote now.

March W T is pretty fair on the whole—honours divided among "Jewels of Gwahlur", "Julhi", & "The Sealed Casket". I don't even try to tackle the serials unless I am assured in advance of their merit. April W T is not so bad, either. Bernal's light science-fiction yarn has a magnificently clever idea—which I wonder no one has used before. I had something similar in my note book, but can't use it now. The "Heald" thing is my own—ghost-written. Klarkash-Ton's "Last Hieroglyph" is impressive, & Howard Wandrei's richly local "Hand of the O'Mecca" is in some ways the most memorable of all—especially in atmosphere. The alleged 'Roman' story[8] is painful in its historical errors. Just to begin with—Rome never heard of such a tribe as the Huns till 300 years after Caligula's time!

Had a delightful visit from Robert Moe (son of our fellow-amateur M. W. Moe) March 2–3. He is 22, & an electrical engineer employed by the Gen. Elec. Co.—recently stationed at Bridgeport, Conn. Extremely brilliant youth—I hadn't seen him since he was 11. Graduate of U. of Wis. He came in his car, & we did considerable antiquarian sightseeing around R.I. I hope to see him again, & he is meanwhile looking up the gang in N.Y. He called on his fellow-electrician Koenig the other day. ¶ One of the youthful science fiction fans—one Kenneth Sterling—has just moved to Providence. Precocious kid—means to become a biologist. ¶ Well—I must get to work. Again, congratulations on your splendid story! ¶ Yrs for the Pnakotic Sign

—Ech-Pi-El

P.S. Have I sent you any old copies of E. H. Cole's splendid amateur journal, *The Olympian?* If not, let me know, & I'll do so. ¶ Just had a card from C A S. He says that *both* his parents are ill, & that he is caring for them single-handed. Poor chap!

Notes

1. "Lovecraft Offers Verse Criticism."
2. "The Cathedral Crypt," *Marvel Tales* 1, No. 4 (March–April 1935): 164–70. John Beynon Harris wrote more commonly under the pseudonym John Wyndham.
3. "Necromancy in Naat" and "The Black Abbot of Puthuum."

4. Fred Anger and Louis C. Smith had hoped to publish HPL's *Fungi from Yuggoth* as a book, but ultimately did not. A. W. Bernal had several stories published in *WT*.

5. DWR did in fact make a linoleum cut silhouette of Robert E. Howard, but it does not appear that FLB ever published his sketch about Howard.

6. A popular jazz song first recorded in 1931 by Cab Calloway and His Orchestra.

7. These would be the novel *The Valley of Fear* and the stories gathered in *His Last Bow* and *The Case-Book of Sherlock Holmes*.

8. "Shadows of Blood."

[28]   [ALS, JHL]

De Land, Florida.
June 30, 1935.

Dear Rhi-Mhel:—

I mourn for the lost Crom! The Kappa Alpha Tau, en masse, mourns with me! And Mr. John Perkins, whose rather unfavourably snapped likeness you'll find amidst the enclosed photographs, adds his plaintive & still juvenile "eeew" to the melancholy chorus. What evil is this which stalks the leaders of the K.A.T., & spans an entire continent with its cryptic malevolence? I have referred the matter to Nimrod, valiant snow-white warrior-chieftain of Many-Pillared Irem, & hope that he will bend all his savage energies toward the extermination of the Unknown Adversary. Enclosed, by the way, is a recent photograph of that Conan among Quadrupeds—in the arms of the invincible Peacock Sultan. Well—you certainly have my unalloyed sympathy! Damn & double-damn the meddlesome idiots whose complaints caused his banishment to uncongenial soil! Iä! Shub-Niggurath! May his alabaster-white sons wax great & vengeful, & sally forth to exterminate all the poultry of the mendacious dastards! Anyhow, I hope you'll acquire one of these sturdy heirs. In the interim, pray extend my greetings to the little grey fellow—who may be regarded as the Regent of the Northwestern Kappa Alpha Tau until the heir of Crom comes to reigning age. Yea—there is surely a new monarch in Ablakar . . . to whom is given the Lordship of the Middle Kingdom, betwixt the lands of his snowy cousin Doodlebug & his duskier fellow-Westerner General Tabasco. To his court shall ofttimes stray Little Sam Perkins, ever young & playful, & legions of other furry companions lost to earth. Hail & farewell, O Crom . . . . . mighty shall be thy memory in Cimmeria!

Of the other absent felidae no trace has been reported. Mr. John Perkins has become almost as great a frequenter of 66 as of his own home across the garden. He loves to chew papers on my desk, curl up in a neighbouring chair, or perch himself like a little basalt sphinx on top of Webster's Unabridged. He plays furiously, & is so pugnacious that he'll probably win the overlordship of the local K.A.T. by the time he's middle-aged. By the time I'm back from De Land he'll be a full-fledged warrior! The enclosed pictures of him &

of Little Sam represent opposite ends of a roll of film started last August & finished in April. To think that these little brothers (*full* brothers, I am certain, for there can be little question about the lithe coal-black troubadour who appears to be their common sire) never existed at the same time!

Hope you'll enjoy the N.A.P.A. 1935–6 may be quite a year of literary upbuilding if the right persons for an enlarged critical bureau can be landed. Meanwhile political battles rage—wasting much energy & developing much acrimony. The only sensible thing to do is to ignore them. The only logical candidate for President is Bradofsky—& as for the editorship, it may be best to vote for Babcock after all unless another really capable candidate appears; despite the rather high-handed tactics he has shewn during his presidency. Hope to see your material in the amateur press before long—*Californian* & *Perspective Review* are the best havens for fiction.

Glad my comment on "The Organ" seemed helpful, & hope the story will land with W T. There's no telling about Wright's editorial policy—he seems guided mainly by caprice. I learn of your further fictional plans with great interest, & imagine that the notebook is gaining some dark & curious entries. Glad the old fisherman is safely down on paper. In the matter of explaining things—it isn't well to make too extensive concessions to popular obtuseness. Your experience with *Fantasy* is certainly more encouraging than otherwise, even if it did not result in an acceptance. Hope you have luck with *Manuscripts*. Sooner or later Crawford will undoubtedly take more of your work. "The Jewels of Charlotte" was easily the best thing in the recent U.S., & I fancy he has been told so from many quarters. The misprints, though, are deplorable. Later there'll be opportunities for illustrating. I think Crawford will try to carry on for some time, even though the financial prospects are none too bright. If he has any sense at all, he will consolidate his two magazines immediately & put all his energies into the task of issuing one good one. Now that you know the mechanical difficulties he encountered in using the linoleum block, you can allow for them. You ought to be able to make a splendid cut for "The Tree". All your cuts in F F & F M have come out delightfully well. Glad there's a chance of Eph-Li's column continuing despite his preference for biography. I was glad to see it—with your cut—transferred to F M. Yes—I thought I missed certain sections of the biography which I had read in MS. F M is a pretty good thing of its kind, & I surely hope it will not be dropped. All my material sent to it by Hornig has been returned—including "The Nameless City." Weird fiction isn't popular with Schwartz! I doubt if my serial article would have interested the dominantly science-fictional clientele of the magazine. Sorry your tales came back.

Up to this writing I have had no further news from Klarkash-Ton save one card. Hope he is all right, & in good shape to receive visitors, since the Peacock Sultan (in a newly purchased successor to old Juggernaut—a rebuilt Essex Terreplane) & young Fred Anger expect to pay him a call before long.

The new Zothique tales *have* landed, I am glad to say. Little Effjay is not in the Bay region this summer, but is in Los Angeles with his grandmother. Louis Smith is planning a mimeograph publishing venture—to include a complex index of W T to date, & perhaps the whole series of my Fungi from Yuggoth . . . 35 in all. All this, though, is tentative.

Glad Eph-Li is still in touch with Asotin—& hope you & he & Petaja can all get together during the summer. Too bad the coach route to Missoula is so indirect. Wish you could find it possible to attend the U. of Montana.

No hurry about "All Fours"—& I have meanwhile sent the later d'Erlette novel, which I trust both you & Eph-Li will enjoy. I'll probably let you lend that van Dine when I get back from De Land. If you've never read the principal Sherlock Holmes tales you certainly ought to. In original form they have a power they could scarcely have on the radio. They ought to be in almost any library—even Asotin's disappointing specimen. By the way— lacking a definite new address of Eph-Li, I took the liberty of sending his "Man With Red Hair" to you instead of to him. Trust the passing-along will give you no inconvenience. I certainly enjoyed it—& hope you'll thank Eph-Li on my behalf for the loan. No hurry about the astronomical books—& hope you can get hold of a planisphere. "Green Mansions" ought indeed to make a good cinema.[1] About the Hodgson books—I'm still prodding those damn'd delinquent D's—Derleth & Dwyer. Hope you'll reap the results thereof before long. Meanwhile you'll probably receive Barlow's copy of "The Golem" (a truly great novel) before long from Margaret Sylvester. Better let Eph-Li & Petaja have a chance to read it—& ask Klarkash-Ton if he'd like to see it. As for L & M & my MSS.—things look very unfavourable. I expect my junk back before long. Crawford has some sort of an idea of publishing "Innsmouth" & "Mts. of Madness", but I doubt if he'll ever do it. *Home Brew* came safely back. I doubt if the differences between magazine & book versions of "Creep, Shadow" are really vital. I shall be interested to see Salammbo's new binding—for which I thank you & Eph-Li most abundantly. I'll send you some *Olympians* as soon as I can get some more duplicates from Cole. Hope you'll enjoy "The Blessing of Pan"[2] despite a certain tameness. I own this volume.

I set Petaja right anent "Out of the Æons". The tale is virtually 100% mine—hence I feel a certain amusement at its capture of the readers' vote. May & June W T are very mediocre, although Two-Gun's "Beyond the Black River" is a good adventure story. I was glad to see "Arthur Jermyn" in print again—& am surprised that you & Eph-Li didn't see it before. I thought I had lent you *all* my MSS! When originally printed in 1924 the editor (Edwin Baird) changed the title without my knowledge & consent . . . . for which I gave him hell! The May Bloch story is an old one, & not representative of R B at his best. Yes—he's placing things right along. Just had a new one, dedicated to *me*, accepted.[3]

I've had only a couple of the popular chain letters.[4] I made a few copies of both to please the senders, but didn't send them all out. The dodge is really worked to death now. Some—including Howard Wandrei—went in for the game in a big way . . . but I don't know how much they've netted. I've had *no* returns to date! At present the only sensible thing to do with such things is to chuck 'em in the waste basket.

Yes—young Sterling is one of the 10 first members of the Science Fiction League. Quite a boy. He returns to N.Y. later this month. Glad you're finding the Lewiston chapter enjoyable, & hope the picnic will materialise pleasantly. A good many science fiction devotees also like weird stories.

I finished "The Shadow out of Time" Feby. 22 & sent it to Derleth, but he has not read it. I am now asking him to pass it on to Bloch, who wanted to try his hand at deciphering it. I'll surely see that it gets your way in the end—in either its present form or a better one.

Spring was badly delayed in R.I.—the brief warm spell noted in a former letter being a deceptive mockery which soon deserted us. Glad you've had better luck! The cherry-blossoms must have been exquisite. My outings were few after those which I described—though one of them, involving the *second* visit of young Robert Moe, was made delightful by the temporary presence of some really *hot* weather.

The welcome visitor blew in on Saturday morning, April 27—in his faithful 1928 Ford—& we put in a strenuous 2 days in that time-tried vehicle. Saturday we visited old Newport—seeing 2 ancient windmills; a flock of sheep with sportive lambkins in the best pastoral tradition; "Whitehall", the 1729–31 home of Dean (later Bishop) Berkeley (whose famous line "westward the course of empire takes its way"[5] caused the California town to be named for him); the Hanging Rocks, where that good cleric composed his well-known "Alciphron; or, the Minute Philosopher"; the lofty cliffs; the strange rock cleft called "Purgatory", where the ocean pounds thunderously in; the Overing farmhouse where a small rowboat party of rebels under Col. Wm. Barton captured Genl. Prescott of the regulars in 1777; & the venerable town itself—with 1698 Quaker Meeting-House, 1726 Anglican church, 1737 Colony-House, 1749 library, 1760 market-house, 1763 Jews' synagogue, & private dwellings as old as 1675. It was a glorious hot day—up to 82° in Providence, though not quite so good in Newport.

Sunday the 28th we went to ancient New Bedford—Nantucket's successor as the world's great whaling centre, whose last lone exemplar of the industry put to sea only 11 or 12 years ago. The marine museum was closed—but after a tour of the centuried waterfront we set off southward to sample something still better. This was the Round Hills estate of Col. E. H. R. Green (son of the noted female financier & miser Hetty Green) in S. Dartmouth, where the old whaling barque *Charles W. Morgan* (built 1841) is preserved at a realistic-looking wharf—but solidly embedded in concrete as a permanent exhibit. We went all over the vessel—which is tremendously fascinating—&

snapped some pictures of it. On the Green estate is also an ancient windmill moved from Rhode Island. We then explored a region—where S. Mass. adjoins southeastern R.I.—which I had never seen before in my life. Splendid unspoiled countryside with rambling stone walls & idyllic white-steepled villages of the old New England type. Of the latter the best two specimens—Adamsville & Little Compton Commons—are both in Rhode Island. Adamsville contains the world's only known monument to a *hen*—perpetuating the fame of the Rhode Island Red, a breed developed in that village from East Indian & Chinese gallinaceous forbears. At Little Compton Commons can be found the home & grave of Elizabeth Alden Pabodie—daughter of the famed John Alden & Priscilla Mullins of Plymouth, & first white woman born in New England. This region was once the seat of the Sakonnet Indians—whose squaw-sachem Awashonks was persuaded by the noted old warrior Capt. Benjamin Church not to join King Philip's conspiracy in 1675. It was settled from Plymouth about 1673, & (like Barrington, Warren, & Bristol) came into Massachusetts in 1691 & into Rhode Island (when a boundary dispute was settled by George II) in 1747. Capt. Church lies buried not far from Little Compton Commons. Well—at last we turned north through Tiverton, where on our left we had some marvellous vistas of low-lying fields & blue water. Here we passed the home of the navigator Capt. Robert Gray, who in 1792 discovered your own Columbia River in the far-off Oregon country—naming it after his stout Rhode Island barque. Then back home via Fall River (an ugly mill city across the line in Mass.) & ancient Warren . . . . at which latter place we paused at the famous Maxfield's (a rendezvous of Morton, Cook, Wandrei, & other visitors of mine) for a dinner consisting entirely of ice cream—a pint & a half each (6 varieties: Moe—chocolate, coffee, banana, caramel, ginger, pistachio. H P L—chocolate, coffee, banana, caramel, lemon, strawberry.) Finally back to #66—after which I regretfully guided the guest out of town & took a 4-mile rural & suburban walk before returning home. All in all, quite a session!

The next week-end—May 3–4–5—I visited Cole in the Boston zone, but cold weather seriously hampered our sightseeing. We covered ancient Marblehead, however—which is attractive under any conceivable set of conditions!

On May 25 I had an interesting visit from young Hornig, erstwhile publisher of the F F. He is a very pleasant & intelligent youth—reminding one slightly of Donald Wandrei, though with a vaguely, quasi-Semitic turn of features. He seemed to appreciate quite keenly the archaic charm of venerable Providence—which is in some respects not unlike his own town of Elizabeth, N.J. I shewed him most of the historic high spots, including the hidden churchyard on the ancient hill which I have probably described to you at one time or another. (Snaps enclosed) Young Sterling (who, as mentioned, will soon return to N.Y.) was also on hand most of the time, making quite a convention of the event. The weather was providentially warm & sunny. I like Hornig very much—& certainly admire the competence which enables him to serve as editor of a full-fledged magazine—*Wonder Stories*—at the age of 18. He is a very mature, assured sort of person—I'd take him for 22 or 23 at first sight.

I've just learned with sorrow that *another* row of ancient buildings in my vicinity is about to feel the vandal's hand. I probably told you of my rage at the destruction of the S. Water St. warehouses (1816) in 1929.[6] This time the scene of devastation is College St. itself—the doomed row being that huddle of quaint houses & archways reaching from Benefit St. downward to the foot of the hill—on the same (N) side as the court leading to 66, but beginning ¾ of a block lower down. Included in the cataclysm are the house of the first President of Brown (1771), a fine old 1750 specimen, & one of those rare old archways leading under parts of a building to inner courtyards [cf. my dream of "Old Man", related not long ago] . . . of which the only perfect survivors in America are those on Providence's ancient hill. (There is a bricked-up specimen in Richmond, & a boarded-up specimen in Phila.) On this site will ascend the new main building of the R.I. School of Design. Two palliating & consoling features exist: (a) The preservation, restoration, & incorporation into the new building of the bottom (& only brick) house of the ancient row—the old Franklin Inn, with its quaint inn-yard archway. Thus the survival of *one* of the archways is assured. And (b) the choice of a splendid Providence–Georgian design for the new edifice. The structure's lower units will harmonise with the surviving Franklin Inn, while the upper units will blend in pattern with the residential buildings higher up on the hill. One part will even have a "monitor roof" like #66—a form especially typical of Providence in the 1790–1820 period. The change is regrettable, yet it is fortunate that the character of the new building will be the same. Obviously, Providence is remaining dominantly true to its traditional Georgian heritage, & avoiding the 'modernistic' epidemic from which even Boston is not quite immune.

Well—as you see, the Southern trip *did* materialise despite all misgivings. Barlow got home June 3d, & I started on Wednesday the 5th. Cut out N.Y. & Washington, & made my first stop in ancient Fredericksburg—a Virginia town of the 18th century where Washington virtually grew up. Had 7 hours there, & saw all my favourite spots. Then straight down to my beloved Charleston, where I likewise went the antiquarian rounds. The moment I struck the steady heat of South Carolina I became stronger & more active—indeed, this southern trip has caused me to feel really comfortable for the first time in 1935. Had 2 days in Charleston, then down to De Land via Jacksonville. Am now repeating my visit of 1934 with minor variations. The Johnstons have moved up the road, & Bob's elder brother Lieut. Wayne Barlow has been here on a furlough from Texas. The colonel—Bob's father—is also home. I mourn the absence of Doodlebug, but High & Jack are great big boys now. Jack's neck is still a bit askew from his mishap of last year. New cats are the yellow Persians—Cyrus & Darius—& two kittens named Henry

Clay & Popeye. Also a little dog—who got slightly hit by a motor the other night. Bob's new cabin is going up in the oak grove across the lake, & presents a fine appearance even in half-finished form. It will be occupiable before long. We are planning a number of things to do before I leave—perhaps some printing project connected with amateurdom. Bob has an excellent press. But time will tell what—if anything—we shall accomplish. I have quite a bit of piled-up work & correspondence to dispose of—& a group of poems to criticise for Derleth. No strikingly new developments to report thus far. ¶ With sincerest regards to you & Eph-Li—

Yrs in the Brotherhood of Zoth

—Ech-Pi-El.

[P.S.] Thanks tremendously for the attractive portrait, which goes appreciatively into my gallery.

[P.P.S.] Am enclosing snapshots of recent things of interest. Please return ultimately, though there is no hurry. Shew these to Eph-Li if convenient.

[P.P.P.S. on envelope, which is stamped with RHB's hand stamps:]

There is a pleasing report that old white Doodlebug is *not dead*—but that he has 'gone native' & is joyously roaming the subtropical jungle. Many rumours of a strange white cat—glimpsed fleetingly by the roadside—have become current along the countryside. ¶ Just saw a magnificent tropical river—Black Water Creek—reminding one of the Congo or Amazon. It winds through a steaming jungle of tall, moss-draped cypresses whose grotesque, twisted roots writhe curiously at the water's edge. Palms lean precariously over the brink, & vines & creepers strow the black, dank earth of the bordering forest aisles. Sinister sunken logs loom up at various points, & in the forest pallid flowers & leprous fungi gleam whitely through the perpetual twilight. Each bend of the tortuous stream brought to light some unexpected vista of tropical luxuriance.

Like the river at Silver Springs, about which I wrote you last year, I liked it even better because of more leisurely observing conditions.

Notes

1. *Green Mansions* (MGM, 1959) directed by Mel Ferrer, starring Audrey Hepburn, Anthony Perkins, and Lee J. Cobb.
2. By Lord Dunsany.
3. "The Shambler from the Stars."
4. See *OFF* 266–67, or *Letters to Robert Bloch and Others* 236–37.
5. George Berkeley (1685–1753), "On the Prospect of Planting Arts and Learning in America," l. 1.

6. See HPL's verses "The East India Brick Row" and his letter to the editor of the *Providence Sunday Journal* (submitted under the signature of James F. Morton).

[29]   [ALS, JHL]

% Barlow, Box 88,
De Land, Florida,
August 4, 1935.

Dear Rhi-Mhel:—

Very glad indeed to receive yours of July 24 with interesting enclosures. The new linoleum blocks are magnificent, & I'm sure the editor & readers of F M ought to thank you profoundly for them. I recognised the portrait of Two-Gun Bob the moment it emerged from the envelope— before seeing any identifying reference in the letter. You certainly have hit his attitude & expression splendidly. Petaja lately sent me some specimens of his linoleum work—which is refreshingly excellent—but you hold your own in any competitive array!

I mourn afresh at Crom's continued absence—& to think his sons & his grey successor have likewise vanished into the mists of Aklakar! Here's hoping you have better luck with the little black boy—perhaps your change of residence will help to break the evil spell. If misery loves company, here's some bad news to cheer you up—*High & Jack have both disappeared within the last fortnight.* It is pretty well agreed, however, that they are not dead. Cats have a tendency to revert to wild nature in this region—inhabitants of backwoods cottages reporting whole troops of them in the jungle. Probably High, Jack, & old white Doodlebug are all alive & enjoying themselves as free men— emancipated for ever from servitude to the whims of the irrational biped *homo sapiens.* Back at #66 little Johnny Perkins is growing up to be a formidable fighting man—even attempting at times to intimidate the august elders of the Kappa Alpha Tau. He has a little black & white sister or half-sister now— who looks just like their mother, & who will be given away as soon as she is able to leave the maternal bosom. She may be gone before my return—but I trust Johnny will be on hand to give the old gentleman a cordial & purring welcome. Well—let us hope that the little black boy at Asotin will grow up plump, valiant, & wise, & in time be ready to take his place as Supreme Regent of the Kappa Alpha Tau's Northwestern Chapter. Just south of you, Nimrod is prospering in accustomed fashion—despite various mysterious absences as long as 5 & 6 days each. He goes on dark & cryptic quests—but always comes back. Sultan Malik now has a second feline at the many-pillar'd palace of Irem—a tiny yellow kitten, tiger-striped, with whom old Nim is reluctantly making friends. May they all live long & flourish!

Congratulations on your change of residence—nearer the centre of things, & away from the meddlesome foes of the Kappa Alpha Tau! Moving is always an arduous business, but sometimes the results justify the trouble. I hope in time to see snapshots of your new abode—& trust you will find it up to all expectations. The absence of a garden is unfortunate, but possibly there is a bit of lawn which in time will form quite an acceptable substitute.

Glad the N.A.P.A. is proving of interest. The recent *Californian* is the best paper in recent years, & Bradofsky's election to the presidency is an occasion for rejoicing. Another excellent sign is the reawakening of interest among some of the high-grade old-timers—survivors of the Golden Age of the 80's & early 90's. Ernest A. Edkins has written several splendid articles & poems, & Truman J. Spencer has accepted the Chairmanship of the Critical Bureau. Spencer wants me to continue with verse criticism—which I've said I'll do if no one else can be found. I am at the same time urging the enlargement of the bureau according to the plan endorsed by Bradofsky. Yes—the actual membership of the N.A.P.A. does seem small as compared with the number of persons actually connected with amateurdom, since the current papers include members of the United Association, Alumni, & others who have never officially belonged to any society. In commenting on amateur verse I have often noticed how few of the bards' names occur on the membership list. Regarding stories—there is no question but that all your work will eventually find a hearty welcome in the amateur press. *Californian* & *Perspective Review* are sure havens, & plenty of others would be glad of shorter pieces. If Barlow successfully launches his paper, there will be still another "market" for good material. This will, I think, be a year of renaissance in amateur journalism. Young Bradley recently came into direct correspondence with Edkins, & received valuable ideas which will later be embodied in *The Perspective Review*—while Bradofsky is always seeking improvement.

Sorry Wright didn't take "The Organ". We're all in the same boat—Loring & Mussey having definitely turned down my MSS. a couple of weeks ago. Don't let such things discourage you—just go ahead & develop that new idea! Derleth didn't finish "The Shadow Out of Time", so I recalled it to shew Barlow . . . & now *he* hasn't finished it. The bad handwriting is perhaps partly responsible for their inattention; but in addition to that the story must lack interest, else they would be carried along in spite of the difficult text. I am therefore crossing the yarn off the list—with the possibility of using the plot (& perhaps part of the action) in some later attempt. Sorry some of your things have come back from the small magazines—but as you know, they all go in primarily for realism, so that the fantaisiste is consistently handicapped. Hope Crawford will use "The Silver Sail" soon—he certainly needs good material badly enough! The last issue of his paper, though surprisingly ambitious in size, is utterly unreadable as to general contents. Petaja's poem is the only thing of value in the entire issue. Hope "The Organ" lands with *The Galleon*—but don't be discouraged if it doesn't, since they are at present overstocked with material. They've just rejected a truly splendid story of Barlow's—on the ground that it didn't have enough plot! By the way—I agree with you in preferring the small to the larger size in M T.

I'll be interested to see your portrait of Sultan Malik—which will have to go some to excel the silhouette of Two-Gun Bob. The Peacock Sultan is certainly liberal enough in his arrangements regarding the picture—but I trust you won't emphasise the element of caricature. Malik is really a very attractive-looking chap—to whom a portrait can't do full justice. His expression & animation are what contribute largely to his general charm. Sorry Eph-Li is less interested in the weird than formerly, but hope he'll eventually return to the fold. I seem to have heard of Alvin Earl Perry before—guess he's had letters in The Eyrie.[1] Glad Eph-Li gets around to Asotin now & then, & hope he'll be available later on for coöperation in printing & other projects.

Your idea of a successor to the F F is a splendid one, & I certainly hope it can be brought to fruition. Petaja mentioned it some time ago, & in replying to him I was enthusiastically favourable. You have surely been thorough in your investigation of practical conditions; & it would seem as if your chances of moderate success—breaking even, that is—were greater than those of any of the others who have dreamed of filling Hornig's place. Among those who have considered & abandoned the idea of a new F F are little Kenneth Sterling, Hill-Billy Crawford, & Louis C. Smith of California. A somewhat more solid venture—your only potential rival—is *The Phantagraph*, official organ of a correspondence society something like the Science Fiction League—called "The Terrestrial Fantascience Guild". This society is rather a poor makeshift—headed by one Wilson Shepard [*sic*] of Alabama, who Barlow says is a distinctly unreliable cuss[2]—but recently it has been improved by the affiliation of a very capable youth who has a grudge against the Gernsback-sponsored S.F.L.—Donald A. Wollheim of 801 West End Ave., N.Y. City. Wollheim is the author of a very sharp pamphlet exposing Gernsback's shady financial tactics.[3] He has now assumed the editorship of *The Phantagraph*, & is determined to make something of it if he possibly can . . . . this ambition involving a design to follow the general F F policy. Whether he will succeed or not is very doubtful—since from the outset he has the opposition of Hornig & all connected with the Science Fiction League. Also, he will not be able to do his own printing. We shall see as the weeks go by. Without question, the odds are in favour of a magazine free from any connexion with any society, & having the good will of Hornig & the "fans" all around.

Your calculations all look sound & logical to me, although I'm rather poor on the practical details of printing enterprises. You realise of course the difficulty & hard work involved. In doing the printing you really ought to have an assistant to speed things up—a matter you might bring up with Eph-Li. Regarding circulation—a clientele is a damned hard thing to assemble. Hornig had only *60* paid subscribers to the F F, & you can recognise the trouble anyone else would have in surpassing him. Barlow points out that your yearly subscription rate ought to be *lower* than the sum of single-copy prices, so that people will find it to their advantage to subscribe. That, however, certainly would bring down the annual rate to a discouragingly low figure. And if you boosted the price of single copies to 15¢, you might find the enterprise harder to launch—since the old F F was a dime. Assuredly, the prosaic business struggle connected with these matters is often more trying than the literary struggle of editorship or the mechanical struggle of printing. You'd better get considerable advice from Hornig—& others with semi-professional experience—before deciding on a permanent price schedule.

8-point type is certainly the appropriate size for any page-size as small as yours will be. Hope you can make advantageous arrangements for a second-hand press & type. Be sure to have plenty of accessories—leads, quads, &c.— & a *composing stick* for setting up the type. Barlow began without a stick, but soon had to order one. At best it will be slow, gruelling work—& you must not try to hurry with it or let it become a burden. Discuss the matter with as many prominent amateur printers as possible.

As for the editorial end—most certainly you are welcome to the rest of "Supernatural Horror in Literature." Just say when you want the copy, & I'll send Petaja the same doctored-up *Recluse* that Hornig had. I've already had my aunt send him "The Nameless City." I am absolutely certain that you could line up the same group of contributors that Hornig had—Derleth, Two-Gun Bob, old Bill Lumley, Barlow, Klarkash-Ton, &c. &c. &c. Robert Nelson, alas, is unavailable as a permanent contributor—for he died on July 22 after an illness of 17 days. His mother recently sent Barlow 5 more "Lost Excerpts" which he had meant to send himself—& I have revised them into a shape fairly fit for publication. If you'd care to use them, I think Ar-Ech-Bei would be glad to send them along. Poor Nelson was quite a case—nervous, excitable, uneasy, & ill-adjusted. I had a letter from him shortly before his death—so late that I don't know whether he was able to read my reply. His work was crude & formless, but he had a sense of colour, atmosphere, & strangeness which seemed to me very promising. What he needed was literary discipline—wider reading & closer study of rhetorical principles. He knew his limitations & would probably have progressed vastly—perhaps amounting to a good deal—but various hints in letters of his about throat trouble & drinking milk make me think it must have been tuberculosis.

Well, anyhow, you have the most enthusiastic good wishes of Barlow & myself for your coming enterprise. Hope Koenig can furnish helpful suggestions. By the way—what have you decided about *paper stock*? It seems to me that something slightly better than the Hornig–Schwartz–Crawford grade is desirable. Nothing luxurious or elaborate, but something like the stock used in certain middle-grade amateur publications like Hanson's *Proof-Sheet* or the first couple of *Californians*. One thing more—Barlow suggests that you do not issue circulars till your first issue is ready to accompany them as a sample. He argues that Hill-Billy's grandiose prospectus—followed by the wretched rag & atrocious delays which actually appeared—has given rise to a popular scepticism & distrust of promises, so that an advance circular would actually harm rather than help a new enterprise. I really don't know how much weight to attach to such an argument—but I pass it on for whatever it may be worth. About the Yuggothian Fungi—would you want to use anything that had been used before? After giving two to Barlow last month for his future paper,[4] I find that the range of *absolutely unpublished* sonnets is wholly exhausted. I could, however, let you have items used years ago in local or amateur papers—forgotten by all, & never seen by the bulk of your prospective readers. How about it? And would the possible booklet publication of all the Fungi (by Louis C. Smith of Oakland, Cal.) be a drawback? Think it over.

About C A S—his parents *were* better, & Sultan Malik & An-Ghah were all ready to visit him on July 12th, when a sudden relapse on his father's part set everything awry. Price & Anger cancelled the trip, & I've had no bulletins from Indian Hill since. Anyhow, it is obvious that Klarkash-Ton is in a tight place—with heavy responsibilities—so that we can't expect any prompt correspondence from him for some time.

I surely hope that you & Petaja can stage a get-together before the summer is over. $12.00 surely is a heavy 'bus rate for a 200-mile round trip—the price for the similar Providence-New York round trip being $5.40. It would certainly be delightful if you, Eph-Li, & Petaja could all assemble in Missoula!

No hurry about the return of anything—take your time, & let Eph-Li read anything he wishes. If "The Golem" has not reached you already, it soon will—though it has been successively delayed at the last two places. Its future itinerary should be as follows:

F. Lee Baldwin, Genl. Delivery, Lewiston, Idaho.
Emil Petaja, Box 85, Milltown, Montana.
R. F. Searight, 19946 Derby Ave., Detroit, Mich.
R. H. Barlow, Box 88, De Land, Florida.

I hope to hades that something can be done soon toward loosening the joint hold of Derleth & Dwyer on those Hodgson books. Their delay has passed all bounds of excusability—for if they can't find time to read the items, they should give the matter up & pass the material along. I shall suggest to Koenig that he drop the two offenders drastic notes.

Yes—the sky down here is delightful. Wide horizons, no electric lights, & the southern constellations riding high in the sky. Not quite far south enough, though, to reveal any bright stars unknown to northern latitudes. I wish I had a telescope to use on Jupiter & Venus, now so prominent in the evening sky. Nothing better here than Col. Barlow's $5\frac{1}{2}$ power field glasses. We couldn't see the total lunar eclipse of last month because of clouds. Hope the astronomical books continue to be of interest to you & your father—& pray give the latter my sincerest regards.

I'll get you some *Olympians* as soon as I return to New England & pay Cole a visit. It is easier to dig them out of him in person than to induce him to hunt them up & mail them himself. You won't be disappointed in this paper—which is the finest thing, editorially & typographically, to be produced in amateurdom in the last 40 years.

About the name of your new magazine—of those suggested, it seems to me that THE FANTAISISTE'S MIRROR is best. But pay careful attention to the spelling & pronunciation of the main word in this title. So far as I know, the only word of this description which is in any way correct is FANTAISISTE—pronounced Fahn-tay-seest´—a French expression which was taken over into English about 20 years ago, when the critic Ernest Boyd published a rather popular monograph called "Lord Dunsany—Fantaisiste". The word signifies "a writer of fantasy"—& is perhaps the only single word having this meaning. I'm repeating this information to Petaja. However, don't decide on a title till you've talked with a large number of qualified persons—Koenig, Malik, Two-Gun, Klarkash-Ton, Ar-E'ch-Bei, & others.

Yes—I've read "The Snake Mother" (= "The Face in the Abyss") & "The Dwellers in the Mirage". Indeed, I own both . . . the latter in the form of collated instalments. Not bad for pulp stuff. The opening section of the "Dwellers"—the scene among the Nighirs—is the best.

July W T is pretty mediocre—though it was refreshing to see Hectograph Eddie with a new plot. The Moore item was excellent—even though it seems to shew a tendency of C L M's to drop into a rut. Haven't yet seen the August issue—things are very backward about getting on the stands in De Land.

I read the weather reports with extreme interest & envy. Congratulate Eph-Li for me on the record set by his new home town. *116! Ædepol!* Yuggoth! Nyarlathotep! And *88°* is the highest De Land has had! Talk about the "balmy tropics" versus the "frozen north"! Well—the truth is that what makes a subtropical climate is not temperatures higher than those of the northern summer, but the *absence of low temperatures* at any time. For instance, it hasn't been over 88° here this summer—but on the other hand it hasn't been lower than 80° except on a few occasions, & won't be below 40° more than 2 or 3 days all winter. That's what keeps the palms & other tropical flora alive. Florida's climate is more equable than that of most continental regions, since the sea is present on both sides to turn down extremes. The summers here are certainly not as warm as those of the middle west—though of course they lack the occasional cold nights. This is supposedly the rainy season, though all it amounts to is a sharp shower near noon on most days. One thing you wouldn't like is the plenitude of insects. Here's the size of a mosquito I got yesterday over at Bob's cabin. Do you have them that big in the Snake River Country?

Black Water Creek surely is a great place. Here's a card which shews pretty well what the landscape is like. We've had several trips since then—twice visiting a highly interesting spot called Rock Springs, about 20 m. S.W. of the Barlow Estate. There, amidst a picturesque wooded valley, a crystal stream issues forth from twin black tunnels in the side of a lofty tree-crowned cliff of hard-packed clay. About 60 feet inside the larger of these tunnels there is a vast hidden chamber of eternal night—once used by the Indians as a refuge from their foes—beyond which is a remoter aperture leading back to unplumbed & inconceivable abysses of inner earth. The stream at one point widens out into a bathing pool—in which, on both occasions, the Barlows disported [I don't swim—never having learned because of the paralysing chill of my native northern waters] while I roamed the neighbouring woodlands & enjoyed the spectacle of the cliff & tunnels. The public is not allowed to crawl into the tunnels & see the hidden cave—although this prohibition is a relatively recent one. I hope to see this spot again very soon.

The date of my visit's end is still unsettled. The Barlows are now urging me to stay *all winter,* but I fear I couldn't be away from my books & files that long, since my library is necessary to any serious work. Nevertheless I wish I could stay—for the northern winter surely does reduce me to a helpless jelly. At present I'm feeling so well that I scarcely know myself! Glad you've had a picturesque vacation. Blue Mt. Park must be a delectable place—& the bears surely add colour. I was once bitten (very slightly—near the knee) by a bear—at Roger Williams Park in Providence.

Yes—my spring trips with young Moe were highly interesting. I was sorry not to be able to meet his father during the latter's eastern sojourn. Old Moe had a great time with his son—& meeting the gang around N.Y. About ice-cream flavours—*coffee* has been one of the most popular kinds in New England for 50 or 60 years. Its use is slowly creeping west—see if it doesn't hit Asotin soon! About the building replacement in Providence—Old Man's archway (which is in Thomas—not College—St.) will *not* be disturbed. ¶ Ar-Ech-Bei seems to have shelved the Whitehead letter project for the time being. He still intends to bind & distribute "The Shunned House"—though I can't say when.

¶ Well—congratulations once more on your new linoleum work . . . & best wishes for your coming magazine enterprise. Give my regards to Eph-Li when you see him. Hope the new residence will prove comfortable, & that the little black boy will prosper there. ¶ Yrs under the Seal of Yuggoth— E'ch-Pi-El

Notes

1. HPL's only surviving letter to Perry contains much the same content provided in DWR 13.
2. See HPL's "Correspondence between R. H. Barlow and Wilson Shepherd . . ."

3. The pamphlet is unidentified. But see Wollheim's "My Experience with Wonder Stories," *Bulletin of the Terrestrial Fantascience Guild* 3, No. 2 (April 1935): 2f.

4. What these are is uncertain. RHB published no individual sonnets in a journal, and the items in question are not discussed in HPL's letters to him. They may have discussed the matter in person when HPL visited RHB only weeks before.

[30]   [ANS, JHL][1]

[Postmarked St. Augustine, FL,
25 August 1935]

On my way at last! Accompanied the Barlows to Daytona & helped them settle in the flat they are to occupy for a fortnight, then took the coach for ancient St. Augustine. It surely is good to see centuried gables & facades & balconies & garden walls—& hear the sound of tinkling fountains at twilight, & of cathedral chimes cast in 1682—after 2 m. & 9 d. amidst rural modernity! Am revelling in the atmosphere of a 370-year-old city—a city founded when Shakespeare was a year old, & still containing homes which had 50 years behind them when the Pilgrims landed on Plymouth Rock. ¶ Am staying a week at my usual hotel—the Rio Vista on the bay front—& cutting my food bill down to a minimum. Spend most of my time absorbing ancient vistas & writing atop the venerable fort. Moving north Aug. 25—& will get a few hours in Savannah before striking ancient Charleston. Am so short of cash that my stay in Charleston will be badly cut down—& hope of stopping anywhere north of there gets slimmer & slimmer. It will probably be impossible to pause in N.Y. except for a brief call on Long. ¶ How goes the programme of the *Fantaisiste's Mirror*? Petaja reported safe receipt of "The Nameless City." All good wishes—
H P L

Notes

1. *Front:* Old Curiosity Shop, St. George Street, St. Augustine, Florida.

[31]   [ANS, JHL postcard][1]

[Postmarked Charleston, SC,
29 August 1935]

Greetings from the most fascinating of all towns! Ancient Charleston makes even St. Augustine seem pallid! It is 115 years younger, but has kept so much of its 18th century architecture that it *seems* vastly older. White steeples, fanlighted colonial doorways, railed double flights of steps, mouldering churchyards—in truth, it is the very spirit of antiquity! No place except Providence seems so utterly homelike to me. Here only 4 days, but wish like the devil I could stay longer. It seems oddly *northern* after Florida—less moss on the live-oaks, fewer

& smaller palmettos, no jungle effects, no rainy season, &c. Am absorbing antiquity & enjoying the scene to the full. Many ancient buildings here are being finely restored as a F.I.R.A. [*sic*] project.[2] ¶ Richmond Aug. 30, Washington the 31st, Philadelphia Sept. 1st.—then a short visit with Wandrei in N.Y.—then home. I dread the coming northern autumn, but shall be glad to see my books & files & familiar things again. ¶ Have just written a section of a composite story which Schwartz is concocting for F M—previous parts by C. L. Moore & A. Merritt.[3] ¶ Hope plans for the magazine are flourishing—
Regards—
Ech-Pi-El

[P.S.] While in St. Aug I had a pleasant visit from Barlow, who came up from Daytona to bid a second adieu!

Notes

1. *Front:* Pink House, Pre-Revolutionary Tavern, Charleston, S.C.

2. The Federal Emergency Relief Administration, created by Herbert Hoover in 1932 as the Emergency Relief Administration, ultimately replaced by the Works Progress Administration in 1935.

3. "The Challenge from Beyond."

[32]   [ANS, JHL][1]

[Postmarked, Providence, RI
13 September 1935]

Found the joint card from you & Petaja upon my arrival home yesterday. Glad to hear that you finally got together! Thanks for the message. Spokane would seem to have some vivid beauty-spots! ¶ I had a pleasant journey northward, though the cold rather sapped my energy. A day in Richmond, another in Washington, a morning in Philadelphia, & then a fortnight in New York as guest of Donald Wandrei. Saw all the gang—Long, Koenig, young Sterling, Hornig, &c.—& really had an excellent time. ¶ Was glad to get home at last, despite the appalling accumulation of work awaiting me. Pres. Randall of the K.A.T. greeted me with many purrs, & young Mr. Perkins—now a huge fighter—has spent most of his time with me since my return. I may spend the next week-end in Boston, visiting & riding with my friend Cole. ¶ All good wishes—
Ech–Pi–El

Notes

1. *Front:* Public Library and Elks Home, Providence, R.I.

[33]   [ALS, JHL]

66 College St.,
Providence, R.I.,
Septr. 28, 1935

Dear Rhi-Mhel:—

Through a really singular coincidence, yours of the 16ᵗʰ arrived the selfsame day on which I received (through Barlow) your sorely delayed letter & MS. of August 26. Nothing is lost—all's well that ends well!

First of all, let me congratulate you on the story.[1] Really, it's *splendid*—one of your best so far! The suspense & atmosphere of dread are admirable, & the scenes are very vividly managed. I like the climax—& the note of indefiniteness as to *what thing* formed the substitute body of the hapless victim. That last touch was very skilfully managed. If Wright has a grain of sense left, this ought to be a sure-fire hit with him—but one never can tell. I've gone over the MS. very carefully with a view to improving the smoothness of the prose style—& I hope you'll find the slight verbal changes acceptable. If the reason for any of them is not self-evident, don't hesitate to bring the matter up. This is a fine yarn, & you certainly have no reason to be dissatisfied with it. It is just as original as *any* weird yarn can be (you can see for yourself the wide difference between this dread-filled, atmospheric chronicle, with its hints of utterly unknown monstrosity, & the ordinary tale of transplantation like Bassett Morgan's),[2] & has a convincing cumulative power utterly lacking in anything which follows the pulp tradition. Don't fail to try it on Wright—even though he may be too dense & capricious to recognise its merit. I was vastly glad of the chance to read it, & shall look forward eagerly to its publication somewhere. Once more, my sincerest congratulations!

Price's letter interests me tremendously, & I feel sure there is much in what he says regarding the playing-out of commercial fiction. All the stock plots certainly have been worked into the ground, & all the actual folklore myths are done to death. Quinn alone has run the gamut of popular superstitions. Thus the task of finding a fresh theme is made vastly difficult for any weird writer *who depends on plot & incident* . . . . that is, for any writer working in the common pulp tradition. The sincere artist, however, is certainly not quite so badly driven to the wall. A *really serious* weird story does not depend on plot or incident at all, but puts all its emphasis on *mood* or *atmosphere*. What it sets out to be is simply *a picture of a mood,* & if it weaves the elements of suggestion with sufficient skill, it matters relatively little what fictitious events the mood is based on. Of course, the more obviously worn-out cliches (in *method* even more than in *subject-matter*) had better be avoided—but a true master of atmosphere & suggestion can do wonders with even the commonest sort of theme. It is well to avoid actually recognised myths such as vampirism, reincarnation, &c., & invent one's own obscure violations of cosmic law. What common myth, for example, does Blackwood use in "The Willows"? Or

Chambers in "The Yellow Sign"? Or Hodgson in "The House on the Border-land"? These writers create a sort of distinctive aura of their own & manage to say something fresh despite all that has been said before. Of course Wright would probably reject any such original stuff—but that's what makes good weird fiction! Naturally it is not always easy to achieve such distinctive expression. Individual writers burn out now & then, & it is harder & harder to be original (though not even comparably as hard as in pulp formula fiction) as the bulk of weird literature grows . . . covering every sort of typical weird mood in human nature. But there is always *a chance* for new material—or at least convincingly fresh material—as there is not in the field of hackneyed "plot & action" fiction. As for *me* in particular—I'm pretty well burned out in the lines I've been following . . . that's why I'm experimenting around for new ways to capture the moods I wish to depict. Price, I think, is a little premature in saying that my newer tales all concentrate on weird aspects of human character. He gets that idea from "The Thing on the Doorstep", which he liked especially, but this story is not by any means typical of my whole output. It is only one of many *experiments*—each different from the other. "The Shadow Out of Time", for example, is nothing at all like this—being a straight *phenom-enon* story close to the borders of science-fiction. *Nothing* is really "typical" of my efforts at this stage. I'm simply casting about for better ways to crystallise & capture certain strong impressions (involving elements of *time, the unknown, cause & effect, fear, scenic & architectural beauty*, & other seemingly ill-assorted things) which persist in clamouring for expression. Perhaps the case is hope-less—that is, I may be experimenting in the wrong medium altogether. It may be that poetry instead of fiction is the only effective vehicle to put such expression across. But the only real way to find out is to try. At any rate, the point is that while the commonplace commercial weird field is certainly wear-ing thin, there is *always* plenty of scope for the sincere artist who has some-thing weird to say in his own way. I don't think the pulp problem need bother you much, since all your tales seem to deal with original phases of weirdness & keep away from the hackneyed forms. My advice to you would be just to keep steadily along in the way you're going. Regarding an extension course—or other systematic instruction in the fictional field—there is really much to be said on both sides. On the one hand, such courses do help immensely in smoothing out a writer's style & teaching certain effective forms of expres-sion—that is, helping the author do to his MSS. what I've just done to "The Disinterment". But on the other hand, it must be admitted that most of them teach the popular commercial type of writing rather than the art of sincere expression. What they tend to aim at is not the artistic fiction of Blackwood & Machen, but the glib, machine-made fiction of the Saturday Evening Post & its congeners. They regard story-writing as a business & not an art—just as pulp agents & critics like Otis Adelbert Kline do. If anyone is aiming at artis-tic writing, an average fiction course would include a great deal that he would have to unlearn later on. And yet in many cases he might be a gainer in the end—the valuable material overbalancing the deleterious material. Much depends on the individual himself—what his temperament is, & how he learns best. Of the members of our group, Frank B. Long is the one who has taken the most thorough short story courses. Klarkash-Ton, Two-Gun Bob, Price, & myself have never had any short story instruction. If I were in your place I wouldn't be excessively anxious to take a course (which would, naturally, repeat much that you already know, although it would also contain new material), but would perhaps do so if some excellent & relatively inexpensive opportunity presented itself. There is undeniably much to be learned from such instruction—& an alert student can always accept with large reservations the phases obviously involving commercial rather than artistic writing. The matter of credit toward a regular college course is also to be considered if you have any intention of taking such a thing later on. Possibly the best thing to do is to investigate the matter—ascertaining rates, & learning something of the specific contents of the course. If the prices are well within your reach, & the synopsis of topics looks sound according to your best judgment, it might be just as well to try it. With what you already know of fiction & its diverse ideals, it couldn't conceivably do you any harm—& it might do you a vast amount of good. Anyhow, better get whatever leaflets or other information the university has to offer.[3]

Yes—I agree that Sultan Malik's letter ought to be published, & I believe that *The Fantaisiste's Mirror* is the place to publish it. I shall keep it safely for the present—perhaps lending to certain members of the group—& have it ready whenever you can use it. Of course it will require editing—transformation into article form—though I don't see how any *real* anonymity can be secured, since so much of the text is bound up inextricably with the Lilith tales whose authorship is universally known throughout the circle. The cracks at science-fiction will undoubtedly be a hard pill for kids like Sterling, Wollheim, Hill-Billy Crawford, &c. to swallow!

About that composite story—my section does *not* conclude it. It is a five-author affair, in the following order: Moore, Merritt, H P L, Two-Gun Bob, Frank B. Long. My section was probably the most difficult, since I had to plan out the general rationale & plot of the whole thing. All that Miss Moore & Abie did was to sketch out the background & plaster on atmosphere. There was no *story* up to the point where I was expected to begin, & at that stage (the 3d instalment out of 5—i.e., the *central* section) it was imperative that somebody start something & give an idea of what it was all about. I fear I made a mess of it. The assignment reached me just as I was leaving St. Augustine, & I did the job in odd moments of Charleston sightseeing. There was no chance for original creation, so I fell very reprehensibly into a hackneyed pattern. I surely hope that no one will judge me by this attempt! Amusingly enough, Abe Merritt very boldly dodged the hard job of a central assignment.

Schwartz had originally given Long the second part to do, & Belknap had prepared a rather clever development. That put Merritt third—where he would have had to build from Long's section. Well—when it came to that, he squirmed out in what both Long & I (& the Wandreis & others as well) think was a distinctly unsportsmanlike way. Claiming that Long had veered away from the subject-matter specified in the title, he refused to "play" unless Schwartz would kill Belknap's section & give *him* second place! That would of course give him a "snap" assignment—with no difficult threads to pick up, & no responsibility in developing the plot. Schwartz gave in & let him have his way—but I'll be damned if I'd have done so, despite his prominence. It was clearly up to him to abide by the rules of the game as originally laid down, no matter what difficult problems they may have created. That is the very essence of sport—& of course a composite yarn like this (*no* composite tale can have any real literary value) is nothing more or less than sport. Instead, Abie demanded that the rules be arbitrarily changed in his favour! Well—he got away with it—& as a result the third & most difficult section was wished on me! For a while Long refused to have anything more to do with the enterprise, but ultimately Schwartz & I persuaded him to tackle the concluding chapter. I shall be anxious to see the completed tale, & learn what Two-Gun & Belknap did with their respective sections. Schwartz tried to get Edmond Hamilton to participate, but could not. C A S was also unable to furnish a section because of the grave illness in his home.

By this time you have my card acknowledging the Spokane postal. I was surely glad to hear of your meeting with Petaja, & can imagine what a festive time you had. Too bad Eph-Li couldn't have participated in the conclave. Spokane would seem to be a very pleasant town—& the park looks delightful in the view you sent. Glad Petaja is getting to the U. of Mont. this year, & wish you could have done likewise.

Meanwhile, good luck with *The Fantaisiste's Mirror!* No hurry, surely. Better to go slowly & make no false moves. I think all Barlow's suggestions are good. Glad you appreciate all the difficulties & allow for them in advance. Your great advantage will be the possession of a press, so that the heavy item of a printer's bill can be eliminated. Having a friend in a printing office is also a fortunate circumstance.

As for contents—you'll have no lack of good material. You can discuss Nelson's "Lost Excerpts" with Ar-Ech-Bei. They are not, of course, of the very first rank—but they will pass muster. If you care for already-printed "Fungi" you can have plenty. I let Wollheim have some for *The Phantagraph*, but there are plenty left. The Smith–Anger booklet of them will *not* appear. Barlow plans a later printing of them—but heaven only knows when that will be. Wollheim asked about my historical article, but I told him it was more or less spoken for. By the way—I am told that *The Phantagraph* is now out, though I have not yet seen a copy. Just what it will amount to, I don't know.

All the small "fan" magazines are in a very shaky position, & I wouldn't be surprised to hear of some failures or consolidations before long.

About Nelson's age—I think it was 22 or 23. Did you ever see a picture of him? I can let you see one if you haven't. He had a curiously strained or worried expression—which apparently did not belie his temperament. It's a pity he couldn't have lived to develop his writing & arrive at a better adjustment to his environment.

You'll be sorry to hear that Klarkash-Ton's mother recently died. While the event had long been expected, it is no less a blow on that account. Mrs. Smith had had a shock last March, which very considerably impaired her speech & memory. This will be a severe jolt for C A S's father, who is in feeble health & of advanced years. Yes—I knew of Klarkash-Ton's new sculptural activities—indeed, he sent a small grotesque image apiece to Barlow & me last July. The best ones are still in his possession, & I am anxious to see photographs of them.

Congratulations on the new fountain pen. I wish I could get a less coarse point that would write easily & flow freely—my script would probably be slightly less illegible if the strokes were finer.

Your linoleum blocks continue to excite my amazement & admiration. Once again I recognised a face before reading any title—for you have caught Price's expression with uncanny skill. The only criticism I could make is that the face seemed just a bit full-jowled for Sultan Malik as I remember him. Probably the effect is due to the angle of the photograph from which the cut is taken—but actually the Peacock Sultan is lean & sharply sculptured, with no fat whatever around the cheeks & jaws. Enclosed is one of the prints doctored to look like Price *as I remember him*. However—this is merely a 2-year-old impression, & the lines may bely the especial effect presented by the photograph-model. People often actually present a very unfamiliar & uncharacteristic aspects when viewed from particular angles. In real life we don't notice it, because we seldom see anybody from exactly the same angle for more than a few moments at a time; but in certain photographs it becomes very apparent. All in all, you've caught the Sultan's expression astonishingly well. I don't see how you do it in as rough-hewn a medium as linoleum. The fact that you *repeat* this resemblance-getting with different subjects proves that it's no mere luck shot. Schwartz paid you quite a tribute in pirating your "Echoes" cut[4] for a general decoration! Glad you're making another—which I know will be splendid, & of which I hope to see a print in due season.

Johnny Perkins welcomed me upon my return—but it took me some time to recognise the overgrown young rascal! Bless me, what a boy! He's going to be a huge warrior indeed before he's through. He is just as handsome as ever on an enlarged scale, & his coat is the sleekest, purest black I have seen in many an age. His late brother Sam had tiger-stripes shewing through, but John is absolute polished ebony except for his little snow-white necktie.

He has been over at 66 a good part of the time since my arrival—purring & drowsing & playing. We've got some catnip for him, which he has learned to relish exceedingly. News of his diminutive half-sister is tragic. She departed for her new home in mid-August—but fell a victim to motor traffic only about a week after the removal. The speeding car surely is the Kappa Alpha Tau's greatest enemy! Glad to hear of the fast-growing little nigger at Box 100! I think *Sotho* would be a most appropriate name for him . . . as a cryptic daemon allied to the vast, engulfing, & immemorial night. There is no such name as *Stygia* . . . the adjective *Stygian* being derived from the name *Styx*—the River of the Dead. Two-Gun Bob misuses the word-root when he speaks of a country called "Stygia". Indeed, he takes frequent & unwarranted liberties with classical names (or variants of names) in devising a nomenclature for his prehistoric world. Price & I have laboured with him in vain on that point. Glad Sotho likes his new home. I still mourn the vanished Crom, & hope he may be roaming jungles of wonder & beauty with all his accustomed grace. The whereabouts of Doodlebug, Gen. Tabasco, High, & Jack remain equally shrouded in mystery.

Amateurdom is plodding along slowly but surely. Have you seen the ambitious Fall *Californian?* The critical bureau is tardy in getting started, but when it is running I fancy an improvement will be noticed. Bradley is planning the radical improvement of his paper, & Barlow has 9 pages of his high-grade *Dragon-Fly* printed. Hope you'll keep the various journals stocked with good material—they need it. When I can pry some *Olympians* out of Cole I'll send them along. This paper was only a 5 × 7, but was very select in contents, typography, & editing. Its contents did not surpass the best material in *The Californian*, but it would not admit the poorer items which the latter occasionally harbours. If it had any fault, such lay in the large amount of space devoted to amateurdom's political history. No—I never had anything in it. Most of the issues preceded my advent to amateurdom.

I shall await news of "The Organ" with much interest. Too bad it met with so many rejections—for it certainly is a darned good story. Hope Kline can put it over somewhere—with or without changes. Kline is a wizard at placing things—though he thinks wholly in terms of commercial pulp fiction. Odd how "choosey" *The Galleon* is getting to be. I haven't had time to go through the issue containing "Iranon", which arrived during my absence.

About "The Shadow Out of Time" . . . Ædepol, what a surprise Ar-Ech-Bei put over on the old gentleman! You'll remember my telling you that he was apparently not finishing it . . . since he was keeping it so long & saying so little about it . . . . but Yuggoth! what that blessed child was actually doing! *He was secretly typing me a copy all the time*—little by little, & with marvellous accuracy in view of the almost illegible script. Early [on the day] I left he presented it to me as a surprise—& you can imagine how veritably knocked out I was! I don't see how he ever had the energy to do it—though the generosity is characteristic of him. It came to 88 double-spaced pages—making it longer than "Innsmouth" but not as long as "Mts. of Madness." Wandrei liked it when I shewed it to him in N.Y., & I have now started it on a circulation list.

Well—I'm glad some of the Hodgson books have come at last! It's about time! Hope the bunch from Dwyer will shew up before long. You'll find "The House on the Borderland" stupendous in its way. Enclosed is the future circulation list so far as I know it. The names are in order of application for the loan—irrespective of geography. If you want to slip Petaja in ahead of Hill-Billy Crawford—so that both editors-to-be of the *Fantaisiste's Mirror* can have the benefit of an early acquaintance with Hodgson—I don't believe there's any law to stop you. Also let Eph-Li read the volumes if he cares to do so.

No hurry about any books. Interested to hear of your father's new Arizona picture . . . pray give him my best regards.

August W T wasn't bad as recent issues go, but the Sept. issue seems to me more than ordinarily mediocre. "Vulthoom" is good, & young Bloch's story has its points—but most of the contents is pure junk. In one tale New Orleans is described as a full-fledged city in *1720,* when at that date the site had scarcely been cleared! I can't read the "Dr. Satan" junk—or any of the wretched serials, for that matter.[5]

Florida is indeed a great place, & I miss its genial warmth. So your mosquitoes are *black?* In New England they tend to be medium or light *brown.* I noticed the different colouration of some of the southern ones—but they seem to vary. It is hard work getting used to the north again, & I haven't half the energy I had in the south. There have, however, been quite a few warm days recently—& the steam is now going. Hope the cold season won't affect your own health too acutely—that rheumatism must be a wretched nuisance!

My trip home had many interesting spots, as I no doubt mentioned on my cards. In Philadelphia I visited for the first time since 1924 the picturesque botanic gardens & ancient stone house (1731) of the eminent naturalist Bartram, who in 1763 made the first scientific study of Florida plants. The estate is owned by the city, & maintained in good condition as a public park. It lies on the high bluff overlooking the Schuylkill—once a fine location, but now hemmed in by factories & cheap suburban developments. The house—built by Bartram with his own hands—is a curious affair with many rather crude features. It shews in certain places the influence of rural Pennsylvania's German architectural tradition. The gardens are extremely attractive—so that the place forms a veritable 18th century oasis in the midst of a sordid modernity.

In New York, as I wrote you, I was the guest of Donald Wandrei—in the flat at 155 W. 10th St. which he has just given up. I had his artist-brother's room—the gifted occupant being home in St. Paul preparatory to his wedding, which took place last Tuesday. Most of my meals were taken up at Long's. I saw most of the weird & amateur groups—Loveman, Koenig, Leeds, Kleiner, Sterling, Hornig, Schwartz, & the young son of Otis Adelbert

Kline, who acts as his father's N.Y. representative. I visited Morton at his museum, & went the usual round of museums & ancient places. Had a really enjoyable time, much as I dislike the city.

Home Sept. 14—& what a devastating pile of papers, packages, mail, &c. &c. confronted me! Tasks of every sort accumulated—3½ months of old papers to read up .... revision jobs ... books to classify ... hades! my programme won't be back to normal for weeks! And yet I played hookey from this insistent chaos on Sept. 20–23 inclusive—visiting my friend Cole in Wollaston & taking sundry Chevrolet trips with him. We visited Swampscott, Nahant, & Marblehead, & on Sept. 21 made a pilgrimage to the "Dunwich" country to deposit the ashes of the late Mrs. Dowe (amateur journalist—Mrs. Miniter's mother) on her native soil in accordance with her lifelong wish.[6] The Wilbraham region looked much as it did when I visited there in 1928—& I regretted that our stay could not have been longer. The leaves in that region were perceptibly turned. On the 22nd we sent to Cape Cod & revelled in a vastly different type of scenery—the gentle, level seaside landscape of southern New England. Here, as in Rhode Island, the leaves were scarcely turned. We had lunch in a pine grove near Hyannis, & loafed at length on the sands of Chatham with only the blue Atlantic between us & Spain. After my long absence, it was good to receive such a representative dose of the various types of New England scenery. There is a bare possibility that I may get one more trip—over the Mohawk Trail & up into Vermont a bit—before the winter closes in, but this remains highly tentative. My year's travel record is pretty ample as it is!

Well—here's wishing you good luck in all your ventures—including *The Fantaisiste's Mirror*. And once more, congratulations on "The Disinterment"— & thanks for letting me see it.

Yrs by the tentacles of Sotho—

E'ch-Pi-El

Notes

1. HPL refers to "The Disinterment," in which he may have had a small revisory hand.

2. Morgan's "*one* basic plot-idea" (as HPL described it; see p. 114) was the transplanting of human brains into the skulls of apes.

3. Portions of the preceding paragraph were published in the *Phantagraph* under the title "What's the Trouble with Weird Fiction?"

4. See DWR 35n8.

5. The New Orleans story is "One Chance" by Ethel Helene Coen. Paul Ernst wrote recurring Doctor Satan tales.

6. HPL and Edward H. Cole went to Wilbraham, MA, for the purpose of scattering the ashes of Jennie E. T. Dowe (1840–1919), mother of Edith Miniter (1867–1934).

HPL had written memorial poems to both women. Edith Miniter and her remote cousin Evanore Olds Beebe (1858–1935) showed HPL the Wilbraham area in 1928.

[34]   [ALS, JHL]

Citadel of Leng—
Nov. 12, 1935

Dear Rhi-Mhel:—

Very glad to receive your communication of Sabbat-Eve, & to digest all the interesting enclosures. I had seen brief press notices of that Salmon River expedition, & was quite fascinated by it—not only because of the Idaho locale, but because of the mysterious & little-known nature of the country traversed. It is curious how many relatively unexplored spots exist in the United States today, despite the general spread of settlement. This Salem River region seems to be a highly remarkable place all apart from its inaccessibility. The majesty of the scenery, & the presence of ancient pictured rocks, give it an intrinsic charm which may be exploited later on. Still, one hopes it will never be overrun & cheapened by casual tourists. There are many rocks with Indian carvings in Rhode Island & adjacent spots, but none with figures as distinct as those here portrayed. The scientific nature of this expedition is especially gratifying—& I fancy in the end some valuable facts will be deduced from it. I am returning the cuttings as per request, & must thank you exceedingly for the loan. The general Associated Press items were tantalisingly brief & without illustrations.

And so Eph-Li is now located on the Salmon himself—or rather, *near* it, since I believe Grangeville is not actually *on* the stream. Of the various places where he has mentioned playing, I believe *Whitebird* is the only genuine Salmon River port. Glad he likes the town, but sorry the climate is harsher than that of Asotin & Lewiston. Hope he is able to get around your way now & then. Give him my best regards.

Sorry "The Disinterment" didn't land with Wright—but I honestly think he doesn't want *really weird* material these days. "Abstruse" . . . nonsense! Does the fellow want an explanatory chart with every story? No question but that he'd reject almost anything of mine today. Well—there's nothing to do but keep trying. Sooner or later the small "fan" magazines will certainly be glad of any contribution of yours. And meanwhile there's no harm in letting Kline try his luck with anything he's willing to handle. He knows all sorts of markets that others overlook, & has a persuasive power with editors—even if he didn't succeed with Wright in the case of "The Organ". Does he charge a fee even when he *doesn't* place a story? If not, you really ought to let him try "The Disinterment"—which might easily land where "The Organ" didn't. Kline's son is a very nice chap—about your age, I should judge, & extremely bright & capable. He & Long are getting to be very cordial friends. Good luck with the "Blue Stone" revision—it ought to be a notable piece of work before you're through with it. But here let me very humbly correct a mistake *of my own* which has been embodied into this & other tales. You'll recall that I corrected the last name of your Greek detective to *Theunis*. Well—upon further research I don't think *that* is much better Greek than what you had originally! I must have got misled by the pseudo-Hellenic sound of a name which is actually *Flemish*—Dutch & Belgian—instead! I am vastly humiliated, & hope you can pardon the false advice. Let me repair my error by furnishing some names (I'll stick to those beginning with T, to avoid radical change) which *undoubtedly are* authentically modern-Greek. No mistake this time— these come out of the Encyclopaedia Britannica (art. Greece) without change: *Tantalides, Tricoupis,* Triantaphyllis, Tepharikis, . . . well, I guess these are enough for a while! Of all these, I think TRICOUPIS sounds about the neatest. It is the name of an eminent historian of the 19th century. "Constantine Tricoupis" . . . doesn't sound so bad! Since only one of the tales has been published—& that in a fan magazine—it is not really too late to make the change. Again I apologise for my carelessness—which was especially inexcusable in one making an alleged correction! Hope you have good luck with *Direction*. The *Galleon*, I'm sorry to say, has withdrawn from the general magazine field. It is now purely a regional Pennsylvania enterprise, & Eshbach has resigned from the editorship. My sonnet "Harbour Whistles" was returned with regret.

I'll return Price's letter in my next epistle. It certainly ought to make a splendid article, & I hope he won't mind having it published in spite of the identity-revealing remarks. Glad my comment proved clarifying. Yes—you could make an article of that if you wished—maintaining anonymity to have it match the other. You might let me see both articles after they are edited, de-personalised, & cast in formal shape. I'll be glad to add whatever touches of formulation & emendation I think they need.

Regarding the extension course—I really think it would be of net benefit in the end. There is no question but that it would help you in dealing with fine points of language & narration, & I doubt if it could do you any harm through its possibly commercial slant. The price seems very reasonable indeed—more so than that of the correspondence courses advertised in various magazines.

About the composite story for F M—the task of plot-building wasn't specifically assigned me. It was merely that anybody who has the 3d part of a 5-part story has got to plan something or else the thing will get nowhere. A mere introduction can't take 3/5 of a tale! Merritt undoubtedly saw this—& acted with more shrewdness than scrupulousness. Of course I suppose he justified the procedure to himself. He's an enormously busy man, & it was probably quite a favour for him to contribute anything at all. But in his place I should have done what Klarkash-Ton (who was asked, but was unable to swing the assignment in his harassed state of last summer) did—simply say I couldn't participate. I certainly wouldn't ask to have the rules of the game changed. I criticise Schwartz for letting Abie get away with his procedure— but then again, I can see how it was. Merritt is a big drawing card, & it does mean a lot to get something from the author of "The Moon Pool." The incident need not affect anyone's estimate of Merritt as an author. He is, manifestly, gifted with a very remarkable power of evoking weird atmosphere—& would have been comparable to Machen & Blackwood if he hadn't let the pulps sidetrack him. Schwartz wanted Hamilton because of the latter's popular association with interplanetary tales. H., however, couldn't furnish anything in time . . . . for which I'm heartily glad, since the instalment was then given to Two-Gun Bob, an incomparably better author! Belknap did very generously consent to do the final instalment. Schwartz thought of Comte d'Erlette, but decided his work didn't have enough of the cosmic element. I suggested young Bloch, but S. didn't seem to think he was well known enough as yet, despite his promise. As a matter of fact, I also suggested you & Barlow & Petaja, but I guess a line was drawn against those with no material professionally (as if that meant anything in view of pulp standards!!) published. I see the story is advertised in the current W T—although in the advertisement the two separate yarns (the weird & the science tales developed from the same title) are mixed up. Wandrei, E. E. Smith, & various others did the science one. And now, after all, the Sept. F M containing the stuff is not yet issued . . . delayed because of Ruppert's crowded programme.

I'm sure your meeting with Æmilius Petaia must have been a pleasing event on both sides. Spokane certainly seems to be a very attractive place with its lakes, its parks, & its surviving traces of primeval forest. I was indeed pleased to hear from the Lord of Shamure about his university course, & hope he can go right head & graduate four years hence. I hope, too, that some unexpected stroke of good fortune will accord you a similar privilege!

Sorry conditions are against The Fantaisiste's Mirror—but the whole situation may be different at some later time. Meanwhile it's a good idea to get back of The Phantagraph, since the latter seems very earnestly trying to fill the place of the departed F F. Glad "The Forbidden Room" & "Its Prayer" are to appear in the P.[1] Incidentally, those linoleum designs of yours are splendid, & Wollheim ought to be extremely grateful for them. You really lead the group in linoleum work, & I don't wonder that your productions are in wide demand! You really caught Sultan Malik's expression magnificently— the detail of the jowl being obviously a mere result of the especial snap you were working from. Any isolated shot can give a very unrepresentative impression if it happens to catch the subject at just the wrong angle. The only sure guide to an unseen person's appearance is a whole set of views displaying the subject as seen from different directions. Incidentally, you're the only linoleum artist I know who has accomplished anything in the line of serious portraits. The cut for "Its Prayer" has admirably weird suggestions—& the

Service Dept. heading is equally adequate in its different field. I'll be interested to see the new "Echoes" cut when it's done. Petaja is doing good work, too, & surely deserves your coöperation in the delicate business of mounting. Why not ask Belknap & Derleth for biographical data & pictures? I'm sure you could do admirably on both the writing & artistic ends—& either of these writers would be very popular subjects with the readers.

As for a booklet-printing programme—such a thing would surely be feasible in many cases when the regular issuance of a magazine wouldn't. Hope you can manage it sooner or later—& when you do, the "Colour" & "Nameless City" will surely be at your disposal. Would you mind the previous publication of the latter in The Phantagraph? As a matter of actual fact, there are better tales of mine than the N.C.—though of course there is plenty of time in which to decide on details. Some day I hope the long-dreamed-of high-grade weird magazine can appear—& perhaps your future press can pave the way to it!

Enclosed is the picture of Nelson which I mentioned—taken shortly before his death. Something in the expression seems to indicate the highly nervous temperament of the subject. Return this some time, but no hurry. It surely is a pity that Nelson did not live to develop the talent which seemed latent in his work. If Barlow doesn't publish the posthumous "Excerpts" himself, I presume he'll let The Phantagraph have them.

Klarkash-Ton is gradually marshalling his energies after the shock of his bereavement. He has written no more stories, but has done quite a bit of work in his new line of grotesque miniature sculpture. He is sending me a new specimen called "The Outsider" & based on my tale of that name, & is presenting Ar-Ech-Bei with another called "The Serpent-Eater of Hyperborea." Later he intends to send around photographs of his best products—& still later to lend a representative assortment to members of the gang. Meanwhile Barlow means to make C A S's "Incantations" (a volume of collected verse) the next item of his publishing programme.[2]

Which reminds me that Ar-Ech-Bei has just surprised Belknap with a finely-bound edition of the latter's recent poems—called "The Goblin Tower" after one of the verses included. I helped with the printing last summer, but lack of materials delayed the binding till now. Long is of course delighted & grateful—though the surprise comes at rather a tragic time for him, his only aunt (who took great interest in his writing, & financed his first book of poems) having been instantly killed in a motor accident near Miami Oct. 20. There is a sad irony in the fact that Barlow was binding a copy of "The Goblin Tower" to present to her.[3]

Glad the new pen is in the main satisfactory, & hope that some adjustment of the feed will soon make it 100% perfect. It isn't always the most expensive pens that give the best results. My latest experiment is in the direction of ink economy—seeing if I can manage to use a cheaper fluid than Skrip, whose repeated purchase at 25¢ per bottle is quite a drain on my alarmingly flattened purse. It is the manuscripts which eat up the ink like hell. Sometimes I do these in pencil, but that smudges so badly that text is occasionally blurred to the point of loss. Well—what I've tried is to use cheap 5¢-a-bottle Woolworth ink (obtainable only in the blue euphemistically called "blue-black") in the Waterman pen which has the exaggeratedly free flow. I don't think this Parker could handle it well, but the Waterman gets by very tolerably—observe a specimen! With this ink I can scribble as freely as I like, & at a cost really less than that of pencil-writing—my first nickel bottle having lasted over a month. The ink is rather non-absorbent, hence cheap pad paper will take it pretty well—& this Waterman can cope with such paper without scratching too badly. However, the Parker fits my hand much better. What I wish I could get is a finer point—without sacrifice of this free flow. If I weren't so broke, I'd experiment with the newer makes; but as it is, I simply take advantage of the exchange privileges connected with the makes I have. Sheaffer & Wahl are two makes especially well regarded today.

Regards to Sotho—both from me & from the drowsy mountain of black fur which purrs intermittently in the semicircular chair on my left! I'd surely like to see a picture of the little imp of darkness when you get a good one. I can imagine the texture of his coat. Johnny Perkins's is also of that intense, glistening, unvaried, & almost bluish lustre—in contrast to his late brother Sam's, which revealed faint traces of a latent tiger heredity. Glad Sotho & his pa get on well together—I'll bet the old gentleman is proud of his boy! Johnny's (& I think Sam's) father is a lean, restless gentleman of the neighbourhood; coal-black, & rather reluctant to make friends with the human species. Johnny has certain characteristic postures which precisely duplicate those of his 1934 brother. Well—to make up for bereavements, Johnny now has 3 new little brothers (or sisters, or both—I don't know), for all of whom good homes have been found. One coal-black, two black & white. They will be delightful companions until the time comes to deliver them to their respective new abodes. Johnny spends a good deal of his time over here, & seems to appreciate the catnip he gets. (Catnip also grows wild in New England, but I don't know of any place to find it.) No further Kappa Alpha Tau disasters in Providence—or in De Land at last reports. Here's hoping that both Sotho & Mr. Perkins may grow into patriarchs as venerable as Old Man & Pres. Peter Randall!

Amateur journalism is making a slow start this term, but I hope the handicap can be overcome. No Sept. N.A. as yet—though I feel sure there is an adequate reason for the delay. The critical bureau was likewise slow in getting started, though all December reports are now in. E. H. Smith is causing a bit of bother by making a complaint (based on technicalities) against last July's story & history laureate awards, but I trust the matter can be adjusted without too great a waste of energy. Hope your recruiting will turn out well. I'm still trying to worm some more Olympians out of Cole, & when I do, you'll head the list of recipients. By this time Barlow's Dragon Fly ought to have reached you. To my mind, it is one of the most creditable products of the season—with absolutely nothing crude in it.

Well—I'm glad the cream of the Hodgsoniana reached you at last. I thought you'd see the peculiar power & originality of this material! Yes— "The Ghost Pirates" was surely powerful, though I still choose "The House on the Borderland" as the high spot. Later I hope Eph-Li can see these items—& I know Æmilius will appreciate Hodgson. Hill-Billy is a nice chap, but literary taste is something which has managed to remain wholly outside his composition! Glad you've come across "Hieroglyphics"[4]—which is an interesting venture in criticism, though of course unconnected with weird fiction. I used to own a copy, but it came to grief with a borrower. I don't entirely agree with Machen's dicta, though it seems to me there is a grain of sense in his pointing out a particular sort of driving force of "ecstasy" as the primary determinant of good literature. Too bad the local library is so weak on weird material—but that's the case everywhere. The weird enthusiast who has to depend on public libraries is simply out of luck! Glad you're going to borrow the Birkhead & Summers volumes. Summers is a peculiar case—a man of vast scholarship, but with the credulousness of a child . . . he really believes in ghosts, witches, vampires, &c.! In reading his work one has to discount this tendency in him. His arrays of facts are always valuable, but it never does to accept his own interpretations of them. Ignore him, & draw your own conclusions! Fortunately he has the sheer honesty to set down all the various interpretations of others—although he generally relegates them to footnotes, & piles the bitterest abuse on the sensible scientific explanations which are probably the correct ones. Summers—a Catholic priest—is not only the most scholarly modern author in his field, but is the sole English translator of the standard mediaeval & Renaissance works on witchcraft & allied subjects. Koenig has several of these translations. Anent Stoker—I read "The Jewel of Seven Stars" years ago, & thought it not at all bad. On the other hand, "The Lair of the White Worm" is almost the worst novel I have ever seen in cloth covers! Whitehead used to insist that Stoker wrote this latter as a joke or parody—it is so much worse than anything else of his—but I convinced him that the case is probably somewhat different. The fact is, that all his successful works were drastically revised—I knew an old lady, now dead, who in 1893 was offered the job of revising "Dracula" (a frightful mess in MS.) but turned it down because of the inadequate pay offered. Probably the "Lair" (his last book, published just before he died) forms his one single attempt to get across a book without revision—hence the abysmal difference from all his former tales. The idea is a splendid one, but he spoils it in the telling. I wish somebody else would write a novel on this theme! Don't worry about returning any of my books. Let everybody get full reading value out of them. My library has received a few accessions—including Sir E. Wallis Budge's translation of "The Book of the Dead"—a gift from old Bill Lumley, one of whose stories I lately touched up. Too bad "The Golem" & the other Hodgsoniana (& Williams books) are delayed. I'll prod the respective offenders. Dwyer has whatever Williams volumes are in circulation—& I can't understand his exaggerated & inexcusable laxity in this matter. I'm beginning to have a sickening fear (its acuteness based on the fact that I recommended Dwyer to Ech-Si-Kheh as a responsible borrower) that something may have happened to the books . . . . but we shall see.

Oct. W T certainly beat the Sept. issue. I liked the Flanders tale exceedingly, & believe the author will be worth watching. He had another good thing some months ago—"The Graveyard Duchess." 5 The Nov. issue, I think, is the best in some months. Paul Frederick Stern's[6] "The Way Home" is great stuff, & I shall certainly keep my eye on its creator—of whom I never heard before. I like Sultan Malik's "Hand of Wrath" better than any other recent thing of his—& of course Two-Gun is always good. Have also received the new Unusual from Crawford. Pretty good—excellent stories by Bloch & Petaja, & one by Dilbeck which could be a damn sight worse.[7]

Well—luck is a queer thing! I was, as may well be imagined, highly elated over the acceptance of the "Mountains" (which I had let Schwartz, at his own insistence, handle as agent, though I thought it a forlorn hope)—when lo! look at the second pleasing jolt I have received! Astounding has also taken "The Shadow Out of Time"—which Wandrei, unknown to me, had submitted to it!! The career of the "Shadow" has certainly been one of surprises. First Bobby Barlow flabbergasted me with the typed copy—& now Wandrei has just put one over on Grandpa by marketing that selfsame copy! Of course this perforce removes the copy from circulation, but when the tale appears (a 2-parter, I suppose) I'll see that everybody gets a look at it. Naturally, I realise that this dual acceptance is simply a coincidence-bred luck shot, & that I can't depend on Astounding to take things right along. However, the occurrence is distinctly encouraging, & may start me on a new period of intensive writing. Indeed, it has done so already—since last week I wrote a 26-page bit of horror whose typing I've just finished. Prompted by one of the letters in the Eyrie, I've dedicated this to young Bloch in exchange for his dedication of the "Shambler." He left me as a splotch of ensanguined jelly—& now I've left him as a glassy-eyed corpse whose expression of cosmic, unutterable fear turns the spectators sick! I doubt if this tale will land anywhere professionally, but am circulating two carbons among the gang. Your copy will come from Two-Gun Bob, & is to be passed on to Æmilius Petaia—unless Eph-Li would like to see it also, in which case please let him do so. There is a good deal of actual Providence colour in this story. The house inhabited by "Blake" is none other than #66, & the view of Federal Hill is also genuine. However, there's no such church as the one I describe. The nearest prototype is a Victorian brick edifice which lost its steeple in a storm last summer while I was away.[8] Oh, yes—I am letting Crawford try "Innsmouth" on Astounding as he suggested, though there really is almost no chance of acceptance. This tale could hardly be grouped as "science fiction" by any stretching of the term—& in addition, Street & Smith now have two long novelettes of mine on their hands. But it's just as well to leave no stone unturned.

Sultan Malik is just getting back from Mexico, where he saw some impressive Aztec temples & pyramids, & encountered some picturesque misadventures (ran into a landslide, lived 4 days on native fare, took a rocky detour & ripped his gasoline tank so that it had to be mended with chewing-gum, &c.). Hope he was able to work in a call on Two-Gun.

Sorry to hear of your premature cold spell—which must have seemed singular in its advent during the season of green leaves! And snow! Bless me, but even Rhode Island, in subarctic New England, has never had a snowfall before late November! Hope your late autumn will be mild in compensation for this bad early start. Incidentally, your present all-masculine household must have a delightfully free-&-easy air! Glad you enjoy cooking. I hate to bother with culinary operations, & am content to get things in cans or at the delicatessen when the preparation of meals devolves upon me. I usually get my own meals except when I eat out—my aunt doing the same for herself. My hours are so irregular that I prefer to be absolute czar of my eating.

New England, after the chilliness of early autumn, turned around & gave us the warmest later autumn in years! Only in 1920 & 1928 do I recall anything like it . . . . . it was 80° on Oct. 29! Naturally, my season of hibernation was radically postponed—nearly every October afternoon giving me a chance to take my work out to the woods & fields. Nor were longer trips wholly absent—although the Mohawk Trail expedition didn't materialise. On Oct. 8 my aunt & I had a trip to New Haven in a friend's car—which gave me 7½ hrs. for exploration (I'd never been off a moving vehicle in the town before) while my aunt did some visiting. The day was ideally sunny (though I could have wished it warmer), & the ride through autumnal Connecticut scenery (foliage at its gorgeous best) delightful. New Haven is not as rich in colonial antiquities as Providence, but has a peculiar charm of its own. Streets are broad & well-kept, & in the residential sections (some of which involve hills & fine views) there are endless stately mansions a century old, with generous grounds & gardens, & an almost continuous overarching canopy of great elms. I visited ancient Connecticut Hall (1752—oldest Yale College building, where Nathan Hale of the class of 1773 roomed), old Centre Church (1812—with an interesting crypt containing the grave of Benedict Arnold's first wife), the Pierpont house (1767—now Yale Faculty Club), the historical, art, & natural history museums, the Farnam & Marsh botanic gardens, & various other points of interest—crowding as much as possible into the limited time available.

Most impressive of all the sights, perhaps, were the great new quadrangles of Yale University—each an absolutely faithful reproduction of old-time architecture & atmosphere, & forming a self-contained little world in itself.

The Gothic courtyards transport one in fancy to mediaeval Oxford or Cambridge—spires, oriels, pointed arches, mullioned windows, arcades with groined roofs, climbing ivy, sundials, lawns, gardens, vine-clad walls & flagstoned walks—everything to give the young occupants that massed impression of their accumulated cultural heritage which they might obtain in Old England itself. To stroll through these quadrangles in the golden light of late afternoon; at dusk, when the candles behind the diamond-paned casements flicker up one by one; or in the beams of a mellow Hunter's Moon; is to walk bodily into an enchanted region of dream. It is the past & the ancient mother land brought magically to the present time & place. The choicest of these Gothic quadrangles is Calhoun College—named for the great Carolinian (whose grave in St. Philip's churchyard, Charleston, I had visited less than two months before), who was a graduate of Yale. Nor are the Georgian quadrangles less glamourous—each being a magical summoning-up of the world of two centuries ago. Many distinct types of Georgian architecture are represented, & the buildings & landscaping alike reflect the finest taste which European civilisation has yet evolved or is likely to evolve. Lucky is the youth whose formative years are spent amid such scenes! I wandered for hours through this limitless labyrinth of unexpected elder microcosms, & mourned the lack of further time. Certainly, I must visit New Haven again, since many of its treasures would require weeks for proper inspection & appreciation.

But this trip did not quite end my 1935 travels. On Oct. 16 at 6 a.m. my friend Samuel Loveman (poet—whose collected verse is shortly to be issued by the Caxton Printers of Caldwell, Idaho) blew into town on the New York boat, & after a session at #66 we both started out for Boston to absorb bookstalls, museums, & general antiquities. We stayed 2 days—at Technology Chambers in Irvington St.—& managed to take in quite a few sights. Most of our time was spent in the Egyptian & Greek sections of the Museum of Fine Arts. Back to Providence on the 18th, & did all the local bookstalls. Discovered one so good that Loveman may be back in a month or so to patronise it. On the evening of the 18th Loveman left for N.Y. on the boat. This probably ends the travel season—though the weather is still mild.

Recently my aunt & I attended several lectures on art & allied subjects at Brown University—only a stone's throw from our door. One of them—on "Art, Economics, & the American Future"—was by Prof. H. A. Overstreet of the College of the City of N.Y. (which young Schwartz attends), author of several interesting works on philosophy & psychology; & during the question period the speaker got into quite a spirited (indeed, almost acrimonious!) debate with the Governor of Rhode Island, Theodore Francis Green, who sat in the seat directly behind me. Green argued that the highest art must be international & non-racial (he himself is a noted collector of Sino-Japanese prints & porcelain); but Overstreet shewed clearly that every artist, in order to rise to truly universal & international heights, must work through the medium of his own cultural inheritance.

Picturesque fog today—gives the outspread roofs of the town a dreamlike & spectral aspect. President & Vice-President of Kappa Alpha Tau taking the air (or the mist) on the clubhouse roof, & Johnny Perkins here calling on me.

Thanks again for the glimpse of those cuttings. Hope you'll be able to get a glimpse of the Salmon River gorge & the painted rocks some day. Did you get any reverberations of the recent earthquakes? Petaja was relatively near the centre of activity. Providence had a tremor early this month, but it wasn't manifest here on the hill. I've felt only one earthquake in the course of my existence—the shock of Feb. 28, 1925, when I was in New York. ¶ Every good wish, & regards to Sotho—

Yrs by the Pnakotic Seal—

Ech-Pi-El

[P.S. on envelope:] Carved images just came from CAS. Magnificent!

Notes

1. Neither piece appeared in the *Phantagraph*.

2. See FLB 26n4.

3. Mrs. Cassie Doty Symmes. HPL ghostwrote the preface to her book, *Old World Footprints,* for Frank Belknap Long.

4. By Arthur Machen.

5. I.e., John Flanders, pseudonym of Jean-Raymond De Kremer (1887–1964), Belgian journalist and writer. "The Graveyard Duchess" appeared in December 1934.

6. Stern was a pseudonym of Paul [Frederick] Ernst, who had another story in the same issue of *WT*.

7. *Unusual Stories* 1, No 2 (Winter 1935): Robert Bloch, "The Black Lotus"; E. Theodore Pine [Emil Petaja], "The Two Doors"; Lionel Dilbeck, "The River Dwellers."

8. St. John's Roman Catholic Church (1871), 352 Atwells Avenue, the edifice that became the Free-Will Church of the Starry Wisdom sect in "The Haunter of the Dark." The steeple fell in 1935, and the church was razed in 1992.

[35]   [ALS, JHL]

Dec. 15, 1935.

Dear Rhi-Mhel:—

I'm speeding up this reply in order to set your mind at rest regarding the amateur situation. Bless me, but I'm sorry you drew so drastic an inference from that "discarded" list! By this time Bradofsky may have written you—but here goes in case he hasn't. Know, then, that those groups of names labelled "discarded" do *not* indicate persons dropped from *membership!* They refer, instead, to those members whose *proxy ballots* were "discarded" at the election of July 5th. In your case the discarding of the ballot was caused by a technicality which possibly included an out-&-out mistake.

According to the constitution no member may cast a vote unless he has had some contribution printed in an amateur paper since the preceding convention—or unless he has published a paper of his own. Now it is possible that nothing of yours was *printed* in time to be recorded by the secretary & included in his list of members qualified to vote. Each member is given the responsibility of seeing that some printed item of his gets into the secretary's hands before the convention—though in practice most neglect this procedure on the assumption that the secretary sees & records everything without being reminded. Not all secretaries are careful to go over all the papers, & a member who *has* had something printed fails to be officially credited with it. I don't know how it was in your case—whether you had nothing in print before July, or whether you did & it failed to get recorded. In either case, however, your membership *is not in the slightest degree affected.* Dozens of the oldest & most prominent members often have their ballots discarded at an election for one reason or another. Therefore I hope you will not let the incident weaken your interest & enjoyment in amateurdom. There is nothing to feel "humiliated" or even irritated about. Now that you are beginning to be well represented in the amateur press, there will be no doubt about your status at the next election.

I might add that this technicality about having voting-credentials *printed* seems to me a lot of hooey. It makes me tired—as do all technicalities & red tape—& if I were writing a new constitution I'd leave it out. The old United association (not the "United" now surviving) had no such rule—indeed, we did not demand the printing of a credential before considering a recruit a full member. In those days—15 to 20 years ago—I could give more time to amateur affairs than I can now, & was very active in the organising field. I succeeded in getting a lot of red tape out of the United's constitution, & had many needless offices eliminated—also, had many formerly elective offices (including the Off. Ed.) made appointive. But alas, the association did not survive—& now I haven't time to be fully active in the National.

I am, though, doing a bit of quiet anti-red-tape fighting in the National right now. Edwin Hadley Smith, as part of his feud with Babcock, has filed a complaint against the legality of the story & history laureateship awards on the thin technical ground that the May *Red Rooster*[1] containing them *was not published before May 1st.* Now I refuse to give a decision on this matter as Exec. Judge until I have more evidence, & as a result old Hadley is about ready to slit my throat or demand my impeachment or expulsion! The situation is really very complex, & Smith's case depends upon so slavishly literal an interpretation of the constitution that I will not consider it a single moment. I mean to have *real* evidence of the very definite non-publication of the *Rooster* last spring before I will cast my vote against the entries. Of course, the final evidence may force me to vote as Smith wishes—but if it does, my ballot will be based on real reasons & not on any attenuated technicalities!

The fact is, that the *fully developed* "May" *Red Rooster* was not indeed issued till September. However, this was labelled "Second Edition", & there are strong indications that a smaller first edition was issued before May 1st. I dimly recall seeing one, though recall no details about it. The laureate entries were submitted to the judges as separate printed pages. Smith claims that whatever was printed last April was "incomplete", & that the entries were therefore technically unpublished & ineligible at the time of the contest. This involves an exact definition of *just what an amateur paper is.* In the constitution there is a definition of just what kind of paper (size, circulation, response, &c.) is needed to give voting-credential status to matter published in it, & Smith would like to see this definition (4 pages, 100 copies mailed, &c.) applied to the kind of paper needed to legalise a laureate entry. Babcock denies that it can be so applied—& there is certainly nothing in the constitution to indicate it. For my part, I refuse to consider such technicalities at all. If the "first edition" *Red Rooster* last spring had a genuine paper's format & date-line, & reached a reasonable number of members, then it was a real paper so far as I am concerned, & the entries printed in it are legal. If, on the other hand, it was a mere set of page-proofs sent only to 2 or 3 persons, we can scarcely call it a "paper". I am now looking for evidence on this point—& wish I could get hold of an actual copy of what was circulated as a *Red Rooster* last spring. Babcock himself is not as prompt with evidence as one might wish.

I consider as wholly absurd Smith's claim that a large final edition of a periodical invalidates any earlier edition bearing the same date—making that smaller & earlier edition legally "incomplete" & "not a paper." Probably the *Spokane Spokesman-Review* has a small noon edition & also an ampler 5 o'clock edition with late news. Would you say that the appearance of the latter instantly gave the former a legally non-existent status or made it technically "incomplete"? I certainly would *not,* & therefore I count the May–Sept. issue of the R.R. out of the present matter. My verdict will be based on the one *real* question—whether or not any sort of genuine paper bearing the given entries was issued around May 1st.

Smith's use of legal technicalities reminds me of the man who invokes some forgotten but still theoretically legal blue-law of 1740 to further a private grudge or check a business rival. It may be valid literally—but is ridiculous in point of equity & justice. I am against allowing such procedure to 'get by' in amateurdom.

Old Hadley is trying to bulldoze me into giving an early decision in his favour—for it appears that my vote would be decisive. In response, I urbanely tell him to go to hell. Mrs. Plaisier—the chairman of the judges—seems to be in his favour, while Haggerty refuses to act because he was laureate judge of the disputed history entry. Smith seems to excuse Haggerty's non-action, but when *I* tell him I won't act till I get some real evidence he insists that I ought to resign & make way for a judge who *will* give a quick vote! I wish I *could* resign without having that act constitute a shirking of responsibility— but I don't want to set a precedent of condoning the intimidation of the judiciary. It may be that a hopeless deadlock of judges will ensue—thus putting the matter up to the next convention.[2] Perhaps the fairest & most representative of all verdicts could be secured that way. But I shall continue to fight against red tape & ultra-constitutionalism in amateurdom, just as I have done throughout the 21 years of my activity.

Oddly, though, I tend to sympathise with Smith so far as his Babcock feud goes. Babcock is just as unscrupulous & given to technical sharpness as he is—nor has he the long record of amateur service which distinguishes his rival. But that is no reason to excuse the fighting of the devil with fire. Smith is a living paradox. On the one hand he has been one of the greatest regenerating influences in post-1929 amateurdom, but on the other hand he retains the cynical trickiness of a ward-heeler. Last spring he "bought" Barlow's vote for his ticket by promising Ar-E'ch-Bei a rare old magazine if he'd "vote right"! Barlow *did* "vote right"—but only because he was pledged to the given ticket anyhow for other & more creditable reasons!

Well—enough of greasy politics! I was glad to see the Sept. & Dec. N.A.'s at last. Hinrichs certainly had a frightful handicap to deal with, but it is possible that he ought to have transferred the editorship sooner when he saw how late he would have to be. Spink will make an ideal editor—he served nobly in that capacity 5 years ago.[3] I liked the critical material of Spencer & Kleiner, & believe there may be some chance of starting the long-wished literary renaissance after all. Bradofsky is planning a monster *Californian*, to which I'm going to contribute a long architectural article that I wrote a year ago.[4] I'll see that you get a copy of *The Dragon Fly* sooner or later. Barlow is abominably careless about mailing. I was glad to see your lines "To the Snake" in print,[5] & hope the amateur press will contain more & more of your work. And—as I said before—don't take that ballot-disqualification business too seriously. Damned technical nonsense—& I'm sure it won't happen again!

I was certainly interested in that Salmon River exploration, & hope the results will appear in detail in the *Geographic*.[6] Glad the region isn't likely to be spoiled. Scenic boat trips wouldn't be such a bad idea—like the one I took last year down that tropical river in Florida, or like the more recent rowing trip along Black Water Creek. Glad Eph-Li finds the Grangeville climate better. I didn't get the postal you mentioned, but dropped him a Christmas card yesterday.

Here's hoping "The Disinterment" lands somewhere. Too bad Kline charges a fee when he doesn't succeed with a story—but for all that he's probably about the best agent in the business. Young Schwartz is doing some agenting nowadays—as witness the "Mts. of Madness"—but of course he hasn't the influence Kline has. He charges no fee. Hope the "Blue Stone" revision is coming along well. Quite an idea to give the astute Constantine a Flemish background & keep the name which I supplied out of the depths of my ignorance! There really was no especial reason for having him Greek—& Constantine is a name which occasionally occurs in other national nomenclatures. Surely a Nordic is more appropriate than a Mediterranean as a delver into cosmic mysteries! Glad the revision of the original Theunis tale permits you to adjust this matter & start the series right.

And now let me congratulate you upon your professional debut! I surely want to see the tale in *Progressive Youth*, & hope you can make this periodical a steady market. Juvenile fiction is an art in itself, requiring a skill fully as great as anything required by adult fiction. If you can secure a foothold in this field, you will be lucky indeed. Glad you've also landed a Linoleum Block article—which you are surely well qualified to write! Meanwhile that extension course will be an excellent thing. Glad you have such good facilities at your disposal.

Enclosed is the Price material which you so kindly lent, & which I hope will form the basis of a published article before very long. As I said before, I'll be glad to look over both this, & any article which might be made of my own random remarks, before their submission to the press.

Glad you found the F M composite interesting. My section was so badly misprinted that the text looks queer in spots, but most readers can puzzle out some sense. The science-fiction mosaic was a good parody of that species of writing. The weird one was by no means as bad as I expected it would be. It is amusing to see how each different writer expressed his personality in his instalment. Two-Gun immediately transformed the scholarly & mild-mannered professor into a raging & sanguinary Conan, while Belknap aired his pet theory concerning man's profound innate savagery. The current issue of F M is a pretty good one on the whole, though the poor taste shewn in the Fantasy Fiction Ratings always exasperates me. This month they are so bad that I couldn't resist discussing the matter in a letter to Schwartz. He hasn't replied as yet—hope he isn't offended. Changing printers for F M will be quite a step. Hope some satisfactory arrangement can soon be made.

I must subscribe to *The Phantagraph* soon. With you & Æmilius actively collaborating, this enterprise will in many ways be a kind of *Fantaisiste's Mirror* in itself! Your "Sun Spot" heading[7] is delightful—say what you will, you hold the record so far for diverse & effective linoleum work! Too bad Sultan Malik's picture didn't come out 100% clear. My 2 copies are about like those which you describe, so I guess the impression was rather uniform. Yes—the blurred impression certainly disposes of the jowl question with tragic finality! I'm eager to see your new "Ebon Isles" design.[8] It would be a very good idea to get biographical material & pictures from Long & Derleth, & I'm sure you could do justice to both the literary & linoleum-block aspects of the matter. If you'd like a *variety* of views of these two, so that you might gain a more thorough impression of their appearance than any one portrait could give, I'll be glad to lend you the different snap-shots in my possession. Too bad the booklet-printing programme seems impracticable, but that may come later even if not now.

That book of Long's verse—"The Goblin Tower"—was printed during my sojourn in De Land—in fact, I set up most of the type myself. The printing is crude—it being a first job for both—but it was valuable practice work. What delayed it was the lack of binding apparatus—which Ar-Ech-Bei could secure only gradually. He is now binding up copies to fill orders as they come in—& I've told him to see about supplying you. I've also told him to see that you get *The Dragon Fly*.

Sorry the new pen doesn't feed freely, but hope that cleaning & continued use will limber it up. One *can*, of course, overdo the matter of a fine point. Certainly, no fine point will write well on poor paper. Hope you'll get a really satisfactory pen some day. As you see, I'm using that 5¢ Woolworth ink very freely now—& without any trouble until I get near the bottom of each bottle. Then (as with Waterman's ink in the old days) I have to finish up by dipping the pen. The air inside the bottle causes chemical change & thickens the ink. That's why I prefer many small bottles to one large bottle. Yes—I know that paper makes a vast difference in the performance of a pen. Possibly you can notice that I'm back on Woolworth's Cavalier pad now. I had a dozen of a slightly better grade which I got in De Land, but finished the last of them yesterday. This coarse, free-flowing Waterman does very well on a Cavalier pad—& indeed, it will work on cheap nickel pad paper also. I am using it almost wholly for MSS., since I find that pencil tends to blur & rub out.

The Providence chapter of the K.A.T. extends its most cordial regards to Sotho & his sire. Johnny Perkins's little brothers are now divided—two given away, & one (a fascinating black-&-white devil who doesn't seem to mind Johnny's cuffing him around) still here. I shall hate to see the dispersal completed. The old patriarchs of the shed roof aren't seen much now that the weather is colder, though the tiger vice-president shews himself briefly now & then.

"The Two Magics" & "Hill of Dreams" duly reached me—pardon me for failure to acknowledge these before. Glad "The Golem" has arrived, & that you duly enjoyed & appreciated its unique power. I'm sure Eph-Li won't be disappointed in it. I've just finished F. Marion Crawford's "Witch of Prague", which Searight lent me. Although full of the false psychology & romantic hokum of the 1880's, it does succeed in conveying something of the shadowy eeriness & brooding mystery of the ancient Bohemian capital. About the books from Dwyer—I advise you to get in touch with him if they haven't shewed up yet. Address *Bernard Dwyer, C.C.C. Camp 25, Peekskill, N.Y.* He claims that he left the books at home over a month ago, with careful instructions to his sister—a very practical & dependable person—to wrap & send them to you. Presumably he gave her your correct address. If he made any blunder—or if she or the post office did—it certainly will be hellishly embarrassing for him—& for me too, since I recommended him to Koenig as a worthy recipient for the loan. But let us hope for the best. You & Dwyer could file tracing forms at the post office—describing the contents of the package, date of mailing, &c. But first of all you ought to get in touch with Dwyer.

December W T is a rotten issue—nothing any good except Klarkash-Ton's "Aforgomon" & the reprint . . . . & probably Two-Gun's serial, though I don't read serials till they are finished. Yes—I noticed that "Stern" is "Ernst"—which clearly goes to shew what some of these hacks could do if they only had some encouragement & opportunities. I've seen good work of Ernst's before—2 or 3 years ago—but then the pulp tradition & the commercial urge got him.

I was certainly pleased by the recent dual acceptance of my novelettes. That new story is "The Haunter of the *DARK*" (not "Dead"). Schwartz must have misread my rotten handwriting or made some other sort of mistake. You'll be getting the circulated carbon before long—& I hope it won't disappoint you too badly. I greatly doubt whether "Innsmouth" will land professionally.

Glad to hear that the cold spell gave place to some more civilised weather. I wouldn't mind *fog* at all—we've had quite a bit—but *cold* is the one enemy which has me down & out every time. Rhode Island had one short, sharp spell of intense cold—down to 15° or so—around Dec. 3–4–5, but has otherwise not been below normal. Naturally, the outdoor season is over for me—but I get around to lectures & the like occasionally. Have heard some pretty good things recently—Sir Norman Angell on international problems, H. A. Dyer on contemporary British art (in connexion with a loan exhibition of paintings at the museum), Prof. Robert Yerkes on the Yale experiments with chimpanzees in the fields of biology & psychology, & Dean Laing[9] of Chicago on the poet Horace—in connexion with the 2000th anniversary of the latter's birth. I had to pass up one that I wanted to hear—on the latest excavations in the Athenian agora—because it came right in the midst of that wretched cold spell. No more trips—& doubt if I shall attempt any soon. So many different things are crowding my programme lately that I scarcely have time for any one of them.

Thanks exceedingly for the article describing Whitman College—which must surely be a delightful institution. I had always realised that something of the transplanted New England atmosphere lingered around the older parts of the "Oregon" country, but did not know how perfectly the spirit had become embodied in a single university. I have seen Williams College in Western Massachusetts—it lies on the scenic Mohawk Trail route. Its standing has always been very high despite its relatively small size. It was developed in 1793 out of a previously existing school. The location is very beautiful—within sight of Mt. Greylock of the picturesque Berkshire Hills—& there are some fine new buildings of an architecture perfectly reproducing the colonial. In recent years Williams has become famous for the conferences on political sci-

ence & international policy held each summer & drawing speakers of prominence from all over the world. Walla Walla must be a very interesting & cultivated town—with its mellowness, historic memories, & 2 or 3 colleges.
Whitman has certainly become an admirable cultural centre, & its atmosphere
& physical appearance must alike be vastly attractive. Sorry its good old president emeritus has lost his sight. The distinction of academic recognition by
Oxford is surely a high one, & must give southeastern Washington a justified
feeling of pride. Hope you can make a trip to Walla-Walla some time—&
wish you could arrange for a course at Whitman. Thanks for permission to
retain the cutting for my files.

Good idea to include some local atmosphere in the revised "Blue Stone".
Almost any kind of story gains power & convincingness through attachment
to the soil of some particular place. One does not have to be too literal in
reproducing local scenes, so long as the general spirit is reflected. No—I
haven't yet written that Arkham graveyard tale I spoke of—so many other
things have intervened. Sometimes I think a story is helped by letting a good
long period elapse between incubation & writing out.

Well—I must finish this up & get it off in order to reassure you about
that amateur matter. Forget about it! ¶ Best holiday wishes to everybody—
        Yrs most sincerely—Ech-Pi-El

Notes

1. Ralph Babcock's magazine.

2. HPL gave his official report, with Vincent B. Haggerty and Jennie K. Plaisier, in
"Report of the Executive Judges." He also discusses the matter in "Some Current
Motives and Practices."

3. HPL refers to O. W. Hinrichs, official editor of the NAPA (1934–35), and Helm C.
Spink, who held the same office in 1939–31 and 1935–36.

4. "A Living Heritage: Roman Architecture in Today's America." One segment of the
article had already been published in the Summer 1935 *Californian* as "Heritage or
Modernism: Common Sense in Art Forms."

5. HPL presumably refers to the poem published as "The Snake."

6. See Philip J. Shenon and John C. Reed, "Down Idaho's River of No Return," *National Geographic* 70, No. 1 (July 1936): 94–136.

7. For Donald A. Wollheim's column in the *Phantagraph*.

8. It appears Rimel worked up an illustration for Petaja's poem "Echo from the Ebon
Isles," dedicated to Robert E. Howard, but the poem was not published.

9. Gordon Jennings Laing (1869–1945) was coeditor with Paul Shorey of *Horace: Odes
and Epodes* (Boston: Benj. H. Sanborn & Co., 1919).

[36]   [ALS, JHL]

66 College St.,
Providence, R.I.,
Feby. 12, 1936.

Dear Rhi-Mhel:—

My delay in acknowledging yours of just a month ago, & in congratulating you upon the acceptance of "The Disinterment" (for which three cheers!!!), may perhaps be excused in view of the handicaps under which I have laboured. A maddening & altogether unprecedented flood of exacting tasks has been engulfing me since early January—added to which I have had a most debilitating touch of grippe. For a week I was "all in"— eating almost nothing, & up very little. I am now around again—but feeling detestably weak, & with eyes which give out (producing a whirling effect that makes reading or writing impossible) after a very little continuous application. Damn *winter,* & all its attributes & effects! The weather, as the papers may have informed you, has turned to arctic & long-continued bitterness in the east—Nantucket being ice-bound on two occasions. There has been no temperature here lower than +4.8°, & that only once. Usually it stays around +20°. But it is the *continuousness* of the thing which makes it so devastating. Very seldom above freezing for the past month—an almost unparallelled phenomenon for Providence. I haven't been out of the house since Jany. 13—not since your letter came, or since King Edward has been on the throne![1] Much snow on the ground, & very slippery going everywhere.

Well—congratulations afresh upon the beginning of your W T career! I shall watch for the story in the months to come—though right now I haven't had a chance to read either Jan. or Feb. issue! Hope the changes aren't too radical & flattening—it is at least fortunate that you could tinker with the text yourself instead of having an unsympathetic editor do it. Wright's insistence on diagram-like explanations is very discouraging to the serious weird writer. It's a bad stylistic influence, too; for after one has listened to his repeated urgings for a year or two, one tends to acquire an unconscious habit of overexplaining. I've done it myself, as the critic at Putnam's pointed out in 1931.

Kline has surely proved a good agent. By the way—his son (though still in N.Y. studying music) has been supplanted by Otto Binder (of the "Eando" team) as his Manhattan agent. Yes—Schwartz specialises in science fiction, though I believe he'll handle any kind. Naturally, he has not Kline's wide market knowledge & editorial pull. I shall take pleasure in seeing Theunis in a new story—& with his lighter complexion & more Nordic features. The revised—or completely metamorphosed "Blue Stone" seems to me very effective, & I read it with much pleasure. I like the touch of realistic localism, & am glad you're giving Lewiston its place in the literary sun. Thanks for the glimpse. The style shews much improvement, & I've touched it up in only a few places—especially just at the end. I hope it will fare well in the professional market, & that Wright won't ask to have all the details explained in words of one syllable. Incidentally—I haven't done enough for this MS. to make it a professional job. Sometime, if you want something thoroughly re-cast, I'll quote what I think are reasonable rates after examining it. Naturally, the fee would vary with the amount of labour needed.

I read the story in *Progressive Youth* with great interest, & am glad to see that you have such a market available. The tale has a few rough spots in lan-guage & structure, & is the least bit conventional in plot & motivation, but for all that is vivid & dramatic. Congratulations—& keep it up! I'm eager to see the linoleum block article when it appears, & hope the illustration or illus-trations will turn out well. I presume a metal reproduction of your linoleum cut would be scarcely distinguishable from the original.

Your version of Sultan Malik's epistle is ideal, & I hope you will send it to *The Phantagraph.* Too bad so many vivid specific touches had to be cut out, but I suppose there was no way around it. The Peacock Sultan identified his work so thoroughly that anonymity would have been impossible without the dele-tions. Enough is certainly left to make it still powerful & significant. I strongly hope it may see the light. Yes—it would be a good idea to let the Sultan have a look at the text & give it his official imprimatur. No hurry about the corre-sponding article (which should also be anonymous) from my letter. You really do this kind of work splendidly—articles seem to give you no trouble at all.

The composite story could have been worse—but it was not much to brag about, at that. Hope Eph-Li enjoyed it. I had a pleasant card from him last month, & hope he will gradually gravitate back to the fantastic field. I've now subscribed for *The Phantagraph,* & have seen the second issue with your block prints. The pictures came out pretty well—though Shepherd's typogra-phy is distressingly primitive. He is as much worse than Crawford as Craw-ford is worse than Ruppert. This, I believe, is his first job—so let us hope he'll improve. Some of his misprints are evidently caused by sheer ignorance rather than carelessness—as when he *repeats* the misprinting of MEMNON as "MEMMON" both in the table of contents & in the title of the sketch.[2] Well—I wish the venture utmost luck, & hope its mechanical difficulties will soon be overcome. You & Æmilius Petaia will do much to keep the standards at a high level. By the way—an article on *weird music* seems an excellent idea, & I hope you & Æmilius will go to it. Have you thought of getting in touch with that weird composer who made a musical version of two of my Fungi? His name is *Harold S. Farnese, 4001 S. Harvard Blvd., Los Angeles, California.* Hope to see the new "Echoes" cut when you do it—& to hear of progress on the Long & Derleth biographies. Anent the latter—here's an envelope of photographs which may be of some small help. There weren't as many as I'd hope to find, but they'll furnish at least a start. Since I've never seen Derleth, I can't say which of the three shots is most typical of him. The best of the Long pictures is the 1934 one—though he is not quite as stout as that now.

The broken 1932 one is pretty good—shewing the bushy way the little dude wears his hair. I'd like to organise a conspiracy with Price & Two-Gun & other hard he-guys to tie Belknap up & give him a regular grown man's haircut! And while I was about it I'd probably run a Gillette over the fuzz on his upper lip! The picture taken with me—which you've probably seen before—isn't very good, but is the only *profile* of Belknap that I know of. The more views you see, the better you can visualise your subject.

Glad Barlow sent you the Ulthar booklet—which was a complete surprise to me. No misprints at all. He's going to send you a "Goblin Tower" C.O.D. ($1.00) before long, since I believe you said you wished to buy one. I haven't yet got a well-bound copy. Incidentally—Crawford is going to issue my "Shadow over Innsmouth" as a book or booklet (besides using it in M T), & is trying to get a few illustrations (woodcuts) from *Utpatel*—the gifted chap who has drawn so much for Comte d'Erlette. Hope it all comes out well—I recently read the first set of proofs. Glad you saw "Mts. of Madness" in *Astounding*. Some bad misprints (like "palaeocene" for *palaeogean*), but tolerable on the whole. The illustrations are far from bad—even the Nameless Things looking much like the original conception of them . . . . as you may see by consulting that sketch which I sent either to you or Eph-Li a year or two ago. Belknap's story in the same issue wouldn't have been bad if he'd left out the cheap pulp devices—the bee-yew-tiful heroine, the sloppy sentiment, & the convenient killing-off of the fiendish madman by a single, providential ray. But I can't forgive him for killing off a Kappa Alpha Tau member! Two or three of the other items in the magazine are tolerable. "The Shapes" has a certain haunting atmosphere, & the *idea* in "Buried Moon" could be used to great advantage. "Mathematica" is ambitious—but too abstract & conventional to be convincing.[3] Haven't had a chance to read either Jan. or Feb. W T as yet—but I mentioned that before. I see I have reprints in *both*—rather an uncommon sort of crowding! The first Crawford-printed *Fantasy* came, but doesn't equal the Ruppert product. One longs for the period of 2 years ago, when both F M & F F were in their heyday!

Well—I'm glad at least *some* of the Dwyer material came. These Williams books are only part of what ought to reach you, & I hope the rest have since come. The principal item is W. H. Hodgson's "The Night Land"—& I guess his "Carnacki, the Ghost Finder" ought to be along also. Then there is a paperbound (& now rather dilapidated, I fear) book of very short tales by Barry Pain—"Shapes After Dark", I think the title is. This seems to complete the list. I've had not a moment for reading—though a mountain of borrowed books reaches almost to the ceiling. Three of these are Williams books from Koenig—to be sent along to Klarkash-Ton. If you like the first two by C W, you might let me (or C A S) know & get in the borrowing line for the rest. Speaking of circulated material—what C A S sent me were only *sketches* of his new statuettes. The actual crated exhibit will come later . . . . its circulation probably starting with the gang in N.Y. Another circulation item—"The Haunter of the Dark" had quite a panning from Sultan Malik, & I may withdraw & cancel it. If not, you'll see it soon—being next after Two-Gun on the list.

Amateurdom seems to be worrying along tolerably well despite the usual red tape, official tangles, & political squabbles. I suppose you received the massive *Californian*—which is certainly a monument to Bradofsky's devotion to the cause.[4] With his admirable services to amateurdom in mind, I can't excuse the smart alecs who have been hampering & ridiculing him during his term. He has some amusingly crude spots—his temperamental touchiness, his naively slipshod & incoherent style, & his painfully flat fictional attempts—but these deserve to be overlooked in estimating him as a whole. Ar-Ech-Bei expects to issue a second *Dragon-Fly* before the year is over—& another important event is the advent of a paper from that greatest veteran of them all—Ernest A. Edkins, acknowledged literary leader in the 1880's & 1890's.[5] 68 years old—but you can't kill off a real old-time amateur. Look at 83-year-old Tryout! Glad you now see the inner workings of that preliminary credential mess. I wish I had time to draw up & submit for voting a really practical & effective constitution—with the nonsense & technicalities all cleared away. Most of the proposed amendments are worse than the original! The Babcock–Smith mess still simmers—& looks as though Babcock weren't coming out so well. It appears that the History Section of the *Rooster* didn't get much of a circulation last spring after all—& indeed, Babcock is considering the withdrawal of his claim to the history laureateship. The question of the story laureateship hangs fire, awaiting evidence as to the circulation of the "Feature Section" containing it. The rights of the winner, Richard Foster, must be safeguarded as far as possible. I am losing sympathy with Babcock because of his high-handed tactics. He persists in ignoring certain members when he mails his papers, & has an unpleasant habit of not sending copies to persons he attacks in them. To excoriate or ridicule a man behind his back, & not send him the text of what is said, is certainly damned bad ethics! Thus Bradofsky received no copy of the recent *Enterprise* in which his poor story attempt is so cruelly pulled to pieces. Well—Babcock is young, & will probably live to mend his ways. He needs a sharp rebuke now & then, though there is no need of hounding & crushing him as Smith would like to do. Live & let live. Some of these sour-tempered churls need to be taught certain elementary rules of fairness, good taste, social consciousness, proportion, & civilised non-encroachment.

Hope we'll see the Salmon River write-up in the *Geographic* in the course of time. Some day you surely must visit Walla-Walla & enjoy the mellow atmosphere to be found there. Glad you had a pleasant holiday visit—& hope you can manage to get some skating before the winter is over. Commiserations on the rheumatic twinges—which I hope suitable weather will dispel. I envy you the springlike weather mentioned on your postcard!

The local Kappa Alpha Tau has sustained a devastating blow—though not from the stern hand of death. Old Pres. Randall & his tiger brother have *moved away* with their human family, leaving the clubhouse roof lone & desolate. I mourn, with many a wistful glance out the window! There will have to be a new election of officers in the spring, & I shall nominate Mr. John Perkins for President. Mr. Perkins—now a huge gentleman indeed—will be a year old day after tomorrow. For Vice-President I shall nominate his sprightly little brother—Gilbert John Murray Kynymond Elliot, 4th Earl of Minto. Lord Minto is getting to be a great boy!

Glad the pen is tolerably satisfactory on Cavalier pads. This is the last of my black ink—though I may get some more for occasional use. I dropped this Parker pen the other day & bent the point all out of shape, but managed to bend it back after a fashion. It will probably, however, need professional attention. When the black ink is gone, I'll see how the Parker compares with the Waterman in handling Woolworth's 5¢ blue!

Had a good Christmas—with a tree, as last year. Young Sterling was in town that week, & we had many colloquies. Around New Year's I visited Long for a week, & saw most of the gang except Schwartz, Koenig (who was tied up whenever I was free), & Hornig (who was on a trip to New Orleans[)]. I met for the first time Arthur J. Burks, young Wollheim, Otto Binder, & Maurice J. Kaplan ("Philip Jacques Bartel"),[6] & saw good old Seabury Quinn for the first time since 1931. We had several gatherings, & I attended a dinner of the Am. Fiction Guild. Saw Long, Loveman, the Wandrei boys, Talman, Kirk, Kleiner, Leeds, young Kline, Morton, Sterling, & the usual crowd. On two occasions I visited the new Hayden Planetarium of the Am. Mus. of Nat. Hist., & found it a highly impressive device. It consists of a round, domed building of 2 storeys, joined at one point to the museum edifice. On the lower floor is a circular hall whose ceiling is a gigantic orrery—shewing the planets revolving around the sun at their proper relative speeds. Above it is another circular hall whose roof is the great dome, & whose edge is made to represent the horizon of N.Y. as seen from Central Park. In the middle of this upper hall is a projector (that looks like a "space ship" or like one of the armoured Martians in "The War of the Worlds")[7] which casts on the whitened concave surface of the dome a perfect image of the sky—capable of duplicating the natural apparent motions of the celestial vault, & of depicticting [*sic*] the heavens as seen at any hour, in any season, from any latitude, & at any period of history. Other parts of the projector can cast suitably movable images of the sun, moon, & planets, & diagrammatic arrows & circles for explanatory purposes. The effect is infinitely lifelike—as if one were outdoors beneath the sky. Lectures—different each month (I heard both Dec. & Jan. ones)—are given in connexion with this apparatus. In the annular corridors on each floor are niches containing typical astronomical instruments of all ages—telescopes, transits, celestial globes, armillaries, spheres, &c.—& cases to display books, meteorites, & other miscellany. Astronomical pictures line the walls (I enclose a postcard of one) & at the desk may be obtained useful pamphlets, books, planispheres, &c. I never saw planispheres so cheap—good ones only 25¢! I got one apiece for Belknap & Donald Wandrei, so that they'll make fewer constellation mistakes in their future stories! The institution holds classes in elementary astronomy, & sponsors clubs of amateur observers. Altogether, it forms the most complete & active popular astronomical centre imaginable. It seems to be crowded at all hours—attesting a public interest in astronomy which did not exist when I was young.

And now the long hibernation. Well—the Vernal Equinox ought to be on hand in a month & 8 days! A theoretical comfort. All good wishes, & congratulations again on your W T placement. May this be only the beginning of a long & fertile career of magazine writing! ¶ Yrs by the Knell of Thun—E'ch-Pi-El

[P.S.] Here's a circular of Loveman's book—published not so far from your region. Hope it gets good reviews.

[P.P.S.] B. C. Black has turned up after a couple of years. He is connected with an author's magazine in Upland, Indiana, & wants me to write an article on horror fiction for it. I may try.

Notes

1. The coronation of Edward VIII, King of England, occurred on January 20.
2. Referring to CAS's "The Memnons of the Night," *Phantagraph* 4, No. 2 (December 1935): [9].
3. *Astounding Stories,* 16, No. 6 (February 1936) contained the first installment of *At the Mountains of Madness,* illustrated by Harold V. Brown; Frank Belknap Long, "Cones"; R. DeWitt Miller, "The Shapes"; John Russell Fearn, "Mathematica"; and Raymond Z. Gallun, "Buried Moon."
4. The Winter 1935 and Spring 1936 issues both had more than 100 pages.
5. HPL writes of the 15 May 1936 issue (no. 2) of the *Dragon-Fly.* Edkins launched his amateur journal *Causerie,* which published HPL's "Continuity" from *Fungi from Yuggoth.*
6. Bartel wrote science fiction stories for *Amazing Stories, Wonder Stories,* and other pulps. His legal name was in fact Maurice Myron Kaplan (1904–1983).
7. By H. G. Wells.

[37]   [ALS, JHL]

66 College St.,
Providence, R.I.,
April 1, 1936

Dear Rhi-Mhel:—

First of all, let me explain most apologetically the delayed date & probable inadequacy of the present epistle. Veritably, my programme is in utter chaos! No sooner had I half-recovered from the grippe, than my aunt came down with a vastly more severe attack of the same malady—which tied me up altogether as a sort of combined nurse, secretary, butler, market-man, & errand-boy. As weeks progressed, the trouble grew worse—& in mid-March complications sent the patient to a hospital, where she is now slowly but surely recovering. All my own affairs have had to be suspended—letters left unopened, revision jobs returned unperformed, amateur duties trans-ferred, &c. The loss has been enormous, & I don't know when I'll ever get back to normal. But at that, my aunt is having a far worse time than I am!

Sorry you've had a rheumatic spell, & hope all traces will disappear amidst the spring weather. Asotin certainly was hard hit by the frost demon—for even Providence had no lower winter temperature than +4°. Now—to pay for the bad winter—we're having an early spring. 72° yesterday, & burst-ing buds on the trees. The season wasn't as advanced as this last year till April 15th or 20th.

Hope all your literary work is progressing well. You are improving all the time, & each of your tales helps you to surmount some new problem in the field of narration. I am watching W T for announcements of "The Disinter-ment." Yes—the sale of *Wonder Stories* is a good thing, for while Gernsback was a virtual crook, Margolies[1] is famous for his fair dealings. He is Long's favourite editor. The one unfortunate thing about the sale is that it has thrown Hornig out of a job. Hope your new science-fiction tale worked out well—also the weird one. Glad Eph-Li enjoyed the composite tale, & hope he'll be back within the circle sooner or later. Your collaborated article on music with Æmilius Petaja ought to be tremendously interesting[2]—especially if you can drag some data out of Farnese. I believe it was with a weird piece that he won the 1911 Grand Prix at the Paris Conservatory. All right about mentioning "Erich Zann"—though I'm afraid I was not very explicit in the story about just what the gentleman was playing!

Delighted to hear that you are doing a "Nameless City" illustration. No one could catch the spirit better than yourself. Also glad you will illustrate your own "Forbidden Room". Hope you can devise good likenesses of Long & Derleth. There is a biography of the latter in the current Fantasy; but it doesn't say much, & I think an ampler illustrated one from you will be none the less welcome.

Hope you have by this time received your copy of "The Goblin Tower". Crawford seems to be going slowly ahead with his "Innsmouth" project—I've had two sets of proofs, & Utpatel has done four illustrations. Have skimmed recent W T issues—though I suppose another is out today. Jan. & Feb. poor—each redeemed only by a Moore story. March surprisingly good—Binder, Klarkash-Ton, & (wonder of wonders) *Hamilton* being creditably repre-sented. Everyone thinks—until I correct them—that I ghost-wrote Kuttner's "Graveyard Rats", but such is *not* the case. I never heard of K. until after it was accepted by Wright. Since then the young newcomer has written me, & I find him a very bright & interesting youth. He has modelled his weird style after mine, but will probably break away from it. Outside the weird field he has made several professional placements. Hope the pulp style won't "get" him.

About *Fantasy*—yes, Schwartz's "Science Fiction Ratings" are utterly ridiculous. I once wrote him about them, but he wouldn't see the light. At first I thought he had personal grudges against some authors, but later I decided he hasn't—for in rating several tales by *the same author* he usually praises the bad & condemns the good. Simply a case of crude taste—he has the standards of the small boys who write their immature opinions in *Astounding's* "Brass Tacks" column.[3]

Now about the books Dwyer was to send—there seems to have been a misunderstanding. Dwyer now writes me that his sister duly sent the books *to the two addresses I gave*. On racking my memory I recall that I thought you might not care for the *Williams* books, so told D. to send them *back to Koenig*. Then Æmilius said he might like to see them, so I switched my directions & told him to send them to Milltown. Confusion all along the line. D's sister has sent *you* the lot that was *not* to come to you, while *somebody else* has got the volumes (Hodgson's "Night Land" & "Carnacki") which *were meant for you*. Amidst this misunderstanding I don't know which recipient—Petaja or Koenig—has the missing volumes. You might drop cards & find out. What a mess! About the future route of the Williams books—& the others when you get them—here is the list. You might copy it for each batch you pass along. I'll put you in line for the later Williams books—which I haven't yet read. Amidst my present chaos, dozens of borrowed books are piled up unread. I may have to give up reading some of them, lest I detain them outrageously long.

Glad you got *The Dragon Fly*. The extra copy was doubtless a mistake, since there was a shortage rather than a plenitude, but you can use it in recruiting. #2 ought to be along any time. But the real N.A.P.A. event is *Causerie*. What a paper! That's the kind of thing which existed plentifully in amateurdom 50 years ago. The "Goblin Tower" review would have been a bit fairer were Edkins less indifferent toward the weird.[4] Another issue of *Causerie* ought to be along in about a month. No—Babcock isn't the villain that many try to accuse him of being. He's simply a bit "fresh" & egotistical & callous & unscrupulous at times. He'll probably mature into a useful amateur. But old E. H. Smith is certainly hot on his trail, having just filed charges that he accepted $15.00 for printing laureateship certificates without ever delivering the goods! This really seems to shew up a bad bit of carelessness or delay on Babcock's part.

Glad you've heard from Morse. He is a very gifted & cultivated young fellow, & has a remarkably fine book of poems to his credit. One of his especial hobbies is *weird pictorial art*—& he has a rather impressive library pertaining to the subject. Yes—I met him in person at Loveman's in 1932. He has written weird prose-poems, like the one you recall,[5] but I doubt whether he has ever seriously attempted a weird *story*.

New candidate for presidency of K.A.T. has appeared—a rather gruff black gentleman with broad cheeks & tattered fur who has recently moved into the neighbourhood. But I shall vote for John Perkins just the same.

Congratulations on your coming of age! A 21st birthday—purely because of legal tradition—always does seem like an impressive landmark. Too bad Eph-Li couldn't have been on hand for the festivities. I celebrated my 21st birthday—Aug. 20, 1911—by taking an all-day electric car ride.[6]

About that article of mine on interplanetary fiction—I also wish it might get in *The Phantagraph*, but Crawford has had a copy for two years with the intention of printing it himself. I may ask him to pass it on to Wollheim if he doesn't intend to use it within a reasonable time. Glad you like it.

Price's Mexican notes are indeed interesting—I had a carbon of the first section some time ago. By the way—I may *see* Sultan Malik next month, since he plans a brief trip east. I surely hope it pans out! Speaking of trips—Miss Moore & her mother dropped in on Barlow in February when travelling in Florida & Ar-E'ch-Bei found them very congenial. Rather sad circumstances, though. C L M's fiance had just met death by accident, & the trip was to ease the shock. Barlow hopes for a second & less immediately tragic visit next summer. Speaking of tragedy & near-tragedy—little Kenneth Sterling, the science fiction prodigy, has had a close call. Gravely ill with abscess of lower colon, & operated on last month. Required blood-transfusion & intra-venous injection of food. He has *dictated* two notes to me recently, & is evidently pulling through all right. It would have been a calamity if such a tremendously promising career had been cut short!

No doubt you've kept up with the recent flood news. Providence escaped, but four miles south of here in Norwood streets were under water. Hartford—only 60 miles away—suffered a major calamity. Haverhill was under 10 feet of water—that is, the business district was. A rise of one foot more in the Merrimack would have inundated our venerable fellow-amateur "Tryout" Smith.

I may possibly have a call from Edkins—whom I've never seen in person—later this month, if he decides to do some touring on his return north. I certainly hope he'll get around!

Well—this a [*sic*] poor & fragmentary epistle, but I'm sure you can excuse it under the circumstances. Hope the present chaos will be cleared up in the next few weeks. ¶ All good wishes—Yrs most sincerely—H P L

Notes

1. Leo Margulies (1900–1975), American editor and publisher of science fiction and fantasy pulp magazines. At one time in the 1930s, he reputedly edited 46 magazines, including *Thrilling Wonder Stories* and *Startling Stories*. He once wrote to HPL requesting a story to publish, but HPL professed to have nothing available.

2. Their joint article, "Weird Music," appeared in the *Phantagraph*. See appendix.

3. Indeed, HPL's stories in *Astounding* were pilloried in "Brass Tacks," although several letter-writers praised or defended HPL. For the complete text of all articles about HPL in *Astounding*, see *A Weird Writer in Our Midst*, ed. S. T. Joshi (New York: Hippocampus Press, 2010), 110–18.

4. [Ernest A. Edkins], "The Goblin Tower," *Causerie* (February 1936): 2–4.

5. Richard Ely Morse, "Ebony and Ash," *FF* 1, No. 12 (August 1934): 189–90.

6. See pp. 54–55 for a description of the trip.

[38]   [ALS, JHL][1]

66 College St.,

Providence, R.I.,

May 18, 1936

Dear Rhi-Mhel:—

Yours of the 29th ult. would have been acknowledged sooner but for the chaos & crowdedness still prevailing hereabouts. On April 7 my aunt left the hospital for a convalescent home, & on the 21st she returned to 66. She is now up & about—taking walks each sunny afternoon—though requiring some coöperation in household tasks. My own programme remains totally shot to pieces, & I feel like the very devil—nervous & run down. Some warmer weather & outdoor activities will be giving me a little more energy later on. After a mild March—& the floods—there came a sickeningly chilly April. Not till the 28th was there a really warm day. Since then I have been able to take my work out to Prospect Terrace several times—& on April 30 my aunt & I were treated to a delightful motor ride through the awakening countryside to Westport Point, Mass. The landscape is now a captivating spectacle with its new verdure & abundant blossoms, & I hope to find time for some rural walks ere long. Barlow has invited me to De Land again, but I greatly doubt my ability to accept.

On May 4 the R.I. Tercentenary observances began with a parade in colonial costume which started at the college gate—just a stone's throw from here. Later there was a mock-session of the rebel legislature of May 4, 1776—held in costume in the selfsame room of the ancient colony-house (1761) where the original session was held. In this, each old-time deputy was impersonated by a lineal descendant. The acting & costuming were so excellent that one might easily have fancied the bygone period returned—with the intervening 160 years merely a bad dream. I was one of the relatively few spectators lucky enough to get into the colony-house & witness the proceedings. In the afternoon—in a ceremony at the State-House which I did not attend—Gov. Curley of Mass. presented to Gov. Green of R.I. a copy of the recent resolution of the Mass. General Court, rescinding the banishment imposed by that august body upon Roger Williams in Oct. 1635. After 300½ years Mr. Williams no doubt highly appreciates this delicate mark of consideration!

Sorry to hear you've had another rheumatic siege—but glad you've found a specialist able to get at the root of the trouble. Hope the good results may prove permanent—which is very probable, since the other doctors were doubtless aiming in the wrong direction. Congratulations on your ability to keep your musical engagements. Now I trust you'll stick faithfully to the diet & regimen mapped out by your new physician.

Glad to hear of your good weather, & of the moving of the Rimel household to more spacious quarters. The tree-girt, creek-side location sounds very picturesque, & I should think you would find it an ideal place to work. I'll surely be grateful for the loan of any sketches of the new place which your father may make. Hope Sotho will soon be used to it—though he will doubtless retain a reminiscent fondness for his earlier abode. Glad he holds his own as local K.A.T. president. The Providence Chapter is flourishing under the leadership of Mr. Perkins (a year old last February) & his younger black & white brother the Earl of Minto. The spirited playing of the brothers in the garden is a delectable sight—& I fancy little Minto's influence helps to keep John in a kitten-like mood. Both the boys often come over to visit Grandpa—& I enjoy it especially when the two of them call at once & transfer their friendly gambols & graceful slumbering to my study.

Interested in hearing all the literary news, & hope "The Blue Stone" will land in its present form. Just as well to save Hermes Trismegistus for another story—you'll have plenty of chances to use him. Good luck with "The Metal Chamber", & with the weird story not yet written. Glad you've placed something more in *Progressive Youth*—but sorry the music article for *The Phantagraph* had to be abridged.

Well—*I have seen* your block prints for "The Forbidden Room" & "The Nameless City" (sent me by Shepherd as proofs), & am delighted with both of them. The malign *suggestion* in the "Nameless City" one is tremendously impressive, & the "Forbidden Room" design puts a curiously sinister quality in apparently mundane objects. [By the way, though—*the horns of the crescent moon never point downward.* (i.e.—at night) The round side (illuminated) is the one toward the sun, & when the moon is a crescent the sun is always comparatively close by (in apparent place), below the horizon. Therefore the *round side* is always the *lower one*. In the evening after sunset (when the moon is waxing) the position is like this: ☽. In the morning before sunrise (moon waning) it is like this: ☾. However—in the land of fantasy & disordered dream some liberties may be allowed!] You certainly have a genius with linoleum. Shepherd's proofs are very good—& thank Yuggoth he's settling down to the use of black ink! Incidentally—*Phantagraph* #2 certainly shews vast improvement. Wollheim is very much interested in the N.A.P.A., & is getting out an amateur paper or leaflet. Hope *Fanciful Tales* will be a success—though Crawford's experience doesn't set a very encouraging precedent. By the way—when I last heard from C. "Innsmouth" orders had crept up to 15. Not so good—but even so, they can't be filled for months. Crawford & delay are hopelessly synonymous—& when it isn't C's fault it's his printer's! Yes—he spoke of that new printing arrangement for M T—I hope it will work! About "The Goblin Tower"—I've jogged Barlow's memory with a note. He's rather a bad hand for delays, too—although this time he has the excuse of having been ill. His throat always gives him trouble, & this spring it is veritably raising hell—demanding daily painting with nitrate of silver, &c.

I haven't followed the "Brass Tacks" references to the "Mts."—in fact, I haven't seen the May A S. I suppose the June issue with "The Shadow Out of Time" ought to be on the stands now, but I haven't had time to get down town since the 15ᵗʰ. Enclosed is your first sheet of the "Mts.", duly scribbled on. The serial is undoubtedly full of typographical errors, & if I ever get time I shall correct my three copies from the original MS. (which is promised to Barlow).

Yes—the book problem seems solved . . . although I must tell Æmilius Petaia that "The Golem" is not to follow the route of the rest, but is to go to *Searight* & then back to Barlow. Hope both you & Æmilius will enjoy "The Night Land" et al. This novel has grave drawbacks—an almost insanely absurd attempt to reproduce archaic (presumably XVII cent.) English which resembles no English ever spoken or written on this planet; occasional touches of sickening sentimentality; & a verboseness which gravely taxes the reader's patience—but for all that is a stupendous piece of imagination. It was Hodgson's own favourite among his works, although I believe "The House on the Borderland" averages better. Koenig, by the way, has uncovered a good deal more biographical data about Hodgson, & is going to send it to *The Phantagraph*. To accompany it, I am sending a brief article on H's novels[2]—adapted from the paragraphs I had meant to insert in the F F serial. I've heard of that new Blackwood item, but believe it has a juvenile slant.[3] Possibly it's on the order of "Jimbo." Hope to see it sooner or later. By the way—"Salammbo" & the "Monk & H. D." safely returned, & I am indeed grateful for the cover supplied to the former. I haven't read "Asylum", but I read "The Magic Island" in 1931. Long has read Seabrook's African book.[4] I haven't seen that volume "Living Authors",[5] & imagine it could tell me a good deal I don't know about my favourites. I have Bierstadt's life of Dunsany, & quasi-autobiographical volumes by Machen & Blackwood[6] have given many hints on these authors. There is, as you suggest, a vague autobiographical element in the hero of "The Hill of Dreams."

Spink is printing the second *Causerie*, & you ought to see it before long. I enjoyed your brief tale in *The Californian*,[7] even though it was not one of your more elaborately planned specimens. Glad to see your verses—& the paragraph introducing you—in the *Cockerel*. Amateur feuds & charges simmer annoyingly as usual. Smith's latest dig at Babcock—the charges about the certificates—has developed into a complex mess involving a misunderstanding of the original order. Possibly it will have to go over to next year's board of judges. That was a curious misapprehension about the cuts in the *Cocker-el*—but I trust that Coleman will be as appreciative of your real work as he was of the work imputed to you. I've never been in touch with him, & am surprised to hear of his standing in the outside world as an artistic printer.[8] He ought to be drafted into service as a typographical critic to help Spink! By the way—leaping to the subject of your future Derleth article & cut—here's a new photograph which A W just sent me, & which may surpass all the others as a guide. No hurry about it—just put it with the rest for ultimate return after the cuts are made. Hope you'll hear from Long soon. He's been having a very bad time—both parents ill with grippe, & his hack-writing schedule unmanageably crowded. The whole family is now at Atlantic City trying to recuperate.

Speaking of the woes of the gang—Robert E. Howard is worried about his mother's health; Klarkash-Ton is having a fearful struggle attending to the place (including care of 40 hens) & caring for his increasingly feeble father; Wandrei has had influenza & dysentery; & young Sterling, slowly recovering from his operation, is tutoring like mad in a desperate attempt to qualify for Harvard in the autumn despite his setback. Verily, 1936 is proving a tough year all around!

Morse is indeed a very nice chap—& a real connoisseur of weird art. His library is an enviable one—especially the pictorial section. He sent me a catalogue of his books in 1932, but there have doubtless been numerous accessions since then. His volume of verse, "Winter Garden", is really splendid. He has a peculiar aptitude for capturing the melancholy of frozen & desolate nature—the icy sterility of winter, & the dank brown soddenness of leafless late autumn. Glad he is appreciative of the felidae!

Sultan Malik's eastern trip, unfortunately, seems to be off for financial reasons. The very thing obtained to make the trip—the mighty Hudson steed—proved such a drain on the treasury that the voyage had to be postponed! However, there is a ray of hope for the autumn or later. Edkins' eastern trip also seems to be cancelled—since it will probably conflict with a journey to Canada which he feels he must make.

Roget's Thesaurus is a wise acquisition. I've always had one edition or another of it around, & last year replaced a tattered copy (which I gave to Barlow—he can re-bind it without expense) with the new Grosset & Dunlap dollar reprint. Long also has this. Glad you have a Webster's Unabridged. I've had several copies—inherited from various branches of the family—including editions of 1847, 1864, 1885, & 1890. I'm now down to the last one—the 1890 one—which is still in good condition. For all ordinary purposes it is about as useful as the latest edition, though of course one must look elsewhere for contemporary terms.

Stumbled on an interesting genealogical discovery recently—when I learned for the first time that I am a great-great-great-great-great-great-great-great-great-grandson of the Elizabethan astronomer who introduced the Copernican theory into England! For one who has always been a keen amateur astronomer, this was quite a find. Ordinarily I'm not much at genealogy, being content to take what existing charts tell me & let it go at that. The other day I ran into a caller of my aunt's—an old lady related to us in the Field & Wilcox lines—& she mentioned how proud I ought to be of our common ancestor, the astronomer John Field or Felde who died in 1587. That had me quite floored, since our charts carried the Field line back only to the original Providence settler John Field, who died in 1686, & I knew he was no stargazer! Well—it soon turned out that the ancestry of this settler has been known for ages among genealogists, though I never had the least inkling of it. The 16th century astronomer (whose 1557 Ephemeris contained the first English account of the Copernican system, & who has been called "The Proto-Copernican of England") was the Prov. colonist's own grandfather—hence my 9-times great-grandfather. It certainly gave me a kick to get a real man of science in my pedigree, which as a general thing is overpopulated with clergymen but short on straight thinkers. [But I'm hanged if this new discovery hasn't added one more divine to the bunch—for it seems that the Prov. colonist's maternal grandfather was the Rev. John Sotwell, Vicar of Peniston in Yorkshire!] Later I looked up the standard Field genealogy (by F. C. Pierce—1901) & found out all about the line. It comes from Sir Hubertus de la Feld [of the family of the Counts de la Feld, seated near Colmar in Alsace], a follower of William the Conqueror who took lands in Lancashire in 1069; the Prov. stock springing from the Yorkshire branch centreing around Sowerby, Ardsley, & Thurnscoe. I've copied a lot of notes & now have my Field linkage straight back—in exactly 20 generations—to Roger de la Feld of Sowerby, born in 1240. But it's the astronomer who chiefly interests me . . . . & about whom I mean to seek more information. I have a triple dose of Field blood, being descended from no less than three of the Providence settler's grandchildren.

I guess I mentioned how much above the average the March & April W Ts seemed to be. Haven't had a moment in which to read the May issue, but hope it doesn't represent to great a falling-off. In the amateur world, bundles from Michigan & Oakland have arrived—though neither seems heavily freighted with material of literary value.

With all good wishes, & hoping your health will stay improved—
Yrs by the Blue Stone—
E'ch-Pi-El

Notes

1. "Paragraph on last page relative to H.P.L.'s remote ancestry—R"
2. "The Weird Work of William Hope Hodgson."
3. *How the Circus Came to Tea*, a children's book.
4. *Jungle Ways* (1931).
5. By Stanley Kunitz.

6. Machen wrote *Far Off Things* (1922), *Things Near and Far* (1923), and *The London Adventure: An Essay in Wandering* (1924), Blackwood *Episodes Before Thirty* (1923).

7. "The Man on the Rail."

8. Carroll D. Coleman (1904–1989) was proprietor of Prairie Press, and a printer of fine editions of poetry known for their elegant typography and small print runs. He published twelve books by August Derleth between 1939 and 1970.

[39]   [ALS, JHL]

June 20, 1936.

Dear Rhi-Mhel:—

I fear this will be a very inadequate line—but pressure & congestion are still the order of the day hereabouts. I haven't been so close to a nervous collapse in 25 years—but the warm weather helps some. Hope your local drought won't prove widely injurious to farms & orchards. I presume the new shore-line you speak of is the result of previous floods. Not much hope of any major trips on my part this year. Your Idaho centenary observances must have been very pleasant & interesting, & I'm sorry you missed part of them. (For that matter, though, I shan't see a third or a quarter of the local tercentenary events!) I'd have liked to see them myself, since (as I've mentioned) my maternal grandfather had so close a connexion with the Snake River country in his latter years. Glad you continue to like your new location—& thanks indeed for the attractive sketch by your father. Pray thank & congratulate him for me. Glad, too, that Sotho takes kindly to the change. Your tailless neighbour ought to make a good friend for Sotho. Are you sure his caudal deficiency is *artificial?* As you know, the Manx cat is naturally tailless—& many cats in America have Manx strains. When I visited my ancestral region in western Rhode Island in 1926 & 1929 I was impressed by the prevalence of tailless cats there. Evidently a Manx litter were imported there some time in the last 60 years, so that the local feline population is thickly permeated with the strain.

But speaking of the felidae—I have the very worst of news to record. At one fell stroke I have lost all my best friends. Some nameless doom—either an epidemic or the work of some contemptible poisoner—has been invading the neighbourhood, & both John Perkins & the Earl of Minto have succumbed. Few recent events have given me so painful a shock—or contributed more to my nervous exhaustion.

File-cleaning (4 days of continuous work—including 2 nights of cut-out sleep) was another exhausting influence, albeit a stern necessity. My archives had got completely beyond control, & I was at a standstill until systematisation could occur. Now—for the first time in years—I know how to get hold of various cuttings, papers, &c. when I need to use them. I threw away about a ton of junk—& have tentatively marked out nearly another ton for kindred disposition. There is no hope of keeping an infinite array of letters & records except in a public institution. The sets of drawers I bought last year were only a sort of palliative.

Glad your rheumatism remains cured, & hope there will be no further return. Barlow's throat seems a little better—but it is an obscure bronchial affair, not to be reached by anything so definite as tonsil removal. Sterling is virtually all right again—& my aunt is pretty well back to her usual routine. But just to sustain 1936's bad record—Edkins is now shadowed by an operation.

Hope you'll have good news from both "Blue Stone" & "Metal Chamber" before long . . . . & that "The Black Idol" will prove satisfying. Thanks extremely for the glimpse of "The Sable Garden"—which I return herewith as per request. The atmosphere is splendid, & there is really no change which I could suggest. A few pencilled points on the MS. are doubtless more or less self-explanatory. I like this story tremendously, & hope it can be published somewhere or other—professionally or otherwise. Glad the musical article is slated for the next *Phantagraph*. Your linoleum cuts are splendid—& that moon matter is really very minor. Hundreds of artists in all ages have pulled just the same sort of astronomical boners now & then . . . & so have hundreds of *authors* in describing the night sky.

Glad you weren't too badly disappointed in the "Shadow out of Time"—which some have panned so badly that I almost resolved to quit writing. It was made rather worse by the by the careless printing—the crazy "stylesheet" of A.S., with its irresponsible overcapitalisation (*Moon, Moonlight,* &c.!) & overpunctuation (redundant commas by the bushel!), & the occasional outright misprints. This story wasn't intentionally mangled, but the "Mts. of Madness" was a beastly mess which sickened me when I read the text. Common names changed to pedantic scientific equivalents (as *dinosaurs* to *Dinosauria*), good spelling made bad (*subterrene* changed to *subterrAne*—which has no existence as an adjective), dozens of sentences spoiled, & paragraphs chopped up into small bits in imitation of juvenile pulp action style . . . a process destroying original rhythms, emotional modulations, & minor climactic effects. Important passages are also deleted—especially toward the end—thus decreasing vitality & colour, & making the action baldly mechanical. So many significant details & impressions are missing from the concluding parts, that the effect is that of a flat ending. After all the adventure & detail *before* the encounter with the shoggoths in the abyss, the characters are shot up to the surface without any of the gradual experiences & emotions which make the reader *feel* their return to the world of men from the nighted, aeon-dead world of The Others. All sense of the *duration & difficulty* of the exhausted climb is lost when it is dismissed objectively in only a few words, with no adequate hint of the fugitives' responses to the scenes through which they pass. Among actual *plot* points omitted is one where the explorers notice (through a dropped battery) that the revived Old Ones have been pausing perplexedly before that ominous & grotesquely crude *palimpsest carving* in the passage to the sunken sea. I had the devil's own time correcting 3 printed copies of the serial—joining up the dissected paragraphs & restoring the dropped passages . . . . the latter feat accomplished by very fine pencil printing on the margins, with proper carets & leading-lines.

Thanks for setting "The Golem" on the right track. Hope you & Æmilius will like "The Night Land" in spite of all its defects. It certainly is a great novel, after all the demerits are reckoned. No hurry about any of the other books. If Morse doesn't send "Winter Garden" I'll lend you my copy. Glad Roget is a help—I never could have got along without him in the early days. Pleased that Comte d'Erlette's new likeness is a help.

Hope you'll duly receive *Causerie* #2, as well as the second *Dragon-Fly*. In a circular[1] accompanying the latter I'm saying a word or two about the current orgy of unpleasant personalities—especially the absurd & vicious persecution of poor Bradofsky. I've just voted the complete Michigan ticket— including Bradofsky for Off. Ed. Glad Wollheim has roped little Sterling in— a thing I tried to do myself last winter.

Too bad Eph-Li (to whom please send my regards) hasn't been able to visit Asotin as yet. Hope Sultan Malik will get around in the course of time— you'll find him tremendously likeable. Hornig has gone to San Francisco—on a newspaper job secured for him by good old Abe Merritt—& stopped off in Indianapolis en route to see Miss Moore. Hope the job turns out well. C D H is a fine chap, & he surely got a raw deal (as everybody does!) from Hugo the Rat!

Among the recent items in my attempted conquest of chaos has been a reading-up of contemporary W T issues. Two-Gun's serial is really splendid. Yuggoth! how he can surround ancient megalithic cities with an aura of aeon-old fear & necromancy! His "Black Canaan" is likewise magnificent in a more realistic way—reflecting a genuine regional background & giving a clutchingly powerful picture of the horror that stalks through the moss-hung, shadow-cursed, serpent-ridden swamps of the farther south. Bloch is doing well— following up his "Druidic Doom" with the "Faceless God" & "Grinning Ghoul." Comte d'Erlette's "Telephone in the Library" has real strength, & Hamilton continues to seek originality in "Child of the Winds". Burks spoils his "Room of Shadows" with a certain hack treatment. M. J. Bardine's "Harbour of Ghosts" has promise & atmosphere—& so has Harold G. Shane's "Lethe". But the recent average is not high. Of all the items here listed, only Two-Gun's work is really vital & first-rate.

Genealogy, though a minor pursuit, has its own sort of interest & rewards. The amount which an expert (such as my friend Morton has become) can dig up is astonishing. People leave traces on public records wherever they go—& it is the genealogist's job to know how to find & correlate these. The notes you give are very interesting—& I'll wager Morton could trace a connected pedigree from them in 3 months. He recently did wonders for a Clevelander named Pabody,[2] whom I turned over to him. Pabody had noticed the name "Pabodie" in my "Mts. of Madness", & wondered if I could give him any ancestral data. Too bad your great-uncle didn't secure patents & reap the fruits of his own inventiveness. And so Eph-Li comes from the Lees of Virginia! He ought to travel there & see the ancestral manor-houses (Stratford, built in 1727, & Arlington, of the 1800 period) which are open as public museums. I, by the way, have just visited the oldest house in R.I. (the Thomas Clemence house—built 1654—with a great stone chimney), from whose builder I am descended in the 8th generation.

Well—I hope my next bulletin will be less dull & fragmentary. Again thanks to you et pater for the sketch.

Yrs by the Claw of Yeguggon—
Ech-Pi-El

[P.S.] Just had a most staggering message—a report that Robert E. Howard has committed suicide. It seems incredible—I had a long normal letter from him May 13. He was worried about his mother's health, but otherwise seemed quite all right. '36 certainly is an unlucky year! This is amateurdom's worst blow since the passing of Whitehead in '32.

Notes

1. *Some Current Motives and Practices.*
2. Frederic Jay Pabody, a late correspondent of HPL.

[40]   [ALS, JHL postcard][1]

[Postmarked Providence, RI,
9 August 1936]

Your card recd. Congratulations on the Shelby engagement, & on the highly interesting trip. Sorry you couldn't see Æmilius in Missoula. ¶ Some friends of Klarkash-Ton's were in the Snake River country a month or so ago, but I couldn't get them word in time to steer them to Asotin. ¶ I had a miserable summer until mid-July—nervous exhaustion & bad digestion—but then a wave of 90° weather put me on my feet. Took a Newport trip, had an interesting visit from Moe & his son, & got out in the open air a bit. Then on July 28 young *Barlow* blew in for an indefinite sojourn. He's here still—at the boarding-house across the back garden, & absorbing old Providence bit by bit. On Aug 6 still another visitor arrived—old Adolphe de Castro (Ambrose Bierce's friend), about whom I've undoubtedly told you. He is now about to depart. Yesterday Barlow, de Castro & I sat in the spectral hidden churchyard just north of here & composed rhymed acrostics on Poe.[2] ¶ All this entertaining is playing hell with my work—I don't know how I'll ever catch up. ¶ Haven't had a chance to read the latest W T, although I've bought it. Did I mention that Wright has taken my last 2 stories?[3]

Best wishes—
Ech-Pi-El

[*On front:*] After winning, Bradofsky has resigned the editorship. Spink will publish the Sept. N.A.

Notes

1. *Front:* Betsy Williams Cottage, Roger Williams Park, Providence, R.I.
2. The three acrostic poems, and others by M. W. Moe and Henry Kuttner, were published in David E. Schultz, "In a Sequester'd Churchyard," *Crypt of Cthulhu* No. 57 (St. John's Eve 1988): 26–29.
3. I.e., "The Thing on the Doorstep" and "The Haunter of the Dark."

[41]   [ALS, JHL]

66 College St.,
Providence, R.I.,
Aug. 27, 1936.

Dear Rhi-Mhel:—

By this time you doubtless have the card which I sent to Asotin in answer to your two. I didn't know how long your stay in Shelby was to be. Glad you had an enjoyable trip, & hope you'll like the town throughout your stay. You'll doubtless grow accustomed to the altitude as time passes. Passing a time belt is rather an entertaining phenomenon—I've been out of Eastern into Central (which New Orleans keeps) once or twice. Here's wishing you a pleasant & profitable sojourn—& I hope you'll find a good library. Congratulations on the continued absence of rheumatism! Trust you'll make Canada before your return.

My card doubtless outlined the latest Prov. news. Barlow forms a very welcome visitor, & is getting quite used to Providence. His genealogical researches have disclosed him to be a *6th cousin* of mine—both he & I being descended in the 7th generation from one John Rathbone of Block Island, born in 1658. Old de Castro's advent was quite a surprise. He stayed 5 days, so that I shewed him quite a bit of the town. On one occasion he, Barlow, & I sat on a tombstone in the hidden hillside churchyard just north of here, writing rhymed acrostics on the name of *Edgar Allan Poe* . . . who 90 years ago roamed in that selfsame churchyard while on visits to Providence. Old 'Dolph tried to saddle me with a lot of unprofitable revisory work, but I managed to dodge it without mortally offending him. Moe's earlier visit (July 18–19) was a delightful event. He came with his son, & we covered quite a bit of scenic & historic ground. On July 11 I took a lone boat trip to ancient Newport, greatly enjoying the venerable town & the rugged sea-cliffs. The hot spell beginning July 8 tended to put me on my feet, & wholly banished the digestive trouble I had been having. July 22 I saw the new Peltier comet at the Ladd Observatory of Brown University (on high ground a mile N. of here)—a place I used to haunt in youth. The object shewed merely a minute disc from which issued a fanlike haze of luminosity.

Sorry to hear of the death of Sotho's new companion. Some hellish cosmic force seems to be an enemy of the Kappa Alpha Tau! By the way—it is *not* in *Providence* cats that a tailless Manx strain exists, but in the cats of the western Rhode Island countryside where my maternal ancestors came from. The times I particularly noticed this peculiarity were in 1926 & 1929, when I visited the region in question.

Sorry Wright didn't like "The Blue Stone"—but better luck next time. Much to my surprise, he has taken my "Thing on the Doorstep" & "Haunter of the Dark", which I sent him as a mere formality before letting Schwartz have them for some British reprinting project (in which I have no confidence). Good luck with the development of "The Sable Garden"—a subtly atmospheric story of that kind is always the better for careful consideration. Yes—I saw & enjoyed the musical article in *The Phantagraph*, & wish it could have been of greater length. *Fanciful* & *Marvel* are surely slow in appearing, but will doubtless be worth waiting for. Did I tell you of the *new* fan magazine which is welcoming contributions? It is the *Science-Fantasy Correspondent,* edited by one Willis Conover, Jun., 27 High St., Cambridge, Maryland. I'll let you see "Winter Garden" whenever you like. Hope the additional Hodgsoniana has now arrived. Glad the other has gone along. No hurry about the Long biography, but glad you have the material.

Pleased to hear that Eph-Li got around at last. Give him my regards when writing. Hope you can see Æmilius before you get back to Asotin. Hornig's job didn't pan out, so after an attempt to secure work in Los Angeles he returned east for a similar quest. His present address is 121 Jefferson Ave., Elizabeth, N.J. Young Sterling is now in Lynn, Mass.—close to "Arkham" & "Kingsport." He is steadily recovering, although a rubber tube is still inside him. He was here June 30. Since then he has brilliantly passed his Harvard entrance examinations, & he now seems definitely headed toward a substantial career a biologist.

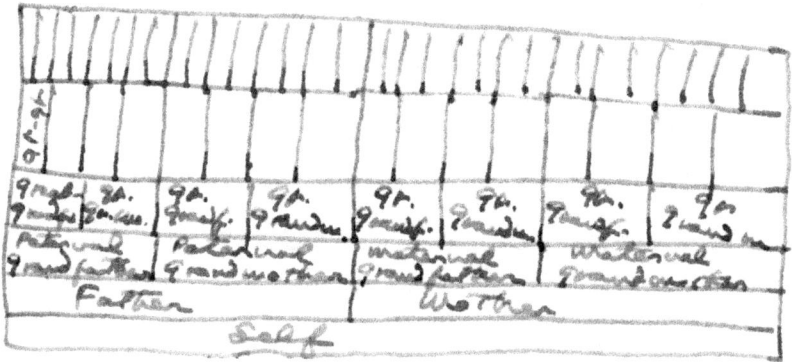

Glad you've dug up some new genealogical facts. Barlow is assembling considerable ancestral data in the local libraries, & has quite a set of charts under construction. These charts are easy to make, & help one to keep his data in compact & understandable form. Their principle is something like the following—in which the lowest rectangle represents the individual himself. In general, every space has 2 spaces above it for the parents of the person whom it represents. When one starts a chart, one fills it in as far as one can, & leaves the other spaces blank for future use. It is fascinating to come upon a "new" ancestor in the course of researches, & be able to fill in previously unused space. What one puts in a space is usually merely essential dates & information, saving ampler biographical matter for separate notes. Thus one of my chart spaces goes this way: When a chart gets rather far back from oneself the spaces become inconveniently narrow & have to be made very long, so that an ordinary piece of paper won't take many generations. For remote ancestors it is better to construct separate charts which *begin* far back. Indeed, since one usually knows all about oneself, it is usually wisest to start with a set of 2 charts, one for one's father & the other for one's mother.

Two-Gun Bob's sad end is surely a major tragedy for the gang. The motive, however, is no longer a mystery. He shot himself in an excess 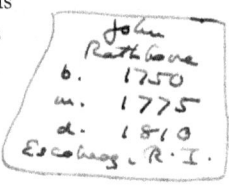 of filial devotion when told that his mother (gravely ill for over a year) could not live more than 48 hours more. 30 hours later Mrs. Howard died without knowing of her son's rash act. Evidently R E H was far more sensitive & neurotic than we ever realised, for most persons accept a parental bereavement philosophically—knowing that in the normal course of nature the elder generation must go first. The blow to old Dr. Howard must be frightful—with wife & only child gone at one stroke—but he is bearing up like a true Texas pioneer. He has presented Two-Gun's library to the latter's alma mater—Howard Payne College in Brownwood—as the nucleus of a Robert E. Howard collection of books & MSS. Further contributions (to be sent to Dr. I. M. Howard, Box 313, Cross Plains, Texas) are solicited from R E H's friends—in the form of books or MSS. in any way connected with him & his dominant interests. I'm going to send a copy of "The Shunned House" which Barlow has bound for the purpose. Poor old Two-Gun! He will be long remembered, & his place will never be filled. No other pulp writer had half his zest & sincerity & convincingness—& he was really far greater than his published work would imply. His scholarship was really profound in certain historical lines, & his epistolary comments on Texas history sometimes approach the province of epic & lyric literature. His account of his imaginary prehistoric world—"The Hyborean Age"—comes into print with tragic opportuneness.[1] Another sadly timely item is P. Schuyler Miller's chronological outline of Conan's career—in which the appearance &

growth of that hero are treated in chronological order—a list of the stories in their time-sequence being given, together with a stream of running comment on Conan & his progress. This was shewn to Two-Gun Bob last March, & he gave considerable help to Miller in correcting it. It is not yet published, though I hope it will be, either in W T or a fan magazine. Miller sent it to Wright, & Wright lent it to me without saying what he was going to do with it. I urged him to publish it when I returned it.

Petaja's sonnet to Two-Gun—which I am tremendously glad R E H saw & appreciated—surely has a significant ending in the light of recent events.[2] There will be plenty of elegies & obituaries—a fine sonnet of Barlow's having been accepted by W T. This marks Ar-E'ch-Bei's first professional acceptance—& it is surely melancholy that his debut should have so tragic a background. Sultan Malik—the only one of us who ever met Two-Gun in person—may write a set of reminiscences for one of the fan magazines. I've prepared a sort of obituary which Schwartz will probably use in *Fantasy Magazine*.

Daniels' suicide was surely regrettable.[3] He was quite a correspondent of young Sterling's. Other items in 1936's necrology are M. R. James at the age of 73 & George Allan England at 59. A grim year!

Amateurdom is jogging along. Entire Michigan ticket elected, but Bradofsky resigned because of fancied non-coöperation. He's really too touchy to be a good office-holder—although that doesn't excuse his really vicious persecution last year. Clyde G. Townsend—a dependable ex-president—has been appointed in his place. Spencer is critical chairman again, & we hope for a fairish year despite the probable loss of the best papers. Edkins' illness (another operation now, poor chap!) makes another *Causerie* unlikely, while Ar-Ech-Bei's possible removal from De Land imperils *The Dragon-Fly*. I hope that Bradofsky will continue *The Californian*.

The loan-exhibit of Klarkash-Ton's grotesque miniature sculpture has reached here, & many of the pieces are tremendously impressive. Wish I could buy some of these carven horrors!

Barlow & I visited Newport Aug. 15, & on the 20th we went the rounds of Salem & Marblehead in company with young Sterling. The old towns seemed fully as impressive as usual. On Sept. 1. Barlow leaves for Kansas City, stopping at N.Y., Washington, & Indianapolis en route. ¶ Regards—Ech-Pi-El

[On envelope:] Wandrei is back home in St. Paul for an indefinite period.

Notes

1. Howard's "The Hyborian Age" was published in part in the *Phantagraph* "Supplement" (October–November 1936), then issued as a booklet (1938).
2. Howard acknowledged seeing "Echo from the Ebon Isles" in a letter to Petaja dat-

ed 17 December 1934. The poem is published in *As Dream and Shadow* (SISU, 1977).
3. David R. Daniels, a young science fiction writer.

[42]   [ANS, JHL]¹

[Postmarked Providence, RI,
5 September 1936]

Card just recd. Sorry the Shelby climate didn't suit you. Hope the letter sent to Shelby about a week ago was duly forwarded. If not, I suppose it will come back to me. Glad the home climate has dispelled the rheumatism. The scenery from the train must have been delightful. ¶ Barlow left here Sept. 1, & has been spending a few days in N.Y.—where Sterling also is. Long & Koenig, however, were away on vacations & couldn't meet them. R H B is now heading west, & may stop in Indianapolis to see Miss Moore. His future address will be ℅ GEORGE H. GEIGER, 104 THIRD AVE., LEAVENWORTH, KANSAS. ¶ I expect Morton here next Friday & look forward to a pleasant session. Work very much behind hand, though, & must let the good part of reading & correspondence go in order to cope with a troublesome professional job.² ¶ Yes—the tales to appear in W T are "Thing" & "Haunter". The new luminary Virgil Finlay is illustrating the "Haunter", & I had a very pleasant letter from him the other day. ¶ Hope you'll be able to study in Lewiston this winter. It would certainly be profitable in the long run. ¶ Yes—the last W T was the poorest in a long time. *Nothing* good in it! Haven't yet seen the Oct. issue. ¶ Weather getting too cold for me these days—indeed, it seems as though there has been no real continuous summer. Need my oil heater almost every evening now. ¶ All best wishes, & I hope my letter will be duly forwarded.
Yrs by the Blue Stone—
E'ch-Pi-El

Notes

1. *Front:* Campus, Brown University, Providence, R.I.
2. *Well Bred Speech* by Anne Tillery Renshaw.

[43]   [ALS, JHL]

66 College St.,
Providence, R.I.,
Oct. 24, 1936.

Dear Rhi-Mhel:—

I note your urban removal with great interest, & hope that you will soon come to like Clarkston even better than Asotin. Glad the new quarters are commodious & convenient. After all, a stretch of merely seven miles doesn't separate you radically from your native scenes .... & the close proximity to Lewiston must surely be welcome. In the end, I fancy you may find the move a distinctly advantageous one. Sorry library facilities aren't better—but they could be worse, as the case of Shelby proves! Hope a warm spell will succeed in banishing the rheumatism which Montana brought back on you.

I learn with genuine sorry [sic] & dismay of Sotho's vanishment. If he does not turn up eventually, I shall suspect some especially potent league of malign powers against the Kappa Alpha Tau! Crom . . . Nimrod . . . Doodle-bug . . . . . . Sam & Johnny Perkins . . . Lord Minto . . . General Tabasco . . . . I shall ask Klarkash-Ton to have the venerable Mother Simaetha invoke a particularly potent counter-curse at the coming Hallowmass Sabbat! Incidentally—Sultan Malik has a fine new member for the Redwood City Chapter of the K.A.T. . . . . a coal-black young gentleman 4 months of age, known as "Pot-Likker", & a half-brother to the already-installed tiger member known variously as Ki-Ki, Battle-Axe, & the Conquering Lion of Judah. With the intermediation of Battle-Axe, I fancy the newcomer will be taught to carry on the noble martial traditions of the lost Nimrod.

By this time you've doubtless received another *Phantagraph*—& perhaps other belated specimens of "fan" editorship. I had heard about the *Fantascience Digest*[1] from Sterling, but haven't seen it. Conover's coming *Correspondent* promises well—& we'll see how it performs. Still another projected periodical is *Supramundane Stories,* to be launched by one Nils H. Frome, Box 3, Fraser Mills, British Columbia. If the various boy editors can't somehow get together & work in coöperation, these innumerable fly-by-night sheets will soon kill one another off! Frome is very anxious for short stories. Why not send him something if you have an item or two on hand? Encourage the journalism of the Northwest! I haven't anything whatever to send—except my blessing & best wishes.

Glad Eph-Li is congenially situated, & hope you can manage the Grangeville trip. His activities are now surely diversified!

Two-Gun Bob's passing still evokes painful echoes. As for the memorial collection—no need of worrying about that unless you happen to have something especially appropriate on hand.

Amateurdom isn't producing anything brilliant just now—but one may continue to hope for the best. I think Bradofsky will still publish *The Californian*—& you have by this time seen the Sept. N.A. I fear I shall be a complete flop as critic—no time at all! The other day (or *days!*) I had to work 60 hours continuously without sleep in order to make the deadline of an especially exacting revision job.

The Klarkash-Ton images were admired by all beholders, & have now regretfully gone back to their gifted creator. Barlow started westward Sept. 1st, & saw Long, Sterling, Koenig, Howard Wandrei (Donald is back home in St. Paul) & others in N.Y.—narrowly missing old Dr. Kuntz & Margaret Sylvester, who arrived just too late to connect. Kuntz is having a great eastern vacation, with side-trips as far as Montreal. At a later stage of his journey Barlow paused in Indianapolis for a congenial call on Miss Moore. He is now permanently settled in the west, & is to be addressed ℅ *H. M. LANGWORTHY, 810 W. 57TH ST. TERRACE, KANSAS CITY, MO.* Sterling escaped (at least, for the present) the second operation, & is now busy getting adjusted to his Harvard courses. Address: Room A-11, Lionel Hall, Cambridge, Mass.

That half-hour's churchyard pastime of Barlow, old de Castro, & myself—the Poe acrostic written last August—has had an amusing series of echoes . . . more of which, perhaps, are still to come. Although it would have never occurred to Barlow & me to submit our results for publication, Old 'Dolph *did*—& secured an acceptance from Satrap Pharnabazus! After that, Ar-E'ch-Bei & I did send our acrostics in—but they were turned down because de Castro's had already been taken. Now that the ball has started rolling, we'll probably let one or another of the fan magazines have our specimens. Meanwhile correspondents began to emulate. Henry Kuttner has devised a splendidly poetic acrostic—best of all because written at leisure.[2] And good old Moe prepared a very clever acrostic variant—& is about to incorporate *all* the acrostics into a hectographed booklet for use in his English classes. Nor is that all. Derleth is editing a Wisconsin Poetry Anthology for the publisher Henry Harrison, & having seen Moe's acrostic decided to include it in the volume.[3] All this from Ar-E'ch-Bei's idle notion of writing an acrostic (his original idea was to have each of us contribute parts to a single poem, but this soon proved impracticable) while seated on a tombstone on a summer's afternoon!

Edkins is now pulling rapidly out of his frightful surgical ordeal—being able to take neighbourhood walks, & contemplating an early start for Florida. Moe—whose nervous & heat breakdown after reaching home I believe I mentioned—is also on the upgrade, having returned to his classroom work despite a good deal of residual feebleness.

At last I have read the Oct. W T—but heaven only knows when I'll ever get at the Nov. issue. The Oct. issue is certainly an improvement on the one before, even though the opening Eshbach story is a frightful piece of tripe. Bloch's tale may not be his best, but it has some good menace & suspense, & the right kind of atmosphere. The same is true of Kuttner's. "The Lost Door" is mediocre, but could be a lot worse. "House of "Duryea" [*sic*] starts out like a routine specimen but develops a potent surprise climax. "Tree of Life" runs a bit to the Moore formula, but is distinctive for all that. "Doors of Death" distinctly dull. Two-Gun's closing Conan serial is not up to the best R E H standard, but is surely average. Finlay keeps up his high standard of drawing—& I hope he won't peter out like Brosnatch & even Rankin. I've been hearing more from him, & find him a very remarkable youth. Only 22, but gifted in poetry as well as pictorial art, & even attempting fiction nowadays. He lives in Rochester, N.Y. He has an idea of illustrating a lot of my stories with a view to increasing their saleability for book use, but I doubt whether I'll let him waste his energy on such a forlorn hope unless he really wants to do it for the sake of practice. Certainly, if I ever *did* have a published collection, I'd be glad enough of Finlay illustrations!

Not making much headway with borrowed books, but finished Hamlin Garland's "Forty Years of Psychic Research" the other day. Curious stuff, & enough to make one credulous of "occult" phenomena if one did not stop to analyse both the evidence & the narrator's attitude.

Had a pleasant visit from James F. Morton Sept. 11–12–13. We indulged in the usual discussion & ice-cream-eating, & had a pleasant call one evening on young Brobst. Morton was fresh from Boston, where at a convention of the Puzzlers' League he had just won that organisation's crossword puzzle championship—an honour which brought him a silver loving-cup. After his visit he returned to the Boston zone to attend the Harvard Tercentenary exercises. Sept. 19–20 Moe's son Robert was here—partly to call on a brilliant & prepossessing young gentlewoman from Milwaukee who is entering Brown as a graduate student of philosophy. I guided them about quite a bit in Bob's car. With this added attraction, Providence will no doubt see more of young Moe than it did last year! I don't welcome the autumn weather, but the steam heat is nobly doing its part. I still get out for occasional rural walks, though it's too late for any real sessions of reading or writing in the open.

The other night I attended a meeting of the local organisation of amateur astronomers—"The Skyscrapers", which functions more or less under the auspices of Brown University—& was astonished at its degree of development. Some of the members are almost serious scientific observers, & the society is contemplating the purchase of a well-known observatory (the Seagrave Observatory, whose private owner & director died recently) with an 8″ refractor in the western part of the state.[4] It has separate meteor, variable star, moon, planet, comet, &c. sections, which hold meetings of their own & report to the general society as units, & enjoys the use of the college observatory. Surprisingly systematic work is done—largely in the variable star & meteor fields—& the enthusiasm of the 70 or 80 members seems to be immense. It brings back my early astronomical interests so vividly that I'm half-tempted to apply for membership! At the recent meeting there was an address on early Rhode Island astronomy, & the reflecting telescope of Joseph Brown—used to observe the transit of Venus on June 3, 1769 & owned by the college since 1780 or so—was exhibited. It is really curious how radically the general public's interest in astronomy has increased since my day. When I was young no layman seemed to give a damn about the universe & its mechanism & phenomena!

Pres. Roosevelt was here Oct. 21, & I had several fine glimpses of him. He spoke from the terrace in front of the State House. That day & the day before were so warm that I took long afternoon rambles in the woods.

All good wishes—

Yrs by the Eye of Ranorada[5]—
Ech-Pi-El

Notes

1. A science fiction fanzine edited by Robert Madle, published by Comet Publications in Philadelphia.

2. "Where He Walked." In David E. Schultz, "In a Sequester'd Churchyard," *Crypt of Cthulhu* No. 57 (St. John's Eve): 26–29. The article contains all five acrostic poems.

3. "In a Providence Churchyard." In August Derleth and Raymond E. F. Larson, ed., *Poetry out of Wisconsin* (New York: Henry Harrison, 1937), 191.

4. The private observatory of Frank Evans Seagrave (1859–1934) was located at 119 Benefit Street; it is now at 47 Peeptoad Road, North Scituate, RI. Seagrave died on 15 August 1934. His executor, Wayne F. Angell, died on 7 July 1936.

5. A "living hill" in the story "The Eye in the Waste" by Lord Dunsany; in *The Gods of Pegāna.*

[44]   [ALS, JHL]

66 College St.,
Providence, R.I.,
Dec. 20, 1936.

Dear Rhi-Mhel:—

Glad to hear that you are becoming gradually adjusted to the Clarkston environment, that local library facilities are revealing redeeming features, & that rheumatism has been abating despite the chill & gloomy weather. Your region has surely seen some meteorological vicissitudes—& I hope the early December snowfall does not presage a bad winter. We had almost unprecedently early snowfalls here—Nov. 24 & 28—but each melted off within two days.

Commiserations on Sotho's continued absence—the remnants of the K.A.T.'s Providence Chapter transmit their sincere & mournful miaows! My previous bulletin has told you of the similar blow sustained by the Redwood City chapter—indeed, the past few years have dealt the mighty fraternity some lethal strokes all over the country! We must call some sort of convention of witches & sorcerers like Mother Simaetha to invoke fresh & additionally potent forms of retributive magic against the Outer Things whose ravages have been so cruel!

Glad to know that *The Phantagraph* has been arriving regularly. It has some highly interesting items—& I noted Anger's "muckraking" article in the recent issue. This article exaggerates considerably, although it does point to certain actual financial conditions which have alienated many writers. Of course, if these writers were primarily interested *in weird fiction for its own sake,* they would not be so easily led away by better economic arrangements in other fields—but as it happens, they are *not* essentially weirdists. Quinn never professed any aim save to make money, & Long, Price, Wandrei, & others are becoming increasingly like him. They go where the cash comes quickest—& that is not in W T. Of course Anger makes a mistake in attributing *all* decreased productivity to W T's financial policy. Actually, other reasons have slowed down many old-timers, including myself. As you probably read elsewhere in the same issue, Wright will have a personal reply to Anger in the next issue. The real truth will probably lie about half way betwixt what he will say & what Anger has said.

All of which reminds me of your article quoting my letter—which I return herewith.[1] Thanks very much for sending it, but I don't believe I'll make any essential change. The one tiny adjustment I am making is probably the rectification of some passage where my wretched script was obscure in the original letter. This series of comments will be very useful in shedding light on existing conditions in the weird field.

I suppose you have by this time seen *Fanciful Tales*—with your attractive art work & your splendid story "The Forbidden Room". I believe I told you before—when Shepherd sent me proofs—how much I like the linoleum designs. I haven't yet looked through your story for misprints—but my "Nameless City" has *59* bad ones. These amateur editors ought somehow to be jolted into a realisation of their laxity. That they don't *need* to be so slovenly is well exemplified by little Corwin Stickney—a kid of 14—who prints *The Science-Fantasy Correspondent*. In the whole first issue of that promising publication there are only 5 or 6 misprints. Compare that record with 59 in a single contribution! I'm damned glad now that Wollheim didn't accept my offer to use the rest of "Sup. Horror in Lit"—although his partner couldn't have messed it up any worse than Hornig's printer did! As it is, assuming the S F C survives to use it, the balance of the text has a chance of appearing in reasonably legible form! I was glad to see the cordial notice given to the S F C in the Eyrie. Have you seen the newcomer as yet? Frome's new magazine (which I think will be mimeographed) has been delayed, but I've sent him a couple of items exhumed from ancient amateur files. I've also sent similar material to a newcomer in San Francisco (C. Hamilton Bloomer, Jr.—also a N.A.P.A. member[2]), & to one of the East Orange N.J. publishers. I never see the magazines these kids issue, & hope they don't misprint my stuff too badly. The number of amateur "fan" magazines is now so vast as to be almost a joke. Indeed, fantasy fandom is becoming a sort of specialised N.A.P.A.! Glad you've received "Innsmouth" at last—although the general appearance of the volume is nothing to brag about. Please make the following changes in the list of errata which accompanies the book:

p. 36, l. 3. (put word *alighted* in quotation marks)
insert under this line the following: *p. 36, l. 9, insert "l" in explained".*
p. 115, l. 11 (change *115* to *120*)

This last error, I was horrified to discover, is *my own*. I was fatigued when I prepared the list, & the *114* on the line above doubtless suggested *115* as the next! [In margin: Yes—I'll be glad to scrawl up your copy if you wish it!] Utpatel's illustrations came out well, but the binding is as bad as the printing. Not so hot as a first published book! If I can ever get hold of the "Shunned House" sheets—now in storage in a bank in De Land—I shall try to have a few copies cheaply bound up for distribution. Meanwhile Hill-Billy is having a hard time financing *Marvel Tales*. He tried to borrow $150.00 from me—but being stone broke, I could refuse with a clear conscience! *Fantasy Magazine*, I think, will justify renewal. You ought to have the large (Sept.) Anniversary Issue anyhow.

It will be long ere the mourning at good old Two-Gun's death subsides. Each new posthumous tale evokes a sigh that the source is no longer functioning. Glad you sent the Collection an Ulthar copy—though I had previously done so myself. I'll be sending an "Innsmouth" copy—for I'm taking out my earlier royalties in copies of the book.

Glad the "Haunter" & "Doorstep" looked good in print. Finlay's illustration to the latter is remarkably fine & imaginative. Recent W T issues have perhaps shewn a slight qualitative upturn. Nov. had a R E H tale with powerful touches, & unexpectedly good stuff by McClusky, Bloch, & Whipple. In Dec. there was a still better tale by Two-Gun, a good Haitian yarn by Bloch, & an excellent Kuttner item. "The Album" alienated me because of anachronisms—a tacit assumption that *photography* existed in the 18th century (permanent photographs do not antedate Niepce's achievement of 1814), & a hash of Chaucerio-Elizabethan near-English which professed to be the language of the late 18th century. I can't understand this gross ignorance of the living speech of only 150 or 200 years ago. As you've seen from "The Night Land" & "The Boats of the Glen Carrig", Hodgson is even worse in this respect than the W T hacks! Haven't yet had a chance to read the Jan. issue, but am glad to see "The Disinterment" in print. Old Farny lately got generous & shot me some extras of issues with my stuff in them. They include this one—& when I dismember it to get the sheets of the "Doorstep" I'll send you the sheets of your tale. I always do that with members of the gang when I dissect a magazine containing their work. Your story involves a slice of Kuttner's—but I'm sending him his story in the preceding issue, so all is fair & equitable! Incidentally, I trust you safely received the MS. of "Doorstep". In looking it over I was surprised to see how few changes I had made in the text. Most of the tale had taken form in my head before I began the actual writing. Glad "Pickman's Model" stood up well under re-reading. The other day I read galley-proofs of "The Picture in the House", which will be reprinted before very long. About sending cards of notification to friends of authors represented in each issue—that is an old policy of W T, going back at least to 1925. It is of course designed to sell more copies of the magazine—the idea being that many might buy the issue for the sake of reading a friend's story even if they weren't interested in the weird. I let Wright have a lot of names years ago—& checked off still others on a N.A.P.A. list. Since then several of the persons have died—but ol' Farny is apparently using the same list, to judge from the reports of survivors. Yes—Finlay is surely *the* illustrative 'find' of 1936! His work does suggest Howard Wandrei's in certain ways—they both inherit the tradition of fantastic art crystallised by Beardsley, Sime, & Harry Clarke—yet is very distinctive for all that. For one thing—despite Finlay's lesser age, he is more influenced by classical art than is Wandrei. In general, I think his remoter artistic heritages are Graeco-Roman where Wandrei's are Gothic. Not long ago, when Finlay expressed regret at the decline of the old-time custom of writing verses on contemporary works of art, I wrote a bit of verse on his splendid drawing for Bloch's "Faceless God." If it doesn't get published somewhere before long I'll copy it for you—together with a similar thing (both in Shakespearian sonnet form) which I addressed to good old Klarkash-Ton.

Meanwhile amateurdom jogs along in the usual way. Sorry you didn't get the Sept. N.A., but I fear it's partly your own fault in not keeping the Secy. in touch with your new address. Better shoot your present address at once to the following:

(Off. Ed.) Clyde G. Townsend, 118 Henry Clay Ave., Pontiac, Mich.
(Secy.) Walter Stevenson, 47 S. Washington St., Tarrytown, N.Y.

The mailing manager—John B. Schlarb,[3] 5757 University Ave. Chicago—reported you as of "address unknown", but I notified him at once of your Clarkston whereabouts. If you fail to receive the two bundles due you, drop Schlarb a line. Barlow & others have been equally cut off through the non-circulation of their new addresses. Anyhow, I'm glad you received *The Californian* (which is more than Ar-E'ch-Bei has done to date) & have noted its diversified contents. Edkins's operation is now a thing of the past, the doctors having at last certified him as 100% sound. Now all he has to do is to let the Florida climate build up his general health. The amateur year will probably prove a rather mediocre one. Bradofsky has generously offered critical space in *The Californian*, but I fear that Spencer may not be able to round up enough critics to cover all the current output. Whether there will be more political squabbling remains to be seen. Bradofsky has issued a sheet called *Lest We Forget*,[4] full of the belated shrapnel which he ought to have shot at his tormentors a year ago, plus a lot of other belligerent matter not so well aimed. It *could* be a match in the powder-magazine—though some of those attacked are resolving to keep quiet rather than precipitate a war. Whether Babcock can bring himself to this point of tactfulness & forbearance remains to be seen. In any case, poor Hymie will have brought on himself any fresh trouble he may encounter. In the language of the day, he asked for it! I was glad to note Æmilius Petaia's advent to the N.A.P.A., & trust his assimilation may be rapid. His new college work is surely pleasant & valuable in the extreme, & I hope you'll be able to indulge in long-distance participation in the way he suggests. Too bad you can't be actually on the spot!

I note with interest your current reading—& must acknowledge safe receipt of the returned books. Don't hurry about the astronomies as long as you can get anything fresh out of them. Glad you've waded through the Hodgsoniana, & that the miserable tediousness & ludicrous pseudo-archaic style didn't blind you to the powerful setting & occasional high points of "The Night Land." The Summers treatise, like all scholarly folklore compilations, undeniably has its dull aspects—nor is the matter remedied by the childish belief in the supernatural professed by the author. As to disposing of the Koenig loan shipment—it *is* supposed to go to Crawford, but poor Hill-Billy is so indifferent toward real literature & scholarship (he didn't know, really, what he was asking for when he sought a place on the loan-list) that I really believe it would be wiser to skip him & shoot the stuff direct to William Lumley, 742 William St., Buffalo, N.Y. Old Bill is a quaint & appreciative soul, & would get full value out of all of these. At the same time you'd better prepare a future loan list, since some of the addresses have changed. Here is the list of recipients, to date, after Old Bill Lumley:

> Mrs. Natalie H. Wooley, 18 S. Mill St., Rosedale Sta., Kansas City, Kansas.
> R. H. Barlow, 810 W. 57th St. Terrace, Kansas City, Mo.
> Richard Ely Morse, 40 Princeton Ave., Princeton, N.J.
> Frank B. Long, Jr., 230 W. 97th St., New York, N.Y.
> Donald Wandrei, 1152 Portland Ave., St. Paul, Minn.
> Miss C. L. Moore, 2547 Brookside Parkway, S. Drive, Indianapolis, Ind.
> R. F. Searight, 19946 Derby Ave., Detroit, Mich.

Before the books get to Searight there may be other names on the list. If not, they naturally go back to their owner. I haven't read the occult stuff you mention, but all of it is pretty much alike. Man's capacity for hallucination, self-delusion, & unconscious mendacity is limitless! Yes, indeed—I've not only *read* "The Purple Cloud", but *own* it—thanks to the kindness of young Morse. The first half is one of the most powerful pictures of its kind in literature, but in the second half it perceptibly flags—sinking into the popular romantic tradition. I envy you the sight of that cinema—"Things to Come".[5] I missed it when it visited Providence last June, but thought surely it would be back soon for a second run. Contrary to expectations, it has not returned to date! I was warned about the disappointing quality of the "Burn, Witch, Burn"[6] thing, & let it slip by.

Sorry you haven't been able to get to Grangeville, but hope Eph-Li can get up to your region before very long. For me the season of outings ended early in November, & the long hibernation is now on. I get to hear lectures now & then, but spend as little time as possible away from steam heat!

Glad to hear that you've been literarily active, & hope "The Sable Garden" may meet with success in its new form. I'm also curious to behold "From the Sea"—whose central idea would seem to be rich in possibilities. I've had no time for any new writing—indeed, I quite despair of ever getting my programme in order!

With best holiday wishes, & renewed congratulations on your professional debut, I remain

Yrs by the Tentacles of Nug—

E'ch-Pi-El

P.S. "Pickman's Model" is to be reprinted again—this time in a "Not at Night" omnibus to be published in London next spring.

Notes

1. "What's the Trouble with Weird Fiction?" See DWR 33n3.
2. Editor of *Tesseract*.
3. Schlarb wrote an article, "Thorton Wilder," that appeared in *Californian* 3, No. 2 (Fall 1935): 32–33.
4. Bradofsky's paper published HPL's "[Letter to the N.A.P.A]" dated 22 June 1936.
5. *Things to Come* (London Film Productions, 1936); directed by William Cameron Menzies; starring Raymond Massey, Edward Chapman, and Ralph Richardson. Based on H. G. Wells's novel *The Shape of Things to Come* (1933). Wells wrote the screenplay.
6. A. Merritt's novel was filmed as *The Devil-Doll* (MGM, 1936), directed by Tod Browning, starring Lionel Barrymore and Maureen O'Sullivan.

[45]   [TLS]

The Ancient Hill—

[20 February 1937?]

Dear Rhi-Mhel:—

Driven to this nerve-racking machine by the grippe aftermath (or whatever it is) which keeps my strength at too low an ebb to let me write legibly for long at a time. The current winter's ills have been varied—involving my old swollen-foot trouble (now better) and some odd intestinal quirks probably related to grippe. The net result is a general weakness which has wrecked most of my programme and made my bewilderingly growing correspondence almost too much for me to cope with. My writing has become such a weak scrawl that I dare not use it much—in two cases puzzling mistakes have arisen lately from mis-readings.

I read "From the Sea" with keen interest, and am returning it with such minor changes as I think are needed.[1] The general effect is splendid, and the growing atmospheric tension communicates itself subtly to the reader. As the end drew near I expected the *more* horrifying tentacular Entity to be the transformed sister—but am not sure but that your arrangement is the better one. The only persistent and definite fault lay in those shiftings of scene and tempo and perspective which I call *transitions*—and in each of these cases I have supplied what I think is required. Thus a definite fresh start had to occur where the father sees the Hoffman item in the paper and transforms the long years of waiting into instant rapid action. Always remember that the way of telling a story is even more important than what is told. In various places I have tried to improve the phraseology and word-choice, but nowhere have I disturbed the plot. I really like this tale enormously, and hope it will land with Wright. Rudolf Yergler and his Chronike and Hermetic Fragments form a welcome addition to the five-foot shelf of imaginary nightmare tomes . . . . . I'll weave them into some tale of mine if I ever get around to writing again. Meanwhile I hope all will ultimately go well with "The Sable Garden" and other current ventures. Thanks for the glimpse of the poem, which I return. It surely captures the spell of the elusively unknown as suggested by distant landscapes under the appropriate conditions. If I had more time I might point out places where the phraseology might be made smoother—but time and practice will correct all these things much better than I could. Congratulations on an excellent piece of verse . . . . which, it occurs to me, you might well try on some of the little fantasy sheets despite its newspaper appearance.

Glad you're getting used to Clarkston—but commiserations on the cold winter! Ours here has averaged very warm, though latterly some cold days have been interspersed. Had the season been a severe one, my health would have been even worse than it is. Congratulations on the survival of Sotho, even though he will not leave his ancient habitat. When the weather permits you to visit him, I'll wager he will be overjoyed! Too bad Eph-Li couldn't get around, and trust that better luck may ensue.

Wright rather dodged the issue in replying to Anger—and in denying that he holds MSS. excessively long he forgot about the two-year (or more) wait still delaying poor old Bill Lumley's "Alonzo Typer", and an earlier three-year wait with one of Belknap's yarns! However, I think he's slowly reforming financially, for I received the first half of my Haunter pay on Jany. 7—only two months after publication. Glad you've sent in the anonymous article to Wollheim. As for a Blackwood tale in THRILLING MYSTERY—without question it's either merely a reprint or a syndicating of something published elsewhere in England.[2] Once in a while, when a British author leaves something in the hands of an agent, some cheap American magazine picks it up for syndicate reprinting—as in the case of E. F. Benson's stuff in W T a few years ago. I've never seen the magazine you mention, but knew that Belknap contributed often to it. Yes—Wandrei told me of the tale in ESQUIRE.[3] This magazine is of rather good grade, I'm told, though not of the serious quality of HARPERS. Wandrei seems destined to be quite a professional success . . . . though none of them can keep within sight of Derleth. Hope you'll get the

SCIENCE-FANTASY CORRESPONDENT before long. Conover has an idea of reprinting my treatise from the start, instead of beginning where Hornig left off., [*sic*] since he argues that comparatively few of his prospective readers will ever have seen the F F. By the way—I suppose you know that the S F C will absorb Schwartz's F M after the next issue. The resulting publication will resemble the S F C more than F M, although it will probably carry the name of the latter. I still await the first issue of Frome's publication—and of Weir's.[4] These East Orange boys, Blish and Miller, seem to promise more than they produce. I've sent them many items in the course of the past year, but have never seen any paper from their press.[5] Now I believe Wollheim–Shepherd have taken over at least one of their enterprises. Meanwhile Hill-Billy blunders along in his typical way—still intending to issue MARVEL in some de luxe or triumphant fashion. Yes—"The Picture in the House" will appear in an early issue of W T. I've even read the galley-proofs—and wrung from Wright the privilege of having "phantom" spelled right instead of in the fashion of his damnable style-sheet (fantom). Haven't had time to read any W T after Jan'y.—in which I think your "Disinterment" leads. "Kobold's Keep" has a certain atmosphere, but is rather ineptly handled. Before long I'll be sending the first of the "Disinterment" sheets—and will naturally be grateful for any sets of "Doorstep" sheets which you may be able to spare.

Hope your new address is gradually getting on the N.A.P.A. records. Did you receive the December official organ? If not, notify Townsend. It listed your old address, but the mailing may have taken place after rectification. Hope you got the Winter CALIFORNIAN with Barlow's magnificent "Night Ocean". That kid is coming along—indeed, the N.O. is one of the most truly artistic weird tales I've ever read. Amateur papers aren't very numerous this year, but it's well to get addresses straightened out and receive all that are coming.

I've heard of Machen and Bierce items in the Blue Books, although I've never seen the volumes in question. The stories, I fancy, are reprints of those found in standard collections. You'll find many valuable items among the Haldeman-Julius publications, though in company with a lot of junk, and in some cases handicapped by flashy sales titles which obscure the identity of the material. Thus Mrs. Whitman's "Edgar Poe and His Critics" masquerades as "Was Poe Immoral?".

Despite my current ills I haven't* been laid absolutely flat as yet, and manage to get around somehow—tottering forth for afternoon walks when the weather is warm enough and occasionally taking in lectures on subjects as varied as Peruvian antiquities, Italian Romanesque architecture, biological concepts in philosophy, and Greek astronomical hypotheses. This last came very opportune-

---

*later—down at last! Doc has me taking 3 nostrums at once, & am up only a little while at a time. I shall have to curtail my programme drastically during the rest of the winter.

ly, since I'm trying to brush up on astronomy after 20 or 30 years. The progress of the science has left me absurdly behind—but not long ago I received a request for some articles which forced me to cover the lost decades as best I might.[6] Our public library has some excellent new books on the subject—the text-book by J. C. Duncan and the layman's manuals by Bartky and Stokeley [*sic*] being apparently the best short cuts for the utterly non-mathematical amateur. For constellation-study and immediate planet data the little monthly magazine called THE MONTHLY EVENING SKY MAP is a boon. It is issued ($1.50 per year) by Leon Barritt, 244 Adams St., Brooklyn, N.Y.—a hale old veteran of 86, from whom I bought a planisphere 30 years ago.

Wright lately gave me the Finlay originals of the headings of my two recent stories, and I found them infinitely better than the reproductions. The "Doorstep" one is really quite a fantastic triumph in its way.

Well—again let me congratulate you on your story, and wish you success in its placement. It has the real atmosphere—and if Wright retains the least scrap of discrimination he'll appreciate the fact.

Yrs by the Beard of Yergler—
Ech-Pi-El

[P.S.] Your sketch of Long is splendidly graphic, & you have cleverly combined the evidence of the different snaps. His hair *is* usually bushy. I wish I could persuade the young rascal to get a real haircut!

Notes

1. HPL's note in his 1937 diary (the so-called "death diary") notes, "Finish Rimel revision" (January 28).

2. "The Man-Eater." The appearance in *Thrilling Mystery* was in fact its first.

3. "The Eye and the Finger." *Esquire* 6, No. 6 (December 1936): 70, 319–20.

4. Frome's magazine was *Supramundane Stories*, Weir's *Fantasmagoria* (or *Phantasmagoria*).

5. James Blish and William Miller, Jr., living in East Orange, NJ, edited a mimeographed magazine called the *Planeteer*. Several issues appeared in 1935–36. Although they printed some sheets that included HPL's poem "The Wood" (2, No. 1 [September 1936]: 5–6), the issue was not completed nor published.

6. Charles Blackburn Johnston, the Barlows' handyman in DeLand, Florida, now "connected" with Stetson University and its astronomical society, asked HPL for a series of "elementary articles on the heavens for the local paper" (see *SL* 5.422). HPL resurrected his series, "Mysteries of the Heavens" (1915) for that purpose, but never revised the articles.

Nils Frome (courtesy Kenneth W. Faig, Jr.)

Letters to Nils Frome

[1]   [AHT]

66 College St.,
Providence, R.I.,
Oct. 15, 1936

Dear Mr. Frome:—

[. . .]

About the "Necronomicon"—I'm sorry to disillusion you, but there is no such book. It is merely a bit of colour which I thought up for my stories some sixteen years ago, and which has been since used by myself and others as a reference-basis. I might add that the "Book of Eibon" (devised by Clark Ashton Smith), Von Junzt's *Unaussprechlichen Kulten* (an invention of the late Robert E. Howard), Ludvig Prinn's *De Vermis Mysteriis* (a creation of Robert Bloch's), the Eltdown Shards (a concept of R. F. Searight's), and the Pnakotic Manuscripts (another concoction of my own) are equally mythical. Others in the same class exist—but their names elude me for the moment. The idea of inventing mysterious book titles for use as background-material in fiction is an old one, and has been employed by a wide variety of standard authors including Poe, Machen, Chambers, Bierce, M. R. James, and any number of others. It would be unfortunate if many took these things seriously and bothered to look them up, since genuine scholarship is hard enough without having fakes and wild-goose-chases added. We have never tried to put across our imaginary gods and daemons and books as real bits of folklore and bibliography, and would be very sorry if anybody accepted them as such. I trust you realise that entities like Cthulhu, Yog-Sothoth, Nyarlathotep, Shub-Niggurath, Tsathoggua, &c. &c. are merely names devised by the various W T authors—largely Smith and myself.

The nearest things in real life to books of the "Necronomicon" type are the scattered bits of magical incantation and description which have come down from the superstitious past in such forms as the Hindoo myths used (and added to) by the Theosophists, the Jewish Cabbala, the writings of Paracelsus, and the isolated rituals and other scraps collected by such indefatigable (and sometimes credulous) scholars as Alphonse-Louis Constant (Eliphas Levi), Arthur Edward Waite, the Rev. Montague Summers, and Lewis Spence.

[. . .]

Yrs most sincerely,
H P Lovecraft

347

[2]

December 19, 1936

[. . .]

No—I don't think interplanetary travel will ever become a fact. The obstacles—thousands of separate ones—are vaster than most laymen can ever dream of, & no voyager would be likely to return alive. But it's a great theme for stories none the less.

About my "Haunter of the Dark"—all the Providence geographical details are correct. The College Hill house described is this one, & the westward view is precisely what I'm looking at now. The old church is a reality—though actually there are no sinister anecdotes connected with it. The real church has been vacant for only a year & a half.

[. . .]

[H. P. Lovecraft]

[3]

Jany. 20, 1937

[. . .]

As for fortune-telling—I won't try to argue the matter, but believe your continued studies in the various sciences will eventually cause you to abandon belief. Authentic psychology is one thing, but irresponsible prophecy is another. A careful analysis of cause & effect as they operate in all the fields around us would do much to destroy the myth of wholesale event-prediction. Certain phenomena like the seasons, eclipses, etc. do indeed result from traceable antecedent causes; but everything in the realm of human action is so infinitely complex, & so dependent upon thousands of separate & non-identifiable factors, that all prophetic efforts are futile. We may roughly guess at certain social & economic trends—though even here some unforeseen element is liable to crop up & set all our estimates awry. We cannot tell in advance when or how or to what extent our present civilization will collapse—what will be carried into the next civilization—how future geologic developments will affect the habitability of the earth—what will happen to human & other organic germ-plasm in the course of millions of years—etc., etc., etc. It is all a mystery, despite the jaunty assurances of such predictors as Wells & J. B. S. Haldane. Regarding interplanetary travel—as I said, I'm not calling it *impossible*. I merely regard it as highly *improbable*. There are tremendous obstacles which no layman can grasp, & there are no good reasons for desperate attempts involving heavy sacrifice. Of course, pure intellectual curiosity is a powerful stimulus—but there are limits to it. Practically speaking, there is no reason why any species should try to get from an environment to which it *is* adapted to one to which it *is not* adapted. Fishes (or rather, amphibians) didn't take to the land because they wanted to, but because in certain times & places the sea went back on them & further marine existence became impossible. However—all this is purely academic matter. There may be *attempts* at interplanetary travel within the next few centuries if the present mechanical civilisation persists with any degree of continuity.

As for *physiognomy*—I imagine we differ quite a bit on that. So far as I can see—aside from such marks of disease, deformity, & degeneration as a biologist could recognise—a human face can tell nothing of its possessor's character *except for those flexions of the skin & tissue which depend on habitual muscle-movements in turn caused by nerve-reactions & typical emotions*[1] (expression of eyes & mouth, etc.), & perhaps one or two touches of contour caused by typical endocrine gland functioning. Otherwise, most typical features come from *heredity*, and any biologist could tell you that we don't often chance to inherit our mental & emotional predispositions from the same genes which give us certain characteristic facial features. We may inherit most of our temperamental traits from ancestors wholly different from the ones who gave us our physical features. Read various popular works on biology—especially Wells's "Science of Life".

[. . .]

About *reincarnation*—of course that is simply nonsense along with all other notions of "soul" & "immortality". Mammals—including man—are simply physico-chemical phenomena . . . . Carbon compounds activated by some quasi-electrical form of energy. When the energy ceases and the body disintegrates, that's the end of it.

All good wishes for 1937—
Yrs. most sincerely—
H. P. Lovecraft

Notes

1. Cf. "The Shadow out of Time."

[4]

February 8, 1937

[. . .]

Regarding views of the universe & its phenomena—my ideas certainly do seem to differ quite diametrically from those which you have so far possessed. However, I can assure you that they are merely the normal ideas held by serious students of science & reflected in the majority of books by responsible authorities. You must realize that what the cheap pulp science-fiction magazines present is not real science. It is simply romance & day-dreaming based on thin scientific theories—the latter often badly twisted & strained. You will not find any real information about life and the universe in the circle of adolescent "fans" which has grown up around these magazines. Those boys are all day-dreamers—who will forget all about science when they grow up. The place to get real facts about man & the world & the universe is in serious books written by careful, thorough researchers & scientific scholars of today—men who do not try to write romance or invent fanciful ideas or keep alive the dead myths of the past; but who are interested only in setting down, so far as they know, the cold facts as they are. Virtually all serious students—biologists, physicists, chemists, astronomers—agree in their estimate of *life* as a very minor phenomenon. It is, of course, the most *highly organised* form of matter & energy which we know; but it is probably of very rare occurrence in the cosmos (since it requires special conditions involving what we must regard as an accident in order to produce the sort of planetary system adapted to its appearance & growth), & we have certain knowledge that its development to complex forms like man & other mammals depends wholly on an intricate chain of accidents extending over hundreds of thousands of years & so utterly peculiar to the one planet in question that nothing similar could possibly occur anywhere else. That is not to say that *some* highly complex form of life could not grow on some other planet in some other galaxy; but merely to say that it is impossible for such an alien form of life to be anything like *our* terrestrial higher forms. Every feature of human life & appearance & thought that we know is determined solely by the chance environmental conditions peculiar to this one planet. Biologists can trace the origin of any phase of life, & see how it grew out of the accidents of terrestrial existence. There is no warrant for reading any such thing as "purpose" into the universe as a whole—indeed, the whole psychological attitude implied in the word "purpose" is merely a chance human characteristic. People who claim that the universe as a whole has "purpose" are merely perpetuating primitive man's crude myth-making process (called "animism") of imagining that abstract or inarticulate objects have the same thoughts & feelings as man. The "soul" is a purely mythical thing. Man's *consciousness* is a material reality—a definite electromechanical process in a biological organism—and the concept of a "soul" is only a primitive & superstitious way of regarding this consciousness with its thoughts & feelings. The notion of anything "immortal" about man or any biological organism—that is, the notion of qualities not dependent upon the cells of the material body—is in the light of today's knowledge wholly untenable. But there is no need of getting depressed about man's insignificance. Who really *wants* to be cosmically important anyhow? What good would it do us if we actually were? There is plenty to keep us comfortably busy during the brief period of our individual existence—& when the momentary phenomenon called life vanishes from our planet we'll never know the difference. Instead of fretting about being insignificant, it's up to us to enjoy the faculties we have—exercising our intellectual curiosity in study & our aesthetic sense in imagination & artistic creation. And if our egos need a stimulus, we can at least reflect that we represent the most complex form or organization within the radius of our knowledge. We are only a momentary accident—& even so, we typify far subtler & more delicate energy-transformation processes than any other objects within our field of view. We may also conjecture that the basic principle of life exists (though sparingly) elsewhere, & that under the usual shifting of planetary conditions it probably evolves to a considerable complexity—albeit a complexity wholly unlike ours—in many cases. Thus we may assume that life as a principle is perhaps eternal; although each local planetary manifestation of it is accidental & momentary, & will never know of any such manifestation elsewhere in the universe. Two or more planetary life-streams can never know of each other unless they occur on neighbouring bodies of the same solar system. The only life outside our earth of which we know is the primitive vegetation which probably exists on Mars—& it is very unlikely that (barring primitive life-forms in meteorites, if such are ever found) we shall ever know of any more. You can get an excellent idea of life, its development, place, nature & psychological attributes in H. G. Wells' large volume "The Science of Life." Wells, like all sober men of science, has no illusions about man's importance in the universe; but believes that much can be made of man just as he is on this planet. We are temporary—but what of it? Let us live while we live—& there are probably hundreds of millions of years ahead for some form of life (perhaps ourselves, perhaps the descendants of some other terrestrial life-form which will supplant us) on this planet.

As to fortune-telling—all one can do is to urge you to use your common sense. You must be aware that every happening on this earth, or in all the universe, for that matter, is the result of *an infinitely vast number of wholly unrelated causes*. If any one of these causes were different, the thing would not happen. If a man stubs his toe in a certain place on a certain day, it is because of an infinity of antecedent elements—hereditary factors, etc.—which have caused him to be in the given place when he is: which have caused the obstacle to exist where it does; and which have caused the man to react to the obstacle as he does. If the man had had another great-great-great grandfather, or if a certain glacier had not been at a certain stage of plasticity when encountering a mountain 200 miles to the north 25,000 years ago; or if the man's great-great-grandmother in a wholly different line of heredity, then unknown to any of his lines, had not died when she did instead of a year later, etc., etc., this particular incident, involving as it does a particular conjunction of elements, could not possibly occur. And all happenings depend upon just as wide a conjunction of totally unrelated circumstances. Any event involving human beings depends on the *total heredity* of each one; and the average person has 4 grandparents, 8 great-grandparents, 16 great-great-grandparents, and so on. Two hundred years ago the ancestors of any one person were so scattered that only a minority are likely to have known of the others' existence; and even then, some who knew each other never knew their descendants would join in marriage. How do you suppose anybody in 1737 could predict what his descendants in 1937 would do? He didn't even know when his great-great-grandchildren were going to marry, or what part of the globe they were going to move to. There is absolutely no clue to the future, because the events are taking place all unknown to the spectators of any other. In our present, which is the future's past, we can know of only one or two factors which will enter into any event of the future. There is no way of finding out the others, because *we don't know what to look for*. Indeed, no one can know that there *will* be any "event" until such future time as the previously-unknown factors shall, by combining, have caused it to occur.

There is no getting around this, and I can assure you that fortune-telling has no place in the belief of educated adults. As for fakes like "numerology"—these things are simply the product of infantile ignorance. I can scarcely believe that this chap Loeffler (from whom I've heard twice) accepts such hilarious nonsense, although I recall his bringing up some of the pedantic geometrical mysticism of Claude Bragdon.[1] Any mental adult knows that people are named by chance, and long after the conjunction of hereditary factors which determine personality. But really—"numerology" is too silly for anybody over four years old to talk about.

There is no sense in invoking ideas of possible cosmic *recurrence* as a justification for fortune-telling—first, because all such ideas are improbable in the extreme; and second, because if such a recurrence cycle *did* occur in the universe, the successive reappearance-phases would be so infinitely far apart that no memories could ever hold over from one to the other. Indeed—no one planet with its resident organisms could ever hold over from one to the other . . . so that there wouldn't be any line of beings to remember. Let me advise you in all good faith to do a lot of serious reading in the sciences. You need it—and you are so keenly interested in the subject that you'll find it highly enjoyable and worth your while. You must get a lot of primitive myths and pseudo-scientific nothing out of your head. For example—there is no such thing as "perpetual motion" (in the sense of anything producible on earth by machinery) *and can never be*. Telepathy is another very doubtful thing. The only apparent evidence in its favour is that of the recent Rhine experiments at the U. of N. C.,[2] and even these experiments are not universally accepted. (By the way—Hugo Gernsback is a notorious sharper who ought never to be trusted. He tries to sensationalise pseudo-science, and is so dishonest in his non-payment of contributors that reputable authors have virtually blacklisted his magazines.)

Here's a list of really solid books on the sciences you should read:

Bartky	High Lights of Astronomy
Stokeley	Stars & Telescopes
Moulton	Consider the Heavens
Duncan	Astronomy
Eddington	The Nature of the Physical World

Jeans	The Universe Around Us
Swann	Architecture of the Universe
Darwin	New Conception of Matter
Jeans	New Background of Science
Reichenbach	Atoms & Cosmos
Infeld	World in Modern Science
Foster	Romance of Chemistry
Findlay	Spirit of Chemistry
Longwell	Foundation of Geology
Norton	Elements of Geology
Moon	Biology for Beginners
Clendening	The Human Body
Dorsey	Why We Behave Like Human Beings
	Various volumes by H. A. Overstreet[3] & W. J. Fielding
Kroeber	Anthropology
Lowie	Introduction to Cultural Anthropology
Frazer	The Golden Bough

Also try to get the four-volume "Outline of Science" by Professor J. Arthur Thomson, & various volumes by Sir Arthur Keith, Sir G. Elliot Smith, Marcelin Boule, & W. K. Gregory. You may not be able to get ahold of all of these, but even a few of them would prove an eye-opener. These are the solid products of real scholars, & would help to counteract the irresponsible daydreaming which clusters around the pseudo-science-fiction magazines.

But don't think that I'm not interested in fantastic speculations about the universe and like, even if I don't believe them. Indeed, they are all the more interesting—like the shadowy dreams I write about in my weird stories—because I don't believe in them.

About physiognomy—some day I'll dig up a snapshot to send you, and let you see how well the facts live up to your conjecture. I have a medium forehead and eyebrows, and a long, thin face with prominent nose. Long chin, average lips—the upper lip is *indented* under the nose, but not *cleft* like a hare-lip. My height is 5 feet 11 inches. Hair dark brown, turning grey. Complexion very light. All these things, however, come from remote hereditary causes and have not the least relation to my tastes or temperament.

[. . .]

Yrs most sincerely—

H P L

Notes

1. Claude Fayette Bragdon (1866–1946), American architect, writer, and stage designer, advocated a theosophical approach to building design. He also wrote books on spiritual topics, including Eastern religions.

2. Actually, the experiments were conducted at Duke University (Durham, NC) by J. B. Rhine (1895–1980) beginning in 1931. Although the experiments were thought to provide some evidence for the existence of telepathy, subsequent researchers (including Rhine himself) were unable to replicate the results, and his findings are now regarded as dubious at best.

3. See DWR 34 (p. 301–2).

Appendix

F. Lee Baldwin

Writings in the *Fantasy Fan*

The Boiling Point

What does this Ackerman guy know about weird and fantastic fiction? From the way he writes, he must be an unimaginative person unable to stretch his mind away from space-ships and foreign star-clusters. I get that he is an egotistical radical and one who doesn't like something that is not even intended for him. So far, in telling about his collection, he has described a sort of madhouse. However, I certainly would like to see this madhouse, as I can appreciate a thing or two that is connected with stf. At heart, I am truly a weird and fantastic fiction fan.

December 1933

Side Glances

R. H. Barlow is getting out a fine book of the late Rev. Henry S. Whitehead's letters. It will contain some fifty extremely interesting letters to the editor of Weird Tales and various other important persons in the fantastic group. The entire edition will consist of but thirty-five copies.

H. P. Lovecraft has written a story in collaboration with E. Hoffmann Price—"Through the Gates of the Silver Key" which will appear in the July issue of Weird Tales.

Seabury Quinn, who was formerly a lawyer, is now editor of a trade journal.

A 1927 issue of Amazing Stories contained a fan letter of 2300 words and a 1928 number presented one of 2600. How have you been doing, Forrie?

April 1934

Side Glances

Frank B. Long, Jr. has studied at New York University and Columbia College. Writing is his sole occupation and he lives with his father and mother, the former being a dentist. Long Jr. is 31.

E. Hoffman[n] Price is 35, a World War veteran, a West Pointer, and a former cavalry officer; also superintendent of an acetylene gas machinery plant until 2 years ago. He now has a garage in Pawhuska, Okla., and writes fiction at leisure.

May 1934

Within the Circle

Two different issues of *Weird Tales* are labeled Volume 19, Number 3. (Look on Index Page.)

E. Hoffmann Price is touring the Southwest and is planning to call on Robert E. Howard, dip into Mexico, stop at Clark Ashton Smith's and finally wind up in San Francisco. His beloved rugs are with him.

"The Curse of Yig" by Zealia Brown Reed has been reprinted in the S & B (London) "Not at Night" anthology a few years ago.

Forrest Ackerman on binding stf: "—Place together evenly all pages to be bound into one booklet; with thumbtack, press two holes through pages, holes being as far apart as the wire clips removed from original copies of magazines containing the stories or parts of serial; push clip through these two holes near top of magazine and bend together at back, then repeating operation near bottom. Story is now clipped together. Backs and covers can now easily be put on by use of adhesive paper.—Does that help you?"

"The Horror in the Museum," by Hazel Heald is scheduled for reprinting this year.

Here's one about Edgar Allan Poe: Mrs. Whitman, poetess, suggested that Poe remove the last stanza from his poem "Ulalume" as she thought it detracted from the work. He did, and there are very few of the younger Poe admirers who have seen it. Modern standard Editions don't contain this bit; it is only the older ones that do.

Howard Wandrei, Don's brother, is a weird painter of the most unusual order. His work is far beyond that of any weird illustrator employed by magazines, in my opinion.........Have a look some time you Editors who want to be surprised! Howard illustrated Donald's "Dark Odyssey."

Here are the stories in the "Randolph Carter Series" by H. P. Lovecraft. They were written as follows: "The Statement of Randolph Carter" (1919), "The Silver Key" (1926), "The Dream-Quest of Unknown Kadath" (1926–7, unpublished), and the collaboration with E. Hoffmann Price, "Through the Gates of the Silver Key" ...... "At the Mountains of Madness" was written in the Spring of 1831 [*sic*] and "The Shadow over Innsmouth" was written in November of the same year. His latest tale is "The Thing on the Doorstep" written in August, 1933.

For those who would like to read some of the classics of weird fiction try "John Silence" by Algernon Blackwood, "The Willows" by the same author (found in "The Best Ghost Stories" edited by Bohun Lynch), "The Three Imposters'" by Arthur Machen (Alfred A. Knopf, Publisher, N.Y.), "The

Turn of the Screw" by Henry James (found in "The Two Magics" by the same author), "The White People" by Arthur Machen (found in "The House of Souls" published by Alfred A. Knopf), and "Portrait of a Man With Red Hair" by Hugh Walpole (found in a public library).

June 1934

Within the Circle

R. H. Barlow is a very talented youth. He is a pianist, painter, sculptor in clay, landscape gardener and book collector. He has completed a clay bas-relief of Cthulhu and a statuette of Ganesa, the Hindoo Elephant God. One of his favorite bindings for his books is snake skin. He shoots many snakes around his home in Florida and tans the skin.

"The Last Hieroglyph" by Clark Ashton Smith, which is scheduled in WT[,] is the last of a series of stories of the fabulous land of Zothique. The first of the series was "The Empire of the Necromancers." WT has on hand another story of Zothique—"The Dark Eidolon" ... William Crawford, Editor of Marvel Tales, holds another for publication [—] "The Coming of the White Worm." It may be issued in a separate booklet. This is the first chapter of The Book of Eibon.

Do you remember Loretta Burrough who wrote "Creeping Fingers"? She had a yarn titled "What Waits in Darkness" slated for a future WT.

H. P. Lovecraft is touring the South. He is making Savannah, St. Augustine, Charleston, and other places that were founded in the *early* days of this country, and also visiting R. H. Barlow of De Land, Fla.

Clark Ashton Smith wrote and published at 17 a book of poems called "The Star Tr[e]ader."

July 1934

Within the Circle

Richard F. Searight has had accepted by WT a short story titled "The Sealed Casket" and a poem "The Wizard's Death."

Wright expects to reprint H. P. Lovecraft's "Arthur Jermyn."

Forrest Ackerman's foreign correspondence runs something like this: one Canada, one Philippine Islands; several New Zealand; four or five Great Britain; two Ireland; one Switzerland; one Hungarian.

Here's a "new" word: *Fantastiac.* One who goes in for the weird and grotesque in life; also one who likes weird fiction.

R. H. Barlow is planning on issuing "The Shunned House" by H. P. Lovecraft sometime in the fall.

Clark Ashton Smith is about 40 and has been a weird poet since boyhood. He is a protege of the late George Sterling and a fantastic painter of great power. He has translated "Bandelaire." [*sic*]

Donald Wandrei is 25 and a U. of Minn. graduate. His sole occupation is fiction-writing—comes from St. Paul but lives in New York.

August 1934

Within the Circle

Forrest Ackerman says he really had that "surprise of one's life" when Linus Hogenmiller of Missouri, his first correspondent, unexpectedly dropped in on him in Los Angeles.

A well known editor who has been recently collecting old Weird Tales had the good fortune of purchasing quite a few for two and a half cents a copy. Just imagine!

C. L. Moore has had some of her own illustrations accepted by Weird Tales.

A. Merritt calls his "The Metal Monster" his "best and worst" story.

The youthful Robert Bloch of Milwaukee has sold his first story to Weird Tales. It is titled "The Secret of the Tomb."

On his way North from Florida, H. P. Lovecraft stopt in Washington D.C. and "did several things I had never done before" ... His "The Rats in the Walls" was first submitted to Argosy but was rejected as being too horrible ... His "The Shunned House" is to be bound and issued by R. H. Barlow. The edition consists of about 225 copies and will appear some time in the fall.

Two of H. P. Lovecraft's "Fungi from Yuggoth" ("Mirage" and "The Elder Pharos") have been set to music by Harold S. Farnese of the Los Angeles Inst. of Musical Education.

A. Merritt is an authority on folklore and mythology and has made a study of ancient sorcery and witchcraft, past and modern.

Forrest J. Ackerman often wonders what *would* happen to him if an earthquake came and splattered up the room where his collection is situated.

September 1934

Side Glances

In a sale conducted by Linus Hogenmiller he sold the Weird Tales Anniversary number for only one dollar.

Stories by Gaston Leroux that have appeared in Weird Tales are translated in the office of Jacques Chambrun, New York literary agent who represents Gaston Leroux's agent in this country. Some of the translating was done by Mildred Gleasson Prochet. "The Crime on Christmas Night" was translated by Morris Bentinck.

R. H. Barlow won the National Amateur Press Association Laureateship for the year 1933.

September 1934

Within the Circle

At one time Forrest Ackerman had a complete collection of *Ghost Stories*—the old large-size magazine of the photographic illustrations, featuring strange stories by Victor Rousseau, Ray Cummings, Frank Belknap Long Jr., etc.—but disposed of them all upon coming across science fiction. This was when he saw his first Amazing Stories—Vol. 2, No. 6, the September 1926 number. Incidentally, this issue contains the only story by H. P. Lovecraft ever to appear in Amazing—"The Colour Out of Space."

Farnsworth Wright is a former music critic of *The Chicago American.*

This seems to be quite a season with our authors for travelling, E. Hoffmann Price has just recently paid a second visit to Clark Ashton Smith of Auburn, Calif.; Robert E. Howard spent some time exploring the gigantic Carlsbad Caverns in New Mexico. Perhaps we'll be getting some tales along that line, after a while. Richard F. Searight spent some time amid the scenic grandeur in Houghton, Michigan; H. P. Lovecraft has just returned from a visit with R. H. Barlow of De Land, Florida and is now taking a trip to ancient Nantucket Island, off the coast of Massachusetts; Jack Williamson has also returned from a sojourn in Key West where he met Edmond Hamilton; Donal[d] Wandrei has been on a fishing trip in the woods of his native state, Minnesota.

H. P. Lovecraft denies all connections with the [*sic*] "The Battle that Ended the Century" (Ms. found in a time machine). He was in De Land or in St. Augustine at the time it was mailed, and by the time he was in Washington, D.C., the Eastern readers had received their copies.

Richard Ely Morse is the son of an Amherst professor and an assistant librarian at Princeton.

Louis C. Smith of Oakland, Calif. is a collector of weird and fantastic books and has a library of over two hundred volumes.

October 1934

Within the Circle

"The Red Brain" by Donald Wandrei is one of a long cosmic series most of which is unpublished.

H. P. Lovecraft wrote 35 "Fungi from Yuggoth" in 1929 and 1930. *The Fantasy Fan* is going to print some of those which WT didn't take.

Farnsworth Wright has been a visitor in Seattle, Washington.

During the month of August, Clark Ashton Smith fought a terrible wood and grass fire on his ranch ... He wrote fiction—of a more realistic cast than some of his present work—as early as 1910 and 1911; some of it appearing in the defunct *Black Cat.* He dropped prose entirely until 1925 when he wrote "The Abominations of Yondo" (rejected by WT and published in the *Overland Monthly*) and "Sadastor" (also rejected by WT but later accepted by them and published).

Weird Tales has on hand "The Hand of Wrath" by E. Hoffmann Price ... He and Otis Adelbert Kline have collaborated in a Mexican weird novelette. It features Bart Leslie—Two Gun Bart—one of Kline's heroes. You will recall that he was featured in "The Demon of Tlaxpam" in WT a few years ago ... Price has also collaborated with Frank Belknap Long, Jr., on a weird novelette which is on a "visit" to *Astounding Stories*. He is about to write a serial and a novelette, interplanetary, and Far East, respectively.

Forrest Ackerman can produce, at his pleasure, hour long programs, of weird and fantastic voices and sequences. He has recently added to his set of sound-discs from "Dr. Jekyll and Mr. Hyde", the complete set of records from the weird-scientific film drama, "Frankenstein". He also possesses the thrilling story of Im-Ho-Tep—the Egyptian, dead 26 centuries, returned to life—featuring the weird voice of Boris Karloff; "Murders in the Rue Morgue" and the grotesque "Old Dark House"[.]

Two youthful Merritt fans burglarized the basement of a certain Carnegie Library and made off with old *Science and Inventions* containing "The Metal Emperor".

Robert E. Howard's occupation is fiction-writing, though he helps his father (a physician) attend to a small farm on the outskirts of Cross Plains, Texas. He is 27 years old and has led a somewhat roving and adventurous life. He is an amateur athlete and boxer; is very fond of fighting and believes barbarism to be preferable to civilization. He is a profound historic student, and an authority on the folklore and tradition of the Southwest.

August W. Derleth is 24—U. of Wis. graduate and lives in Souk [*sic*] City, Wis. He is gaining fame in magazines of select quality with serious reminiscent regional fiction and poetry. He writes mystery books besides fantasy.

November 1934

Within the Circle

"The Ghoul," British weird tale of the screen, disappeared from Los Angeles screens the day Forrest J. Ackerman arrived there, playing no theater during all the summer months he looked for it. The morning he left, it came on again!

Jack Williamson is recuperating from an appendix operation and has done no writing for quite a while. He says: "—My drugged slumbers in the first few days after the operation bred some of the weirdest dreams yet, and I'm anxious to get back to writing" ...... When in Key West last winter, he and Edmond Hamilton had a few adventures such as capsizing a skiff out in the Atlantic and towing it behind them as they swam back to shore. Hamilton caught a monster jew fish.

Wright has bought "The Cyclops of Xoatl," featuring Two-Gun Bart Leslie and his pursuit of a cannibal monster in Mexico. The tale is by E. Hoffmann Price and Otis Adelbert Kline ...... The two are now planning a story of Burma, about leopard men ...... Pierre d'Artois, Price's veteran swordsman, is more or less a picture of his old fencing-master of long ago during his academic days ...... Price says about "Queen of the Lilin": I ploughed through a good deal of research in order to present Lilith authentically. A good deal of the Lilith lore had to be cut out in the interests of brevity, which I regretted, as I felt that some of the fans would enjoy a closer acquiantance [*sic*] with the fascinating Queen of Zemargad."

R. H. Barlow is in Washington taking treatment for his eyes. He is also taking a light art course at the Corcoran Gallery.

Alonzo Leonard, who appeared sometime ago in "Believe It Or Not" for inventing a private language, is an authority on culis, [*sic*] ancient languages, superstitions, and strange beliefs. He has compiled a set of "books," 48 volumes, of all strange happenings and things of unusual nature. The collection is called "Encyclopedia Satanic."

January 1935

Within the Circle

A. Merritt is contemplating a sequel to "Thru the Dragon Glass."

Robert Bloch recently sold his second story to WT. Title: "The Feast in the Abbey."

H. P. Lovecraft is working on a tale called "The Shadow Out of Time."

Adolph[e] de Castro, author of "The Last Test" and "The Electric Executioner," is 74 years old, a graduate of Bonn, and master of 7 languages. He has had published work of undoubted importance. Some of his unpublished books are of great potential interest and value .... He lived in Mexico from 1922 to 1925 and had interviews with Villa and his generals in 1923; from whom he derived an account of the end of his associate and colleague Ambrose Bierce at the hand of these revolutionists. There are three slightly differing reports as to Bierce's death, all of which are probably carelessly transmitted variants of the actual facts. De Castro's original name is Gustav Adolf Danziger—he changed it during the World War, taking the name of a remote Spanish ancestor. He came to America in 1886 and was a dentist for a long period. Also pursued politics to some extent and was American consul at Madrid for a time. The piece of work he did with Bierce was translating the German novel of Richard Voss—"The Monk and the Hangman's Daughter." He was German-speaking and (1889) was not fluent in English. Bierce, on the other hand, was a master of English but knew no German. De Castro—or Danziger—admired the Voss novel and made a rough translation, with certain modifications, into such English as he knew. Then Bierce took that crude translation and made the present admirable English novelette out of it. The book as it stands is a curious three-man job. It is not a weird tale.

February 1935

H. P. Lovecraft: A Biographical Sketch

Howard Phillips Lovecraft was born August 20th, 1890, in Providence, Rhode Island, about a mile east of 66 College Street, where he now lives. Began to read at four; Grimm's Fairy Tales and Arabian Nights being among the first volumes he seized upon. Later, he came across books about Greek and Roman Mythology and was still more fascinated by them. He first tried writing at six and his earliest story was written at seven—about a cave of robbers—called "The Noble Eavesdropper." At eight he began to take an interest in science—first chemistry—then geography, astronomy, and other subjects, but his first love for mythology and mystery never diminished. Was about nine when he got his first volume of Poe and adopted him as a model. Virtually all his tales are weird, for nothing has ever fascinated him half so much as the mystery of time and space and the unknown. Remote and inaccessible places like the Antarctic (*At the Mountains of Madness*) and other worlds enthralled his imagination.

Astronomy in particular attracted him and when thirteen began to edit and publish a very small hectographed paper called *The Rhode Island Journal of Astronomy*. He continued this little publication for a few years and at the age of sixteen (while still in school) broke into print for the first time with a monthly article on astronomical phenomena in a new local daily, and followed this with other astronomical articles in the local press.

At eighteen he became dissatisfied with all of his fiction and destroyed most of the tales he had written. His time was used exclusively for verse, essays, and criticism, and did not write another tale for nine years. In 1914 he joined the nation-wide United Amateur Press Association, and his first tale to appear anywhere was 'The Alchemist' in *The United Amateur* in 1916. This story was written in 1908. The next was "The Beast in the Cave," written in 1905 and appearing in W. Paul Cook's *Vagrant* sometime in 1917. In this same year, 1917, he wrote "The Tomb" and "Dagon"; in 1918 "Polaris," and in 1919 "Beyond the Wall of Sleep," "The White Ship," "The Doom that Came to Sarnath," and "The Statement of Randolph Carter."

His first tale to be professionally printed was "Herbert West—

Reanimator" in 1922. This appeared in the now defunct *Home Brew* in six parts, each a separate episode. Later in 1922, *Home Brew* published "The Lurking Fear" as a four-part serial with illustrations by Clark Ashton Smith, whom he met through amateur journalism. In 1923 *Weird Tales* was founded, and "Dagon" was published in October.

"The Horror at Red Hook" was written while Mr. Lovecraft lived in New York, where he got much of the local color for the tale. "He" was based on the old Greenwich Village section of New York. Like "The Horror at Red Hook," it expresses the author's detestation of the metropolis. "The Shunned House" was written in Brooklyn. It is about a house in Benefit Street, Providence, not far from his present home. In reality, the place has no sinister connection. The tale was printed by the Recluse Press (W. Paul Cook) of Athol, Mass., as a brochure, but the loose sheets were never put together. R. H. Barlow of De Land, Florida, now has them in his possession and plans to present the story sometime in the future. It was twice rejected by *Weird Tales*. Frank Belknap Long, Jr., has written a preface for it. The tale "Cool Air," which WT also rejected, was published in 1927 in the short-lived Philadelphia magazine called *Tales of Magic and Mystery*. Of all his tales Mr. Lovecraft likes best "The Colour Out of Space," and next best "The Music of Erich Zann." Edward J. O'Brien gave "The Colour Out of Space" a three-star rating in "Best Short Stories of 1928." "The Music of Erich Zann" was reprinted in the *London Evening Standard* and also in an anthology, then again in WT. "The Rats in the Walls" was first submitted to *Argosy* in 1923 but was rejected as being too horrible. However, it twice appeared in WT, and in 1931 was included in the British anthology "Not at Night." "The Dunwich Horror" was given a three-star rating by Edward J. O'Brien, the only tale besides "The Colour Out of Space" to be so honored. "The Strange High House in the Mist" was given first class rating in the "O. Henry Memorial Year Book." "In the Vault," "Pickman's Model," and "The Silver Key" were given minor year book mention.

His favorite authors—aside from the Græco-Roman classics and the English poets and essayists of the18th century—are Poe, Dunsany, Machen, Blackwood, M. R. James, and Walter de la Mare. Of the pulp writers he prefers A. Merritt, E. Hoffmann Price, C. L. Moore, Robert E. Howard, Clark Ashton Smith, and Frank Belknap Long, Jr. Apart from fantasy, he likes realism in fiction—Balzac, de Maupassant, Zola and Proust, etc.; believes the French are better adapted than we to the reflection of life as a whole; dislikes nearly all Victorian literature and believes that such very recent material as escapes freakishness has more promise than most of the stuff immediately preceding it; regards ultra-modernism mainly as a blind alley; likes conservatism in style and thinks recent prose tends to be slipshod and inartistic. In music—disavowing all genuine classical taste—he unashamedly prefers Victor Herbert, and also likes the old colored "cake walk" songs. In painting he prefers landscapes as subjects. In architecture he favors Georgian and classic types, but feels strongly the charm of Gothic. He is greatly interested in archæology and anthropology. His principal hobbies are early American architecture and general antiquarianism. His library, only the weird section of which is catalogued, contains over 2000 volumes. This includes a *complete set of Weird Tales.*

He usually does his best work at night and prefers two meals a day on a flexible schedule. He dotes on cheese, chocolate and ice cream, but abhors all sea food; doesn't care for tobacco and has never tasted intoxicating liquor; has great fondness for cats of all kinds, and likes conversation. Letter-writing holds the place of the latter to quite an extent with him, and he has 51 or 52 regular correspondents, with about 25 more as long-term occasionals. Some are of 20 years' standing.

In many of Mr. Lovecraft's tales the cities of "Arkham" and "Kingsport" are much in evidence. These are his somewhat modified reflections of Salem and Marblehead, Massachusetts. He has even made a map of the "imaginary" city of Arkham, marking all the streets, buildings, rivers, bridges and cemeteries so that there will be no chance of a slip-up in the locations and landmarks. To us, the readers of his tales, the names "Dunwich," "Kingsport," and "Arkham" are synonymous with the sequestered and sometimes decadent towns of old Mass.

Ideas for stories come from almost anywhere—dreams, pictures, another story, a happening on the street—anything. The idea for Frank Belknap Long, Jr.'s tale, "The Horror from the Hills," came while he and Lovecraft were looking at a reproduction of an elephant-god statuette in the Louvre lately added to Long's collection. Lovecraft exclaimed: "What do you suppose would cause a Chinaman to fall screaming to the floor in front of that statue's original in the Louvre?" That sentence caused the spark and Long wrote the tale.

The length of time taken by Lovecraft to write a story depends largely on the difficulty of the theme. "The Whisperer in Darkness" took about a fortnight, "The Dreams in the Witch House" took a little less than a week. A story of average length takes about three days.

The idea for "Cassius" was given to Henry S. Whitehead by Lovecraft, and H. S. W. wanted him to collaborate on it. But of course, he didn't, as his way of developing the tale differed widely from Whitehead's . . . The idea for the yarn came from seeing an actual case of the undeveloped-twin anomaly in a freak show in New York . . . As Lovecraft puts it, "The man in question had a little anthropoid excrescence growing out of his abdomen that looked hellishly gruesome when uncovered. Clothed, he looked like any ordinary 'pot bellied' individual. He looked so essentially refined and high-grade that I wondered at his willingness to be exploited as a freak, and speculated as to what he would do if a stroke of luck removed him from the need of such an ignominious occupation. The first thing he would do, I argued, would be to have the excrescence cut off—and then and there the idea of the story came. This was in 1924 or 1925. The odd and amazing thing is this: Years after-

ward—after I had given the idea to Whitehead and was awaiting the appearance of 'Cassius'—I chanced to mention the matter to my old friend Arthur
Leeds of New York, who has had extensive dealings with freaks and other
amusement enterprises. Fancy my surprise when he told me that he knows
the man well, and that the latter is a person of much education and intelligence. More—that he is interested in everything *weird,* and (believe it or not—
it's the actual truth!) that he is especially fond of *my* work in WT!! Leeds was
going to introduce me to him; but something prevented, so the meeting never
came off. It certainly would have seemed odd to meet one of my plot-germs
in the flesh . . . the flesh of *two* bodies, or a body and a half, at that!"

Preface to the *Fantasy Fan Index**

It was a small green, square-shaped announcement and it came enclosed in a
letter from H. P. Lovecraft. This green announcement's arrival led me into
closer contact with one of the finest hobbies I know, and was my open-
sesame into the pages of *The Fantasy Fan,* one of the very early amateur publications devoted solely to the interests of the fantasy enthusiast.

The general tone of the magazine is of a sober nature and features the
work of many professional writers as well as the finest work of the hobbyists
themselves. In comparing current amateur publications of this type with *The
Fantasy Fan,* it is obvious that in that comparatively early era, the average quality of the writing and selection of subject matter of these amateur writers has
seldom if ever been equalled by those of today.

The Fantasy Fan—September 1933 thru February 1935—ran 18 issues. It
was printed on newsprint by Conrad Ruppert, hand set, and cost a dime a
copy or a dollar per annum. 250 copies of Number One were printed but only part of that number was circulated. Today, it is virtually an impossibility to
procure any of those 18 issues from any of the older fans who have complete
files. Most of these complete sets thru the passing years have had the duplicates segregated (these have either been sold or traded off) and now repose
on the shelves as bound volumes, having been made into book form by professional binders or by the collector himself, who might have a flare for
working with cloth and paste. An aura of sentiment surrounds these volumes.
One of these sets *if* available, brings about $25. Separate numbers of the early
issues bring about $2 each.

Among the professionals who contributed material were Clark Ashton
Smith and H. P. Lovecraft. These two literary giants had started their own
careers by way of amateur journalism, and *The Fantasy Fan* found favor with
them. Their work acted as a profound inspiration to the younger, less prac-

---

*Bloomington, Illinois: Bob [Wilson] Tucker, July 1945.

ticed contributors, who reveled in the fact that they were appearing with such figures as these paragons of the weird and grotesque.

Raymond A. Palmer, Mort Weisinger, Julius Schwartz, Duane Rimel, Emil Petaja, and R. H. Barlow are names you will see listed in this indexing. Palmer is now editor of *Amazing Stories*. Mort Weisinger earned money while attending college by writing science-fiction, and has recently been appearing in the slicks with many fine articles. His material has appeared in both *Writer's Digest* and *The Reader's Digest*.

Petaja is coming on very well in the detective and weird field. Thruout the past years Rimel has sold to *Weird Tales, Future Fiction, Detective and Murder Mysteries, Jungle Stories, Progress Guide, Author & Journalist,* as well as newspaper syndicates and various verse magazines. Julius Schwartz is a literary agent; and as of 1943–44, R. H. Barlow was engaged in research work pertaining to pre-Hispanic history which included doing a map with exact boundaries of the so-called "Aztec Empire," the empire of Montezuma *2nd*—as Cortez found it in 1519—based on original documents.

Three items of non-professional authorship which stand out by dint of their own merit are Rimel's "Dreams of Yith", Barlow's series "Annals of the Jinns", and Robert Nelson's unforgettable "Trilogy of Death" (". . . death is a dollar bill.").

. . . . . .It was the third issue of *The Fantasy Fan* which punctured a golden bubble; the belief held by most weirdists that strange books like *The Necronomicon* and The *Book of Eibon* actually existed. So skilfully had the inventors woven these volumes into their yarns that fans wrote letters asking where they could be had, and this writer heard of at least one instance where a fan queried a public library.

Clark Ashton Smith (in November 1933) proposed to partly rectify matters by writing one complete chapter of The Book of *Eibon*, which he said would be entitled "The Coming of the White Worm". A Smith story by this name eventually appeared in the April 1941 *Stirring Science Stories*, and was reprinted in the December 1941 issue of the Canadian magazine, *Uncanny Tales*.

. . . .

Only three issues of *The Fantasy Fan* bore formal covers. The remainder carried a masthead and editorial matter, as well as readers' letters, on page one, where the cover would normally appear.

Charles D. Hornig was quite young—around 17 or 18—when he launched *The Fantasy Fan*. His was a labor of love—a passionate love hampered more and more as time passed by ever-decreasing funds. But he gave freely to the last, knowing that thru his ideals he was bringing to others of the same bent a magazine indeed pertinent to a wonderful avocation. After seeing the initial issue of *The Fantasy Fan*, Hugo Gernsback immediately hired young Hornig as managing editor of *Wonder Stories*. In letters, Hornig recounts how Gernsback asked him to come to the *Wonder Stories* offices for an interview.

He did, and left with the job. It seems that first issue made quite an impression. To the best of my knowledge this is the only instance of a fan magazine bringing about a professional editorship.

Should you, at some future date, be moved by the insatiable urge to possess a complete file of this sterling amateur magazine, you will be embarking upon a very Herculean venture. But it *can* be accomplished—yes, it can.

Grangeville, Idaho
April 21, 1945

Duane W. Rimel

H. P. Lovecraft As I Knew Him

I was recuperating slowly from a bout with typhoid fever at the age of fifteen, having started my sophomore year at Asotin High School, when my friend at the time, Lee Baldwin, brought some stories he wanted me to read, taken from a pulp magazine called *Weird Tales*.

They were by an author with the rather improbable name of H. P. Lovecraft, which I assumed was a pen name. Since I had been reading Poe, and liked to listen to radio dramas of that day, 1930, called "The City of the Dead," and a few others I can't remember, Lee had guessed I would like Lovecraft.

The first one was "The Outsider." I was instantly overwhelmed by an obsession that has lasted most of a lifetime. The next one I read was "The Dunwich Horror." I was hooked.

I missed the first half of my sophomore year, and during this recovery period Lee used to visit, and since I had been trying to learn to play the piano, which he was working on, too, we would sit and listen to Earl Hines, direct from The Grand Terrace Cafe in south Chicago, and marvel at his mastery of the keyboard.

And of course, Lovecraft was discussed. When I learned that Lee had written him, in care of *Weird Tales*, and had received a warm reply, I was so envious I could have screamed. Like being in contact with God!

I finally screwed up enough courage to write him, too, having gotten his address from Baldwin. Here came an answer that I treasured for decades! It was after this, in my youthful ignorance, that I sent him several amateurish attempts at verse and fiction. I had no idea then that he gleaned part of his precarious living by ghost writing.

He encouraged me. He was too much of a gentleman to even suggest remuneration for such "touching up." I could not have afforded it, anyway. Times were very hard. The family lost the old home, along with the Majestic radio and the electrically powered Thor washing machine, quite a luxury those days, and moved into a rented place.

My father went on WPA. I made a few bucks thumping piano and tooting a trumpet at weekend dances. We had to move again, into an old house down near town, which rented for $5 per month. Meanwhile I was writing as best I could.

I managed to sell two stories and one article to a youth magazine, the check for the first tale amounting to $8! These Lovecraft never saw; they were not weird or fantasy, they were adventure. The article was about making linoleum blocks, and this dubious skill of mine was used in *Fantasy Fan*.

Baldwin and I were members of a sort of "inner circle." I'd already had letters from Clark Ashton Smith, who assisted with "Dreams of Yith," and E. Hoffmann Price, among others. Smith once gave me a recipe for making homemade wine, which included honey. I never tried it. Price sent me carbon copies of some stories he was doing then for *Spicy Adventure* and several other "Spicy" pulps of the time. When I found out what he was earning from them I turned green with envy.

About this time—I was still in high school because I'd had to graduate with the class of '34 instead of in '33, after missing half a year—along came the original manuscript of *At the Mountains of Madness*. HPL was having some of his correspondents read it and make comments.

I told him it was a winner. Several of those who read it were not so optimistic. I recall one of Price's comments. "You can't whip a dead horse to life." I was very gratified when it sold to *Astounding*. He never forgot my faith in it.

HPL's letters were looked forward to with such fervor my family considered me slightly daft. I stopped trying to write for youth magazines, which I realize I should not have done; they paid cash on acceptance! I concentrated on weird and fantasy.

Lovecraft opened up whole new vistas of learning for me. He sent me books on astronomy, a subject never even hinted at in high school, and I began reading more widely. I finally sold a story ("The Disinterment!") to *Weird Tales*. HPL did very little to that story, in spite of what some of my detractors claim.

The "Yith" thing has been gone into so thoroughly that I won't belabor readers with the ramifications. Of course, HPL assisted me! And with other poems, too. I did send for a little booklet he recommended about basics of writing poetry, and still have it.

What wonderful years those were! To make money, however, I picked cherries, tooted trumpet in a band, played piano when I could, worked on ranches. My health had improved, but the fever had left me with an ailment that had no name then, to my knowledge. Osteomyelitis, or a disease of the bone. It was a constant drain, literally, from the hips and legs and feet. It colored all my life for years. HPL was a rock during those fragile, hard-time years, a source of hope and inspiration, even though, in my case, rather misdirected.

Although in later years I managed to sell another story to *Weird Tales*, I was learning that this narrow market was not for me. At least "The Metal

Chamber" proved, once and for all, that I could write a story without HPL's "touches." He had been dead more than a year when it was written.

After much struggling I worked into the mystery and suspense book markets. But that is another tale . . .

His trip to visit Barlow was highly fascinating, as his postcards and letters show most vividly. For part of that time I was in Shelby, Montana, playing piano in a joint and making very good money, considering the year, 1936. HPL's letters and cards livened my days.

And to think that in another year or so he would be dead.

In later years, when I showed HPL's letters to my friend, Francis T. Laney, he said they were equal to a college education. Laney, bright and energetic, edited *The Acolyte*, one of the best fan magazines of that period. I started him by loaning him my copies of *The Outsider and Others* and *Beyond the Wall of Sleep*. He was instantly converted, as I had been, as hundreds had been before us.

Much better read and educated than me, he still was swept off his feet, as though he had been waiting for something like HPL and fandom to ignite him into furious energy. Copies of that fanzine are very valuable today.

To sum up, briefly. HPL convinced me that there could be no life after death, a proposition that offended my very religious father until he died. By his example I became a better human being, more tolerant, more open to new views and opinions.

He transformed the life of a rather thick-headed young man living out in the boondocks and made him into something like a civilized person. I will take Derleth's view of him above those views held by certain biographers and critics.

In this world there are the doers and knockers. Let them berate HPL all they like, let them dig into his ancestry looking for faulted genes and alcoholics or venereal diseases.

Yes, he was a cove writer—but what a remarkable cove he created! If his writings are not considered literature, they come damn close. They thrilled and informed; they entertain even to this day.

Knowing him, even for a few brief years, was one of the highlights of my life.

He was a doer. And what pains me most is that certain of his correspondents are holding onto his letters for the purpose of selling them to the highest bidder. What a malfunction of trust! What a crime against all that HPL himself stood for!

Let's don't pick his bones clean, let's let him rest in peace. He deserves that.

Addenda

It is quite likely that some of the dates just given may be awry. I haven't seen any of those letters from HPL to me since 1967, when they were given to the Collection at Brown University. I've never asked for copies.

Some events from 1933 to 1937 are foggy at best. Fifty years can cloud one's memory. But of course the good things stand out; we would all go crazy if everything wrong and evil and nasty were to haunt the mind continually.

A few additional notes might be of interest.

I should not be too harsh on people trying to eke a few dollars out of HPL's letters, etc. Along in the seventies before the IRS stopped the practice of taking deductions for valuable papers donated, I asked the Brown University people to have an estimate made on the value of the material I had donated to the Lovecraft Collection.

This they did promptly, and my tax accountant used the estimate in figuring my taxes for that year. August Derleth also sold for me an autographed copy of *At the Mountains of Madness,* printed in *Astounding.*

Shortly before Derleth died I asked him what he thought the original script of "The Thing on the Doorstep," autographed to me, which I had donated to the Collection, might be worth. He said at least $1,000. I am not an Indian giver. I didn't ask for it back.

I wonder what it would be worth today?

A Fan Looks Back

How well I remember my first encounter with a fellow-fan! Away back in 1934, when I was still going to High School, corresponding with Lovecraft, Clark Ashton Smith, and trying my hand at a few weird stories and poems, I happened to be lounging in the summer shade of a big maple in front of the Rimel domicile, in Asotin, Washington. Asotin was a small town, and you noticed strangers. Two of them were coming up the sidewalk, headed, apparently, straight at me. They looked younger than I by a few years, but not many, and one youth had white, flaxenish hair; the other dark hair. Coming nearer, they stopped.

"Could you tell us where Duane Rimel lives?" one of them said.

"Right here," I answered, puzzled.

"Is he home now," the white-hair said eagerly, grinning.

"I'm it," I said.

They looked rather crestfallen and exchanged glances. They seemed to doubt me.

"Are you the guy who has poetry in *Fantasy Fan?*"

I nodded. "Who'd you expect to see, a graybeard?"

At last they seemed convinced, and we began talking like troopers. It seems they expected to find a middle-aged person with bushy hair and receding forehead, but soon it didn't matter, as the words continued flying at a great rate.

It turned out that their names were Dwight Edwards, of the fair hair, and Stuart Ayers, two avid fans from Lewiston, Idaho, a city seven miles distant. Their principal interest was science fiction, however; but we found much common ground for discussion. They told me about their big collection of fan mags, prozines, and so on. They had seen my name in *Fantasy Fan*, and in the Eyrie, *Weird Tales*. They thought I was quite a poet, and insisted on getting an autograph! As time went by, they discovered I was just another guy and not a prodigy or something.

(Right now I must mention that Baldwin was the first fan I knew; we both lived in Asotin, so our meeting and friendship came about gradually. This one with Edwards and Ayers was full of surprises for me, especially in regards to science fiction.)

Later Edwards and Ayers persuaded Baldwin and me to come to meetings of their stf club, one of those sponsored by the old *Wonder Stories*, and several such gatherings were written up in the gossip columns of that magazine. They showed us their collection of autographs, very impressive, and piles of books and magazines. We had a lot of fun while it lasted, but the old gang split up. Ayers joined the Marines, where he still is, and Edwards moved to Seattle. Baldwin went to Grangeville, and I was left alone.

After moving to Clarkston, I ran into a chap who had never heard of fan doings, and quickly began converting him. What happened after that is now history. Laney became a sensation. But to go back again to Baldwin, in the very early days.

As I said, Lee and I lived in the same small town, and although he was older than I and further along in school, our paths crossed occasionally, and we were acquainted well. At that time I was a Freshman in high school, and Lee was a Junior. I was wild about fishing and hunting those days, and while returning down Asotin creek from a fishing expedition one evening, I ran into Lee near his home, which was right beside the creek. His mother was gone, and he invited me over to his house. I had some trout in my basket, and Baldwin said we ought to cook up a feed. So we did.

After stuffing ourselves on trout and other food, we relaxed awhile and Lee showed me some stories in the old *Amazing*. (Lee was reading stf when volume 1 No. 1 came out, and he still owns the copy). Having read a lot of Poe, and having written a few childish themes for the HS paper, this was meaty stuff for me! Then he brought out *Weird Tales*, and my eyes bulged. What a treasure-trove he had! He loaned me copies of some mags, and from then on I was a convert. I read "The Horror from the Hills," by F. B. Long, Jr., "The Outsider," by Lovecraft, and was held entranced.

Then Baldwin and I conceived the idea of writing to some of these superb writers for autographs. Lee sent a letter to Lovecraft, and received a nice reply. So did I, and also received a fine epistle in return. We were flabbergasted that a man of such talent would write to a couple of interested kids in a small town. But I kept up my correspondence with HPL until his death in 1937, and his letters are one of my most valued items in my collection. One other item I prize highly is the original pencil Ms. of "The Thing on the

Doorstep," autographed to me. The association with him was invaluable in shaping my future life and ambitions. Lovecraft had much the same effect on Baldwin, inspiring him to do things he never dreamed of before. HPL encouraged me to write, gave me valuable pointers and advice, and was quite as tickled as I when I sold my first yarn to *Weird Tales*.

Then there was the time when Emil Petaja and I arranged a meeting in Spokane. We had been corresponding energetically for several months, when the idea struck us. He lived in Milltown, Montana, not far from Missoula, and would have further to come than I, but he was willing. We met as arranged, and had quite a day talking, haunting book-stores, and so on. Baldwin had left Asotin then, so there was just the two of us in a big town.

At one time we planned to put out a fan magazine, but lack of funds and being so far apart was in the way. Lovecraft even sent us material for the project—none other than "The Nameless City."* At that time mimeographing fan magazines wasn't being done—*Fantasy Fan* and *Fantasy* were both printed sheets.

We had a lot of fun then, even if times were hard. I still call those "the good old days."

Lee Baldwin—A Fan's Fan

Having known Franklin Lee Baldwin as a youthful acquaintance, high school companion, fellow musician and ardent admirer of Lovecraft; having been his friend for many long years, I feel able to let other fans know just what kind of person he is.

First of all, Baldwin is a fan for the pure joy of it; he started reading fantasy and science fiction when a lot of present day "hot-shots" were still in swaddling clothes. He knew no other fans—in fact the word *fantasy fan* had not yet been coined—when he started to sample the delights of other-world fiction, first in *Argosy,* about 1923, *Weird Tales* in 1924–25 and *Amazing Stories* in 1926. Before that he had read all of Poe and a few others. Naturally, Lee read Edgar Rice Burroughs at an early age; and as I said in a previous article first got me interested in fantasy and the supernatural in literature. This friendship began while I was the tender age of 14—Lee was older, of course. Baldwin remembers vividly the first yarn he ever read in *Weird Tales;* it was in our home town of Asotin, Washington, (population about 600) while parked behind the magazine rack in the village drug store, and the title was "Just Bones" by (he believes) Arthur J. Burks.†

Lee's interest in fantasy and science fiction has never waned since, although he has been inactive several times when busy with other things. He has one of

---

*Actually "The Colour out of Space."—ED.

†Actually by Samuel Stewart Mims. *WT* 4. No. 2 (May–June–July 1924): 91–94. —ED.

the largest and best collections of magazines and books in [the] whole fan king-dom—also included in his library are mysteries (detective) and historic novels.

While yet in high school, Baldwin began learning to play the banjo (plec-trum—four string) where he often regaled the boys with original parodies of "Minnie the Moocher" and other such vocals, accompanying them on his in-strument. I was quite awed in my youth by his rendition of "Willie the Weep-er—the hashish eater" or something like that! Baldwin never went in for sports, but he spent a lot of time writing out-of-the-world themes, much to the astonishment of his English teacher.

Later, before graduating, Baldwin became interested in the piano, and encouraged by his mother, who is a very accomplished musician and vocal teacher, learned rapidly. None of the classics for him, however. He liked jazz, has ever since. He is now one of the best boogie-woogie men I have heard outside of big time—and plays a mean piano in most other swing depart-ments as well.

For many years, Lee made his livelihood in the music game, having played with many fine groups around Lewiston and northern Idaho—and still beats out a job once in a while just for the fun of it.

His idol (and mine, incidentally) on the blacks and whites is Earl Hines, and Lee has in his record collection nearly every platter the "Father" ever cut, alone or with different bands. Other records he owns cover every phase of jazz and boogie—from Pine-top Smith to Lux Lewis.

He has a remarkable collection of letters from Lovecraft, covering a pe-riod of several years—and dating back to the days of *Fantasy Fan*, when Lee contributed a news column to that and other fan mags called "Within the Circle", more recently continued in *The Acolyte*, where he is an assistant editor. To get news in his column, Baldwin kept in touch with E. Hoffman Price, Lovecraft, R. H. Barlow, and many others of the period. He corresponds with all kinds of people and contributes to a number of fan sheets. He recently sold a poem to *Hobo News*.

Baldwin is deceptively non-scholarly in appearance, rather broad-shouldered and husky. He has a wide, friendly smile and a firm hand-clasp. While not as tall as lot of people, you don't really notice Lee's height unless very close to him. At least, I never do. His hands are small and deft; but with-all, he is able to reach ten keys on the piano. (Try it [some] time.)

Baldwin is persistent and tenacious. An example is his search for a copy of *The Golem*, which he finally found after several years writing book stores and putting ads in various magazines. His fine collection is largely due to this quality. Married now, for a good many years, Lee lives in Grangeville, Idaho. He is one of the few fans who corresponded with the late A. Merritt, and has many autographed volumes by the old master. It was through his efforts that *Acolyte* was able to feature a cover by Howard Wandrei, which Lee financed, incidentally. A true believer in fantasy for its own sake, and not for the promotion of personalities, Lee is truly a fan's fan—one of those rare connoisseurs of imaginative literature with grown-up tastes and mature outlook.

It's too bad there aren't more like Baldwin these days. As with Laney, the bickerings and arguments in various fan groups gives him a good belly laugh—and one of his fondest hopes is to see, someday, a quality fantasy publication that will feature artistic stuff rather than the regimented hackbound writing of today; and fewer rabble-rousing fan sheets. When Laney and I first plunged into the *Acolyte,* Baldwin gave much valued support, and although he is now separated from its source, as I am also, his spirit is ever with it. I salute a real, honest-to-God fan!

Weird Music
With Emil Petaja

Since the dawn of civilization and probably long before, the soul of man has thrilled and trembled to strange music of one type or another. The savage voodoo drums of Africa; the harsh strains of Oriental rhythms; the tango of South America, the classics, and even much modern jazz—are filled in varying degrees with an unmistakable weirdness. There is something about a melody or succession of harmonic changes portraying intense fear, sorrow, remorse, or other gloomy moods of human nature that is easily recognizable, yet quite undefinable. They awaken queer thoughts and emotions which no mere language or tongue can interpret.

One of the most fantastic compositions is Danse Macabre, the ghostly *Dance of Death* by Saint-Saens. Music such as Rimsky-Korsakov's *Scheherazade* Suite which is filled with the glamour and exotic charm of the Arabian Nights, and his fairy tale operas, is replete with fantastic atmosphere. The Gounod *Faust* Ballet music conjures up a strange scene in a dark castle high in the mountains of Germany on Walpurgis night. Mephistopheles causes all the dead beauties—Helen of Troy, Cleopatra, etc.—to appear and dance before Faust, who may take his choice from among them. Such music evokes a weird and wonderful panorama. Edvard Grieg's *Peer Gynt Suite* is a masterpiece of fanciful, sensuous and sinister rhythm-patterns. Tschaikowsky is the God of sad and sombre themes, often heart-rending in their pathos—sometimes welling up in sudden intense orchestral sobs—sometimes low and passionate in exquisite depths of sorrow; while Rachmaninoff's compositions like *Isle of the Dead* are spine-chilling in their vividness. There are countless other weird compositions in the classics, and even such modern songs as George Gershwin's *Rhapsody in Blue* and Ferde Grofé's *Grand Canyon Suite* possess more than a touch of fancy, and it would take many volumes to cover and adequately describe all of the music of this type.

In literature we find that many masterpieces have been inspired by or written about weird music. Poe's great poem "The Bells" catches some of the elusive charm that only eerie sounds can evoke. Some of the best stories in *Weird Tales* have dealt with the subject: H. P. Lovecraft's "The Music of Erich Zann" ably portrays a genuine mood of outré terror by the wild suggestive notes of a bass viol. "Bells of Oceana" by Arthur J. Burks brings to the reader a sense of the unknown horror inspired by unearthly music. The rites of Pan are climaxed to the accompaniment of weird, piping strains, and we have all read stories in which the Pipes of Pan are heard, reminding some one of the drowsy Aeolian measures of Debussy's [*Prelude to the*] *Afternoon of a Faun*. Much weird verse is closely akin to music of the same nature—and the two are very often combined with marvelous results. As an example, two of H. P. Lovecraft's verses [from] *Fungi from Yuggoth* were set to music by a composer of Los Angeles, Harold S. Farnese. Readers of *Weird Tales* will remember "Sable Reverie" by Robert Nelson, for which music had been written.

Certainly when great masters like Richard Wagner, Felix Mendelsohn, and Jan Sibelius and others have expressed themselves through the medium of weird, haunting music, it is at once raised to immortal levels.

The Forbidden Room

Bony footprints in the earth—

It is said that an old pirate once dwelt in Hampdon; but why he chose that secluded and decadent village no one ever knew, for the place is many miles from the sea, hidden among the hills of Nurbyshire. His motive has been interpreted in numerous ways. Some have said it was to escape the sight of the ocean which had been his home, while others have suggested that certain seamen might want to reckon with the aged pirate, were he to inhabit the haunts of a sailor. His name was Exer Jones: that name symbolized wealth; enormous, hidden fortunes, which, though none had ever seen them, formed part of the legend. When Jones is mentioned natives will point to a tall, three-story dwelling which, with one other, rises from amidst a mouldering group of hovels, and will explain to travelers who happen to stop at the decrepit hotel, that such was his house. But unless they know the visitor well, they will tell no more, for the people of Hampdon do not like to have their stories ridiculed—as would certainly happen were they to tell all they know of Exer Jones.

The edifice has been deserted for many years—no one knows the exact number—and strangers who are attracted to the quaint but sinister place are warned against renting it. Beside the ancient, gabled dwelling is another house of enormous proportions, brick-made and ivy-crested, where once lived another man of strange and evil character. The second person, one Hiram Shell, had also been rich, but his existence covered a later span of years than that of Exer Jones, and one which people knew more about. The source of his wealth seemed questionable as well.

Before the arrival of Shell in Hampdon, and following a rapid decline in

Jones' health, the latter was ever seen to have a lamp burning in the upper story of his dwelling. It gleamed into the small hours, as the legend goes, and people passing by the forbidding house thought they heard the muffled clink of coins and queer mumbling noises, as if Pirate Jones were counting again and again his ill-gotten wealth. This went on indefinitely, till at last, one winter morning the old fellow was found, quite stiff and cold at the bottom of the long flight of steps which leads to the upper rooms.

They buried him back of the queer dwelling in which he had died, and when the will was read it was discovered that he had given the property to the township; but of his money not one word was said, At the close of the brief document they found a warning—and to this day it is a whispered tale, surviving the fleeting years. It ran thus:

> Pass not beyond the stairway door;
> My cursed wealth has left me poor.

Ordinarily, such a fatuous couplet would have provoked a hearty laugh from Hampdon townspeople, but when they remembered that the "stairway door" was the one opening on the room from whence the strange noises had come, there were none who wished to venture so far within the house. And too, some argued, the position of Jones' body when discovered was not a pleasant one. For though no marks of violence were found on the corpse, it was possible that instead of falling from the stairs, as was generally supposed, the deceased had leaped purposely to the landing below. But such rumors were not encouraged.

The property then lawfully became a part of the township; but though repeated efforts were made by the council to dispose of it at ridiculously low prices, no buyer was ever found. That is, until the advent of Hiram Shell.

When this individual settled in Hampdon he chanced to secure a lot adjoining that of the forbidding house, where he plied a meagre trade of cobbling. However, his fiery tongue and irascible temperament soon drove away most of the slim clientele which he had begun to secure, till he was reduced to miserable poverty. As the years passed he began to assimilate portions of the neighborhood gossip. Just how much or how little he picked up no one could say, but at night he was often seen prowling about in the vicinity of the ancient Pirate house. Age, too, was creeping rapidly upon the man.

Then one day Hampdon was surprised to see Hiram Shell displaying signs of uncommon wealth. He bought the best span of horses available, dressed in stylish clothes and to crown it all, built an enormous brick mansion on his lot—the house which is there today, if Hampdon still lives. Accompanying this paradox came another burst of whispered gossip, for it was learned that his purchases were paid for with strange-looking gold coins. And still another incentive for talking was raised when it was revealed that he had bought the ancient and mouldy Pirate house on Beacon Street. Whether he knew of the warning against the upper room was a question no one could answer—nor did anyone care to enlighten him either, for Hiram had become even more captious and litigious, and people shunned him as they might some poisonous reptile.

About a year later Sam Perkins, in passing the deserted house one night at 12, saw a light burning in the topmost story of the dwelling. And when he perceived that it shone from a window of the forbidden room, and heard strange clinking sounds which he remembered from years gone by, he ran trembling from the place and spread the news.

It was early morning before the gossip got about, and several of the townspeople strolled by the place to see if anything had gone amiss. Noticing no object out of the ordinary, they moved on, not caring to loiter about the house any longer than was necessary. When the day had passed and no Hiram put in an appearance and no smoke was seen to rise from his chimneys, people again began their whispering.

Here the legend becomes varied and indistinct, and the listener is warned against asking too many questions concerning Hiram Shell. But of what remains, a partial conclusion may be drawn. The man was never found after that, though a diligent search was made. Only one place in town was not explored—for local authorities were loath to enter that stairway door. But it was reasoned that if he had died in the forbidden room, the neighbors would soon become aware of his presence; so the door was never opened.

The last bit of evidence as to Shell's disappearance was a messy trail which some of the people noticed. It led down the steps away from the locked room and around to the back of the house; being formed, some said, of peculiar footprints and bits of debris as if something heavy had been dragged behind the marks, partly obliterating them. The path went straight to the grave of Exer Jones, and ended abruptly while the sod about the marker seemed recently disturbed. These facts were kept from the authorities however, for people did not want Jones' grave uncovered. . . .

Of the fragments of tracks which were yet half-visible, the old men will say little. But some have hinted that they were unlike ordinary footprints in that the outline had the appearance of being formed by *bones* pressing upon the ground instead of flesh.

The Pirate house still stands beside the great ivy-covered mansion, and to this day natives of Hampdon say that at midnight queer lights gleam from the third story window and strange clinking sounds are heard, as if Exer Jones were once again mumbling and counting his money.

The Sorcery of Aphlar

The council of twelve seated on the jeweled celestial dais ordered that Aphlar be cast from the gates of Bel-haz-en. He sat too much alone, they decreed, and brooded when toil should have been his lot. And in his obscure and hidden delvings he read all too frequently those papyri of Elder aeons which reposed in the Guothic shrine and were to be consulted only for rare and special purposes.

The twilight city of Bel-haz-en had climbed backward in its knowledge. No longer did philosophers sit upon street corners speaking wise words to the populace, for stupid ignorance ruled within the crumbling and immemorially ancient walls. Where once the wisdom of the stars abounded, only feebleness and desolation now lay upon the place, spreading like a monstrous blight and sucking foul nurture from the stupid dwellers. And out of the waters of the Oll that meandered from the mountains of Azlakka to pass by the aged city, there rose often great clouds of pestilence that racked the people sorely, leaving them pale and near to dying. All this their loss of wisdom brought. And now the council had sent their last and greatest wise man from them.

Aphlar wandered to the mountains far above the city and built a cavern for protection from the summer heat and winter chill. There he read his scrolls in silence and told his mighty wisdom to the wind about the crags and to the swallows on the wing. All day he sat and watched below or drew queer drawings on small bits of stone and chanted to them, for he knew that some day men would seek the cave and slay him. The cunning of the twelve did not mislead him. Had not the last exiled wise man's screams rent the night two moon-rounds before when people thought him safely gone? Had not his own eyes seen the priest's sword-slashed form floating by in the poison waters? He knew no lion had killed old Azik, let the council say what they might. Does a lion slash with a sword and leave his prey uneaten?

Through many seasons Aphlar sat upon the mountain, gazing at the muddy Oll as it wound into the misty distance to the land where none ever ventured. He spoke his words of wisdom to the snails that worked in the ground by his feet. They seemed to understand, and waved their slimy feelers before they sank beneath the sand again. On moonlight nights he climbed the hill above his cave and made strange offerings to the moon-God Alo; and when the night-birds heard the sound they drew close and listened to the whispering. And when queer winged things flapped across the darkened sky and loomed up dimly against the moon Aphlar was content. Those which he had addressed had heeded his beckoning. His thoughts were always far away, and his prayers were offered to the pale fancies of dusk.

Then one day past noontide Aphlar rose from his earthen chair and strode down the rock mountain-side. His eyes, heeding not the rotten, stone-walled city, held steadfast to the river. When he drew near its muddy brink he paused and looked up the bosom of the stream. A small object floated near the rushes, and this Aphlar rescued with tender and curious care. Then, wrapping the thing in the folds of his robe, he climbed up again to his cave in the hills. All day he sat and gazed upon the object; rummaging now and then in his musty chronicles, and muttering awful syllables as he drew faint figures on a piece of parchment.

That night the gibbous moon rose high, but Aphlar did not climb above his dwelling. Queer night-birds flew past the cavern's mouth, chirped eerily, and fled away into the shadows.

Many days passed before the council sent their messengers of murder; but at last the time was thought ripe, and seven dark-browed men stole away to the hills. Yet when that grim seven ventured within the cave they saw not the wise man Aphlar. Instead, small blades of grass were sprouting in his natural chair of earth. All about lay papyri dim and musty, with faint figures drawn upon them. The seven shuddered and left forthwith when they beheld these things, but as the last man tremblingly withdrew he saw a round and unknown thing lying on the ground. He picked it up, and his fellows drew close in curiosity; but they saw upon it only alien symbols which they could not read, yet which made them shrink and quaver without knowing why. Then he who had found it cast it quickly over the steep precipice beside him, but no sound came from the slope below whereon it should have fallen. And the thrower trembled, fearing many things that are not known but only whispered about. Then, when he told how the sphere he had held was without the weight a thing of stone should have; how it was like to have floated on air as the thistledown floats; he and the six with him slunk as one from the spot and swore it was a place accursed.

But after they had gone a snail crawled slowly from a sandy crevice and slid intently over to where the blades of grass were growing. And when it reached the spot, two slimy feelers stretched forth and bent oddly downward, as if eager to watch forever the winding river.

Dreams of Yid

Black Sacrifice

On blasted hillsides covered with foul moss
    Of that dim spawning strange to our clean Earth,
Close by a ragged rampart dread hands toss
    A nightmare shadow of archaean birth
Upon an altar stretching damp across
    A daemon-fane that echoes with mad mirth,
And in that realm sane eyes may never see—
    For black light streams from skies of ebony.

Dreams of Yith

I.

In distant Yith past crested, ragged peaks;
    On far-flung islands lost to worldly eyes,
A shadow from the ancient star-void seeks
    Some being which in caverns shrilly cries
A challenge; and the hairy dweller speaks
    From that deep hole where slimy Sotho lies.
But when those night-winds crept about the place,
They fled—for Sotho had no human face!

II.

Beyond the valleys of the sun which lie
    In misty chaos past the reach of time;
And brood beneath the ice as aeons fly,
    Long waiting for some brighter, warmer clime;
There is a vision, as I vainly try
    To glimpse the madness that must some day climb
From age-old tombs in dim dimensions hid,
And push all angles back—unseal the lid!

III.

Beside the city that once lived there wound
    A stream of putrefaction writhing black;
Reflecting crumbling spires stuck in the ground
    That glow through hov'ring mist whence no stray track
Can lead to those dead gates, where once was found
    The secret that would bring the dwellers back.
And still that pitch-black current eddies by
Those silver gates of Yith to sea-beds dry.

IV.

On rounded turrets rising through the visne
    Of cloud-veiled aeons that the Old Ones knew;
On tablets deeply worn and fingered clean
    By tentacles that dreamers seldom view;
In space-hung Yith, on clammy walls obscene
    That writhe and crumble and are built anew;
There is a figure carved; but God! those eyes,
That sway on fungoid stems at leaden skies!

V.

Around the place of ancient, waiting blight;
    On walls of sheerest opal rearing high,
That move as planets beckon in the night
    To faded realms where nothing sane can lie;
A deathless guard tramps by in feeble light
    Emitting to the stars a sobbing cry.
But on that path where footsteps should have led
There rolled an eyeless, huge and bloated head.

VI.

Amid dim hills that poison mosses blast,
    Far from the lands and seas of our clean earth,
Dread nightmare shadows dance—obscenely cast
    By twisted talons of archaean birth
On rows of slimy pillars stretching past
    A daemon-fane that echoes with mad mirth.
And in that realm sane eyes may never see—
For black light streams from skies of ebony.

VII.

On those queer mountains which hold back the horde
    That lie in waiting in their mouldy graves,
Who groan and mumble to a hidden lord
    Still waiting for the time-worn key that saves;
There dwells a watcher who can ill afford
    To let invaders by those hoary caves.
But some day then may dreamers find the way
That leads down elfin-painted paths of gray.

VIII.

And past those unclean spires that ever lean
    Above the windings of unpeopled streets;
And far beyond the walls and silver screen
    That veils the secrets of those dim retreats,
A scarlet pathway leads that some have seen
    In wildest visions that no mortal greets.
And down that dimming path in fearful flight
Queer beings squirm and hasten in the night.

IX.

High in the ebon skies on scaly wings
    Dread batlike beasts soar past those towers gray
To peer in greedy longing at the things
    Which sprawl in every twisted passageway.
And when their gruesome flight a shadow brings
    The dwellers lift dim eyes above the clay.
But lidded bulbs close heavily once more;
They wait—for Sotho to unlatch the door!

X.

Now, though the veil of troubled visions deep
    Is draped to blind me to the secret ways
Leading through blackness to the realm of sleep
    That haunts me all my jumbled nights and days,
I feel the dim path that will let me keep
    That rendezvous in Yith where Sotho plays.
At last I see a glowing turret shine,
And I am coming, for the key is mine!

The Ship

In clouded mists a ship came sailing by
    On star-flecked seas the Elders swam apace;
Dream sails all furled, and outlined in the sky
    Were dim horizons strangely out of place.
I climbed aboard and knew the hulk would fly
    From vague auroras into boundless space.
And when I turned to face the fading shore,
    I knew that life had fled—forevermore!

Late Revenge

Spawn of the cellars, rising black,
Midst darkened doorways, out a crack;
To wither each bright blade of grass,
And smother flying souls that pass.

Spawns of the cellars; evil slime;
Heed not their calling, lest they climb
As rays of light upon thy face,
And steal thy spirit's resting place.

Wraiths of corruption, creep not in;
For though their minds be steeped in sin,
They hold a germ of terror yet,
That baffles every evil met.

Seed of the tombstone, enter now;
Their house is darkened to the mow.
Your chance has come to right the wrong,
That you have waited all too long.

Spawn of the cellars, rising fast,
To seek the hell-hounds out at last:
They cloudlike through the window creep,
On those who sprawl in drunken sleep.

Dread putrefactions, find your breed;
That you may pay that awful deed;
That you may spread your bloating jaws,
And sap their entrals through your maws.

Germ of corruption, speed ye fast.
A thing is rising to its last;
For greedy claws to grip around,
And carry back to that mouldy mound.

Spawn of the cellars, get ye back
To gulfs of darkness where no track,
Can trace you to that worming brood;
Or toss your bones in darkened mood.

Seed of the tombstone, floating black,
Back to the cellar through that crack
And beings stare with sightless eyes,
Down black steps where a brother lies.

The Snake

Churning, gurgling, twisting river
Filled with secrets yet untold;
Winding, writhing through deep canyons,
Over granite gray and cold.

Idling by a wind-torn narrow,
Sweeping through some cavern black;
Taking seaward in its clutches
Things that never will come back.

Gliding past a brightened meadow,
Past a field of waving grain;
Moaning endlessly in eddies
As if stung by hate or pain.

Through a tunnel dim and musty
Hewn from stone to help it on;
By a rock whose ancient carving
Greeted many a primal dawn.

Muddy waters passing ever
In procession by the sand,
Like a march of endless soldiers
Moved by nature's great command.

Dark and brooding then at nightfall,
Whisp'ring thoughts no mind can read;
Striving to reveal in horror
Some remote and nameless deed.

But those tales go all unuttered;
Those dark mysteries it will hold
'Till that deep and muddy bosom
Lingers dry in ages old.

Yet its silent voice is calling
As it stretches pleading hands;
Calling me to cross the border—
Past the rim to other lands.

Its Prayer

A grisly hand raised to the sky
    In awful supplication,
Weaving dreams of elder worlds
    With rhythmic incantation.

Spectral fingers clutched in vain
    At entities unbounded;
Where star-spawn swirls in endless night
    Through spaces yet unsounded.

Weak limbs rise and sway and fall
    Upon a lightless planet,
And strive with fruitless straining arms
    To reach the void and span it.

The hand is graven in the earth,
    In mould that never darkens
Save when it wrenches free its hold,
    Or to the west wind harkens.

It flaps about and stretches up
    Into the cloudy distance,
But cannot reach those nightmare realms
    Without a ghoul's assistance,

And yet at last it soared indeed,
    All stars and worlds eluding—
This Thing men thought a wind-torn weed
    Through to long weeks of brooding!

Chronology

FLB 1	2 October 33
FLB 2	16 October 33
FLB 3	14 November 33
FLB 4	13 December 33
FLB 5	10 January 34
DWR 1	10 January 34
FLB 6	13 January 34
DWR 2	22 January 34
FLB 7	31 January 34
DWR 3	2 February 34
FLB 8	13 February 34
DWR 4	14 February 34
DWR 5	15 February 34
DWR 6	4 March 34
FLB 9	5 March 34
DWR 7	16 March 34
DWR 8	19 March 34
FLB 10	27 March 34
DWR 9	29 March 34
DWR 10	13 April 34
FLB 11	29 April 34
DWR 11	13 May 34
FLB 12	16 May 34
DWR 12	1 June 34
FLB 13	3 June 34
DWR 13	17 June 34
DWR 14	18 June 34
DWR 15	23 July 34
FLB 14	27 July 34
DWR 16	10 August 34
FLB 15	21 August 34

DWR 17	23 August 34
DWR 18	12 September 34
DWR 19	14 September 34
FLB 16	1 October 34
DWR 20	8 October 34
FLB 17	17 October 34
DWR 21	30 October 34
FLB 18	2 November 34
DWR 22	19 November 34
FLB 19	7 December 34
DWR 23	22 December 34
FLB 20	23 December 34
DWR 24	30 December 34
FLB 21	10 January 35
DWR 25	28 January 35
FLB 22	13 February 35
FLB 23	16 February 35
DWR 26	10 March 35
FLB 24	20 {26?} March 1935
DWR 27	16 April 35
DWR 28	30 June 35
DWR 29	4 August 35
FLB 25	20 August 35
DWR 30	25 August 35
DWR 31	29 August 35
DWR 32	13 September 35
DWR 33	28 September 35
DWR 34	12 November 35
DWR 35	15 December 35
FLB 26	18 January 1936
DWR 36	12 February 36
DWR 37	1 April 36
DWR 38	18 May 36
DWR 39	20 June 36

DWR 40	9 August 36
DWR 41	27 August 36
DWR 42	5 September 36
NF 1	15 October 1936
DWR 43	24 October 36
NF 2	19 December 1936
DWR 44	20 December 36
NF 3	20 January 1937
NF 4	8 February 1937
DWR 45	20 February 37

Glossary of Frequently Mentioned Names

Ackerman, Forrest J (1916–2008), American agent, author, editor. Ackerman had been a science fiction fan since the late '20s; he corresponded sporadically with HPL from around 1931 onward.

Anger, William Frederick (1921–1982), weird fiction fan and late correspondent of HPL.

Babcock, Ralph W., Jr. (1914–2003), a lifelong writer and printer (since the age of seven). Was active in amateur journalism (NAPA President 1934-35 and Official Editor 1939-40), and publisher of the *Scarlet Cockerel* and and other papers.

Barlow, R[obert] H[ayward] (1918–1951), author and collector. As a teenager he corresponded with HPL and acted as his host during two long visits in the summers of 1934 and 1935. In the 1930s he wrote several works of weird and fantasy fiction, some in collaboration with HPL. HPL appointed him his literary executor. He assisted AWD and DAW in preparing the early HPL volumes for Arkham House. In the 1940s he went to Mexico and became a distinguished anthropologist. He died by suicide.

Bates, Harry (1900–1981), editor of *Strange Tales* and *Astounding Stories*.

Bierce, Ambrose (1842–1914?), American author and journalist. His collections of horror and Civil War tales, *Tales of Soldiers and Civilians* (1891; later titled *In the Midst of Life*) and *Can Such Things Be?* (1893) are landmarks. He was also the author of *The Devil's Dictionary* (1906 [as *The Cynic's Word Book*]) and enormous quantities of journalism, chiefly for the Hearst papers.

Blackwood, Algernon (1869–1951), prolific British author of weird and fantasy tales whose work HPL greatly admired when he read it in 1924.

Bloch, Robert (1917–1994), author of weird and suspense fiction who came into correspondence with HPL in 1933. HPL tutored him in the craft of writing during their four-year association.

Bradofsky, Hyman (1906–2002), correspondent of HPL (1934–37). He was president of the NAPA (1935–36) and edited the *Californian* (1933f.), one of the most distinguished and voluminous amateur journals of the period.

Cave, Hugh B[arnett] (1910–2004), prolific author of stories for the pulp magazines. Lived for a time near HPL in Pawtucket, RI. They corresponded briefly but never met.

Coates, Walter J[ohn] (1880–1941), editor of *Driftwind*.

Cole, Edward H[arold] (1892–1966), longtime amateur associate of HPL, living in the Boston area.

Conover, Willis (1920–1996), weird fiction fan who edited *Science-Fantasy Correspondent* (1936–37) and was a late correspondent of HPL.

Cook, W. Paul (1880–1948), publisher of the *Monadnock Monthly*, the *Vagrant*, and other amateur journals; a longtime amateur journalist, printer, and life-long friend of HPL. He first visited HPL in 1917, and it was he who urged HPL to resume writing fiction after a hiatus of nine years. In 1927 Cook published the *Recluse*, containing HPL's "Supernatural Horror in Literature."

Crawford, William L[evy] (1911–1984), editor of *Marvel Tales* and *Unusual Stories* and publisher of the Visionary Publishing Company, which issued HPL's *The Shadow over Innsmouth* (1936).

Davis, Robert H[obart] (1869–1942), American journalist, editor, dramatist, and photographer. Editor of *Munsey's Magazine* from 1904 to 1925, columnist for the *New York Sun* from 1925 to 1942.

de Castro, Adolphe (Danziger) (1859–1959), author, co-translator with Ambrose Bierce of Richard Voss's *The Monk and the Hangman's Daughter*, and correspondent of HPL. HPL revised his "The Last Test" and "The Electric Executioner."

de la Mare, Walter (1873–1956), British author and poet who wrote occasional weird tales much admired by HPL for their subtlety and allusiveness.

Derleth, August W[illiam] (1909–1971), author of weird tales and also a long series of regional and historical works set in his native Wisconsin. After HPL's death, he and Donald Wandrei founded the publishing firm of Arkham House to preserve HPL's work in book form.

Dunsany, Lord (Edward John Moreton Drax Plunkett) (1878–1957), Irish writer of fantasy tales whose work notably influenced HPL after HPL read it in 1919.

Edkins, Ernest A[rthur] (1867–1946), amateur journalist associated with the "halcyon days" of the National Amateur Press Association (1885–95). He came in touch with HPL in 1932.

Eshbach, Lloyd Arthur (1910–2003), editor of a little magazine (not devoted to the weird) entitled the *Galleon*.

Farnese, Harold S. (1885–1945), musical composer and sporadic correspondent of HPL. It was he who provided AWD with the spurious "Black Magic" quotation attributed to HPL.

Finlay, Virgil (1914–1971), one of the great weird artists of his time and a prolific contributor of artwork to the pulps; late correspondent of HPL.

Flagg, Francis. *See* Weiss, Henry George

Gamwell, Annie E[meline] P[hillips] (1866–1941), HPL's younger aunt, living with him at 66 College Street (1933–37).

Gernsback, Hugo (1884–1967), editor of *Amazing Stories, Wonder Stories,* and other pioneering science fiction pulps.

Harré, T[homas] Everett (1884–1948), American journalist who edited the horror anthology *Beware After Dark!* (1929), containing HPL's "The Call of Cthulhu." HPL met him on a few occasions in New York in the 1930s.

Hodgson, William Hope (1877–1918), British author of weird fiction whose work had fallen into obscurity until it was rediscovered in the 1930s, largely through the efforts of H. C. Koenig.

Hornig, Charles D[erwin] (1916–1999), editor of the *Fantasy Fan* (1933–35) and associate editor of *Wonder Stories.*

Houdini, Harry (stage name of Erik Weisz) (1874–1926), Hungarian-American illusionist, magician, escape artist, and debunker. HPL did ghost-writing for him.

Howard, Robert E[rvin] (1906–1936), prolific Texas author of weird and adventure tales for *Weird Tales* and other pulp magazines; creator of the adventure hero Conan the Cimmerian. He and HPL corresponded voluminously from 1930 to 1936. He committed suicide when he heard of his mother's impending death.

James, M[ontague] R[hodes] (1862–1936), celebrated British writer of ghost stories much admired by HPL. His *Collected Ghost Stories* appeared in 1931.

Kirk, George [Willard] (1898–1962), member of the Kalem Club. He published *Twenty-one Letters of Ambrose Bierce* (1922) and ran the Chelsea Bookshop in New York.

Kleiner, Rheinhart (1882–1949), amateur poet and longtime friend of HPL. He visited HPL in Providence in 1918, 1919, and 1920, and met him frequently during the heyday of the Kalem Club (1924–26).

Koenig, H[erman] C[harles] (1893–1959), late associate of HPL who spearheaded the rediscovery of the work of William Hope Hodgson.

Long, Frank Belknap (1901–1994), fiction writer and poet and one of HPL's closest friends and correspondents. Late in life he wrote the memoir, *Howard Phillips Lovecraft: Dreamer on the Nightside* (1975).

Loveman, Samuel E. (1887–1976), poet and longtime friend of HPL and DAW as well as of Ambrose Bierce, Hart Crane, George Sterling, and Clark Ashton Smith. He wrote *The Hermaphrodite* (1926) and other works.

Lumley, William (1880–1960), eccentric late associate of HPL for whom HPL ghostwrote "The Diary of Alonzo Typer" (1935).

Machen, Arthur (1863–1947), Welsh author of weird fiction. He corresponded sporadically with AWD.

Merritt, A[braham] (1884–1943), writer of fantasy and horror tales for the pulps. His work was much admired by HPL in spite of its concessions to pulp formulae. His late novel, *Dwellers in the Mirage* (1932), may have been influenced by HPL.

Moe, Maurice W[inter] (1882–1940), of Appleton and Milwaukee, WI. Amateur journalist, English teacher, and longtime friend and correspondent of HPL.

Moe, Robert Ellis (1912–1992), one of Maurice W. Moe's two sons (the other was Donald), who began corresponding with HPL in 1934 and met him on several occasions.

Moore, C[atherine] L[ucile] (1911–1987), late associate of HPL who later married Henry Kuttner and became a leading figure in science fiction and fantasy.

Morse, Richard Ely (1909–1986), poet, librarian, and late correspondent of Lovecraft.

Morton, James Ferdinand (1870–1941), amateur journalist, author of many tracts on race prejudice, free thought, and taxation, and longtime friend of HPL.

Munn, H[arold] Warner (1903–1981), prolific contributor to the pulp magazines, living near W. Paul Cook in Athol, MA.

Nelson, Robert (1912–1935), young poet and weird fiction writer who committed suicide shortly after coming into correspondence with HPL.

Petaja, Emil (1915–2000), science fiction fan and late associate of HPL's; later a prolific author and editor.

Phillips, Whipple Van Buren (1833–1904), HPL's maternal grandfather. A wealthy industrialist, he established the Owyhee Land and Irrigation Company in Idaho. He provided strong guidance to HPL in the absence of HPL's father. His death in 1904 and the subsequent mismanagement of his estate forced HPL and his mother to move from 454 Angell Street to smaller quarters at 598 Angell Street.

Price, E[dgar] Hoffmann (1898–1988), prolific pulp writer of weird and adventure tales. HPL met him in New Orleans in 1932 and corresponded extensively with him thereafter.

Quinn, Seabury (1889–1969), prolific author of weird and detective tales to the pulps, notably a series of tales involving the psychic detective Jules de Grandin.

Rankin, Hugh Doak (1878–1956), illustrator for *WT*.

Ruppert, Conrad (1912–1997), publisher of the *Fantasy Fan* (1933–35).

Schwartz, Julius (1915–2004), editor of *Fantasy Magazine* who acted as HPL's agent in marketing *At the Mountains of Madness* to *Astounding Stories*.

Searight, Richard F[ranklyn] (1902–1975), sporadic contributor of weird and science fiction tales to the pulp magazines. He corresponded with HPL from 1933 to 1937.

Shepherd, Wilson (1917–1985), amateur printer and publisher of the *Phantagraph*, *Fanciful Tales*, and HPL's *A History of the Necronomicon* (Rebel Press, 1937).

Smith, Charles W. ("Tryout") (1852–1940), longtime amateur journalist, editor of the *Tryout*, and friend and correspondent of HPL.

Smith, Clark Ashton (1893–1961), prolific California poet and writer of fantasy tales. He received a "fan" letter from HPL in 1922 and corresponded with him until HPL's death.

Sterling, Kenneth (1920–1995), young science fiction fan who came into contact with HPL in 1934. He later became a distinguished physician.

Stickney, Corwin F. (1921–1998), copublisher with Willis Conover of *Science-Fantasy Correspondent* (1936–37), later titled *Amateur Correspondent* (1937f.), edited by Stickney alone.

Sully, Helen V. (1904–1997), friend of CAS who visited HPL in Providence in 1933, then saw DAW and others in New York.

Sylvester [Ronan], Margaret (1918–2010), correspondent of HPL (1934–37). She had written to HPL in care of *WT*, asking him to explain the origin and meaning of the term *Walpurgisnacht*. She married and became Margaret Ronan, writing the preface to a school edition of HPL's tales, *The Shadow over Innsmouth and Other Stories of Horror* (Scholastic Books, 1971).

Talman, Wilfred Blanch (1904–1986), correspondent of HPL and late member of the Kalem Club. HPL assisted Talman on his story "Two Black Bottles" (1926) and wrote "Some Dutch Footprints in New England" for Talman to publish in *De Halve Maen*, the journal of the Holland Society of New York. Late in life he wrote the memoir *The Normal Lovecraft* (1973).

Wandrei, Donald (1908–1987), poet and author of weird fiction, science fiction, and detective tales. He corresponded with HPL from 1926 to 1937, visited HPL in Providence in 1927 and 1932, and met HPL occasionally in New York during the 1930s. He helped HPL get "The Shadow out of Time" published in *Astounding Stories*. After HPL's death he and AWD founded the publishing firm Arkham House to preserve HPL's work. For their joint correspondence, see *Mysteries of Time and Spirit* (Night Shade Books, 2002).

Wandrei, Howard (1909–1956), younger brother of Donald Wandrei, premier weird artist and prolific author of weird fiction, science fiction, and detective stories; correspondent of HPL.

Weiss, Henry George (1898–1946) American poet, writer and novelist. His science fiction stories and poetry appeared under the pseudonym "Francis Flagg" in *Amazing Stories, Astounding, Tales of Wonder, Weird Tales*, and others.

Whitehead, Henry S[t. Clair] (1882–1932), author of weird and adventure tales, many of them set in the Virgin Islands. HPL corresponded with him and visited him in Florida in 1931. HPL wrote a brief eulogy of Whitehead for *WT*.

Wollheim, Donald A. (1914–1990), editor of the *Phantagraph* and *Fanciful Tales* and prolific author and editor in the science fiction field.

Wooley, Natalie H. (1904–1973), amateur poet and story writer, and late correspondent of HPL.

Wright, Farnsworth (1888–1940), editor of *Weird Tales* (1924–40). He rejected some of HPL's best work of the 1930s, only to publish it after HPL's death upon submittal by AWD.

Bibliography

Works by H. P. Lovecraft

Books

The Ancient Track: Complete Poetical Works. Edited by S. T. Joshi. 2nd ed. New York: Hippocampus Press, 2013.

The Annotated Supernatural Horror in Literature. Edited by S. T. Joshi. 2nd ed. New York: Hippocampus Press, 2012.

The Cats of Ulthar. Cassia, FL: The Dragon-Fly Press, Christmas 1935. (*LL* 547)

Collected Essays. Edited by S. T. Joshi. New York: Hippocampus Press, 2004–06. 5 vols.

Collected Fiction: A Variorum Edition. Edited by S. T. Joshi. New York: Hippocampus Press, 2015 (Volumes 1–3), 2016 (Volume 4).

Commonplace Book. Edited by David E. Schultz. West Warwick, RI: Necronomicon Press, 1987.

Essential Solitude: The Letters of H. P. Lovecraft and August Derleth. Edited by David E. Schultz and S. T. Joshi. New York: Hippocampus Press, 2008. 2 vols.

Fungi from Yuggoth. Edited by David E. Schultz. New York: Hippocampus Press, 2016.

Further Criticism of Poetry. [Louisville, KY: Printed on the Press of George G. Fetter Co, 1932.] In *CE* 2.

Letters to Alfred Galpin. Edited by S. T. Joshi and David E. Schultz. New York: Hippocampus Press, 2003.

Letters to Robert Bloch and Others. Edited by David E. Schultz and S. T. Joshi. New York: Hippocampus Press, 2015.

Lovecraft at Last (with Willis Conover). Arlington, VA: Carrollton-Clark, 1975. New York: Cooper Square Press, 2002.

A Means to Freedom: The Letters of H. P. Lovecraft and Robert E. Howard. Edited by S. T. Joshi, David E. Schultz, and Rusty Burke. New York: Hippocampus Press, 2009. 2 vols.

Mysteries of Time and Spirit: The Letters of H. P. Lovecraft and Donald Wandrei. Edited by S. T. Joshi and David E. Schultz. San Francisco: Night Shade Books, 2002.

O Fortunate Floridian: H. P. Lovecraft's Letters to R. H. Barlow. Edited by S. T. Joshi and David E. Schultz. Tampa: University of Tampa Press, 2007.

The Outsider and Others. Collected by August Derleth and Donald Wandrei. Sauk City, WI: Arkham House, 1939.

Selected Letters. Edited by August Derleth, Donald Wandrei, and James Turner. Sauk City, WI: Arkham House, 1965–76. 5 vols. [*SL*]

Some Current Motives and Practices. [De Land, FL: R. H. Barlow, 1936.]

The Shadow over Innsmouth. Everett, PA: Visionary Publishing Co., 1936.

The Shunned House. Athol, MA: Recluse Press, 1928 (printed but not bound or distributed until 1959–61).

Stories

"The Alchemist." *United Amateur* 16, No. 4 (November 1916): 53–57. In *CF* 1.

"Arthur Jermyn." See "Facts concerning the Late Arthur Jermyn and His Family."

At the Mountains of Madness. Astounding Stories 16, No. (February 1936): 8–32; 17, No. 1 (March 1936): 125–55; 17, No. 2 (April 1936): 132–50. In *CF* 3.

"The Beast in the Cave." *Vagrant* No. 7 (June 1918): 113–20. In *CF* 1.

"Beyond the Wall of Sleep." *Pine Cones* 1, No. 6 (October 1919): 2–10. *Fantasy Fan,* 2, No. 2 (October 1934): 25–32. In *CF* 1.

"The Call of Cthulhu." *WT* 11, No. 2 (February 1928): 159–78, 287. In *Beware After Dark! The World's Most Stupendous Tales of Mystery, Horror, Thrills and Terror,* ed. T. Everett Harré. New York: Macaulay, 1929. 223–59. In *CF* 2.

The Case of Charles Dexter Ward. First published in *Beyond the Wall of Sleep.* Sauk City, WI: Arkham House, 1943. In *CF* 3.

"The Cats of Ulthar." *Tryout* 6, No. 11 (November 1920): [6–11]. *WT* 7, No. 2 (February 1926): 252–54. In *CF* 1.

"Celephaïs." *Rainbow* No. 2 (May 1922): 10–12. *Marvel Tales* 1, No. 1 (May 1934): 26, 28–32. In *CF* 1.

"The Colour out of Space." *Amazing Stories* 2, No. 6 (September 1927): 557–67. In *CF* 2

"Cool Air." *Tales of Magic and Mystery* 1, No. 4 (March 1928): 29–34. In *CF* 1.

"Dagon." *Vagrant* No. 11 (November 1919): 23–29. *WT* 2, No. 3 (October 1923): 23–25. In *CF* 1.

"The Doom That Came to Sarnath." *Scot* No. 44 (June 1920): 90–98. *Marvel Tales of Science and Fantasy* 1, No. 4 (March–April 1935): 157–63. In *CF* 1.

The Dream-Quest of Unknown Kadath. First published in *Beyond the Wall of Sleep.* Sauk City, WI: Arkham House, 1943. In *CF* 3.

"The Dreams in the Witch House.'" *WT* 22, No. 1 (July 1933): 86–111. In *CF* 3.

"The Dunwich Horror." *WT* 13, No. 4 (April 1929): 481–508. In *CF* 2.

"Facts concerning the Late Arthur Jermyn and His Family." *Wolverine* No. 9 (March 1921): 3–11. *WT* 3, No. 4 (April 1924): 15–18 (as "The White Ape"). *WT* 25, No. 5 (May 1935): 642–48 (as "Arthur Jermyn"). In *CF* 1.

"The Festival." *WT* 5, No. 1 (January 1925): 169–74. *WT* 22, No. 4 (October 1933): 519–20, 522–28. In *CF* 1.

"From Beyond." *Fantasy Fan* 1, No. 10 (June 1934): 147–51, 160. In *CF* 1.

"The Haunter of the Dark." *WT* 28, No. 5 (December 1936): 538–53. In *CF* 3.

"He." *WT* 8, No. 3 (September 1926): 373–80. In *CF* 1.

"Herbert West—Reanimator" (as "Grewsome Tales"). *Home Brew:* 1, No. 1

(February 1922): 84–88 ("From the Dark"); 1, No. 2 (March 1922): 45–50 ("The Plague Demon"); 1, No. 3 (April 1922): 21–26 ("Six Shots by Moonlight"); 1, No. 4 (May 1922): 53–58 ("The Scream of the Dead"); 1, No. 5 (June 1922): 45–50 ("The Horror from the Shadows,"); 1, No. 6 (July 1922): 57–62 ("The Tomb-Legions,"). In *CF* 1.

"The Horror at Red Hook." *WT* 9, No. 1 (January 1927): 59–73. In *You'll Need a Night Light*, ed. Christine Campbell Thomson. London: Selwyn & Blount, 1927, pp. 228–54. In *CF* 1.

"The Hound." *WT* 3, No. 2 (February 1924): 50–52, 78. *WT* 14, No. 3 (September 1929): 421–25, 432. In *CF* 1.

"Hypnos." *National Amateur* 45, No. 5 (May 1923): 1–3; *WT* 4, No. 2 (May–June–July 1924): 33–35: *WT* 30, No. 5 (November 1937): 626–31. In *CF* 1.

"In the Vault." *Tryout* 10, No. 6 (November 1925): [3–17]. *WT* 19, No. 4 (Apr. 1932): 459–65. In *CF* 1.

"The Lurking Fear." *Home Brew* 2, No. 6 (January 1923): 4–10; 3, No. 1 (February 1923): 18–23; 3, No. 2 (March 1923): 31–37, 44, 48; 3, No. 3 (April 1923): 35–42. *WT* 11, No. 6 (June 1928): 791–804. In *CF* 1.

"The Moon-Bog." *WT* 7, No. 6 (June 1926): 805–10. In *CF* 1.

"The Music of Erich Zann." *National Amateur* 44, No. 4 (March 1922): 38–40. *WT* 5, No. 5 (May 1925): 219–34. In *Creeps by Night: Chills and Thrills*, ed. Dashiell Hammett. New York: John Day Co., 1931. 347–63. In *Modern Tales of Horror*, ed. Dashiell Hammett. London: Victor Gollancz, 1932. 301–17. *Evening Standard* (London) (24 October 1932): 20–21. *WT* 24, No. 5 (November 1934): 644–48, 655–56. In *CF* 1.

"The Mysterious Ship." In *CF* 3.

"The Mystery of the Grave-yard." In *CF* 3.

"The Nameless City." *Wolverine* No. 11 (Nov. 1921): 3–15. *Fanciful Tales* 1, No. 1 (Fall 1936): 5–18. In *CF* 1.

"The Noble Eavesdropper." Nonextant.

"The Other Gods." *Fantasy Fan* 1, No. 3 (November 1933): 35–38. *Weird Tales* 32, No. 4 (October 1938): 489–92.

"The Outsider." *WT* 7, No. 4 (April 1926): 449–53. *WT* 17, No. 4 (June–July 1931): 566–71. In *CF* 1.

"Pickman's Model." *WT* 10, No. 4 (October 1927): 505–14. In *By Daylight Only*, ed. Christine Campbell Thomson. London: Selwyn & Blount, 1929. 37–52. *WT* 28, No. 4 (November 1936): 495–505. In *The "Not at Night" Omnibus*, ed. Christine Campbell Thomson. London: Selwyn & Blount, [1937]. 279–307. In *CF* 2.

"The Picture in the House." *National Amateur* 41, No. 6 (July 1919 [*sic*]): 246–49. *WT* 3, No. 1 (January 1924): 40–42. *WT* 29, No. 3 (March 1937): 370–73. In *CF* 1.

"Polaris." *Philosopher* 1, No. 1 (December 1920): 3–5. *National Amateur* 48, No. 5 (May 1926): 48–49. *Fantasy Fan* 1, No. 6 (February 1934): 83–85. In *CF* 1.

"The Quest of Iranon." *Galleon* 1, No. 5 (July–August 1935): 12–20. In *CF* 1.

"The Rats in the Walls." *WT* 3, No. 3 (March 1924): 25–31. *WT* 15, No. 6 (June 1930): 841–53. In *Switch On the Light,* ed. Christine Campbell Thomson. London: Selwyn & Blount, 1931. 141–65. In *CF* 1.

"The Secret of the Grave." See "The Mystery of the Grave-yard."

"The Shadow out of Time."*Astounding Stories* 17, No. 4 (June 1936): 110–54. In *CF* 3.

The Shadow over Innsmouth. Everett, PA: Visionary Publishing Co., 1936. In *CF* 3.

"The Shunned House." In *CF* 1.

"The Silver Key." *WT* 13, No. 1 (January 1929): 41–49, 144. In *CF* 2.

"The Statement of Randolph Carter." *Vagrant* No. 13 (May 1920): 41–48. *WT* 5, No. 2 (February 1925): 149–53. In *CF* 1.

"Strange High House in the Mist." *WT* 18, No. 3 (October 1931): 394–400. In *CF* 1.

"The Terrible Old Man." *Tryout* 7, No. 4 (July 1921): [10–14]. *WT* 8, No. 2 (August 1926): 191–92. In *CF* 1.

"The Temple." *WT* 6, No. 3 (September 1925): 329–36, 429–31; *WT* 27, No. 2 (February 1936): 239–44, 246–49. In *CF* 1.

"The Thing on the Doorstep." *WT* 29, No. 1 (January 1937): 52–70. In *CF* 3.

"The Tomb." *Vagrant* No. 14 (March 1922): 50–64. In *CF* 1.

"The Tree." *Tryout* 7, No. 7 (October 1921): [3–10]. In *CF* 1.

"The Unnamable." *WT* 6, no. 1 (July 1925): 78–82. In *CF* 1.

"The Very Old Folk." *Scienti-Snaps* 3, No. 3 (Summer 1940): 4–8. In *CF* 4.

"The Whisperer in Darkness." *WT* 18, No. 1 (August 1931): 32–73. In *CF* 2.

"The White Ship." *United Amateur* 19, No. 2 (November 1919): 30–33. *WT* 9, No. 3 (March 1927): 386–89. In *CF* 1.

Revisions and Collaborations

Barlow, R. H. "The Battle That Ended the Century." In *CF* 4.

———. "The Night Ocean." *Californian* 4, No. 3 (Winter 1936): 41–56. In *CF* 4.

Bishop, Zealia. "The Curse of Yig." *WT* 14, No. 5 (November 1929): 625–36. In *Switch On the Light,* ed. Christine Campbell Thomson. London: Selwyn & Blount, 1931. 9–31. In *The "Not at Night" Omnibus,* ed. Christine Campbell Thomson. London: Selwyn & Blount, [1937]. 13–29. In *CF* 4.

———. "The Mound." *WT* 35, No. 6 (November 1940): 98–120 (abridged). In *CF* 4.

de Castro, Adolphe. "The Electric Executioner" [orig. "The Automatic Executioner"]. *WT* 16, No. 2 (August 1930): 223–36. In *CF* 4.

———. "The Last Test" [orig. "A Sacrifice to Science"]. *WT* 12, No. 5 (November 1928): 625–56. In *CF* 4.

Eddy, C. M., Jr. "The Loved Dead." *WT* 4, No. 2 (May–June–July 1924): 54–57. In *CF* 4.

Heald, Hazel. "The Horror in the Museum." *WT* 22, No. 1 (July 1933): 49–68. In *Terror by Night,* ed. Christine Campbell Thomson. London: Selwyn &

Blount, [1934]. 111–41. In. *The "Not at Night" Omnibus,* ed. Christine Campbell Thomson. London: Selwyn & Blount, [1937]. 279–307. In *CF* 4.

———. "Out of the Aeons." *WT* 25, No. 4 (April 1935): 478–96. In *CF* 4.

Houdini, Harry. "Under the Pyramids." *WT* 4, No. 2 (May–June–July 1924): 3–12 (as "Imprisoned with the Pharaohs"; as by "Houdini"). In *CF* 1.

Lumley, William. "The Diary of Alonzo Typer." *WT* 31, No. 2 (February 1938): 152–66. In *CF* 4.

Moore, C. L., A. Merritt, Robert E. Howard, and Frank Belknap Long. *Fantasy Magazine* 5, No. 4 (September 1935): 221–29 (HPL portion on 223–27). In *CF* 4.

Price, E. Hoffmann. "Through the Gates of the Silver Key." *WT* 24, No. 1 (July 1934): 60–85. In *CF* 3.

Rimel, Duane W. "The Disinterment." *Weird Tales* 29, No. 1 (January 1937): 95–102. *TYB* 11–18. In *CF* 4.

———. "The Tree on the Hill." *Polaris* (September 1940): 4–11. *CC* No. 16 (Michaelmas 1983): 5–12. In *CF* 4.

Nonfiction

"An Account of a Trip to the Antient Fairbanks House, in Dedham, and to the Red Horse Tavern in Sudbury, in the Province of the Massachusetts-Bay." In *CE* 4.

"Chairman of the Bureau of Critics Reports on Poetry." *National Amateur* 57, No. 1 (5 September 1934): Sec. 2, p. 3. In *CE* 1.

"Correspondence between R. H. Barlow and Wilson Shepherd of Oakman, Alabama—September–November 1932." *Lovecraft Studies* No. 13 (Fall 1986): 68–71. In *CE* 5.

"Homes and Shrines of Poe." *Californian* 2, no. 3 (Winter 1934): 8–10.

"A Living Heritage: Roman Architecture in Today's America." *Californian* 3, No. 1 (Summer 1935): 23–28 (abridged; as "Heritage or Modernism: Common Sense in Art Forms"). In *CE* 5.

"[List of Correspondents to Whom Postcards Have Been Sent]." *CE* 5.

"Lovecraft Offers Verse Criticism." *National Amateur* 57, No. 4 (June 1935): 5–6. In *CE* 1.

"Notes on Writing Weird Fiction." *Amateur Correspondent* 2, No. 1 (May–June 1937): 7–10. *Supramundane Stories* 1, No. 2 (Spring 1938): 11–13 (as "Notes on Weird Fiction-Writing—The 'Why' and 'How'"). In *CE* 2.

"Report of the Bureau of Critics—Verse Department." *National Amateur* 57, No. 2 (December 1934): 1. In *CE* 1.

"Report of the Executive Judges." *National Amateur* 58, No. 4 (June 1936): 2–3.

"Science and Charlatanry." In *CE* 3.

"Some Dutch Footprints in New England." *De Halve Maen* 9, No. 1 (18 October 1933): 2, 4. In *CE* 4.

"Some Notes on a Nonentity." In *Beyond the Wall of Sleep.* Sauk City: WI: Arkham House, 1943. xi–xiv. In *CE* 5.

"Some Notes on Interplanetary Fiction." *Californian* 3, No. 3 (Winter 1935): 39–42. In *CE* 2.

"Suggestions for Writing Story"; part of "[Notes on Writing Fiction]". In *CE* 2.

"Supernatural Horror in Literature." *Recluse* No. 1 (1927): 23–59. Rev. ed. in *Fantasy Fan* (October 1933–February 1935). In *CE* 2.

"The Unknown City in the Ocean." *Perspective Review* (Winter 1934 [Fourth Anniversary Number]): 7–8. In *CE* 4.

"The Weird Work of William Hope Hodgson." *Phantagraph* 5, No. 5 (February 1937): 5–7. Incorporated into "Supernatural Horror in Literature."

Poems [all poems are in *The Ancient Track*]

"The Ancient Track." *WT* 15, No. 3 (March 1930): 300.

"The East India Brick Row." *Providence Journal* (8 January 1930): 13.

"Festival." *Weird Tales* 8, No. 6 (December 1926): 846 (without final stanza; as "Yule Horror").

Fungi from Yuggoth.

XXIII. "Mirage." *Weird Tales* 17, No. 2 (February–March 1931): 175

XXVII. "The Elder Pharos." *Weird Tales* 17, No. 2 (February–March 1931): 175.

XXXIII. "Harbour Whistles." *Silver Fern* 1, No. 5 (May 1930): [1]. *L'Alouette* 3, No. 6 (September–October 1930): 161. *Phantagraph* 5, No. 2 (November 1936): 1.

"In a Sequester'd Providence Churchyard Where Once Poe Walk'd." *Science-Fantasy Correspondent* 1, No. 3 (March–April 1937): 16–17. *WT* 31, No. 5 (May 1938): 578 (as "Where Poe Once Walked: An Acrostic Sonnet"). In *Four Acrostic Sonnets on Poe* (1936), ed. Maurice W. Moe.

"[Little Sam Perkins.]" *Olympian* No. 35 (Autumn 1940): 36.

"Nemesis." *Vagrant* No. 7 (June 1918): 41–43; *WT* 3, No. 4 (April 1924): 78.

"The Outpost." *Bacon's Essays* 3, No. 1 (Spring 1930): 7. *Fantasy Magazine* 3, No. 3 (May 1934): 24–25.

"Psychopompos: A Tale in Rhyme." *Vagrant* No. 10 (October 1919): 13–22.

"To Clark Ashton Smith, Esq., upon his Fantastic Tales, Verses, Pictures, & Sculptures." *WT* 31, No. 4 (April 1938): 392 (as "To Clark Ashton Smith").

"To Mr. Finlay, upon his Drawing for Mr. Bloch's Tale, 'The Faceless God.'" *Phantagraph* 6, No. 1 (May 1937). *Weird Tales* 30, No. 1 (July 1937): 17.

"Yule Horror." See "Festival."

Letters

"Excerpts from the Letters of H. P. Lovecraft." *Acolyte* 1, No. 1 (Fall 1942): 4–5, 15. *Contains:* Letters to Duane W. Rimel, 19 November 1934, p. 4; 10 March 1935, pp. 4–5; 16 April 1935, p. 5; 12 November 1935, pp. 5, 15.

Letter to the N.A.P.A. (22 June 1936). *Lest We Forget* (October 1936): 28. In *CF* 1.

"Six Letters." *Science Fiction Critic* 2, No. 2 (March 1938): 3–10 (contains extracts from three letters to Nils Frome); in *Uncollected Letters*, ed. S. T. Joshi (West Warwick, RI: Necronomicon Press, 1986): 38–42; in *Howard Phillips Lovecraft and Nils Helmer Frome: A Recollection of One of Canada's Earliest Science Fiction Fans*. Ed. Sam Moskowitz. (Glenview, IL: Moshassuck Press, 1989): 79–84 (as "Letters to Nils Helmer Frome").

"Lovecraft as an Illustrator." *Acolyte* 1, No 4 (Summer 1944): 21–23. An extract from Lovecraft's letter to F. Lee Baldwin of 27 March 1934.

"Save the Old Brick Row." *Providence Sunday Journal* (22 December 1929): Section A, p. 5 (as "Praises Beauty of 'Old Brick Row': Removal of Ancient Warehouses Along South Water Street Would Mean Needless Destruction of Notable Architectural Asset That Should Be Prevented"; as by James F. Morton).

To Alvin Earl Perry (4 October 1935). *Whispers* 2, Nos. 2/3 (June 1975): 80–84 (as "Story-Writing: A Letter from HPL"); published in part in *SL* 5.201–4.

To Charles D. Hornig. *FF* 1, No. 7 (March 1934): 105.

To Duane W. Rimel (28 September 1935). *Phantagraph* 5, No. 5 (February 1937): 4–8 (as "What's the Trouble with Weird Fiction?"; unsigned).

To Ralph E. Babcock. *Scarlet Cockerel* No. 15 (January 1941): 15–19 (as "A Voice from the Grave").

Works by Lovecraft's Correspondents

F. Lee Baldwin

Crime Stalks the Fan World. Entropy (1960, published by Terry Carr). *Contents:* Crime Stalks the Fan World; The Girl With The Muddy Eyes.

Nonfiction

"H. P. Lovecraft: A Biographical Sketch." *Fantasy Magazine* 4, No. 5 (April 1935): 108–10, 132. In *Lovecraft at Last* (q.v.). In Richardson, *Within the Circle* (q.v.).

"Side Glances." *Fantasy Fan* 1, No. 8 (April 1934): 116; 1, No. 9 (May 1934): 136; 2, No. 1 (September 1934): 13.

"Some Lovecraft Sidelights." *Fantasy Commentator* 2, No. 6 (Spring 1948): 219–20 (revised version of "H. P. Lovecraft: A Biographical Sketch."

"A Stribling 'Unknown.'" *The Fanscient* 2, No. 1 (Spring 1948): 30.

"Within the Circle." *Fantasy Fan* 1, No. 10 (June 1934): 156; 1, No. 11 (July 1934): 164; 1, No. 12 (August 1934): 180; 2, No. 1 (September 1934): 7; 2, No. 2 (October 1934): 19; 2, No. 3 (November 1934): 36; 2, No. 4 (January 1935): 71; and 2, No. 5 (February 1935): 90; *Acolyte* 1, No. 4 (Summer 1943): 2.

Fiction

"Crime Stalks the Fan World." *Shangri-L'affaires* (January 1945);

"The Fox and I." *The Fanscient* 2, No. 2 (Summer 1948): 4–5.

"The Girl With The Muddy Eyes." *Shangri-L'affaires* (December 1946).

"Island Bees." *Star Rover* 6 (November–December 1948).

"Poker—Texas Style." *Famous Western* 9, No. 1 (January 1948): 84–86.

Letters

In "The Boiling Point." *Fantasy Fan* 1, No. 4 (December 1933): 63; and 1, No. 6 (February 1934): 93. In *The Boiling Point,* [ed. Marc A. Michaud]. West Warwick, RI: Necronomicon Press, 1985).

The following are all reprinted in Richardson, *Within the Circle* (q.v.):

Fantasy Fan 1, No. 4 (December 1933): 51.

Fantasy Fan 1, No. 8 (April 1934): 115.

Fantasy Fan 1, No. 9 (May 1934): 129, 130.

Fantasy Fan 1, No. 10 (June 1934): 146.

Fantasy Fan 1, No. 11 (July 1934): 162.

Fantasy Magazine 3, No. 5 (July 1934).

Fantasy Fan 2, No. 1 (September 1934): 2, 16.

Fantasy Fan 2, No. 2 (October 1934): 18–19.

Fantasy Fan 2, No. 3 (November 1934): 35.

Fantasy Fan 2, No. 4 (December 1934): 49.

Duane W. Rimel

Collections

The Many Worlds of Duane Rimel: Prose, Poetry, & Art. Edited by Ralph Vaughn. Chula Vista, CA: Running Dinosaur, 1988. *Contents:* Duane W. Rimel [unsigned]; Wings of Dream [v]; The Guardian [v]; The Librarian; The Ship [v]; Dreams of Yith [v]; The Snake [v]; The Runner [v]; Shadow on the Wall [v]; The Little Ones [v]; The Tale of Rondo and Ilana; [assorted linoleum cuts]; The Dollmaker; Lost [v]; The Whisperer [v]; The Worm [v]; The Key [v]; Ennui [v]; Reverie [v]; Fatality [v];Wind from the River [v]; Strange Flowers Bloom [v]; Across the River [v]; Fantasy Fandom (Late 1930–Early 1940) [nf]; Goodbye, Bill [v]; [assorted linoleum cuts on back cover].

The Second Book of Rimel. Edited by Ralph Vaughn. Chula Vista, CA: Running Dinosaur, 1989. *Contents:* Introduction, by Ralph E. Vaughn; About Hampdon [nf]; Its Prayer [v]; The Hills Beyond Hampdon; The Man at the Rail; The Jewels of Charlotte; The Forbidden Room; Music of the Stars; About Yith [nf].

To Yith and Beyond. Edited by Kenneth W. Faig, Jr. Glenview, IL: Moshassuck Press, 1990. *Contents:* INTRODUCTION; BIOGRAPHY: My Grandparents; My Parents; A Brief Autobiography; My Siblings; My Children; PROFESSIONAL STORIES: The Disinterment; The Metal Chamber; The City Un-

der the Sea; Jungle Princess; ARTICLES: A Fan Looks Back; Joshua II: He
Shocked Corvallis; AMATEUR FICTION: Norton and I; The Tale of Rondo
and Ilana; The Small, Dark Thing; The Sorcery of Aphlar; POETRY: Con-
tradiction; Mood; The Snake; Across the River; Estranged; Fatality; The
Little Ones; The Runner; The Whisperer; Wind from the River; Reverie;
Dreams of Yith; Late Revenge; TWO CLASSIC PRINTINGS OF "Dreams of
Yith": Charles D. Hornig (1934); Francis T. Laney (1943).

Crypt of Cthulhu No. 79 (Hallowmass 1991) was an all-Rimel issue. *Contents:*
The Sorcery of Aphlar; The Metal Chamber; The Last Scientist; Norton
and I; The Small, Dark Thing; Two in a Dungeon; The Wrong Night;
Contradiction [v]; Mood [v]; Estranged [v].

Novels

Carnal Psycho. Chicago: Novel Books, 1961.

The Curse of Cain. Philadelphia: David McKay, 1945. Rpt. in *The Duane Rimel
Noir Crime Megapack* (q.v.). Tr. as *Un Meurtrier chasse l'autre* (*Le Masque*):
Paris: Librairie Des Champs-Élysées, 1976.

The Duane Rimel Noir Crime Megapack. Rockville, MD: Wildside Press, 2015
(eBook). Contains: *The Jury Is Out; Motive for Murder; The Curse of Cain;* and
The River Is Cold.

Hot Package. Chicago: Novel Books, 1961.

The Jury Is Out. London: Withy Grove Press, 1947. Rpt. in *The Duane Rimel
Noir Crime Megapack* (q.v.).

Motive for Murder. London: Withy Grove Press, 1945. Rpt. in *The Duane Rimel
Noir Crime Megapack* (q.v.).

The River Is Cold. Clovis, CA: Vega Books, 1962 (bound with *Beauty Can Kill* by
Michael McCretton). Rpt. in *The Duane Rimel Noir Crime Megapack* (q.v.).

As by Rex Weldon

Arouse Me! Chicago: Novel Books, 1962.

Babe in Blue Jeans. Las Vegas: Neva Books, 1967.

Bed Slave. North Hollywood CA: Brandon House, 1966.

Bedroom Bingo. Las Vegas: Playtime, 1966.

Black Thighs. San Diego: Publisher's Export Co., 1969.

Brothers and Sisters. San Diego: Greenleaf Classics, 1971.

A Carnival of Swappers. North Hollywood, CA: Brandon House, 1970.

Daughter's Dilemma. San Diego: Chelsea Library Press, 1975.

Depraved Family. San Diego: Greenleaf Classics, 1973.

Double Swap. Publishers Export Company, Inc., 1969.

Erotic Encounter. Chicago: Novel Books, 1964.

Everloving Father. San Diego: Greenleaf Classics, 1972.

Free Love Resort. Chicago: Novel Books, 1963.

Gas Station Girls. Olympia Press.

Gone with the Storm. New York: Bee-Line, 1966

Harem House. San Diego: Greenleaf Classics, 1972.
Heather's Big Brother. New York: Carlyle Communications (Beeline), 1976.
Her Sexual Debut. New York: Carlyle Communications, 1978.
Her Uncle Charley's Answer. San Diego: Greenleaf Classics, 1971.
Hot to Swap. San Diego: Greenleaf Classics, 1973.
In Tre e Meglio. Italy: Olympia Press, 1985.
The Innocent Lesbian. North Hollywood, CA: Brandon House, 1965.
The Lavender House. North Hollywood, CA: Brandon House, 1965.
Lesbian Lessons. New York: Carlyle Communications (Beeline), 1977.
The Limit for Laura. North Hollywood, CA: Brandon House, 1967.
Love Me Wild. North Hollywood, CA: Brandon House, 1965.
Master in Bed. Las Vegas: Neva Paperbacks, 1967.
Mom's Dirty Sis. New York: Carlyle Communications. 1975.
Monstrous Passion. Chicago: Novel Books, 1962.
More Than a Mother. San Diego: Greenleaf Classics, 1973.
Mrs. Field's Frenzy. San Diego: Greenleaf Classics, 1972.
A Naïve Maid. Late Night Library, 1975.
Neighborhood Swap. El Cajon, CA: Publisher's Export Co., 1968.
New Wine. 1967.
A Night at the Orgy. New York: Carlyle Communications, 1979.
No Bed of Her Own. North Hollywood, CA: Brandon House, 1969.
Party Wife. North Hollywood, CA: Brandon House, 1967.
Passion Pool. San Diego: Publishers Export Co., 1966.
Peculiarly Passionate Pair. Chicago: Novel Books, 1963.
The Pussy Machine. n.p.: [No imprint,] 1970.
Reluctant Lesbian. North Hollywood, CA: Brandon House, 1969.
Satisfaction. North Hollywood, CA: Nitely Books.
Seduction Induction. New York: Carlyle Communications, 1978.
Sex Schedule Playtime. Las Vegas: Neva Paperbacks, 1964.
Sex Secret. Las Vegas: Neva Paperbacks, 1967
Sex Spy. Las Vegas: Neva Paperbacks, 1965.
Sex Week. North Hollywood, CA: Brandon House, 1965.
Sexmates. Fresno, CA: Saber Books, 1964.
Stud for Hire. Las Vegas: Neva Paperbacks, 1965.
The Peeping Swapper. El Cajon, CA: Publishers Export Co., 1968.
The Shy One. North Hollywood, CA: Brandon House, 1966.
Swap Hole. San Diego: Publishers Export Co. 1968.
Swap Picnic. San Diego: Publishers Export Co. n.d.
Sweet Saphic Scene. New York: Carlyle Communications.
Ted's Bisexual Wife. San Diego: Greenleaf Classics, 1971.
Thrill Seekers. North Hollywood, CA: Brandon House, 1965.
Time Swap. El Cajon, CA: Publishers Export Co., 1969.
TONI Obeliskos Classic. N.p., 1970.

Try Me Again. North Hollywood, CA: Brandon House, 1967.

Twin Stud Swap. San Diego: Publishers Export Co., 1970.

Twin Switchers. Beeline. 1976.

The Two-way Amazon. North Hollywood, CA: Brandon House, 1965.

Untamed Desires. Fresno, CA: Saber Books, 1963.

Wake Up, My Love. North Hollywood, CA: Brandon House, 1966.

Wet Lips. New York: Carlyle Communications, 1976.

With a Nephew Like Don. San Diego, CA: Greenleaf Classics, 1971.

Woman Fever. Olympia Press, 2013.

Your Wife for Mine. North Hollywood, CA: Brandon House, 1967.

As by Peter Biggs

A Man's Woman. Las Vegas: Neva Paperbacks, 1968.

As by Andre Lemir

Erotic Woman. Chicago: Camerarts Pub. Co., 1964.

Nonfiction

The Forbidden Room and How the Forbidden Room Happened. Glenview, IL: Moshassuck Press, 1988.

Poetry

Dreams of Yith. Clarkston, WA: Francis T. Laney, 1943 ("An 'Acolyte' Publication," for FAPA). Ill. Rosco E. Wright. In *TYB* 99–111.

Short Fiction

"The Black Idol." Nontextant.

"The Bride of the Robot." *Vulcan* 1, No. 6 (March 1944).

"Chief White Cloud." *CC* No. 31 (Roodmas 1985): 20.

"The City under the Sea." *Future Fiction* (July 1940): 55–65. *TYB* 25–35.

"The Dollmaker." *MW* 22–30.

"The Forbidden Room." *Fanciful Tales* 1, No. 1 (Fall 1936): 21–25. *SB* 24–27. Glenview, IL: Moshassuck Press, 1988.

"From the Sea" (revised by HPL?). Nontextant.

"The Gift." *Risqué Stories* No. 3 (July 1985): 37–38.

"Goodbye, Joe." *CC* No. 29 (Candlemas 1985): 34–36.

"The Green Door." *Queen City Amateur* (1930s); *Moshassuck Review* (November 1997): 11–12.

"The Hampdon Horror." *CC* No. 25 (Michaelmas 1984): 41–46.

"The Hills Beyond Hampdon." *Etchings and Odysseys* No. 9 (1986): 70–71. *SB* 4–9.

"The Jewels of Charlotte." *Unusual Stories* 1, No. 1 (May/June 1935): 24–33. *SB* 13–23. In *Acolytes of Cthulhu*, ed. Robert M. Price. Minneapolis, MN: Fedogan & Bremer, 2001. 46–52. In *The Yith Cycle: Lovecraftian Tales of the*

Great Race and Time Travel, ed. Robert M. Price. Heyward, CA: Chaosium, 2010. 204–10.

"June, 4683." *Risqué Stories* No. 1 (March 1984): 28–30, 32–34.

"Jungle Princess." *Jungle Stories* (Winter 1944): 116–28. *TYB* 36–48.

"The Kiss of Zak." Nonextant.

"The Ladder of Thought." Nonextant.

"The Last Scientist." *Polaris* 2, No. 1 (December 1940); *CC* No. 79 (Hallowmas 1991): 11–16.

"The Librarian." *Etchings and Odysseys* No. 10 (1987): 96–97. *MW* 3–9.

"The Man on at the Rail." *Californian* 3, No. 4 (Spring 1936): 72–73. *SB* 10–12.

"The Metal Chamber." *Weird Tales* 33, No. 3 (March 1939): 7–12. *CC* No. 79 (Hallowmass 1991): 6–10. *TYB* 19–24.

"The Midnight Visitor." *Supramundane Stories* 1, No. 2 (February 1938): 8–9.

"Music of the Stars." *Acolyte* 1, No. 3 (Spring 1943): 7–12. *SB* 28–39.

"Norton and I." *Acolyte* 1, No. 1 (Fall 1942): 6–14. *TYB* 55–62. *CC* No. 79 (Hallowmass 1991): 17–22, 10.

"The Organ." Nonextant. Possible alternate titles: "At the Morning Service"; "Diana."

"Rehearsal for the Morgue." *Detective and Murder Mysteries* 1, No. 4 (November 1939): 65–68.

"The Room of Pictures." Nonextant.

"The Sable Garden." Nonextant.

"The Silver Sail." Nonextant

"The Small, Dark Thing." *Acolyte* (Summer 1944): 20–24. *TYB* 66–71. *CC* No. 79 (Hallowmass 1991): 23–27.

"The Sorcery of Aphlar." *Fantasy Fan* 2, No. 4 (December 1934): 57–58. *Tri-State* [NY] *Times* 1, No. 1 (Spring 1937): 3–4 (as "The Sourcery of Alphar"). *CC* No. 10 (Yuletide 1982) [*Ashes and Others* by H. P. Lovecraft & divers hands): 16–17 (as by Duane W. Rimel and H. P. Lovecraft). *CC* No. 79 (Hallowmass 1991): 4–5. *TYB* 72–73. In *CF* 4.

"The Spell of the Blue Stone." Nonextant.

"The Tale of Rondo and Ilana." *Acolyte* 1, No. 2 (Winter 1942): 3–5. *MW* 16–19. *TYB* 63–65.

"The Tenth Brick." Nonextant.

"Two in a Dungeon." *Literary Newsette* (12 April 1944). *CC* No. 79 (Hallowmass 1991): 27.

"The Waterfall." Nonextant.

"The Wrong Night." *Lazarette* (December 1944). *CC* No. 79 (Hallowmass 1991): 28–29.

Poems

"Across the River." *Acolyte* 1, No. 4 (Summer 1943): 14. In *TYB* 77. In *MW* 37.

"Contradiction." *Acolyte* 1, No. 1 (Fall 1942): 20. In *TYB* 74. *CC* No. 79 (Hallowmass 1991): 30.

"The Dreams of Yid." *CC* No. 10 (Yuletide 1982) [*Ashes and Others* by H. P. Lovecraft & divers hands]: 20 (as "Dreams of Yid"). In *The Yith Cycle: Lovecraftian Tales of the Great Race and Time Travel,* ed. Robert M. Price. Heyward, CA: Chaosium, 2010. 198.

"Dreams of Yith" (I–X). *Fantasy Fan* 1, No. 11 (July 1934): 170–71 (I–V); 2, No. 1 (September 1934): 8–9 (VI–X). *Acolyte* 1, No. 1 (Fall 1942): 2–3. In *Dreams of Yith* (1943). In *Dark of the Moon: Poems of Fantasy and the Macabre,* ed. August Derleth. Sauk City, WI: Arkham House, 1947. 401–403. *CC* 10 (Yuletide 1982) [*Ashes and Others* by H. P. Lovecraft & divers hands]: 18–19 (as by Duane W. Rimel and H. P. Lovecraft). *MW* 10–12. *TYB* 95–98. In *The Yith Cycle: Lovecraftian Tales of the Great Race and Time Travel,* ed. Robert M. Price. Heyward, CA: Chaosium, 2010. 198–202. In *The Ancient Track* 472–74.

"Ennui." *MW* 34.

"Estranged." *Acolyte* 2, No. 1 (Fall 1943): 21. *TYB* 78. *CC* No. 79 (Hallowmass 1991): 31.

"Fatality." *Acolyte* 2, No. 2 (Spring) 1944: 14. *MW* 35. *TYB* 79.

"Goodbye, Bill." *MW* 40.

"The Guardian." *MW* 2.

"Its Prayer." *Californian* 3, No. 2 (Fall 1935): 16. *Phantagraph* 4, No. 2 (November–December 1935): 12. *SB* 3.

"The Key." *Arkham Collector* No. 1 (Summer 1967): 12. *MW* 33.

"Late Revenge." *Fantasy Fan* 2, No. 5 (January 1935): 73. *TYB* 88.

"The Little Ones." *Acolyte* 2, No. 3 (Summer 1944): 7. *MW* 15. *TYB* 89.

"Lost." *MW* 30.

"Midnight Fancy." Nonextant.

"Mood." *Acolyte* 1, No. 2 (Winter 1942): 27. *TYB* 75. *CC* No. 79 (Hallowmass 1991): 31.

"Reverie." *Scarlet Cockerel* No. 2 ("Somewhat Later A. O. 13 April 1936"): 17. *Phantagraph* 5, No. 4 (January 1937): 3. *MW* 34. *TYB* 84.

"The Room of Pictures." Nonextant.

"The Runner." *Acolyte* 3, No. 1 (Winter 1945): 22. *TYB* 81. *MW* 13.

"Shadow on the Wall." *Arkham Collector* No. 5 (Summer 1969): 133. *MW* 14.

"The Ship." *Marvel Tales* 1, No. 3 (Winter 1934): 80. *MW* 9.

"The Snake." First appearance in Lewiston (ID) newspaper not found. *Acolyte* 1, No. 3 (Spring 1943): 12. *MW* 12. *TYB* 76.

"Strange Flowers Bloom." *Arkham Collector* No. 8 (Winter 1971): 247. *MW* 36.

"The Whisperer." *Acolyte* 3, No. 2 (Spring 1945): 5. *MW* 31. *TYB* 82.

"Wind from the River." *Arcana* 1, No. 1 (1944). *MW* 36. *TYB* 83.

"Wings of Dream." 1984. *MW* 2.

"The Worm." *MW* 32.

Nonfiction

"About Hampdon." *SB* 2.

"About Yith." *SB* 40.

"The Acolyte Years." *Etchings and Odysseys* No. 10 (1987): 88.

"F. Lee Baldwin—A Fan's Fan." *Concept* No. 5 (20 February 1945). Rpt. in Richardson, *Within the Circle* xiv–xv.

"A Fan Looks Back." *New Concept* 1, No. 3 (December 1944) 3–4. *TYB* 50–51. In Richardson, *Within the Circle* xvi–xix.

"Fan Magazinitis." *Fantasmagoria: The Literary Fan Magazine* 1, No. 1 (March 1937): 4-6.

"Fantasy and Music." *Utopia* 1, No. 1 (May 1945): 8, 16.

"Fantasy Fandom." (late 1930–early 1940). *MW* 38–39.

"H. P. Lovecraft as I Knew Him." *CC* No. 18 (Yuletide 1983): 9–11.

"A History of The Chronicle of Nath." *Etchings and Odysseys* No. 9 (1986): 80.

"Joshua II: He Shocked Corvallis." First appearance unknown. *TYB* 52–54.

"The Lovecraft Years I." *Etchings and Odysseys* No. 9 (1986): 17.

"Weird Music" (with Emil Petaja). *Phantagraph* 4, No. 4 (July 1936): 6–7. In *Operation Phantasy*, ed. Donald A. Wollheim. Rego Park, NY: Phantagraph Press, 1967. 24–26.

Letters

Fantasy Fan. 1, No. 2 (October 1933): 16.

Weird Tales 22, No. 4 (October 1933): 517.

Fantasy Fan 1, No. 5 (January 1934): 77–78.

Fantasy Fan 1, No. 6 (February 1934): [80]–81.

Fantasy Fan 1, No. 7 (March 1934): [97].

Weird Tales 23, No. 3 (March 1934): 390.

Fantasy Fan 1, No. 8 (April 1934): 114–15; another on 124.

Fantasy Fan 1, No. 9 (May 1934): 130.

Fantasy Fan 1, No. 10 (June 1934): 145.

Fantasy Fan 1, No. 11 (July 1934): 161.

Fantasy Fan 1, No. 12 (August 1934): 178.

Fantasy Fan 2, No. 2 (October 1934): 18.

Fantasy Fan 2, No. 3 (November 1934): 35.

Weird Tales 25, No. 2 (February 1935): 272.

Astounding Stories 17, No. 4 (June 1936): 157.

CC No. 17 (1983): 48.

CC No. 28 (1984): 36.

CC No. 32. (1985): 51.

Nils Frome

Fiction
"The Alien Pictures." In *NHF.*
"Blurred Worlds." *Supramundane Stories* 1, No. 2 (Spring 1938): 5–6. In *NHF.*
"The Cloud People." In *NHF.*
"Devolution." *Spaceways* 4, No. 6 Whole No. 29 (July 1942).
"The Eyes of Paul Cordney." *Fantascience Digest* 1, No. 4 May–June 1938.
"The Flaming Sword of Yucatan." *Supramundane Stories* 1, No. 1 (Spring 1937): 25–26, 24. In *NHF.*
"Ghoul of Selem." In *NHF.*
"Into the Violet Flame." In *NHF.*
"The Mirror." *Canadian Fandom* 10 (May 1946): 17–.
"The Mother." *Scienti-Snaps* 2, No. 1 (February 1939): 4–.
"Spectrum Shift." *Helios* 1, No. 5 (January–February 1938). In *NHF.*

Nonfiction
"But the Stars Still Shine!" *Golden Atom* 1, No. 6 (March 1940). In *NHF.*
"[Editorial.]" *Supramundane Stories* 1, No. 2 (Spring 1938): 3–4. In *NHF.*
"The Editor's Word." *Supramundane Stories* 1, No. 1 (Spring 1937): [22], 16. In *NHF.*
"The Enigma of Thought." In *NHF.*
"Letters to Claire Beck." In *NHF.*
"Letters to Sam Moskowitz." In *NHF.*
"A Message from Nils H. Frome." Helios 1, No. 3 (August–September 1937).
"Notes on Writing Science Fiction." *Tesseract* 1, No. 3 (May 1936); 1, No. 4 (June 1936). Adapted [i.e., written] by Jim Blish.
"A Portfolio of Laer Drawings by Hils Helmer Frome." In *NHF.*
"Possibilities Galore." *Supramundane Stories* 1, No. 1 (Spring 1937): 13. In *NHF.*
"Stf Intelligence." *Supramundane Stories* 1, No. 1 (Spring 1937): 24, 26. In *NHF.*
"Wonderscope No. 1." *Supramundane Stories* 1, No. 1 (Spring 1937): 16. In *NHF.*

Letters
Canadian Fandom No. 13 (September 1947).
Famous Fantastic Mysteries 4, No. 4 (August 1942): 142.
Weird Tales 27, No. 6 (June 1936).
Weird Tales 28, No. 2 (August/September 1936): 252. (apparently written by Jim Blish, given East Orange, NJ address).
Weird Tales. 31, No. 1 (January 1938).
Weird Tales 32, No. 1 (July 1938): 128.

Works by Others

Dates in angular brackets indicate first publication.

Alden, Abner (1758?–1820). *The Reader: Containing the Art of Delivery, Articulation, Accent, Pronunciation, [etc.].* <1797> 3rd ed. Boston, Printed by J. T. Buckingham for Thomas & Andrews, 1808. (*LL* 16)

Ahlhauser, William C. *Ex-Presidents of the National Amateur Press Association: Sketches.* Athol, MA: W. Paul Cook, 1919. (*LL*)

Allen, Hervey (1889–1949). *Anthony Adverse.* New York: Holt, Rinehart & Winston, 1933.

Andrews, Roy Chapman (1884–1960). *On the Trail of Ancient Man: A Narrative of the Field Work of the Central Asiatic Expeditions.* New York: G. P. Putnam's Sons, 1926.

Anger, Fred. "Phantastic Bread & Butter; or, The Mystery of the Missing Authors." *Phantagraph* 5, No. 2 (November 1936): 4–8. In *Letters to Robert Bloch* 456–59.

Barlow, R. H. (1918–1951). "The Flower God." *Fantasy Fan,* 1, No. 9 (May 1934): 139–40, 144. Part VI. of "The Annals of the Jinns." In *Eyes of the God: The Weird Fiction and Poetry of R. H. Barlow.* Ed. S. T. Joshi, Douglas A. Anderson, and David E. Schultz. New York: Hippocampus Press, 2002. 20–21.

———. "R. E. H." *WT* 28, No. 3 (October 1936): 353. In *Eyes of the God* 148.

Bartky, Walter (1901–1958). *Highlights of Astronomy.* Chicago: University of Chicago Press, 1935.

Baudelaire, Charles Pierre (1821–1867). *Baudelaire: His Prose and Poetry.* Ed. T. R. Smith. New York: Boni & Liveright (Modern Library), [1919]. (*LL* 69)

Bayne, Samuel G. (1844–1924). *The Pith of Astronomy (without Mathematics): The Latest Facts and Figures as Developed by the Giant Telescopes.* New York: Harper & Brothers, 1903. (*LL*)

Bierce, Ambrose (1842–1914?). *Can Such Things Be?* <1893> New York: Boni & Liveright (Modern Library), 1918. (*LL* 87)

———. *The Devil's Dictionary.* <1906/1911> Girard, KS: Haldeman-Julius, [1926?].

———. *Extraordinary Opinions on Commonplace Subjects.* Girard, KS: Haldeman-Julius, [1927?].

———. *Fantastic Debunking Fables.* Girard, KS: Haldeman-Julius, [1927?].

———. *The Horseman in the Sky and Other Stories.* Girard, KS: Haldeman-Julius, [1926?].

———. *In the Midst of Life: Tales of Soldiers and Civilians.* <1891? Introduction by George Sterling. New York: Modern Library, [1927]. (*LL* 88)

———. *The Monk and the Hangman's Daughter; Fantastic Fables; [etc.].* New York: Albert & Charles Boni, 1925. (*LL* 90)

———. *My Favorite Murder and Other Stories.* Girard, KS: Haldeman-Julius, [1927?].

———. *An Occurrence at Owl Creek Bridge and Other Stories.* Girard, KS: Haldeman-Julius, [1926?].

———. *Tales of Ghouls and Ghosts.* Girard, KS: Haldeman-Julius, [1927?].

———. *Tales of Haunted Houses.* Girard, KS: Haldeman-Julius, [1927?].

Bierstadt, Edward Hale (1891–1970). *Dunsany the Dramatist.* Boston: Little, Brown, 1917 (rev. ed. 1919). (*LL* 91)

Birkhead, Edith (1889–1951). *The Tale of Terror: A Study of the Gothic Romance.* New York: E. P. Dutton, 1921. (*LL* 94)

Blackwood, Algernon (1869–1951). *Episodes Bfore Thirty.* London & New York: Cassell & Co., 1923.

———. *How the Circus Came to Tea.* Oxford: Basil Blackwell, 1936.

———. *John Silence—Physician Extraordinary.* London: Eveleigh Nash, 1908. Boston: John W. Luce, 1909. London: Macmillan, 1912. New York: Vaughan & Gomme, 1914. New York: Knopf, 1917. New York, E. P. Dutton, [1920]. (*LL* 96, 97)

———. "The Man-Eater." *Thrilling Mystery* 6, No. 2 (March 1937): 32–41

———. "The Willows." In *The Listener and Other Stories.* London: Eveleigh Nash, 1907. In *The Best Ghost Stories,* ed. John Gilbert Bohun Lynch. Boston: Small, Maynard, 1924. (*LL* 543)

Boguet, Henri (d. 1619). *An Examen of Witches.* Tr. E. Allen Ashwin. Ed. Montague Summers. Bungay, UK: John Rodker, 1929.

The Book of the Dead. An English Translation of the Chapters, Hymns, etc. of the Theban Recension, with Introduction, Notes, etc., by Sir E. A. Wallis Budge (1857–1934). 2nd ed., rev. & enl. London: Kegan Paul, Trench, Trübner; New York: E. P. Dutton, 1923. 3 vols. in 1. (*LL* 110)

Boyd, Ernest A. (1887–1946). "Lord Dunsany—Fantaisiste." In *Appreciations and Depreciations.* New York: John Lane, 1918. Freeport, NY: Books for Libraries Press, 1968. 71–100.

Brewer, Ebenezer Cobham (1810–1897). *Dictionary of Phrase and Fable.* London: Cassell, Petter & Galpin, 1870.

Bryk, Felix (1882–1957). *Voodoo-Eros: Ethnological Studies in the Sex-Life of the African Aborigines.* New York: Privately printed for subscribers, 1933.

Bullen, John Ravenor (1886–1927). *White Fire.* Edited by H. P. Lovecraft. Athol, MA: Recluse Press, 1927 [actually January 1928]. (*LL* 131)

Burritt, Elijah Hinsdale (1794–1838). *The Geography of the Heavens, and Classbook of Astronomy: Accompanied by a Celestial Atlas.* A New Edition, Revised and Illustrated by Hiram Mattison. New York: F. J. Huntington, 1853. (*LL* 139)

Clendening, Logan (1884–1945). *The Human Body.* New York: Knopf, 1927.

Cornebise, Alfred Emile. *The CCC Chronicles: Camp Newspapers of the Civilian Conservation Corps, 1933–1942.* Jefferson NC: McFarland, 2004.

Crawford, F. Marion (1854–1909). *The Witch of Prague: A Fantastic Tale.* London & New York: Macmillan, 1891.

Cummings, Ray (1887–1957). "The Girl in the Golden Atom." *All-Story Weekly* (15 March 1919). In *The Girl in the Golden Atom.* New York: Harper & Brothers, 1923.

Damon, S. Foster (1893–1971). *Thomas Holley Chivers, Friend of Poe, with Selections from His Poems: A Strange Chapter in American Literary History.* New York: Harper & Brothers, 1930.

Darwin, C[harles] G[alton] (1887–1962). *The New Conception of Matter.* London: G. Bell & Sons, 1931.

De Castro, Adolphe Danziger (1859–1959). *Portrait of Ambrose Bierce.* New York: Century Co., 1929.

Derleth, August (1909–1971). "Crows Fly High." *Scribner's Magazine* 96, No. 6 (December 1934): 358–62.

———. *The Man on All Fours.* New York: Loring & Mussey, 1934.

———. *Murder Stalks the Wakely Family.* New York: Loring & Mussey, 1934.

———. *Place of Hawks.* Illustrated with wood engravings by George Barford. New York: Loring & Mussey, 1935. (*LL* 235)

———. *Sign of Fear: A Judge Peck Mystery.* New York: Loring & Mussey, 1935. (*LL* 236)

———. *Three Who Died.* New York: Loring & Mussey, 1935. (*LL* 237)

Dorsey, George A. (1868–1931). *Why We Behave Like Human Beings.* New York: Blue Ribbon Books, 1925.

Doyle, Arthur Conan (1859–1930). *The Case-Book of Sherlock Holmes.* John Murray, 1927.

———. *His Last Bow.* London: John Murray, 1917.

———. *The Valley of Fear.* Garden City, NY: George H. Doran, 1915.

Duncan, John Charles (1882–1967). *Astronomy.* New York: Harper & Brothers, 1926; 3rd ed. 1935.

Dunsany, Edward John Moreton Drax Plunkett, 18th baron (1878–1957). *The Blessing of Pan.* London: G. P. Putnam's Sons, 1927. (*LL* 270)

———. *The Curse of the Wise Woman.* London: William Heinemann, 1933. New York: Longmans, Green, 1933.

———. *A Dreamer's Tales and Other Stories.* <1910> Introduction by Padraic Colum. New York: Boni & Liveright (Modern Library), [1917], [1919], or [1921]. (*LL* 273)

———. *Mr. Jorkens Remembers Africa.* London: William Heinemann, 1934. New York: Longmans, Green, 1934 (as *Jorkens Remembers Africa*).

Eddington, Sir Arthur Stanley (1882–1944). *The Nature of the Physical World.* New York: Macmillan; Cambridge: Cambridge University Press, 1928.

England, George Allan (1877–1937) *Darkness and Dawn.* Boston: Small, Maynard, 1914.

Faig, Kenneth W., Jr. *The Unknown Lovecraft.* New York: Hippocampus Press, 2009.

"Whipple V. Phillips and the Owyhee Land and Irrigation Company." *Owyhee Outpost* No. 19 (May 1988): 21–30.

Findlay, Alexander (1874–1966). *The Spirit of Chemistry.* New York: Longmans, Green, 1931.

Flaubert, Gustave (1821–1880). *Salammbô: A Romance of Ancient Carthage.* <1862> (*LL* 320)

Foster, William (1869–1937). *The Romance of Chemistry.* New York: Century Co., 1927.

Frazer, Sir James George (1854–1941). *The Golden Bough: A Study in Magic and Religion.* <1890–1915> New York: Macmillan, 1930.

Garland, Hamlin (1860–1940). *Forty Years of Psychic Research: A Plain Narrative of Fact.* New York: Macmillan, 1936.

Gawsworth, John [pseud. of Terence Ian Fytton Armstrong] (1912–1970), ed. *Strange Assembly.* London: Unicorn Press, 1932. (*LL* 42)

Grattan, C. Hartley. *Bitter Bierce: A Mystery of American Letters.* Garden City, NY: Doubleday, Doran, 1929. (*LL* 370)

Haldeman-Julius, E. (1889–1951), ed. *Tales of the Mysterious and Weird.* Girard, KS: Haldeman-Julius, n.d. Contains Machen's "The Inmost Light."

Hall, Austin (1882?–1933), and Homer Eon Flint (1892–1924). *The Blind Spot. Argosy* (14 May–18 June 1921). Philadelphia: Prime, 1953.

———. *The Spot of Life. Argosy* (13 August–10 September 1932). New York: Ace, 1964.

Harré, T. Everett (1884–1948), ed. *Beware After Dark! The World's Most Stupendous Tales of Mystery, Horror, Thrills and Terror.* New York: Macaulay, 1929. (*LL* 397)

Hawthorne, Nathaniel (1804–1864). *Dr. Grimshawe's Secret.* Boston: Houghton Mifflin, 1882.

Hoag, Jonathan E. (1831–1927). *The Poetical Works of Jonathan E. Hoag.* New York: [Privately printed], 1923.

Hodgson, William Hope (1877–1918). *Carnacki the Ghost-Finder.* London: Eveleigh Nash, 1913.

———. *The Boats of the "Glen Carrig."* London: Chapman & Hall, 1907.

———. *The Ghost Pirates.* London: Stanley Paul, 1909.

———. *The House on the Borderland.* London: Chapman & Hall, 1908.

———. *The Night Land.* London: Eveleigh Nash, 1912.

———. "The Voice in the Night." In *They Walk Again,* ed. Colin de la Mare. London: Faber & Faber, 1931. 236–52.

Howard, Robert E. (1906–1936). *The Hyborian Age.* Los Angeles: LANY Cooperative Publications, 1938.

Hudson, W. H. (1841–1922). *Green Mansions.* New York: G. P. Putnam's Sons, 1904. London, Duckworth & Co., 1904 (rpt. 1934).

Infeld, Leopold (1888–1968). *The World in Modern Science: Matter and Quanta.* London: Victor Gollancz, 1934.

James, Henry (1843–1916). *Portrait of a Lady.* Boston: Houghton, Mifflin, 1881.

———. *The Turn of the Screw.* <1898?> New York: Modern Library, 1930.

———. *The Two Magics: The Turn of the Screw; Covering End.* <1898> New York: Macmillan, 1911. (*LL* 467)

James, M[ontague] R[hodes] (1862–1936). *Ghost-Stories of an Antiquary.* London: Edward Arnold, 1904. (*LL* 468)

Jeans, James Hopwood (1877–1946). *The New Background of Science.* New York: Macmillan, 1933.

———. *The Universe Around Us.* Cambridge: Cambridge University Press, 1929.

Keller, David H. (1880–1966). "The Dead Woman." *Fantasy Magazine* 3, No. 2 (whole no. 20) (April 1934): 1–5. *Strange Stories* (April 1939).

Khun de Prorok, Byron (1896–1954?). *Digging for Lost African Gods: The Record of Five Years Archaeological Excavation in North Africa.* New York: G. P. Putnam's Sons, 1926.

Koenig, H. C. "The Intellectual Shocker." *Fantasy Fan* 2, No. 1 (September 1934): 10, 15.

———. "William Hope Hodgson." *Fantasy Fan,* 2, No. 4 (December 1934): 56, 64.

Kremer, Heinrich (1430–1505), and Jakob Sprenger (1436?–1495). *Malleus Maleficarum.* Tr. Montague Summers. London: J. Rodker, 1928.

Kroeber, A[lfred] L[ouis] (1876–1960). *Anthropology.* New York: Harcourt, Brace, 1923.

Kunitz, Stanley. *Living Authors: A Book of Book of Biographies.* New York: H. W. Wilson Co., 1931.

———, Howard Haycraft, and Wilbur C Hadden. *Authors Today and Yesterday: A Companion Volume to Living Authors.* New York: H. W. Wilson Co., 1931.

Kurath, Hans (1891–1992), ed. *Linguistic Atlas of New England.* Providence, RI: Brown University, 1939–43. 3 vols. in 6.

Laney, Francis T (1914–1958). "The Acolyte Gang." In Richardson, xi–xiii [an extract from Chapter 3 of Laney's *Ah! Sweet Idiocy* (13–14).

———. *Ah! Sweet Idiocy!: The Fan Memoirs of Francis T. Laney.* Los Angeles: Published by F. T. Laney and C. Burbee for FAPA, 1948.

——— and William H. Evans. *Howard Phillips Lovecraft—1890–1937: A Tentative Bibliography.* Los Angeles: An "Acoylte" Publication [for FAPA], Winter 1943.

Lévi, Eliphas (pseud. of Alphonse Louis Constnat, 1810–1875). *The History of Magic: Including a Clear and Precise Exposition of Its Procedure, Its Rites and Its Mysteries.* Tr. A. E. Waite. London: W. Rider & Son, 1913.

Lewis, Matthew Gregory (1775–1818). *The Monk.* <1796> London: Brentano's, [1924]. 3 vols. in 1. (*LL* 531)

Long, Frank Belknap (1901–1994). *The Goblin Tower.* Cassia, FL: Dragon-Fly Press, 1935.

———. *The Horror from the Hills. Weird Tales* 7, No. 1 (January 1931); 7, No. 2 (February–March 1931). Sauk City, WI: Arkham House, 1963.

Longwell, Chester R. (1887–1975), and Charles Schuchert (1858–1942). *Foundations of Geology: Being a Combination of Outlines of Physical Geology & Outlines of Historical Geology.* New York: John Wiley & Sons, 1931.

Loveman, Samuel (1887–1976). *The Hermaphrodite and Other Poems.* Caldwell, ID: Caxton Printers, 1936. (*LL* 550)

Lowie, Robert Heinrich (1883–1957). *An Introduction to Cultural Anthropology.* London: Harrap, 1934.

Lynch, John Gilbert Bohun (1884–1928), ed. *The Best Ghost Stories.* Boston: Small, Maynard, [1924]. (*LL* 558)

Machen, Arthur (1863–1947). "The Coming of the Terror." *Century* 94, No. 6 (October 1917): 801–25. (*LL* 157)

———. *Far Off Things.* <1922> New York: Alfred A. Knopf, 1923. (*LL* 570)

———. *The Great God Pan and The Inmost Light.* London: John Lane; Boston: Roberts Brothers, 1894, 1895. London: Grant Richards, 1913.

———. *The Green Round.* London: Ernest Benn, 1933. Sauk City, WI: Arkham House, 1968.

———. *Hieroglyphics: A Note upon Ecstasy in Literature.* <1902> (*LL* 571)

———. *The Hill of Dreams.* London: E. Grant Richards, 1907. (*LL* 572); or *The Hill of Dreams* (blue paper edition). London: Martin Secker, [1922].

———. *The House of Souls.* London: Grant Richards, 1906. New York: Knopf, 1922. *Contents:* "A Fragment of Life"; "The White People"; "The Great God Pan"; "The Inmost Light." (*LL* 573)

———. *The London Adventure: An Essay in Wandering.* New York: Knopf, 1924. (*LL* 574)

———. *Out of the Earth and Other Sketches.* Girard, KS: Haldeman-Julius, [1925?]. Contains "Out of the Earth," "The Spagyric Quest of Beroaldus Cosmopolita," "The Hidden Mystery," "The Art of Dickens," and "Unconscious Magic."

———. *The Shining Pyramid.* London, Martin Secker, 1925. (*LL* 576)

———. *Tales of the Strange and Supernatural.* Girard, KS: Haldeman-Julius, [1925?]. *Contains:* "The Priest and the Barber"; "The Lost Club"; "A Wonderful Woman"; and "The Shining Pyramid."

———. *The Terror.* London: Duckworth, 1917. New York: McBride, 1917.

———. *Things Near and Far.* New York: Knopf, 1923. (*LL* 577)

———. *The Three Impostors.* <1895> New York: Knopf, 1930. (*LL* 578)

———. "The White People." *Horlick's Magazine* 1 (January 1904): 57–78. In *The House of Souls* (q.v.).

MacLeish, Archibald (1892–1982). *Conquistador.* Boston: Houghton Mifflin, 1932.

McNeil, Everett (1862–1929). *Tonty of the Iron Hand.* New York: E. P. Dutton, 1925.

———. *The Totem of Black Hawk.* New York: E. P. Dutton, 1921.

McWilliams, Carey (1905–1980). *Ambrose Bierce: A Biography.* New York: A. & C. Boni, 1929.

Maturin, Charles Robert (1782?–1824). *Melmoth the Wanderer.* <1820> London: Richard Bentley & Son, 1892. 3 vols. (*LL* 599)

Merritt, A. (1884–1943). *Burn, Witch, Burn! Argosy* (22 October–26 November 1932). New York: Liveright, 1933.

————. *The Conquest of the Moon Pool. All-Story Weekly* (15 February–22 March 1919). Incorporated into *The Moon Pool* (q.v.).

————. *Creep, Shadow! Argosy* (8 September–20 October 1934). Garden City, NY: Doubleday, 1934. (*LL* 40)

————. "The Drone." *Fantasy Magazine*, 4, No. 1 (September 1934): 1–10.

————. *The Dwellers in the Mirage. Argosy* (23 January–27 February 1932). New York: Liveright, 1932.

————. *The Face in the Abyss. Argosy* (8 September 1923). New York: Liveright, 1931 (combined with *The Snake Mother*). (*LL* 603)

————. *The Metal Emperor. Science and Invention* (October 1927–August 1928).

————. *The Metal Monster. Argosy* (7 August–25 September 1920). New York: Hippocampus Press, 2002.

————. "The Moon Pool." *All-Story Weekly* (22 June 1918) (*LL* 17). Expanded as *The Moon Pool*. New York: G. P. Putnam's Sons, 1919. *Amazing Stories* (May–July 1927).

————. "The People of the Pit." *All-Story Weekly* (5 January 1918). *Amazing Stories Annual* (1927).

————. *The Snake Mother. Argosy* (25 October–6 December 1930).

Meyrink, Gustav (1868–1932). *Der Golem.* <1915> Tr. Madge Pemberton as *The Golem*. London: Gollancz, 1928. Boston: Houghton Mifflin, 1928.

Miller, P. Schuyler, and John D. Clark. *A Probable Outline of Conan's Career*. Los Angeles: LANY Coöperative Publications, 1938. In Robert E. Howard. *The Coming of Conan*. New York: Gnome Press, 1953.

Moon, Truman J. (1879–1946). *Biology for Beginners*. New York: Henry Holt, 1926.

Morse, Richard Ely (1909–1986). *Winter Garden*. Amherst, MA: Poetry Society of Amherst College, 1931.

Moskowitz, Sam, ed. *Howard Phillips Lovecraft and Nils Helmer Frome: A Recollection of One of Canada's Earliwest Science Fiction Fans*. Glenview, IL: Moshassuck Press, 1989. *Contents:* Kenneth W. Faig, Jr., "Publisher's Preface"; Sam Moskowitz, "Nils Frome: Making The Unknown Known"; Sam Moskowitz, "On Nils Frome and Blish, Lovecraft, et al."; Sam Moskowitz, "Nils Frome in *The Golden Atom*"; Sam Moskowitz, "The Frome Finale"; Michael Dann, with Brenda Yvonne Hallack [*sic:* Halak], "Nils Helmer Frome Found And Lost"; Nils H. Frome, "But The Stars Still Shine"; Nils H. Frome, "The Cloud People"; Nils H. Frome, "Spectrum Shift"; Nils H. Frome, "Ghoul of Selem"; Nils H. Frome, "Into the Violet Flame"; Nils H. Frome, "The Alien Pictures"; "The Alien Pictures" (Manuscript Facsimile, Claire Beck Collection); Nils H. Frome, "The Enigma of Thought"; H. P. Lovecraft, "Letters to Nils Helmer Frome"; Nils H. Frome, "Letters to Claire Beck"; Nils H. Frome, "Letters to Sam Moskowitz"; Kenneth W. Faig, Jr., "Nils Frome's Two Favorite Actresses"; Claire Beck, "On the Multigraph"; Sam Moskowitz, "Fantasy Artists Numbers 1 and 2"; Nils H. Frome, "*Supramundane Stories* in Facsimile Reproduction"; "Three

Photographs of Nils Helmer Frome" (Alice Frome Collection); "A Port-folio of Later Drawings by Nils Helmer Frome" (Alice Frome Collec-tion); Brenda Yvonne Hallack, "Published Work by Nils Helmer Frome."

Moulton, Forest Ray (1872–1952). *Consider the Heavens.* Garden City, NY: Doubleday, Doran, 1925.

Munroe, Kirk (1850–1930). *The Fur Seal's Tooth: A Story of Alaska Adventure.* New York: Harper & Brothers, 1894.

———. *Rick Dale: A Story of the Northwest Coast.* New York: Harper & Broth-ers, 1896.

———. *Snow Shoes and Sledges.* New York: Harper & Brothers, 11923.

Murray, Margaret A. (1863–1963). *The Witch-Cult in Western Europe.* Oxford: Clarendon Press, 1921.

Norton, William Harmon (1856–1944). *The Elements of Geology.* Boston: Ginn, 1905.

O'Brien, Edward J., ed. *The Best Short Stories of 1924 and the Yearbook of the American Short Story.* Boston: Small, Maynard, 1924.

———. *The Best Short Stories of 1928 and the Yearbook of the American Short Story.* New York: Dodd, Mead, 1928.

———. *The Best Short Stories of 1929 and the Yearbook of the American Short Story.* New York: Dodd, Mead, 1929.

Pain, Barry (1864–1928). *Stories in the Dark.* London: Grant Richards, 1901. [Contains "The Undying Thing."]

Palgrave, Francis T. (1824–1897), ed. *The Golden Treasury: Selected from the Best Songs and Lyrical Poems in the English Language.* London: Macmillan, 1861. (LL 671)

Pierce, Frederick Clifton (1855–1904). *Field Genealogy.* Chicago: W. B. Conkey, 1901.

Radcliffe, Ann (1764–1823). *The Mysteries of Udolpho: A Romance.* <1794> London: George Routledge & Sons, [1882]–[192-]. (LL 718)

Railo, Eino (1884–1948). *The Haunted Castle: A Study of the Elements of English Romanticism.* New York: E. P. Dutton, 1927.

Reichenbach, Hans (1891–1953). *Atom and Cosmos: The World of Modern Physics.* London: George Allen & Unwin, 1930.

Renshaw, Anne Tillery. *Well Bred Speech: A Brief, Intensive Aid for English Stu-dents.* Washington, DC: Standard Press, 1936. (LL 726)

Reynolds, George W. M. (1814–1879). *Faust and the Demon: A Romance of the Secret Tribunals.* London: G. Vickers, 1847.

———. *Wagner the Wehr-Wolf.* London: J. Dicks, 1848, 1857, 1872.

Richardson, Josephine, and Divers Hands. *Within the Circle—In Memoriam: Franklyn Lee Baldwin, Born March 26, 1913 Asotin Washington, Died August 30 1987 Moscow, Idaho.* Ed. Kenneth W. Faig, Jr. Evanston, IL: Moshas-suck Press, 1988. *Contains:* Kenneth W. Faig, Jr., "Publisher's Preface"; Josephine Richardson, "Some Memories of Franklin Lee Baldwin";

Francis T. Laney, "The Acolyte Gang"; Duane W. Rimel, "Lee Baldwin—A Fan's Fan"; Duane W. Rimel, "A Fan Looks Back"; F. Lee Baldwin, "Preface to the *Fantasy Fan Index*"; F. Lee Baldwin, "*Fantasy Fan* Columns"; "Dear Editor: The Letters of F. Lee Baldwin to the *Fantasy Fan*"; F. Lee Baldwin, "H. P. Lovecraft: A Biographical Sketch"; F. Lee Baldwin, "*Acolyte* Columns"; Duane W. Rimel, "Music of the Stars"; Ed McBride [F. Lee Baldwin], "Re-creation"; F. Lee Baldwin, "Letters to The Antipodes"; F. Lee Baldwin, "Dealer and Trader [A Sampling of Advertisements Placed by F. Lee Baldwin over the Years]"; August W. Derleth, "Hoax Walter Dunkelberger: A Dissenting Viewpoint on *The Outsider and Others* as a Collector's Item"; F. Lee Baldwin, "Things Past and Things Present: A Letter From the Seventies"; F. Lee Baldwin, "A Flame Still Burning: Letters to the Editor of *Xenophile*"; "Final Farewell: *The Lewiston Tribune*, September 2, 1987."

Roget, Peter Mark (1779–1869). *Thesaurus of English Words and Phrases.* New ed., enlarged & improved, partly from the author's notes, & with a full index, by John Lewis Roget. New York: John R. Anderson, 1882. (*LL* 741)

Rohmer, Sax (pseud. of Arthur Sarsfield Ward, 1883–1959). *The Romance of Sorcery.* New York: E. P. Dutton, 1914.

Scott, Sir Walter (1771–1832). *Letters on Demonology and Witchcraft.* <1830> London: George Routledge & Sons, 1884. (*LL* 770)

Seabrook, William B. (1887–1945). *Asylum.* New York: Harcourt, Brace, 1935.

———. *Jungle Ways.* New York: Harcourt, Brace, 1931.

———. *The Magic Island.* New York: Harcourt, Brace, 1929.

Shiel, M. P. (1865–1947). *The Purple Cloud.* <1901> New York: Vanguard Press, [1930]. (*LL* 800)

Smith, Clark Ashton (1893–1961). "The Abominations of Yondo." *Overland Monthly* 84, No. 4 (April 1926): 100–101, 114, 126. *Celephaïs* 1, No. 1 (March 1944): 4–7.

———. "The City of the Singing Flame." *Wonder Stories,* 3, No. 2 (July 1931): 202–13.

———. "The Coming of the White Worm." *Stirring Fantasy Fiction* 1, No. 2 (April 1941): 105–14. *Uncanny Tales* 2. No. 11 (December 1941): 10–17.

———. *The Double Shadow and Other Fantasies.* [Auburn, CA]: Auburn Journal, 1933. (*LL* 810)

———. *Ebony and Crystal: Poems in Verse and Prose.* Auburn, CA: Auburn Journal, [1922]. (*LL* 811)

———. "The Epiphany of Death." *Fantasy Fan* 1, No. 11 (July 1934): 165–68.

———. "The Ninth Skeleton." *WT* 12, No. 3 (September 1928): 363–66.

———. "Sadastor." *WT* 16, No. 1 (July 1930): 133–35.

———. *The Star-Treader and Other Poems.* San Francisco: A. M. Robertson, 1912. (*LL* 814)

———, and David H. Keller. *The White Sibyl and Men of Avalon.* Everett, PA:

Fantasy Publications, 1934.

Steele, Joel Dorman (1836–1866). *A Fourteen Weeks Course in Descriptive Astronomy.* New York: A. S. Barnes; Boston: Woolworth, Ainsworth, 1873. (*LL* 836)

———. *Fourteen Weeks in Chemistry.* <1873>. (*LL*)

———. *Fourteen Weeks in Human Physiology.* New York: A. S. Barnes, 1873. (*LL* 837)

———. *Fourteen Weeks in Physics.* <1878>. (*LL*)

———. *Fourteen Weeks in Zoology.* New York: A. S. Barnes, 1877. (*LL* 838)

———. *The Story of the Rocks: Fourteen Weeks in Popular Geology.* Rev. ed. New York: A. S. Barnes, 1877. (*LL* 839)

Stoker, Bram (1847–1912). *Dracula.* <1897> Garden City, NY: Doubleday, Page, 1925. (*LL* 848)

———. *The Jewel of Seven Stars.* London: Heinemann, 1903. London: William Rider & Son, 1912, 1919.

———. *The Lair of the White Worm.* London: Rider, 1911.

Stokley, James (1900–1989). *Stars and Telescopes.* New York: Harper & Brothers, 1936.

Stormonth, James (1824–1882). *A Dictionary of the English Language,* The Pronunciation Carefully Revised by the Rev. P. H. Help <1871>. New York: Harper & Brothers, 1885. (*LL* 850)

Summers, Montague (1880–1948). *The Geography of Witchcraft.* London: Kegan Paul, Trench, Trübner; New York: Alfred A. Knopf, 1927.

———. *The Vampire in Europe.* London: Kegan Paul, Trench, Trübner, 1929.

———. *The Vampire: His Kith and Kin.* London: Kegan Paul, Trench, Trübner, 1928.

Swann, W. F. G. (1884–1962). *The Architecture of the Universe.* New York: Macmillan, 1934.

Teter, George E. (1877–1940) *An Introduction to Some Elements of Poetry.* Wauwatosa, WI: Kenyon Press, 1927. (*LL* 868)

Thomson, J. Arthur (1861–1933). *The Outline of Science: A Plain Story Simply Told.* New York: G. P. Putnam's Sons, 1922.

Todd, David Peck (1855–1939). *Astronomy: The Science of the Heavenly Bodies.* New York: Harper & Brothers, 1922. (*LL*)

Tolstoi, Leo (1828–1910). *War and Peace.* Tr. into French by a Russian Lady, and from the French by Clara Bell. New York: W. S. Gottsberger, 1887. 2 vols. (*LL* 888)

Upton, Winslow (1853–1914). *Star Atlas.* Boston: Ginn, 1896. (*LL* 900)

Van Dine, S. S. (pseud. of Willard Huntington Wright, 1888–1939). *The Kennel Murder Case: A Philo Vance Story.* New York: Charles Scribner's Sons, 1933.

Vechten, Carl Van (1880–1964). *Lords of the Housetops.* New York: Knopf, 1921.

Walpole, Hugh (1884–1941). *Portrait of a Man with Red Hair.* London: Macmillan, 1925.

Wandrei, Donald (1908–1987). "The Chuckler." *Fantasy Magazine* 4, No. 1

(September 1934): 26–27. (Written in 1926.)

———. *Dark Odyssey*. St. Paul, MN: Webb Publishing Co., (1931). (*LL* 917)

———. *Ecstasy and Other Poems*. Athol, MA: Recluse Press, 1928. (*LL* 918)

———. "The Eye and the Finger." *Esquire* 6, No. 6 (December 1936): 70, 319–20.

———. "The Red Brain." *WT* 10, No. 4 (October 1927): 531–37. *WT* 27, No. 5 (May 1936): 626–28, 630–33.

Warren, David M. (1820–1861). *A Primary Geography*. Philadelphia: H. Cowperthwait, 1864). (*LL* 924)

Wasso, John, Jr. (1906–1987). *Fantasy Magazine* 3, No. 6 (August 1934): 10–12.

Webster, Noah (1758–1834). *Webster's International Dictionary of the English Language*, Now Thoroughly Revised and Enlarged under the Supervision of Noah Porter. Springfield, MA: G. & C. Merriam, 1891. (*LL* 932)

Wells, H[erbert] G[eorge] (1866–1946), Julian Huxley, and G. P. Wells. *The Science of Life: A Summary of Contemporary Knowledge about Life and Its Possibilities*. London: Amalgamated Press, 1930. 2 vols. New York: Doubleday, 1931. 4 vols.

———. *The War of the Worlds*. London: Heinemann; New York: Harper & Brothers, 1898.

Whitehead, Henry S. (1882–1932). "The Black Beast." *Adventure* 79, No. 3 (15 July 1931): 136–57.

———. "Cassius." *Strange Tales of Mystery and Terror* 1, No. 2 (November 1931).

Whitman, Sarah Helen. *Was Poe Immortal?* Girard, KS: Haldeman-Julius, n.d.

Wood, Clement. *Hints on Writing Poetry*. Girard, KS: Haldeman-Julius, [1924].

Wright, Farnsworth. "An Answer to Mr. Anger." *Phantagraph* 5, No. 2 (December 1936): 4–6. In *Letters to Robert Bloch* 459–60.

Young, Charles Augustus (1834–1908). *Lessons in Astronomy Including Uranography*. Boston: Ginn, 1893. (*LL* 979)

Items Published in *Weird Tales*

Items mentioned by HPL in the correspondence.

23, No. 1 (January 1934)
In the Triangle	Howard Wandrei

23, No. 3 (March 1934)
The Charnel God	Clark Ashton Smith

23, No. 4 (April 1934)
The Bells of Oceana (rpt)	Arthur Burks
Black Thirst	C. L. Moore
The Death of Malygris	Clark Ashton Smith
Shadows in the Moonlight	Robert E. Howard

23, No. 5 (May 1934)
Queen of the Black Coast   Robert E. Howard
Scarlet Dream   C. L. Moore
The Tomb Spawn   Clark Ashton Smith

23, No. 6 (June 1934)
The Colossus of Ylourgne   Clark Ashton Smith
The Haunter of the Ring   Robert E. Howard
They Called Him Ghost   Laurence J. Cahill

24, No. 1 (July 1934)
The Disinterment of Venus   Clark Ashton Smith
Through the Gates of the Silver Key   H. P. Lovecraft and E. Hoffmann Price
The Thunderstones of Nuflo   Ralph Allen Lang
The Trail of the Cloven Hoof [1/7]   Arlton Eadie

24, No. 2 (August 1934)
The Devil in Iron   Robert E. Howard
The Distortion Out of Space   Francis Flagg
Dust of the Gods   C. L. Moore
The Isle of Black Magic   Hugh B. Cave
The Trail of the Cloven Hoof [2/7]   Arlton Eadie

24, No. 3 (September 1934)
The People of the Black Circle [1/3]   Robert E. Howard
The Trail of the Cloven Hoof [3/7]   Arlton Eadie

24, No. 4 (October 1934)
The People of the Black Circle [2/3]   Robert E. Howard
The Trail of the Cloven Hoof [4/7]   Arlton Eadie

24, No. 5 (November1934)
Feigman's Beard   August W. Derleth
The Music of Erich Zann   H. P. Lovecraft
The People of the Black Circle [3/3]   Robert E. Howard
Queen of the Lilin   E. Hoffmann Price
The Trail of the Cloven Hoof [5/7]   Arlton Eadie

24, No. 6 (December 1934)
The Black God's Shadow   C. L. Moore
The Graveyard Duchess   John Flanders
A Matter of Faith   August Derleth and Mark Schorer
Pale Pink Porcelain   Frank Owen [Roswell Williams]
The Trail of the Cloven Hoof [6/7]   Arlton Eadie
The Vengeance of Ti Fong   Bassett Morgan

The Werewolf's Howl	Brooke Byrne
A Witch Shall Be Born	Robert E. Howard
Xeethra	Clark Ashton Smith

25, No. 1 (January 1935)
The Dark Eidolon	Clark Ashton Smith
The Feast in the Abbey	Robert Bloch
The Trail of the Cloven Hoof [7/7]	Arlton Eadie

25, No. 2 (February 1935)
| The Dinner Set | Fanny Kemble Johnson |
| The Fireplace | Henry S. Whitehead |

25, No. 3 (March 1935)
Jewels of Gwahlur	Robert E. Howard
Julhi	C. L. Moore
The Sealed Casket	Richard F. Searight

25, No. 4 (April 1935)
Dream-Stair	Robert Nelson
The Hand of the O'Mecca	Howard Wandrei
The Last Hieroglyph	Clark Ashton Smith
The Man Who Was Two Men	Arthur William Bernal
Out of the Aeons	Hazel Heald
Shadows of Blood	Eando Binder

25, No. 5 (May 1935)
| Beyond the Black River [1/2] | Robert E. Howard |
| The Secret of the Tomb | Robert Bloch |

25, No. 6 (June 1935)
Arthur Jermyn	H. P. Lovecraft
Beyond the Black River [2/2]	Robert E. Howard
Satan in Exile [1/4]	Arthur William Bernal

26, No. 1 (July 1935)
The Avenger from Atlantis	Edmond Hamilton
Jirel Meets Magic	C. L. Moore
Satan in Exile [2/4]	Arthur William Bernal

26, No. 2 (August 1935)
| Satan in Exile [3/4] | Arthur William Bernal |

26, No. 3 (September 1935)
| The Man Who Chained the Lightning | Paul Ernst |
| The Monster God of Mamurth | Edmond Hamilton |

One Chance	Ethel Helene Coen
Satan in Exile [4/4]	Arthur William Bernal
The Shambler from the Stars	Robert Bloch
Vulthoom	Clark Ashton Smith

26, No. 4 (October 1935)

The Mystery of the Last Guest	John Flanders

26, No. 5 (November 1935)

The Consuming Flame	Paul Ernst
The Hand of Wrath	E. Hoffmann Price
Shadows in Zamboula	Robert E. Howard
The Way Home	Paul Frederick Stern

26, No. 6 (December 1935)

The Chain of Aforgomon	Clark Ashton Smith
The Hour of the Dragon [1/5]	Robert E. Howard
Lukundoo	Edward Lucas White

27, No. 1 (January 1936)

Dagon	H. P. Lovecraft
The Dark Land	C. L. Moore
The Hour of the Dragon [2/5]	Robert E. Howard

27, No. 2 (February 1936)

The Hour of the Dragon [3/5]	Robert E. Howard
The Temple	H. P. Lovecraft
Yvala	C. L. Moore

27, No. 3 (March 1936)

The Black Abbott of Puthuum	Clark Ashton Smith
The Crystal Curse	Eando Binder
The Graveyard Rats	Henry Kuttner
The Hour of the Dragon [4/5]	Robert E. Howard
In the World's Dusk	Edmond Hamilton

27, No. 4 (April 1936)

The Druidic Doom	Robert Bloch
The Hour of the Dragon [5/5]	Robert E. Howard

27, No. 5 (May 1936)

Child of the Winds	Edmond Hamilton
The Faceless God	Robert Bloch
The Room of Shadows	Arthur J. Burks

27, No. 6 (June 1936)

Black Canaan	Robert E. Howard
The Grinning Ghoul	Robert Bloch
The Harbour of Ghosts	M. J. Bardine
Lethe	Harold G. Shane
The Telephone in the Library	August W. Derleth

28, No. 1 (July 1936)

Red Nails [1/3]	Robert E. Howard

28, No. 2 (August/September 1936)

Red Nails [2/3]	Robert E. Howard

28, No. 3 (October 1936)

Isle of the Undead	Lloyd Arthur Eschbach
The Opener of the Way	Robert Bloch
The Lost Door	Dorothy Quick
Doom of the House of Duryea	Earl Peirce, Jr.
The Tree of Life	C. L. Moore
Red Nails [3/3]	Robert E. Howard
The Doors of Death	Arthur B. Waltermire
The Secret of Kralitz	Henry Kuttner

28, No. 4 (November 1936)

Black Hound of Death	Robert E. Howard
Brother Lucifer	Chandler H. Whipple
The Crawling Horror	Thorp McClusky
The Dark Demon	Robert Bloch

28, No. 5 (December 1936)

The Album	Amelia Reynolds Long
The Fire of Asshurbanipal	Robert E. Howard
The Haunter of the Dark	H. P. Lovecraft
It Walks by Night	Henry Kuttner
Mother of Serpents	Robert Bloch

29, No. 1 (January 1937)

The Disinterment	Duane W. Rimel
The Headless Miller of Kobold's Keep	G. Garnet
The Thing on the Doorstep	H. P. Lovecraft

29, No. 3 (March 1937)

The Picture in the House	H. P. Lovecraft

Index

www.ingramcontent.com/pod-product-compliance
Lightning Source LLC
Chambersburg PA
CBHW070800030726
47504CB00003B/635